THE GOVT SOLUTION

STUDENT RESOURCES

- Interactive eBook
- Graded Quizzes
- New Practice Quiz Generator
- New Interactive Exhibits
- Video Quizzes
- Flashcards

- Animated Learning Modules and Simulations
- Primary Source Activities
- American Government NewsWatch
- Glossary
- Review Cards

Students sign in at **www.cengagebrain.com**

INSTRUCTOR RESOURCES

- All Student Resources
- Engagement Tracker
- LMS Integration
- Instructor's Manual
- PowerPoint® Slides
- Test Bank
- Prep Cards
- Discussion Questions

Instructors log in at **www.cengage.com/login**

Print

GOVT7 delivers all the key terms and all the content for the **Principles of American Government** course through a visually engaging and easy-to-reference print experience.

CourseMate

CourseMate provides access to the full **GOVT7** narrative, alongside a rich assortment of quizzing, flashcards, and interactive resources for convenient reading and studying.

GOVT7

Edward Sidlow • Beth Henschen

Vice President, General Manager, 4LTR Press and the Student Experience: Neil Marquardt

Product Director, 4LTR Press: Steven E. Joos

Content Developer: Victoria Castrucci

Product Assistant: Mandira Jacob

Marketing Manager: Valerie Hartman

Senior Content Project Manager: Ann Borman

Manufacturing Planner: Ron Montgomery

Sr. Art Director: Stacy Shirley

Cover and Internal Designer: KeDesign, Mason, OH

Cover Image: © Tom Grill/Corbis

Intellectual Property:
  Analyst: Alex Ricciardi
  Project Manager: Betsy Hathaway

Indexer: Terry Casey

Production Service: Parkwood Composition Service, Inc.

For product information and technology assistance, contact us at
Cengage Learning Customer & Sales Support
1-800-354-9706

For permission to use material from this text or product, submit all requests online at
www.cengage.com/permissions.

Further permissions questions can be e-mailed to
permissionrequest@cengage.com.

Library of Congress Control Number: 2014950621

ISBN-13: 978-1-285-87029-8

Cengage Learning
20 Channel Center Street
Boston, MA 02210
USA

Cengage Learning is a leading provider of customized learning solutions with office locations around the globe, including Singapore, the United Kingdom, Australia, Mexico, Brazil, and Japan. Locate your local office at: **www.cengage.com/global**.

Cengage Learning products are represented in Canada by Nelson Education, Ltd.

To learn more about Cengage Learning Solutions, visit **www.cengage.com**.

Purchase any of our products at your local college store or at our preferred online store **www.cengagebrain.com**.

Printed in the United States of America
Print Number: 01   Print Year: 2014

SIDLOW / HENSCHEN

GOVT⁷

BRIEF CONTENTS

© STILLFX/Shutterstock 139345961

CONTENTS

Part I
THE FOUNDATIONS OF OUR AMERICAN SYSTEM 2

Part II
OUR LIBERTIES AND RIGHTS 72

© Scott Olson/Getty Images

Part III
THE POLITICS OF DEMOCRACY 122

© Marlon Correa / The Washington Post / Getty Images

Part IV
INSTITUTIONS 238

© Patsy Lynch/Retna Ltd./Corbis.

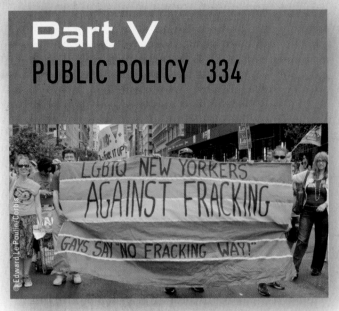

Part V
PUBLIC POLICY 334

15 Domestic Policy 334

16 Foreign Policy 356

© Creativa/Shutterstock

SKILL PREP

A Study Skills Module

Welcome! With this course and this textbook, you've begun what we hope will be a fun, stimulating, and thought-provoking journey into the world of American government and politics.

In this course, you will learn all about the foundation of the American system, culture and diversity, interest groups, political parties, campaigns, elections, the media, our governing institutions, public policy, and foreign policy. Knowledge of these basics will help you think critically about political issues and become an active citizen.

To help you get the most out of this course, and this textbook, we have developed this study skills module. You may be a recent high school graduate, or a working professional continuing your education, or an adult making your way back to the classroom after a few years. Whatever type of student you are, you want RESULTS when you study. You want to be able to understand the

issues and ideas presented in the textbook, to be able to talk about them intelligently during class discussions, and to be able to remember them as you prepare for exams and papers.

This kind of knowledge doesn't just come from natural talent. Instead, it comes from the use of good study skills. This module is designed to help you develop the skills and habits you'll need to get the results that you want from this course. With tips on how to be more engaged when you study, how to get the most out of your textbook, how to prepare for exams, and how to write papers, this guide will help you become the best learner you can be!

STUDY PREP

What does it take to be a successful student? Like many people, you may think that success depends on how naturally smart you are, that some people are just better at school than others. But in reality, successful students aren't born, they're made. What this means is that even if you don't consider yourself naturally "book smart," you can do well in this course by developing study skills that will help you understand, remember, and apply key concepts.

Reading for Learning

Your textbook is the foundation for information in a course. It contains key concepts and terms that are important to your understanding of the subject. For this reason, it is essential that you develop good reading skills. As you read your textbook with the goal of learning as much of the information as possible, work on establishing the following habits:

FOCUS

Make an effort to focus on the book and tune out other distractions so that you can understand and remember the information it presents.

TAKE TIME

To learn the key concepts presented in each chapter, you need to read slowly, carefully, and with great attention.

REPEAT

To read for learning, you have to read your textbook a number of times. Follow a preview-read-review process:

1. **PREVIEW: Look over the chapter title, section headings, and highlighted or bold words. This will give you a good preview of important ideas in the chapter.** Notice that each major section heading in this textbook has a corresponding **Learning Outcome**. By turning headings or subheadings in all of your textbooks into questions or learning objectives—and then answering them—you will increase your understanding of the material. Note graphs, pictures, and other visual illustrations of important concepts. Pay special attention to the headings and subheadings within each Learning Outcome.

   QUICK TIP! Log in to the CourseMate Web site with the access code in the front of your textbook to find interactive figures and tables from the chapters!

2. **READ: During this phase, it is important to read with a few questions in mind:** What is the main point of this paragraph or section? What does the author want me to learn from this? How does this relate to what I read before? Keeping these questions in mind will help you to be an attentive reader who is actively focusing on the main ideas of the passage.

   It is helpful to take notes while reading in detail. You can mark your text or write an outline, as explained next. Taking notes will help you read actively, identify important concepts, and remember them. Then when it comes time to review for the exam, the notes you've made will make your studying more efficient.

3. REVIEW: Review each section of the text and the notes you made, asking this question: **What was this section about?** You'll want to answer the question in some detail, readily identifying the important points. Use the Learning Outcomes in the text to help focus your review.

A reading group is a great way to review the chapter. After completing the reading individually, group members should meet and take turns sharing what they learned. Explaining the material to others will reinforce and clarify what you already know. Getting a different perspective on a passage will increase your knowledge, since different people will find different things important during a reading.

© Diego Cervo/Shutterstock

Ask Questions

If you are really engaged in your American government course, you will ask a question or two whenever you do not understand something. You can also ask a question to get your instructor to share her or his opinion on a subject. However you do it, true engagement requires you to be a participant in your class. The more you participate, the more you will learn (and the more your instructor will know who you are!).

Take Notes

Being *engaged* means listening to discover (and remember) something. One way to make sure that you are listening attentively is to take notes. Doing so will help you focus on the professor's words and will help you identify the most important parts of the lecture.

The physical act of writing makes you a more efficient learner. In addition, your notes provide a guide to what your instructor thinks is important. That means you will have a better idea of what to study before the next exam if you have a set of notes that you took during class.

Make an Outline

As you read through each chapter of your textbook, you might want to make an outline—a simple method for organizing information. You can create an outline as part of your reading or at the end of your reading. Or you can make an outline when you reread a section before moving on to the next one. The act of physically writing an outline for a chapter will help you retain the material in this text and master it, thereby obtaining a higher grade in class.

To make an effective outline, you have to be selective. Your objectives in outlining are, first, to identify the main concepts and, then, to add the details that support those main concepts.

Your outline should consist of several levels written in a standard format. The most important concepts are assigned Roman numerals; the second most important, capital letters; and the third most important, numbers. Here is a quick example:

I. What Are Politics and Government?
   A. Defining Politics and Government
      1. Politics and Conflict
      2. Government and Authority
   B. Resolving Conflicts
   C. Providing Public Services
      1. Services for All and Services for Some
      2. Managing the Economy
   D. Defending the Nation and Its Culture
II. Different Systems of Government
   A. Undemocratic Systems
      1. Monarchy
      2. Dictatorship
   B. Democratic Systems
      1. The Athenian Model of Direct Democracy
      2. Direct Democracy Today
      3. Representative Democracy
      4. Types of Representative Democracy
   C. Other Forms of Government

Mark Your Text

If you own your own textbook for this course, you can greatly improve your learning by marking your text. By doing so, you will identify the most important concepts of each chapter, and at the same time, you'll be making a handy study guide for reviewing material at a later time. It allows you to become an active participant in the mastery of the material. Researchers have shown that the physical act of marking, just like the physical acts of note-taking during class and outlining, increases concentration and helps you better retain the material.

> Researchers have shown that the physical act of marking, just like the physical acts of note-taking during class and outlining, increases concentration and helps you better retain the material.

WAYS OF MARKING

The most common form of marking is to underline important points. The second most commonly used method is to use a felt-tipped highlighter, or marker, in yellow or some other transparent color. Put a check mark next to material that you do not understand. Work on better comprehension of the checkmarked material after you've finished the chapter. Marking also includes circling, numbering, using arrows, jotting brief notes, or any other method that allows you to remember things when you go back to skim the pages in your textbook prior to an exam.

QUICK TIP! Go to the MindTap Reader eBook in your CourseMate Web site to highlight your notes and access for later study online.

TWO POINTS TO REMEMBER WHEN MARKING

▸ **Read one section at a time before you do any extensive marking.** You can't mark a section until you know what is important, and you can't know what is important until you read the whole section.

▸ **Don't overmark.** Don't fool yourself into thinking that you have done a good job just because each page is filled up with arrows, circles, and underlines. The key to marking is selective activity. Mark each page in a way that allows you to see the most important points at a glance. You can follow up your marking by writing out more in your subject outline.

Try These Tips

Here are a few more hints that will help you develop effective study skills.

▸ **Do schoolwork as soon as possible after class.** The longer you wait, the more likely you will be distracted by television, video games, texts from friends, or social networking.

▸ **Set aside time and a quiet, comfortable space where you can focus on reading.** Your school library is often the best place to work. Set aside several hours a week of "library time" to study in peace and quiet. A neat, organized study space is also important. The only work items that should be on your desk are those that you are working on that day.

▸ **Reward yourself for studying!** Rest your eyes and your mind by taking a short break every twenty to thirty minutes. From time to time, allow yourself a break for doing something else that you enjoy. These interludes will refresh your mind, give you more energy required for concentration, and enable you to study longer and more efficiently.

▸ **To memorize terms or facts, create flash (or note) cards.** On one side of the card, write the question or term. On the other side, write the answer or definition. Then, use the cards to test yourself or have a friend quiz you on the material.

QUICK TIP! Review the electronic flashcards for GOVT found when you log on to the CourseMate Web site.

▸ **Mnemonic (pronounced ne-mon-ik) devices are tricks that increase our ability to memorize.** A well-known mnemonic device is the phrase ROY G BIV, which helps people remember the colors of the rainbow—Red, Orange, Yellow, Green, Blue, Indigo, Violet. You can create your own for whatever you need to memorize. The more fun you have coming up with mnemonics for yourself, the more useful they will be.

▸ **Take notes twice.** First, take notes in class. Then, when you have a chance, rewrite your notes. The rewrite will act as a study session by forcing you to think about the material again.

© Vladyslav Danilin/Shutterstock

TEST PREP

You have worked hard throughout the term, reading the book, paying close attention in class, and taking good notes. Now it's test time, when all that hard work pays off. To do well on an exam, of course, it is important that you learn the concepts in each chapter as thoroughly as possible, but there are additional strategies for taking exams. You should know which reading materials and lectures will be covered. You should also know in advance what type of exam you are going to take—essay or objective or both. Finally, you should know how much time will be allowed for the exam. By taking these steps, you will reduce any anxiety you feel as you begin the exam, and you'll be better prepared to work through the entire exam.

Follow Directions

Students are often in a hurry to start an exam, so they take little time to read the instructions. The instructions can be critical, however. In a multiple-choice exam, for example, if there is no indication that there is a penalty for guessing, then you should never leave a question unanswered. Even if only a few minutes are left at the end of an exam, you should guess on the questions that you remain uncertain about.

Additionally, you need to know the weight given to each section of an exam. In a typical multiple-choice exam, all questions have equal weight. In other types of exams, particularly those with essay questions, different parts of the exam carry different weights. You should use these weights to apportion your time accordingly. If the essay portion of an exam accounts for 20 percent of the total points on the exam, you should not spend 60 percent of your time on the essay.

Finally, you need to make sure you are marking the answers correctly. Some exams require a No. 2 pencil to fill in the dots on a machine-graded answer sheet. Other exams require underlining or circling. In short, you have to read and follow the instructions carefully.

Objective Exams

An objective exam consists of multiple-choice, true/false, fill-in-the-blank, or matching questions that have only one correct answer. Students usually commit one of two errors when they read objective exam questions: (1) they read things into the questions that do not exist, or (2) they skip over words or phrases. Most test questions include key words such as:

> >ALL   >NEVER
> >ALWAYS   >ONLY

If you miss any of these key words, you may answer the question wrong even if you know the information.

Whenever the answer to an objective question is not obvious, start with the process of elimination. Throw out the answers that are clearly incorrect. Typically, the easiest way to eliminate incorrect answers is to look for those that are meaningless, illogical, or inconsistent. Often, test authors put in choices that make perfect sense and are indeed true, but they are not the answer to the question under study.

Here are a few more tips that will help you become an efficient, results-oriented student.

▶ **Review your notes thoroughly** as part of your exam preparation. Instructors usually lecture on subjects they think are important, so those same subjects are also likely to be on the exam.

- **Create a study schedule** to reduce stress and give yourself the best chance for success. At times, you will find yourself studying for several exams at once. When this happens, make a list of each study topic and the amount of time needed to prepare for that topic.

- **Get together a small group for a study session.** Discussing a topic out loud can improve your understanding of that topic and will help you remember the key points that often come up on exams.

- **Study from old exams.** Some professors make old exams available, either by posting them online or by putting them on file in the library. Old tests can give you an idea of the kinds of questions the professor likes to ask.

- **Avoid cramming just before an exam.** Cramming tires the brain unnecessarily and adds to stress, which can severely hamper your testing performance. If you've studied wisely, have confidence that the information will be available to you when you need it.

- **Be prepared.** Make sure you have everything you will need for the exam, such as a pen or pencil. Arrive at the exam early to avoid having to rush, which will only add to your stress. Good preparation helps you focus on the task at hand.

- **When you first receive your exam, make sure that you have all the pages.** If you are uncertain, ask your professor or exam proctor. This initial scan may uncover other problems as well, such as illegible print or unclear instructions.

- **With essay questions, look for key words** such as "compare," "contrast," and "explain." These will guide your answer. Most important, get to the point without wasting your time (or your professor's) with statements such as "There are many possible reasons for . . . ."

- **Review your answers** when you finish a test early. You may find a mistake or an area where some extra writing will improve your grade.

- **Be sure to eat** before taking a test so you will have the energy you need to concentrate.

- **Keep exams in perspective.** Worrying too much about a single exam can have a negative effect on your performance. If you do poorly on one test, it's not the end of the world. Rather, it should motivate you to do better on the next one.

WRITE PREP

A key part of succeeding as a student is learning how to write well. Whether writing papers, presentations, essays, or even e-mails to your instructor, you have to be able to put your thoughts into words and do so with force, clarity, and precision. In this section, we outline a three-phase process that you can use to write almost anything.

Phase 1: Getting Ready to Write

First, make a list. Divide the ultimate goal—a finished paper—into smaller steps that you can tackle right away. Estimate how long it will take to complete each step. Start with the date your paper is due and work backward to the present: For example, if the due date is December 1, and you have about three months to write the paper, give yourself a cushion and schedule November 20 as your targeted completion date. Plan what you want to get done by November 1, and then list what you want to get done by October 1.

PICK A TOPIC

To generate ideas for a topic, any of the following approaches work well:

- **Brainstorm with a group.** There is no need to create in isolation. You can harness the energy and the natural creative power of a group to assist you.

- **Speak it.** To get ideas flowing, start talking. Admit your confusion or lack of clear ideas. Then just speak. By putting your thoughts into words, you'll start thinking more clearly.

- **Use free writing.** Free writing, a technique championed by writing teacher Peter Elbow, is also very effective when trying to come up with a topic. There's only one rule in free writing: Write without stopping. Set a time limit—say, ten minutes—and keep your fingers dancing across the keyboard the whole time. Ignore the urge to stop and rewrite. There is no need to worry about spelling, punctuation, or grammar during this process.

> There is no need to create in isolation. Brainstorm ideas for a topic with a group. Ask for feedback from your instructor or a friend as you prepare an outline and revise your first draft.

REFINE YOUR IDEA

After you've come up with some initial ideas, it's time to refine them:

- **Select a topic and working title.** Using your instructor's guidelines for the paper, write down a list of topics that interest you. Write down all of the ideas you think of in two minutes. Then choose one topic. The most common pitfall is selecting a topic that is too broad. "Political Campaigns" is probably not a useful topic for your paper. Instead, consider "The Financing of Political Campaigns."

- **Write a thesis statement.** Clarify what you want to say by summarizing it in one concise sentence. This sentence, called a *thesis statement*, refines your working title. A thesis is the main point of the paper— it is a declaration of some sort. You might write a thesis statement such as "Recent decisions by the Supreme Court have dramatically changed the way that political campaigns are funded."

SET GOALS

Effective writing flows from a purpose. Think about how you'd like your reader or listener to respond after considering your ideas.

- If you want someone to think differently, make your writing clear and logical. Support your assertions with evidence.

- If your purpose is to move the reader into action, explain exactly what steps to take and offer solid benefits for doing so.

To clarify your purpose, state it in one sentence—for example, "The purpose of this paper is to discuss and analyze the various explanations for the increasing partisanship in Congress."

BEGIN RESEARCH

At the initial stage, the objective of your research is not to uncover specific facts about your topic. That comes later. First, you want to gain an overview of the subject. Say that you want to persuade the reader to vote against a voter ID requirement in your state. You must first learn enough about voter ID laws to summarize for your reader the problems such laws may cause for some voters and whether the laws actually deter voting fraud.

MAKE AN OUTLINE

An outline is a kind of map. When you follow a map, you avoid getting lost. Likewise, an outline keeps you from wandering off topic. To create your outline, follow these steps:

1. **Review your thesis statement** and identify the three to five main points you need to address in your paper to support or prove your thesis.

2. **Next, focus on the three to five major points** that support your argument and think about what minor points or subtopics you want to cover in your paper.

Your major points are your big ideas. Your minor points are the details you need to fill in under each of those ideas.

3. **Ask for feedback.** Have your instructor or a classmate review your outline and offer suggestions for improvement. Did you choose the right points to support your thesis? Do you need more detail anywhere? Does the flow from idea to idea make sense?

DO IN-DEPTH RESEARCH

Dig in and start reading. Keep a notebook, tablet, or laptop handy and make notes as you read. It can help to organize your research into three main categories:

1. **Sources** (bibliographical information for a source),
2. **Information** (nuggets of information from a correctly quoted source), and
3. **Ideas** (brilliant thoughts that occur to you as you research, written in your own words).

You might want to use these categories to create three separate documents as you work. This will make it easy to find what you need when you write your first draft.

When taking research notes, be sure to:

▶ Copy all of the information correctly.

▶ Always include the source and page number while gathering information. With Internet searches, you must also record the date a site was accessed.

▶ Stay organized, and refer to your outline as you work.

Phase 2: Writing a First Draft

To create your draft, gather your notes and your outline (which often undergoes revision during the research

© Digital Vision/Getty Images

```
If you get stuck, get
help. All schools
have writing resource
centers where you can
go for assistance and
guidance.
```

process). Then write about the ideas in your notes. It's that simple. Just start writing. Write in paragraphs, with one idea per paragraph. As you complete this task, keep the following suggestions in mind:

▶ **Remember that the first draft is not for keeps.** You can worry about quality later. Your goal at this point is simply to generate words and ideas.

▶ **Write freely.** Many writers prefer to get their first draft down quickly and would advise you to keep writing, much as in free writing. You may pause to glance at your notes and outline, but avoid stopping to edit your work.

▶ **Be yourself.** Let go of the urge to sound "scholarly" and avoid using unnecessary big words or phrases. Instead, write in a natural voice.

▶ **Make writing a habit.** Don't wait for inspiration to strike. Make a habit of writing at a certain time each day.

▶ **Get physical.** While working on the first draft, take breaks. Go for a walk. From time to time, practice relaxation techniques and breathe deeply.

▶ **Put the draft away for a day.** Schedule time for rewrites, and schedule at least one day between revisions so that you can let the material sit. After a break, problems with the paper or ideas for improvement will become more evident.

Phase 3: Revising Your Draft

During this phase, keep in mind the saying, "Write in haste; revise at leisure." When you are working on your first draft, the goal is to produce ideas and write them down. During the revision phase, however, you need to slow down and take a close look at your work. One guideline is to allow 50 percent of writing time for planning, researching, and writing the first draft. Then use the remaining 50 percent for revising.

Here are some good ways to revise your paper:

1. **READ IT OUT LOUD.** The combination of voice and ears forces us to pay attention to the details. Is the thesis statement clear and supported by enough evidence? Does the introduction tell your reader what's coming? Do you end with a strong conclusion that expands on what's in your introduction rather than just restating it?

2. **HAVE A FRIEND LOOK OVER YOUR PAPER.** This is never a substitute for your own review, but a friend can often see mistakes you miss. With a little practice, you will learn to welcome feedback because it is one of the fastest ways to approach the revision process.

3. **CUT.** Look for excess baggage. Also, look for places where two (or more sentences) could be rewritten as one. By cutting text you are actually gaining a clearer, more polished product. For maximum efficiency, make the larger cuts first—sections, chapters, pages. Then go for the smaller cuts—paragraphs, sentences, phrases, words.

4. **PASTE.** The next task is to rearrange what's left of your paper so that it flows logically. Look for consistency within paragraphs and for transitions from paragraph to paragraph and section to section.

5. **FIX.** Now it's time to look at individual words and phrases. Define any terms that the reader might not know. In general, focus on nouns and verbs. Too many adjectives and adverbs weaken your message and add unnecessary bulk to your writing. Write about the details, and be specific. Also, check your writing to ensure that you:

   ▸ **Use the active voice.** Write *"The research team began the project"* rather than (passively) *"A project was initiated."*

   ▸ **Write concisely.** Instead of *"After making a timely arrival and observing the unfolding events, I emerged totally and gloriously victorious,"* be concise with *"I came, I saw, I conquered."*

   ▸ **Communicate clearly.** Instead of *"The speaker made effective use of the television medium, asking in no uncertain terms that we change our belief systems,"* you can write specifically, *"The senatorial candidate stared straight into the television camera and said, 'Take a good look at what my opponent is doing! Do you really want six more years of this?'"*

6. **PREPARE.** Format your paper following accepted standards for margin widths, endnotes, title pages,

© Izabela Habur/iStockphoto.com

and other details. Ask your instructor for specific instructions on how to cite the sources used in writing your paper. You can find useful guidelines in the *MLA Handbook for Writers of Research Papers*. If you are submitting a hard copy (rather than turning it in online) use quality paper for the final version. For an even more professional appearance, bind your paper with a plastic or paper cover.

7. **PROOFREAD.** As you ease down the home stretch, read your revised paper one more time, and look for the following:

   ▸ A clear thesis statement.

   ▸ Sentences that introduce your topic, guide the reader through the major sections of your paper, and summarize your conclusions.

   ▸ Details—such as quotations, examples, and statistics—that support your conclusions.

   ▸ Lean sentences that have been purged of needless words.

   ▸ Plenty of action verbs and concrete, specific nouns.

   ▸ Finally, look over your paper with an eye for spelling and grammar mistakes. Use contractions sparingly if at all. Use spell-check by all means, but do not rely on it completely as it will not catch everything.

Academic Integrity: Avoiding Plagiarism

Using another person's words, images, or other original creations without giving proper credit is called *plagiarism.* Plagiarism amounts to taking someone else's work and presenting it as your own—the equivalent of cheating on a test. The consequences of plagiarism can range from a failing grade to expulsion from school.

To avoid plagiarism, ask an instructor where you can find your school's written policy on this issue. Don't assume that you can resubmit a paper you wrote for another class for a current class. Many schools will regard this as plagiarism even though you wrote the paper. The basic guidelines for preventing plagiarism are to cite a source for each phrase, sequence of ideas, or visual image created by another person. While ideas cannot be copyrighted, the specific way that an idea is *expressed* can be. You also need to list a source for any idea that is closely identified with a particular person. The goal is to clearly distinguish your own work from the work of others. There are several ways to ensure that you do this consistently:

- **Identify direct quotes.** If you use a direct quote from another source, put those words in quotation marks. If you do research online, you might copy text from a Web page and paste it directly into your notes. This is the same as taking direct quotes from your source. Always identify such passages in an obvious way.

- **Paraphrase carefully.** Paraphrasing means restating the original passage in your own words, usually making it shorter and simpler. Students who copy a passage word for word and then just rearrange or delete a few phrases are running a serious risk of plagiarism. Remember to cite a source for paraphrases, just as you do for direct quotes. When you use the same sequence of ideas as one of your sources—even if you have not paraphrased or directly quoted—cite that source.

- **Note details about each source.** For books, include the author, title, publisher, publication date, location of publisher, and page number. For articles from print sources, record the author, date, article title, and the name of the magazine or journal as well. If you found the article in an academic or technical journal, also include the volume and number of the publication. A librarian can help identify these details.

- **Most professors don't regard Wikipedia as a legitimate source.** If your source is a Web page, record as many identifying details as you can find— author, title, sponsoring organization, URL, publication date, and revision date. In addition, list the date that you accessed the page. Be careful when using Web resources, as not all Web sites are considered legitimate sources.

- **Cite your sources as endnotes or footnotes to your paper.** Ask your instructor for examples of the format to use. You do not need to credit wording that is wholly your own. Nor do you need to credit general ideas, such as the suggestion that people use a to-do list to plan their time. When you use your own words to describe such an idea, there's no need to credit a source. But if you borrow someone else's words or images to explain the idea, do give credit.

- **When in doubt, don't.** Sometimes you will find yourself working against a deadline for a paper, and in a panic you might be tempted to take "shortcuts." You'll find a source that expressed your idea perfectly, but you must cite it or completely rephrase the idea in your own words. Professors are experts at noticing a change in tone or vocabulary that signals plagiarism. Often, they can simply Google a phrase to find its source online. Do not let a moment's temptation cause you to fail the course or face an academic integrity hearing.

TAKE ACTION

A Guide to Political Participation

It's easy to think of politics as a spectator sport—something that politicians do, pundits analyze, and citizens watch. But there are many ways to get engaged with politics, to interact with the political world and participate in it, and even to effect change.

GET INFORMED

Find Out Where You Fit and What You Know

- You already have some opinions about a variety of political issues. Do you have a sense of where your views place you on the political map? Get a feel for your ideological leanings by taking *The World's Smallest Political Quiz:* **www.theadvocates.org/quiz/**.

- Which Founder Are You? The National Constitutional Center can help you with that. Go to **constitutioncenter. org/foundersquiz/** to discover which Founding Father's personality most resembles your own.

- The U.S. Constitution is an important part of the context in which American politics takes place. Do you know what the Constitution says? *Take the Constitution I.Q. Quiz:* **www.constitutionfacts.com/**. Was your score higher than the national average?

- At the National Constitution Center, you can explore the interactive Constitution and learn more about the provisions in that document: **constitutioncenter. org/**.

- Find out what those who want to become U.S. citizens have to do—and what they have to know. Go to the U.S. Citizenship and Immigration Services Web site at **www.uscis.gov/**. What is involved in applying for citizenship? Take the *Naturalization Self-Test*. How did you do?

Think about How Your Political Views Have Been Shaped

- Giving some thought to how agents of political socialization—your family, your schools, your peers, for example—have contributed to your political beliefs and attitudes may help you understand why others might *not* share your views on politics. Have some conversations with people in your classes or in your residence hall about the people, institutions, and experiences that influenced the way they view the political world.

- Now explore how your views on political issues compare with those of a majority of Americans. There are a number of good polling sites that report public opinion on a range of topics.

    o The Pew Research Center for the People & the Press conducts monthly polls on politics and policy issues: **www.people-press.org/**.

    o Public Agenda reports poll data and material on major issues: **publicagenda.org/**.

    o The results of recent polls and an archive of past polls can be found at Gallup: **www.gallup.com/**.

    o The Roper Center for Public Opinion Research is a leading archive of data from surveys of public opinion: **www.ropercenter.uconn.edu/**.

    o PollingReport organizes public opinion data from various sources by keyword: **pollingreport.com/**.

GET CONNECTED

News

Keep up with news—print and broadcast. Remember that different news organizations (or media brands) will report the same information in different ways. Don't avoid certain news sources because you think you might not agree with the way they report the news. It's just as important to know how people are talking about issues as it is to know about the issues themselves.

- One of the best ways to get to the source of the news is to get your information from the same place that journalists do. Often they take their cues or are alerted to news events by news agencies like the nonprofit cooperative Associated Press: **ap.org/**.

- Installing a few key apps on your phone or tablet can make all the difference in being informed. Try downloading the Associated Press (AP) app for short updates from news around the world, as they happen. There are tons of other great political apps—some that are fairly polarized, others that are neutral, and still others that are just plain silly.

Blogs

The blogosphere affords views of politics that may be presented differently than the way the mainstream media do it.

- **Shortformblog.com** provides snippets of news and information from the White House and around the world in small, digestible amounts.

- **Technorati.com/politics** is a great place to explore hundreds of blogs about politics (or anything else you want), rated by political authority.

Social Media

Staying connected can be as simple as following local, national, or international politics on social media. President Barack Obama, Senator Elizabeth Warren, House Speaker John Boehner, and even the White House have Instagram accounts worth following. Most politicians and political outlets are also on Twitter and Facebook.

Check the Data

- It's not always easy to figure out if what newsmakers are saying is accurate. Politifact, a project of the Tampa Bay Times, is a good place to go to get the facts: **www.politifact.com/**. Check out the Truth-O-Meter, and get it on your smartphone or tablet.
- A project of the Annenberg Public Policy Center, **www.factcheck.org/** is a nonpartisan, nonprofit "consumer advocate" for voters that monitors the factual accuracy of what political players are saying in TV ads, speeches, and interviews.

Keep Up During Election Season

- Project Vote Smart offers information on elections and candidates: **votesmart.org/**.
- Nate Silver's FiveThirtyEight features election analysis, in addition to covering sports and economics: **www.fivethirtyeight.com/**.
- Stay connected to the horse-race aspect of electoral politics by tracking election polls. There are many good sources:
    - For a comprehensive collection of election polls, go to the RealClearPolitics Web site: **realclearpolitics.com/polls/**. RealClearPolitics is a good source for other political news and opinions as well.
    - Polls for U.S. federal elections, including state-by-state polls, can be found at **electoral-vote.com/**.
    - HuffPost Pollster publishes pre-election poll results combined into interactive charts: **elections.huffingtonpost.com/pollster/**. During presidential elections, additional maps and electoral vote counts can be found at HuffPost Politics Election Dashboard.
    - Interactive electoral vote maps are available at 270 to Win: **www.270towin.com/**.

- If you have the opportunity, attend a speech by a candidate you're interested in.

Monitor Money and Influence in Politics

The Center for Responsive Politics Web site is an excellent source for information about who's contributing what amounts to which candidates: **www.open secrets.org/**. You can also use the lobbying database to identify the top lobbying firms, the agencies most frequently lobbied, and the industries that spend the most on lobbying activities.

Connect with Congress

You can, of course, learn a lot about what's going on in Congress from the Web sites of the House of Representatives and the Senate: **www.house.gov/** and **www.senate.gov/**. Look up the names and contact information for the senators and the representative from your area. If you want your voice to be heard, simply phone or e-mail your senators or your representative. Your chances of influencing your members of Congress will be greater if you can convince others, including your friends and family members, to do likewise. Members of Congress do listen to their constituents and often do act in response to their constituents' wishes. Indeed, next to voting, contacting those who represent you in Congress is probably the most effective way to influence government decision making.

Check GovTrack to find out where your representative and senators fall on the leadership and ideology charts, as well as their most recently sponsored bills and votes on legislation: **www.govtrack.us/**.

GET INVOLVED

Take an Interest in Your Community— However You Define It. Offer to Help.

Every community—large or small—can use energetic people willing to help where there is a need. Local non-profit agencies serving the homeless, or battered women, or troubled teens often welcome volunteers who are willing to pitch in. You can learn a lot about the public policies that focus on social services while doing some good for others.

The Internet also has abundant resources about nonprofits and charities and how you can get involved:

- **Idealist.org** is a great place to find organizations and events that are looking for employees, interns, and volunteers. Filter by type and area of focus (women, disaster relief, animals, etc.) to find a cause that fits you.

- **Tinyspark.org** is a watchdog for nonprofits and charity organizations. It highlights individuals and groups that are doing good things in communities and around the globe and checks on those who may not be doing as much good as you'd think. Tinyspark also has a podcast.

- **Charitynavigator.org** is another tool for checking on charities. It reports on charities in terms of how much of their donations go to the cause, which charities are in the red, which are worth promoting, and the like—it's kind of like *opensecrets.org* for charities.

Design your own ways to take action

- Are there people on your campus who, because of disability or recent injury, need someone to help carry belongings, open doors, or push wheelchairs? Start a network to match those who need assistance and those who want to help.

- Do you want to raise awareness about an issue? Is there a cause that you think needs attention? Talk with friends. Find out if they share your concerns. Turn your discussions into a blog. Create videos of events you think are newsworthy and share them online. Sign or start a petition.

Join a Group on Campus

You see flyers promoting groups and recruiting members posted all over campus—in the student center, in the residence halls, in classroom buildings. Chances are, there's a group organized around something you're interested in or care about.

Maybe it's an organization that works to bring clean water to remote parts of the world. Perhaps it's an organization that works to foster tolerance on campus. The American Civil Liberties Union may have a chapter on your campus. The American Red Cross may be there, too. You'll find College Republicans, College Democrats, groups organized around race or culture, groups that go on alternative spring break trips to give direct service to communities in need, service organizations of all kinds, groups that serve to create community among culturally underrepresented students, and groups that care about the environment. The list goes on and on.

If you have an interest that isn't represented by the groups on your campus, start your own. Your college or university has an office of campus life (or something similar) that can help you navigate the process for establishing a student organization.

Remember, too, that there are hundreds of political interest groups with national reach. Check out their Web sites to see if you want to join.

Vote (But First You Have to Register)

- You can learn about the laws governing voting in your state—and all of the others—by going to the Web site of the National Conference of State Legislatures and its link to Voter Identification Requirements: **www. ncsl.org/research/elections-and-campaigns/ voter-id/.**

- Register: Enter "register to vote in [your state]" in a search engine. The office in your state that administers voting and elections (in some states it's the office of the secretary of state, in others it might be the State Board of Elections) will have a Web site that outlines the steps you will need to follow. If you need to vote absentee, you'll find out how to do that here, too.

- If you want to view a sample ballot to familiarize yourself with what you'll be looking at when you go to the polls, you will probably be able to view one online. Just enter "sample ballot" in a search engine. Your local election board, the League of Women Voters, or your district library often post a sample ballot online.

- Vote: Familiarize yourself with the candidates and issues before you go to the polls. If you'd like to influence the way things are done in your community, state, or Washington, D.C., you can do so by helping to elect state and local officials, a president, and members of Congress whose views you endorse and who you think would do a good job of running the government. Make sure you know the location and hours for your polling place.

© LHF Graphics/Shutterstock

Support a Political Party

Getting involved in political parties is as simple as going to the polls and casting your vote for the candidate of one of the major parties—or of a third party. You can also consider becoming a delegate to a party convention. Depending on the state, parties may hold conventions by U.S. House district, by county, or by state legislative district. In many states, the lowest-level conventions are open to anyone who shows up. Voting rights at a convention, however, may be restricted to those who are elected as precinct delegates in a party primary.

In much of the country, precinct delegate slots go unfilled. If this is true in your area, you can become a precinct delegate with a simple write-in campaign, writing in your own name and persuading a handful of friends or neighbors to write you in as well. Whether you attend a convention as a voting delegate or as a guest, you'll have a firsthand look at how politics operates. You'll hear debates on resolutions. You might participate in electing delegates to higher-level conventions—perhaps even the national convention if it is a presidential election year.

Work for a Campaign

Candidates welcome energetic volunteers. So do groups that are supporting (or opposing) ballot measures. While sometimes tiring and frustrating, working in campaign politics can also be exhilarating and very rewarding.

Find the contact information for a campaign you're interested in on its Web site and inquire about volunteer opportunities. Volunteers can assemble mailings, answer the telephone, or make calls to encourage voters to support their candidate or cause. Even if you have little free time or are not comfortable talking to strangers, most campaigns can find a way for you to participate.

Be Part of Campus Media

Do you have a nose for news and do you write well? Try reporting for the university newspaper. Work your way up to an editor's position. If broadcast media are your thing, get involved with your college radio station or go on air on campus TV.

© franckreporter/iStockphoto.com

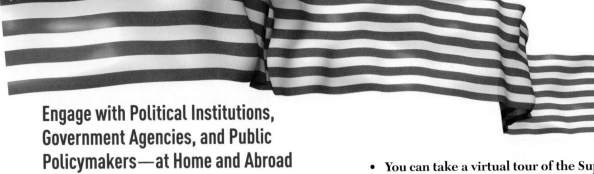

Engage with Political Institutions, Government Agencies, and Public Policymakers—at Home and Abroad

- **Visit the government Web sites for your state and community and learn about your representatives.** Contact them with your thoughts on the matters that are important to you. Attend a city council meeting. You can find date, location, and agenda information on the Web site for your city. And if you're passionate about a local issue, you can even sign up to speak.

- **Check to see if internships or volunteer opportunities are available close to home.** Your U.S. representatives have district offices—one may be in the town in which you live. Your U.S. senators also have offices in various locations around the state. If you plan to be in Washington, D.C., and want to visit Capitol Hill, you can book a tour in advance through your senators' or representative's offices. That's where you get gallery passes, too.

- **Spend some time in Washington, D.C.** Many colleges and universities have established internship programs with government agencies and institutions. Some have semester-long programs that will bring you into contact with policymakers in Congress and in the bureaucracy, with journalists, and with a variety of other prominent newsmakers. Politics and government come alive, and the contacts you make while participating in such programs can often lead to jobs after graduation.

- **If you're interested in the Supreme Court** and you're planning a trip to Washington, try to watch oral arguments. Go to the Court's Web site to access the link for oral arguments: **www.supremecourt.gov/**. You'll find the argument calendar and a visitor's guide. (The secret is to get in line early.)

- **Become a virtual tourist.** If you can't make it to Washington, D.C., for a semester-long program or even a few days, take the U.S. Capitol Virtual Tour: **www.senate.gov/vtour/**.

- **You can take a virtual tour of the Supreme Court** at the Web site of the Oyez Project at IIT Chicago-Kent College of Law: **www.oyez.org/**. And you can listen to Supreme Court oral arguments wherever you are. Go to the Oyez site and check out ISCOTUSnow.

- **Check with the study-abroad office** at your college or university. Studying abroad is a great way to expand your horizons and to get a feel for different cultures and the global nature of politics and the economy. There are programs that will take you almost anywhere in the world.

- **Participate in the Model UN Club** on your campus (or start a Model UN Club if there isn't one). By participating in Model UN, you will become aware of international issues and conflicts and recognize the role that the United Nations can play in forging collective responses to global concerns. Model UN conferences are simulations of a session of the United Nations; your work as part of a country's UN delegation will give you hands-on experience in diplomacy.

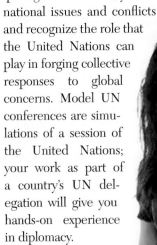

GET INFORMED. GET CONNECTED. GET INVOLVED.

1 | America in the Twenty-First Century

LEARNING OUTCOMES After reading this chapter, you should be able to:

1-1 Explain what is meant by the terms *politics* and *government*.

1-2 Identify the various types of government systems.

1-3 Summarize some of the basic principles of American democracy and basic American political values.

1-4 Define common American ideological positions, such as "conservatism" and "liberalism."

After finishing this chapter go to **PAGE 21** for **STUDY TOOLS**.

AMERICA AT ODDS

© Semmick Photo/Shutterstock

Has Our Government Grown Too Large?

For much of America's history, there was little discussion about whether our government had grown too large. The government, after all, wasn't that big. Since the Great Depression of the 1930s, however, the government has grown by leaps and bounds.

Americans are at odds over the proper size of government. Indeed, the size of government lies at the very heart of the differences between Republicans and Democrats. Republicans have called for trillions of dollars in federal budget cuts over the next decade. Democrats, however, believe that cuts of this size may endanger important programs such as Medicare and Medicaid. (Medicare provides health-care funding to the elderly, and Medicaid provides it to low-income persons.) Following the 2014 elections, both the U.S. Senate and U.S. House were in the hands of the Republicans, while the Democrats continued to control the Presidency. Under such circumstances, arguments over the size of the government should continue for the foreseeable future.

Big Government Must Shrink

Many of those who believe that big government must shrink admit that government programs can help many people in need of, for example, medical care or better education. The problem is that once government programs are in place, they expand. The result is an "assisted society." Opponents of big government believe that too many people spend too much time seeking government assistance rather than taking care of their problems by themselves or with the help of family and friends.

Conservatives argue that government spending must be held back to avoid higher taxes. Even if the government supports its spending by borrowing, it will have to make up the difference by imposing new taxes at some time in the future. The federal budget deficit cannot rise forever, and most Americans know that. Further, the government is inefficient. Private citizens can almost always make better use of funds than the government can, so taxing the people to allow government spending wastes resources. Finally, taxing some people to support other people is just fundamentally unfair.

We Need What the Government Does

Liberals reject the argument that taxation must injure the economy. In the 1990s, President Bill Clinton raised taxes to reduce the federal budget deficit. Conservatives predicted disaster. In fact, America then experienced some of the strongest economic growth in its history.

More generally, liberals argue that we need the programs that a big government can provide. Medicare, Medicaid, Social Security, and national defense together make up well over half of all federal spending. The first three programs assist people who cannot get by just with the help of family or friends. Most of the smaller programs, such as education and veterans' benefits, serve equally important purposes.

Liberals agree that we should do whatever we can to limit wasteful spending and get more "bang" for the taxpayer's buck. But when we must choose between higher taxes and eliminating crucial services, then we will simply have to pay for the benefits we need. We can do this. Until December 2012, when some taxes increased, taxes were lower as a share of our economy than in any year since the 1950s.

Where do you stand?

1. Is big government necessary in times of crisis, such as after the terrorist attacks of 9/11 and during the Great Recession that began in December 2007? Explain your answer.

2. Would you favor a law that reduced the budget of every federal, state, and local agency by, say, 15 percent? What would be the consequences?

Explore this issue online

- The issue of big government divides liberals and conservatives. For examples of conservative views, visit the Web site of *National Review,* a conservative magazine, at www.nationalreview.com. For a liberal take on the issues, go to the Think Progress Web site at thinkprogress.org.

INTRODUCTION

Regardless of how Americans feel about government, one thing is certain: they can't live without it. James Madison (1751–1836) once said, "If men were angels, no government would be necessary." Today, his statement still holds true. People are not perfect. People need an organized form of government and a set of rules by which to live.

Government performs a wide range of extremely important functions. From the time we are born until the day we die, we constantly interact with various levels of government. Most (although not all) students attend government-run schools. All of us travel on government-owned streets and highways. Many of us serve in the military—a completely government-controlled environment. A few of us get into trouble and meet up with the government's law enforcement system. Every citizen after reaching the age of sixty-five can expect the government to help with medical and living expenses. To fund all these functions, the government collects taxes.

In a representative democracy such as ours, it is politics that controls what the government decides to do. As discussed in this chapter's opening *America at Odds* feature, the primary question is: How big should the government be? This leads to other questions, including the following: What combination of taxes and government services is best? When should our leaders use military force against foreign nations or rebellions in foreign countries? How the nation answers these and many other questions will have a major impact on your life—and participation in politics is the only way you can influence what happens.

> "The Ultimate Rulers of our democracy are . . . the voters of this country."
>
> ~ **Franklin D. Roosevelt**
> Thirty-Second President of the United States 1933–1945

Even if—contrary to Madison's observation—people were perfect, they would still need to establish rules to guide their behavior. They would somehow have to agree on how to divide up a society's resources, such as its land, among themselves and how to balance individual needs and wants against those of society generally.

These perfect people would also have to decide *how* to make these decisions. They would need to create a process for making rules and a form of government to enforce those rules. It is thus not difficult to understand why government is one of humanity's oldest and most universal **institutions.**

As you will read in this chapter, a number of different systems of government exist in the world today. In the United States, we have a democracy in which decisions about pressing issues ultimately are made politically by the people's representatives in government.

Because people rarely have identical thoughts and feelings about issues, it is not surprising that in any democracy citizens are often at odds over many political and social problems. Throughout this book, you will read about contemporary controversies that have brought various groups of Americans into conflict with one another.

Differences in political opinion are part and parcel of a democratic government. Ultimately, these differences are resolved, one way or another, through the American political process and our government institutions.

1–1a Defining Politics and Government

Politics means many things to many people. There are also many different notions about the meaning of government. How should we define these two central concepts?

POLITICS AND CONFLICT To some, politics is an expensive and extravagant game played in Washington, D.C., in state capitols, and in city halls, particularly during election time. To others, politics involves all of the tactics and maneuvers carried out by the president and Congress. Most formal definitions of politics, however, begin with the assumption that **social conflict**—disagreements among people in a society over what the society's priorities should be—is inevitable. Conflicts will naturally arise over how the society should use its scarce resources and who should receive various benefits, such as status, health care, and higher education. Resolving such conflicts is the essence of **politics.** Political scientist Harold Lasswell perhaps said it best when he defined politics as the process of determining "who gets what, when, and how" in a society.[1]

1–1 WHAT ARE POLITICS AND GOVERNMENT?

> **LO** Explain what is meant by the terms *politics* and *government*.

institution An ongoing organization that performs certain functions for society.

social conflict Disagreements among people in a society over what the society's priorities should be.

politics The process of resolving conflicts over how society should use its scarce resources and who should receive various benefits, such as public health care and public higher education.

GOVERNMENT AND AUTHORITY

From the perspective of political science, **government** can best be defined as the individuals and institutions that make society's rules and also possess the *power* and *authority* to enforce those rules. Although this definition of government sounds remote and abstract, what the government does is very real indeed. As one scholar put it, "Make no mistake. What Congress does directly and powerfully affects our daily lives."[2] The same can be said for decisions made by state legislators and local government officials, as well as for decisions rendered by the courts—the judicial branch of government.

Of course, a key question remains: How do specific individuals obtain the power and authority to govern? As you will read shortly, the answer to this question varies from one type of political system to another.

To understand what government is, you need to understand what it actually does for people and society. Generally, in any country government serves at least three essential purposes: (1) it resolves conflicts, (2) it provides public services, and (3) it defends the nation and its culture against attacks by other nations.

An instructor helps a college student. *In what ways are college faculty members different from other government employees?*

© moodboard/Corbis

> ## "The thing about democracy,
> beloveds, is that it is not neat, orderly or quiet. It requires a certain relish for confusion."
>
> ~ **Molly Ivins**, American Journalist, 1944–2007

of force (often called coercion), persuasion, or rewards. Governments typically also have **authority,** which they can exercise only if their power is legitimate. As used here, the term *authority* means the ability to use power that is collectively recognized and accepted by society as legally and morally correct. Power and authority are central to a government's ability to resolve conflicts by making and enforcing laws, placing limits on what people can do, and developing court systems to make final decisions.

For example, the judicial branch of government—specifically, the United States Supreme Court—resolved the highly controversial question of whether the Second Amendment to the Constitution grants individuals the right to bear arms. In 2008 and 2010, the Court affirmed that such a right does exist. Because of the Court's stature and authority as a government body, there was little resistance to its decision, even from gun control advocates.

1–1b Resolving Conflicts

Even though people have lived together in groups since the beginning of time, none of these groups has been free of social conflict. Disputes over how to distribute a society's resources inevitably arise because valued resources, such as property, are limited, while people's wants are unlimited. To resolve such disputes, people need ways to determine who wins and who loses, and how to get the losers to accept those decisions. Who has the legitimate power—the authority—to make such decisions? This is where governments step in.

Governments decide how conflicts will be resolved so that public order can be maintained. Governments have **power**—the ability to influence the behavior of others. Power is getting someone to do something that he or she would not otherwise do. Power may involve the use

government The individuals and institutions that make society's rules and possess the power and authority to enforce those rules.

power The ability to influence the behavior of others, usually through the use of force, persuasion, or rewards.

authority The ability to legitimately exercise power, such as the power to make and enforce laws.

1–1c Providing Public Services

Another important purpose of government is to provide **public services**—essential services that many individuals cannot provide for themselves. Governments undertake projects that individuals usually would not or could not carry out on their own, such as building and maintaining roads, establishing welfare programs, operating public schools, and preserving national parks. Governments also provide such services as law enforcement, fire protection, and public health and safety programs. As Abraham Lincoln once stated:

U.S. paratroopers practice in Estonia in July 2014. Estonia, a U.S. ally, borders Russia and has a large Russian minority. *How likely is it that Russia might attack such a country?*

© Sgt. John L. Carkeet IV/U.S. Army Reserve

> The legitimate object of government is to do for a community of people, whatever they need to have done, but cannot do, *at all*, or cannot, *so well* do, for themselves—in their separate, individual capacities. In all that the people can individually do as well for themselves, government ought not to interfere.[3]

SERVICES FOR ALL AND SERVICES FOR SOME

Some public services are provided equally to all citizens of the United States. For example, government services such as national defense and domestic law enforcement allow all citizens, at least in theory, to feel that their lives and property are safe. Laws governing clean air and safe drinking water benefit all Americans.

Other services are provided only to citizens who are in need at a particular time, even though they are paid for by all citizens through taxes. Examples of such services include health and welfare benefits. Laws such as the Americans with Disabilities Act explicitly protect the rights of people with disabilities, although all Americans pay for such protections whether they have disabilities or not.

MANAGING THE ECONOMY
One of the most crucial public services that the government is expected to provide is protection from hardship caused by economic recessions or depressions. From 2008 on, this governmental objective became more important than almost any other, due to the severity of the recession that began in December 2007.

One of the most damaging consequences of the recession has been high rates of unemployment, which have continued into the present, even though the recession officially ended in June 2009 when economic growth resumed. True, the official unemployment rate was about 6 percent in mid-2014, down from a high of 10 percent. Yet large numbers of discouraged workers remained out of the workforce and were not counted in the unemployment figures. The nation's economic problems have doubtless contributed to increasingly negative views about government in recent years.

1–1d Defending the Nation and Its Culture

Historically, matters of national security and defense have been given high priority by governments and have demanded considerable time, effort, and expense. The U.S. government provides for the common defense and national security with its Army, Navy, Marines, Air Force, and Coast Guard. The departments of State, Defense, and Homeland Security, plus the Central Intelligence Agency, National Security Agency, and other agencies, also contribute to this defense network.

As part of an ongoing policy of national security, many departments and agencies in the federal government are constantly dealing with other nations. The Constitution gives our national government exclusive power over relations with foreign nations. No individual state can negotiate a treaty with a foreign nation.

Of course, in defending the nation against attacks by other nations, a government helps to preserve the

public services Essential services that individuals cannot provide for themselves, such as building and maintaining roads, establishing welfare programs, operating public schools, and preserving national parks.

nation's culture, as well as its integrity as an independent unit. Failure to defend successfully against foreign attacks may have significant consequences for a nation's culture. For example, consider what happened in Tibet in the 1950s. When that country was taken over by the People's Republic of China, the conquering Chinese set out on a systematic program, the effective result of which was large-scale cultural destruction.

Since the terrorist attacks on the World Trade Center and the Pentagon in 2001, defending the homeland against future terrorist attacks has become a priority of our government.

CRITICAL THINKING

▶ Young Americans have the lowest voter-turnout rate of any group in the country. Some believe that if voting were made easier, young Americans would turn out in greater numbers. Others believe that America's youth stay away from the polls because they are not interested in politics. What is your position on this issue?

1-2 DIFFERENT SYSTEMS OF GOVERNMENT

LO Identify the various types of government systems.

Through the centuries, the functions of government just discussed have been performed by many different types of structures. A government's structure is influenced by a number of factors, such as a country's history, customs, values, geography, resources, and human experiences and needs. No two nations have exactly the same form of government. Over time, however, political analysts have developed ways to classify different systems of government. One of the most meaningful ways is according to *who* governs. Who has the power to make the rules and laws that all must obey?

1-2a Undemocratic Systems

Before the development of democratic systems, the power of the government was typically in the hands of an authoritarian individual or group. When such power is exercised by an individual, the system is called **autocracy.** Autocrats can gain power by traditional or nontraditional means.

MONARCHY One form of autocracy, known as a **monarchy,** is government by a king, queen, emperor, empress, tsar, or tsarina. In a monarchy, the monarch, who usually acquires power through inheritance, is the highest authority in the government.

Historically, many monarchies were *absolute monarchies,* in which the ruler held complete and unlimited power. Until the eighteenth century, the theory of "divine right" was widely accepted in Europe. This **divine right theory,** variations of which had existed since ancient times, held that God gave those of royal birth the unlimited right to govern other men and women. In other words, those of royal birth had a "divine right" to rule, and only God could judge them. Thus, all citizens were bound to obey their monarchs, no matter how unfair or unjust they seemed to be. Challenging this power was regarded not only as treason against the government but also as a sin against God.

Most modern monarchies, however, are *constitutional monarchies,* in which the monarch shares governmental power with elected lawmakers. Over time, the monarch's power has come to be limited, or checked, by other government leaders and perhaps by a constitution or a bill of rights. Most constitutional monarchs today serve merely as ceremonial leaders of their nations, as in Spain, Sweden, and the United Kingdom (Britain).

DICTATORSHIP Undemocratic systems that are not supported by tradition are called **dictatorships.** Often, a dictator is a single individual, although dictatorial power can be exercised by a group, such as the Communist Party of China. Dictators are not accountable to anyone else.

A dictatorship can also be *totalitarian,* which means that a leader or group of leaders seeks to control almost all aspects of social and economic life. The needs of the nation come before the needs of individuals, and all citizens must work for the common goals established by the government.

Examples of the totalitarian form of government include Adolf Hitler's Nazi regime in Germany from 1933 to 1945 and Joseph Stalin's dictatorship in the Soviet Union (Russia) from 1929 to 1953. A more contemporary example

autocracy A form of government in which the power and authority of the government are in the hands of a single person.

monarchy A form of autocracy in which a king, queen, emperor, empress, tsar, or tsarina is the highest authority in the government. Monarchs usually obtain their power through inheritance.

divine right theory The theory that a monarch's right to rule was derived directly from God rather than from the consent of the people.

dictatorship A form of government in which absolute power is exercised by an individual or group whose power is not supported by tradition.

of a totalitarian dictator is the latest leader of North Korea, Kim Jong Un.

1–2b Democratic Systems

The most familiar form of government to Americans is **democracy,** in which the supreme political authority rests with the people. The word *democracy* comes from the Greek *demos*, meaning "the people," and *kratia*, meaning "rule." The main idea of democracy is that government exists only by the consent of the people and reflects the will of the majority. Figure 1–1, which follows, shows the extent of democracy in the world today—with "democratic" defined as "free."

> "People often say that, in a democracy, decisions are made by a majority of the people. Of course, that is not true.
> # Decisions
> are made by a majority of . . . the people who vote— a very different thing."
>
> ~ Walter H. Judd,
> U.S. Representative from Minnesota 1943–1963

democracy A system of government in which the people have ultimate political authority. The word is derived from the Greek *demos* ("the people") and *kratia* ("rule").

direct democracy A system of government in which political decisions are made by the people themselves rather than by elected representatives. This form of government was practiced in some parts of ancient Greece.

THE ATHENIAN MODEL OF DIRECT DEMOCRACY

Democracy as a form of government began long ago. In its earliest form, democracy was simpler than the system we know today. What we now call **direct democracy** exists when the people participate directly in government decision making. In its purest form, direct democracy was practiced in Athens and several other ancient Greek city-states about 2,500 years ago. Every Athenian citizen participated in the governing assembly and voted on all major issues. Some consider the Athenian form of direct democracy ideal because it demanded a high degree of citizen participation. Others point out that most residents in the Athenian city-state (women, foreigners, and slaves) were not considered citizens. Thus, were not allowed to participate in government.

DIRECT DEMOCRACY TODAY Clearly, direct democracy is possible only in small communities in which citizens can meet in a chosen place and decide key issues and policies. Nowhere in the world does pure direct democracy exist today. Some New England towns, though, and a few of the smaller political subunits, or cantons, of Switzerland still use a modified form of direct democracy.

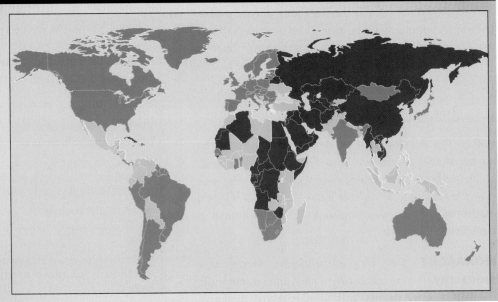

FIGURE 1–1 FREE AND UNFREE NATIONS OF THE WORLD, JANUARY 2014

In this classification of nations by Freedom House, green means free, yellow means partly free, and purple means unfree. Bear in mind that these are the assessments of a single organization. *Why might another organization come up with a different system of classification?*

Sources: Arch Puddington, *Freedom in the World 2014: The Democratic Leadership Gap* (Washington, D.C.: Freedom House, 2014). Outline map adapted from Wikimedia.

These voters are listening to a debate at a town hall meeting in Plainfield, Vermont. Some New England towns use such meetings to engage in a form of direct democracy. *Why doesn't the United States as a nation have direct democracy?*

racy would deteriorate into mob rule. They thought that large groups of people meeting together would ignore the rights and opinions of people in the minority and would make decisions without careful thought. They believed that representative assemblies were superior because they would enable public decisions to be made in a calmer and more deliberate manner.

In a **representative democracy,** the will of the majority is expressed through smaller groups of individuals elected by the people to act as their representatives. These representatives are responsible to the people for their conduct and can be voted out of office. Our founders preferred to use the term **republic,** which means essentially a representative democracy—with one qualification.

A republic, by definition, has no king or queen. Rather, the people are sovereign. In contrast, a representative democracy may be headed by a monarch. For example, as Britain evolved into a representative democracy, it retained its monarch as the head of state (but with no real power).

TYPES OF REPRESENTATIVE DEMOCRACY In the modern world, there are basically two forms of representative democracy: presidential and parliamentary. In a *presidential democracy*, the lawmaking and law-enforcing branches of government are separate but equal. For example, in the United States, Congress is charged with the power to make laws, and the president is charged with the power to carry them out.

In a *parliamentary democracy*, the lawmaking and law-enforcing branches of government are united. In Britain, for example, the prime minister and the cabinet are members of the legislature, called Parliament, and are responsible to that body. A **parliament** thus both enacts the laws and carries them out.

1–2c Other Forms of Government

Monarchy, dictatorship, and *democracy* are three of the most common terms for describing systems of government, but there are others. For example, the term *aristocracy*, which in Greek means "rule by the best,"

Another modern institution with some of the characteristics of direct democracy is the ballot proposal, in which the voters themselves decide a specific question rather than letting their elected officials resolve the issue. Ballot proposals are used in many American states. They include the *referendum*, in which the legislature sends a ballot proposal to the voters. In an *initiative*, a question is placed on the ballot by gathering signatures, not by action of the legislature. A related process is *recall*, an initiative to recall an elected official immediately, before his or her term of office comes to an end. For more about referendums and initiatives, see the *Join the Debate* feature, which follows.

REPRESENTATIVE DEMOCRACY Although the founders of the United States were aware of the Athenian model and agreed that government should be based on the consent of the governed, they believed that direct democ-

representative democracy A form of democracy in which the will of the majority is expressed through groups of individuals elected by the people to act as their representatives.

republic Essentially, a representative democracy in which there is no king or queen and the people are sovereign.

parliament The name of the national legislative body in countries governed by a parliamentary system, such as Britain and Canada.

Join the Debate

Do Ballot Proposals Help or Hurt Our Democracy?

As the text explains, many states offer several forms of direct democracy: the referendum, the initiative, and the recall. The referendum and the initiative allow voters either to make new laws or to amend the state constitution. A referendum is sent to the voters by the legislature. For an initiative to qualify for a state ballot, petition gatherers must obtain a prescribed number of signatures from registered voters. In most states, successful referendums and initiatives are binding on the legislature and on the governor.

Here is a sample of proposals on state ballots in the November 2014 elections:

- Define the unborn as legal persons in Colorado and North Dakota (both failed).
- Abolish cruel methods of hunting bears in Maine (it failed).
- Legalize the recreational use of marijuana in Alaska, the District of Columbia, and Oregon (all passed).
- Legalize medical marijuana in Florida (it failed).

Direct Democracy Is Always Good

State ballot proposals help our democracy by allowing voters to make decisions on public policy issues. Citizens therefore feel—and

are—empowered. Initiatives and referendums are enormously popular with the voters. Initiatives in particular are an important check on the power of the legislative branch. Often, the only effective way to change government is through an initiative. Also, history has shown that citizens take this responsibility seriously. When they are unsure about the effects of a ballot proposal, they usually vote "no."

Finally, lobbyists often have less influence on ballot proposals than they do on state legislation. Consider some current examples. In recent elections, voters have been far more willing than state legislators to legalize medical marijuana. Lawmakers have to fear negative campaigns by a zealous anti-marijuana minority. Voters, in contrast, can decide this issue for themselves. Another example—even in conservative states, voters have regularly knocked down ballot proposals aimed at restricting the availability of abortion. Legislators are much more likely to pass such laws because of the influence of the religious right.

Direct Democracy Can Make a State Ungovernable

The initiative was originally meant as a way for ordinary citizens to make

their voices heard. In reality, it is special interests that have the resources to mount initiative campaigns. In many states, it is impossible to gather enough signatures using volunteers. Proposal campaigns must have wealthy backers to hire the staff needed to gather signatures. Special interests also have the funds to run statewide advertising. Finally, unlike contributions to the campaigns of individuals running for office, contributions to ballot measure campaigns are not limited. All this gives wealthy individuals and special interests too much control over the ballot process.

Often, initiatives require the state to spend money, but do not provide a mechanism for raising the needed sums. California, to name one state, tied its finances in knots for years with proposals that cut taxes even as other proposals increased spending. (True, voters did recently endorse a tax increase proposed by the legislature that eased the situation somewhat.) Americans may hold politicians in low regard, but politicians perform a necessary function—balancing the costs and benefits of all the different things that government does.

CRITICAL ANALYSIS — Could the initiative or referendum work at the nationwide level? Why or why not?

describes a government run by members of old, noble families. Aristocracies have rarely had complete power, but have usually shared power with other forces, such as a monarch. *Plutocracy*, a somewhat similar form, means "government by the wealthy." The term typically refers to systems in which the rich have a disproportionate influence.

A difficult form of government for Americans to understand is *theocracy*—a term derived from the Greek words meaning "rule by the deity" or "rule by God." In a theocracy, there is no separation of church and state. Rather, the government rules according to religious precepts. In Iran, the Council of Guardians, an unelected group of religious leaders, ensures that laws and lawmakers conform to their interpretation of the teachings of Islam.

CRITICAL THINKING

▶ Chinese Communist leader Mao Zedong (1893–1976) once said, "Political power grows out of the barrel of a gun." Are there governments in today's world that tend to confirm Mao's point? Are there forms of government that disprove his statement?

1-3 AMERICAN DEMOCRACY

LO Summarize some of the basic principles of American democracy and basic American political values.

This country, with all its institutions, belongs to the people who inhabit it. Whenever they shall grow weary of the existing government, they can exercise their constitutional right to amend it, or their revolutionary right to dismember or overthrow it.[4]

With these words, Abraham Lincoln underscored the most fundamental concept of American government: that the people, not the government, are ultimately in control.

1-3a The British Legacy

In writing the U.S. Constitution, the framers incorporated two basic principles of government that had evolved in England: *limited government* and *representative government*. In a sense, then, the beginnings of our form of government are linked to events that occurred centuries earlier in England. They are also linked to the writings of European philosophers, particularly the English political philosopher John Locke. From these writings, the founders of our nation derived ideas to justify their rebellion against Britain and their establishment of a "government by the people."

LIMITED GOVERNMENT At one time, the English monarch claimed to have almost unrestricted powers. This changed in 1215, when King John was forced by his nobles to accept the Magna Carta, or the Great Charter. This monumental document provided for a trial by a jury of one's peers (equals). It prohibited the taking of a free man's life, liberty, or property except through due process of law. The Magna Carta also forced the king to obtain the nobles' approval of any taxes he imposed on them. Government thus became a contract between the king and his subjects.

The importance of the Magna Carta to England cannot be overemphasized, because it clearly established the principle of **limited government**—a government on which strict limits are placed, usually by a constitution. This form of government is characterized by institutional checks to ensure that it serves public rather than private interests. Hence, the Magna Carta signaled the end of the monarch's absolute power. Although many of the rights provided under the original Magna Carta applied only to the nobility, the document formed the basis of the future constitutional government for England and eventually the United States.

THE ENGLISH BILL OF RIGHTS In 1689, the English Parliament passed the English Bill of Rights, which further extended the concept of limited government. This document included several important ideas:

▶ The king or queen could not interfere with parliamentary elections.

▶ The king or queen had to have Parliament's approval to levy (collect) taxes or to maintain an army.

▶ The king or queen had to rule with the consent of the people's representatives in Parliament.

The English colonists in North America were also English citizens, and nearly all of the major concepts in the English Bill of Rights became part of the American system of government.

REPRESENTATIVE GOVERNMENT In a representative government, the people, by whatever means, elect individuals to make governmental decisions for all of the citizens. Usually, these representatives of the people are elected to their offices for specific periods of time. In England, as mentioned earlier, this group of representatives is called a *parliament*. The English form of government provided a model for Americans to follow. Each of the American colonies established its own legislature.

POLITICAL PHILOSOPHY: SOCIAL CONTRACTS AND NATURAL RIGHTS Our democracy resulted from what can be viewed as a type of **social contract** among early Americans to create and abide by a set of governing rules. Social-contract theory was developed in the seventeenth and eighteenth centuries by

limited government A form of government based on the principle that the powers of government should be clearly limited either through a written document or through wide public understanding. It is characterized by institutional checks to ensure that government serves public rather than private interests.

social contract A voluntary agreement among individuals to create a government and to give that government adequate power to secure the mutual protection and welfare of all individuals.

philosophers such as John Locke (1632–1704). According to this theory, individuals voluntarily agree with one another, in a "social contract," to give up some of their freedoms to obtain the benefits of orderly government. The government is given adequate power to secure the mutual protection and welfare of all individuals.

Locke also argued that people are born with **natural rights** to life, liberty, and property. He theorized that the purpose of government was to protect those rights. If it did not, it would lose its legitimacy and need not be obeyed. As you will read in Chapter 2, when the American colonists rebelled against British rule, such concepts as natural rights and a government based on a social contract became important theoretical tools in justifying the rebellion.

1–3b Principles of American Democracy

We can say that American democracy is based on at least five fundamental principles:

▸ *Equality in voting.* Citizens need equal opportunities to express their preferences about policies and leaders.

▸ *Individual freedom.* All individuals must have the greatest amount of freedom possible without interfering with the rights of others.

▸ *Equal protection of the law.* The law must entitle all persons to equal protection.

▸ *Majority rule and minority rights.* The majority should rule, while guaranteeing the rights of minorities.

▸ *Voluntary consent to be governed.* The people who make up a democracy must collectively agree to be governed by the rules laid down by their representatives.

These principles frame many of the political issues that you will read about in this book. They also frequently lie at the heart of America's political conflicts. Does the principle of minority rights mean that minorities should receive preferential treatment in hiring and firing decisions to make up for past mistreat-

natural rights Rights that are not bestowed by governments but are inherent within every man, woman, and child by virtue of the fact that he or she is a human being.

political culture The set of ideas, values, and attitudes about government and the political process held by a community or a nation.

ment? Does the principle of individual freedom mean that individuals can express whatever they want on the Internet, including hateful, racist comments? Such conflicts over individual rights and freedoms and over society's priorities are natural and inevitable. Resolving these conflicts is what politics is all about. The key point is that Americans are frequently able to reach acceptable compromises because of their common political heritage.

1–3c American Political Values

Historically, as the nations of the world emerged, the boundaries of each nation normally coincided with the boundaries of a population that shared a common ethnic heritage, language, and culture.

From its beginnings as a nation, however, America has been defined less by the culture shared by its diverse population than by a set of ideas, or its political culture. A **political culture** can be defined as a patterned set of ideas, values, and ways of thinking about government and politics.

Our political culture is passed from one generation to another through families, schools, and the media. This culture is powerful enough to win over most new immigrants. Indeed, some immigrants come to America precisely because they are attracted by American values.

The ideals and standards that constitute American political culture are embodied in the Declaration of Independence, one of the founding documents of this nation, which will be discussed further in Chapter 2 and presented in its entirety in Appendix A. The political values outlined in the Declaration of Independence include natural rights (to life, liberty, and the pursuit of happiness), equality under the law, government by the consent of the governed, and limited government powers. In some ways, the Declaration of Independence defines Americans' sense of right and wrong. It presents a challenge to anyone who might wish to overthrow our democratic processes or deny our citizens their natural rights.

The rights to liberty, equality, and property are fundamental political values shared by most Americans. These values provide a basic framework for American political discourse and debate because they are shared, yet Americans often interpret their meanings quite differently. The result of these differences can be sharp conflict in the political arena.

Corbis Yellow/RF

Elections 2014

The economy may have been improving by November 2014, but ordinary citizens did not feel the benefits. Indeed, the national mood was sour, with worries about Ebola, the ISIS terrorists in Iraq, Russian actions in Ukraine, and racial tensions in Missouri. When the dust settled after the midterm elections and runoffs, the Republicans had gained control of the U.S. Senate with 54 seats to the Democrats' 46. That was a swing of nine seats to the Republicans. In the U.S. House, the Republicans had 249 seats to 186 for the Democrats, a swing to the Republicans of fifteen. These were very good results for the Republicans. In the House, they now had a larger margin than in any election year since 1928. Republicans also did well in the races for governor, and won control of an exceptionally large number of state legislative bodies.

The Republicans sought to make President Barack Obama the issue, and they largely succeeded. Six years into his presidency, the nation was experiencing "Obama fatigue." (To be sure, the president's party historically experiences losses in year six.) Another factor contributing to the results: Republican leaders tried hard to ensure that the party had strong candidates. Weak candidates had been a problem in years past. In 2014, good candidates probably delivered Senate seats to the Republicans in Colorado and Iowa. The Republicans also benefited from the low voter turnout that is common in midterm elections. Low turnout means voters are older and more conservative than in presidential election years.

LIBERTY The term *liberty* refers to a state of being free from external controls or restrictions. In the United States, the Constitution sets forth our *civil liberties* (see Chapter 4), including the freedom to practice whatever religion we choose and to be free from any state-imposed religion. Our liberties also include the freedom to speak freely on any topic and issue. Because people cannot govern themselves unless they are free to voice their opinions, freedom of speech is a basic requirement in a true democracy.

Clearly, though, if we are to live together with others, there have to be some restrictions on individual liberties. If people were allowed to do whatever they wished, without regard for the rights or liberties of others, pandemonium would result. Hence, a more accurate definition of **liberty** would be as follows: *liberty is the freedom of individuals to believe, act, and express themselves as they choose so long as doing so does not infringe on the rights of other individuals in the society.*

While almost all Americans believe strongly in liberty, differing ideas of what, in practice, liberty should mean have led to some of our most heated political disputes. Should women be free to obtain abortions? Should employers be free to set the wages and working conditions of their employees? Should individuals be free to smoke marijuana? Over the years, Americans have been at odds over these and many other issues that concern liberty.

EQUALITY The goal of **equality** has always been a central part of American political culture. The Declaration of Independence confirmed the importance of equality to early Americans by stating, "We hold these Truths to be self-evident, that all Men are created equal." Because of the goal of equality, the Constitution prohibited the government from granting titles of nobility. Article I, Section 9, of the Constitution states, "No Title of Nobility shall be granted by the United States." (The Constitution did not prohibit slavery, however—see Chapter 2.)

But what, exactly, does equality mean? Does it mean simply political equality—the right to vote and run for political office? Does it mean that individuals should have equal opportunities to develop their talents and skills? What about those who are poor, suffer from disabilities, or are otherwise at a competitive disadvantage? Should it be the government's responsibility to ensure that such individuals also have equal opportunities?

Although most Americans believe that all persons should have the opportunity to fulfill their potential,

liberty The freedom of individuals to believe, act, and express themselves as they choose so long as doing so does not infringe on the rights of other individuals in the society.

equality A concept that holds, at a minimum, that all people are entitled to equal protection under the law.

© Ariel Skelley/PhotoLibrary

Young girls celebrate the Fourth of July. *What function does "flag waving" have?*

Property and Capitalism. Private property in America is not limited to personal possessions such as automobiles and houses. Property also consists of assets that can be used to create and sell goods and services, such as factories, farms, and shops. Private ownership of wealth-producing property is at the heart of our capitalist economic system. **Capitalism** enjoys such widespread support in the United States that we can reasonably call it one of the nation's fundamental political values. In addition to the private ownership of productive property, capitalism is based on *free markets*—markets in which people can freely buy and sell goods, services, and financial investments without undue constraint by the government. Freedom to make binding contracts is another element of the capitalist system. The preeminent capitalist institution is the privately owned corporation.

Capitalism and Government. Although capitalism is supported by almost all Americans, there is no equivalent agreement on the relationship between capitalism and the government. Is it best for the government to leave businesses alone in almost all circumstances—or would this lead to excessive inequality and unethical business practices that injure consumers? As with the values of liberty and equality, Americans are divided over what the right to property should mean.

1–3d **Political Values and a Divided Electorate**

Differences among Americans in interpreting our collectively held values underlie the division between the Republican and Democratic parties. Recent election results suggest that the voters are split right down the middle. Elections have often been close. In 2000, for example, Republican George W. Bush narrowly won the presidency in a contested election. Since then, support for the parties has swung back and forth without giving either one a long-term advantage.

THE DEMOCRATS IN POWER Public rejection of the war in Iraq was enough to give the Democrats control of Congress in the 2006 elections. The economic crisis of 2008 then handed Democrat Barack Obama the presidency and gave the Democrats large margins in the U.S. House and Senate. Within a year, many voters had turned away from the Democrats, believing that they had failed to heal the economy and were letting the government grow too fast. In 2010, Republicans took control of the House, gained six senators and six governors, and won control of many state legislatures.

few contend that it is the government's responsibility to totally eliminate the economic and social differences that lead to unequal opportunities. Indeed, some contend that efforts to achieve equality, in the sense of equal treatment for all, are fundamentally incompatible with the value of liberty.

PROPERTY As noted earlier, the English philosopher John Locke asserted that people are born with natural rights and that among these rights are life, liberty, and *property*. The Declaration of Independence makes a similar assertion: people are born with certain "unalienable" rights, including the right to life, liberty, and the pursuit of happiness. For Americans, property and the *pursuit of happiness* are closely related. Americans place a great value on home ownership, on material possessions, and on their businesses. Property gives its owners political power and the liberty to do what they want—within limits.

capitalism An economic system based on the private ownership of wealth-producing property, free markets, and freedom of contract. The privately owned corporation is the preeminent capitalist institution.

REPUBLICAN AMBITIONS Some argue that the Democrats overreached in 2009 and 2010, but the Republicans may have done the same in the following years. For example, House Republicans, many of them aligned with the **Tea Party movement,** proposed changes to the government's Medicare and Medicaid programs that would have made them less generous. (Founded after Barack Obama became president, the grass-roots Tea Party movement opposes current levels of government and taxation, and also resists compromise.) By 2012, many moderate voters were apparently concerned that Republican threats to popular social programs outweighed worries about Democratic fondness for "big government." In the end, President Obama won reelection by a comfortable margin. The Democrats, however, were not able to take control of the U.S. House back from the Republicans.

THE 2014 ELECTIONS In 2014, the fierce antipathy between the parties continued unabated. Public opinion polls reported that increasing numbers of Republicans and Democrats considered the other party to be not merely misguided, but a threat to the very nature of the country. The Republicans had high hopes of winning control of the U.S. Senate, in part because their older, more prosperous supporters might be more likely than Democratic groups to turn out and vote. Still, the outcome of the election remained uncertain. We reported the actual results in the *Elections 2014* feature earlier in this chapter.

1–3e **Political Values in a Changing Society**

From the earliest English and European settlers to the many cultural groups that today call America their home, American society has always been multicultural. Until recently, most Americans accepted that American society included numerous ethnic and cultural groups, but they expected that the members of these groups would abandon their cultural distinctions and assimilate the language and customs of earlier Americans. One of the outgrowths of the civil rights movement of the 1960s, however, was an emphasis on *multiculturalism,* the belief that the many cultures that make up American society should remain distinct and be protected—and even encouraged—by our laws.

Despite the growth in multiculturalism, Americans of all backgrounds remain committed to the values described in the last few sections of this text. Inevitably, however, different groups will interpret these values in varying ways, thus adding to our political divisions. African Americans, for example, given their collective history, will often have a different sense of what equality means than do Americans whose ancestors came from Europe.

RACE AND ETHNICITY The racial and ethnic makeup of the United States has changed dramatically in the last two decades and will continue to change (see Figure 1–2, which follows). Already, non-Hispanic whites are a minority in California. For the nation as a whole, non-Hispanic whites will be in the minority before 2050. Some Americans

> **Tea Party movement** A grassroots conservative movement that arose in 2009 after Barack Obama became president. The movement opposes big government and current levels of taxation, and also rejects political compromise.

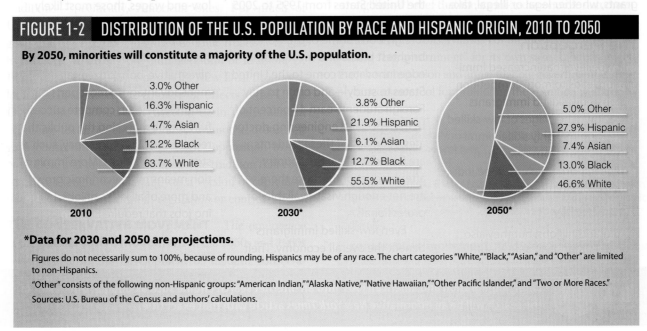

FIGURE 1-2 **DISTRIBUTION OF THE U.S. POPULATION BY RACE AND HISPANIC ORIGIN, 2010 TO 2050**

By 2050, minorities will constitute a majority of the U.S. population.

2010
- 3.0% Other
- 16.3% Hispanic
- 4.7% Asian
- 12.2% Black
- 63.7% White

2030*
- 3.8% Other
- 21.9% Hispanic
- 6.1% Asian
- 12.7% Black
- 55.5% White

2050*
- 5.0% Other
- 27.9% Hispanic
- 7.4% Asian
- 13.0% Black
- 46.6% White

*Data for 2030 and 2050 are projections.

Figures do not necessarily sum to 100%, because of rounding. Hispanics may be of any race. The chart categories "White," "Black," "Asian," and "Other" are limited to non-Hispanics.

"Other" consists of the following non-Hispanic groups: "American Indian," "Alaska Native," "Native Hawaiian," "Other Pacific Islander," and "Two or More Races."

Sources: U.S. Bureau of the Census and authors' calculations.

strong. Libertarians oppose almost all government regulation of the economy and government redistribution of income.

Many ardent conservatives, such as the members of the Tea Party movement, share these beliefs. What distinguishes true libertarians from Tea Party supporters, however, is that libertarians also oppose government involvement in issues of private morality. In this belief, they often have more in common with liberals than they do with conservatives. For most people, however, economic issues remain the more important ones, and a majority of libertarians ally with conservatives politically and support the Republicans.

ECONOMIC PROGRESSIVES, SOCIAL CONSERVATIVES Many other voters are liberal on economic issues even as they favor conservative positions on social matters. These people favor government intervention to promote both economic "fairness" *and* moral values. Low-income people frequently are economic progressives and social conservatives. A large number of African Americans and Hispanics fall into this camp. While it is widespread within the electorate, this "anti-libertarian" point of view has no agreed-upon name.

In sum, millions of Americans do not fit neatly into the traditional liberal-conservative spectrum. We illustrate an alternative, two-dimensional political classification in Figure 1–4.

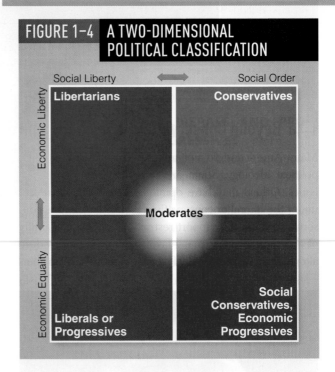

FIGURE 1–4 A TWO-DIMENSIONAL POLITICAL CLASSIFICATION

AMERICA AT ODDS
Key Conflicts in America in the Twenty-First Century

As you learned in this chapter, Americans are united by a common political culture. At the same time, however, Americans are at odds over how much weight should be given to various fundamental principles. We can summarize these most basic disputes as follows:

• **How large should our government be?** *Should it offer a wide range of services, along with the resulting taxes—or should it provide relatively few services and collect less in taxes?*

• *Should businesses be strictly regulated to ensure the common good—or should regulation be minimized to promote economic freedom and growth?*

• *More generally, should we place a greater value on economic liberty and property rights—or on economic egalitarianism and improving the condition of those who are less well off?*

• **How active should the government be in promoting moral behavior?** *Should the government support traditional values—or place a high value on social liberty?*

• **Are progressive or liberal policies best for the nation—or does conservatism provide better answers?** *Alternatively, is libertarianism the solution—or social conservatism combined with progressive economic policies?*

Internet Resources

- The U.S. government's official Web site is a gateway to information on the national government and the services it provides to citizens. To access it, go to www.usa.gov.

- The Associated Press is one of the nation's leading providers of news. Check out its breaking news Web site at hosted.ap.org.

- The Pew Research Center offers survey data online on a number of topics, including American politics and government, the media, Hispanics, and religion. For the center's home page, visit www.pewresearch.org.

- Real Clear Politics collects opinion and news articles and also polling data on U.S. elections. The site is run by conservatives, but it attempts to match conservative opinion pieces with liberal articles on the same topic. See it at www.realclearpolitics.com.

- Founded in 2014, Vox is a useful news site run by Ezra Klein and several of his colleagues. While Vox attempts to offer in-depth news, as opposed to opinion, its politics are without a doubt moderately liberal. Find it at www.vox.com.

- Wikipedia, the giant online encyclopedia written by volunteers, is a valuable source of information on almost any conceivable topic, including politics and government. Note that Wikipedia is occasionally attacked by vandals who insert false information into articles. Such vandalism is usually detected and deleted quickly, however.

STUDY TOOLS 1

READY TO STUDY?

- ☐ Review what you've read with the quiz below.
- ☐ Check your answers in Appendix D at the back of the book.
- ☐ For any questions you miss, read the corresponding Learning Outcome section again to prepare for class and your exam.
- ☐ Rip out and study the Chapter in Review card (at the back of the book).

VISIT WWW.CENGAGEBRAIN.COM:

- ☐ Interactive Quizzes
- ☐ Key Term Flashcards or Crossword Puzzles
- ☐ Audio Summaries
- ☐ Simulations, Animated Learning Modules, and Interactive Timelines
- ☐ Videos
- ☐ American Government NewsWatch

FILL-IN

LearningOutcome 1–1

1. _____ can best be defined as the individuals and institutions that make society's rules and also possess the power and authority to enforce those rules.

2. In any country, government generally serves at least three essential purposes: _____.

LearningOutcome 1–2

3. In an _____, the power and authority of the government are in the hands of a single person.

4. In a _____, the will of the majority is expressed through groups of individuals elected by the people to act as their representatives.

LearningOutcome 1–3

5. The philosopher John Locke argued that people are born with natural rights to _____.

6. American democracy is based on five fundamental principles: _____.

LearningOutcome 1–4

7. When it comes to ideology, Americans are often placed in two broad political camps: _____.

8. People whose views fall in the middle of the traditional political spectrum are generally called _____.

9. _____ oppose almost all government regulation of the economy and government redistribution of income, while also opposing government involvement in issues of private morality.

MULTIPLE CHOICE

LearningOutcome 1–1

10. Political scientist Harold Lasswell defined _____ as the process of determining "who gets what, when, and how" in a society.
    a. government   **b.** power   **c.** politics

LearningOutcome 1–2

11. The system of government in the United States is best described as a _____ democracy.
    a. parliamentary   **b.** presidential   **c.** direct

12. In _____, there is no separation of church and state. Rather, the government rules according to religious precepts.
    a. a plutocracy   **b.** an aristocracy   **c.** a theocracy

LearningOutcome 1–3

13. Which of the following best describes a social contract?
    a. The set of ideas, values, and attitudes about government and the political process held by a community or a nation.
    b. A voluntary agreement among individuals to create a government and to give that government adequate power to secure the mutual protection and welfare of all individuals.
    c. An economic system based on the private ownership of wealth-producing property, free markets, and freedom of contract.

14. Because of the political value of _____, Article I, Section 9, of the U.S. Constitution prohibits the government from granting titles of nobility.
    a. equality   **b.** liberty   **c.** multiculturalism

LearningOutcome 1–4

15. American liberalism took its fully modern form in the
    a. 1960s, during the administration of Lyndon Johnson.
    b. 1990s, during the administration of Bill Clinton.
    c. 2000s, during the administration of Barack Obama.

4LTR Press solutions are designed for today's learners through the continuous feedback of students like you. Tell us what you think about **GOVT7** and help us improve the learning experience for future students.

YOUR FEEDBACK MATTERS.

Complete the Speak Up
survey in CourseMate at
www.cengagebrain.com

 Follow us at
www.facebook.com/4ltrpress

2 | The Constitution

LEARNING OUTCOMES After reading this chapter, you should be able to:

2-1 Point out some of the influences on the American political tradition in the colonial years.

2-2 Explain why the American colonies rebelled against Britain.

2-3 Describe the structure of government established by the Articles of Confederation and some of the strengths and weaknesses of the Articles.

2-4 List some of the major compromises made by the delegates at the Constitutional Convention, and discuss the Federalist and Anti-Federalist positions on ratifying the Constitution.

2-5 Summarize the Constitution's major principles of government, and describe how the Constitution can be amended.

After finishing this chapter go to **PAGE 48** for **STUDY TOOLS.**

AMERICA AT ODDS

© Steven Frame/Shutterstock

Was the United States Meant to Be a Christian Nation?

The Pilgrims sought to establish a religious colony when they landed in New England. In early Virginia, failure to attend Church of England services was a serious crime. By the time the Constitution was written, several states still had established (state-supported) churches. Christian beliefs were strong among the general population in that era. Most Americans considered themselves to be part of a Christian—indeed, a Protestant—people. Anti-Catholicism was widespread.

Yet the Declaration of Independence never refers to Christ. The Constitution does not contain the word *God.* It refers to religion twice. Article VI states: "no religious Test shall ever be required as a Qualification to any Office or public Trust under the United States." The world-famous First Amendment begins: "Congress shall make no law respecting an establishment of religion, or prohibiting the free exercise thereof."

Considering these facts, was the United States meant to be a Christian nation—or not? The answer to that question depends in part on what we mean by "Christian nation."

Yes, America Is a Christian Nation

By *nation,* do we mean a country's government or its people? If we say "people," it is hard to deny that the United States has been a Christian nation. Today, 78.5 percent of all Americans consider themselves to be Christians. Some conservatives, however, have argued that "Christian nation" should mean more than that. Most of the founders, even those whose private commitment to Christianity was questionable, agreed that religion was essential to a just and harmonious society. The founders would have been astonished to learn that public school teachers today may not lead their students in prayer. According to Christian conservatives, students should also learn that America has a divine mission in the world. In this view, constitutional principles are inseparable from Christianity, and the First Amendment means only that the government must not pick and choose among Christian denominations. Limits on "anti-Western" religions—such as bans on Islamic mosques—are appropriate.

The "Christian Nation" Idea Would Violate Our Rights

It is hard to imagine how the founders could have sought to establish a Christian nation when many of them were not Christians at all, in any modern sense. Consider our first five presidents. George Washington never took communion or referred to Christ in his speeches and correspondence. John Adams was a Unitarian—that is, he did not believe that Jesus was divine. Thomas Jefferson thought likewise. It is impossible to say what James Madison and James Monroe believed, because they avoided issues of doctrine even in their private correspondence. Not until Andrew Jackson (1829–1837) did we have a president who openly endorsed Christianity in the way we now expect of political candidates.

Opponents of the Christian nation concept argue that the First Amendment should be interpreted strictly. Whatever the beliefs of the majority, it is essential to tolerate the adherents of all religions—including Muslims and, for that matter, atheists. This is an issue about which the founders were quite explicit.

Where do you stand?

1. Christian conservatives argue that discrimination against Christians is widespread in modern America. Is anti-Christian discrimination a problem? Why or why not?

2. Should religiously affiliated colleges or hospitals have a right to reject health-insurance programs that pay for contraception? Should profit-making businesses have such a right?

Explore this issue online

- For a wealth of information about the religious beliefs and practices of Americans, visit the Web site of the Pew Forum on Religion and Public Life at www.pewforum.org.

- The First Amendment Center is a resource for information on First Amendment issues, including issues of religious freedom. Find its site at www.firstamendmentcenter.org.

INTRODUCTION

The Constitution, which was written more than two hundred years ago, continues to be the supreme law of the land. Time and again, its provisions have been adapted to the changing needs and conditions of society. The challenge before today's citizens and political leaders is to find a way to apply those provisions to a society and an economy that could not possibly have been anticipated by the founders. Will the Constitution survive this challenge? Most Americans assume that it will—and with good reason: no other written constitution in the world today is as old as the U.S. Constitution.

To understand the principles of government set forth in the Constitution, you have to go back to the beginnings of our nation's history.

2–1 THE BEGINNINGS OF AMERICAN GOVERNMENT

LO Point out some of the influences on the American political tradition in the colonial years.

When the framers of the Constitution met in Philadelphia in 1787, they brought with them some valuable political assets. One asset was their English political heritage (see Chapter 1). Another was the hands-on political experience they had acquired during the colonial era. Their political knowledge and experience enabled them to establish a constitution that could meet not only the needs of their own time but also the needs of generations to come.

The American colonies had been settled by individuals from many nations, including France, Germany, Ireland, the Netherlands, Spain, and Sweden. The majority of the colonists, though, came from England and Scotland. The British colonies in North America were established by private individuals and private trading companies, and were under the rule of the British Crown. The colonies, which were located along the Atlantic seaboard of today's United States, eventually numbered thirteen.

Mayflower Compact A document drawn up by Pilgrim leaders in 1620 on the ship *Mayflower*. The document stated that laws were to be made for the general good of the people.

Although American politics owes much to the English political tradition, the colonists actually derived most of their understanding of social compacts, the rights of the people, limited government, and representative government from their own experiences. Years before Parliament adopted the English Bill of Rights or John Locke wrote his *Two Treatises on Government* (1690), the American colonists were putting the ideas expressed in those documents into practice.

2–1a The First English Settlements

The first permanent English settlement in North America was Jamestown, in what is now Virginia.[1] Jamestown was established in 1607 as a trading post of the Virginia Company of London.[2]

PLYMOUTH COLONY The first New England colony was founded by the Plymouth Company in 1620 at Plymouth, Massachusetts. Most of the settlers at Plymouth were Pilgrims, a group of English Protestants who came to the New World on the ship *Mayflower*. (We discussed religion and the Constitution in the chapter-opening *America at Odds* feature.) Even before the Pilgrims went ashore, they drew up the **Mayflower Compact,** in which they set up a government and promised to obey its laws.

The reason for the compact was that the group was outside the territory assigned to the Virginia Company, which had arranged for them to settle in what is now New York, not Massachusetts. Fearing that some of the passengers might decide that they were no longer subject to any rules of civil order, the leaders on board the *Mayflower* agreed that some form of governmental authority was necessary.

The Mayflower Compact was essentially a social contract. It has historical significance because it was the first of a series of similar contracts among the colonists to establish fundamental rules of government.[3]

MORE COLONIES, MORE CONSTITUTIONS The Massachusetts Bay Colony was established as another trading outpost in New England in 1630. In 1639, some of the Pilgrims at Plymouth, who felt that they were being persecuted by the Massachusetts Bay Colony, left Plymouth and settled in what is now Connecticut. They developed America's first written constitution, which was called the Fundamental Orders of Connecticut. This document called for the laws to be made by an assembly of elected representatives from each town. The document also provided for the popular election of a governor and judges.

Other colonies, in turn, established fundamental governing rules. The Massachusetts Body of Liberties protected individual rights. The Pennsylvania Frame of Government, passed in 1682, and the Pennsylvania Charter of Privileges of 1701 established principles that were later expressed in the U.S. Constitution and **Bill of Rights** (the first ten amendments to the Constitution). By 1732, all thirteen colonies had been established, each with its own political documents and constitution (see Figure 2–1, nearby).

2–1b Colonial Legislatures

As mentioned, the British colonies in America were under the rule of the British monarchy. Britain, however, was thousands of miles away—it took two months to sail across the Atlantic. Thus, to a significant extent, colonial legislatures carried on the "nuts and bolts" of colonial government. These legislatures, or *representative assemblies*, consisted of representatives elected by the colonists. The earliest colonial legislature was the Virginia House of Burgesses, established in 1619. By the time of the American Revolution, all of the colonies had representative assemblies. Many had been in existence for more than a hundred years.

Through their participation in colonial governments, the colonists gained crucial political experience. Colonial leaders became familiar with the practical problems of governing. They learned how to build coalitions among groups with diverse interests and how to make compromises. Indeed, by the time of the American Revolution in 1776, Americans had formed a complex, sophisticated political system.

The colonists benefited from their political experiences. They were quickly able to establish their own constitutions and state systems of government after they declared their independence from Britain in 1776. Eventually, they were able to set up a national government as well.

FIGURE 2–1   THE THIRTEEN COLONIES BEFORE THE AMERICAN REVOLUTION

The western boundary of the colonies was set by the Proclamation Line of 1763, which banned European settlement in western territories that were reserved for Native Americans. Note that Vermont, which is cross-hatched, was claimed by both New York and New Hampshire.

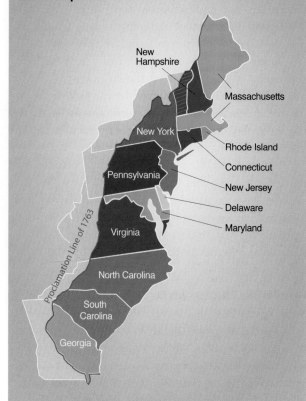

CRITICAL THINKING

▸ When first founded, each of the colonies had very few people. How might that have made it easier to draw up founding documents?

2–2 THE REBELLION OF THE COLONISTS

LO Explain why the American colonies rebelled against Britain.

Scholars of the American Revolution point out that by and large, the American colonists did not want to become independent of Britain. For the majority of the colonists, Britain was the homeland, and ties of loyalty were strong. Why, then, did the colonists revolt against Britain and declare their independence? What happened to sever the political, economic, and emotional bonds that tied the colonists to Britain? The answers to these questions lie in a series of events in the mid-1700s that culminated in a change in British policy toward the colonies. Table 2–1, which follows, shows some major political events in early U.S. history.

Bill of Rights The first ten amendments to the U.S. Constitution. They list the freedoms—such as the freedoms of speech, press, and religion—that a citizen enjoys and that cannot be infringed on by the government.

TABLE 2-1	SIGNIFICANT EVENTS IN EARLY U.S. POLITICAL HISTORY
1607	Jamestown established; Virginia Company lands settlers.
1620	Mayflower Compact signed.
1630	Massachusetts Bay Colony set up.
1639	Fundamental Orders of Connecticut adopted.
1641	Massachusetts Body of Liberties adopted.
1682	Pennsylvania Frame of Government passed.
1701	Pennsylvania Charter of Privileges written.
1732	Last of thirteen colonies established (Georgia).
1756	French and Indian War declared.
1765	Stamp Act; Stamp Act Congress meets.
1773	Boston Tea Party.
1774	First Continental Congress meets.
1775	Second Continental Congress; Revolutionary War begins.
1776	Declaration of Independence signed.
1777	Articles of Confederation drafted.
1781	Last state signs Articles of Confederation.
1783	"Critical period" in U.S. history begins; weak national government until 1789.
1786	Shays' Rebellion.
1787	Constitutional Convention held.
1788	Constitution ratified.
1791	Bill of Rights ratified.

One of these events was the Seven Years' War (1756–1763) between Britain and France, which Americans often refer to as the French and Indian War. The British victory in the Seven Years' War permanently altered the relationship between Britain and its American colonies. After successfully ousting the French from North America, the British expanded their authority over the colonies. To pay its war debts and to finance the defense of its expanded North American empire, Britain needed revenues. The British government decided to obtain some of these revenues by imposing taxes on the American colonists and exercising more direct control over colonial trade.

At the same time, Americans were beginning to distrust the expanding British presence in the colonies. Having fought alongside British forces, Americans thought that they deserved more credit for the victory. The British, however, attributed the victory solely to their own effort.

Furthermore, the colonists began to develop a sense of identity separate from the British. Americans were shocked at the behavior of some of the British soldiers and the cruel punishments meted out to enforce discipline among the British troops. The British, in turn, had little good to say about the colonists alongside whom they had fought. They considered them brutish, uncivilized, and undisciplined. It was during this time that the colonists began to use the word *American* to describe themselves.

2–2a "Taxation without Representation"

In 1764, the British Parliament passed the Sugar Act, which imposed a tax on all sugar imported into the American colonies. Some colonists, particularly in Massachusetts, vigorously opposed this tax and proposed a boycott of certain British imports. This boycott developed into a "nonimportation" movement that soon spread to other colonies.

THE STAMP ACT OF 1765 The following year, in 1765, Parliament passed the Stamp Act, which imposed the first direct tax on the colonists. Under the act, all legal documents and newspapers, as well as certain other items, including playing cards and dice, had to use specially embossed (stamped) paper that was purchased from the government.

The Stamp Act generated even stronger resentment among the colonists than the Sugar Act. James Otis, Jr., a Massachusetts attorney, declared that there could be "no taxation without representation." The American colonists were not represented in the British Parliament. They viewed Parliament's attempts to tax them as contrary to the principle of representative government. The British saw the matter differently. From the British perspective, it was only fair that the colonists pay taxes to help support the costs incurred by the British government in defending its American territories and maintaining the troops that were permanently stationed in the colonies following the Seven Years' War.

In October 1765, nine of the thirteen colonies sent delegates to the Stamp Act Congress in New York City. The delegates prepared a declaration of rights and grievances, which they sent to King George III. This action marked the first time that a majority of the colonies had joined together to oppose British rule. The British Parliament repealed the Stamp Act.

FURTHER TAXES AND THE COERCIVE ACTS Soon, however, Parliament passed new laws designed to bind the colonies more tightly to the central government in London. Laws that imposed taxes on glass, paint, lead, and many other items were passed in 1767. The colonists protested by boycotting all British goods. In 1773, anger over taxation reached a powerful climax at the Boston

An artist's depiction of the Boston Tea party of 1773, when tax protesters dropped chests of British tea into Boston Harbor. *Why did the colonists object to British taxes?*

Tea Party, in which colonists dressed as Mohawk Indians dumped almost 350 chests of British tea into Boston Harbor as a gesture of tax protest.[4]

The British Parliament was quick to respond to the Tea Party. In 1774, Parliament passed the Coercive Acts (sometimes called the "Intolerable Acts"), which closed Boston Harbor and placed the government of Massachusetts under direct British control.

2–2b The Continental Congresses

In response to the "Intolerable Acts," New York, Pennsylvania, and Rhode Island proposed a colonial congress. The Massachusetts House of Representatives requested that all colonies select delegates to send to Philadelphia for the congress.

THE FIRST CONTINENTAL CONGRESS The **First Continental Congress** met on September 5, 1774, at Carpenter's Hall in Philadelphia. Of the thirteen colonies, only Georgia did not participate. The congress decided that the colonies should send a petition to King George III to explain their grievances, which they did. The congress also called for a continued boycott of British goods and required each colony to establish an army.

To enforce the boycott and other acts of resistance against Britain, the delegates to the First Continental Congress urged that "a committee be chosen in every county, city and town . . . whose business it shall be attentively to observe the conduct of all persons." The committees of "safety" or "observation," as they were called, organized militias, held special courts, and suppressed the opinions of those who remained loyal to the British

Crown. Committee members spied on neighbors' activities and reported to the press the names of those who violated the boycott against Britain. The names were then printed in the local papers, and the transgressors were harassed and ridiculed in their communities.

THE SECOND CONTINENTAL CONGRESS Almost immediately after receiving the petition from the First Continental Congress, the British government condemned the actions of the congress as open acts of rebellion. Britain responded with even stricter and more repressive measures. On April 19, 1775, British soldiers (Redcoats) fought against colonial citizen soldiers (Minutemen) in the towns of Lexington and Concord in Massachusetts—the first battles of the American Revolution.

Less than a month later, delegates from all thirteen colonies gathered in Pennsylvania for the **Second Continental Congress,** which immediately assumed the powers of a central government. The Second Continental Congress declared that the militiamen who had gathered around Boston were now a full army. It also named George Washington, a delegate to the congress who had some military experience, as its commander in chief.

The delegates to the Second Continental Congress still intended to reach a peaceful settlement with the British Parliament. One declaration stated specifically that "we [the congress] have not raised armies with ambitious designs of separating from Britain, and establishing independent States." The continued attempts to effect a reconciliation with Britain, even after the outbreak of fighting, underscore the colonists' reluctance to sever their relationship with the home country.

2–2c Breaking the Ties: Independence

Public debate about the problems with Britain continued to rage, but the stage had been set for declaring independence. One of the most rousing arguments in favor of independence was presented by Thomas Paine,

First Continental Congress A gathering of delegates from twelve of the thirteen colonies, held in 1774 to protest the Coercive Acts.

Second Continental Congress The congress of the colonies that met in 1775 to assume the powers of a central government and to establish an army.

a former English schoolmaster and corset maker, who wrote a pamphlet called *Common Sense*.

PAINE'S *COMMON SENSE* Paine's pamphlet was published in Philadelphia in January 1776. In it, Paine addressed the crisis using "simple fact, plain argument, and common sense." He mocked King George III and attacked every argument that favored loyalty to the king. He called the king a "royal brute" and a "hardened, sullen-tempered Pharaoh [Egyptian king in ancient times]."[5]

Paine's writing went beyond a personal attack on the king. He contended that America could survive economically on its own and no longer needed its British connection. He wanted the developing colonies to become a model republic in a world in which other nations were oppressed by strong central governments.

None of Paine's arguments was new. In fact, most of them were commonly heard in tavern debates throughout the land. Instead, it was the wit and eloquence of Paine's words that made *Common Sense* so effective:

> A government of our own is our natural right: and when a man seriously reflects on the precariousness of human affairs, he will become convinced, that it is infinitely wiser and safer, to form a constitution of our own in a cool and deliberate manner, while we have it in our power, than to trust such an interesting event to time and chance.[6]

REVOLUTION AND THE POPULAR MIND Many historians regard Paine's *Common Sense* as the single most important publication of the American Revolution. The pamphlet became a best seller. More than one hundred thousand copies were sold within a few months after its publication.[7] It put independence squarely on the agenda. Above all, *Common Sense* helped sever the remaining ties of loyalty to the British monarch, thus removing the final psychological barrier to independence. Indeed, later John Adams would ask,

> What do we mean by the Revolution? The War? That was no part of the Revolution. It was only an effect and consequence of it. The Revolution was in the minds of the people, and this was effected, from 1760 to 1775, in the course of fifteen years before a drop of blood was drawn at Lexington.[8]

INDEPENDENCE FROM BRITAIN—THE FIRST STEP By June 1776, the Second Continental Congress had voted for free trade at all American ports with all countries except Britain. The congress had also suggested that all colonies establish state governments separate from Britain. The colonists realized that a formal separation from Britain was necessary if the new nation was to obtain supplies for its armies and commitments of military aid from foreign governments. On June 7, 1776, the first formal step toward independence was taken when Richard Henry Lee of Virginia placed the following resolution before the congress:

> RESOLVED, That these United Colonies are, and of right ought to be, free and independent States, that they are absolved from allegiance to the British Crown, and that all political connection between them and the state of Great Britain is, and ought to be, totally dissolved.

The congress postponed consideration of Lee's resolution until a formal statement of independence could be drafted. On June 11, a "Committee of Five" was appointed to draft a declaration that would present to the world the colonies' case for independence.

THE SIGNIFICANCE OF THE DECLARATION OF INDEPENDENCE Adopted on July 4, 1776, the Declaration of Independence is one of the world's most famous documents. Like Paine, Thomas Jefferson, who wrote most of the document, elevated the dispute between Britain and the American colonies to a universal level. Jefferson opened the second paragraph of the declaration with the following words, which have since been memorized by countless American schoolchildren and admired the world over:

> We hold these Truths to be self-evident, that all Men are created equal, that they are endowed by their Creator with certain unalienable Rights, that among these are Life, Liberty, and the Pursuit of Happiness—That to secure these Rights, Governments are instituted among Men, deriving their just Powers from the Consent of the Governed, that whenever any Form of Government becomes destructive of these Ends, it is the Right of the People to alter or to abolish it, and to institute new Government.

The concepts expressed in the Declaration of Independence clearly reflect Jefferson's familiarity with European political philosophy, particularly the works of John Locke.[9] Locke's philosophy provided philosophical underpinnings by which the revolution could be justified.

FROM COLONIES TO STATES Even before the Declaration of Independence, some of the colonies had transformed themselves into sovereign states with their own permanent governments. In May 1776, the Second

> "We have it in our power to begin the world over again."
>
> ~ Patrick Henry
> American planter and politician
> 1736–1799

Three members of the committee chosen to draft a declaration of independence are shown here: Benjamin Franklin, John Adams, and Thomas Jefferson. *What would the British have done if they had managed to arrest these people?*

Continental Congress had directed each of the colonies to form "such government as shall . . . best be conducive to the happiness and safety of their constituents [those represented by the government]."

Before long, all thirteen colonies had created constitutions. Eleven of the colonies had completely new constitutions. The other two, Rhode Island and Connecticut, made minor modifications to old royal charters. Seven of the new constitutions contained bills of rights that defined the personal liberties of all state citizens. All constitutions called for limited governments.

REPUBLICANISM Many citizens were fearful of a strong central government because of their recent experiences under the British Crown. They opposed any form of government that resembled monarchy in any way. This anti-royalist—or *republican*—sentiment pervaded the colonies.

The Impact of Republicanism. Wherever antiroyalist sentiment was strong, the legislature—composed of elected representatives—became all-powerful. In

Pennsylvania and Georgia, for example, **unicameral** (one-chamber) **legislatures** were unchecked by any executive authority. Indeed, the executive branch was extremely weak in all thirteen states.

The republican spirit was strong enough to seriously interfere with the ability of the new nation to win the Revolutionary War. (For example, republican sentiments made it difficult for the national government to raise the funds needed to adequately supply General Washington's army.) Republicans of the Revolutionary Era (not to be confused with supporters of the later Republican Party) were suspicious not only of executive authority in their own states but also of national authority as represented by the Continental Congress. This anti-authoritarian, localist impulse contrasted with the *nationalist* sentiments of many of the nation's founders, especially such leaders as George Washington and Alexander Hamilton. Nationalists favored an effective central authority. Of course, many founders, such as Thomas Jefferson, harbored both republican and nationalist impulses.

Who Were the Republicans? Like all political movements of the time, the republicans were led by men of "property and standing." Leaders who were strongly republican, however, tended to be less prominent than their nationalist or moderate counterparts. Small farmers may have been the one group that was disproportionately republican. Significantly, small farmers made up a majority of the voters in every state.

CRITICAL THINKING

▶ The American colonists did not have the right to elect members of the British Parliament. How might American history have been different if the British had permitted such representation?

2–3 THE CONFEDERATION OF STATES

LO Describe the structure of government established by the Articles of Confederation and some of the strengths and weaknesses of the Articles.

Republican sentiments influenced the thinking of the delegates to the Second Continental Congress, who formed a committee to draft a plan of confederation.

unicameral legislature A legislature with only one chamber.

Confederation had been the lack of an independent executive authority. The Constitution remedied this problem by creating an independent executive—the president—and by making the president the commander in chief of the army and navy and of the state militias when called into national service. The president was also given extensive appointment powers, although Senate approval was required for major appointments. To insulate the presidency from the masses, the position was to be filled by members of an *electoral college*, not directly by the people. For more about the electoral college, see the *Join the Debate* feature that follows.

Another problem under the Confederation was the lack of a judiciary that was independent of the state courts. The Constitution established the United States Supreme Court and authorized Congress to establish other "inferior" federal courts.

To protect against possible wrongdoing, the Constitution also provided a way to remove federal officials from office—through the impeachment process. The Constitution provides that a federal official who commits "Treason, Bribery, or other high Crimes and Misdemeanors" may be *impeached* (accused of, or charged with, wrongdoing) by the House of Representatives and tried by the Senate. If found guilty of the charges by a two-thirds vote in the Senate, the official can be removed from office and prevented from ever assuming another federal government post.

2–4f The Final Draft Is Approved

A five-man Committee of Detail handled the executive and judicial issues, plus other remaining work. In August, it presented a rough draft to the convention. In September, a committee was named to "revise the stile [style] of, and arrange the Articles which had been agreed to" by the convention. The Committee of Style was headed by Gouverneur Morris of Pennsylvania.[15] On September 17, 1787, the final draft of the Constitution was approved by thirty-nine of the remaining forty-two delegates (some delegates had left early).

As we look back on the drafting of the Constitution, an obvious question emerges: Why didn't the founders ban slavery outright? Certainly, many of the delegates thought that slavery was morally wrong and that the

Federalists A political group, led by Alexander Hamilton and John Adams, that supported the adoption of the Constitution and the creation of a federal form of government.

Anti-Federalists A political group that opposed the adoption of the Constitution.

Constitution should ban it entirely. Many Americans have since regarded the framers' failure to deal with the slavery issue as a betrayal of the Declaration of Independence, which proclaimed that "all Men are created equal."

A common argument supporting the framers' action (or lack of it) with respect to slavery is that they had no alternative but to ignore the issue. If they had taken a stand on slavery, the Constitution certainly would not have been ratified. Indeed, if the antislavery delegates had insisted on banning slavery, the delegates from the southern states might have walked out of the convention—and there would have been no Constitution to ratify. For another look at this issue, however, see this chapter's *Perception versus Reality* feature.

2–4g The Debate over Ratification

The ratification of the Constitution set off a national debate of unprecedented proportions. The battle was fought chiefly by two opposing groups—the **Federalists** (those who favored a strong central government and the new Constitution) and the **Anti-Federalists** (those who opposed a strong central government and the new Constitution).

In the debate over ratification, the Federalists had several advantages. They assumed a positive name, leaving their opposition with a negative label. (Instead, the Anti-Federalists could well have called themselves republicans and their opponents nationalists.) The Federalists also had attended the Constitutional Convention and thus were familiar with the arguments both in favor of and against various constitutional provisions. The Anti-Federalists, in contrast, had no actual knowledge of those discussions because they had not attended the convention.

The Federalists also had time, funding, and prestige on their side. Their impressive list of political thinkers and writers included Alexander Hamilton, John Jay, and James Madison. The Federalists could communicate with one another more readily because many of them were bankers, lawyers, and merchants who lived in urban areas, where communication was easier. Accordingly, the Federalists organized a quick and effective ratification campaign to elect themselves as delegates to each state's ratifying convention.

THE FEDERALISTS ARGUE FOR RATIFICATION
Alexander Hamilton, a leading Federalist, enlisted John Jay and James Madison to help him write newspaper columns in support of the new Constitution. In a period of less than a year, these three men wrote a series of eighty-

Should We Elect the President by Popular Vote?

When Americans go to the polls every four years to cast their ballots for president, many are unaware that they are not, in fact, voting directly for the candidates. Rather, they are voting for electors—persons chosen in each state by political parties to cast the state's electoral votes for the candidate who wins that state's popular vote. This system is known as the *electoral college*.

Each state has as many electoral votes as it has members in the U.S. Senate and House of Representatives. Each state has two senators, and the number of representatives it has is determined by the size of its population. There are currently 538 electoral votes.[16] To win, a presidential candidate must win 270 of these votes.

Most states have a "winner-take-all" system in which the candidate who receives more of the popular votes than any other candidate receives all of that state's electoral votes, even if the margin of victory is slight. A candidate who wins the popular vote nationally may yet lose in the electoral college. Many Americans believe that we should let the popular vote, not the electoral college, decide who becomes president.[17] Others are not so sure.

Let the People Elect Our President

In 2000, Democratic candidate Al Gore won the popular vote yet narrowly lost to Republican George W. Bush in the electoral college. Many Americans questioned the legitimacy of Bush's election. This situation could happen again.

The electoral college was designed to protect the interests of the smaller states. Yet the college gives these smaller states a disproportionate amount of clout. Consider, for example, that one electoral vote in California now corresponds to roughly 715,000 people, while an electoral vote in more sparsely settled Wyoming represents only about 174,000. Clearly, the votes of Americans are not weighted equally, and this voting inequality is contrary to the "one person, one vote" principle of our democracy.

The Electoral College Ensures Stability

Supporters of the electoral college argue that it helps to protect the small states from being overwhelmed by the large states. The electoral college also helps to maintain a relatively stable party system. If the president were elected by popular vote, we might have multiple parties vying for the nation's highest office—as occurs in such nations as France, Germany, and Italy.

The current system helps to discourage single-issue or regional candidates—candidates who are not focused on the interests of the nation as a whole. To prevail in the electoral college, a candidate must build a national coalition. Finally, the electoral college vote has diverged from the popular vote in only three elections during our nation's history—in 1876, 1888, and 2000. These exceptions do not justify abolishing the system. There is a relevant saying: "If it ain't broke, don't fix it."

CRITICAL ANALYSIS Do you believe that a candidate elected by popular vote would be more representative of the entire nation than a candidate elected by the electoral college? Why or why not?

five essays in defense of the Constitution. These essays, which were printed in newspapers throughout the states, are known collectively as the *Federalist Papers.*

Generally, the papers attempted to allay the fears expressed by the Constitution's critics. One fear was that the rights of those in the minority would not be protected. Many critics also feared that a republican form of government would not work in a nation the size of the United States. Various groups, or **factions,** would struggle for power, and chaos would result.

Madison responded to the latter argument in *Federalist Paper* No. 10 (see Appendix C), which is considered a classic in political theory. Among other things, Madison argued that the nation's size was actually an advantage in controlling factions: in a large nation, there would be so many diverse interests and factions that no one faction would be able to gain control of the government.[18]

faction A group of persons forming a cohesive minority.

2–5e Limited versus Effective Government

Such American constitutional principles as the separation of powers and a system of checks and balances are not universal among representative democracies. Compared with the United States, many countries place less emphasis on limited government and a higher value on "effective government." The *parliamentary system* is a constitutional form that reflects such values. We describe it in this chapter's *The Rest of the World* feature, which follows.

The Rest of the World

The Parliamentary Alternative

An alternative to our form of government is the *parliamentary system*. Britain—the United Kingdom—has a typical parliamentary system. In contrast to the American system, the British one is based on the *fusion* of powers rather than the *separation* of powers.

First, a Few Basics

Members of Parliament (MPs) are elected just as we elect members of Congress. Here the similarity ends. British voters do not directly choose a chief executive, as we do when we vote for president. Rather, the chief executive is chosen by the lower house of Parliament—the House of Commons, analogous to our House of Representatives. (There is an upper house, the House of Lords, but it has little power.)

Each political party selects a leader well before the general elections. The leader then chooses other MPs who, if the party wins, will take cabinet posts, such as minister of defense or minister of justice. If one party wins a majority of the seats in the House of Commons, it can name its leader as the *prime minister*—the chief executive of the nation.

The Fusion of Powers

MPs who join the cabinet keep their seats in Parliament. The prime minister is both the chief executive of the nation and the leader of his or her party in the legislature. The legislature and the executive are fused, not separated. In contrast, the U.S. Constitution explicitly requires members of Congress who join the president's administration to resign from Congress.

Americans often view the parliamentary system as undemocratic because voters cannot choose the chief executive. Citizens of parliamentary countries do not see the system in quite that way, however. Voters know who the party leaders are in advance of the elections. When they vote, they are choosing a party and its leader. The identity of their own local MP usually has little impact on how they cast their ballots.

What the parliamentary system really does is prevent voters from choosing a chief executive from one party and a legislative representative from another. In America after the 2010 and 2012 elections, for example, Democratic president Barack Obama faced a House of Representatives controlled by the Republicans. That kind of divided government is impossible under the parliamentary system.

Coalition Governments

The parliamentary system does foster a different kind of divided government. It encourages the formation of multiple major parties, thus providing voters with more options than is common in America. But what if no party wins a majority in the lower house of Parliament? Two options are possible. The largest party can form a *minority government* with the acquiescence of other parties. Alternatively, two, three, or more parties can agree to form a *coalition government*.

Many countries that use the parliamentary system are normally governed by coalitions, but until 2010 Britain had not had one for decades. Following the elections in that year, the Conservative Party formed a coalition with the Liberal Democratic Party. The Labour Party then became "Her Majesty's Loyal Opposition."

CRITICAL ANALYSIS **Why is it so hard to form effective third parties in the United States?**

Demonstrators support a 2014 Supreme Court decision. Hobby Lobby, a craft store chain, objected to part of the Affordable Care Act (Obamacare) that requires health-care insurance for certain birth control methods. The Court ruled that the government could not require family-owned companies to provide the coverage if they objected on religious grounds. The chapter-opening *America at Odds* feature described how the Bill of Rights guarantees freedom of religion. *Was the Supreme Court right to extend this freedom to a corporation?*

2–5f The Bill of Rights

To secure the ratification of the Constitution in several important states, the Federalists had to provide assurances that amendments would be passed to protect individual liberties against violations by the national government. At the state ratifying conventions, delegates set forth specific rights that should be protected. James Madison considered these recommendations as he labored to draft what became the Bill of Rights.

After sorting through more than two hundred state recommendations, Madison came up with sixteen amendments. Congress tightened the language somewhat and eliminated four of the amendments. Of the remaining twelve, two—one dealing with the apportionment of representatives and the other with the compensation of the members of Congress—were not ratified by the states during the ratification process.[24] By 1791, all of the states had ratified the ten amendments that now constitute our Bill of Rights. We discuss the Bill of Rights in depth in Chapter 4.

2–5g Amending the Constitution

Since the Constitution was written, more than eleven thousand amendments have been introduced in Congress. Nonetheless, in the years since the ratification of the Bill of Rights, the first ten amendments to the Constitution, only seventeen proposed amendments have actually survived the amendment process and become a part of our Constitution. It is often contended that members of Congress use the amendment process simply as a political ploy. By introducing an amendment, a member of Congress can show her or his position on an issue, knowing that the odds against the amendment's being adopted are high.

One of the reasons there are so few amendments is that the framers, in Article V, made the formal amendment process difficult (although it was easier than it had been under the Articles of Confederation). There are two ways to propose an amendment and two ways to ratify one. As a result, there are four possible ways for an amendment to be added to the Constitution.

METHODS OF PROPOSING AN AMENDMENT

The two methods of proposing an amendment are as follows:

1. **A two-thirds vote in the Senate and in the House of Representatives is required. All of the twenty-seven existing amendments have been proposed in this way.**

2. **If two-thirds of the state legislatures request that Congress call a national amendment convention, then Congress must call one. The convention may propose amendments to the states for ratification. No such convention has ever been convened.**

The notion of a national amendment convention is exciting to many people. Many leaders, however, are uneasy about the prospect of convening a body that conceivably could do what the Constitutional Convention did—create a new form of government.

METHODS OF RATIFYING AN AMENDMENT

There are two methods of ratifying a proposed amendment:

1. **Three-fourths of the state legislatures can vote in favor of the proposed amendment. This method is considered the "traditional" ratification method and has been used twenty-six times.**

2. **The states can call special conventions to ratify the proposed amendment. If three-fourths of the states approve, the amendment is ratified. This method has been used only once—to ratify the Twenty-first Amendment.[25]**

You can see the four methods for proposing and ratifying amendments in Figure 2–6, which follows. As you can imagine, to meet the requirements for proposal and ratification, any amendment must have wide popular support throughout the country.

CRITICAL THINKING

▶ Is amending the Constitution too difficult? Why or why not?

FIGURE 2–6   THE PROCESS OF AMENDING THE CONSTITUTION

What kind of a constitution might a runaway national constitutional convention try to write?

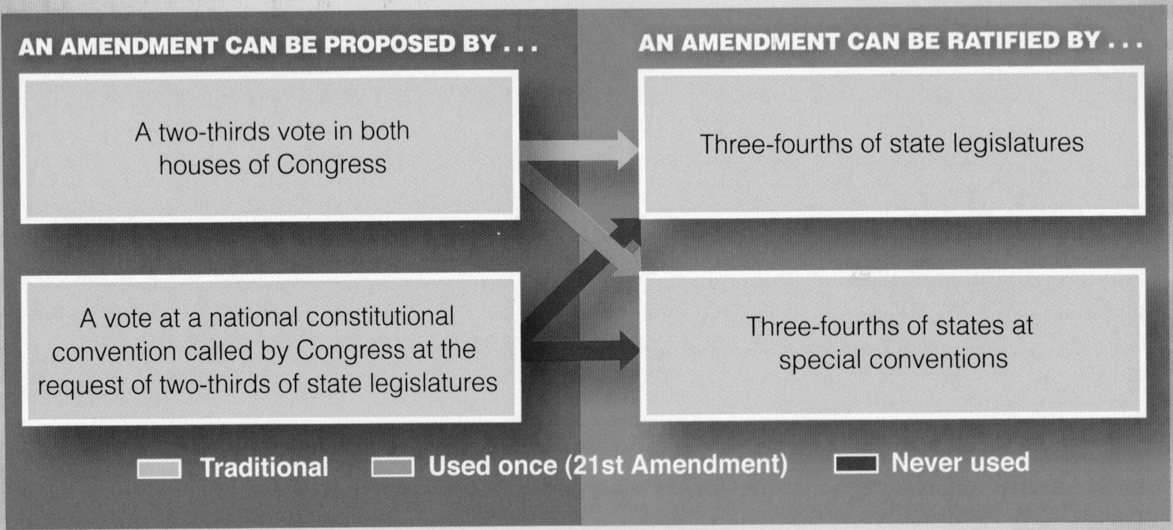

AN AMENDMENT CAN BE PROPOSED BY . . .

A two-thirds vote in both houses of Congress

A vote at a national constitutional convention called by Congress at the request of two-thirds of state legislatures

AN AMENDMENT CAN BE RATIFIED BY . . .

Three-fourths of state legislatures

Three-fourths of states at special conventions

☐ Traditional   ☐ Used once (21st Amendment)   ☐ Never used

AMERICA ★ AT ODDS
The Constitution

Americans engaged in intense disputes about the ratification of the Constitution, as you have learned in this chapter. The most important of these disputes was over the relative power of the states and the national government. This dispute is central to the topic of federalism, which we will take up in Chapter 3. Proposed constitutional amendments have also been the source of many controversies throughout U.S. history. These controversies include the following:

- **The Equal Rights Amendment of 1972 stated, "Equality of rights under the law shall not be denied or abridged by the United States or** by any state on account of sex." The amendment failed to win approval from enough states. *Should it be revived—or are equal rights for women unacceptable because women could not then be exempted from a military draft?*

- **Members of the Tea Party movement have advocated the repeal of the Seventeenth Amendment, which transferred the election of U.S. senators from state legislatures to the people of the respective states. The argument is that giving the choice of senators back to state legislatures would strengthen the relative power of the states.** *Is this a good argument—or is popular election of senators the superior system?*

- **Conservatives have campaigned for a constitutional amendment to require the federal government to balance its budget.** *Would such a measure be desirable—or would it introduce a disastrous lack of flexibility into national finances?*

- **What about an amendment to ban the destruction of the American flag as an act of protest?** *Is such a ban important to the dignity of our fallen soldiers—or would it be an unacceptable limit on free speech?*

Internet Resources

- An online version of the Constitution provides hypertext links to amendments and other changes. Go to www.law.cornell.edu/constitution.

- The National Constitution Center in Philadelphia has a Web page at constitutioncenter.org. The site offers basic facts about the Constitution, including many videos.

- James Madison's notes are one of our most important sources for the debates and exchanges that took place during the Constitutional Convention. These notes are now online at www.thisnation.com/library/madison.

- The constitutions of almost all of the states are online. You can find them by visiting www.findlaw.com/casecode and clicking on the appropriate state.

- You can find constitutions of other countries at www.servat.unibe.ch/icl.

- For information on the workings of the electoral college, visit Dave Leip's Atlas of U.S. Presidential Elections at uselectionatlas.org. An electoral college calculator lets you experiment with possible election outcomes.

STUDY TOOLS 2

READY TO STUDY?

- ☐ Review what you've read with the quiz below.
- ☐ Check your answers in Appendix D at the back of the book.
- ☐ For any questions you miss, read the corresponding Learning Outcome section again to prepare for class and your exam.
- ☐ Rip out and study the Chapter in Review card (at the back of the book).

VISIT WWW.CENGAGEBRAIN.COM:

- ☐ Interactive Quizzes
- ☐ Key Term Flashcards or Crossword Puzzles
- ☐ Audio Summaries
- ☐ Simulations, Animated Learning Modules, and Interactive Timelines
- ☐ Videos
- ☐ American Government NewsWatch

FILL-IN

LearningOutcome 2–1

1. Even before the Pilgrims went ashore, they drew up the _____, in which they set up a government and promised to obey its laws.

LearningOutcome 2–2

2. After the Seven Years' War, the British government decided to obtain revenues to pay its war debts and to finance the defense of its North American empire by _____.

3. The British Parliament imposed several taxes on the colonists, including the _____.

LearningOutcome 2–3

4. The Articles of Confederation established the _____ as the central governing body.

5. _____, a rebellion of angry farmers in western Massachusetts in 1786, along with similar uprisings throughout most of the New England states, emphasized the need for a true national government.

LearningOutcome 2–4

6. At the Constitutional Convention in 1787, the delegates forged the Great Compromise, which established a bicameral legislature composed of the _____.

7. The Constitution provides that a federal official who commits "_____" may be impeached by the House of Representatives and tried by the Senate.

8. During the debate over ratification, the Anti-Federalists argued that the Constitution needed a _____ because a strong national government might take away the political rights won during the American Revolution.

LearningOutcome 2–5

9. The principle of dividing governmental powers among the legislative, the executive, and the judicial branches of government is known as the _____.

10. Among the checks and balances built into the American system of government is the court's power of _____.

MULTIPLE CHOICE

LearningOutcome 2–1

11. The majority of American colonists came from
    a. Germany and Spain.
    b. France and Ireland.
    c. England and Scotland.

LearningOutcome 2–2

12. Before the mid-1700s, the majority of American colonists were
    a. secretly planning to declare their independence from Britain.
    b. loyal to the British monarch and viewed Britain as their homeland.
    c. loyal to France.

LearningOutcome 2–3

13. Under the Articles of Confederation, the new nation
    a. could not declare war.
    b. could enter into treaties and alliances.
    c. regulated interstate commerce.

LearningOutcome 2–4

14. The three-fifths compromise reached at the Constitutional Convention had to do with
    a. how slaves would be counted in determining representation in Congress.
    b. the imposition of export taxes.
    c. the regulation of commerce.

LearningOutcome 2–5

15. All of the existing amendments to the Constitution have been proposed
    a. by a two-thirds vote in the Senate and in the House of Representatives.
    b. by a vote in three-fourths of the state legislatures.
    c. at national constitutional conventions.

WHY CHOOSE?

Every 4LTR Press solution comes complete with a visually engaging textbook in addition to an interactive eBook. Go to CourseMate for **GOVT7** to begin using the eBook. Access at **www.cengagebrain.com**

INTRODUCTION

Clearly, those who work for the national government would like the states to cooperate fully in the implementation of national policies. At the same time, those who work in state government don't like to be told what to do by the national government, especially when the implementation of a national policy is costly for the states. (Sometimes, this attitude can lead to unrealistic proposals, such as the one described in the chapter-opening *America at Odds* feature.) Finally, those who work in local governments would like to run their affairs with the least amount of interference from both their state governments and the national government.

Such conflicts arise because our government is based on the principle of **federalism,** which means that government powers are shared by the national government and the states. When the founders of this nation opted for federalism, they created a practical and flexible form of government capable of enduring for centuries. At the same time, however, they planted the seeds for future conflict between the states and the national government over how government powers should be shared. As you will read in this chapter—and throughout this book—many of today's most pressing issues have to do with which level of government should exercise certain powers.

3-1 FEDERALISM AND ITS ALTERNATIVES

> **LO** Explain what federalism means, how federalism differs from other systems of government, and why it exists in the United States.

There are various ways of ordering relations between central governments and local units. Federalism is one of these ways. Learning about federalism and how it differs from other forms of government is important to understanding the American political system.

3-1a What Is Federalism?

Nowhere in the Constitution does the word *federalism* appear. This is understandable, given that the concept of

federalism A system of shared sovereignty between two levels of government—one national and one subnational—occupying the same geographic region.

federalism was an invention of the founders. Since the Federalists and the Anti-Federalists argued more than two hundred years ago about what form of government we should have, hundreds of definitions of federalism have been offered. Basically, as mentioned in Chapter 2, government powers in a *federal system* are divided between a central government and regional, or subdivisional, governments.

DEFINING *FEDERALISM* Although the definition given here seems straightforward, its application certainly is not. After all, almost all nations—even the most repressive totalitarian regimes—have some kind of subnational governmental units. Thus, the existence of national and subnational governmental units by itself does not make a system federal. *For a system to be truly federal, the powers of both the national units and the subnational units must be specified and limited.*

Under true federalism, individuals are governed by two separate governmental authorities (national and state authorities) whose expressly designated powers cannot be altered without changing the fundamental nature of the system—for example, by amending a written constitution. Table 3–1, which follows, lists some of the countries that have a federal system of government.[3]

TABLE 3-1 COUNTRIES THAT HAVE A FEDERAL SYSTEM TODAY	
What influence might the example of the United States have had on the adoption of federal systems in other countries?	
Country	**Population (in Millions)**
Argentina	42.7
Australia	23.6
Austria	8.5
Brazil	202.9
Canada	35.4
Ethiopia	88.0
Germany	80.7
India	1,247.1
Malaysia	30.2
Mexico	119.7
Nigeria	172.5
Pakistan	188.0
Switzerland	8.2
United States	318.4

Source: Official estimates by governments of the listed nations or by the United Nations.

U.S. FEDERALISM IN PRACTICE Federalism in theory is one thing—federalism in practice is another. As you will read shortly, the Constitution sets forth specific powers that can be exercised by the national government and provides that the national government has the implied power to undertake actions necessary to carry out its expressly designated powers. All other powers are "reserved" to the states. The broad language of the Constitution, though, has left much room for debate over the specific nature and scope of certain powers, such as the national government's implied powers and the powers reserved to the states. Thus, the actual workings of our federal form of government have depended, to a great extent, on the historical application of the broad principles outlined in the Constitution.

To further complicate matters, the term *federal government,* as it is used today, refers to the national, or central, government. When individuals talk of the federal government, they mean the national government based in Washington, D.C. They are *not* referring to the federal *system* of government, which is made up of both the national government and the state governments.

3–1b Alternatives to Federalism

Perhaps an easier way to define federalism is to discuss what it is *not.* Most of the nations in the world today have a **unitary system** of government. In such a system, the constitution vests all powers in the national government. If the national government so chooses, it can delegate certain activities to subnational units. The reverse is also true: the national government can take away, at will, powers delegated to subnational governmental units. In a unitary system, any subnational government is a "creature of the national government." The governments of Britain, France, Israel, Japan, and the Philippines are examples of unitary systems.

In the United States, because the Constitution does not mention local governments (cities and counties), we say that city and county governmental units are "creatures of state government." That means that state governments can—and do—both give powers to and take powers from local governments.

The Articles of Confederation, discussed in Chapter 2, created a confederal system. In a **confederal system,** the national government exists and operates only at the direction of the subnational governments. Few true confederal systems are in existence today, although some people contend that the European Union—a group of twenty-eight European nations that has established many common institutions—qualifies as such a system.

3–1c Federalism—An Optimal Choice for the United States?

The Articles of Confederation failed because they did not allow for a sufficiently strong central government. The framers of the Constitution, however, were fearful of tyranny and a too-powerful central government. The outcome had to be a compromise—a federal system.

The appeal of federalism was that it retained state powers and local traditions while establishing a strong national government capable of handling common problems, such as national defense. A federal form of government also furthered the goal of creating a division of powers (to be discussed shortly). There are other reasons why the founders opted for a federal system, and a federal structure of government continues to offer many advantages (as well as some disadvantages) for U.S. citizens.

ADVANTAGES OF FEDERALISM: SIZE One of the reasons a federal form of government is well suited to the United States is our country's large size. Even in the days when the United States consisted of only thirteen states, its geographic area was larger than that of England or France. In those days, travel was slow and communication was difficult, so people in outlying areas were isolated. The news of any particular political decision could take several weeks to reach everyone. Therefore, even if the framers of the Constitution had wanted a more centralized system (which most of them did not), such a system would have been unworkable.

Look at Figure 3–1, which follows. As you can see, to a great extent the practical business of governing this country takes place in state and local governmental units. Indeed, the most common type of governmental unit in the United States is the special district, which is generally concerned with a specific issue such as solid waste disposal, mass transportation, or fire protection.

Often, the jurisdiction of special districts crosses the boundaries of other governmental units, such as cities or counties. Special districts also tend to have fewer restrictions than other local governments as to how much debt they can incur and so are created to finance large building projects.

unitary system A centralized governmental system in which local or subdivisional governments exercise only those powers given to them by the central government.

confederal system A league of independent sovereign states, joined together by a central government that has only limited powers over them.

FIGURE 3–1 GOVERNMENTAL UNITS IN THE UNITED STATES TODAY

How could the number of governments in the United States create problems for voters?

THE NUMBER OF GOVERNMENTS IN THE UNITED STATES TODAY

Government	Number
Federal government	1
State governments and District of Columbia	51
Local governments	
Counties	3,031
Municipalities (mainly cities or towns)	19,522
Townships (less extensive powers)	16,364
Special districts (water, sewer, and so on)	37,203
School districts	12,884
Subtotal local governments	89,004
Total	**89,056**

PERCENTAGE OF ALL GOVERNMENTS IN THE UNITED STATES TODAY

Townships 18.4%
School districts 14.5%
Counties 3.4%
States (& D.C.) 0.06%
Federal 0.001%

Municipalities 21.9%
Special districts 41.8%

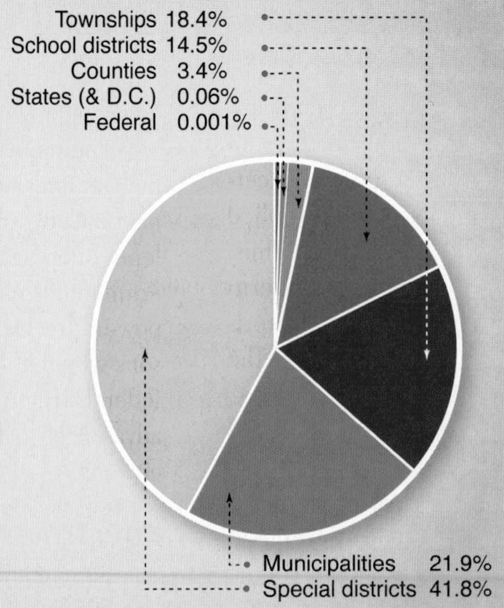

Source: U.S. Census Bureau, 2012

ADVANTAGES OF FEDERALISM: EXPERIMENTATION

The existence of numerous government subunits in the United States also makes it possible to experiment with innovative policies and programs at the state or local level. Many observers, including Supreme Court justice Louis Brandeis (1856–1941), have emphasized that in a federal system, state governments can act as "laboratories" for public-policy experimentation. For example, many states have adopted minimum-wage laws that establish a higher minimum wage than the one set by national legislation. State governments also have a wide variety of policies on how or whether state employees can form labor unions.

Depending on the outcome of a specific experiment, other states may (or may not) implement similar programs. State innovations can also serve as models for federal programs. For instance, California was a pioneer in air-pollution control. Many of that state's regulations were later adapted by other states and eventually by the federal government.

ADVANTAGES OF FEDERALISM: SUBCULTURES

We have always been a nation of different political subcultures. The Pilgrims who founded New England were different from the settlers who established the agricultural society of the South. Both of these groups were different from those who populated the Middle Atlantic states.

The groups that founded New England had a religious focus, while those who populated the Middle Atlantic states were more business oriented. Those who settled in the South were more individualistic than the other groups. That is, they were less inclined to act as a collective and more inclined to act independently of each other. A federal system of government allows the political and cultural interests of regional groups to be reflected in the laws governing those groups.

As we noted earlier, nations other than the United States have benefited from the principle of federalism. One of them is Canada. Because federalism permits the expression of varying regional cultures, Canadian federalism naturally differs from the American version, as you will discover in this chapter's *The Rest of the World* feature, which follows.

SOME DRAWBACKS TO FEDERALISM

Federalism offers many advantages, but it also has some drawbacks. Consider that although federalism in many ways promotes greater self-rule, or democracy, some scholars point out that local self-rule may not always be in society's best interests. These observers argue that the smaller the political unit, the higher the probability that it will be dominated by a single political group, which may or may not be concerned with the welfare of many of the local unit's citizens. For example, entrenched segregationist politicians in southern states denied African Americans their civil rights and voting rights for decades, as we discuss further in Chapter 5.

Powerful state and local interests can block progress and impede national plans. State and local interests often diverge from those of the national government. For example, several of the states have recently been at odds with the national government over implementing health-care reform. Finding acceptable solutions to such conflicts has not always been easy. Indeed, as will be discussed shortly, in the 1860s, war—not politics—decided the outcome of a struggle over states' rights.

The Rest of the World

Canadian versus American Federalism

By land area, Canada is the second-largest country in the world. Physically, the country seems designed for a federal system of government. And indeed, Canada has a federal system similar in some ways to that of the United States—but also with some big differences. When the 1867 Constitution Act created modern Canada, the United States had just concluded the Civil War. Canada's founders blamed that war on the weakness of the U.S. central government. Therefore, the Canadian Constitution gave far more power to the central government than did the U.S. Constitution.

The Powers of Lower-Level Governments

Our lower levels of government are called states, whereas in Canada they are called provinces. Right there, the powers of the central government are emphasized. The word *state* implies sovereignty. A *province,* however, is never sovereign and is typically set up for the convenience of the central government.

In the United States, the powers of the national government are limited to those listed in the Constitution. In the Canadian Constitution, it is the powers of the provinces that are limited by a list. The Tenth Amendment to the U.S. Constitution reserves residual powers to the states or to the people. In Canada, residual powers rest with the national government. Under the 1867 Canadian Constitution, the central government could veto any provincial legislation. No such clause appears in the U.S. Constitution.

The Provinces Gain Strength

Over time, the powers of the U.S. federal government grew at the expense of the states. The opposite happened in Canada. By the end of the nineteenth century, the Canadian government in practice had abandoned the power to veto provincial legislation. The Great Depression of the 1930s strengthened the national government in the United States. In Canada, it strengthened the provinces.

Two Languages

Another striking difference between Canada and the United States is that Canada has two national languages. A majority of Canadians speak English, but most of the population of Québec speak French. The Parti Québécois (PQ), which wants Québec to be a separate country, gained power in that province in 1976 and 1994. Both times, it held referendums on whether Québec should demand "sovereignty-association," a euphemism for independence. In 1995, the PQ almost obtained a majority vote for its position. The PQ returned to power in 2012 but without enough votes to hold another referendum. In 2014, it was defeated by the Liberal Party. Nevertheless, the possibility exists that Canada could actually break apart someday.

CRITICAL ANALYSIS The Canadian Constitution is based on the principles of "peace, order, and good government." Contrast that phrase with the words in the Declaration of Independence—"life, liberty, and the pursuit of happiness." How do the statements differ?

Federalism has other drawbacks as well. One of them is the lack of uniformity of state laws, which can complicate business transactions that cross state borders. Another problem is the difficulty of coordinating government policies at the national, state, and local levels. Additionally, the simultaneous regulation of business by all levels of government creates red tape that imposes substantial costs on the business community.

In a federal system, there is always the danger that national power will be expanded at the expense of the states. President Ronald Reagan (1981–1989) once said, "The Founding Fathers saw the federalist system as constructed something like a masonry wall. The States are the bricks, the national government is the mortar. . . . Unfortunately, over the years, many people have increasingly come to believe that Washington is the whole wall."[4]

3–2 THE CONSTITUTIONAL DIVISION OF POWERS

LO Indicate how the Constitution divides governing powers in our federal system.

The founders created a federal form of government by dividing sovereign powers into powers that could be exercised by the national government and powers that were reserved to the states. Although there is no systematic explanation of this **division of powers** between the national and state governments, the original Constitution, along with its amendments, provides statements on what the national and state governments can (and cannot) do.

3–2a The Powers of the National Government

The Constitution delegates certain powers to the national government. It also prohibits the national government from exercising certain powers.

POWERS DELEGATED TO THE NATIONAL GOVERNMENT The national government possesses three types of powers: expressed powers, implied powers, and inherent powers.

division of powers A basic principle of federalism established by the U.S. Constitution, by which powers are divided between the national and state governments.

expressed powers Constitutional or statutory powers that are expressly provided for by the U.S. Constitution; also called *enumerated powers.*

implied powers The powers of the federal government that are implied by the expressed powers in the Constitution, particularly in Article I, Section 8.

necessary and proper clause Article I, Section 8, Clause 18, of the Constitution, which gives Congress the power to make all laws "necessary and proper" for the federal government to carry out its responsibilities; also called the *elastic clause.*

inherent powers The powers of the national government that, although not always expressly granted by the Constitution, are necessary to ensure the nation's integrity and survival as a political unit.

Expressed Powers. Article I, Section 8, of the Constitution expressly enumerates twenty-seven powers that Congress may exercise. Two of these **expressed powers,** or *enumerated powers,* are the power to coin money and the power to regulate interstate commerce. Constitutional amendments have provided for other expressed powers. For example, the Sixteenth Amendment, added in 1913, gives Congress the power to impose a federal income tax.

One power expressly granted to the national government is the right to regulate commerce not only among the states, but also "with the Indian Tribes." As a result, relations between Native American tribal governments and the rest of the country have always been a national responsibility. A further consequence is that state governments face significant limits on their authority over Indian reservations within their borders.

Implied Powers. The constitutional basis for the **implied powers** of the national government is found in Article I, Section 8, Clause 18, often called the **necessary and proper clause.** This clause states that Congress has the power to make "all Laws which shall be necessary and proper for carrying into Execution the foregoing [expressed] Powers, and all other Powers vested by this Constitution in the Government of the United States, or in any Department or Officer thereof." The necessary and proper clause is often referred to as the *elastic clause,* because it gives elasticity to our constitutional system.

Inherent Powers. The national government also enjoys certain **inherent powers**—powers that governments must have simply to ensure the nation's integrity and survival as a political unit. For example, any national government must have the inherent ability to make treaties, regulate immigration, acquire territory, wage war, and make peace. While some inherent powers are also enumerated in the Constitution, such as the powers to wage war and make treaties, others are not. For example, the Constitution does not speak of regulating immigration or acquiring new territory. Although the national government's inherent powers are few, they are important.

Federal Lands. One inherent power is older than the Constitution itself—the power to own land. The United States collectively owned various western lands under the Articles of Confederation. The Northwest Territory, which included the modern states of Illinois, Indiana, Michigan, Ohio, Wisconsin, and part of Minnesota, joined United States' lands together with lands given up by New York and Virginia. The Northwest Territory

> # "The great difficulty lies in this:
> you must first enable the government to control the governed; and in the next place, oblige it to control itself."
>
> ~ **James Madison,** Fourth President of the United States 1809–1817

was organized during the ratification of the Constitution. Indeed, establishing the territory as the collective property of the entire Union was necessary to secure support for ratification in several states, including Maryland.

The United States then sold land to new settlers—land sales were a major source of national government income throughout much of the 1800s. To this day, the national government owns most of the acres in many far western states, a fact that annoys many Westerners.

POWERS PROHIBITED TO THE NATIONAL GOVERNMENT
The Constitution expressly prohibits the national government from undertaking certain actions, such as imposing taxes on exports, and from passing laws restraining certain liberties, such as the freedom of speech or religion. Most of these prohibited powers are listed in Article I, Section 9, and in the first eight amendments to the Constitution. Additionally, the national government is implicitly prohibited from exercising certain powers. For example, most authorities believe that the federal government does not have the power to create a national public school system, because such power is not included among those that are expressed and implied.

3–2b The Powers of the States

The Tenth Amendment to the Constitution states that powers that are not delegated to the national government by the Constitution nor prohibited to the states "are reserved to the States respectively, or to the people." The Tenth Amendment thus gives numerous powers to the states, including the power to regulate commerce within their borders and the power to maintain a state militia.

POLICE POWERS
In principle, each state has the ability to regulate its internal affairs and to enact whatever laws are necessary to protect the health, safety, welfare, and morals of its people. These powers of the states

are called **police powers.** The establishment of public schools and the regulation of marriage and divorce have traditionally been considered to be entirely within the purview of state and local governments.

Because the Tenth Amendment does not specify what powers are reserved to the states, these powers have been defined differently at different times in our history. In periods of widespread support for increased regulation by the national government, the Tenth Amendment tends to recede into the background. When the tide of support turns, the Tenth Amendment is resurrected to justify arguments supporting increased states' rights (see, for example, the discussion of the new federalism later in this chapter). Because the United States Supreme Court is the ultimate arbiter of the Constitution, the outcome of disputes over the extent of state powers often rests with the Court.

POWERS PROHIBITED TO THE STATES
Article I, Section 10, denies certain powers to state governments, such as the power to tax goods that are transported across state lines. States are also prohibited from entering into treaties with other countries. In addition, the Thirteenth, Fourteenth, Fifteenth, Nineteenth, Twenty-fourth, and Twenty-sixth Amendments prohibit certain state actions. (The complete text of these amendments is included in Appendix B.)

3–2c Interstate Relations

The Constitution also contains provisions relating to interstate relations. The states have constant commercial and social interactions among themselves, and these interactions often do not directly involve the national government. The relationships among the states in our federal system of government are sometimes referred to as *horizontal federalism.*

THE FULL FAITH AND CREDIT CLAUSE
The Constitution's full faith and credit clause requires each state to honor every other state's public acts, records, and judicial proceedings. The issue of gay marriage, however, has made this constitutional mandate difficult to follow. If a gay couple legally married in Massachusetts moves to a state that bans same-sex marriage, which state's law takes priority? The federal government attempted to answer that question through the 1996 Defense of Marriage Act (DOMA), which provided that no state is *required* to

---

police powers The powers of a government body that enable it to create laws for the protection of the health, safety, welfare, and morals of the people. In the United States, most police powers are reserved to the states.

In May 2014, these two women became the first same-sex couple to be married in Oregon. *Why is same-sex marriage an issue for our federal system?*

states where it was currently illegal. All of the rulings cited *Windsor*. These rulings were initially *stayed* (suspended) pending action by higher courts. In October 2014, the Supreme Court refused to take up these rulings, and the stays were lifted. By late October, thirty states permitted same-sex marriage. Lawsuits were pending in all other states. Of course, if gay marriages become legal in all the states, the full faith and credit clause will no longer be a problem in the area of gay marriage.

INTERSTATE COMPACTS Horizontal federalism also includes agreements, known as *interstate compacts*, among two or more states to regulate the use or protection of certain resources, such as water or oil and gas. California and Nevada, for example, have formed an interstate compact to regulate the use and protection of Lake Tahoe, which lies on the border between those states.

3–2d Concurrent Powers

Concurrent powers can be exercised by both the state governments and the federal government. Generally, a state's concurrent powers apply only within the geographic area of the state and do not include functions that the Constitution delegates exclusively to the national government, such as the coinage of money and the negotiation of treaties.

An example of a concurrent power is the power to tax. Both the states and the national government have the power to impose income taxes—and a variety of other taxes. States, however, are prohibited from imposing tariffs (taxes on imported goods), and, as noted, the federal government may not tax articles exported by any state.

Figure 3–2, which follows, summarizes the powers granted and denied by the Constitution and lists other concurrent powers.

3–2e The Supremacy Clause

The Constitution makes it clear that the federal government holds ultimate power. Article VI, Clause 2, known as the **supremacy clause,** states that the U.S. Constitution and the laws of the federal government "shall be the supreme Law of the Land." In other words, states

treat a relationship between persons of the same sex as a marriage, even if the relationship is considered a marriage in another state.

A second part of the law barred the national government from recognizing same-sex marriages in states that legalize them. From 2010 through 2012, however, U.S. district and appellate courts ruled repeatedly that this part of DOMA was unconstitutional. The federal government, in other words, was required to provide marriage-based benefits to couples who have been married in states where such unions are legal. In 2013, the United States Supreme Court, in *United States v. Windsor*, backed the lower courts on this issue.[5]

By mid-2014, judges had ruled that same-sex marriage should be permitted in fourteen of the thirty-one

concurrent powers Powers held by both the federal and the state governments in a federal system.

supremacy clause Article VI, Clause 2, of the Constitution, which makes the Constitution and federal laws superior to all conflicting state and local laws.

FIGURE 3–2   THE CONSTITUTIONAL DIVISION OF POWERS

The Constitution grants certain powers to the national government and certain powers to the state governments, while denying them other powers. Some powers, called *concurrent powers,* can be exercised at either the national or the state level, but generally the states can exercise these powers only within their own borders. *Should states be allowed to collect sales tax on items that their residents purchase through the Internet? Why or why not?*

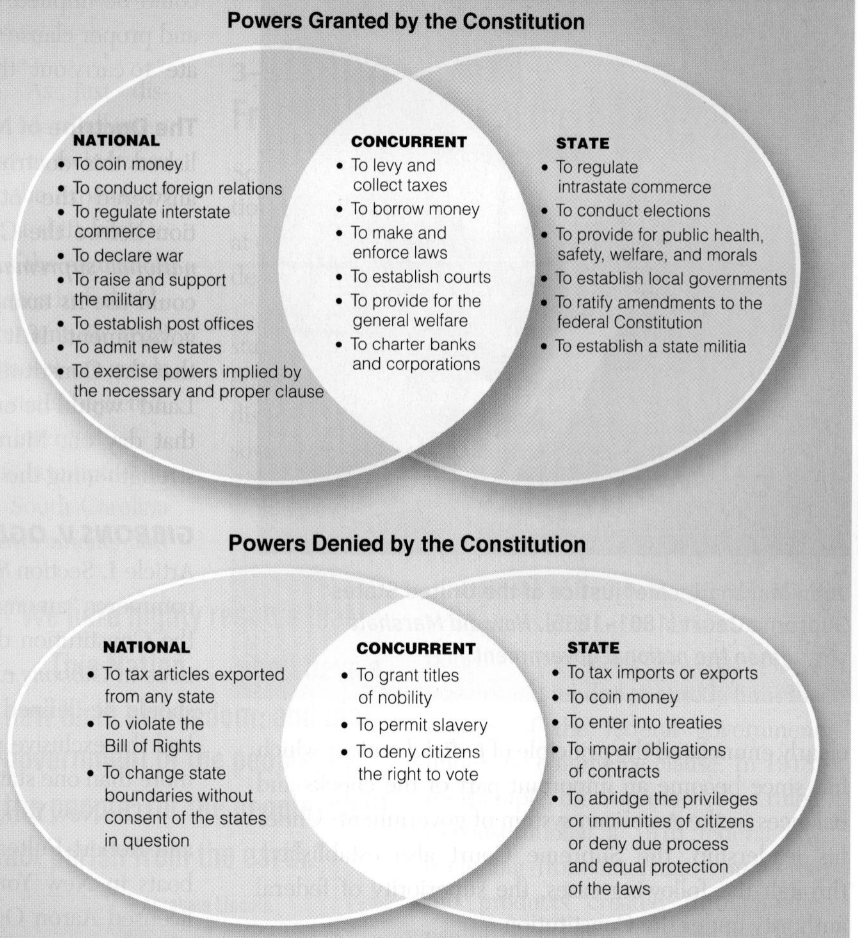

Powers Granted by the Constitution

NATIONAL
- To coin money
- To conduct foreign relations
- To regulate interstate commerce
- To declare war
- To raise and support the military
- To establish post offices
- To admit new states
- To exercise powers implied by the necessary and proper clause

CONCURRENT
- To levy and collect taxes
- To borrow money
- To make and enforce laws
- To establish courts
- To provide for the general welfare
- To charter banks and corporations

STATE
- To regulate intrastate commerce
- To conduct elections
- To provide for public health, safety, welfare, and morals
- To establish local governments
- To ratify amendments to the federal Constitution
- To establish a state militia

Powers Denied by the Constitution

NATIONAL
- To tax articles exported from any state
- To violate the Bill of Rights
- To change state boundaries without consent of the states in question

CONCURRENT
- To grant titles of nobility
- To permit slavery
- To deny citizens the right to vote

STATE
- To tax imports or exports
- To coin money
- To enter into treaties
- To impair obligations of contracts
- To abridge the privileges or immunities of citizens or deny due process and equal protection of the laws

cannot use their reserved or concurrent powers to counter national policies. Whenever state or local officers, such as judges or sheriffs, take office, they become bound by an oath to support the U.S. Constitution. National government power always takes precedence over any conflicting state action.[6]

> **CRITICAL THINKING**
>
> ▶ The national government also exercises police powers, such as environmental regulation. Name some other federal activities that might fall into this category.

3–3

THE STRUGGLE FOR SUPREMACY

LO Summarize the evolution of federal–state relationships in the United States over time.

Much of the political and legal history of the United States has involved conflicts between the supremacy of the national government and the desire of the states to preserve their sovereignty. The most extreme example of this conflict was the Civil War in the 1860s. Through the years, because of the Civil War and several important Supreme Court decisions, the national government has increased its power.

3–3a Early United States Supreme Court Decisions

Two Supreme Court cases, both of which were decided in the early 1800s, played a key role in establishing the constitutional foundations for the supremacy of the national government. Both decisions were issued while John Marshall was chief justice of the Supreme Court. In his thirty-four years as chief justice (1801–1835), Marshall did much to establish the prestige and the independence of the Court. In *Marbury v. Madison,*[7] he

President Franklin D. Roosevelt proposed many new federal programs during the Great Depression. *How did our conception of federalism change during his presidency?*

facing the entire United States. For example, federal law enforcement agencies, such as the Federal Bureau of Investigation, lend technical expertise to solve local crimes, and local officials cooperate with federal agencies.

ROOSEVELT'S NEW DEAL Cooperative federalism grew out of the desire to solve the pressing national problems caused by the Great Depression, which began in 1929. In an attempt to bring the United States out of the Depression, President Franklin D. Roosevelt (1933–1945) launched his **New Deal,** which involved many government spending and public-assistance programs. Roosevelt's New Deal legislation not only ushered in an era of cooperative federalism, which has more or less continued until the present day, but also marked the real beginning of an era of national supremacy.

Before the period of cooperative federalism could be truly established, it was necessary to obtain the concurrence of the United States Supreme Court. As mentioned, in the early part of the twentieth century, the Court held a very restrictive view of what the fed-

---

New Deal The policies ushered in by the Roosevelt administration in 1933 in an attempt to bring the United States out of the Great Depression.

picket-fence federalism A model of federalism in which specific policies and programs are administered by all levels of government — national, state, and local.

---

eral government could do under the commerce clause. In the 1930s, the Court ruled again and again that various economic measures were unconstitutional.

In 1937, Roosevelt threatened to "pack" the Court with up to six new members who presumably would be more favorable to federal action. This move was widely considered to be an assault on the Constitution, and Congress refused to support it. Later that year, however, Roosevelt had the opportunity—for the first time since taking office—to appoint a new member of the Supreme Court. Hugo Black, the new justice, tipped the balance on the Court. After 1937, the Court ceased its attempts to limit the scope of the commerce clause.

COOPERATIVE FEDERALISM AND THE "GREAT SOCIETY" The 1960s and 1970s saw an even greater expansion of the national government's role in domestic policy. The Great Society legislation of President Lyndon B. Johnson (1963–1969) created Medicaid, Medicare, the Job Corps, Operation Head Start, and other programs. The Civil Rights Act of 1964 prohibited discrimination in public accommodations, employment, and other areas on the basis of race, color, national origin, religion, or gender. In the 1970s, national laws protecting consumers, employees, and the environment imposed further regulations on the economy. Today, few activities are beyond the reach of the regulatory arm of the national government.

Nonetheless, the massive social programs undertaken in the 1960s and 1970s also resulted in greater involvement by state and local governments. The national government simply could not implement those programs alone. For example, Head Start, a program that provides preschool services to children of low-income families, is administered by local nonprofit organizations and school systems, although it is funded by federal grants.

The model in which every level of government is involved in implementing a policy is sometimes referred to as **picket-fence federalism.** In this model, the policy area is the vertical picket on the fence, while the levels of government are the horizontal support boards.

THE COMMERCE CLAUSE AND COOPERATIVE FEDERALISM The two United States Supreme Court decisions discussed earlier, *McCulloch v. Maryland* and *Gibbons v. Ogden,* became the constitutional cornerstone of the regulatory powers that the national government enjoys today. From 1937 on, the Supreme Court consistently upheld Congress's power to regulate domestic policy under the commerce clause. Even activities that occur entirely within a state were rarely considered to be outside the regulatory power of the national government. For example, in 1942 the Supreme Court held that wheat production by an individual farmer intended wholly for consumption on his own farm was subject to federal regulation because the home consumption of wheat reduced the demand for wheat and thus could have an effect on interstate commerce.[11]

In 1980, the Supreme Court acknowledged that the commerce clause had "long been interpreted to extend beyond activities actually in interstate commerce to reach other activities that, while wholly local in nature, nevertheless substantially affect interstate commerce."[12] Today, Congress can regulate almost any kind of economic activity, no matter where it occurs. In recent years, though, the Supreme Court has, for the first time since the 1930s, occasionally curbed Congress's regulatory powers under the commerce clause. You will read more about this development shortly.

FEDERAL PREEMPTION AND COOPERATIVE FEDERALISM John Marshall's validation of the supremacy clause of the Constitution has also had significant consequences for federalism. One important effect of the supremacy clause today is that the clause allows for federal **preemption** of certain areas in which the national government and the states have concurrent powers. When Congress chooses to act exclusively in an area in which the states and the national government have concurrent powers, Congress is said to have *preempted* the area. In such cases, the courts have held that a valid federal law or regulation takes precedence over a conflicting state or local law or regulation covering the same general activity.

CRITICAL THINKING

▶ Although marijuana is illegal under national law, Colorado and Washington have moved to legalize and tax it. Should the federal government take a hands-off approach or crack down on these states? In either case, why?

3–4 FEDERALISM TODAY

LO Describe developments in federalism in recent years.

By the 1970s, some Americans had begun to question whether the national government had acquired too many powers. Had the national government gotten too big? Had it become, in fact, a threat to the power of the states and the liberties of the people? Should steps be taken to reduce the regulatory power and scope of the national government? Since that time, the model of federalism has evolved in ways that reflect these and other concerns.

3–4a The New Federalism—More Power to the States

Starting in the 1970s, several administrations attempted to revitalize the doctrine of dual federalism, which they renamed the "new federalism." The **new federalism** involved a shift from *nation-centered* federalism to *state-centered* federalism. One of the major goals of the new federalism was to return to the states certain powers that had been exercised by the national government since the 1930s. The term **devolution**—the transfer

preemption A doctrine rooted in the supremacy clause of the Constitution that provides that national laws or regulations governing a certain area take precedence over conflicting state laws or regulations governing that same area.

new federalism A plan to limit the federal government's role in regulating state governments and to give the states increased power in deciding how they should spend government revenues.

devolution The surrender or transfer of powers to local authorities by a central government.

A shopkeeper greets customers on the first day that recreational marijuana could be sold legally under state law in Colorado—January 1, 2014. *Should Colorado be a model for other states? Why or why not?*

© Joe Amon/The Denver Post/Getty Images

Activists attend a rally in favor of voting rights in Washington, D.C. The rally marked the one-year anniversary of the Supreme Court decision that found part of the Voting Rights Act of 1965 to be unconstitutional. *How could Congress respond to this decision?*

the states to provide persons with disabilities with access to public buildings, sidewalks, and other areas; to establish minimum water-purity and air-purity standards; and to extend Medicaid coverage to all poor children.

To help the states pay for some of the costs associated with implementing national policies, the national government gives back some of the tax dollars it collects to the states in the form of grants. As you will see, the states have come to depend on grants as an important source of revenue. When taxes are collected by one level of government (typically the national government) and spent by another level (typically state or local governments), we call the process **fiscal federalism.**

3–5 THE FISCAL SIDE OF FEDERALISM

LO Explain what is meant by the term *fiscal federalism.*

Since the advent of cooperative federalism in the 1930s, the national government and the states have worked hand in hand to implement programs mandated by the national government. Whenever Congress passes a law that preempts a certain area, the states are, of course, obligated to comply with the requirements of that law. As already noted, a requirement that a state provide a service or undertake some activity to meet standards specified by a federal law is called a *federal mandate.*

Many federal mandates concern civil rights or environmental protection. Recent federal mandates require

fiscal federalism The allocation of taxes collected by one level of government (typically the national government) to another level (typically state or local governments).

categorical grant A federal grant targeted for a specific purpose as defined by federal law.

3–5a Federal Grants

Even before the Constitution was adopted, the national government granted lands to the states to finance education. Using the proceeds from the sale of these lands, the states were able to establish elementary schools and, later, *land-grant colleges.* Cash grants started in 1808, when Congress gave funds to the states to pay for the state militias. Federal grants were also made available for other purposes, such as building roads and railroads.

Only in the twentieth century, though, did federal grants become an important source of funds to the states. The major growth began in the 1960s, when the dollar amount of grants quadrupled to help pay for the Great Society programs of the Johnson administration. Grants became available for education, pollution control, conservation, recreation, highway construction and maintenance, and other purposes. There are two basic types of federal grants: categorical grants and block grants.

CATEGORICAL GRANTS A **categorical grant** is targeted for a specific purpose as defined by federal law—the federal government defines hundreds of categories of state and local spending. Categorical grants give the national government control over how states use the funds by imposing certain conditions. For example, a categorical grant may require that the funds must be used for the purpose of repairing interstate highways and that the projects cannot pay below the local prevailing wage. Depending on the project, the government might require that an environmental impact statement be prepared.

BLOCK GRANTS   A **block grant** is given for a broad area, such as criminal justice or mental-health programs. The term *block grant* was coined in 1966 to describe a series of programs initiated by President Johnson, although a number of federal grants issued earlier in our history shared some of the characteristics of modern block grants. Block grants now constitute a growing percentage of all federal aid programs.

A block grant gives the states more discretion over how the funds will be spent. Nonetheless, the federal government can exercise control over state decision making through these grants by using *cross-cutting requirements,* or requirements that apply to all federal grants. Title VI of the 1964 Civil Rights Act, for example, bars racial discrimination in the use of all federal funds, regardless of their source.

3–5b Federal Grants and State Budgets

Currently, about one-fifth of state and local revenue comes from the national government. In fiscal year 2014, the federal government transferred about $602 billion to state and local governments—more than half a trillion dollars. By far, the largest transfer was for Medicaid, the health-care program for the poor. It totaled $309 billion. The federal government provided the states with about $67 billion for education. Highway grants ran about $45 billion.

GENERAL FUND BUDGETS   When the media discuss state and local budgets, they typically refer just to the general fund budgets, which are largely supported by state and local taxes. But, in fact, state and local taxes support just under half of state and local spending. Federal funds aren't listed in general fund budgets. Further, more than one-third of state and local spending goes to fee-for-service operations, in which governments charge for the services they provide. This spending applies to functions such as water supply, sewers, and other public utilities; fees charged by government-owned hospitals and airports; college tuition; and much else. Typically, these operations are also excluded from general fund budgets.

FEDERALISM AND THE ECONOMIC CRISIS   Unlike the federal government, state governments are

supposed to balance their budgets. A practical result is that when a major recession occurs, the states are faced with severe budget problems. Because state citizens are earning and spending less, state income and sales taxes fall. During a recession, state governments may be forced either to reduce spending and lay off staff—or to raise taxes. Either choice helps make the recession worse. State spending patterns tend to make economic booms more energetic and busts more painful—in a word, they are *procyclical.*

The federal government has no difficulty in spending more on welfare, unemployment compensation, and Medicaid during a recession. Also, the federal government often cuts tax rates in a recession to spur the economy. It makes up the difference by going further into debt. In a recession, the actions of the federal government are normally *anticyclical.*

One method of dealing with the procyclical nature of state spending is to increase federal grants to the states during a recession. Such grants were included in the February 2009 stimulus legislation championed by President Obama. By the middle of 2010, however, the grants had largely dried up. From 2010 through 2012, the states laid off a substantial number of employees.

3–5c Using Federal Grants to Control the States

Grants of funds to the states from the national government are one way that the Tenth Amendment to the U.S. Constitution can be bridged. Remember that the Tenth Amendment reserves all powers not delegated to the national government to the states and to the people. You might well wonder, then, how the federal government has

block grant   A federal grant given to a state for a broad area, such as criminal justice or mental-health programs.

Elementary school children in South Dakota. The federal government has given this state a waiver allowing it more time to meet the requirements of the No Child Left Behind legislation. *Why doesn't the federal government operate schools directly?*

been able to exercise control over matters that traditionally have been under the authority of state governments, such as the minimum drinking age. The answer involves the giving or withholding of federal grant dollars.

For example, as noted in the *Join the Debate* feature, which follows, the national government forced the states to raise the minimum drinking age to twenty-one by threatening to withhold federal highway funds from states that did not comply. Obamacare also raised questions about forcing the states to expand Medicaid, as mentioned earlier in this chapter. The education reforms embodied in the No Child Left Behind Act rely on federal funding for their implementation as well. The states receive block grants for educational purposes and, in return, must meet federally imposed standards for testing and accountability.

3–5d The Cost of Federal Mandates

As mentioned earlier, when the national government passes a law preempting an area in which the states and the national government have concurrent powers, the states must comply with that law in accordance with the supremacy clause of the Constitution. Thus, when such laws require the states to implement certain programs, the states must comply—but compliance with federal mandates can be costly. The cost of compliance has been estimated by some at $29 bil-

lion annually, and some believe the true figure to be much higher. Although Congress passed legislation in 1995 to curb the use of unfunded federal mandates, that legislation was more rhetoric than reality.

Even when funding is provided, it may be insufficient, resulting in an *underfunded* federal mandate. As mentioned earlier, for example, states receive block grants for educational purposes in return for meeting standards imposed by the federal No Child Left Behind Act. Critics argue that the national government does not supply the states with enough funds to implement the act properly.

3–5e Competitive Federalism

The debate over federalism is sometimes reduced to a debate over taxes. Which level of government will raise taxes to pay for government programs, and which will cut services to avoid raising taxes?

THE RIGHT TO MOVE How states answer that question gives citizens an option: they can move to a state with fewer services and lower taxes, or to a state with more services but higher taxes. Political scientist Thomas R. Dye calls this model of federalism **competitive federalism.** State and local governments compete for businesses and citizens. If the state of Ohio offers tax advantages for locating a factory there, for example, a business may be more likely to build its factory in Ohio, thereby providing more jobs for Ohio residents.

If Ohio has very strict environmental regulations, however, that same business may choose not to build there, no matter how beneficial the tax advantages, because complying with the regulations would be costly. Although Ohio citizens lose the opportunity for more jobs, they may enjoy better air and water quality than citizens of the state where the new factory is ultimately built.

ADVANTAGES AND DISADVANTAGES OF COMPETITION Some observers consider such competition an advantage: Americans have several variables to consider when they choose a state in which to live. Others

competitive federalism A model of federalism in which state and local governments compete for businesses and citizens, who in effect "vote with their feet" by moving to jurisdictions that offer a competitive advantage.

Join the Debate

Should the States Lower the Drinking Age?

The Tenth Amendment to the U.S. Constitution reserves all powers not delegated to the national government to the states and to the people. Nonetheless, the national government has often been able to exercise power over matters that traditionally have been under the control of the states. It has been able to do so because of its ability to give or withhold federal grants. In the 1980s, for example, the national government wanted the states to raise the minimum drinking age to twenty-one years. States that refused to do so would lose federal highway construction funds. It was not long before all of the states had changed their minimum drinking age laws.

It's Time to End the Charade

Underage drinking did not disappear when the minimum drinking age requirement was raised to twenty-one years. Indeed, the problem got worse. Millions of young people today are, in effect, criminals, because they are breaking the law by drinking. The minimum drinking age of twenty-one years has not prevented teenagers from driving drunk—in part because it is largely unenforceable. Additionally, it has bred contempt for the law in general among teenagers. That is why a group of 135 U.S. college presidents and chancellors endorsed the Amethyst Initiative, a movement calling for the reconsideration of U.S. drinking age laws. Prohibition did not work in the 1920s, and prohibiting those under twenty-one from drinking will not work in the twenty-first century. Almost no other country has such a high minimum drinking age. It is time to lower the drinking age everywhere in the United States. Responsible drinking can be taught through role modeling by parents and through educational programs.

The Age-Twenty-One Requirement Is Working

Mothers Against Drunk Driving (MADD) leads the opposition to lowering the drinking age. That group contends that the current drinking age laws have saved more than twenty thousand lives. The National Transportation Safety Board, the American Medical Association, and the Insurance Institute for Highway Safety all agree. After all, young persons' brains are not fully developed, so they are more susceptible to alcohol. Teenagers who drink are a danger not only to themselves but also to others—particularly when driving. Young people away at college must deal with enough new responsibilities. They don't need drinking as yet another problem. Further, teenagers who drink are a danger not only to themselves but also to others—particularly when driving. Fatalities involving eighteen-to-twenty-year-old drivers have decreased since the laws establishing the minimum drinking age of twenty-one were enacted. These laws are working as planned, so we should keep them.

CRITICAL ANALYSIS Would most parents be against the Amethyst Initiative? Why or why not?

---

consider it a disadvantage: A state that offers more social services or lower taxes may experience an increase in population as people "vote with their feet" to take advantage of that state's laws. The resulting population increases can overwhelm the state's resources and force it to cut social services or raise taxes. Regulations that make it easier to build new housing may also draw in new residents. Recent studies suggest that much of the difference in population growth rates among states in recent decades may be due to differences in the cost of housing.

It appears likely, then, that the debate over how our federal system functions, as well as the battle for control between the states and the federal government, will continue. The Supreme Court, which has played umpire in this battle, will also likely continue to issue rulings that influence the balance of power.

CRITICAL THINKING

▶ What kinds of factors might cause you to consider moving to a different state? Are any of these factors under the control of state governments?

AMERICA ⚑ AT ODDS
Federalism

The topic of federalism raises one of the most enduring disputes in American history—the relative power of the national government versus that of the governments of the states. As you read in the last two chapters, Americans have been at odds over the strength of the central government since well before the American Revolution. The issue of centralization versus decentralization has taken a number of specific forms:

- *Is it right for the national government to use its financial strength to pressure states into taking actions such as raising the drinking age by threatening to withhold subsidies—or are such pressures an abuse of the federal system?*

- *Should the national government intervene in the issue of legalizing or banning same-sex marriages—or leave such matters strictly to the states?*

- *Should the commerce clause be interpreted broadly, granting the federal government much power to regulate the economy—or should it be interpreted as narrowly as possible to keep the government from interfering with the rights of business owners?*

- *Should the federal government have a role in setting national policies for public education—or should that be left entirely to the states?*

- *Should the federal government establish a national system for funding health care—or should that, too, be left to the states or to the private sector?*

Internet Resources

- Searching on "The New York Times - Civil War" in Facebook brings up the Civil War page of the *New York Times*. This page includes a wealth of historical information plus popular discussions about these crucial events.

- Supreme Court opinions, including those discussed in this chapter, can be found at the Court's official Web site. Go to www.supremecourt.gov.

- *The Federalist Papers,* by Alexander Hamilton, John Jay, and James Madison, is a key resource on federalism and other characteristics of our political system. It is not under copyright and is therefore part of the vast Project Gutenberg collection of free e-books. Find it in multiple formats at www.gutenberg.org/ebooks/1404.

- A good source of information on state governments and issues concerning federalism is the Web site of the Council of State Governments. See it at www.csg.org.

- The Web site of the National Governors Association offers information on many issues affecting the nation, ranging from health-care reform, to education, to new and innovative state programs. You can access information on these issues at www.nga.org.

- *Governing* magazine, an excellent source of state and local news, can be found online at www.governing.com.

STUDY TOOLS 3

READY TO STUDY?

- ☐ Review what you've read with the quiz below.
- ☐ Check your answers in Appendix D in the back of the book.
- ☐ For any questions you miss, read the corresponding Learning Outcome section again to prepare for class and your exam.
- ☐ Rip out the Chapter in Review card in the back.

VISIT WWW.CENGAGEBRAIN.COM:

- ☐ Interactive Quizzes
- ☐ Key Term Flashcards or Crossword Puzzles
- ☐ Audio Summaries
- ☐ Simulations, Animated Learning & Interactive Timelines
- ☐ Videos
- ☐ American Government NewsWatch

FILL-IN

LearningOutcome 3–1

1. The advantages of a federal system of government in the United States include _____.

LearningOutcome 3–2

2. The constitutional basis for the implied powers of the national government is the _____ clause.

3. The Constitution's _____ clause requires each state to honor every other state's public acts, records, and judicial proceedings.

LearningOutcome 3–3

4. In *McCulloch v. Maryland,* a case decided in 1819, the United States Supreme Court established the doctrines of _____.

5. Cooperative federalism grew out of the need to solve the pressing problems caused by _____.

LearningOutcome 3–4

6. The relationship of national, state, and local levels of government in implementing massive social programs in the 1960s and 1970s is often referred to as _____ federalism.

7. A _____ is a requirement in federal legislation that forces states and municipalities to comply with certain rules.

LearningOutcome 3–5

8. The national government forced the states to raise the minimum drinking age to twenty-one by _____.

MULTIPLE CHOICE

LearningOutcome 3–1

9. In a unitary system,
   a. subdivisional governments exercise only those powers given to them by the central government.
   b. sovereign states are joined together by a central government that has only limited powers over them.
   c. there are no local or subdivisional governments.

10. There are ____ governmental units in the United States today.
   a. 51   b. nearly 3,000   c. almost 90,000

LearningOutcome 3–2

11. Article I, Section 8, of the U.S. Constitution enumerates twenty-seven powers that Congress may exercise. Two of these _____ powers are the power to coin money and the power to regulate interstate commerce.
   a. concurrent   b. expressed   c. inherent

12. The relationships among the states in our federal system of government are sometimes referred to as _____ federalism.
   a. picket-fence   b. cooperative   c. horizontal

LearningOutcome 3–3

13. The era of _____ federalism came to an end in the 1930s.
   a. dual   b. new   c. competitive

LearningOutcome 3–4

14. The welfare reform legislation passed by Congress in 1996 is an example of _____ federalism.
   a. dual   b. cooperative   c. new

LearningOutcome 3–5

15. Block grants
   a. are targeted for specific purposes as defined by federal law.
   b. are federal grants given to a state for broad areas, such as criminal justice or mental-health programs.
   c. give the states less discretion than categorical grants over how funds will be spent.

4 | Civil Liberties

© Mark Wilson/Getty Images

LEARNING OUTCOMES After reading this chapter, you should be able to:

4-1 Define the term *civil liberties*, explain how civil liberties differ from civil rights, and state the constitutional basis for our civil liberties.

4-2 List and describe the freedoms guaranteed by the First Amendment and explain how the courts have interpreted and applied these freedoms.

4-3 Discuss why Americans are increasingly concerned about privacy rights.

4-4 Summarize how the Constitution and the Bill of Rights protect the rights of accused persons.

After finishing
this chapter go to
PAGE 94 for
STUDY TOOLS.

AMERICA AT ODDS

© Melanie Stetson Freeman/
The *Christian Science Monitor*/Getty Images

Do U.S. Citizens Really Need Military-Style Rifles?

The Second Amendment to the U.S. Constitution states that the people have the right "to keep and bear arms." The Supreme Court has ruled that this right is enjoyed by individuals, not just state militias. In these rulings, however, the Court has also said that the national and state governments may limit the types of weapons that individuals may hold. Should ordinary citizens have a right to own rifles based on military weapons?

This issue came to the fore after a shooter killed twenty-six children and teachers in December 2012 at the Sandy Hook Elementary School in Connecticut. The shooter used a semiautomatic rifle based on the military's M4 carbine. Earlier that year, a shooter used a similar rifle with a hundred-round magazine in a movie theater in Colorado. He killed twelve people and wounded fifty-eight. Proposed gun control legislation to ban such weapons and magazines failed to pass Congress in 2013. Nevertheless, Americans remain at odds about whether military-style rifles and high-round magazines should be legal.

The Second Amendment Means What It Says

Those who do not believe that Congress should ban military-style rifles maintain that such weapons are fully covered by the constitutional right to bear arms. The most popular military-style rifle is the AR-15, based on the military's M16. Other rifles are based on the similar but lighter M4. These civilian rifles are semi-automatic, which means that the trigger must be pulled once for each shot. That makes these weapons different from fully automatic military weapons that can spray bullets like water from a hose. Plenty of civilian weapons other than the AR-15 are semiautomatic, including many handguns and deer rifles. Yet they were exempt from the recent proposed legislation.

From 1994 to 2004, the Federal Assault Weapons Ban outlawed military-style semiautomatic rifles. This law did not reduce the national murder rate. Although the murder rate fell throughout this period, the decline would have occurred even if these weapons had not been banned. After all, only 2.6 percent of all murders are committed using any type of rifle.

Citizens Don't Need Military-Style Rifles

Although the National Rifle Association claims that semiautomatic military-style rifles are useful for hunting, target practice, and home defense, they are not. The AR-15's .223 caliber ammunition is too light for deer hunting and useless for waterfowl. The low-power .22 rimfire cartridge—not the high-power .223—is the international standard for target competition. An ordinary 12-gauge shotgun is vastly superior for home protection, and a handgun is best for self-defense in other circumstances.

The AR-15/M16 was designed in 1957 for the U.S. Army. This rifle, and its more recent M4 version, is optimized for one purpose only—killing the largest number of enemy possible on the battlefield. How can such a weapon be legitimate in a civilian context? Let's face it: military-style rifles are popular because they appeal to owners' dangerous fantasies of domestic chaos or insurrection. *World War Z* is not an acceptable basis for national policy.

Where do you stand?

1. **Should the Second Amendment be interpreted to mean that anyone can own any weapon anywhere at anytime? Why or why not?**

2. **Could a citizens' militia possibly be effective against an attempt to install a dictator?**

Explore this issue online

- For a defense of the right to bear the AR-15, search on "lott wsj assault weapons" for an article by John Lott.

- Justin Peters criticizes the usefulness of the AR-15—enter "slate peters hunting."

- Finally, Matt Steinglass attacks the fantasies of AR-15 owners at "economist gun treason."

INTRODUCTION

The debate over military-style rifles, discussed in the chapter-opening *America at Odds* feature, is but one of many controversies concerning our civil liberties. **Civil liberties** are legal and constitutional rights that protect citizens from government actions.

Perhaps the best way to understand what civil liberties are and why they are important to Americans is to look at what might happen if we did not have them. If you were a student in China, for example, you would have to exercise some care in what you said and did. That country prohibits a variety of kinds of speech, notably any criticism of the leading role of the Communist Party. If you criticized the government in e-mail messages to your friends or on your Web site, you could end up in court on charges that you had violated the law—and perhaps even go to prison.

Note that some Americans confuse *civil liberties* (discussed in this chapter) with *civil rights* (discussed in the next chapter) and use the terms interchangeably. Scholars, however, make a distinction between the two. They point out that whereas civil liberties are limitations on government action, setting forth what the government *cannot* do, civil rights specify what the government *must* do—for example, ensure equal protection under the law for all Americans.

4–1 THE CONSTITUTIONAL BASIS FOR OUR CIVIL LIBERTIES

> **LO** Define the term *civil liberties*, explain how civil liberties differ from civil rights, and state the constitutional basis for our civil liberties.

The founders believed that the constitutions of the individual states contained ample provisions to protect citizens from government actions. Therefore, the founders

civil liberties Individual rights protected by the Constitution against the powers of the government.

writ of *habeas corpus* An order that requires an official to bring a specified prisoner into court and explain to the judge why the person is being held in jail.

bill of attainder A legislative act that inflicts punishment on particular persons or groups without granting them the right to a trial.

***ex post facto* law** A criminal law that punishes individuals for committing an act that was legal when the act was committed.

did not include many references to individual civil liberties in the original version of the Constitution. Many of our liberties were added by the Bill of Rights, ratified in 1791. Nonetheless, the original Constitution did include some safeguards to protect citizens against an overly powerful government.

4–1a Safeguards in the Original Constitution

Article I, Section 9, of the Constitution provides that the writ of *habeas corpus* (a Latin phrase that roughly means "produce the body") will be available to all citizens except in times of rebellion or national invasion. A **writ of *habeas corpus*** is an order requiring that an official bring a specified prisoner into court and explain to the judge why the prisoner is being held in jail. If the court finds that the imprisonment is unlawful, it orders the prisoner to be released. If our country did not have such a constitutional provision, political leaders could jail their opponents without giving them the opportunity to plead their cases before a judge. Without this opportunity, many opponents might conveniently be left to rot away in prison.

The Constitution also prohibits Congress and the state legislatures from passing bills of attainder. A **bill of attainder** is a legislative act that directly punishes a specifically named individual (or a group or class of individuals) without a trial. For example, no legislature can pass a law that punishes a named Hollywood celebrity for unpatriotic statements.

Finally, the Constitution also prohibits Congress from passing *ex post facto laws*. The Latin term *ex post facto* roughly means "after the fact." An ***ex post facto* law** punishes individuals for committing an act that was legal when it was committed.

4–1b The Bill of Rights

As you read in Chapter 2, one of the contentious issues in the debate over ratification of the Constitution was the lack of protections for citizens from government actions. Although many state constitutions provided such protections, the Anti-Federalists wanted more. The promise of the addition of a bill of rights to the Constitution ensured its ratification.

The Bill of Rights was ratified by the states and became part of the Constitution on December 15, 1791. Look at the text of the Bill of Rights in Table 4–1, which follows. As you can see, the first eight amendments grant the people specific rights and liberties. The remaining two amendments reserve certain rights and powers to the people and to the states.

TABLE 4–1 **THE BILL OF RIGHTS**

Amendment I.
Religion, Speech, Press, Assembly, and Petition

Congress shall make no law respecting an establishment of religion, or prohibiting the free exercise thereof; or abridging the freedom of speech, or of the press; or the right of the people peaceably to assemble, and to petition the Government for a redress of grievances.

Congress may not create an official church or enact laws limiting the freedom of religion, speech, the press, assembly, and petition. These guarantees, like the others in the Bill of Rights (the first ten amendments), are not absolute—each right may be exercised only with regard to the rights of other persons.

Amendment II.
Militia and the Right to Bear Arms

A well regulated Militia, being necessary to the security of a free State, the right of the people to keep and bear Arms, shall not be infringed.

Each state has the right to maintain a volunteer armed force. Although individuals have the right to bear arms, states and the federal government may regulate the possession and use of firearms by individuals.

Amendment III.
The Quartering of Soldiers

No Soldier shall, in time of peace be quartered in any house, without the consent of the Owner, nor in time of war, but in a manner to be prescribed by law.

Before the Revolutionary War, it had been common British practice to quarter soldiers in colonists' homes. Military troops do not have the power to take over private houses during peacetime.

Amendment IV.
Searches and Seizures

The right of the people to be secure in their persons, houses, papers, and effects, against unreasonable searches and seizures, shall not be violated, and no Warrants shall issue, but upon probable cause, supported by Oath or affirmation, and particularly describing the place to be searched, and the persons or things to be seized.

Here, the word warrant refers to a document issued by a magistrate or judge indicating the name, address, and possible offense committed. Anyone asking for a warrant, such as a police officer, must be able to convince the magistrate or judge that an offense probably has been committed.

Amendment V.
Grand Juries, Self-Incrimination, Double Jeopardy, Due Process, and Eminent Domain

No person shall be held to answer for a capital, or otherwise infamous crime, unless on a presentment or indictment of a Grand Jury, except in cases arising in the land or naval forces, or in the Militia, when in actual service in time of War or public danger; nor shall any person be subject for the same offense to be twice put in jeopardy of life or limb; nor shall be compelled in any criminal case to be a witness against himself, nor be deprived of life, liberty, or property, without due process of law; nor shall private property be taken for public use, without just compensation.

There are two types of juries. A grand jury considers physical evidence and the testimony of witnesses and decides whether there is sufficient reason to bring a case to trial. A petit jury hears the case at trial and decides it. "For the same offense to be twice put in jeopardy of life or limb" means to be tried twice for the same crime. A person may not be tried for the same crime twice or forced to give evidence against herself or himself. No person's right to life, liberty, or property may be taken away except by lawful means, called the due process of law. Private property taken for public purposes must be paid for by the government.

Amendment VI.
Criminal Court Procedures

In all criminal prosecutions, the accused shall enjoy the right to a speedy and public trial, by an impartial jury of the State and district wherein the crime shall have been committed, which district shall have been previously ascertained by law, and to be informed of the nature and cause of the accusation; to be confronted with the witnesses against him; to have compulsory process for obtaining witnesses in his favor, and to have the Assistance of Counsel for his defence.

Any person accused of a crime has the right to a fair and public trial by a jury in the state in which the crime took place. The charges against that person must be made clear. Any accused person has the right to a lawyer to defend him or her and to question those who testify against him or her, as well as the right to call people to speak in his or her favor at trial.

Amendment VII.
Trial by Jury in Civil Cases

In Suits at common law, where the value in controversy shall exceed twenty dollars, the right of trial by jury shall be preserved, and no fact tried by a jury, shall be otherwise re-examined in any Court of the United States, than according to the rules of the common law.

A jury trial may be requested by either party in a dispute in any case involving more than $20. If both parties agree to a trial by a judge without a jury, the right to a jury trial may be put aside.

Amendment VIII.
Bail, Cruel and Unusual Punishment

Excessive bail shall not be required, nor excessive fines imposed, nor cruel and unusual punishments inflicted.

Bail is that amount of money that a person accused of a crime may be required to deposit with the court as a guarantee that she or he will appear in court when requested. The amount of bail required or the fine imposed as punishment for a crime must be reasonable compared with the seriousness of the crime involved. Any punishment judged to be too harsh or too severe for a crime shall be prohibited.

Amendment IX.
The Rights Retained by the People

The enumeration in the Constitution, of certain rights, shall not be construed to deny or disparage others retained by the people.

Many civil rights that are not explicitly enumerated in the Constitution are still held by the people.

Amendment X.
Reserved Powers of the States

The powers not delegated to the United States by the Constitution, nor prohibited by it to the States, are reserved to the States respectively, or to the people.

Those powers not delegated by the Constitution to the federal government or expressly denied to the states belong to the states and to the people. This clause in essence allows the states to pass laws under their "police powers."

Basically, in a democracy, government policy tends to reflect the view of the majority. A key function of the Bill of Rights, therefore, is to protect the rights of those in the minority against the will of the majority. When there is disagreement over how to interpret the Bill of Rights, the courts step in.

The United States Supreme Court, as our nation's highest court, has the final say as to how the Constitution, including the Bill of Rights, should be interpreted. The civil liberties that you will read about in this chapter have all been shaped over time by Supreme Court decisions. For example, it is the Supreme Court that determines where freedom of speech ends and the right of society to be protected from certain forms of speech begins.

4–1c The Incorporation Principle

For many years, the courts assumed that the Bill of Rights limited only the actions of the national government, not the actions of state or local governments. In other words, if a state or local law was contrary to a basic freedom, such as the freedom of speech or the right to due process of law, the federal Bill of Rights did not come into play. The founders believed that the states, being closer to the people, would be less likely to violate their own citizens' liberties. Moreover, state constitutions, most of which contain bills of rights, protect citizens against state government actions. The United States Supreme Court upheld this view when it decided, in *Barron v. Baltimore* (1833), that the Bill of Rights did not apply to state laws.[1]

Eventually, however, the Supreme Court began to take a different view. Because the Fourteenth Amendment played a key role in this development, we look next at the provisions of that amendment.

THE RIGHT TO DUE PROCESS In 1868, three years after the end of the Civil War, the Fourteenth Amendment was added to the Constitution. The **due process clause** of this amendment requires that state governments protect their citizens' rights. (A similar requirement, binding on the federal government, was provided by the Fifth Amendment.) The due process clause reads, in part, as follows:

> No State shall . . . deprive any person of life, liberty, or property, without due process of law.

The right to **due process of law** is simply the right to be treated fairly under the legal system. That system and its officers must follow "rules of fair play" in making decisions, in determining guilt or innocence, and in punishing those who have been found guilty. Due process has two aspects—procedural and substantive.

Procedural Due Process. *Procedural* due process requires that any governmental decision to take life, lib-

erty, or property be made equitably. For example, the government must use "fair procedures" in determining whether a person will be subjected to punishment or have some burden imposed on him or her. Fair procedure has been interpreted as requiring that the person have at least an opportunity to object to a proposed action before an impartial, neutral decision maker (who need not be a judge).

Substantive Due Process. *Substantive* due process focuses on the content, or substance, of legislation. If a law or other governmental action limits a *fundamental right,* it will be held to violate substantive due process, unless it promotes a *compelling* or *overriding state interest.* All First Amendment rights plus the rights to interstate travel, privacy, and voting are considered fundamental. Compelling state interests could include, for example, the public's safety.

OTHER LIBERTIES INCORPORATED The Fourteenth Amendment also states that no state "shall make or enforce any law which shall abridge the privileges or immunities of citizens of the United States." For some time, the Supreme Court considered the "privileges and immunities" referred to in the amendment to be those conferred by state laws or constitutions, not the federal Bill of Rights.

Starting in 1925, however, the Supreme Court gradually began using the due process clause to say that states could not abridge a civil liberty that the national government could not abridge. In other words, the Court *incorporated* the protections guaranteed by the national Bill of Rights into the liberties protected under the Fourteenth Amendment. As you can see in Table 4–2, which follows, the Supreme Court was particularly active during the 1960s in broadening its interpretation of the due process clause to ensure that states and localities could not infringe on civil liberties protected by the Bill of Rights.

Today, the liberties still not incorporated include the right to a grand jury hearing. The right to refuse to quarter soldiers has been affirmed by a U.S. appeals court, but not by the Supreme Court, and so that liberty is fully guaranteed in only a few states. The right to bear arms described in the Second Amendment was incorporated only in 2010.

---

due process clause The constitutional guarantee, set out in the Fifth and Fourteenth Amendments, that the government will not illegally or arbitrarily deprive a person of life, liberty, or property.

due process of law The requirement that the government use fair, reasonable, and standard procedures whenever it takes any legal action against an individual; required by the Fifth and Fourteenth Amendments.

CRITICAL THINKING

▶ Congress often passes laws that are so narrowly defined that only one individual or corporation is covered by the legislation. Should such laws be considered bills of attainder and thus unconstitutional? Why or why not?

TABLE 4-2 INCORPORATING THE BILL OF RIGHTS INTO THE FOURTEENTH AMENDMENT

Year	Issue	Amendment Involved	Court Case
1925	Freedom of speech	I	*Gitlow v. New York*, 268 U.S. 652.
1931	Freedom of the press	I	*Near v. Minnesota*, 283 U.S. 697.
1932	Right to a lawyer in capital punishment cases	VI	*Powell v. Alabama*, 287 U.S. 45.
1937	Freedom of assembly and right to petition	I	*De Jonge v. Oregon*, 299 U.S. 353.
1940	Freedom of religion	I	*Cantwell v. Connecticut*, 310 U.S. 296.
1947	Separation of church and state	I	*Everson v. Board of Education*, 330 U.S. 1.
1948	Right to a public trial	VI	*In re Oliver*, 333 U.S. 257.
1949	No unreasonable searches and seizures	IV	*Wolf v. Colorado*, 338 U.S. 25.
1961	Exclusionary rule	IV	*Mapp v. Ohio*, 367 U.S. 643.
1962	No cruel and unusual punishments	VIII	*Robinson v. California*, 370 U.S. 660.
1963	Right to a lawyer in all criminal felony cases	VI	*Gideon v. Wainwright*, 372 U.S. 335.
1964	No compulsory self-incrimination	V	*Malloy v. Hogan*, 378 U.S. 1.
1965	Right to privacy	Various	*Griswold v. Connecticut*, 381 U.S. 479.
1966	Right to an impartial jury	VI	*Parker v. Gladden*, 385 U.S. 363.
1967	Right to a speedy trial	VI	*Klopfer v. North Carolina*, 386 U.S. 213.
1969	No double jeopardy	V	*Benton v. Maryland*, 395 U.S. 784.
1982	Right to refuse to quarter soldiers	III	*Engblom v. Carey*, 677 F.2d 957 (2d Cir.)
2010	Right to bear arms	II	*McDonald v. Chicago*, 561 U.S. 3025.

4-2 PROTECTIONS UNDER THE FIRST AMENDMENT

LO List and describe the freedoms guaranteed by the First Amendment and explain how the courts have interpreted and applied these freedoms.

The First Amendment sets forth some of our most important civil liberties. Specifically, the First Amendment guarantees the freedoms of religion, speech, the press, and assembly, as well as the right to petition the government. In the pages that follow, we look closely at the first three of these freedoms and discuss how, over time, Supreme Court decisions have defined their meaning and determined their limits.

4-2a Freedom of Religion

The First Amendment prohibits Congress from passing laws "respecting an establishment of religion, or prohibiting the free exercise thereof." The first part of this amendment is known as the **establishment clause.** The second part is called the **free exercise clause.**

LAWS ON RELIGION IN THE COLONIES That freedom of religion was the first freedom mentioned

in the Bill of Rights is not surprising. After all, many colonists came to America to escape religious persecution. Nonetheless, these same colonists showed little tolerance for religious freedom within the communities they established. For example, in 1610 the Jamestown colony enacted a law requiring attendance at religious services on Sunday "both in the morning and the afternoon." Repeat offenders were subjected to particularly harsh punishments. For those who twice violated the law, for example, the punishment was a public whipping. For third-time offenders, the punishment was death. (We provided additional details on religion in the colonies in the *America at Odds* feature at the beginning of Chapter 2.)

These examples of religious laws provide a context that is helpful in understanding why, in 1802, President Thomas Jefferson—a great proponent of religious freedom and tolerance—wanted the establishment clause

establishment clause The section of the First Amendment that prohibits Congress from passing laws "respecting an establishment of religion."

free exercise clause The provision of the First Amendment stating that the government cannot pass laws "prohibiting the free exercise" of religion.

to be "a wall of separation between church and state." The context also helps to explain why even state leaders who supported state religions might have favored the establishment clause—to keep the national government from interfering in such state matters. After all, the First Amendment says only that *Congress* can make no law respecting an establishment of religion. It says nothing about whether the *states* can make such laws.

THE ESTABLISHMENT CLAUSE The establishment clause forbids the government from establishing an official religion or church. This makes the United States different from countries that are ruled by religious governments, such as the Islamic government of Iran. It also makes us different from nations that have in the past strongly discouraged the practice of any religion at all, such as the People's Republic of China.

Limits to the Establishment Clause. What does this separation of church and state mean in practice? For one thing, religion and government, though constitutionally separated in the United States, have never been enemies or strangers. The establishment clause does not prohibit government from supporting religion in *general*. Religion remains a part of public life.

Most government officials take an oath of office in the name of God, and our coins and paper currency carry the motto "In God We Trust." Clergy of different religions serve in each branch of the armed forces. Public meetings and even sessions of Congress open with prayers. (The Supreme Court endorsed such practices as recently as 2014 in *Town of Greece v. Galloway.*)[2] Indeed, the establishment clause often masks the fact that Americans are, by and large, religious and prefer that their political leaders be people of faith.

The Wall of Separation. The "wall of separation" that Thomas Jefferson referred to, however, does exist and has been upheld by the Supreme Court on many occasions. An important ruling by the Supreme Court on the establishment clause came in 1947. The case involved a New Jersey law that allowed the state to pay for bus transportation of students who attended parochial schools (schools run by churches or other religious groups).

The Court stated: "No tax in any amount, large or small, can be levied to support any religious activities or institutions." Nevertheless, the Court upheld the New Jersey law because it did not aid the church *directly* but provided for the safety and benefit of the students.[3] The ruling both affirmed the importance of separating church and state and set the precedent that not *all* forms of state and federal aid to church-related schools are forbidden under the Constitution.

The First Amendment to the Constitution mandates separation of church and state. Nonetheless, references to God are common in public life, as the phrase "In God We Trust" on this coin demonstrates.

A full discussion of the various church–state issues that have arisen in American politics would fill volumes. Here, we examine three of these issues: prayer in the schools, the teaching of evolution versus creationism or intelligent design, and government aid to parochial schools.

PRAYER IN THE SCHOOLS On occasion, some public schools have promoted a general sense of religion without proclaiming allegiance to any particular church or sect. Whether the states have a right to allow this was the main question presented in 1962 in *Engel v. Vitale,*[4] also known as the "Regents' Prayer case." The State Board of Regents in New York had composed a nondenominational prayer (a prayer not associated with any particular church) and urged school districts to use it in classrooms at the start of each day. The prayer read as follows:

> Almighty God, we acknowledge our dependence upon Thee, and we beg Thy blessings upon us, our parents, our teachers, and our Country.

Some parents objected to the prayer, contending that it violated the establishment clause. The Supreme Court agreed and ruled that the Regents' Prayer was unconstitutional. Speaking for the majority, Justice Hugo Black wrote that the First Amendment must at least mean "that in this country it is no part of the business of government to compose official prayers for any group of the American people to recite as a part of a religious program carried on by government."

Prayer in the Schools—The Debate Continues. Since the *Engel v. Vitale* ruling, the Supreme Court has continued to shore up the wall of separation between church and state in a number of decisions. Generally, the Court has walked a fine line between the wishes of those who believe that religion should have a more prominent place in our public institutions and those who do not. For example, in a 1980 case, the Supreme Court ruled that a Kentucky law requiring that the Ten Commandments be posted in all public schools violated the establishment clause.[5] Many groups around the country opposed this ruling.

Moments of Silence and Other Issues. Another controversial issue is whether "moments of silence" in the schools are constitutional. In 1985, the Supreme Court ruled that an Alabama law authorizing a daily one-minute period of silence for meditation and voluntary prayer was unconstitutional. Because the law specifically endorsed prayer, it appeared to support religion.[6]

Since then, the lower courts have generally held that a school may require a moment of silence, but only if it serves a clearly secular purpose (such as to meditate on the day's activities).[7] Yet another issue concerns prayers said before public school sporting events, such as football games. In 2000, the Supreme Court held that student-led pregame prayer using the school's public-address system was unconstitutional.[8]

In sum, the Supreme Court has ruled that public schools, which are agencies of government, cannot sponsor religious activities. It has *not,* however, held that individuals cannot pray, when and as they choose, in schools or in any other place. Nor has it held that the schools

High school students form a prayer circle outside of a school building. *To what extent does the Constitution allow prayers in school?*

are barred from teaching *about* religion, as opposed to engaging in religious practices.

EVOLUTION VERSUS CREATIONISM   Certain religious groups have long opposed the teaching of evolution in public schools. These groups contend that evolutionary theory, a theory with overwhelming scientific support, directly counters their religious belief that human beings did not evolve but were created fully formed, as described in the biblical story of the creation. In fact, surveys have shown that up to one-third of Americans believe that humans were directly created by God rather than having evolved from other species. The Supreme Court, however, has held that state laws forbidding the teaching of evolution in the schools are unconstitutional.

For example, in a case decided in 1968, the Supreme Court held that an Arkansas law prohibiting the teaching of evolution violated the establishment clause because it imposed religious beliefs on students.[9] In 1987, the Supreme Court also held unconstitutional a Louisiana law requiring that the biblical story of the creation be taught along with evolution. The Court deemed the law unconstitutional in part because it had as its primary purpose the promotion of a particular religious belief.[10]

Teaching the Controversy.   Nevertheless, some state and local groups continue their efforts against the teaching of evolution. In 2008, Louisiana adopted the Louisiana Science Education Act, which states, "The teaching of some scientific subjects can cause controversy." It encourages Louisiana teachers to "help students understand, analyze, critique, and review in an objective manner the scientific strengths and scientific weaknesses of existing scientific theories." Debate in the state legislature made it clear that the theories in question included evolution and climate change. Critic John Derbyshire commented, "The act will encourage Louisiana local school boards to unconstitutional behavior. That's what it's *meant* to do." The legislation has not yet been challenged in court, however.

Evolution versus Intelligent Design. Some activists have advocated the concept of "intelligent design" as an alternative to the teaching of evolution. This concept posits that an intelligent cause, rather than an undirected process such as natural selection, lies behind the creation and development of the universe and living things.

Jesse Ventura, author, former pro wrestler, and former independent governor of Minnesota. Ventura recently won a libel suit against the estate of an author who allegedly defamed him. *Why is it harder for celebrities to win such cases than it is for ordinary people?*

obscenity hard to define. In 1973, the Supreme Court finally came up with a three-part test in *California v. Miller.*[24] To be ruled obscene, a work must (1) excite "unwholesome sexual desire" under present-day community standards, (2) offensively depict prohibited sexual conduct, and (3) lack serious literary, artistic, political, or scientific value. Under "community standards," the definition of obscenity could vary from one part of the country to another.

The *Miller* test was handed down at a time when American attitudes toward sexual expression were undergoing a revolution. A few years earlier, major literary works such as *Ulysses* by James Joyce and *Lady Chatterley's Lover* by D. H. Lawrence were illegal. By

obscenity Indecency or offensiveness in speech, expression, behavior, or appearance.

the early 1980s, however, it was possible in almost all parts of the country to rent pornographic videotapes that left nothing to the imagination.

The Internet was the final blow to the concept of obscenity. By the end of the twentieth century, U.S. officials no longer tried to impose obscenity restrictions on printed or visual material. Attempts by Congress in 1996 and 1998 to ban Internet obscenity that might be seen by minors were ruled unconstitutional by the Supreme Court.[25]

Remaining Restrictions on Pornography. Several types of restrictions survive. The First Amendment applies only to governments, so private, voluntary restrictions are possible. Most mainstream movie theaters, for example, will not show a film that has received a "No Child 17 or Under Admitted" (NC-17) rating from the Motion Picture Association of America. In addition, the government retains the right to impose restrictions on activities that it subsidizes or media that it controls, such as the broadcast spectrum. Thus, restrictions on radio and broadcast television remain in effect.

Finally, the courts have upheld laws aimed at protecting children. Making or possessing pornographic videos or photographs of underage persons remains a serious crime, based on the argument that such depictions are acts of child abuse. Ironically, this argument demonstrates the collapse of obscenity as a legal concept—child pornography is *not* banned because it is obscene. Writings or drawings, including animation, that depict underage sexuality are tolerated because no actual children are involved.

FREE SPEECH FOR STUDENTS? America's schools and college campuses experience an ongoing tension between the guarantee of free speech and the desire to restrain speech that is offensive to others. Typically, cases involving free speech in the schools raise the following question: Where should the line between unacceptable speech and merely offensive speech be drawn? Schools at all levels—elementary schools, high schools, and colleges and universities—have grappled with this issue.

Elementary and High Schools. Generally, the courts allow elementary schools wide latitude to define what students may and may not say to other students. At the high school level, the Supreme Court has allowed some restraints to be placed on the freedom of expression. For example, as you will read shortly in the discussion of freedom of the press, the Court allows school officials to exercise some censorship over high school publications. And, in a controversial 2007 case, the Court upheld a school principal's decision to suspend a high school student who unfurled a banner reading "Bong Hits 4 Jesus" at an event off the school premises. School officials maintained that the banner appeared to advocate illegal drug use in violation of school policy. Many legal commentators and scholars strongly criticized this decision.[26]

University Speech Codes. A difficult question that many universities face today is whether the right to free speech includes the right to make hateful remarks about others based on their race, gender, or sexual orientation. Some claim that allowing people with extremist views to voice their opinions can lead to violence. In response to this question, several universities have gone so far as to institute speech codes to minimize the disturbances that hate speech might cause. Speech codes at public colleges have been ruled unconstitutional on the ground that they restrict freedom of speech.[27] Such codes continue to exist on many college campuses, however.

For example, the policy on acceptable e-mail usage at Claremont McKenna College (a private institution) provides that "the College's system must not be used to create or transmit material that is derogatory, defamatory, obscene or offensive. Such material includes, but is not limited to, slurs, epithets or anything that might be construed as harassment or disparagement based on race, color, national origin, sex, sexual orientation, age, disability, or religious or political beliefs." Presumably, under a policy such as this, it would be a violation to say "Democrats are idiots" or "Republicans are insane."

4–2c Freedom of the Press

The framers of the Constitution believed that the press should be free to publish a wide range of opinions and information, and generally the free speech rights just discussed also apply to the press. The courts have placed certain restrictions on freedom of the press, however. Over the years, the Supreme Court has developed various guidelines and doctrines to use in deciding whether freedom of speech and the press can be restrained.

THE PREFERRED-POSITION DOCTRINE One major guideline, called the *preferred-position doctrine,* states that certain freedoms are so essential to a democracy that they hold a preferred position. According to this doctrine, any law that limits these freedoms should be presumed unconstitutional unless the government can show that the law is absolutely necessary. The idea behind this doctrine is that freedom of speech and the press should rarely, if ever, be diminished, because spoken and printed words are the prime tools of the democratic process.

PRIOR RESTRAINT Stopping an activity before it actually happens is known as *prior restraint.* With respect

> "The only security of all is in a **free press. . . .** It is necessary, to keep the waters pure."
>
> ~ **Thomas Jefferson,** Third president of the United States
> 1801–1809

to freedom of the press, prior restraint involves *censorship,* which occurs when an official removes objectionable materials from an item before it is published or broadcast. An example of censorship and prior restraint would be a court's ruling that two paragraphs in an upcoming article in the local newspaper had to be removed before the article could be published. The Supreme Court has generally ruled against prior restraint, arguing that the government cannot curb ideas before they are expressed.

In certain circumstances, however, the Court has allowed prior restraint. For example, in a 1988 case, a high school principal deleted two pages from the school newspaper just before it was printed. The pages contained stories on students' experiences with pregnancy and discussed the impact of divorce on students at the school. The Supreme Court, noting that students in school do not have exactly the same rights as adults in other settings, ruled that high school administrators can censor school publications. The Court said that school newspapers are part of the school curriculum, not a public forum. Therefore, administrators have the right to censor speech that promotes conduct inconsistent with the "shared values of a civilized social order."[28]

CRITICAL THINKING
▶ The establishment of religious chaplains in the armed forces has been justified on the basis that otherwise, service members on active duty would have no access to religious services and counseling. Do you agree with this argument? Why or why not?

4–3 THE RIGHT TO PRIVACY

LO Discuss why Americans are increasingly concerned about privacy rights.

In a dissenting opinion written in 1928, Supreme Court justice Louis Brandeis stated that the right to privacy is "the most comprehensive of rights and the right most valued by civilized men."[29] The majority of the justices on the

Supreme Court at that time did not agree. In the 1960s, however, Court opinion began to change.

In 1965, in the landmark case of *Griswold v. Connecticut*,[30] the Supreme Court held that a right to privacy is implied by other constitutional rights guaranteed in the First, Third, Fourth, Fifth, and Ninth Amendments. For example, consider the words of the Ninth Amendment: "The enumeration in the Constitution, of certain rights, shall not be construed to deny or disparage others retained by the people." In other words, just because the Constitution, including its amendments, does not specifically mention the right to privacy does not mean that this right is denied to the people.

Although Congress and the courts have acknowledged a constitutional right to privacy, the nature and scope of this right are not always clear. For example, Americans continue to debate whether the right to privacy includes the right to have an abortion or the right of terminally ill persons to commit physician-assisted suicide. Since the terrorist attacks of September 11, 2001, another pressing privacy issue has been how to monitor potential terrorists to prevent another attack without violating the privacy rights of all Americans.

4–3a The Abortion Controversy

One of the most divisive and emotionally charged issues debated today is whether the right to privacy means that women can choose to have abortions.

ABORTION AND PRIVACY In 1973, in the landmark case of *Roe v. Wade*,[31] the Supreme Court, using the *Griswold* case as a precedent, held that the "right of privacy . . . is broad enough to encompass a woman's decision whether or not to terminate her pregnancy." The right is not absolute throughout pregnancy, however. The Court also said that any state could impose certain regulations to safeguard the health of the mother after the first three months of

pregnancy and, in the final stages of pregnancy, could act to protect potential life.

Since the *Roe v. Wade* decision, the Supreme Court has adopted a more conservative approach and has upheld restrictive state laws requiring counseling, waiting periods, notification of parents, and other actions prior to abortions.[32] Yet the Court has never overturned the *Roe* decision. In fact, in 1997 and again in 2000, the Supreme Court upheld laws requiring "buffer zones" around abortion clinics to protect those entering the clinics from unwanted counseling or harassment by antiabortion groups.[33] In 2014, however, the Court ruled that a thirty-five-foot buffer zone established by Massachusetts was excessive.[34]

PARTIAL-BIRTH ABORTIONS In 2000, the Supreme Court invalidated a Nebraska statute banning "partial-birth" abortions, a procedure used during the second trimester of pregnancy.[35] Undeterred by the fate of the Nebraska law, President George W. Bush signed the Partial Birth Abortion Ban Act in 2003. In a close (five-to-four) and controversial 2007 decision, the Supreme Court upheld the constitutionality of the 2003 act.[36]

Many were surprised at the Court's decision on partial-birth abortion, given that the federal act banning this practice was quite similar to the Nebraska law that had been struck down by the Court in 2000, just seven years earlier. The Court became more conservative in 2006, however, when President George W. Bush

Pro-choice activists in Washington, D.C., in 2014. *What has the Supreme Court said on the abortion issue?*

appointed Justice Samuel Alito to replace Sandra Day O'Connor. Dissenting from the majority opinion in the case, Justice Ruth Bader Ginsburg said that the ruling was an "alarming" departure from three decades of Supreme Court decisions on abortion.

In reality, how easy is it for women to access abortion services today? We examine that question in the *Perception versus Reality* feature, which follows.

4–3b Do We Have the "Right to Die"?

Whether it is called euthanasia (mercy killing), assisted suicide, or a dignified way to leave this world, it all comes down to one basic question: Do terminally ill persons have, as part of their civil liberties, a right to die and to be assisted in the process by physicians or others? Phrased another way, are state laws banning physician-assisted suicide in such circumstances unconstitutional?

In 1997, the issue came before the Supreme Court, which characterized the question as follows: Does the liberty protected by the Constitution include a right to commit suicide, which itself includes a right to assistance in doing so? The Court's clear and categorical answer to this question was no. To hold otherwise, said the Court, would be "to reverse centuries of legal doctrine and practice, and strike down the considered policy choice of almost every state."[37]

Perception vs. REALITY

The Availability of Abortion

Before 1973, abortion was illegal in much of the United States. In that year, the United States Supreme Court issued its decision in *Roe v. Wade.* The outcome of this landmark case seemed to settle the abortion issue once and for all. Women had the right to terminate their pregnancies.

The Perception

The highest court in the land made it clear—women can have an abortion if they so decide, and no state laws may prevent this, at least during the first trimester of pregnancy. During the second trimester, only state laws that limit the procedure to protect the health of pregnant women are constitutional. It follows that abortion should be freely available throughout the land.

The Reality

The pro-life and pro-choice sides of the abortion debate seem to agree on one thing. In practice, *Roe v. Wade* is no longer the law of the land. From 2011 to mid-2014, states enacted 222 new abortion restrictions, more than in the entire previous decade. Twenty-six states have imposed a waiting period between required counseling and the time an abortion can be performed. Sixteen states require that counseling include statements that the medical profession considers false or unproven. Nineteen place limits on how late in the pregnancy an abortion can be performed that are stricter than the "first trimester" specified in *Roe v. Wade.* Twelve require an ultrasound before an abortion can be performed.

Other legislation is aimed at closing down abortion clinics. Twenty-four states require that abortion facilities must meet structural standards equivalent to those for surgical facilities. In some states, this requirement is easy to meet. In Texas, however, many clinics would have to move into new and expensive custom-built facilities. Eight states require that clinic physicians have admitting privileges at a local hospital. The states can then rely on hospitals to refuse such privileges. (These laws have been blocked by federal judges in four states.)

Most of these new laws violate *Roe v. Wade* and subsequent Supreme Court rulings. Supporters of abortion rights, however, have been reluctant to challenge the laws because they are afraid that the Supreme Court might narrow abortion rights further. Still, recent laws have been so strict that abortion clinics in particular have been forced to defend themselves in court. Already, for all practical purposes, women cannot get an abortion in several small-population Great Plains and Rocky Mountain states.

 For maps showing access to abortion by state, visit the FiveThirtyEight blog at fivethirtyeight.com/datalab/maps-of-access-to-abortion-by-state.

AMERICA 🇺🇸 AT ODDS
Civil Liberties

Civil liberties represent a contentious topic, and Americans are at odds over many of its issues. Almost all Americans claim to believe in individual rights, but how should this freedom be defined? Often, one right appears to interfere with another. Some of the resulting disputes include the following:

- *Should the First Amendment's establishment clause be interpreted strictly, so that no one's rights are infringed on by government sponsorship of religion—or should it be interpreted loosely, to recognize that the United States is a very religious country?*

- **What kinds of religious practices should be allowed under the free exercise clause?** *For example, should religious groups that limit or ban participation by gay men and lesbians receive the same government benefits as any other group—or may they be penalized for discrimination?*

- *Should advertising receive the same free speech rights as any other kind of speech—or should advertisers be held accountable for making false claims?*

- *Has the government gone too far in restricting liberties in an attempt to combat terrorism—or are the restrictions trivial compared with the benefits?*

- *Consider the most intense controversy of all: Should women have a privacy right to terminate a pregnancy for any reason—or should abortion be a crime?*

Internet Resources

- The Web site for the leading civil liberties organization, the American Civil Liberties Union (ACLU), can be found at www.aclu.org.
- The National Coalition against Censorship (NCAC) seeks to oppose censorship in all its forms. Find it at ncac.org.
- Liberty Counsel is "dedicated to advancing religious freedom, the sanctity of life, and the family." Its take on civil liberties is definitely right of center. You can access its home page at www.lc.org.

- For information on online civil liberties and human rights and on keeping the Internet "open, innovative, and free," go to the Center for Democracy and Technology at www.cdt.org.
- For information on privacy issues relating to the Internet, go to the Electronic Privacy Information Center's Web site at epic.org.
- As you might suspect, cyberbullying is a major topic online. Check out www.stompoutbullying.org.

STUDY TOOLS 4

READY TO STUDY?

- ☐ Review what you've read with the quiz below.
- ☐ Check your answers in Appendix D at the back of the book.
- ☐ For any questions you miss, read the corresponding Learning Outcome section again to prepare for class and your exam.
- ☐ Rip out and study the Chapter in Review card (at the back of the book).

VISIT WWW.CENGAGEBRAIN.COM:

- ☐ Interactive Quizzes
- ☐ Key Term Flashcards or Crossword Puzzles
- ☐ Audio Summaries
- ☐ Simulations, Animated Learning Modules, and Interactive Timelines
- ☐ Videos
- ☐ American Government NewsWatch

FILL-IN

Learning Outcome 4-1

1. The _____ clause of the Fourteenth Amendment to the U.S. Constitution guarantees that state governments will not arbitrarily deprive any person of life, liberty, or property.

Learning Outcome 4-2

2. The *Lemon* test, enunciated by the Supreme Court in 1971 to determine whether government aid to parochial schools is constitutional, states that the aid must _____.

3. The current Supreme Court standard for assessing the constitutionality of _____ is the imminent lawless action test.

4. _____ is a published report of a falsehood that tends to injure a person's reputation or character.

5. The Supreme Court's _____ doctrine states that certain freedoms are so essential to a democracy that any law that limits these freedoms should be presumed to be unconstitutional unless the government can show that the law is absolutely necessary.

Learning Outcome 4-3

6. Under the USA Patriot Act of 2001, the FBI is authorized to use _____ to demand personal information about individuals from private companies, such as banks and phone companies.

7. In _____, the Supreme Court held that the "right of privacy . . . is broad enough to encompass a woman's decision whether or not to terminate her pregnancy."

Learning Outcome 4-4

8. The _____ Amendment includes protection from unreasonable searches and seizures.

9. The Eighth Amendment prohibits _____.

MULTIPLE CHOICE

Learning Outcome 4-1

10. A(n) _____ is an order requiring that an official bring a specified prisoner into court and explain to the judge why the prisoner is being held.
    a. *ex post facto* law
    b. writ of *habeas corpus*
    c. bill of attainder

Learning Outcome 4-2

11. Thomas Jefferson wanted the establishment clause of the First Amendment to be a
    a. "bridge connecting government and religion."
    b. "barrier between government and the freedom of speech."
    c. "wall of separation between church and state."

12. The Supreme Court has ruled that public schools
    a. cannot sponsor religious activities.
    b. are allowed to determine for themselves the number of religious exercises they will sponsor.
    c. are barred from teaching about religion.

Learning Outcome 4-3

13. The Supreme Court, in *Griswold v. Connecticut* (1965), held that a right to privacy is implied by other constitutional rights guaranteed in the
    a. Magna Carta.
    b. First, Third, Fourth, Fifth, and Ninth Amendments.
    c. Declaration of Independence.

Learning Outcome 4-4

14 The Fifth Amendment
    a. includes a protection against self-incrimination.
    b. guarantees a speedy trial and a trial by jury.
    c. guarantees the right to counsel at various stages in some criminal proceedings.

15. _____ says that illegally obtained evidence is not admissible in court.
    a. Double jeopardy
    b. The exclusionary rule
    c. Probable cause

5 | Civil Rights

HANDS UP DONT SHOOT
#JusticeForMikeBrown

© Scott Olson/Getty Images

LEARNING OUTCOMES After reading this chapter, you should be able to:

5-1 Explain the constitutional basis for our civil rights and for laws prohibiting discrimination.

5-2 Discuss the reasons for the civil rights movement and the changes it caused in American politics and government.

5-3 Describe the political and economic achievements of women in this country over time and identify some obstacles to equality that women continue to face.

5-4 Summarize the struggles for equality that other groups in America have experienced.

5-5 Explain what affirmative action is and why it has been so controversial.

After finishing this chapter go to **PAGE 120** for **STUDY TOOLS.**

AMERICA AT ODDS

© John Moore/Getty Images

What Should We Do with Unauthorized Immigrant Children?

How to deal with unauthorized immigration has been a problem for years, as we mentioned in Chapter 1. In the last few years, a new problem has arisen—unauthorized minors traveling alone. U.S. Border Control agents apprehended almost eighty thousand unaccompanied children in 2014. The number of children under thirteen crossing the border in 2014 was three times the number in 2013. The United Nations has done a survey of these unaccompanied child migrants. More than 80 percent said that they were immigrating because of better economic opportunities in the United States or to reunite with family members. Many, also cited fear of violent gangs in their home communities.

When unaccompanied minors arrive from Mexico, current U.S. immigration law allows for immediate deportation. In contrast, unaccompanied minors from Central America have the right to an asylum hearing. About half of the unaccompanied minors whose cases have been heard have been allowed to stay in this country.

The immigration system has been overwhelmed by the number of children arriving from Central America. There must be a better way to handle these children than the current system—but what should it be?

Send Them Back So Others Aren't Encouraged to Come

Many conservatives are in favor of "getting tough." They believe that the law should be changed to send all unaccompanied minors back to their home countries immediately. Current law that allows an asylum hearing to unaccompanied Central American children should be rescinded.

Some Republicans have blamed the Obama administration's Deferred Action for Childhood Arrivals (DACA) program for the current increased influx. That program gives provisional protection from deportation—and the right to seek employment—to some illegal child immigrants brought into the United States before 2007. If the word got out that unauthorized immigration by minors would no longer be tolerated, fewer parents would let their children make the dangerous journey from Central America to the American border with Mexico. Conservatives have also advocated sending the National Guard to the border to make it easier for the Border Patrol to prevent entry in the first place.

Helping These Children Is the Right Thing to Do

Many liberals and religious leaders point out that most children in the new wave of immigration are fleeing from some of the most violent nations on earth. El Salvador, Guatemala, and Honduras have the world's highest murder rates. Most of the influx has come from these three countries. The United States has an obligation under international treaties to consider requests for asylum by those who believe their lives would be at risk if they returned home. These children are just as much refugees as the millions who have been forced out of their homes in Afghanistan, Syria, and Iraq.

Congress was wrong to reject Obama's request in 2014 for $3.7 billion to deal with this growing problem. We need the funds to hire more immigration judges to help process cases more quickly. Our immigration services need additional Spanish-speaking staff. More resources are needed to find foster care options for these minors. The United States has always been a nation of immigrants. It should stay that way.

Where do you stand?

1. Is completely securing the border with Mexico an effective method of avoiding additional unauthorized immigrants? Why or why not?

2. What is the best way to take care of unaccompanied minors who have already entered the United States illegally?

Explore this issue online

- The Roman Catholic Church has long supported the rights of unauthorized immigrants. See its positions at www.usccb.org/about/children-and-migration.

- The Federation for American Immigration Reform demands greater restrictions on immigration. Find its views at www.fairus.org.

INTRODUCTION

As noted in Chapter 4, people sometimes confuse civil rights with civil liberties. Generally, though, the term **civil rights** refers to the rights of all Americans to equal treatment under the law, as provided by the Fourteenth Amendment.

As you will read in this chapter, the struggle of various groups in American society to obtain equal treatment has been a long one, and it continues. Latinos make up one such group, and we discussed an issue that concerns them in this chapter's opening *America at Odds* feature.

In a sense, the history of civil rights in the United States is a history of discrimination against various groups. Discrimination against women, African Americans, and Native Americans dates back to the early years of this nation. More recently, other groups, including persons with disabilities and gay men and lesbians, have struggled for equal treatment under the law. This chapter discusses each of these groups. Inevitably, though, a single short chapter must omit discussion of some groups that have experienced discrimination. Two such groups are American Muslims and older Americans.

Central to any discussion of civil rights is the interpretation of the equal protection clause of the Fourteenth Amendment to the Constitution. For that reason, we look first at that clause.

All Americans
are entitled to
**equal
treatment
under
the law,** as
provided by the
Fourteenth Amendment.

civil rights The rights of all Americans to equal treatment under the law, as provided by the Fourteenth Amendment to the Constitution.

equal protection clause Section 1 of the Fourteenth Amendment, which states that no state shall "deny to any person within its jurisdiction the equal protection of the laws."

fundamental right A basic right of all Americans, such as First Amendment rights. Any law or action that prevents some group of persons from exercising a fundamental right is subject to the *strict scrutiny standard*.

strict scrutiny standard A standard under which a law or action must be necessary to promote a compelling state interest and must be narrowly tailored to meet that interest.

suspect classification A classification, such as race, that provides the basis for a discriminatory law. Any law based on a suspect classification is subject to strict scrutiny by the courts, meaning that the law must be justified by a compelling state interest.

5–1 THE EQUAL PROTECTION CLAUSE

LO Explain the constitutional basis for our civil rights and for laws prohibiting discrimination.

You read about the due process clause of the Fourteenth Amendment in Chapter 4. Equal in importance to the due process clause is the **equal protection clause** in Section 1 of that amendment, which reads as follows: "No State shall . . . deny to any person within its jurisdiction the equal protection of the laws." Section 5 of the amendment provides a legal basis for federal civil rights legislation: "The Congress shall have power to enforce, by appropriate legislation, the provisions of this article."

The equal protection clause has been interpreted by the courts, and especially the Supreme Court, to mean that states must treat all persons equally and may not discriminate *unreasonably* against a particular group or class of individuals. The task of distinguishing between reasonable and unreasonable discrimination is difficult. Generally, in deciding this question, the Supreme Court balances the constitutional rights of individuals to equal protection against government interests in protecting the safety and welfare of citizens.

Over time, the Court has developed various tests, or standards, for determining whether the equal protection clause has been violated. These standards are strict scrutiny, intermediate scrutiny, and ordinary scrutiny (the rational basis test).

5–1a Strict Scrutiny

If a law or action prevents some group of persons from exercising a **fundamental right** (such as one of our First Amendment rights), the law or action will be subject to the **strict scrutiny standard.** Under this standard, the law or action must be necessary to promote a *compelling state interest* and must be narrowly tailored to meet that interest. A law based on a **suspect classification,** such as race, is also subject to strict scrutiny by the courts, meaning that the law must be justified by a compelling state interest.

5–1b Intermediate Scrutiny

Because the Supreme Court had difficulty deciding how to judge cases in which men and women were treated differently, another test was developed—the *intermediate scrutiny standard*. Under this standard, also known as *exacting scrutiny*, laws based on gender classifications are permissible if they are "substantially related to the achievement of an important governmental objective."

For example, a law punishing males but not females for statutory rape has been ruled valid by the courts. The reasoning is that there is an important governmental interest in preventing teenage pregnancy in those circumstances and almost all of the harmful consequences of teenage pregnancies fall on young females.[1] A law prohibiting the sale of beer to males under twenty-one years of age and to females under eighteen years would not be valid, however.[2]

DECLARING GENDER-BASED LAWS UNCONSTITUTIONAL Generally, since the 1970s, the Supreme Court has scrutinized gender classifications closely and has declared many gender-based laws unconstitutional. In 1979, the Court held that a state law allowing wives to obtain alimony judgments against husbands but preventing husbands from receiving alimony from wives violated the equal protection clause.[3] In 1982, the Court declared that Mississippi's policy of excluding males from the School of Nursing at Mississippi University for Women was unconstitutional.[4]

THE VIRGINIA MILITARY INSTITUTE CASE In a controversial 1996 case, *United States v. Virginia*,[5] the Court held that Virginia Military Institute, a state-financed institution, violated the equal protection clause by refusing to accept female applicants. The Court said that the state of Virginia had failed to provide sufficient justification for its gender-based classification.

5–1c The Rational Basis Test (Ordinary Scrutiny)

A third test used to decide whether a discriminatory law violates the equal protection clause is the **rational basis test.** This test is employed only when there is no classifica-

© Shane Hansen/Getty Images

Increasingly, women are filling traditionally male jobs, such as police officer. *What benefits can a police force obtain by hiring more women officers?*

tion—such as race or gender—that would require a higher level of scrutiny. When applying this test to a law that classifies or treats people or groups differently, the courts ask whether the discrimination is rational. In other words, is it a reasonable way to achieve a legitimate government objective? Few laws tested under the rational basis test—or the *ordinary scrutiny standard*, as it is also called—are found invalid, because few laws are truly unreasonable.

A municipal ordinance that prohibits certain vendors from selling their wares in a particular area of the city, for example, will be upheld if the city can meet this rational basis test. The rational basis for the ordinance might be the city's legitimate interest in reducing traffic congestion in that particular area.

CRITICAL THINKING

▸ When evaluating cases of discrimination against gay men or lesbians, some judges have employed the rational basis test, while others have applied intermediate scrutiny. Which standard do you consider appropriate, and why?

rational basis test A test (also known as the *ordinary scrutiny standard*) used by the Supreme Court to decide whether a discriminatory law violates the equal protection clause of the Constitution. It is used only when there is no classification—such as race or gender—that would require a higher level of scrutiny.

Civil rights leader the Reverend Dr. Martin Luther King, Jr. (1929–1968) with civil rights marchers at the Alabama capitol building in 1965. *What was King's first important civil rights campaign?*

decision, the Court upheld busing in several northern cities.[10] Proponents believed that busing improved the educational and career opportunities of minority children and also enhanced the ability of children from different ethnic groups to get along with one another.

Nevertheless, busing was unpopular with many groups from its inception. By the mid-1970s, the courts had begun to retreat from their former support for busing. In 1974, the Supreme Court rejected the idea of busing children across school district lines.[11] In 1986, the Court refused to review a lower court decision that ended a desegregation plan in Norfolk, Virginia.[12] Today,

busing orders to end *de facto* segregation are not upheld by the courts. Indeed, *de facto* segregation in America's schools is still widespread.

5-2d The Civil Rights Movement

In 1955, one year after the first *Brown* decision, an African American woman named Rosa Parks, a long-time activist in the NAACP, boarded a public bus in Montgomery, Alabama. When it became crowded, she refused to move to the "colored section" at the rear of the bus. She was arrested and fined for violating local segregation laws. Her arrest spurred the local African American community to organize a year-long boycott of the entire Montgomery bus system.

The protest was led by a twenty-seven-year-old Baptist minister, the Reverend Dr. Martin Luther King, Jr. During the protest period, he was jailed and his house was bombed. Yet, despite white hostility and what appeared to be overwhelming odds against them, the protesters were triumphant in the end.

In 1956, a federal court prohibited the segregation of buses in Montgomery, and the era of the **civil rights movement**—the movement by minorities and concerned whites to end racial segregation—had begun. The movement was led by a number of groups and individuals, including Martin Luther King and his Southern Christian Leadership Conference (SCLC). Other groups, such as the Congress of Racial Equality (CORE), the NAACP, and the Student Nonviolent Coordinating Committee (SNCC), also sought to secure equal rights for African Americans.

NONVIOLENCE AS A TACTIC Civil rights protesters in the 1960s began to apply the tactic of nonviolent **civil disobedience**—the deliberate and public refusal to obey laws considered unjust—in civil rights actions throughout the South. Activists were trained in the tools of nonviolence—how to use nonthreatening body language, how to go limp when dragged or assaulted, and how to protect themselves from clubs and police dogs.

Greensboro: An Example. In 1960, for example, four African American students in Greensboro, North Carolina, sat at the "whites only" lunch counter at Woolworth's and ordered food. The waitress refused to serve them, and the store closed early, but more students returned the next day to sit at the counter, with supporters picketing outside. **Sit-ins** spread to other lunch counters across the South.

In some instances, students participating in sit-ins were heckled or even dragged from Woolworth's by angry whites. But the protesters never reacted with violence.

civil rights movement The movement in the 1950s and 1960s, by minorities and concerned whites, to end racial segregation.

civil disobedience The deliberate and public act of refusing to obey laws thought to be unjust.

sit-in A tactic of nonviolent civil disobedience. Demonstrators enter a business, college building, or other public place and remain seated until they are forcibly removed or until their demands are met.

"Injustice
anywhere is a threat to
justice everywhere."

~ Martin Luther King, Jr.
U.S. Civil Rights Leader 1929–1968

They simply returned to their seats at the counter, day after day. Within months of the first sit-in, lunch counter managers began to reverse their policies of segregation.

The National Reaction. As the civil rights movement gained momentum, media images increasingly showed nonviolent protesters being assaulted by police, sprayed with fire hoses, and attacked by dogs. These pictures shocked and angered Americans across the country. The resulting public backlash led to nationwide demands for reform. The March on Washington for Jobs and Freedom, led by Martin Luther King, Jr. in 1963, aimed in part to demonstrate widespread public support for legislation to ban discrimination in all aspects of public life.

CIVIL RIGHTS LEGISLATION IN THE 1960S
As the civil rights movement demonstrated its strength, Congress began to pass civil rights laws. While the Fourteenth Amendment prevented the *government* from discriminating against individuals or groups, the private sector—businesses, restaurants, and the like—could still freely refuse to employ and serve nonwhites. Therefore, Congress sought to address this issue.

Black Muslim leader Malcolm X speaks at a Harlem rally in 1963. His speech restated the Black Muslim theme of complete separation of whites and African Americans. *Why might some African Americans have been receptive to Malcolm X's appeal?*

© Library of Congress

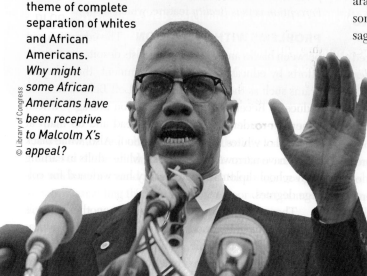

The Civil Rights Act of 1964. The Civil Rights Act of 1964 was the first and most comprehensive civil rights law. It forbade discrimination on the basis of race, color, religion, gender, and national origin. The major provisions of the act were as follows:

▶ It outlawed discrimination in public places of accommodation, such as hotels, restaurants, movie theaters, and public transportation.

▶ It provided that federal funds could be withheld from any federal or state government project or facility that practiced any form of discrimination.

▶ It banned discrimination in employment.

▶ It outlawed arbitrary discrimination in voter registration.

▶ It authorized the federal government to sue to desegregate public schools and facilities.

Voting and Housing Rights. Other significant laws were passed by Congress during the 1960s as well. The Voting Rights Act of 1965 made it illegal to interfere with anyone's right to vote in any election held in this country. (We discuss restrictions on voting rights further in Chapter 8.) The Civil Rights Act of 1968 prohibited discrimination in housing.

THE BLACK POWER MOVEMENT
Not all African Americans embraced nonviolence. Several outspoken leaders in the mid-1960s were outraged at the slow pace of change in the social and economic status of blacks.

Malcolm X, a speaker and organizer for the Nation of Islam (also called the Black Muslims), rejected the goals of integration and racial equality espoused by the civil rights movement. He called instead for black separatism and "black pride." Although he later moderated some of his views, his rhetorical style and powerful message influenced many African American young people.

By the late 1960s, with the assassinations of Malcolm X in 1965 and Martin Luther King in 1968, the era of mass acts of civil disobedience in the name of civil rights had come to an end.

5–2e African Americans in Politics Today

As mentioned earlier, in many jurisdictions African Americans were prevented from voting for years after the Civil War, despite the Fifteenth Amendment (1870). These discriminatory practices persisted in the twentieth century. In the early 1960s, only 22 percent of African Americans of voting age in the South were

In 2013, the Department of Defense ruled that women could apply for front-line combat positions. *Why would some women want to serve in combat units?*

It is estimated that for every dollar earned by men, women earn about 77 cents. Although the wage gap has narrowed significantly since 1963, when the Equal Pay Act was enacted (at that time, women earned 58 cents for every dollar earned by men), it still remains. This is particularly true for women in management positions and older women. Notably, when the workers in a particular occupation include a disproportionately high number of women, the wages that are paid in that occupation tend to be relatively low.

Recent research suggests that wage inequality is concentrated in fields in which staff members are expected to put in very long hours. Finance, where long hours are expected, may have the most unequal pay structure of any industry. In contrast, pay differentials are zero among dental hygienists and advertising salespeople. In effect, women may be penalized because child-care responsibilities make it hard for them to work far more than forty hours a week.[15]

women won races for each of the top five offices in Arizona, the first such occurrence in U.S. history. Generally, women have been more successful politically in the western states than elsewhere. In Washington, more than one-third of the state's legislative seats are now held by women. At the other end of the spectrum are states such as Alabama. In that state, fewer than 10 percent of the lawmakers are women.

5–3d Women in the Workplace

An ongoing challenge for American women is to obtain equal pay and equal opportunity in the workplace. In spite of federal legislation and programs to promote equal treatment of women in the workplace, women continue to face various forms of discrimination.

WAGE DISCRIMINATION   In 1963, Congress passed the Equal Pay Act. The act requires employers to pay an equal wage for substantially equal work—males cannot be paid more than females who perform essentially the same job. The following year, Congress passed the Civil Rights Act of 1964, Title VII of which prohibits employment discrimination on the basis of race, color, national origin, gender, and religion. Women, however, continue to face wage discrimination.

THE GLASS CEILING   Even though an increasing number of women now hold business and professional jobs once held only by men, relatively few of these women are able to rise to the top of the career ladder in their firms due to the lingering bias against women in the workplace. This bias has been described as the **glass ceiling**—an invisible but real discriminatory barrier that prevents women and minorities from rising to top positions of power or responsibility. Today, less than one-sixth of the top executive positions in the largest American corporations are held by women.

SEXUAL HARASSMENT   Title VII's prohibition of gender discrimination has also been extended to prohibit sexual harassment. **Sexual harassment** occurs when job opportunities, promotions, salary increases, or even the ability to retain a job depend on whether an employee complies with demands for sexual favors. A special form of sexual harassment, called *hostile environment harassment*, occurs when an employee is subjected to sexual conduct or comments in the workplace that interfere with the employee's job performance or that create an intimidating, hostile, or offensive environment.

The Supreme Court has upheld the right of persons to be free from sexual harassment on the job on a number of occasions. In 1998, the Court made it clear that sexual harassment includes harassment by members of the same

glass ceiling   An invisible but real discriminatory barrier that prevents women and minorities from rising to top positions of power or responsibility.

sexual harassment   Unwanted physical contact, verbal conduct, or abuse of a sexual nature that interferes with a recipient's job performance, creates a hostile environment, or carries with it an implicit or explicit threat of adverse employment consequences.

sex.[16] In the same year, the Court held that employers are liable for the harassment of employees by supervisors unless the employers can show that (1) they exercised reasonable care in preventing such problems (by implementing antiharassment policies and procedures, for example), and (2) the employees failed to take advantage of any corrective opportunities provided by the employers.[17]

The Civil Rights Act of 1991 greatly expanded the remedies available for victims of sexual harassment. Under the act, victims can seek damages as well as back pay, job reinstatement, and other compensation.

SEXUAL ASSAULT ON CAMPUS Title IX of the Education Amendments of 1972 prohibits gender-based discrimination in schools that receive federal money. Title IX is best known for requiring equal opportunities in sports for men and women. Sexual assault is also considered discrimination under Title IX, however.

Sexual assault on campus, ranging from unwanted touching to acts of violence, is a long-standing problem. Use of alcohol is a major contributing factor. Under the broadest definition, about one in five college women has experienced sexual assault. Yet few women report assault to school authorities, and those who do often receive little help. In some cases, victims have actually been penalized for making complaints.

Beginning in 2011, the Obama administration began cracking down on the problem. By 2014, fifty-five colleges were under investigation for mishandling complaints. Twenty-five were under investigation for retaliating against persons reporting assault. Schools that fail to improve their procedures are at risk of losing federal funds.

CRITICAL THINKING

▶ In recent years, the percentage of young women who have received college diplomas has exceeded the percentage for young men. In the future, how might this development change the social and economic roles of women and men?

5–4 **SECURING RIGHTS FOR OTHER GROUPS**

LO Summarize the struggles for equality that other groups in America have experienced.

In addition to African Americans and women, a number of other groups in U.S. society have faced discriminatory treatment. One lingering result of past discrimination can be that a group suffers from below-average incomes and relatively high rates of poverty. Figure 5–1, which

follows, shows the percentage of persons with incomes below the poverty line for five major racial or ethnic groups. The chart provides statistics for children as well as the overall population. Note that in all groups, children are much more likely than adults to live in poverty. This reality makes poverty that much more damaging.

Next, we look at three groups that have had to struggle for equal treatment—Latinos, Asian Americans, and Native Americans (or American Indians). Then we examine the struggles of several other groups of Americans—persons with disabilities and gay men and lesbians.

5–4a Latinos

Latinos, or Hispanics, constitute the largest ethnic minority in the United States. Whereas African Americans represent 13.1 percent of the U.S. population, Latinos now constitute 16.9 percent. Each year, the Hispanic population grows by nearly 1 million people, one-third of whom are newly arrived legal immigrants. By 2050, Latinos are expected to constitute almost 30 percent of the U.S. population.

FIGURE 5–1 PERSONS IN POVERTY IN THE UNITED STATES BY RACE AND HISPANIC ORIGIN, 2010

Blacks, Hispanics, and American Indians are more likely than whites or Asians to have incomes below the poverty line. *Why are children substantially more likely than adults to live in families with incomes below the poverty line?*

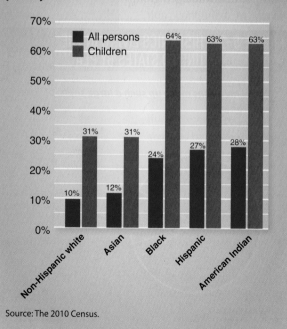

Source: The 2010 Census.

U.S. Representative Tammy Duckworth, Democrat of Illinois. Duckworth lost both legs after her helicopter was shot down in Iraq in 2004.

act also mandates that employers "reasonably accommodate" the needs of workers or job applicants with disabilities who are otherwise qualified for particular jobs unless to do so would cause the employer to suffer an "undue hardship."

The ADA defines persons with disabilities as persons who have physical or mental impairments that "substantially limit" their everyday activities. Health conditions that have been considered disabilities under federal law include blindness, a history of alcoholism, heart disease, cancer, muscular dystrophy, cerebral palsy, paraplegia, diabetes, and acquired immune deficiency syndrome (AIDS). The ADA, however, does not require employers to hire or retain workers who, because of their disabili-

ties, pose a "direct threat to the health or safety" of their co-workers.

LIMITING THE SCOPE OF THE ADA From 1999 to 2002, the Supreme Court handed down a series of rulings that substantially limited the scope of the ADA. The Court found that any limitation that could be remedied by medication or by corrective devices such as eyeglasses did not qualify as a protected disability. According to the Court, even carpal tunnel syndrome was not a disability.[22] In 2008, however, the ADA Amendments Act overturned most of these limits. Carpal tunnel syndrome and other ailments may again qualify as disabilities. (The need for eyeglasses was not, however, covered by the new law.)

In 2001, the Supreme Court reviewed a case raising the question of whether suits under the ADA could be brought against state employers. The Court concluded that states are immune from lawsuits brought to enforce rights under this federal law.[23]

5-4e Gay Men and Lesbians

Today, many Americans—including seven members of Congress—are openly gay, lesbian, or bisexual. Until the late 1960s and early 1970s, though, gay men and lesbians tended to keep quiet about their sexual orientation because exposure usually meant facing harsh consequences. This attitude began to change after a 1969 incident in the Greenwich Village neighborhood of New York City. When the police raided the Stonewall Inn—a bar popular with gay men and lesbians—on June 27 of that year, the bar's patrons responded by throwing beer cans and bottles at the police. The riot continued for two days. The Stonewall Inn uprising launched the "gay power" movement. By the end of the year, gay men and lesbians had formed fifty organizations, including the Gay Activist Alliance and the Gay Liberation Front.

A CHANGING LEGAL LANDSCAPE The number of gay and lesbian organizations has grown from fifty in 1969 to several thousand today. These groups have exerted significant political pressure on legislatures, the media, schools, and churches. In the decades following Stonewall, more than half of the forty-nine states that had sodomy laws repealed them. (*Sodomy laws* prohibit intimate homosexual conduct and certain other forms of sexual activity.) In seven other states, the courts invalidated such laws. Then, in 2003, the United States Supreme Court issued a ruling that effectively invalidated all remaining sodomy laws in the country.

Gaining Legal Status. In *Lawrence v. Texas*,[24] the Court ruled that sodomy laws violated the Fourteenth Amendment's due process clause. According to the

Court, "The liberty protected by the Constitution allows homosexual persons the right to choose to enter upon relationships in the confines of their homes and their own private lives and still retain their dignity as free persons."

Antidiscrimination Laws. Today, twenty-one states and more than 170 cities and counties in the United States have laws prohibiting discrimination against homosexuals in at least some contexts. The laws may prohibit discrimination in housing, education, banking, employment, or public accommodations. In a landmark case in 1996, *Romer v. Evans*,[25] the Supreme Court held that a Colorado constitutional amendment that would have invalidated all state and local laws protecting homosexuals from discrimination violated the equal protection clause of the U.S. Constitution. The Court stated that the amendment would have denied to homosexuals in Colorado—but to no other Colorado residents—"the right to seek specific protection from the law."

A same-sex couple embraces outside the United States Supreme Court on June 26, 2013, after the Court cleared the way for same-sex marriage in California. *What are some of the arguments that have been advanced in favor of same-sex marriage?*

CHANGING ATTITUDES Laws and court decisions protecting the rights of gay men and lesbians reflect social attitudes that are much changed from the 1960s. Liberal political leaders have been supporting gay rights for at least two decades. Even some conservative politicians have softened their stance on the issue. For example, Republican U.S. senators from Alaska, Illinois, and Ohio now support same-sex marriage.

Public support for same-sex marriage, which was endorsed by only 27 percent of Americans in 1996, has risen ever since. In a striking development, several polling organizations reported in mid-2011 that for the first time ever, an absolute majority of those questioned supported same-sex marriage. Support in current polls ranges from 54 to 59 percent.

SAME-SEX MARRIAGE By mid-2014, same-sex marriage had been legalized in nineteen states, the District of Columbia, and ten American Indian tribal jurisdictions. States adopting same-sex marriage were concentrated in the Northeast and on the Pacific Coast, though several Midwestern states legalized the procedure as well. As we noted in Chapter 3, judges ruled in 2013 and 2014 that

same-sex marriage should be permitted in fourteen of the thirty-one states where it was currently illegal. These rulings were initially *stayed* (suspended) pending appeal, however. In October 2014, the Supreme Court refused to take up these rulings, and the stays were lifted. By late October, thirty states permitted same-sex marriage. Lawsuits were pending in all other states. It seemed inevitable that the Court would have to address the issue eventually.

Same-Sex Marriage In the Courts. State supreme courts took the lead in legalizing same-sex marriage, beginning with the Massachusetts Supreme Judicial Court in 2003.[26] In May 2008, California became the second state to legalize gay marriage as a result of a ruling by the state's supreme court. In November of that year, however, California voters approved Proposition 8, which restricted marriage to "one man and one woman." California continued to recognize same-sex marriages conducted between May and Election Day in 2008.

In 2010, a U.S. district court declared that Proposition 8 violated the due process and equal protection clauses of the Fourteenth Amendment to the U.S. Constitution. The Ninth Circuit Court of Appeals upheld this decision in 2012. The inevitable result was to send the matter to the United States Supreme Court. In June 2013, the Court declined to decide the case on the merits, arguing that the private parties who had filed the appeal had no legal grounds for doing so. (The

California state government had refused to appeal the case.) As a result, the district court ruling remained valid, and California immediately resumed conducting same-sex marriages.[27]

A second Supreme Court decision in 2013 had more sweeping consequences. In 1996, Congress passed the Defense of Marriage Act (DOMA). Section 3 of DOMA barred the national government from recognizing same-sex marriages performed under state law. In *United States v. Windsor,* the Court found Section 3 to be unconstitutional under the Fifth Amendment.[28] The result was to make same-sex couples eligible for thousands of federal benefits. As noted, a large number of judges across the country ruled in favor of same-sex marriage in 2013 and 2014. These courts invariably cited *Windsor* as a basis for their decisions.

State Legislators and Referendums. While same-sex marriage has often been established through judicial action, an even larger number of states have adopted the reform by a vote of either the state legislature or the people. The legislatures of Connecticut and Vermont were the first to take such a vote, though the Connecticut legislature was merely affirming an earlier decision by the state supreme court. In the following years, nine other state legislatures and the District of Columbia Council legalized same-sex marriage. In Maine, the legislation was overturned in a referendum. In New Jersey, Governor Chris Christie vetoed that state's law. Christie's veto was later ruled unconstitutional by the state supreme court. In 2012, Maine—in a reversal—plus Maryland and Washington became the first states to endorse same-sex marriage in popular referendums.

In many states, legalization of same-sex marriage was preceded by laws establishing same-sex domestic partnerships. Vermont pioneered this institution in 2000. These partnerships provided many, if not all, of the benefits of marriage under state law, but denied couples the dignity of the marriage title. By 2014, Nevada was the only state in which this status was still relevant. Wisconsin also provided some benefits to same-sex couples, but these fell short of those available under domestic partnership laws.

GAYS AND LESBIANS IN THE MILITARY Gay men and lesbians who wish to join the military have faced a number of obstacles. Until recently, one was the

affirmative action A policy that gives special consideration, in jobs and college admissions, to members of groups that have been discriminated against in the past.

"don't ask, don't tell" policy. This policy, which banned openly gay men and lesbians from the military, was implemented in 1993 by President Bill Clinton when it became clear that more liberal alternatives would not be accepted. During his presidential campaign, Barack Obama pledged to abolish the policy. Later, gay and lesbian rights activists accused him of "putting the issue on a back burner."

The courts forced the issue, however. In September 2010, a U.S. district court ruled that "don't ask, don't tell" was unconstitutional.[29] A U.S. appeals court stayed (suspended) the ruling, but the possibility that "don't ask, don't tell" might be thrown out by the courts forced Congress to take action. In the "lame duck" session between the November 2010 elections and the swearing-in of new members in January 2011, Congress repealed the policy. Full repeal was implemented later in 2011. As a result, gay men and lesbians may now serve openly in the nation's armed forces.

CRITICAL THINKING

▶ The number of Latinos in the United States continues to grow. What impact do you think this will have on American culture and politics?

5-5 BEYOND EQUAL PROTECTION —AFFIRMATIVE ACTION

LO Explain what affirmative action is and why it has been so controversial.

One provision of the Civil Rights Act of 1964 called for prohibiting discrimination in employment. Soon after the act was passed, the federal government began to legislate programs promoting *equal employment opportunity.*

Such programs require that employers' hiring and promotion practices guarantee the same opportunities to all individuals. Experience soon showed that minorities often had fewer opportunities to obtain education and relevant work experience than did whites. Because of this, minorities were still excluded from many jobs. Even though discriminatory practices were made illegal, the change in the law did not make up for the results of years of discrimination. Consequently, under President Lyndon B. Johnson (1963–1969), a new policy was developed.

Called **affirmative action,** this policy required employers to take positive steps to remedy *past* discrimination. Affirmative action programs involved giving special consideration, in jobs and college admissions, to members of groups that were discriminated against in the past.

Until recently, all public and private employers who received federal funds were required to adopt and implement these programs. Thus, the policy of affirmative action was applied to all agencies of the federal, state, and local governments and to all private employers who sell goods to or perform services for any agency of the federal government. In short, it covered nearly all of the nation's major employers and many of its smaller ones.

5-5a Affirmative Action Tested

The Supreme Court first addressed the issue of affirmative action in 1978 in *Regents of the University of California v. Bakke*.[30] Allan Bakke, a white male, had been denied admission to the University of California's medical school at Davis. The school had set aside sixteen of the one hundred seats in each year's entering class for applicants who wished to be considered as members of designated minority groups. Many of the students admitted through this special program had lower test scores than Bakke.

Bakke sued the university, claiming that he was a victim of **reverse discrimination**—discrimination against whites. Bakke argued that the use of a **quota system,** in which a specific number of seats were reserved for minority applicants only, violated the equal protection clause. A majority on the Supreme Court concluded that although both the Constitution and the Civil Rights Act of 1964 allow race to be used as a factor in making admissions decisions, race cannot be the *sole* factor. Because the university's quota system was based solely on race, it was unconstitutional.

5-5b Strict Scrutiny Applied

In 1995, the Supreme Court issued a landmark decision in *Adarand Constructors, Inc. v. Peña*.[31] The Court held that any federal, state, or local affirmative action program that uses racial classifications as the basis for making decisions is subject to "strict scrutiny" by the courts. As discussed earlier in this chapter, this means that, to be constitutional, a discriminatory law or action must be narrowly tailored to meet a *compelling* government interest.

In effect, the *Adarand* decision narrowed the application of affirmative action programs. An affirmative action program can no longer make use of quotas or preferences and cannot be maintained simply to remedy past discrimination by society in general. It must be nar-

A supporter of affirmative action outside the Supreme Court. The Court was hearing arguments on *Fisher v. University of Texas*, an affirmative action case. *Is diversity a legitimate argument in favor of affirmative action? Why or why not?*

rowly tailored to remedy actual discrimination that has occurred, and once the program has succeeded, it must be changed or dropped.

5-5c The Diversity Issue

Following the *Adarand* decision, several lower courts faced cases raising the question of whether affirmative action programs designed to achieve diversity on college campuses were constitutional. In a 1996 case, *Hopwood v. State of Texas,* a federal appellate court challenged the *Bakke* decision by stating that *any* use of race in college admissions, even when diversity was a goal, violated the Fourteenth Amendment.[32]

reverse discrimination Discrimination against those who have no minority status.

quota system A policy under which a specific number of jobs, promotions, or other types of placements, such as university admissions, are given to members of selected groups.

THE UNIVERSITY OF MICHIGAN CASES   In 2003, the United States Supreme Court reviewed two cases involving issues similar to that in the *Hopwood* case. Both cases involved admissions programs at the University of Michigan.

Undergraduate Admissions.   In *Gratz v. Bollinger*,[33] two white applicants who were denied undergraduate admission to the university alleged reverse discrimination. The university's policy gave each applicant a score based on grade point average, standardized test scores, and personal achievements. The system automatically awarded every "underrepresented" minority (African American, Hispanic, and Native American) applicant one-fifth of the points needed to guarantee admission. The Court held that this policy violated the equal protection clause.

Law School Admissions.   In contrast, in *Grutter v. Bollinger*,[34] the Court held that the University of Michigan Law School's admissions policy was constitutional. The significant difference between the two admissions policies, in the Court's view, was that the law school's approach did not apply a mechanical formula giving "diversity bonuses" based on race or ethnicity. In short, the Court concluded that diversity on college campuses was a legitimate goal and that limited affirmative action programs could be used to attain this goal.

THE SUPREME COURT REVISITS THE ISSUE   By 2007, when another case involving affirmative action came before the Court, Justice Samuel Alito, Jr., had replaced Justice Sandra Day O'Connor. She had often been the "swing" vote on the Court, sometimes voting with the more liberal justices and sometimes joining the conservative bloc. Alito was a more conservative jurist than O'Connor, and his appointment moved the Court to the right.

Parents Involved in Community Schools v. Seattle School District No. 1 was decided in 2007, after Justice Alito had joined the Court.[35] The case concerned the policies of two school districts—one in Louisville, Kentucky, and one in Seattle, Washington. Both schools were trying to achieve a more diversified student body by giving preference to minority students if space in the schools was limited and a choice among applicants had to be made.

Parents of white children who were turned away from schools because of these policies sued the school districts, claiming that the policies violated the equal protection clause. Ultimately, the Supreme Court held in favor of the parents. The Court's decision did not overrule the 2003 case involving the University of Michigan Law School, however, for the Court did not deny that race could be used as a factor in university admissions policies. Nonetheless, some claimed that the decision represented a significant change on the Court with respect to affirmative action policies.

5–5d State Actions

Beginning in the mid-1990s, some states have taken actions to ban affirmative action programs or replace them with alternative policies.

BANS ON AFFIRMATIVE ACTION   In 1996, by a ballot initiative, California amended its state constitution to prohibit any "preferential treatment to any individual or group on the basis of race, sex, color, ethnicity, or national origin in the operation of public employment, public education, or public contracting." Two years later, voters in the state of Washington approved a ballot measure ending all state-sponsored affirmative action. Florida has also ended affirmative action.

© AP Photo/Charles Dharapak

Abigail Fisher, who sued the University of Texas alleging reverse discrimination. The Supreme Court's 2013 ruling on *Fisher v. University of Texas* was relatively inconclusive. *Is it time to end affirmative action programs? Why or why not?*

In 2006, a ballot initiative in Michigan banned affirmative action in that state just three years after the Supreme Court decisions discussed above. In the 2008 elections, Nebraska also banned affirmative action, but voters in Colorado rejected such a measure. Arizona banned affirmative action in 2010, and New Hampshire and Oklahoma did so in 2012.

In 2012, a federal appeals court overturned the affirmative action ban approved by Michigan voters in 2006. In April 2014, however, the Supreme Court reversed the appeals court ruling, arguing that state voters had the right to eliminate affirmative action programs.[36] This decision gave support to bans on affirmative action in other states.

"RACE-BLIND" ADMISSIONS In the meantime, many public universities are trying to find "race-blind" ways to attract more minority students to their campuses. For example, Texas has established a program under which the top students at every high school in the state are guaranteed admission to the University of Texas, Austin. Originally, the guarantee applied to students who were in the top 10 percent of their graduating class. Today, the percentage varies from year to year. For 2014, the guarantee was limited to students in the top 7 percent of their class. Beginning in 2005, the university reinstated an affirmative action plan, but it was limited to students who were not admitted as part of the top-student guarantee.

The guarantee ensures that the top students at minority-dominated inner-city schools can attend the state's leading public university. It also assures admission to the best white students from rural, often poor, communities. Previously, many of these students could not have hoped to attend the University of Texas. The losers are students from upscale metropolitan neighborhoods or suburbs who have high test scores but are not the top students at their schools. One result is that more students with high test scores enroll in less famous schools, such as Texas Tech University and the University of Texas, Dallas—to the benefit of these schools' reputations.

CRITICAL THINKING

▶ Is the Texas plan to admit the top students from each high school to the University of Texas fair? Why or why not?

AMERICA AT ODDS
Civil Rights

During the first part of the twentieth century, discrimination against African Americans and members of other minority groups was a social norm in the United States. Indeed, much of the nation's white population believed that the ability to discriminate was a constitutionally protected right. Today, the "right to discriminate" has very few defenders. America's laws—and its culture—now hold that discrimination on the basis of race, gender, religion, national origin, and many other characteristics is flatly unacceptable.

Even if civil rights are now broadly supported and protected by law, however, questions remain as to how far these protections should extend. Americans are at odds over a number of civil rights issues, including the following:

- *If unauthorized immigrants have certain rights as persons under the Fourteenth Amendment to the Constitution, should these rights be construed broadly—or as narrowly as possible?*

- *Should same-sex marriages by lesbians and gay men be recognized—or prohibited?*

- *Should we allow lesbians and gay men to serve openly in the nation's armed forces—or was it a mistake to abandon the "don't ask, don't tell" policy?*

- *Is affirmative action still a necessary policy—or should it be abandoned?*

- *When colleges and universities consider admissions, is it legitimate to promote racial, ethnic, gender, or socioeconomic diversity—or are such considerations just new forms of discrimination?*

Internet Resources

- The home page for the National Association for the Advancement of Colored People (NAACP), which contains extensive information about African American civil rights issues, is www.naacp.org.

- The home page of the National Organization for Women (NOW) has information on the rights and status of women. You can find NOW's home page at www.now.org.

- For discussions about what feminism means to many women, visit www.whoneedsfeminism.com.

- For information on Latinos in the United States, the League of United Latin American Citizens is a good source. You can find it at lulac.org.

- For information on the Americans with Disabilities Act, go to askjan.org.

- The Gay and Lesbian Alliance against Defamation (GLAAD) provides news and information at www.glaad.org.

STUDY TOOLS 5

READY TO STUDY?

- ☐ Review what you've read with the quiz below.
- ☐ Check your answers in Appendix D at the back of the book.
- ☐ For any questions you miss, read the corresponding Learning Outcome section again to prepare for class and your exam.
- ☐ Rip out and study the Chapter in Review card (at the back of the book).

VISIT WWW.CENGAGEBRAIN.COM:

- ☐ Interactive Quizzes
- ☐ Key Term Flashcards or Crossword Puzzles
- ☐ Audio Summaries
- ☐ Simulations, Animated Learning Modules, and Interactive Timelines
- ☐ Videos
- ☐ American Government NewsWatch

FILL-IN

LearningOutcome 5–1

1. A law based on a _____, such as race, is subject to strict scrutiny by the courts.

LearningOutcome 5–2

2. In *Plessy v. Ferguson* (1896), the Supreme Court established the _____ doctrine, which was used to justify racial segregation in many areas of life for nearly sixty years.

3. The Civil Rights Act of 1964 forbade discrimination on the basis of _____.

LearningOutcome 5–3

4. The feminist movement that began in the 1960s sought _____ for women.

5. It is estimated that for every dollar earned by men, women earn about _____.

LearningOutcome 5–4

6. _____ constitute the largest ethnic minority in the United States.

7. Actions taken under an executive order issued by President Franklin D. Roosevelt in 1942 subjected many _____ Americans to curfews and evacuated many of those on the West Coast to "relocation centers."

LearningOutcome 5–5

8. Affirmative action is best defined as a policy _____.

9. In *Adarand Constructors, Inc. v. Peña* (1995), the Supreme Court held that any federal, state, or local affirmative action program that uses racial classifications as the basis for making decisions is subject to _____ scrutiny by the courts.

MULTIPLE CHOICE

LearningOutcome 5–1

10. The equal protection clause of the _____ Amendment reads: "No State shall . . . deny to any person within its jurisdiction the equal protection of the laws."
    a. Fifth   b. Fourteenth   c. Nineteenth

LearningOutcome 5–2

11. "Jim Crow" laws
    a. separated the white community from the black community.
    b. were justified by the Supreme Court's decision in *Brown v. Board of Education of Topeka* (1954).
    c. required an end to segregation.

12. In *Brown II* (1955), the Supreme Court ordered desegregation to begin
    a. "immediately."
    b. "with caution and care."
    c. "with all deliberate speed."

LearningOutcome 5–3

13. _____ appointed the first woman to serve as a justice of the United States Supreme Court.
    a. Ronald Reagan   c. Barack Obama
    b. George W. Bush

LearningOutcome 5–4

14. In 1789, Congress designated the Native American tribes as _____ so that the government could sign land and boundary treaties with them.
    a. enemies
    b. sovereign states composed of American citizens
    c. foreign nations

LearningOutcome 5–5

15. In *Gratz v. Bollinger* (2003), the Supreme Court held that the undergraduate admissions policy at the University of Michigan violated the equal protection clause because it
    a. automatically awarded every "underrepresented" minority applicant one-fifth of the points needed to guarantee admission.
    b. failed to take into account an applicant's race or ethnicity.
    c. failed to take into account an applicant's gender.

6 | Interest Groups

© Marlon Correa/The Washington Post/Getty Images

LEARNING OUTCOMES   After reading this chapter, you should be able to:

6-1 Explain what an interest group is, why interest groups form, and how interest groups function in American politics.

6-2 Identify the various types of interest groups.

6-3 Discuss how the activities of interest groups help to shape government policymaking.

6-4 Describe how interest groups are regulated by government.

After finishing
this chapter go to
PAGE 142 for
STUDY TOOLS.

AMERICA AT ODDS

© Jani Bryson/Getty Images

Are Farmers Getting a Deal That's Too Good?

Many people, including those who live in large cities, have a romantic view of farming and farmers. This view is one of many reasons why interest groups representing farmers are so successful in winning support from the federal government. Over the last five years, about 2 million farmers received subsidies. The federal government's farm program is authorized by five-year farm bills. The last one expired in 2012. Because of the high political polarization of today's Congress, no new farm bill passed until 2014. Farm bills have traditionally passed with bipartisan support because farm programs were in the same bill as the Supplemental Nutrition Assistance Program (SNAP, or food stamps). That ensured that liberals would join with rural legislators to support the bill. In 2013, Tea Party members tried to separate SNAP from the farm program. They failed.

The 2014 bill provides $4.4 billion per year for commodity programs, $5.6 billion per year for conservation, and $9.0 billion per year for crop insurance. *Direct payments* were abolished. These payments went to growers of corn, cotton, rice, soybeans, and wheat regardless of whether they actually planted the crops. Almost all of the funds saved were added back as crop insurance subsidies, however. Are farmers getting too good a deal? Should farm subsidies be cut?

Agriculture Works— Don't Mess with Success

Farming is one of the riskiest businesses around. Farmers are ten times as likely to be killed on the job as the average worker. The weather is a constant worry. Every year, thousands of farmers lose their crops to floods or drought—as in 2012. Further, unlike many businesses, farmers can't set their own prices for what they sell. If you manufacture dishwashers, you expect that you can set a price for them that will cover your costs. Not so in agriculture. Prices are set by world commodity markets, where prices can swing wildly from month to month.

Despite the dangers, agriculture is a success story. Farm exports are booming as poor countries become richer and their people demand better diets—and the United Nations predicts that farmers will need to produce 70 percent more food by 2050 to keep up with population increases. Farm programs are an important safety net that helps keep our farmers in business. At less than half a percent of the federal budget, these programs are also a bargain.

Wealthy Farmers Don't Need These Subsidies

Everybody loves small farmers, but most of the subsidies don't go to these farmers. Under the previous farm bill, large commercial farms amassed 62 percent of all federal payments. The average family income for these farmers exceeded $200,000 per year. Their subsidies averaged about $30,000 per year. These numbers are unlikely to change under the new bill. Why are we giving so much federal aid to people who are that well off?

There's no doubt that farming is risky. That's why the great majority of farmers carry crop insurance, which—as noted above—is subsidized. Typically, two-thirds of the cost of the insurance is covered by the government. Further, the 2014 bill contains an extra provision to cover policy deductibles. How can you lose? Some may claim that we need disaster assistance and conservation programs. But commodity programs and excessive insurance subsidies need to be cut back dramatically. American food consumers and taxpayers have paid too much for too long.

Where do you stand?

1. What effect might farm programs have on rural residents who are not farmers?

2. Soybeans are the nation's second-largest crop, after corn. Half of all U.S. soybeans are exported, many of them to feed Chinese pigs. What benefits might we gain from this trade?

Explore this issue online

- You can find the site of the Environmental Working Group (EWG), a critic of farm subsidies, at www.ewg.org. The EWG has a database that contains a complete record of farm program recipients and what they were paid.

- To find arguments in support of the farm programs, visit the Web site of the Farm Bureau at www.fb.org.

INTRODUCTION

The groups supporting and opposing farm programs provide but one example of how Americans form groups to pursue or protect their interests. All of us have interests that we would like to have represented in government: labor unionists would like it to be easier to organize unions, young people want good educational opportunities, and environmentalists want cleaner air and water, for example.

The old saying that there is strength in numbers is certainly true in American politics. Special interests significantly influence American government and politics. Indeed, some Americans think that this influence is so great that it jeopardizes representative democracy. Others maintain that interest groups are a natural consequence of democracy. After all, throughout our nation's history, people have organized into groups to protect special interests. Because of the important role played by interest groups in the American system of government, we examine such groups in this chapter. We look at what they are, why they are formed, and how they influence policymaking.

6–1 INTEREST GROUPS AND AMERICAN GOVERNMENT

LO Explain what an interest group is, why interest groups form, and how interest groups function in American politics.

An **interest group** is an organized group of people sharing common objectives who actively attempt to influence government policymakers through direct and indirect methods. Whatever their goals—more or fewer social services, higher or lower prices—interest groups pursue these goals on every level and in every branch of government.

On any given day in Washington, D.C., you can see national interest groups in action. If you eat breakfast in the Senate dining room, you might see congressional committee staffers reviewing testimony with representatives from women's groups. Later that morning, you might visit the Supreme Court and watch a civil rights lawyer arguing on behalf of a client in a discrimination suit. Lunch in a popular Washington restaurant might find you listening in

on a conversation between an agricultural lobbyist and a congressional representative.

That afternoon you might visit an executive department, such as the Department of Labor, and watch bureaucrats working out rules and regulations with representatives from a business interest group. Then you might stroll past the headquarters of the National Rifle Association (NRA), AARP (formerly the American Association of Retired Persons), or the National Wildlife Federation.

6–1a The Constitutional Right to Petition the Government

The right to form interest groups and to lobby the government is protected by the Bill of Rights. The First Amendment guarantees the right of the people "to petition the Government for a redress of grievances." This important right sometimes gets lost among the other, more well-known First Amendment guarantees, such as the freedoms of religion, speech, and the press. Nonetheless, the right to petition the government is as important and fundamental to our democracy as the other First Amendment rights.

The right to petition the government allows citizens and groups of citizens to lobby members of Congress and other government officials, to sue the government, and to submit petitions to the government. Whenever someone

Much lobbying takes place in Washington, D.C., inside the U.S. Capitol building.

---

interest group An organized group of individuals sharing common objectives who actively attempt to influence policymakers.

> ## "Politics is about
> # people,
> ## not politicians."
>
> ~ **Scott Simms,** Canadian Politician B. 1969

e-mails her or his congressional representative for help with a problem, such as not receiving a Social Security payment, that person is petitioning the government.

6–1b Why Interest Groups Form

The United States is a vast country of many regions, scores of ethnic groups, and a huge variety of businesses and occupations. The number of potential interests that can be represented is therefore very large. Beyond the sheer size of the country, however, there are a number of specific reasons why the United States has as many interest groups as it does.

BECOMING AN INTEREST GROUP It is worth remembering that not all groups are interest groups. A group becomes an interest group when it seeks to affect the policies or practices of the government. Many groups do not meet this standard. A social group, for example, may be formed to entertain or educate its members, with no broader purpose. Churches, organized to facilitate worship and community, frequently have no political aims. (Indeed, certain political activities, such as campaigning for or against candidates for office, could cost a church its tax-exempt status.)

A group founded with little or no desire to influence the government can become an interest group, however, if its members decide that the government's policies are important to them. Alternatively, lobbying the government may initially be only one of several activities pursued by a group and then grow to become the group's primary purpose.

The National Rifle Association (NRA) provides an example of this process. From its establishment in 1871 until the 1930s, the group took little part in politics. As late as the 1970s, a large share of the NRA's members joined for reasons that had nothing to do with politics. Many joined solely to participate in firearms training programs or to win marksman certifications. The NRA continues to provide such services today, but it is now so heavily politicized that anyone likely to take out a membership is certain to broadly agree with the NRA's political positions.

MORE GOVERNMENT, MORE INTEREST GROUPS Interest groups may form—and existing groups may become more politically active—when the government expands its scope of activities. More government, in other words, means more interest groups. Prior to the 1970s, for example, the various levels of government were not nearly as active in attempting to regulate the use of firearms as they were thereafter. This change provides one explanation of why the NRA is much more politically active today than it was years ago.

Consider another example—AARP, formerly the American Association of Retired Persons. AARP is a major lobbying force that seeks to preserve or enhance Social Security and Medicare benefits for citizens sixty-five years of age and older. Before the creation of Social Security in the 1930s, however, the federal government did not provide income support to the elderly, and there would have been little reason for an organization such as AARP to exist.

DEFENDING THE GROUP'S INTERESTS Interest groups also may come into existence in response to a perceived threat to a group's interests. In the example of the NRA, the threat was an increase in the frequency of attempts to regulate or even ban firearms. This increase threatened the interests of gun owners. As another example, the National Right to Life Committee formed in response to *Roe v. Wade*, the United States Supreme Court's decision that legalized abortion. Interest groups can also form in reaction to the creation of other interest groups, thus pitting two groups against each other. Political scientist David B. Truman coined the term *disturbance theory* for his description of this kind of defensive formation of interest groups.[1]

THE IMPORTANCE OF LEADERS Political scientist Robert H. Salisbury provided another analysis of the organization of interest groups that he dubbed *entrepreneurial theory*. This line of thought focuses on the importance of the leaders who establish the organization. The desire of such individuals to guarantee a viable organization is important to the group's survival.[2] AARP is an example of a group with a committed founder—Dr. Ethel Percy Andrus, a retired high school principal. Andrus organized the group in 1958 to let older Americans purchase healthcare insurance collectively. Like the NRA, AARP did not develop into a lobbying powerhouse until years after it was founded.

INCENTIVES TO JOIN A GROUP The French political observer and traveler Alexis de Tocqueville wrote in 1835 that Americans have a tendency to form "associations" and have perfected "the art of pursuing in common the object of their common desires. . . . In no other country of the world, has the principle of association been more successfully used or applied to a greater multitude of objectives than in America."[3] Of course, Tocqueville could not foresee the thousands of associations that now exist in this country. Surveys show that more than 85 percent of Americans belong to at least one group. Table 6–1, which follows, shows the percentage of Americans who belong to various types of groups today.

Political scientists have identified various reasons why people join interest groups. Often, people have one or more incentives to join such organizations.

▸ If a group stands for something that you believe is very important, you can gain considerable satisfaction in taking action from within that group. Such satisfaction is referred to as a **purposive incentive.**

▸ Some people enjoy the camaraderie and sense of belonging that come from associating with other people who share their interests and goals. That enjoyment can be called a **solidary incentive.**

▸ Some groups offer their members material incentives for joining, such as discounts on products, subscriptions, or group insurance programs. Each of these could be characterized as a **material incentive.**

Sometimes, though, none of these incentives is enough to persuade people to join a group.

THE FREE RIDER PROBLEM The world in which we live is one of scarce resources that can be used to create *private goods* and *public goods.* Most of the goods and services that you use are private goods. If you consume them, no one else can consume them at the same time. If you eat a sandwich, no one else can have it.

With public goods, however, your use of a good does not diminish its use by someone else. National defense is a good example. If this country is protected through its national defense system, your protection from enemy invasion does not reduce any other person's protection.

People cannot be excluded from enjoying a public good, such as national defense, just because they did not pay for it. As a result, public goods are often provided by the government, which can force people to pay for the public good through taxation.

The existence of persons who benefit but do not contribute is called the **free rider problem.** Much of

purposive incentive A reason to join an interest group—satisfaction resulting from working for a cause in which one believes.

solidary incentive A reason to join an interest group—pleasure in associating with like-minded individuals.

material incentive A reason to join an interest group—practical benefits such as discounts, subscriptions, or group insurance.

free rider problem The difficulty that exists when individuals can enjoy the outcome of an interest group's efforts without having to contribute, such as by becoming members of the group.

TABLE 6-1 PERCENTAGE OF AMERICANS BELONGING TO VARIOUS GROUPS	
Social clubs	17%
Neighborhood groups	18
Hobby, garden, and technology clubs	19
PTA and school groups	21
Professional and trade associations	27
Health, sport, and country clubs	30
Religious groups	61

Source: AARP.

what we know about the free rider problem comes from Mancur Olson's classic work of political science, *The Logic of Collective Action.*[4]

Interest Groups and Public Goods. Lobbying, collective bargaining by labor unions, and other forms of representation can also be public goods. If an interest group is successful in lobbying for laws that will improve air quality, for example, everyone who breathes that air will benefit, whether they paid for the lobbying effort or not.

Addressing the Problem. In some instances, the free rider problem can be overcome. For example, social pressure may persuade some people to join or donate to a group for fear of being ostracized. This motivation is more likely to be effective for small, localized groups than for large, widely dispersed groups like AARP, however.

The government can also step in to ensure that the burden of lobbying for the public good is shared by all. When the government classifies interest groups as nonprofit organizations, it confers on them tax-exempt status. The groups' operating costs are reduced because they do not have to pay taxes, and the impact of the government's lost revenue is absorbed by all taxpayers.

6–1c How Interest Groups Function in American Politics

Despite the bad press that interest groups tend to get in the United States, they do serve several purposes in American politics:

▸ Interest groups help bridge the gap between citizens and government and enable citizens to explain their views on policies to public officials.

▸ Interest groups help raise public awareness and inspire action on various issues.

▸ Interest groups often provide public officials with specialized and detailed information that might be difficult to obtain otherwise. This information may be useful in making policy choices.

Alexis de Tocqueville (1805–1859) a French political historian, took a keen interest in the new democracy in America. He toured the United States and collected his observations in *Democracy in America*, published in 1835. *What U.S. institutions would he have seen that were undemocratic?*

▶ Interest groups serve as another check on public officials to make sure that they are carrying out their duties responsibly.

ACCESS TO GOVERNMENT In a sense, the American system of government invites the participation of interest groups by offering many points of access for groups wishing to influence policy. Consider the possibilities at just the federal level.

An interest group can lobby members of Congress to act in the interests of the group. If the Senate passes a bill opposed by the group, the group's lobbying efforts can shift to the House of Representatives. If the House passes the bill, the group can try to influence the new law's application by lobbying the executive agency that is responsible for implementing the law. The group might even challenge the law in court, directly (by filing a lawsuit) or indirectly (by filing a brief as an *amicus curiae*,[5] or "friend of the court").

Interest groups can seek a variety of different benefits when lobbying the government. A frequent goal is favorable treatment under federal or state regulations.

Groups may also seek outright subsidies that benefit their members. An increasingly popular objective is special treatment in the tax code. Tax breaks for a special interest can be easier to obtain than subsidies because the breaks don't look like government spending.

PLURALIST THEORY The **pluralist theory** of American democracy focuses on the participation of groups in a decentralized government structure that offers many points of access to policymakers. According to the pluralist theory, politics is a contest among various interest groups. These groups vie with one another—at all levels of government—to gain benefits for their members. Pluralists maintain that the influence of interest groups on government is not undemocratic because individual interests are indirectly represented in the policymaking process through these groups.

Although not every American belongs to an interest group, inevitably some group will represent at least some of the interests of each individual. Thus, each interest is satisfied to some extent through the compromises made in settling conflicts among competing interest groups.

Pluralists also contend that because of the extensive number of interest groups vying for political benefits, no one group can dominate the political process. Additionally, because most people have more than one interest, conflicts among groups do not divide the nation into hostile camps. Not all scholars agree that this is how American democracy functions, however.

MAJORITARIANISM AND ELITE THEORY Political scientists have two other theories to describe American democracy: majoritarianism and elite theory. *Majoritarianism* is the belief that public policy should be set in accordance with the opinions of a majority of the people. Majoritarianism is highly popular, but political scientists find it to be a startlingly poor description of how politics actually works. *Elite theory* contends that, as a practical matter, the government is controlled by one or more elite groups, typically drawn from the wealthiest members of society. One version of elite theory posits that multiple elites compete for power. It is worth noting that many interest groups are largely funded—or even controlled—by wealthy individuals, so pluralism (described previously) and elite theory may overlap.

EVALUATING THE THEORIES How valid are these three theories as explanations of how policy is made? Many political scientists have long believed that both pluralism

pluralist theory A theory that views politics as a contest among various interest groups—at all levels of government—to gain benefits for their members.

grain, fruit, corn, cotton, beef, and sugar beets, have formed their own organizations.

Interest groups representing farmers have been spectacularly successful in winning subsidies from the federal government, as we explained in the chapter-opening *America at Odds* feature. Subsidies are not the only way in which the federal government can benefit growers of a particular crop. The government can also restrict imports of a specific commodity, such as sugar. The restrictions raise the price of sugar, which benefits sugar beet growers at the expense of consumers.

6–2b Labor and Professional Interest Groups

Interest groups representing labor have been some of the most influential groups in our country's history. They date back to at least 1886, when the American Federation of Labor (AFL) was formed. The largest and most powerful labor interest group today is the AFL-CIO (the American Federation of Labor–Congress of Industrial Organizations), a confederation of fifty-six unions representing 9 million organized workers and 3.2 million community affiliates.

Unions not affiliated with the AFL-CIO also represent millions of members. The Change to Win federation consists of three unions and 4.2 million workers. Dozens of other unions are independent. Examples include the National Education Association, the United Electrical Workers (UE), and the Major League Baseball Players Association. We list some top labor campaign donors in Table 6–3, which follows.

UNION GOALS Like labor unions everywhere, American unions press for policies to improve working conditions and ensure better pay for their members. Unions may compete for new members. In many states, for example, the National Education Association and the AFL-CIO's American Federation of Teachers compete fiercely for members.

THE DECLINE OF UNIONS Although unions were highly influential in the 1930s, 1940s, and 1950s, their strength and political power have waned in the last several decades, as you can see in Figure 6–1, which follows. Today, members of organized labor make up only 11.3 percent of the **labor force**—defined as all of the people over the age of sixteen who are working or actively looking for jobs.

Reasons for Labor's Decline. There are several reasons why the power of organized labor has declined in the

TABLE 6-3	TOP LABOR CAMPAIGN DONORS, 1989–2014	
Union or Group		**Total, 1989–2014**
1. American Fed. of State, County & Municipal Employees		$63,765,415
2. National Education Assn.		$59,702,708
3. Int'l. Brotherhood of Electrical Workers		$46,770,951
4. Carpenters & Joiners Union		$43,655,925
5. United Auto Workers		$42,381,475
6. Service Employees Int'l. Union		$41,184,128
7. Laborers' Union		$39,759,823
8. American Federation of Teachers		$38,030,375
9. Teamsters Union		$37,040,317
10. Communications Workers of America		$36,839,216

Date for 2014 is through July 21 only.

United States. One is the continuing fall in the proportion of the nation's workforce employed in such blue-collar activities as manufacturing and transportation. These sectors have always been among the most heavily unionized.

Another important factor in labor's decline, however, is the general political environment. Forming and maintaining unions is more difficult in the United States than in most other industrial nations. Among the world's wealthy democracies, the United States is one of the most politically conservative, at least on economic issues. Economic conservatives are traditionally hostile to labor unions. Further, many business owners in the United States do not accept unions as legitimate institutions and will make enormous

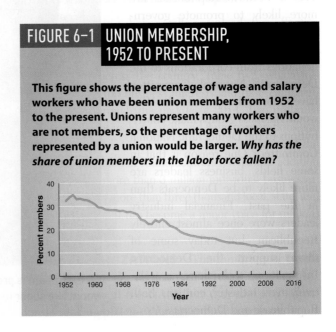

FIGURE 6-1 UNION MEMBERSHIP, 1952 TO PRESENT

This figure shows the percentage of wage and salary workers who have been union members from 1952 to the present. Unions represent many workers who are not members, so the percentage of workers represented by a union would be larger. *Why has the share of union members in the labor force fallen?*

labor force All of the people over the age of sixteen who are working or actively looking for jobs.

efforts to ensure that their own businesses remain ununionized.

Differing State Laws. The impact of the political environment on labor's organizing ability can be easily seen by comparing rates of unionization in various states. These rates are especially low in conservative southern states. Georgia and North Carolina are both major manufacturing states, but unions represent only 6.3 percent of the workforce in Georgia and only 4.8 percent in North Carolina.

Compare these figures with rates in more liberal states, such as California and New York: unions represent 17.4 percent of the workforce in California and 25.8 percent in New York. One factor that depresses unionization rates in many states is the existence of so-called **right-to-work laws.** These laws ban unions from collecting dues or other fees from workers whom they represent but who have not actually joined the union. Such laws create a significant free rider problem for unions. Twenty-four states have right-to-work laws.

PUBLIC-SECTOR UNIONS While organized labor has suffered from declining numbers and a resulting loss in lobbying power, labor has held the line in one industry—government. In the 1960s and 1970s, public-sector unions enjoyed rapid growth. The percentage of government workers who are union members then leveled off, but it remains high. More than one-third of all public-sector workers are union members today.

In contrast to unions in the private sector, public-sector unions do not have the right to strike over wages and working conditions. Still, they are influential. Unlike workers in private industry, public-sector employees—as citizens—have the right to vote for their own bosses. As a result, elected officials are often reluctant to antagonize public-sector unions. One consequence of the influence of these unions is that government workers typically enjoy pension benefits that are substantially more generous than those received by equivalent employees in the private sector.

Following the 2010 elections, several Republican governors attempted to curtail the bargaining rights of state and local employee unions. These governors argued

© Andrew Harrer/Bloomberg via Getty Images

This medical student is lobbying with the American Medical Student Association. He has $190,000 in student debt and one more year to go. *What problems result from these kinds of debts?*

that pension benefits and other perks won by the unions threatened the financial stability of state and local governments. The role and status of state and local unions, therefore, have become important political issues.

PROFESSIONAL INTEREST GROUPS Employees are not the only members of the labor force who find a need to organize interest groups. Most professions that require advanced education or specialized training have organizations to protect and promote their interests. These groups are concerned mainly with the standards of their professions, but they also work to influence government policy.

Major professional groups include the American Medical Association (AMA), representing physicians; the American Bar Association, representing lawyers; and the American Association for Justice, representing trial lawyers. In addition, there are dozens of less well-known and less politically active professional groups, such as the National Association of Social Workers and the American Political Science Association.

Competing interests sometimes divide professional interest groups from one another. For example, medical groups contend that it is too easy for lawyers to sue

right-to-work laws Laws that ban unions from collecting dues or other fees from workers whom they represent but who have not actually joined the union.

TABLE 6-5 DIRECT LOBBYING TECHNIQUES

Technique	Description
Making Personal Contacts with Key Legislators	A lobbyist's personal contacts with key legislators or other government officials—in their offices, in the halls of Congress, or on social occasions such as dinners, boating expeditions, and the like—comprise one of the most effective direct lobbying techniques.
Providing Expertise and Research Results for Legislators	Lobbyists often have knowledge and expertise that are useful in drafting legislation, and this expertise can be a major strength for an interest group. Harried members of Congress cannot possibly be experts on everything they vote on and therefore eagerly seek information to help them make up their minds.
Offering "Expert" Testimony before Congressional Committees	Lobbyists often provide "expert" testimony before congressional committees for or against proposed legislation. Each expert offers as much evidence as possible to support her or his position.
Providing Legal Advice to Legislators	Many lobbyists assist legislators in drafting legislation or prospective regulations. Lobbyists are a source of ideas and sometimes offer legal advice on specific details.
Following Up on Legislation	Because executive agencies responsible for carrying out legislation can often change the scope of the new law, lobbyists may also try to influence the bureaucrats who implement the policy.

6-3 HOW INTEREST GROUPS SHAPE POLICY

LO Discuss how the activities of interest groups help to shape government policymaking.

Interest groups operate at all levels of government and use a variety of strategies to steer policies in ways beneficial to their interests. Sometimes, they attempt to influence policymakers directly, but at other times they try to exert indirect influence on policymakers by shaping public opinion. The extent and nature of the groups' activities depend on their goals and their resources.

6-3a Direct Techniques

Lobbying and providing election support are two important **direct techniques** used by interest groups to influence government policy.

LOBBYING Today, **lobbying** refers to all of the attempts by organizations or by individuals to influence the passage, defeat, or contents of legislation or to influence the administrative decisions of government. (The term *lob-*

direct technique Any method used by an interest group to interact with government officials directly to further the group's goals.

lobbying All of the attempts by organizations or by individuals to influence the passage, defeat, or contents of legislation or to influence the administrative decisions of government.

lobbyist An individual who handles a particular interest group's lobbying efforts.

bying arose because, traditionally, individuals and groups interested in influencing government policy would gather in the foyer, or lobby, of the legislature to corner legislators and express their concerns.) A **lobbyist** is an individual who handles a particular interest group's lobbying efforts. Most of the larger interest groups have lobbyists in Washington, D.C. These lobbyists often include former members of Congress or former employees of executive bureaucracies who are experienced in the methods of political influence and who "know people." Table 6–5, which follows, summarizes some of the basic methods by which lobbyists directly influence legislators and government officials.

Lobbying can be directed at the legislative branch of government, or at administrative agencies. As mentioned earlier, lobbying can also be directed at the courts, through filing a lawsuit or an *amicus curiae* brief. Many lobbyists also work at state and local levels. In fact, lobbying at the state level has increased in recent years as states have begun to play a more significant role in policymaking.

PROVIDING ELECTION SUPPORT Interest groups often become directly involved in the election process. Many group members join and work with political parties to influence party platforms and the nomination of candidates. Interest groups provide campaign support for legislators who favor their policies and sometimes encourage their own members to try to win posts in party organizations.

Most important, interest groups urge their members to vote for candidates who support the views of the group. They can also threaten legislators with the withdrawal of votes. No candidate can expect to have support from all interest groups, but if the candidate is to win, she or he must have support from many of the strongest ones.

Perception vs. Reality

The Unrepresented Poor

America has not eliminated poverty. Indeed, every year we read stories about poor Americans and about Americans who have fallen into poverty. Given that the poor are in no position to lobby for themselves, it seems obvious that rich individuals and major corporations, because they do lots of lobbying, must get all the benefits from government.

The Perception

Because the poor have no access to the halls of government, they are underrepresented. Low-income persons simply do not have the time, funds, or spare energy to compete with moneyed interests, at either the state or the national level.

The Reality

While it may be true that lobbyists are often successful in getting "special deals" for the rich and for big corporations, the tax burden on wealthy individuals remains heavy. The richest 10 percent of Americans pay about half of all federal income and payroll taxes. (Payroll taxes are Social Security and Medicare taxes.) The top 1 percent of Americans pay about one-quarter of these taxes. Low-income taxpayers are largely exempt from the income tax. They pay only payroll taxes, and in many cases, they can get rebates on these. Even without being able to lobby for themselves, low-income families and individuals receive beneficial tax treatment.

Now consider spending. Ron Haskins of the Brookings Institution estimates that all federal low-income programs together cost more than $800 billion a year. One of the most important of these programs is food stamps (now called Supplemental Nutrition Assistance Program, or SNAP). Just since 2007, when the Great Recession struck, the number of food stamp recipients has risen from 26 million to 45 million. The average monthly value of the benefit is close to $300. Other programs for the poor include Medicaid and the refundable portions of the Earned-Income Tax Credit and the Additional Child Tax Credit.

The reality is that for decades, many liberal groups have lobbied on behalf of those suffering from poverty. Mainstream religious groups have done the same—including Catholic organizations, Lutherans, the National Council of Churches, the Friends (Quakers), and many others. Liberal and religious interests have done for the poor what the poor cannot do for themselves. The result: If there were no federal tax and spending programs aimed at low-income persons, as many as 25 percent of U.S. families would have incomes below the official poverty line. If you take into account all benefits that low-income families obtain, that number drops to about 10 percent.

BLOG **ON**
- For a vast collection of data on social services provided by the federal government, see the *Green Book* of the Ways and Means Committee of the U.S. House of Representatives. Find it at greenbook.waysandmeans.house.gov.
- For another source of information, see the Web site of the University of Kentucky Center for Poverty Research. Go to www.ukcpr.org.

Political Action Committees (PACs). Since the 1970s, federal laws governing campaign financing have allowed corporations, labor unions, and special interest groups to raise funds and make campaign contributions through **political action committees (PACs).** Both the number of PACs and the amount of money PACs spend on elections have grown astronomically in recent years. There were about 1,000 PACs in 1976. Today, there are more than 4,500 PACs. In 1973, total spending by PACs amounted to $19 million. In the 2011–2012 election cycle, contributions to federal candidates by PACs totaled about $440 million, and spending in 2013–2014 was similar.

Even with their impressive growth, PACs provided a smaller share of campaign spending in the years after 1988, principally because of the development of other

> **political action committee (PAC)** A committee that is established by a corporation, labor union, or special interest group to raise funds and make campaign contributions on the establishing organization's behalf.

Join the Debate

Should We Let Uber and Lyft Pick Up Pasengers?

Until recently, taxis and, to an extent, limousines have been the only services that would pick you up and take you from one point to another in a car. Today, depending on where you live, you may have other choices—Uber, Lyft, Sidecar, or Haxi. These "transportation network" companies directly compete with taxis. These services are built around the Internet. All you need to summon a car is a smartphone app. You use the app to locate the nearest Lyft, Uber, Sidecar, or Haxi driver. You talk directly with that driver. You must already have a credit card number on file with the company—no cash changes hands. The driver picks you up, and your credit card is automatically charged at the end of your ride. Transportation network companies use both full-time and part-time drivers, all of whom own their own cars.

These competitors to taxis are a completely new service and are therefore unregulated. This fact has provoked controversy. Some city councils have banned the services outright. Others are trying to regulate them. Should they just be left alone instead?

Public Safety Is At Issue and It's Also Unfair Competition

Opponents of Uber, Lyft, and other services point out that taxi services are heavily regulated in most cities. The goal of the regulations is twofold: to ensure public safety and to allow taxi drivers to make a living wage. In many cities, you must pay for a license to own a cab. Drivers for Uber and similar companies do not pay anything. Taxis must also carry expensive vehicle-for-hire insurance. They are regularly inspected to protect public safety. Another point—because you must have a credit card to use Uber or Lyft, these companies discriminate against poor people who don't have credit cards

or smartphones. In sum, these new services do not compete fairly with licensed, regulated taxi drivers.

It's All About the Taxi Lobby

Supporters of the new "ride-share" systems say that talk of unfair competition and public safety is a smokescreen. Taxi lobbies simply want to eliminate competition. Uber, Lyft, and the others perform background checks on their drivers. Passengers have the names and mobile phone numbers of their drivers. They rate the drivers, and those who receive low ratings get fewer and fewer calls. Localities that regulate the new services, such as the state of California, require extra insurance. The ride-share market works just as well as any other market. Banning these services simply guarantees that current taxi owners—not necessarily drivers—make high profits and passengers have fewer choices.

CRITICAL ANALYSIS What might motivate a city council to ban Uber or Lyft services?

6–4c The Lobbying Disclosure Act of 1995

In 1995, Congress passed new expanded lobbying legislation—the Lobbying Disclosure Act—that reformed the 1946 act in the following ways:

▶ Strict definitions now apply to determine who must register with the clerk of the House and the secretary of the Senate as a lobbyist. A lobbyist is anyone who either spends at least 20 percent of his or her time lobbying members of Congress, their staffs, or executive-branch officials, or is paid more than $5,000 in a six-month period for such work. Any organization that spends more than $20,000 in a six-month period conducting such lobbying activity must also register.

These amounts have since been altered to $2,500 and $10,000 per quarter, respectively.

▶ Lobbyists must report their clients, the issues on which they lobbied, and the agency or chamber of Congress they contacted, although they do not need to disclose the names of those they contacted.

Tax-exempt organizations, such as religious groups, were exempted from these provisions, as were organizations that engage in grassroots lobbying, such as a media campaign that asks people to write or call their congressional representative. Nonetheless, the number of registered lobbyists nearly doubled in the first few years after the new legislation.

A Lyft customer gets into a car in San Francisco. The San Francisco Cab Driver Association reports that nearly one third of the city's licensed taxi drivers have stopped driving taxis and have begun driving for ridesharing services. *Why would they switch?*

6–4d Recent Reform Efforts

In 2005, a number of lobbying scandals in Washington, D.C., came to light. As a result, following the midterm elections of 2006, the new Democratic majority in the Senate and House of Representatives undertook a lobbying reform effort. This involved changes to the rules that the two chambers impose on their own members.

Bundled campaign contributions, in which a lobbyist arranges for contributions from a variety of sources, would have to be reported. Expenditures on the sometimes lavish parties to benefit candidates would have to be reported as well. (Of course, partygoers were expected to pay for their food and drink with a check written out to the candidate.) The new rules covered PACs as well as registered lobbyists, which led one lobbyist to observe sourly that this wasn't lobbying reform but campaign-finance reform.

President George W. Bush signed the Honest Leadership and Open Government Act in 2007. The new law increased lobbying disclosure requirements and placed further restrictions on the receipt of gifts and travel by members of Congress paid for by lobbyists and the organizations they represent. The act also included provisions requiring the disclosure of lawmakers' requests for earmarks in legislation. Earmarks are also known as "pork barrel legislation," or simply *pork*.

In March 2010, the Republican-led House Appropriations Committee banned earmarks that benefit profit-making corporations. About a thousand such earmarks had been authorized in the previous year, to the value of $1.7 billion. The ban was renewed in 2012. As it turned out, legislators proved remarkably creative in finding ways around the ban on pork, though the ban did at least limit its prevalence.

CRITICAL THINKING

▶ As noted at the beginning of this chapter, the right to lobby is protected by the Constitution. If that weren't so, would it be a good idea to ban lobbying? Why or why not?

AMERICA ⚑ AT ODDS
Interest Groups

Interest groups are one of the most controversial features of our democratic system. The right to lobby may be protected by the First Amendment, but many people consider lobbying by interest groups to be a source of corruption within the political system. Of course, people can readily see the problems with lobbying when it is done for a cause that they oppose. In contrast, it is easy to support political action for something you believe in, regardless of what others might think of it. Some of the controversies surrounding interest group lobbying include the following:

- *Should labor unions be allowed to organize workplaces by obtaining signed cards—or are secret-ballot elections an essential safeguard?*

- *Are farm subsidies a valid protection for an important industry—or just another giveaway to the politically powerful?*

- *Does lobbying always harm legislation—or can lobbying improve it?*

- *Free riders benefit from a particular activity without paying their share of its costs. Is free riding inherently unfair—or is it only a problem when it is so pervasive that it makes the activity in question (for example, lobbying by consumer groups) unaffordable?*

- *Are there too many lobbyists—or is the real problem that there aren't enough lobbyists for ordinary people?*

Internet Resources

- To find particular interest groups online, a good point of departure is the ipl2 Web site, which resulted from a merger of Internet Public Library and the Librarians' Internet Index. The site provides links to hundreds of professional and trade associations. Go to www.ipl.org/div/aon.

- Find the Web site of the U.S. Chamber of Commerce, the nation's largest business group, at www.uschamber.com.

- To see an example of a labor union Web site, check out the National Education Association at www.nea.org.

- You can access the National Rifle Association online at www.nra.org.

- AARP's Web site can be found at www.aarp.org.

- You can find information on environmental issues and the activities of the Natural Resources Defense Council at www.nrdc.org.

STUDY TOOLS 6

READY TO STUDY?

- ☐ Review what you've read with the quiz below.
- ☐ Check your answers in Appendix D at the back of the book.
- ☐ For any questions you miss, read the corresponding Learning Outcome section again to prepare for class and your exam.
- ☐ Rip out and study the Chapter in Review card (at the back of the book).

VISIT WWW.CENGAGEBRAIN.COM:

- ☐ Interactive Quizzes
- ☐ Key Term Flashcards or Crossword Puzzles
- ☐ Audio Summaries
- ☐ Simulations, Animated Learning Modules and Interactive Timelines
- ☐ Videos
- ☐ American Government NewsWatch

FILL-IN

LearningOutcome 6–1

1. The right to form interest groups and to lobby the government is protected by the _____ Amendment to the U.S. Constitution.

2. _____ theory describes the defensive formation of interest groups.

LearningOutcome 6–2

3. Today, members of organized labor make up only _____ percent of the labor force.

4. _____ laws ban unions from collecting dues or other fees from workers whom they represent but who have not actually joined the union.

LearningOutcome 6–3

5. Lobbying refers to _____.

6. Interest groups can influence the outcome of litigation without being a party to a lawsuit by filing _____.

LearningOutcome 6–4

7. It has become increasingly common for those who leave positions with the federal government to become lobbyists or consultants for the private-interest groups they helped to regulate. This is called the _____ syndrome.

MULTIPLE CHOICE

LearningOutcome 6–1

8. There are various reasons why people join interest groups. Some people find that they gain considerable satisfaction from supporting causes that they agree with. Such satisfaction is referred to as a _____ incentive.
   a. free rider **b.** purposive **c.** material

9. Interest groups
   a. are often policy generalists.
   b. compete for public office.
   c. help bridge the gap between citizens and government.

LearningOutcome 6–2

10. The American Association for Justice represents the interests of
    a. trial lawyers. **b.** children. **c.** senior citizens.

11. MoveOn and the Club for Growth are _____ interest groups.
    a. business **b.** consumer **c.** ideological

LearningOutcome 6–3

12. _____ is a direct technique used by interest groups to influence public policy.
    a. The use of rating systems
    b. Providing election support
    c. Staging demonstrations

13. The Supreme Court has made it clear that the First Amendment's guarantee of free speech
    a. protects interest groups' rights to set forth their positions on issues when they fund such activities through independent expenditures that are not coordinated with a candidate's campaign or a political party.
    b. protects issue advocacy as long as that advocacy is coordinated with a candidate's campaign or a political party.
    c. does not include protection for interest groups to set forth their positions on issues.

14. Lobbying campaigns that masquerade as grassroots mobilizations (but are not) have been labeled _____ lobbying.
    a. *Bluegrass* **b.** *Turfgrass* **c.** *Astroturf*

LearningOutcome 6–4

15. When a benefit is provided to a limited number of people, the enthusiasm gap between recipients of the benefit and everyone else is called:
    a. concentrated costs and dispersed benefits.
    b. the free rider problem.
    c. concentrated benefits and dispersed costs.

7 | Political Parties

MOST PEOPLE COME INTO THE OFFICE WITH GREAT DREAMS THEY LEAVE IT WITH MANY SATISFACTIONS AND SOME DISAPPOINTM

AND AS TO HOW SUCCESSFUL WE'V__ __N IN DOING THE GREATEST GOOD FOR THE GR____ __MBER...

PEOPLE THEMSELVES AND THE_____ULTIMATELY DECI

PRESIDENT LYND

© Brendan Smialowski/Getty Images

LEARNING OUTCOMES   After reading this chapter, you should be able to:

7-1   Summarize the origins and development of the two-party system in the United States.

7-2   Describe the current status of the two major parties.

7-3   Explain how political parties function in our democratic system.

7-4   Discuss the structure of American political parties.

7-5   Describe the different types of third parties and how they function in the American political system.

After finishing this chapter go to **PAGE 165** for **STUDY TOOLS.**

AMERICA AT ODDS

© Cheryl Casey/Shutterstock.com

Does the Republican Party Need a New Strategy?

The Republican Party did very well in the midterm elections of 2010. Conservative Republicans turned out in large numbers, while many Democrats stayed home. As a result, the Republicans took control of the U.S. House away from the Democrats. Republicans also did well in the midterm elections of 2014, and they continue to show great strength at the state and local levels. Yet the Republicans have won fewer popular votes than the Democrats in five of the last six presidential races. The Democrats appear well placed to win the presidency again in 2016. As a result, some Republicans argue that the party should change to attract moderate voters, especially Hispanics. Other Republicans, however, claim that Republican politicians are not conservative enough. Who has the more convincing argument?

Uncompromising Conservatism Is the Only Way Forward

Uncompromising conservatives believe that the Republicans must steer to the political right. Even though only 25 percent of voters call themselves Republicans, 40 percent say that they are conservatives. Support is rising for such conservative positions as the right to bear arms and opposition to abortion.

Conservative activists argue that their values are not only popular but also "correct" in a very deep sense. In their view, values such as religious belief, strong families, and individual self-reliance are the foundation of our civilization. Liberalism erodes these values and paves the road to cultural collapse.

According to some conservative commentators, the Republicans lost the 2012 presidential elections only because white working-class voters in states such as Ohio stayed home—they were turned off by the Republican candidate Mitt Romney, a wealthy financier. If Republicans support causes such as immigration reform, they will just alienate these voters further.

Americans are starting to rebel against big government and a culture of immorality. If the Republicans don't stand firm for true conservatism, these Americans won't have anyone to vote for.

Radical Conservatism Spells Disaster in the Long Run

The face of America is changing. Support for gay rights has risen dramatically. The number of Hispanic voters rises year by year, and by 2050, non-Hispanic whites will be a minority of the U.S. population. Despite these changes, some conservatives seem intent on ensuring that the Republicans are seen as the "nasty party"—the party that hates people.

Republicans require young voters, but tirades against gays are poison to that constituency. If the vast majority of Latinos come to reject the Republicans because of the party's anti-immigrant rhetoric, eventually the Republicans will even fail to carry Texas. If voters conclude that Republicans see large numbers of their fellow Americans as "the enemy," the party will lose future elections, no matter how well it did in 2014.

Finally, a complete refusal to compromise is not a winning formula. Many Americans, especially the independents who decide elections, strongly favor cooperation between the parties. If either party refuses to compromise, in time the voters are likely to take notice. Conservatism can be a winning ideology. (The Democrats are certainly an ideological party as well.) But radicalism is not a winning strategy in American politics.

Where do you stand?

1. Pastor Rick Warren, author of *The Purpose Driven Life*, accepts that homosexuality is a sin, but he also emphasizes his belief in God's love for all people. Why might some members of the religious right reject Warren's formula?

2. What could the Republicans do to win Latino votes?

Explore this issue online

- For full-throttle conservatism, try Rush Limbaugh's site at www.rushlimbaugh.com.

- Reihan Salam and Ross Douthat are columnists who argue for "conservative reform" even as they continue to support the Republican Party. See Salam's blog at www.nationalreview.com/agenda, and follow Douthat at twitter.com/DouthatNYT.

INTRODUCTION

Political ideology can spark heated debates among Americans, as you read in the chapter-opening *America at Odds* feature. Today, political ideologies are typically embodied in political parties. A **political party** can be defined as a group of individuals who organize to win elections, operate the government, and determine policy.

Political parties were an unforeseen development in American political history. The founders defined many other important institutions, such as the presidency and Congress, and described their functions in the Constitution. Political parties, however, are not even mentioned in the Constitution. In fact, the founders decried factions and parties. Thomas Jefferson probably best expressed the founders' antiparty sentiments when he declared, "If I could not go to heaven but with a party, I would not go there at all."[1]

If the founders did not want political parties, though, who was supposed to organize political campaigns and mobilize supporters of political candidates? Clearly, there was a practical need for some kind of organizing group to form a link between citizens and their government. Even our early national leaders, for all their antiparty feelings, soon realized this. Several of them were active in establishing or organizing the first political parties.

> "Both of our political parties . . . agree conscientiously in the same object: the **public good**; but they differ essentially in what they deem the means of promoting that good."
>
> ~ **Thomas Jefferson,** In a Letter to Abigail Adams, 1804

7–1 A SHORT HISTORY OF AMERICAN POLITICAL PARTIES

LO Summarize the origins and development of the two-party system in the United States.

Throughout the course of our history, several parties have formed, and some have disappeared. Even today, although we have only two major political parties, a few others always exist at any one time, as will be discussed later in this chapter.

political party A group of individuals who organize to win elections, operate the government, and determine policy.

7–1a The First Political Parties

The founders rejected the idea of political parties because they believed, as George Washington said in his Farewell Address, that the "spirit of party . . . agitates the community with ill-founded jealousies and false alarms, kindles the animosity of one part against another, foments occasionally riot and insurrection."[2] At some point in the future, the founders feared, a party leader might even seize power as a dictator.

FEDERALISTS AND ANTI-FEDERALISTS In spite of the founders' fears, two major political factions—the Federalists and the Anti-Federalists—were formed even before the Constitution was ratified. Remember from Chapter 2 that the Federalists pushed for the ratification of the Constitution because they wanted a stronger national government than the one that had existed under the Articles of Confederation. The

John Adams (1735–1826) was the Federalists' candidate to succeed George Washington. Adams defeated Thomas Jefferson in 1796, but lost to him in 1800. *What did the Federalists stand for?*

Thomas Jefferson (1743–1826) became our third president and served two terms. Jefferson's Republicans (not to be confused with the later Republican Party of Abraham Lincoln) dominated American politics for more than two decades. *What kinds of people supported this party?*

Library of Congress

Andrew Jackson (1767–1845) led the newly formed Democratic Party. Jackson won the presidential election in 1828, defeating the candidate of the National Republicans. *Which of these two parties was more like the Federalists?*

Library of Congress

Anti-Federalists argued against ratification. They supported states' rights and feared a too-powerful central government.

FEDERALISTS AND REPUBLICANS The Federalist and Anti-Federalist factions continued, in somewhat altered form, after the Constitution was ratified. Alexander Hamilton, the first secretary of the Treasury, became the leader of the Federalist Party, which Vice President John Adams also joined. The Federalists supported a strong central government that would encourage the development of commerce and manufacturing. The Federalists generally thought that a republic should be ruled by its wealthiest and best-educated citizens.

Opponents of the Federalists and Hamilton's policies referred to themselves as Republicans. Today, they are often referred to as Jeffersonian Republicans or Democratic Republicans (names never used at the time), to distinguish this group from the later-established Republican Party. Jefferson's Republicans favored a more limited role for government. They believed that the nation's welfare would be best served if the states had more power than the central government. In their view, Congress should dominate the government, and government policies should serve farming interests rather than promote commerce and manufacturing.

7–1b From 1796 to 1860

The nation's first two parties clashed openly in the elections of 1796, in which John Adams, the Federalists' candidate to succeed George Washington as president, defeated Thomas Jefferson. Over the next four years, Jefferson and James Madison worked to extend the influence of the Republican Party. In the presidential elections of 1800 and 1804, Jefferson won the presidency, and his party also won control of Congress.

TRIUMPH OF THE JEFFERSONIANS The transition of political power from the Federalists to the Jeffersonian party is the first example in American history of what political scientists have called a **realignment.** In a realignment, a substantial number of voters change their political allegiance, which usually also changes the balance of power between the two major parties. In fact, the Federalists never returned to power and thus became the first (but not the last) American party to go out of existence. (See the time line of American political parties in Figure 7–1, which follows.)

Jefferson's Republicans dominated American politics for the next twenty years. Jefferson was succeeded in

realignment A process in which the popular support for and relative strength of the parties shift and the parties are reestablished with different coalitions of supporters.

FIGURE 7–1   A TIME LINE OF U.S. POLITICAL PARTIES

Many of these parties—including the Constitutional Union Party, Henry Wallace's Progressive Party, and the States' Rights Democrats—were important during only one presidential election.

Evolution of the Major American Political Parties and Splinter Groups

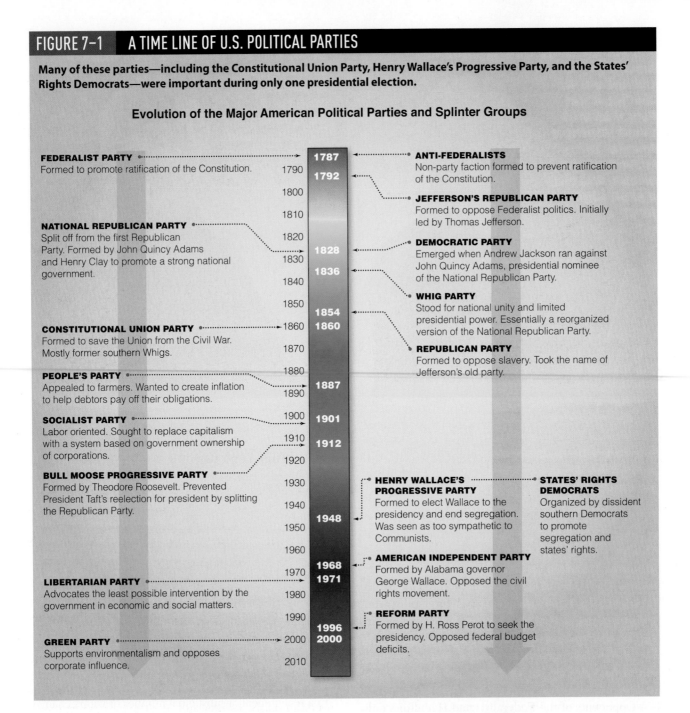

FEDERALIST PARTY
Formed to promote ratification of the Constitution.

1790

1800

1810

NATIONAL REPUBLICAN PARTY
Split off from the first Republican Party. Formed by John Quincy Adams and Henry Clay to promote a strong national government.

1820

1830

1840

1850

CONSTITUTIONAL UNION PARTY
Formed to save the Union from the Civil War. Mostly former southern Whigs.

1870

1880

PEOPLE'S PARTY
Appealed to farmers. Wanted to create inflation to help debtors pay off their obligations.

1890

1900

SOCIALIST PARTY
Labor oriented. Sought to replace capitalism with a system based on government ownership of corporations.

1910

1920

BULL MOOSE PROGRESSIVE PARTY
Formed by Theodore Roosevelt. Prevented President Taft's reelection for president by splitting the Republican Party.

1930

1940

1950

1960

1970

LIBERTARIAN PARTY
Advocates the least possible intervention by the government in economic and social matters.

1980

1990

GREEN PARTY
Supports environmentalism and opposes corporate influence.

2000

2010

1787
1792
1828
1836
1854
1860
1887
1901
1912
1948
1968
1971
1996
2000

ANTI-FEDERALISTS
Non-party faction formed to prevent ratification of the Constitution.

JEFFERSON'S REPUBLICAN PARTY
Formed to oppose Federalist politics. Initially led by Thomas Jefferson.

DEMOCRATIC PARTY
Emerged when Andrew Jackson ran against John Quincy Adams, presidential nominee of the National Republican Party.

WHIG PARTY
Stood for national unity and limited presidential power. Essentially a reorganized version of the National Republican Party.

REPUBLICAN PARTY
Formed to oppose slavery. Took the name of Jefferson's old party.

HENRY WALLACE'S PROGRESSIVE PARTY
Formed to elect Wallace to the presidency and end segregation. Was seen as too sympathetic to Communists.

STATES' RIGHTS DEMOCRATS
Organized by dissident southern Democrats to promote segregation and states' rights.

AMERICAN INDEPENDENT PARTY
Formed by Alabama governor George Wallace. Opposed the civil rights movement.

REFORM PARTY
Formed by H. Ross Perot to seek the presidency. Opposed federal budget deficits.

the White House by two other members of the party— James Madison and James Monroe. In the mid-1820s, however, Jefferson's Republicans split into two groups. This was the second realignment in American history. Supporters of Andrew Jackson, who was elected president in 1828, called themselves Democrats. The Democrats appealed to small farmers and the growing class of urbanized workers. The other group, the National Republicans (later the Whig Party), was led by John Quincy Adams, Henry Clay, and the great orator Daniel Webster. It had the support of bankers, business owners, and many southern planters.

THE IMPENDING CRISIS As the Whigs and Democrats competed for the White House throughout the 1840s and 1850s, the two-party system as we know it today emerged. Both parties were large, with well-known leaders and supporters across the nation. Both had grassroots organizations of party workers committed to winning as many political offices (at all levels of government) for the party as possible. Both the Whigs and the Democrats tried to avoid the issue of slavery.

By the mid-1850s, the Whig coalition had fallen apart. Most northern Whigs were absorbed into the new Republican Party, which opposed the extension of slav-

From the election of Abraham Lincoln in 1860 until the election of Franklin Delano Roosevelt in 1932, the Republican Party was the more successful party in presidential politics. *Where were the Republicans strong?*

The realigning election of 1932 brought Franklin Delano Roosevelt to the presidency and the Democrats back to power at the national level. *Why did the Democrats win in 1932?*

ery into new territories. Campaigning on this platform in 1860, the Republicans succeeded in electing Abraham Lincoln—the first president elected under the banner of the new Republican Party.

7–1c From the Civil War to the Great Depression

When the former Confederate states rejoined the Union after the Civil War, the Republicans and Democrats were roughly even in strength. The Republicans, though, were more successful in presidential contests. It was in this period that the Republicans picked up the nickname **GOP,** for "grand old party."

In the 1890s, however, the Republicans gained a decisive advantage. In that decade, the Democrats allied themselves with the Populist movement, which consisted largely of indebted farmers in the West and South. The Populists—the People's Party—advocated inflation as a way of lessening their debts. Urban workers in the Midwest and East strongly opposed this program, which would erode the value of their paychecks. After the realigning election of 1896, the Republicans established themselves in the minds of many Americans as the party that knew how to manage the nation's economy.

As a result of a Republican split, the Democrats under Woodrow Wilson won power from 1912 to 1920. Otherwise, the Republicans remained dominant in national politics until the onset of the Great Depression.

7–1d After the Great Depression

The Great Depression of the 1930s destroyed the belief that the GOP could better manage the economy and contributed to another realignment in the two-party system. In a realignment, the minority (opposition) party may emerge as the majority party, and this is certainly what happened in 1932. The election of 1932 brought Franklin D. Roosevelt to the presidency and the Democrats back to power at the national level.

A CIVIL RIGHTS PLANK Roosevelt's programs to fight the Depression were called the *New Deal.* Those who joined the Democrats during Roosevelt's New Deal included a substantial share of African Americans—Roosevelt's relief programs were open to people of all races. (Until the 1930s, African Americans had been overwhelmingly Republican.) In 1948, for the first time ever, the Democrats adopted a civil rights plank as part of the party platform at their national convention. A number of southern Democrats revolted and ran a separate States' Rights ticket for president.

In 1964, the Democrats, under incumbent president Lyndon Johnson, won a landslide victory, and liberals held a majority in Congress. In the political environment that produced this election result, a coalition of northern Democrats and Republicans crafted the major civil

GOP A nickname for the Republican Party—"grand old party."

rights legislation that you read about in Chapter 5. The subsequent years were turbulent, with riots and marches in several major cities and student protests against the Vietnam War (1965–1975).

A "ROLLING REALIGNMENT" Conservative Democrats did not like the direction in which their party seemed to be taking them. Under President Richard Nixon, the Republican Party was receptive to these conservative Democrats, and over a period of years, most of them became GOP voters. This was a major alteration in the political landscape, although it was not exclusively associated with a single election. Republican president Ronald Reagan helped cement the new Republican coalition.

Turnover in Congress. The Democrats continued to hold majorities in the House and Senate until 1994, but partisan labels were somewhat misleading. During the 1970s and 1980s, a large bloc of Democrats in Congress, mostly from the South, sided with the Republicans on almost all issues. In time, these conservative Democrats were replaced by conservative Republicans.

A Closely Divided Nation. The result of this "rolling realignment" was that the two major parties were fairly evenly matched. The elections of 2000 were a striking demonstration of how closely the electorate was now divided. Republican George W. Bush won the presidency in that year by carrying Florida with a margin of 537 votes. Democrat Al Gore actually received about half a million more popular votes than Bush. Following the elections, the Senate was made up of 50 Republicans and 50 Democrats. The GOP controlled the House by a razor-thin margin of seven seats.

> **CRITICAL THINKING**
> ▶ If you could create a new party, what would be its most important principles?

7-2 AMERICA'S POLITICAL PARTIES TODAY

> **LO** Describe the current status of the two major parties.

Historically, political parties drew together like-minded individuals. Today, too, individuals with similar characteristics tend to align themselves more often with one or the other major party. Such factors as race, age, income, education, marital status, and geography all influence party identification. For example, upper-income voters

traditionally have been more likely to support the Republican Party. But is this still true today? We examine that question in this chapter's *Perception versus Reality* feature, which follows.

7-2a Red States versus Blue States

Geography is one of the many factors that can determine party identification. Examine the national electoral map shown in Figure 7–2, which follows. In 2012, Republican Mitt Romney did well in the South, in the Great Plains, and in parts of the Midwest and Mountain West. Democrat Barack Obama did well in the Northeast, in parts of the Midwest, and on the West Coast. Beginning with the presidential elections of 2000, the press has made much of the supposed cultural differences between the "blue" states that vote for the Democratic candidate and the "red" states that vote for the Republican.[3] In reality, though, many states could better be described as "purple"—that is, a mixture of red and blue. These states could give their electoral votes to either party.

For another way to consider the influence of geography, see the map of Ohio in Figure 7–3, which follows. Most of Ohio is red, and a quick glance might lead you to believe that Romney carried the state. In fact, Obama carried Ohio by a margin of 3 percentage points. Ohio looks red because Romney carried almost all of the rural parts of the state. The Obama counties had larger populations. This pattern was seen all over the country: the more urban the county, the more likely it was to vote Democratic.

7-2b Trouble for the Parties

As noted earlier, by 2000 the two major parties were very closely matched in terms of support. Public opinion polls reported that voters continued to view the parties with roughly equal favor. But that situation soon began to shift.

TROUBLE FOR THE REPUBLICANS During 2005, the seemingly endless war in Iraq began to cut into support for the Republicans. Even before the start of the Great Recession in December 2007, therefore, the GOP was in trouble. In 2006, the Democrats regained control of the House and Senate. In 2008, in the shadow of a global financial crisis, Americans elected Democrat Barack Obama as president.

Within one year of Obama's inauguration, the Democratic advantage had vanished. Continued high rates of unemployment were one major reason. Also, a sharp increase in government activity during Obama's first two years in office appeared to bother many voters.

FIGURE 7–2   THE 2012 PRESIDENTIAL ELECTION RESULTS

This map shows the 2012 presidential election results by state. While Barack Obama won the election, Mitt Romney picked up two states that Obama carried in 2008.

WA 12 · OR 7 · MT 3 · ID 4 · WY 3 · ND 3 · SD 3 · MN 10 · WI 10 · MI 16 · NV 6 · UT 6 · CO 9 · NE 5 · IA 6 · IL 20 · IN 11 · OH 18 · NY 29 · PA 20 · CA 55 · AZ 11 · NM 5 · KS 6 · MO 10 · KY 8 · WV 5 · VA 13 · OK 7 · AR 6 · TN 11 · NC 15 · SC 9 · MS 6 · AL 9 · GA 16 · TX 38 · LA 8 · FL 29 · AK 3 · HI 4 · VT 3 · NH 4 · ME 4 · MA 11 · RI 4 · CT 7 · NJ 14 · DE 3 · MD 10 · DC 3

■ Won by Barack Obama in 2012
■ Won by Mitt Romney in 2012
■ Won by Obama in 2008 and Romney in 2012

Making the Other Party Look Weak. Ideological uniformity has made it easier for the parties to maintain discipline in Congress. Personal friendships across party lines, once common in Congress, have become rare. The belief has grown that compromise with the other party is a form of betrayal. According to this view, the minority party should not attempt to improve legislation proposed by the majority. Instead, it should oppose majority-party measures in an effort to make the majority appear ineffective. The Republican Party has employed such tactics throughout Obama's term of office.

In November 2010, the voters handed an additional sixty-three seats in the U.S. House to the Republicans, granting that party control of the chamber. (The Democrats still controlled the Senate.)

RECENT ELECTIONS   By 2012, some were beginning to wonder whether the strong conservatism of the newly elected Republicans might be alienating independent voters. In fact, in the 2012 elections, Democratic presidential candidate Barack Obama prevailed by almost 4 percentage points. While these results were better for the Democrats than for the Republicans, they did nothing to change the partisan balance in the nation's capital.

In 2014, the Republicans decisively won the Senate. Still, following these elections the nation's leadership continued to be divided by party.

THE TRIUMPH OF PARTISANSHIP   A key characteristic of recent politics has been the extreme partisanship of party activists and members of Congress. As noted earlier, in the 1960s, party coalitions included a variety of factions with differing politics. The rolling realignment after the elections of 1968 resulted in parties that were much more homogeneous. Political scientists have concluded that already by 2009, the most conservative Democrat in the House was to the left of the most moderate Republican.

The Impact of the Tea Party Movement.   Political polarization grew even more severe after the 2010 elections. Many of the new Republican members of Congress were pledged to the Tea Party philosophy of no-compromise conservatism. These members were fully prepared to revolt if the GOP leadership presented them with legislation that Democrats could support. Given that the Democrats still controlled the Senate and the presidency, political deadlock seemed inevitable.

The Debt-Ceiling Crisis.   A key example of deadlock was the debt-ceiling crisis. Congress regularly must vote to lift the *debt ceiling*, the maximum sum that the federal government can borrow. Failure to lift the ceiling could force the federal government to default on its obligations. In the summer of 2011, House Republicans demanded federal spending cuts in exchange for raising the ceiling. The House leadership and President Obama reached a compromise at the very last moment. In a second confrontation in October 2013, however, House Republicans were forced to back down.

7–2c Realignment, Dealignment, and Tipping

Despite the narrowness of the Republican margin after 2000, Republican strategists dreamed of a new realignment that would force the Democrats into the minority. These hopes were not fulfilled. After 2006,

FIGURE 7–3 THE 2012 PRESIDENTIAL ELECTION RESULTS IN OHIO

This map displays the Ohio counties carried by Barack Obama (blue) and Mitt Romney (red) in the 2012 presidential elections. The cities shown on the map are the ten most populous municipalities in Ohio. Obama did well in urban and suburban counties, but poorly in nonmetropolitan regions. (Note that one nonmetropolitan county that Obama carried contains a major university.)

many Democrats anticipated a realignment that would benefit the Democrats. These dreams were shattered as well. For a major realignment to take place, a large number of voters must conclude that their party is no longer capable of representing their interests and ideals, and that another party can do better. It is hard to identify large groups of voters who could be swayed to support a different party today.

DEALIGNMENT One political development that may rule out realignment is the growth in the number of independent voters. By 2014, fully 42 percent of the electorate claimed to be independent. True, many of these voters admitted to leaning toward the Republicans or the Democrats. Still, anyone claiming to be an independent has a weakened attachment to the parties.

dealignment Among voters, a growing detachment from both major political parties.

Some political scientists argue that with so many independent voters, the concept of realignment becomes irrelevant. Realignment has been replaced by **dealignment.** In such an environment, politics would be unusually volatile, because the large body of unattached independents could easily swing from one party to another. The dramatic changes in fortune experienced by the two major parties in recent years provide some evidence to support the dealignment theory. The parties have recently experienced record-high unfavorable scores in public opinion polls.

TIPPING Realignment is not the only process that can alter the political landscape. What if the various types of voters maintain their political identifications—but one type of voter becomes substantially more numerous? This can happen due to migration between states or between nations, or even due to changes in education levels and occupations. The result could tip a state from one party to another. Many Democratic strategists believe that such *tipping* will benefit their party greatly in the future.

CRITICAL THINKING
▶ Demographers expect that minority group members will be a majority of the U.S. population by 2050. How might this affect the two major parties?

7–3 WHAT DO POLITICAL PARTIES DO?

LO Explain how political parties function in our democratic system.

As noted earlier, the Constitution does not mention political parties. Historically, though, political parties have played a vital role in our democratic system. Their main function has been to link the people's policy preferences to actual government policies. Political parties also perform many other functions.

7–3a Selecting Candidates and Running Campaigns

One of the most important functions of the two political parties is to recruit and nominate candidates for political office. This function simplifies voting choices for the electorate. Political parties take the large number

Perception vs. REALITY

Wealthy People Are Republicans

Many people in the United States, as in most other countries, see the wealthy as conservative (on the political right). Likewise, the poor are seen as liberal (on the political left). In America, that means the wealthiest citizens should be Republicans and the poor should be Democrats.

The Perception

The political left—Democrats and others—is united in favor of policies that help the poor. Democrats also dislike the rich and want to increase taxes on the wealthiest taxpayers. Consequently, the wealthy vote against Democrats because Democrats will raise their taxes. The rich therefore speak with one voice—a Republican voice.

The Reality

Consider the results of exit polling after the 2012 elections, in which Democrat Barack Obama won the presidency. As you move up the income ladder, you indeed see fewer votes for Obama. Families making from $100,000 to $200,000 per year were more Republican than those making $50,000 to $100,000. Moving up to the $200,000 to $250,000 category, however, support for Obama jumped from 44 percent to 47 percent. We all know that many rich and famous Hollywood stars lean toward the left. In addition, many executives in high-tech companies are Democrats. Some are quite liberal indeed.

The fact is, there are conservatives *and* liberals among the rich—particularly among the very rich. Class warfare is not on the American agenda. The cosmopolitan cultural attitudes of the wealthy cause many of them to favor liberal politics. Even when Democrats, including President Obama, talk about raising tax rates for the rich, many of these people believe that such policies are "fair." For example, at a Facebook forum with President Obama, Facebook founder Mark Zuckerberg said that he was "cool" with paying more in taxes.

Note, too, that many of the super-rich are not particularly affected by higher income tax rates. People like Zuckerberg receive most of their income as capital gains—notably as increases in the value of their stocks. Taxes on earned income can reach almost 40 percent. Capital gains are taxed less severely. The rate is only 15 percent for most people. (The rate does go up to 18 percent for families with incomes over $250,000 and 23.6 percent for those with incomes above $450,000.) It is certainly easier for the super-rich to support Democrats who want to raise income tax rates if they know that for the most part they are not going to pay those additional taxes.

BLOG ON You can check out recent exit polls for yourself. You'll see how income, education, race, religion, ideology, and many other variables affect people's votes. For the 2012 polls, search on "exit polls 2012." For 2014, try "exit polls 2014."

---

of people who want to run for office and narrow the field. They accomplish this by the use of the **primary,** which is a preliminary election to choose a party's final candidate. This candidate then runs against the opposing party's candidate in the general election.

PRIMARY ELECTIONS Voter turnout for primaries is lower than it is for general elections. The voters who do go to the polls are often strong supporters of their party. Indeed, in many states, independents cannot participate in primary elections, even if they lean toward one or the other of the two major parties. As a result, the Republican primary electorate is very conservative, and Democratic primary voters are quite liberal. Candidates often find that they must run to the political right or left during the primaries. Traditionally, candidates then often moved to the center during the general election campaign. Chapter 9 provides much more detail on primary and general elections.

primary A preliminary election held for the purpose of choosing a party's final candidate.

Like sports teams, the parties use mascots. The Republican elephant and the Democratic donkey date to the nineteenth century. Both were first drawn by a Republican cartoonist. The elephant was supposed to illustrate the large size of the GOP in the northern states. *Given that the donkey was drawn by a Republican, what do you think it was meant to represent?*

7-4a The Party in the Electorate

Let's look more closely at the largest component of each party—the party in the electorate. What does it mean to belong to a political party? In many European countries, being a party member means that you actually join a political party. You get a membership card to carry in your wallet, you pay dues, and you vote to select your local and national party leaders. In the United States, becoming a member of a political party is far less involved.

In most states, voters may declare a party preference when they register to vote. This declaration allows them to participate in party primaries. Some states do not register party preferences, however. In short, to be a member of a political party, an American citizen has only to think of herself or himself as a Democrat or a Republican (or a member of a third party, such as the Green Party or the Libertarian Party). Members of parties do not have to work for the party or attend party meetings. Nor must they support the party platform.

party identifier A person who identifies himself or herself as being a supporter of a particular political party.

party activist A party member who helps to organize and oversee party functions and planning during and between campaigns, and may even become a candidate for office.

IDENTIFIERS AND ACTIVISTS Generally, the party in the electorate consists of **party identifiers** (those who identify themselves as being members of the party) and **party activists**—party members who choose to work for the party and even become candidates for office. Political parties need year-round support from the latter group to survive. During election campaigns in particular, candidates depend on active party members and volunteers to answer phones, conduct door-to-door canvasses, participate in Web campaigns, organize speeches and appearances, and, of course, donate money.

Between elections, parties also need active members to plan the upcoming elections, organize fundraisers, and stay in touch with party leaders in other communities to keep the party strong. The major functions of American political parties are carried out by the party activists.

ELITE GROUPS Most members of the party in the electorate are ordinary citizens. Even party activists are generally not known outside their own circles. Yet the party in the electorate is not limited to those who lack fortune or fame. It is also made up of elites of various kinds—opinion leaders, media personalities, and prominent persons in all walks of life. It includes fund raisers, former politicians, and nationally famous political operatives.

Consider talk radio personality Rush Limbaugh and deep-pocket campaign contributors Charles and David Koch. These people have no official position in government or in the Republican Party. They may be members of the party in the electorate, but their influence on the GOP is considerable. Likewise, comedian Jon Stewart and Arianna Huffington of the Huffington Post are influential among Democrats. A large number of entertainment celebrities are ardent Democrats, though some are Republicans.

Various interest groups are also considered to be part of the party coalitions. Labor unions are almost always seen as a base of support for the Democrats. Business groups such as the U.S. Chamber of Commerce are likewise viewed as key Republican players.

WHY PEOPLE JOIN POLITICAL PARTIES In a few countries, such as the People's Republic of China, people belong to a political party because they are required to do so to get ahead in life, regardless of whether they agree with the party's ideas and candidates. In the United States, though, people generally belong to a political party because they agree with many of its main ideas and support some of its candidates. Just as with interest groups, people's reasons for choosing one party over another may include solidarity, material, and purposive incentives.

Solidarity Incentives. Some people join a particular party to express their **solidarity,** or mutual agreement, with the views of friends, loved ones, and other like-minded people. People also join parties because they enjoy the excitement of engaging in politics with like-minded others.

Material Incentives. Many believe that by joining a party, they will benefit materially through better employment or personal career advancement. The traditional institution of **patronage**—rewarding the party faithful with government jobs or contracts—lives on, even though it has been limited to prevent abuses.[4] Back in the nineteenth century, when almost all government employees got their jobs through patronage, people spoke of it as the "spoils system," as in "the spoils of war."

Purposive Incentives. Finally, some join political parties because they wish to actively promote a set of ideals and principles that they feel are important to American politics and society. As a rule, people join political parties because of their overall agreement with what a particular party stands for.

Thus, when asked why they support the Democratic Party, people may make such remarks as the following: "The economy is better when the Democrats are in control." "The Democrats are for the working people." People might say about the Republican Party: "The Republicans favor a smaller government." "The Republicans are stronger on national defense."

7–4b The Party Organization

In theory, each of the major American political parties has a standard, pyramid-shaped organization. This theoretical structure is much like that of a large company, in which the bosses are at the top and the employees are at various lower levels.

Georgia delegates at the 2012 Republican National Convention in Tampa, Florida. *What kinds of persons are likely to attend the national conventions of the two major parties?*

Actually, neither major party is a closely knit or highly organized structure. Both parties are fragmented and *decentralized*, which means there is no central power with a direct chain of command. If there were, the national chairperson of the party, along with the national committee, could simply dictate how the organization would be run, just as if it were Apple or Google. In reality, state party organizations are all very different and are only loosely tied to the party's national structure. Local party organizations are often quite independent from the state organization.

In short, no single individual or group directs all party members. Instead, a number of personalities, frequently at odds with one another, form loosely identifiable leadership groups.

STATE ORGANIZATIONS The powers and duties of state party organizations differ from state to state. In general, the state party organization is built around a central committee and a chairperson. The committee works to raise funds, recruit new party members, maintain a strong party organization, and help members running for state offices.

The state chairperson is usually a powerful party member chosen by the committee. In some instances, however, the chairperson is selected by the governor or a senator from that state.

solidarity Mutual agreement among the members of a particular group.

patronage A system of rewarding the party faithful and workers with government jobs or contracts.

major parties have preferred to ignore. Third parties are in a position to take bold stands on issues that major parties avoid because third parties are not trying to be all things to all people.

Some people have argued that third parties are often the unsung heroes of American politics, bringing new issues to the forefront of public debate. Progressive social reforms such as the minimum wage, women's right to vote, railroad and banking legislation, and old-age pensions were first proposed by third parties. The Free Soilers of the 1850s were the first true antislavery party, and the Populists and Progressives put many social reforms on the political agenda. Although some of the ideas proposed by third parties were never accepted, others were taken up by the major parties as those ideas became increasingly popular.

THIRD PARTIES CAN AFFECT THE VOTE Third parties can also influence election outcomes. On occasion, they have taken victory from one major party and given it to another, thus playing the "spoiler" role.

For example, in 1912, when the Progressive Party split from the Republican Party, the result was three major contenders for the presidency: Woodrow Wilson, the Democratic candidate; William Howard Taft, the regular Republican candidate; and Theodore Roosevelt, the Progressive candidate. The presence of the Progressive Party "spoiled" the Republicans' chances for victory and gave the election to Wilson, the Democrat. Without Roosevelt's third party, Taft might have won. Similarly, some commentators contended that Green Party candidate Ralph Nader "spoiled" the chances of Democratic candidate Al Gore in the 2000 elections, because many of those who voted for Nader would have voted Democratic had Nader not been on the ballot.

THIRD PARTIES PROVIDE A VOICE FOR DISSATISFIED AMERICANS Third parties also provide a voice for voters who are frustrated with and alienated from the Republican and Democratic parties. Americans who are unhappy with the two major political parties can still participate in American politics through third parties that reflect their opinions on political issues. For example, many new Minnesota voters turned out during the 1998 elections to vote for Jesse Ventura, a Reform Party candidate for governor in that state. Ventura won.

© Library of Congress

Theodore Roosevelt, who was a Republican president from 1901 to 1909, ran for president on a third-party ticket in 1912. *What effect did his campaign have on the election results?*

Ultimately, third parties in national elections find it difficult to break through in an electoral system that perpetuates their failure. Because third parties normally do not win elections, Americans tend not to vote for them or to contribute to their campaigns, so they continue not to win. As long as Americans hold on to the perception that third parties can never win big in an election, the current two-party system is likely to persist.

AMERICA ⚑ AT ODDS
Political Parties

By their very nature, arguments about the parties are some of the most divisive conflicts in politics. We can list only a sampling of the disputes:

- *Is the Republican Party, through excessive conservatism, driving off voters that it needs—or can it win by upholding basic conservative values? For that matter, are the Democrats too liberal—or not liberal enough?*

- *Is it better when the two chambers of Congress and the presidency are held by the same party, thus guaranteeing effective government—or is it better when Congress and the presidency are held by different parties, so that the two parties can check each other?*

- *Is the increasing importance of political independents a positive development—or is it a sign that citizens are becoming dangerously detached from our political system?*

- *Are political parties desirable and inevitable—or should elections be nonpartisan whenever possible?*

- *Is it better to support a third party when you are in greater agreement with its positions than with those of either major party—or should you avoid wasting your vote and always support the major party that is closer to your politics?*

- *Finally, looking forward, do the Republicans or the Democrats offer the best solutions for our problems?*

Internet Resources

- For a list of political Web sites available on the Internet, sorted by country and with links to parties, organizations, and governments throughout the world, go to www.politicalresources.net.

- Ron Gunzburger's Politics1 Web site contains a vast amount of information on American politics. Click on "Political Parties" in the directory box at the top of the home page to see one of the most complete descriptions of major and minor parties to be found anywhere. Gunzburger's site is at www.politics1.com.

- The Democratic Party is online at www.democrats.org.

- The Republican National Committee is online at www.gop.com.

- The Libertarian Party has a Web site at www.lp.org.

- The Green Party's Web site can be accessed by going to www.greenparty.org.

STUDY TOOLS 7

READY TO STUDY?

- ☐ Review what you've read with the quiz below.
- ☐ Check your answers in Appendix D at the back of the book.
- ☐ For any questions you miss, read the corresponding Learning Outcome section again to prepare for class and your exam.
- ☐ Rip out and study the Chapter in Review card (at the back of the book).

VISIT WWW.CENGAGEBRAIN.COM:

- ☐ Interactive Quizzes
- ☐ Key Term Flashcards or Crossword Puzzles
- ☐ Audio Summaries
- ☐ Simulations, Animated Learning Modules, and Interactive Timelines
- ☐ Videos
- ☐ American Government NewsWatch

FILL-IN

LearningOutcome 7–1

1. The nation's first two political parties, the _____, clashed openly in the elections of 1796.

2. In 1860, Abraham Lincoln became the first president elected under the banner of the new _____ Party.

LearningOutcome 7–2

3. Dealignment among voters refers to _____.

LearningOutcome 7–3

4. Political parties link the people's policy preferences to actual government policies. Parties also perform many other functions, including _____.

5. A _____ is a preliminary election held for the purpose of choosing a party's final candidate.

LearningOutcome 7–4

6. The Republican and Democratic candidates for president and vice president are nominated at each party's _____.

7. A party platform is _____.

LearningOutcome 7–5

8. Third parties have influenced American politics in several ways, including _____.

MULTIPLE CHOICE

LearningOutcome 7–1

9. _____ refers to a process in which a substantial number of voters change their political allegiance, which usually also changes the balance of power between the two major parties.

   a. Realignment   **b.** Dealignment   **c.** Tipping

10. After the election of 1896, the _____ established themselves in the minds of many Americans as the party that knew how to manage the nation's economy, and they remained dominant in national politics until the onset of the Great Depression.

    a. Democrats   **b.** Republicans   **c.** Whigs

LearningOutcome 7–2

11. After the 2010 elections, many of the new Republican members of Congress were pledged to the Tea Party philosophy of

    a. moving the Republican Party toward more liberal positions.

    b. breaking political deadlock in Washington to solve national problems.

    c. no-compromise conservatism.

LearningOutcome 7–3

12. Which of the following statements best describes the way in which political parties perform the function of balancing competing interests?

    a. The political party is usually the major institution through which the executive and legislative branches cooperate with each other.

    b. Political parties are essentially coalitions— alliances of individuals and groups with a variety of concerns and opinions who join together to support the party's platform or parts of it.

    c. Political parties take the large number of people who want to run for office and narrow the field.

LearningOutcome 7–4

13. To be a member of a political party in the United States, a citizen

    a. must join the party and pay membership dues.

    b. must support the party platform.

    c. has only to think of himself or herself as a Democrat or a Republican (or a member of a third party).

LearningOutcome 7–5

14. An issue-oriented third party

    a. supports a particular political doctrine or a set of beliefs.

    b. is formed to promote a particular cause.

    c. is also referred to as a splinter party.

USE THE TOOLS.

- Rip out the Review Cards in the back of your book to study.

Or Visit CourseMate to:

- Read, search, highlight, and take notes in the Interactive eBook
- Review Flashcards (Print or Online) to master key terms
- Test yourself with Auto-Graded Quizzes
- Bring concepts to life with Games, Videos, and Animations!

Go to CourseMate for **GOVT7** to begin using these tools.
Access at **www.cengagebrain.com**

Complete the Speak Up survey in CourseMate at **www.cengagebrain.com**

f Follow us at **www.facebook.com/4ltrpress**

8 | Public Opinion and Voting

LEARNING OUTCOMES   After reading this chapter, you should be able to:

8–1 Describe the political socialization process.

8–2 Explain how public opinion polls are conducted, problems with polls, and how they are used in the political process.

8–3 Discuss the different factors that affect voter choices.

8–4 Indicate some of the factors that affect voter turnout, and discuss what has been done to improve voter turnout and voting procedures.

After finishing
this chapter go to
PAGE 190 for
STUDY TOOLS.

AMERICA AT ODDS

© Jorge Salcedo/Shutterstock

Do New State Laws Interfere with Voting Rights?

In 1965, Congress passed the Voting Rights Act. The goal was to stop efforts by state and local governments, particularly in the South, to keep African Americans from voting. One provision of the act was that state and local governments with a history of violating voters' rights must obtain "preclearance" for changes to voting rules and district boundaries from the federal government.

In 2013, however, the United States Supreme Court threw out the formula in the act that determined which states and localities must obtain preclearance. The Court argued that the formula was unacceptable because it was based on forty-year-old data. State governments in the South and elsewhere quickly implemented new voting laws. The most common change was to require voters to show photo identification at the polls, but other new laws were adopted as well.

The goal of the new state laws, according to state officials, was to reduce voter fraud. While no one is in favor of voter fraud, many argue that the new laws did more harm than good because they restricted voting rights. The Obama administration mounted challenges to many of these new laws under clauses of the Voting Rights Act that remained in effect. Attorney General Eric Holder said that the administration planned to "use every tool" at its disposal to maintain federal oversight of voting, despite the Supreme Court's decision. Did the attorney general overreact? Do new state laws truly interfere with voting rights?

Fewer Eligible Voters Will Vote

According to columnist Harold Meyerson of the *Los Angeles Times,* "Voter fraud is a myth—not an urban or a real myth, as such, but a Republican one." He argues that Republicans have raised the specter of voter fraud to pass laws that make it harder for disadvantaged persons (mostly Democrats) to vote.

For example, Arizona and Kansas now require proof of citizenship, such as a birth certificate or a passport, to vote in state elections. Many poorer citizens—especially minority group members—do not have these documents. Other states have eliminated same-day registration on Election Day. In some states, young citizens lost the right to "preregister" to vote before they turned eighteen. Some states decided to reduce early voting—a practice that minorities have used more than others. North Carolina, for example, eliminated Sunday early voting. In that state, African American church congregations had adopted the practice of marching as a group to polling places at the conclusion of Sunday services.

Much Ado About Nothing

Those who support the new state voting laws argue that photo ID requirements do not restrict anyone's rights. After all, Americans have to show their IDs when they cash a check or board an airplane. Violations of voting laws continue to occur. Felons, for example—who are not allowed to vote in many states—may end up voting anyway. Support for ID requirements exists even within some minority communities. Polls show that Hispanic Texans support the requirement. In Texas, anyone can get the necessary ID free of charge, so poverty cannot be an excuse not to obtain it.

Also, many states have recently passed laws to make voting more convenient. Colorado now allows Election Day registration, as well as preregistration of eligible young people. Maryland has expanded its early voting system. Today, Virginia and West Virginia provide online registration. True, some states have tightened the rules, but overall, it is as easy to vote now as it ever was.

Where do you stand?

1. Given that a photo ID is required to board an airplane, do you think one should be required to vote? If so, why? If not, why not?
2. Some people claim that minority groups can counteract any negative effect of restrictive voting rules by increased turnout at the polls. How easy would it be to do that? Explain.

Explore this issue online

- For a spirited defense of Texas voting laws by the state's attorney general, type "abbott washington times voting" into a search engine.
- The liberal Daily Kos blog opposes legislation that restricts voting—search on "kos voting."

INTRODUCTION

For a democracy to be effective, members of the public must form opinions and openly express them to their elected officials. Only when the opinions of Americans are communicated effectively to elected representatives can those opinions form the basis of government action.

Citizens use many methods to communicate with elected officials, including tweets, e-mail, texting, telephone calls, and attendance at rallies or "town hall" meetings with representatives. The most accurate way of gauging overall public opinion between elections, however, is through public opinion polls, which we describe in this chapter.

The ultimate way that citizens communicate their views, of course, is by casting ballots for their preferred candidates. Many factors affect the political beliefs that motivate voters, and we discuss these factors in this chapter. We also look at the mechanics of voting, which can have a definite impact on election results.

> "A government can be no better than the
> **public opinion**
> that sustains it."
>
> ~ **Franklin Delano Roosevelt,** Thirty-Second President of the United States
> 1933–1945

8–1 HOW DO PEOPLE FORM POLITICAL OPINIONS?

LO Describe the political socialization process.

What exactly is **public opinion?** We define it as the sum total of a complex collection of opinions held by many people on issues in the public arena, such as taxes, health care, Social Security, clean-air legislation, and unemployment. When asked, most Americans are willing to express an opinion on such issues. Not one of us, however, was born with these opinions. Most people acquire their political attitudes, opinions, beliefs, and knowledge through a complex learning process called

public opinion The views of the citizenry about politics, public issues, and public policies; a complex collection of opinions held by many people on issues in the public arena.

political socialization The learning process through which most people acquire their political attitudes, opinions, beliefs, and knowledge.

agents of political socialization People and institutions that influence the political views of others.

political socialization. This process begins in childhood and continues throughout life.

Most political socialization is informal, and it usually begins during early childhood, when the dominant influence on a child is the family. Although parents normally do not sit down and say to their children, "Let us explain to you the virtues of becoming a Republican," their children nevertheless come to know the parents' feelings, beliefs, and attitudes. The strong early influence of the family later gives way to the multiple influences of school, church, peers, television, co-workers, and other groups. People and institutions that influence the political views of others are called **agents of political socialization.**

8–1a The Importance of Family

As just suggested, most parents or caregivers do not deliberately set out to form their children's political ideas and beliefs. They are usually more concerned with the moral, religious, and ethical values of their offspring. Yet a child first sees the political world through the eyes of his or her family, which is perhaps the most important force in political socialization. Children do not "learn" political attitudes the same way they learn to master in-line skating. Rather, they learn by hearing their parents' everyday conversations and stories about politicians and issues and by observing their parents' actions and reactions.

The family's influence is strongest when children can clearly perceive their parents' attitudes, and most can. In one study, more high school students could identify their parents' political party affiliation than their parents' other attitudes or beliefs. The political party of the parents often becomes the political party of the children, particularly if both parents support the same party.

8–1b Schools and Churches

Education also strongly influences an individual's political attitudes. From their earliest days in school, children learn about the American political system. They say the Pledge of Allegiance and sing patriotic songs. They celebrate national holidays, such as Presidents' Day and Veterans' Day, and learn about the history and symbols associated with them. In the upper grades, young people acquire more knowledge about government and democratic pro-

Family support for going to college often matters. *Why might it be important to encourage youth from low-income families to attend college?*

cedures through civics classes and participation in student government and various clubs. They also learn citizenship skills through school rules and regulations. Generally, those with more education have more knowledge about politics and policy than those with less education. The level of education also influences a person's political values, as will be discussed later in this chapter.

A majority of Americans hold strong religious beliefs, and these attitudes can also contribute significantly to political socialization. For example, if a family's church emphasizes that society has a collective obligation to care for the poor, the children in that family may be influenced in a liberal direction. If the church instead depicts the government as irreligious and morally threatening, children will receive a conservative message.

8-1c The Media

The **media**—newspapers, magazines, television, radio, and the Internet—also have an impact on political socialization. The most influential of these media is television, which continues to be a leading source of political information for older voters. As explained later in this chapter, older citizens turn out to vote significantly more often than younger ones.

Still, the Internet—and social media in particular—are extremely important sources of information for younger citizens. Social media are also important for politicians. Consider that President Obama has 16.5 million followers on Twitter, placing him among the top ten worldwide.

Some contend that the media's role in shaping public opinion has increased to the point that the media are as influential as the family, particularly among high school students. For example, in her analysis of the media's role in American politics, media scholar Doris A. Graber points out that high school students, when asked where they obtain the information on which they base their attitudes, mention the Internet and social media far more than they mention their families, friends, and teachers.[1]

Other studies have shown that the media's influence on people's opinions may not be as great as some have thought. Generally, people go online, watch television, or read articles with preconceived ideas about the issues. These preconceived ideas act as a kind of perceptual screen that blocks out information that is not consistent with the ideas. Generally, the media tend to wield the most influence over the views of persons who have not yet formed opinions about various issues or candidates. (See Chapter 10 for a more detailed discussion of the media's role in American politics.)

8-1d Opinion Leaders

Every state or community has well-known citizens who are able to influence the opinions of their fellow citizens. These people may be public officials, religious leaders, teachers, or celebrities. They are the people to whom others listen and from whom others draw ideas and convictions about various issues of public concern. These opinion leaders play a significant role in the formation of public opinion.

Opinion leaders often include politicians or former politicians. For example, President Barack Obama asked former U.S. presidents George W. Bush (2001–2009) and Bill Clinton (1993–2001) to lead a nationwide fundraising drive following the January 2010 earthquake in Haiti, which destroyed much of that country.

Sometimes, however, opinion leaders can fall from grace when they express views radically different from what most Americans believe. One example is former

media Newspapers, magazines, television, radio, the Internet, and any other printed or electronic means of communication.

president Jimmy Carter (1977–1981), who lost much popularity after he published a book that harshly criticized Israel's actions toward the Palestinians.[2] (Most Americans of both parties are strongly pro-Israel.)

8–1e Major Life Events

Often, the political attitudes of an entire generation of Americans are influenced by a major event. For example, consider the Great Depression (1929–1939), the most severe economic depression in modern U.S. history. This event persuaded many Americans who lived through it that the federal government should step in when the economy is in decline. A substantial number of voters came to believe that the New Deal programs and policies of President Franklin Roosevelt showed that the Democratic Party was concerned about the fate of ordinary people. As a result, they became supporters of that party.

The generation that lived through World War II (1939–1945) tends to believe that American intervention in foreign affairs is good. In contrast, the generation that came of age during the Vietnam War (1965–1975) is more skeptical of American interventionism. A national tragedy, such as the terrorist attacks of September 11, 2001, is also likely to influence the political attitudes of a generation. The recent Great Recession and the financial crisis that struck in September 2008 will surely affect popular attitudes in years to come.

8–1f Peer Groups

Once children enter school, the views of friends begin to influence their attitudes and beliefs. From junior high school on, the **peer group**—friends, classmates, co-workers, club members, or religious group members—becomes a significant factor in the political socialization process.

Most of this socialization occurs when the peer group is involved with political activities or other causes. For example, your political beliefs might be influenced by a peer group with which you are working on a common cause, such as cleaning up a local river bank or campaigning for a favorite candidate. Your political beliefs probably are not as strongly influenced by peers with whom you, say, snowboard regularly or attend concerts.

8–1g Economic Status and Occupation

A person's economic status may influence her or his political views. For example, poorer people are more likely to favor government assistance programs. On an issue such as abortion, lower-income people are more likely to be conservative—that is, to be against abortion—than are higher-income groups (of course, there are many exceptions).

Where a person works also affects her or his opinions. Co-workers who spend a great deal of time working together tend to influence one another. For example, labor union members working together for a company may have similar political opinions, at least on issues of government involvement in the economy. Individuals working for a nonprofit agency that depends on government funds will tend to support government spending in that area. Business managers are more likely to favor tax laws helpful to businesses than are factory workers.

> **CRITICAL THINKING**
> ▸ Thinking about your own life, what sources of political socialization were most important to you? How did they influence your beliefs?

8–2 PUBLIC OPINION POLLS

> **LO** Explain how public opinion polls are conducted, problems with polls, and how they are used in the political process.

When you hear a news report or read a magazine article stating that "a significant number of Americans" feel a certain way about an issue, you are probably hearing that a particular opinion is held by a large enough number of people to make government officials listen. Such reports most often come from polls of public opinion.

A **public opinion poll** is a survey of the public's opinion on a particular topic at a particular moment. The results of opinion polls are most often cast in terms of percentages: 62 percent feel this way, 31 percent do not, and 7 percent have no opinion.

Of course, a poll cannot survey the entire U.S. population. Therefore, public opinion pollsters have devised scientific polling techniques for measuring public opinion through the use of **samples**—groups of people who are typical of the general population.

peer group Associates, often close in age to one another; may include friends, classmates, co-workers, club members, or religious group members.

public opinion poll A survey of the public's opinion on a particular topic at a particular moment.

sample In the context of opinion polling, a group of people selected to represent the population being studied.

8–2a Early Polling Efforts

Since the 1800s, magazines and newspapers have often spiced up their articles by conducting **straw polls** of readers' opinions. Straw polls simply ask a large number of people the same question. The problem with straw polls is that the opinions expressed usually represent an atypical subgroup of the population, or a **biased sample.** A survey of those who read *People* will most likely produce different results than a survey of those who read *Sports Illustrated,* for example.

THE *LITERARY DIGEST* FIASCO

The most famous of all straw-polling errors was committed by the *Literary Digest* in 1936 when it tried to predict the outcome of that year's presidential elections. The *Digest* forecast that Republican Alfred Landon would easily defeat Democratic incumbent Franklin D. Roosevelt. Instead, Roosevelt won by a landslide. The editors of the *Digest* had sent mail-in cards to names in telephone directories, to its own subscribers, and to automobile owners—a staggering 2,376,000 people. In the Depression year of 1936, however, people who owned a car or a telephone or who subscribed to the *Digest* were not representative of most Americans. The vast majority of Americans could not afford such luxuries. The sample turned out to be unrepresentative and consequently inaccurate.

THE FIRST SCIENTIFIC POLL TAKERS
Several newcomers to the public opinion poll industry, however, did predict Roosevelt's victory. Two of these organizations are still at the forefront of the polling industry today: the Gallup Organization, started by George Gallup, and Roper Associates, founded by Elmo Roper and now known as the Roper Center.

8–2b Polling Today

Today, polling is used extensively by political candidates and policymakers. Politicians and the news media generally place a great deal of faith in the accuracy of poll results. Polls can be quite accurate when they are conducted properly. In the twenty presidential elections in which Gallup has participated, its polls conducted in late October correctly predicted the winner in six-

Nate Silver appears on *Good Morning America.* While working for the *New York Times,* Silver correctly predicted the 2012 presidential winner in all fifty states. His politics and sports blog, fivethirtyeight.com, is now sponsored by ESPN. *How much does politics resemble sports?*

teen of the races.[3] Even polls taken several months in advance have been able to predict the eventual winner.

TYPES OF POLLS
In the earliest days of scientific polling, interviewers typically went door to door locating respondents. Such in-person surveys were essential in the mid-twentieth century, when a surprisingly large number of homes did not have telephones.

Telephone Polls. In time, the number of homes without phones dwindled, and polling organizations determined that they could obtain satisfactory samples of voters through telephone interviews alone. In recent years, poll takers have even replaced human interviewers with prerecorded messages that solicit responses. Such methods allow companies to conduct very large numbers of polls at little cost. Questions have arisen as to whether automated polling is as accurate as polling that uses live interviewers, however.

Further complications for telephone poll takers include the increase in the use of cell phones—which not all pollsters bother to call. Today, many cell phone users no longer have a landline number. An additional

---

straw poll A nonscientific poll in which there is no way to ensure that the opinions expressed are representative of the larger population.

biased sample A poll sample that does not accurately represent the population.

FIGURE 8-2   VOTING BY GROUPS IN THE 2012 PRESIDENTIAL ELECTIONS

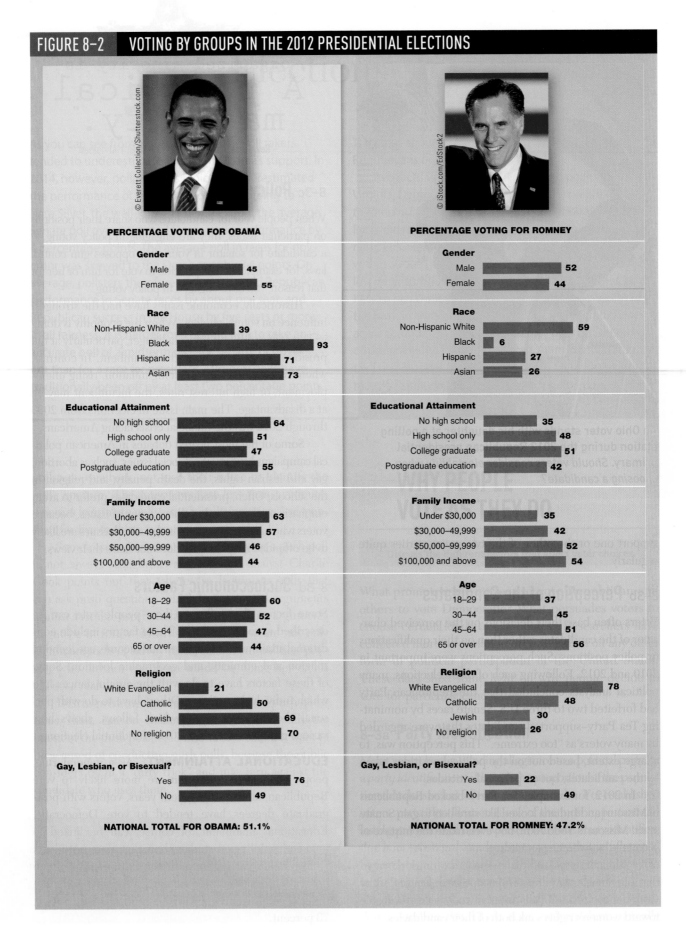

PERCENTAGE VOTING FOR OBAMA

Gender
Male — 45
Female — 55

Race
Non-Hispanic White — 39
Black — 93
Hispanic — 71
Asian — 73

Educational Attainment
No high school — 64
High school only — 51
College graduate — 47
Postgraduate education — 55

Family Income
Under $30,000 — 63
$30,000–49,999 — 57
$50,000–99,999 — 46
$100,000 and above — 44

Age
18–29 — 60
30–44 — 52
45–64 — 47
65 or over — 44

Religion
White Evangelical — 21
Catholic — 50
Jewish — 69
No religion — 70

Gay, Lesbian, or Bisexual?
Yes — 76
No — 49

NATIONAL TOTAL FOR OBAMA: 51.1%

PERCENTAGE VOTING FOR ROMNEY

Gender
Male — 52
Female — 44

Race
Non-Hispanic White — 59
Black — 6
Hispanic — 27
Asian — 26

Educational Attainment
No high school — 35
High school only — 48
College graduate — 51
Postgraduate education — 42

Family Income
Under $30,000 — 35
$30,000–49,999 — 42
$50,000–99,999 — 52
$100,000 and above — 54

Age
18–29 — 37
30–44 — 45
45–64 — 51
65 or over — 56

Religion
White Evangelical — 78
Catholic — 48
Jewish — 30
No religion — 26

Gay, Lesbian, or Bisexual?
Yes — 22
No — 49

NATIONAL TOTAL FOR ROMNEY: 47.2%

OCCUPATION AND INCOME   Businesspersons tend to vote Republican and have done so for many years. This is understandable, given the pro-business stand traditionally adopted by that party. Recently, professionals (such as attorneys, professors, and physicians) have been more likely to vote Democratic than in earlier years. It appears that institutional and social changes have made it less likely that professionals will see themselves as small businesspersons or identify with business interests. Manual laborers, factory workers, and especially union members are more likely to vote for the Democrats, who have a history of pro-labor positions.

In the past, the higher the income, the more likely it was that a person would vote Republican. Conversely, a much larger percentage of low-income individuals voted Democratic. But this pattern is also breaking down. (For more on this topic, see the *Perception versus Reality* feature in Chapter 7.)

AGE   The conventional wisdom is that the young are liberal and the old are conservative. Certainly, younger voters were unusually supportive of Barack Obama in the 2008 and 2012 elections. Yet in years past, age differences in support for the parties have often been quite small.

One age-related effect is that people's attitudes are shaped by the events that unfolded as they grew up. As we observed earlier, many voters who came of age during Franklin Roosevelt's New Deal held on to a preference for the Democrats. Voters who were young when Ronald Reagan was president have had a tendency to prefer the Republicans. Younger voters are noticeably more liberal on one set of issues, however—those dealing with the rights of minorities, women, and gay males and lesbians.

GENDER   In the 1960s and 1970s, there seemed to be no fixed pattern of voter preferences by gender in presidential elections. Women and men tended to vote for the various candidates in roughly equal numbers. Some political analysts believe that a **gender gap** became a major determinant of voter decision making in the 1980 presidential elections, however. In that year, Ronald Reagan outdrew Jimmy Carter by 16 percentage points among male voters, whereas women gave about an equal number of votes to each candidate. In the years since, the gender gap has been a continuing phenomenon. For example, in 2012 Barack Obama carried the female vote by 55 to 44 percentage points, while losing the male vote by a 45 to 52 point margin.

The modern feminist movement and the recognition that women have suffered from various types of discrimination doubtless have something to do with the gender gap. It also appears, however, that compared with men, women on average have a stronger commitment to the liberal value of the common welfare and a weaker belief in the conservative value of self-reliance.

RELIGION AND ETHNIC BACKGROUND   A century ago, at least in the northern states, white Catholic voters were likely to be Democrats, and white Protestant voters were probably Republicans. There are a few places around the country where this pattern continues to hold, but for the most part, non-Hispanic white Catholics are now almost as likely as their Protestant neighbors to support the Republicans.

Regular Church Attendance.   In recent years, a different religious variable has become important in determining voting behavior. Regardless of their denomination, white Christian voters who attend church regularly have favored the Republicans by substantial margins. White Christian voters who attend church rarely or who find religion less important in their lives are more likely to vote Democratic.

Although some churches do promote liberal ways of thinking, the number of churches that promote conservative values is much larger. Note, too, that Jewish voters are strongly Democratic, regardless of whether they attend services.

Minority Group Members.   Most African Americans are Protestants, but African Americans are one of the most solidly Democratic constituencies in the United States. This is a complete reversal of the circumstances that existed a century ago. As noted in Chapter 7, for many years after the Civil War, those African Americans who could vote were overwhelmingly Republican. Not until President Franklin Roosevelt's New Deal did black voters begin to turn to the Democrats. While we would predict that today's African American voters would trend Democratic based on their low average income, black support for the Democrats far exceeds the levels that could be deduced from economics alone.

Latino voters have supported the Democrats by margins of about two to one, with some exceptions: older Cuban Americans are strongly Republican. In contrast to support from African Americans, Hispanic support for the Democrats is only modestly greater than what we would predict based on low average income. This fact

> **gender gap**   The difference between the percentage of votes cast for a particular candidate by women and the percentage of votes cast for the same candidate by men.

states to provide all eligible citizens with the opportunity to register to vote when they apply for or renew a driver's license. The law also requires that states allow mail-in registration. Forms are available at public assistance agencies. The law, which took effect in 1995, has facilitated millions of registrations.

MAIL-IN VOTING In 1998, Oregon voters approved a ballot initiative requiring that all elections in that state, including presidential elections, be conducted exclusively by mail. In the 2012 presidential elections, 65 percent of Oregonians eligible to vote cast ballots, a figure that is somewhat higher than the national average but not exceptionally so.

The state of Washington now also relies almost exclusively on mail-in ballots. Many states have recently made such ballots an option for all voters. In the past, *absentee ballots* were often available only to those who clearly could not make it to a polling place on Election Day. Reasons for an absentee ballot might include military service, business travel, or ill health.

LAWS THAT MAY DISCOURAGE VOTING In recent years, a number of states have passed laws that may have the effect of making it harder to vote, not easier. The most common such law requires that voters produce photographic identification before they are allowed to register or vote. Supporters of such laws contend that they reduce voter fraud. Opponents argue that the net effect is to deter voters—mostly lower income and often minority—who do not have easy access to ID cards. We discussed this issue in the chapter-opening *America at Odds* feature.

8-4d Attempts to Improve Voting Procedures

Because of serious problems in achieving accurate vote counts in recent elections, particularly in the 2000 presidential elections, steps have been taken to attempt to ensure more accuracy in the voting process. In 2002, Congress passed the Help America Vote Act, which, among other things, provided funds to the states to help them purchase new electronic voting equipment. Concerns about the possibility of fraudulent manipulation of electronic voting machines then replaced the worries over inaccurate vote counts caused by the previous equipment.

PROBLEMS IN 2006 In the 2006 elections, about half of the states that were using new electronic voting systems reported problems. Some systems "flipped" votes

from the selected candidate to the opposing candidate. In one Florida district, about eighteen thousand votes apparently were unrecorded by electronic equipment, and this may have changed the outcome of a congressional race. Many experts have demanded that electronic systems create a "paper trail," so that machine errors can be tracked and fixed.

VOTING SYSTEMS IN RECENT ELECTIONS Because of problems with electronic systems, fewer polling places used them in 2008 and 2010. Indeed, more than half of all votes cast in these years used old-fashioned paper ballots. As a result, vote counting was slow.

In 2012, the development of voter-verified paper audit trail (VVPAT) printers led to the reintroduction of electronic machines in many states. Often, however, only a limited number of such machines were installed to serve voters with disabilities. Two-thirds of all votes nationwide were still cast using paper ballots. In seventeen states, some or all of the votes were cast through electronic devices that lacked a paper audit trail. A full quarter of all votes were cast using these questionable systems.[9] The trend toward the reintroduction of electronic systems continued with the 2014 elections.

One feature of the elections was the large number of states that allowed early voting at polling places that opened weeks before Election Day. A benefit of early voting was that it allowed election workers time to ensure that all systems were working properly by Election Day. As we have noted in this chapter, however, since 2012 some states have attempted to cut back on early voting.

8-4e Who Actually Votes

Just because an individual is eligible to vote does not necessarily mean that the person will cast a ballot. Why do some eligible voters go to the polls while others do not? Although nobody can answer this question with absolute conviction, certain factors appear to affect voter turnout.

EDUCATIONAL ATTAINMENT Among the factors affecting voter turnout, education appears to be the most important. The more education a person has, the more likely it is that she or he will be a regular voter. People who graduated from high school vote more regularly than those who dropped out, and college graduates vote more often than high school graduates.

INCOME LEVEL AND AGE Differences in income also lead to differences in voter turnout. Wealthy people tend to be overrepresented among regular voters.

© Charley Gallay/Getty Images

Musician Joe Jonas, actor Bryan Greenberg, and musician Kevin Jonas at the Rock The Vote exclusive apparel kick-off in 2012 in West Hollywood. *Why do young people need extra encouragement to vote?*

voter-turnout figures. In the past, voter turnout was often expressed as a percentage of the **voting-age population,** the number of people residing in the United States who are at least eighteen years old. Due to legal and illegal immigration, however, many people of voting age are not eligible to vote because they are not citizens. Millions more cannot vote because they are felons. Additionally, the voting-age population excludes Americans abroad, who are eligible to cast absentee ballots.

Today, political scientists calculate the **vote-eligible population,** the number of people who are actually entitled to vote in American elections. They have found that there may be 20 million fewer eligible voters than the voting-age population suggests. Therefore, voter turnout is actually greater than the percentages sometimes cited.

Some experts have argued that the relatively low levels of voter turnout often reported for the years between 1972 and 2000 were largely due to immigration.[10] Beginning in 2004, voter turnout has improved by any calculation method.

Generally, older voters turn out to vote more regularly than younger voters do, although participation tends to decline among the very elderly. Participation likely increases with age because older people tend to be more settled, are already registered, and have had more experience with voting.

MINORITY STATUS Racial and ethnic minorities traditionally have been underrepresented among the ranks of voters. In several recent elections, however, participation by these groups, particularly African Americans and Hispanics, has increased. In part because the number of Latino citizens has grown rapidly, the increase in the Hispanic vote has been even larger than the increase in the black vote.

IMMIGRATION AND VOTER TURNOUT The United States has experienced high rates of immigration in recent decades, and that has had an effect on

voting-age population The number of people residing in the United States who are at least eighteen years old.

vote-eligible population The number of people who are actually eligible to vote in an American election.

Public Opinion and Voting

Public opinion polls reveal that Americans are in broad agreement on many issues, such as the basic political structure of our nation. Nevertheless, polls also report that Americans are at odds with one another on many other issues. After all, the questions posed by poll takers are typically divisive ones. Issues surrounding who votes and why can also be contentious. Some examples include the following:

- *Is the disenfranchisement of felons a form of racial discrimination—or a rational part of the punishment process?*

- *Given that historical events shape popular attitudes toward the parties, when all is said and done, will the impact of the Great Recession benefit one of the major parties—or will the effects of the recession prove trivial?*

- *Should legislators follow public opinion as faithfully as they can—or, as the Democrats did on health-care reform, should lawmakers do what they think is best for the country regardless of the polls?*

- We discussed push polls earlier in this chapter. *Should push polls be banned—or would that violate First Amendment guarantees of free speech?*

- *Should voters be more concerned with the policy positions of the presidential candidates—or are the presidential candidates' personalities and personal characteristics of equal or greater concern?*

Internet Resources

- Pollingreport.com has one of the Internet's larger collections of polls on every conceivable topic. Visit it at www.pollingreport.com.

- The Huffington Post Web site offers the HuffPost Pollster, which tracks thousands of polls. Its charts allow you to combine the results of multiple polls on the same topic. See it at elections.huffingtonpost.com/pollster.

- In addition to its large collection of recent articles on politics, the Real Clear Politics Web site has one of the most comprehensive collections of election polls available. For the polls, go to www.realclearpolitics.com/polls.

- At the Gallup Organization's Web site, you can find the results of recent polls, as well as an archive of past polls and information on how polls are conducted. Go to www.gallup.com.

- The highly regarded Pew Research Center conducts polls on politics, the media, social trends, religion, technology, Hispanics, and global issues. Its home page is at www.pewresearch.org.

- The United States Elections Project, now at the University of Florida, has the best voter turnout data available anywhere. The project is led by political scientist Michael McDonald. Visit it at www.electproject.org.

STUDY TOOLS 8

READY TO STUDY?

- ☐ Review what you've read with the quiz below.
- ☐ Check your answers in Appendix D at the back of the book.
- ☐ For any questions you miss, read the corresponding Learning Outcome section again to prepare for class and your exam.
- ☐ Rip out and study the Chapter in Review card (at the back of the book).

VISIT WWW.CENGAGEBRAIN.COM:

- ☐ Interactive Quizzes
- ☐ Key Term Flashcards or Crossword Puzzles
- ☐ Audio Summaries
- ☐ Simulations, Animated Learning Modules, and Interactive Timelines
- ☐ Videos
- ☐ American Government NewsWatch

LearningOutcome 8–1

1. Agents of political socialization include
   _____.

LearningOutcome 8–2

2. A random sample means that _____.

3. When a pollster's results appear to consistently favor a particular political party, polling experts refer to the phenomenon as a _____.

4. A _____ is a campaign tactic used to feed false or misleading information to potential voters, under the guise of conducting an opinion poll.

LearningOutcome 8–3

5. For established voters, _____ is one of the most important and lasting predictors of how a person will vote.

6. When people vote for candidates who share their positions on particular issues, they are engaging in _____.

7. Socioeconomic factors that influence how people vote include _____.

LearningOutcome 8–4

8. Methods used to keep African Americans from voting even after the Fifteenth Amendment to the U.S. Constitution was ratified included _____.

LearningOutcome 8–1

9. Most political socialization is informal, and it usually begins
   a. in college.
   b. in high school.
   c. during early childhood.

10. The family is an important agent of political socialization because
    a. most families deliberately set out to form their children's political ideas and beliefs.
    b. a child first sees the political world through the eyes of his or her family.
    c. parents are responsible for registering their children to vote.

LearningOutcome 8–2

11. A *Literary Digest* poll incorrectly predicted that Alfred Landon would win the presidential election in 1936 because the
    a. pollsters used an unrepresentative sample.
    b. pollsters used a random sample.
    c. sample size was too small.

LearningOutcome 8–3

12. Historically, _____ issues have had the strongest influence on voters' choices.
    a. foreign policy   b. social   c. economic

13. The term *gender gap*
    a. refers to the difference between the percentage of votes cast for a particular candidate by women and the percentage of votes cast for the same candidate by men.
    b. describes the difference in voter turnout between men and women.
    c. describes the differences in the campaign styles of male and female candidates.

LearningOutcome 8–4

14. In 1971, the Twenty-sixth Amendment reduced the minimum voting age to
    a. sixteen.   b. eighteen.   c. twenty-one.

15. Among the factors affecting voter turnout, _____ appears to be the most important.
    a. educational attainment   c. income level
    b. race

9 | Campaigns and Elections

© Jae C. Hong/AP Photo

LEARNING OUTCOMES After reading this chapter, you should be able to:

9–1 Explain how elections are held and how the electoral college functions in presidential elections.

9–2 Discuss how candidates are nominated.

9–3 Indicate what is involved in launching a political campaign today, and describe the structure and functions of a campaign organization.

9–4 Describe how the Internet has transformed political campaigns.

9–5 Summarize the current laws that regulate campaign financing and the role of money in modern political campaigns.

After finishing this chapter go to **PAGE 214** for **STUDY TOOLS.**

AMERICA AT ODDS

© Sean Locke Photography/Shutterstock

Should We Let Political Contributors Conceal Their Identities?

In the run-up to every November general election, television watchers can be certain that they will be bombarded with negative political ads. Such ads must identify their sponsors. If you see an ad by the Committee for the Advancement of Everything Good, how can you tell who actually funded it?

Many such ads are put together by super PACs or 501c organizations, which we describe in this chapter. If you go to the Web sites of these organizations, you are not likely to learn who provided the funds. In some cases, you might be able to find the answer at the Web site of the Federal Election Commission or of a watchdog organization at OpenSecrets. Yet four of the twenty largest independent-expenditure organizations hide the identities of all their donors. Another five offer donors the option of hiding their identities.

Full Disclosure, Please

Polls show that a strong majority of voters are concerned about the role of money in politics. No one believes that special interest money is going to disappear, but most voters from both parties say that we should know who is making the contributions.

Opponents of anonymous contributions point to a number of reasons why they should have no place in our democracy. When voters evaluate a candidate, they have the right to know who stands behind that person. Which unions, corporations, trade associations, or individual billionaires are supporting him or her? How can we battle undue influence on the part of special interests if we don't know which interests are supporting which candidates? Also, those who fund misleading advertisements or even flat-out lies should take responsibility for their messages.

Furthermore, small campaign contributors lose out when they are up against well-funded super PACs with anonymous donors. Candidates can compete fairly for public office only when we eliminate secret funding of political campaigns.

Political Privacy Should be a Civil Right

Not everyone is in favor of forcing secret donors to political campaigns out into the open. Consider that in 1958, the United States Supreme Court ruled that Alabama could not require the NAACP to disclose its membership rolls. Why? Because if segregationists in Alabama were able to identify NAACP members, they could retaliate against the most vulnerable ones. Some members might lose their jobs or be threatened with violence. Publicizing the membership list of an organization such as the NAACP would make a mockery of the constitutional rights to free association and free speech. According to the Court, the privacy of group membership is critical to "effective advocacy of both public and private points of view, particularly controversial ones."

If all political contributions were exposed, what could happen to a supporter of a liberal cause such as gay rights if he or she worked for a conservative employer? In California, supporters of same-sex marriage picketed and boycotted various groups that funded opposition to gay marriage. Banning anonymous donations harms free speech—not the other way around.

Where do you stand?

1. Which kind of donor might be more interested in identity protection— an individual billionaire or a corporation that sells products to the public? Why?

2. Why do you think that the authors of the *Federalist Papers* (see Chapter 2) remained anonymous?

Explore this issue online

- *New York Times* columnist Thomas Edsall examines the arguments and comes down against anonymity. Find his article by searching on "anonymous edsall."

- Republican activist Shoshana Weissman argues for anonymity that is so strict even the candidates won't know where the money came from. Search on "anonymous contributions shoshana weissman."

INTRODUCTION

During elections, candidates vie to become representatives of the people in both national and state offices. Campaigning for election has become an arduous task for every politician. As you will see in this chapter, American campaigns are long and expensive undertakings. The rules that govern our elections can be controversial, as we discussed in the chapter-opening *America at Odds* feature. Yet America's campaigns are an important part of our political process, because it is through campaigns that citizens learn about the candidates and decide how they will cast their votes.

American democracy would be impossible without campaigns and elections. Otherwise, there would be no way for the people to control the government. For freedom to thrive, however, elections are not enough. Democracy also requires the kind of shared political culture that we described in Chapter 1. We explain what can happen in countries that do not enjoy such a political culture in this chapter's *The Rest of the World* feature, which follows.

 9–1 **HOW WE ELECT CANDIDATES**

> **LO** Explain how elections are held and how the electoral college functions in presidential elections.

The ultimate goal of a political campaign and the associated fund-raising efforts is, of course, winning the election. The most familiar kind of election is the **general election,** which is a regularly scheduled election held

---

general election A regularly scheduled election to choose the U.S. president, vice president, and senators and representatives in Congress. General elections are held in even-numbered years on the Tuesday after the first Monday in November.

special election An election that is held at the state or local level when the voters must decide an issue before the next general election or when vacancies occur by reason of death or resignation.

Australian ballot A secret ballot that is prepared, distributed, and counted by government officials at public expense; used by all states in the United States since 1888.

poll watcher A representative from one of the political parties who is allowed to monitor a polling place to make sure that the election is run fairly and that fraud doesn't occur.

elector A member of the electoral college.

electoral college The group of electors who are selected by the voters in each state to officially elect the president and vice president. The number of electors in each state is equal to the number of that state's representatives in both chambers of Congress.

---

in even-numbered years on the Tuesday after the first Monday in November. During general elections, the voters decide who will be the U.S. president, vice president, and senators and representatives in Congress. The president and vice president are elected every four years, senators every six years, and representatives every two years.

General elections are also held to choose state and local government officials, often at the same time as those for national offices. A **special election** is held at the state or local level when the voters must decide an issue before the next general election or when vacancies occur by reason of death or resignation.

9–1a Conducting Elections and Counting the Votes

Since 1888, all states in the United States have used the **Australian ballot**—a secret ballot that is prepared, distributed, and counted by government officials at public expense. As its name implies, this ballot was first developed in Australia.

Recall from Chapter 8 that local units of government, such as cities, are divided into smaller voting districts, or precincts. Within each precinct, voters cast their ballots at a designated polling place.

An election board supervises the polling place and the voting process in each precinct. The board sets hours for the polls to be open according to the laws of the state and sees that ballots or voting machines are available.

In most states, the board provides the list of registered voters and makes certain that only qualified voters cast ballots in each precinct. When the polls close, staff members count the votes and report the results, usually to the county clerk or the board of elections.

Representatives from each party, called **poll watchers,** are allowed at each polling place to make sure the election is run fairly and that fraud doesn't occur.

9–1b Presidential Elections and the Electoral College

When citizens vote for president and vice president, they are not voting directly for the candidates. Instead, they are voting for **electors** who will cast their ballots in the **electoral college.** The electors are selected during each presidential election year by the states' political parties, subject to the laws of the state. Each state has as many electoral votes as it has U.S. senators and representatives (see Figure 9–1, which follows). In addition, there are three electors from the District of Columbia, even though it is not a state.

The Rest of the World

Elections Are Not Enough

In recent decades, more and more nations have sought to choose their leaders through elections. Often, however, elections have done little to address a nation's problems. Most conspicuously, elections in Afghanistan and Iraq that were relatively free and fair have not curbed the violence in those two countries. Russia's Vladimir Putin first came to power in a reasonably fair election, but he is fast turning into an absolute dictator. Apparently, elections are not enough. Why not?

Playing by the Rules

First, consider the obvious: Elections can only settle national questions when most of a country's citizens are willing to accept the election results. Political leaders must be willing to follow the "rules of the game." Voters must be willing to punish rule breakers, even when an offender is a member of their own party. In Iraq and Afghanistan, large groups of citizens are flatly unwilling to accept a loss at the polls. In Russia, Putin has been able to institutionalize lawlessness without effective reprisals from anyone.

On a deeper level, a free society relies on a shared political culture such as the one described in "American Democracy" in Chapter 1. The nation's people must recognize one another as fellow citizens. Furthermore, a free society cannot survive without a broad popular commitment to such values as freedom of expression, the right to personal property, and equality under the law.

Finally, freedom is dependent on the flourishing of *civil society*—that is, all the organizations, businesses, churches, unions, and social groups that bring people together outside of the control of government. When elections fail, one or more of these preconditions for freedom are invariably lacking.

The Example of Egypt

In 2013, Egypt's short experiment with representative democracy collapsed. After huge demonstrations against Mohamed Morsi, the nation's first freely elected president, the military seized power. Elected in 2012, Morsi was a member of the Muslim Brotherhood, Egypt's main Islamist organization. Days after the military coup, security forces broke up pro-Morsi demonstrations, killing hundreds.

Earlier, in 2011, massive demonstrations had forced out the former Egyptian dictator, Hosni Mubarak. Egypt at that time contained three important political forces.

- The weakest group was made up of the often-youthful liberals who led the demonstrations.
- The second group was the Islamists, especially the well-organized Muslim Brotherhood. This group won the 2012 election campaign.
- The third group was the "deep state," the military and government officials who owned or controlled Egypt's most important institutions. This centralized control of social institutions crippled civil society.

Of these forces, only the liberals were committed to democratic values. Yet after a year of disastrously incompetent rule by Morsi, even the liberals had given up on accepting election results. When liberals allied with the deep state against the Brotherhood, Egyptian democracy no longer had any defenders at all.

 CRITICAL ANALYSIS Do you think there are people in the United States who would refuse to abide by election results if they thought they could get away with it?

THE WINNER-TAKE-ALL SYSTEM The electoral college system is primarily a **winner-take-all system,** in which the candidate who receives the largest popular vote in a state is credited with all that state's electoral votes. The only exceptions are Maine and Nebraska.[1]

In December, after the general election, electors (either Republicans or Democrats, depending on which candidate has won the state's popular vote) meet in their state capitals to cast their votes for president and vice

> **winner-take-all system** A system in which the candidate who receives the most votes wins. In contrast, proportional systems allocate votes to multiple winners.

FIGURE 9-1   STATE ELECTORAL VOTES IN 2012

The size of each state reflects the number of electoral votes that state has, following the changes required by the 2010 census. The colors show which party the state voted for in the 2012 presidential elections: red for Republican, blue for Democratic. A candidate must win 270 electoral votes to be elected president.

president. When the Constitution was drafted, the framers intended that the electors would use their own discretion in deciding who would make the best president. Beginning as early as 1796, however, electors have usually voted for the candidates to whom they are pledged. The electoral college ballots are then sent to the U.S. Senate, which counts and certifies them before a joint session of Congress held early in January. The candidates who receive a majority of the electoral votes are officially declared president and vice president.

WHAT IT TAKES TO WIN   To be elected, a candidate must receive more than half of the 538 electoral votes available. Thus, a candidate needs 270 votes to win. If no presidential candidate gets an electoral college majority (which has happened twice—in 1800 and 1824), the House of Representatives votes on the candidates, with each state delegation casting only a single vote. If no candidate for vice president gets a majority of electoral votes, the vice president is chosen by the Senate, with each senator casting one vote.

Even when a presidential candidate wins by a large margin in the electoral college and in the popular vote—a *landslide election*—it does not follow that the candidate has won the support of the majority of those eligible to vote. We explore this paradox in this chapter's *Perception versus Reality* feature, which follows.

CRITICAL THINKING

▶ Should the District of Columbia be admitted as a state—and therefore elect members to the U.S. House and Senate in addition to participating in the electoral college?

9-2 HOW WE NOMINATE CANDIDATES

LO   Discuss how candidates are nominated.

The first step on the long road to winning an election is the nomination process. Nominations narrow the field of possible candidates and limit each political party's choice to one person.

For many local government posts, which are often nonpartisan, self-nomination is the most common way to become a candidate. A self-proclaimed candidate usually files a petition to be listed on the ballot. Each state has laws that specify how many signatures a candidate must obtain to show that he or she has some public support. An alternative is to be a *write-in candidate*—voters write the candidate's name on the ballot on Election Day.

Perception vs. Reality

Presidents and the "Popular Vote"

Some presidential contests are very close, such as the 2000 race between Al Gore and George W. Bush. Others are less so, such as the one between Lyndon B. Johnson and Barry Goldwater in 1964. When a presidential candidate wins the race by a wide margin, as Johnson did, the result is called a landslide victory for the winning candidate.

The Perception

The traditional perception has been that, in general, our presidents are elected by a majority of eligible American voters. A president who has been swept into office by a landslide victory may thus claim to have received a "mandate from the people" to govern the nation. Moreover, a president may assert that his or her landslide victory proves that a policy or program endorsed in campaign speeches is backed by popular support.

The Reality

In reality, the "popular vote" is not all that popular, in the sense of representing the wishes of a majority of American citizens who are eligible to vote. In fact, the president of the United States has never received the votes of a majority of all eligible adults. Lyndon Johnson, in 1964, came the closest of any president in history, and even he won the votes of fewer than 40 percent of those who were eligible to cast a ballot.

The hotly contested presidential elections of 2000 and 2004 were divisive, leaving the millions of Americans who had voted for the losing candidates unhappy with the results. Nonetheless, George W. Bush assumed that his reelection in 2004—in which he received the votes of 30.5 percent of eligible citizens—was a signal from the American people to push his controversial foreign policy and the war on terrorism. Barack Obama likewise claimed a personal mandate based on his strong performance in 2008, and he parlayed it into a sweeping program of domestic initiatives. Yet Obama had won the support of only 32.6 percent of eligible voters. In the 2012 elections, he won just 29.7 percent.

It is useful to keep these figures in mind whenever a president claims to have received a mandate from the people. The truth is, no president has ever been elected with sufficient popular backing to make this a serious claim.

BLOG ON **Dave Leip's Atlas of U.S. Presidential Elections provides detailed figures on presidential election results. Find the Atlas at uselectionatlas.org.**

Candidates for major offices are rarely nominated in these ways, however. As you read in Chapter 7, most candidates for high office are nominated by a political party and receive considerable support from party activists throughout their campaigns.

9–2a Party Control over Nominations

The methods used by political parties to nominate candidates have changed during the course of American history. Broadly speaking, the process has grown more open over the years, with the involvement of ever-greater numbers of local leaders and ordinary citizens. Today, any voter can participate in choosing party candidates. This was not true as recently as 1968, however, and was certainly not possible during the first years of the republic.

THE CAUCUS SYSTEM George Washington was essentially unopposed in the first U.S. presidential elections in 1789—no other candidate was seriously considered in any state. By the end of Washington's eight years in office, however, political divisions among the nation's leaders had solidified into political parties, the Federalists and Jefferson's Republicans (see Chapter 7). These early parties were organized by gatherings of important persons, who often met in secret. The meetings came to be called **caucuses.**[2]

Beginning in 1800, members of Congress who belonged to the two parties held caucuses to nominate

 caucus A meeting held to choose political candidates or delegates.

candidates for president and vice president. The Republican caucus chose Thomas Jefferson in 1800, as expected, and the Federalist caucus nominated the incumbent president, John Adams. By 1816, the Federalist Party had ceased to exist, and the Republican congressional caucus was in complete control of selecting the president of the United States.

THE DEATH OF "KING CAUCUS" The congressional caucus system collapsed in 1824.[3] It was widely seen as undemocratic—opponents derided it as "King Caucus." A much-diminished caucus nominated a presidential candidate who then came in third in the electoral vote. The other three major candidates were essentially self-nominated.[4] The four candidates split the electoral vote so completely that the House of Representatives had to decide the contest. It picked John Quincy Adams, even though Andrew Jackson had won more popular and electoral votes.

In the run-up to the 1828 elections, two new parties grew up around the major candidates. Adams's supporters called themselves the National Republicans (later known as the Whigs). Jackson's supporters organized as the Democratic Party, which won the election.

9–2b A New Method: The Nominating Convention

In 1832, both parties settled on a new method of choosing candidates for president and vice president—the national nominating convention. A number of state parties had already adopted the convention system for choosing state-level candidates. New Jersey held conventions as early as 1800.

NOMINATING CONVENTIONS A **nominating convention** is an official meeting of a political party to choose its candidates. Those who attend the convention are called **delegates,** and they are chosen to represent the people of a particular geographic area. Conventions can take place at multiple levels. A county convention might choose delegates to attend a state convention. The state convention, in turn, might select delegates to the national convention. By 1840, the convention system was the most common method of nominating political party candidates at the state and national levels.

LIMITS OF THE CONVENTION SYSTEM While the convention system drew in a much broader range of leaders than had the caucus, it was not a particularly democratic institution. Convention delegates were rarely chosen by a vote of the party's local members. Typically, they were appointed by local party officials, who were usually, with good reason, called bosses. These local leaders often gained their positions in ways that were far from democratic. Not until 1972 did ordinary voters in all states gain the right to select delegates to the national presidential nominating conventions.

9–2c Primary Elections and the Loss of Party Control

The corruption that so often accompanied the convention system led reformers to call for a new way to choose candidates—the **primary election,** in which voters go to the polls to decide among candidates who seek the nomination of their party. Candidates who win a primary election then go on to compete against the candidates from other parties in the general election.

The first primary election may have been held in 1842 by Democrats in Crawford County, Pennsylvania. The technique was not widely used, however, until the end of the nineteenth century and the beginning of the twentieth. These were years in which reform was a popular cause.

DIRECT AND INDIRECT PRIMARIES The rules for conducting primary elections are highly variable, and a number of different types of primaries exist. One major distinction is between a direct primary and an indirect primary.

In a **direct primary,** voters cast their ballots directly for candidates. The elections that nominate candidates for Congress and for state or local offices are almost always direct primaries.

In an *indirect primary,* voters choose delegates, who in turn choose the candidates. The delegates may be pledged to a particular candidate but sometimes run as *unpledged delegates.* The major parties use indirect primaries to elect delegates to the national nominating conventions that choose candidates for president and vice president.

---

nominating convention An official meeting of a political party to choose its candidates. Nominating conventions at the state and local levels also select delegates to represent the citizens of their geographic areas at a higher-level party convention.

delegate A person selected to represent the people of one geographic area at a party convention.

primary election An election in which voters choose the candidates of their party, who will then run in the general election.

direct primary An election held within each of the two major parties—Democratic and Republican—to choose the party's candidates for the general election. Voters choose the candidate directly, rather than through delegates.

Democratic candidates for governor of Maryland following a debate in 2014. Left to right, they are Lieutenant Governor Anthony Brown, Representative Heather Mizeur, and Attorney General Doug Gansler. Brown won the primary. *Why does Maryland usually lean Democratic?*

THE ROLE OF THE STATES Primary elections are normally conducted by state governments. States set the dates and conduct the elections. They provide polling places, election officials, and registration lists, and they then count the votes. By sponsoring the primaries, state governments have obtained considerable influence over the rules by which the primaries are conducted. The power of the states is limited, however, by the parties' First Amendment right to freedom of association, a right that has been repeatedly confirmed by the United States Supreme Court.[5]

On occasion, parties that object to the rules imposed by state governments have opted out of the state-sponsored primary system altogether.[6] Note that third parties typically do not participate in state-sponsored primaries, but hold nominating conventions instead. The major parties rarely opt out of state elections, however, because the financial—and political—costs of going it alone are high. (When primary elections are used to choose candidates for local *nonpartisan* positions, state control is uncontested.)

PRIMARY VOTERS Voter turnout for primaries is lower than it is in general elections. The voters who do go to the polls are often strong supporters of their party. Indeed, as you will learn shortly, independents cannot participate in primary elections in some states, even if they lean toward one or the other of the two major parties. As a result, the Republican primary elec-

torate is very conservative, and Democratic primary voters are quite liberal. Candidates often find that they must run to the political right or left during the primaries. They may then move to the center during the general election campaign.

INSURGENT CANDIDATES Primary elections were designed to take nominations out of the hands of the party bosses. Indeed, the most important result of the primary system has been to reduce dramatically the power of elected and party officials over the nominating process.

Ever since primary elections were established, the insurgent candidate who runs against the party "establishment" has been a common phenomenon. Running against the "powers that be" is often a very effective campaign strategy, and many insurgents have won victories at the local, state, and national levels.

Occasionally, an insurgent's platform is strikingly different from that of the party as a whole. Yet even when an insurgent's politics are abhorrent to the rest of the party—for example, an insurgent might make an outright appeal to racism—the party has no way of denying the insurgent the right to the party label in the general election.

CLOSED AND OPEN PRIMARIES Primaries can be classified as closed or open.

Closed Primaries. In a **closed primary,** only party members can vote to choose that party's candidates, and they may vote only in the primary of their own party. Thus, only registered Democrats can vote in the Democratic primary, and only registered Republicans can vote for the Republican candidates. A person usually establishes party membership when she or he registers to vote. Some states have a *semiclosed* primary, which allows voters to register with a party or change their party affiliations on Election Day.

Regular party workers favor the closed primary because it promotes party loyalty. Independent voters

closed primary A primary in which only party members can vote to choose that party's candidates.

Hillary Clinton's supporters were organizing well before she made an official announcement as to whether or not she would run. Would many Americans like to see a woman as president? *Why or why not?*

9–3a Responsibilities of the Campaign Staff

To run a successful campaign, a candidate's campaign staff must be able to raise funds, get media coverage, produce and pay for political ads, schedule the candidate's time effectively with constituent groups and potential supporters, convey the candidate's position on the issues, conduct research on the opposing candidate, and persuade the voters to go to the polls.

When party identification was firmer and TV campaigning was still in its infancy, a strong party organization on the local, state, or national level could furnish most of the services and expertise that the candidate needed. Today, party organizations are no longer as important as they once were in providing campaign services. Instead of relying so extensively on political parties, candidates now turn to professionals to manage their campaigns.

The fact that party organizations no longer provide large quantities of campaign services, however, should not lead anyone to believe that the parties are unimportant in campaigns. Because of the intense political polarization that has taken place in recent years, the parties are in some ways more important than ever. Political experts know that today, the party label allows them to predict how a senator or representative will vote on almost all issues. Many voters are also aware of this reality.

9–3b The Professional Campaign Organization

As mentioned, the role of the political party in managing campaigns has declined, although the party continues to play an important role in recruiting volunteers and getting out the vote. Professional **political consultants** now manage nearly all aspects of a presidential candidate's campaign. Most candidates for governor, the House, and the Senate also rely on consultants. Political consultants generally specialize in a particular area of the campaign, such as researching the opposition, conducting polls, developing the candidate's advertising, or organizing "get-out-the-vote" efforts. Nonetheless, most candidates have a campaign manager who coordinates and plans the **campaign strategy.** Figure 9–2, which follows, shows a typical presidential campaign organization.

9–3 THE MODERN POLITICAL CAMPAIGN

LO Indicate what is involved in launching a political campaign today, and describe the structure and functions of a campaign organization.

Once nominated, candidates focus on their campaigns. The term *campaign* originated in the military context. Generals mounted campaigns, using their scarce resources (soldiers and materials) to achieve military objectives. Using the term in a political context is apt. In a political campaign, candidates also use scarce resources (time and funds) in an attempt to defeat their adversaries in the battle for votes.

political consultant A professional political adviser who, for a fee, works on an area of a candidate's campaign. Political consultants include campaign managers, pollsters, media advisers, and "get out the vote" organizers.

campaign strategy The comprehensive plan developed by a candidate and his or her advisers for winning an election.

FIGURE 9–2   A TYPICAL PRESIDENTIAL CAMPAIGN ORGANIZATION

Most aspects of a candidate's campaign are managed by professional political consultants, as this figure illustrates.

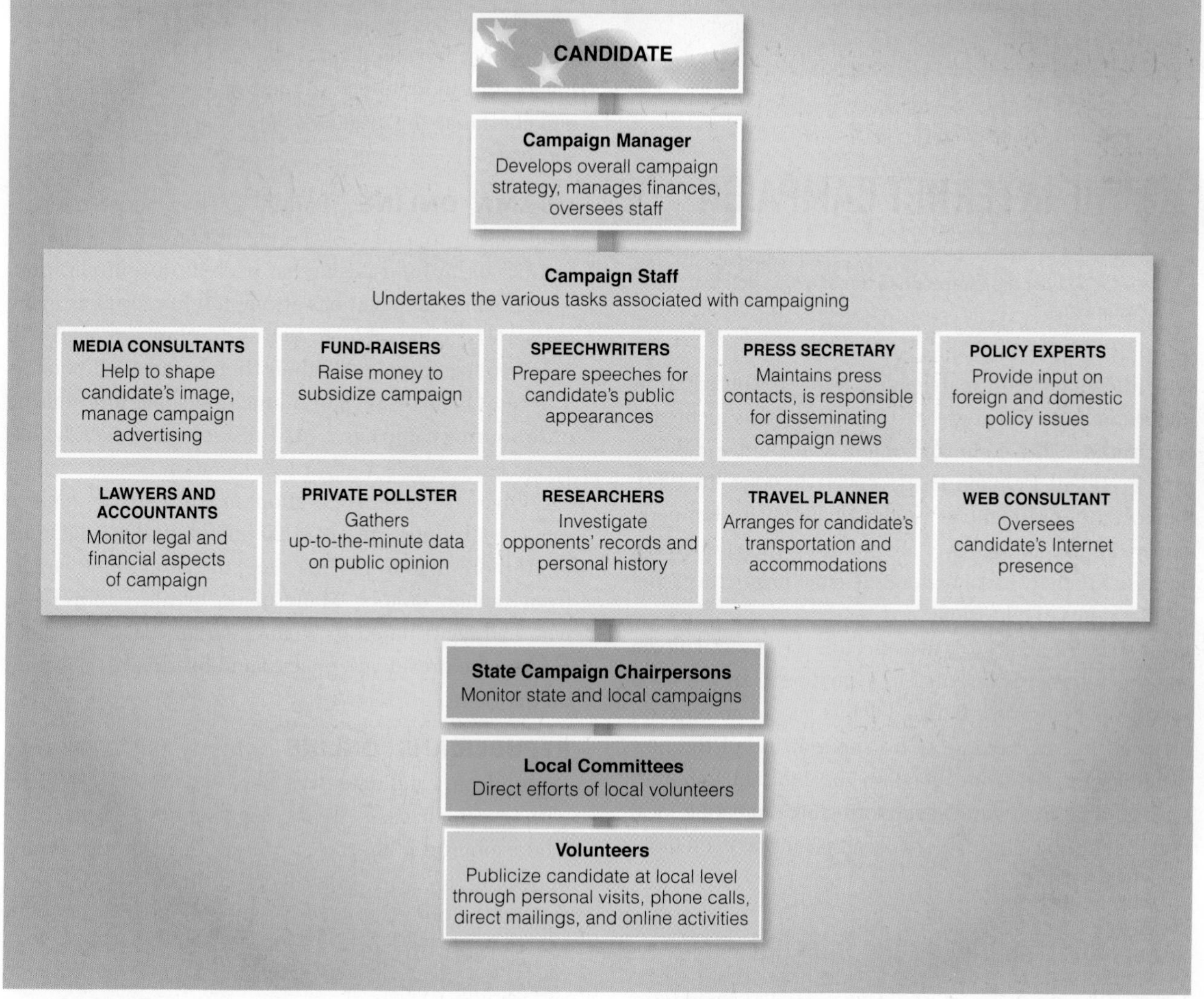

CANDIDATE

Campaign Manager
Develops overall campaign strategy, manages finances, oversees staff

Campaign Staff
Undertakes the various tasks associated with campaigning

MEDIA CONSULTANTS	**FUND-RAISERS**	**SPEECHWRITERS**	**PRESS SECRETARY**	**POLICY EXPERTS**
Help to shape candidate's image, manage campaign advertising	Raise money to subsidize campaign	Prepare speeches for candidate's public appearances	Maintains press contacts, is responsible for disseminating campaign news	Provide input on foreign and domestic policy issues
LAWYERS AND ACCOUNTANTS	**PRIVATE POLLSTER**	**RESEARCHERS**	**TRAVEL PLANNER**	**WEB CONSULTANT**
Monitor legal and financial aspects of campaign	Gathers up-to-the-minute data on public opinion	Investigate opponents' records and personal history	Arranges for candidate's transportation and accommodations	Oversees candidate's Internet presence

State Campaign Chairpersons
Monitor state and local campaigns

Local Committees
Direct efforts of local volunteers

Volunteers
Publicize candidate at local level through personal visits, phone calls, direct mailings, and online activities

A major development in contemporary American politics is the focus on reaching voters through effective use of the media, particularly television. At least half of the budget for a major political campaign is consumed by television advertising. Media consultants are therefore pivotal members of the campaign staff. The nature of political advertising is discussed in more detail in Chapter 10.

9–3c Opposition Research

Major campaigns, such as those for governor, senator, and U.S. president, typically make use of **opposition research.** A staff member—or even an entire team—spends time discovering as much negative information about opposing candidates as possible. Journalists often rely on opposition researchers for their stories.

Republican candidates for president in 2012 had little reason to fund opposition research on President Obama. This research had already been done in the 2008 elections, and there was little prospect of finding anything new. It was necessary only to repeat themes that had been developed earlier, such as Obama's alleged radicalism.

In contrast, opposition research aimed at Mitt Romney was a major activity of the Obama campaign. Obama supporters focused on Romney's time as CEO of Bain Capital, a financial firm. Democrats accused Romney of sabotaging profitable companies and of shipping jobs overseas. Clearly, the intent of these allegations was to define Romney as a cold-hearted businessman with little concern for the problems of ordinary Americans.

opposition research The attempt to learn damaging information about an opponent in a political campaign.

CRITICAL THINKING

▶ Some people have accused political consultants of "managing the candidate" too well, making the candidate appear stilted and unnatural. How could a candidate prevent that from happening?

9-4 THE INTERNET CAMPAIGN

LO Describe how the Internet has transformed political campaigns.

Over the years, political leaders have benefited from understanding and using new communications technologies. In the 1930s, command of a new medium—radio—gave President Franklin D. Roosevelt an edge. In 1960, Democratic presidential candidate John F. Kennedy gained an advantage over Republican Richard Nixon because Kennedy had a better understanding of the visual requirements of television.

Today, the ability to make effective use of social media and the Internet is essential to a candidate. In the 2008 presidential elections, Barack Obama gained an edge on his rivals in part because of his superior use of the new technologies. His team relied on the Internet for fund-raising, targeting potential supporters, and creating local political organizations. His 2012 campaign was even more sophisticated.

9-4a Fund-Raising on the Internet

Internet fund-raising grew out of an earlier technique: the direct-mail campaign. In direct mailings, campaigns send solicitations to large numbers of likely prospects, typically seeking contributions. Developing good lists of prospects is central to an effective direct-mail operation, because postage, printing, and the rental of address lists make the costs of each mailing high. In many direct-mail campaigns, most of the funds raised are used up by the costs of the campaign itself. In contrast to the costs, response rates are low—a 1 percent response rate is a tremendous success. From the 1970s on, conservative organizations became especially adept at managing direct-mail campaigns. For a time, this expertise gave conservative causes and candidates an advantage over liberals.

To understand the old system is to recognize the superiority of the new one. The cost of e-mailing is very low. Lists of prospects need not be prepared as carefully, because e-mail sent to unlikely prospects does not waste

resources. E-mail fund-raising did face one problem when it was new—many people were not yet online. Today, the extent of online participation is no longer a concern.

The new technology brought with it a change in the groups that benefited the most. Conservatives were no longer the most effective fund-raisers. Instead, liberal and libertarian organizations enjoyed some of the greatest successes.

OBAMA ONLINE Barack Obama took Internet fund-raising to a new level. One of the defining characteristics of his fund-raising has been its decentralization. The Obama campaign has attempted to recruit as many supporters as possible to act as fund-raisers who will solicit contributions from their friends and neighbors. As a result, Obama was spared much personal fund-raising effort during campaigns. (As President, however, he has raised large sums for other Democrats).

Obama's online operation in 2011–2012 made a major contribution to his $1.25 billion fund-raising total. Even more than in his first race, the sums came largely from smaller donors. Many of the wealthy individuals who had contributed to Obama earlier had been alienated by the president's policies and his rhetorical attacks on the rich.

REPUBLICANS ONLINE Already in 2008, one Republican candidate was able to use the Internet with great success—Texas representative Ron Paul, who espoused a libertarian philosophy that was highly appealing to many high-tech enthusiasts. Paul pioneered the online *moneybomb* technique, described by the San José *Mercury News* as "a one-day fund-raising frenzy." A moneybomb organized by Paul supporters in December 2007 raised $6.3 million, a new record for one-day fund-raising. (Obama's moneybombs soon bested Paul's totals, however.) Despite Paul's fund-raising prowess, his libertarian politics were sufficiently far from the conservative Republican mainstream that he was able to win only a handful of national convention delegates.

In 2012, Mitt Romney was less reliant on the Internet than many other recent candidates. In part, this was because much of his campaign finance came in large chunks from wealthy individuals—the reverse of Obama's experience. Romney's campaign fund-raising roughly matched Obama's—about $1.25 billion in total.

9-4b Targeting Supporters

In 2004, President George W. Bush's chief political adviser, Karl Rove, pioneered a new campaign technique known as *microtargeting*. The process involves collect-

"In constant pursuit of money to finance campaigns, the political system is simply unable to function. Its deliberative powers are paralyzed."

~ **John Rawls,** American Educator 1921–2000

ing as much information as possible about voters in a gigantic database and then filtering out various groups for special attention.

Through microtargeting, for example, the Bush campaign could identify Republican prospects living in heavily Democratic neighborhoods—potential supporters whom the campaign might otherwise have neglected because the neighborhood as a whole seemed so unpromising. In 2004, the Democrats had nothing to match Republican efforts. In 2012, however, Obama's microtargeting operation vastly outperformed Romney's.

9–4c Support for Local Organizing

Perhaps the most effective use of the Internet has been as an organizing tool. One of the earliest Internet techniques was to use the site Meetup.com to organize real-world meetings. In this way, campaigns were able to gather supporters without relying on the existing party and activist infrastructure.

OBAMA'S CAMPAIGN As with fund-raising, Barack Obama took Web-based organizing to a new level. In 2012, Obama had seven times as many Facebook supporters as Romney (28 million versus 4 million). Although this was a substantial advantage, it was not necessarily as significant as you might think. The problem is that the Facebook demographic is heavily weighted toward young people who either cannot or do not vote. Indeed, surveys in 2012 showed that those least likely to vote supported Obama by a two-to-one margin. The question for the Obama campaign, therefore, was whether it could turn politically disengaged social media participants into actual voters.

THE GROUND GAME A modern campaign collects as much data as it can—in part, through use of Internet resources—to identify the people whose votes it wants.

President Obama sends a tweet during a "Twitter Town Hall" at the White House. *How important was the Internet to Obama's reelection?*

© Mandel Ngan/AFP/Getty Images

The data are used to make human contact more efficient by directing volunteers toward the voters they most need to reach. Such get-out-the-vote drives have been called the *ground game* (as opposed to advertising, called the *air game*).

By 2012, Obama had had years to perfect his ground game, and it showed. The Obama campaign was able to create active local support groups in towns and counties across the country—many in areas that had traditionally supported Republicans. By comparison, Romney's ground game sometimes looked like a comedy of errors. His volunteers often called the wrong voters. The team developed a major Web program called Orca to allocate resources on Election Day. It crashed. A staffer reported, "Orca is lying on the beach with a harpoon in it." Even if Orca had worked perfectly, Election Day would have been far too late for it to be effective.

CRITICAL THINKING

▶ Some candidates are more successful than others in using the Internet. Do such candidates have any traits in common? If so, what might these be?

the vote, and holding fund-raising events. Contributions to political parties were called **soft money.**

By 2000, the parties were raising nearly $463 million per election season through soft money contributions. Soft dollars became the main source of campaign money in the presidential race until after the 2002 elections, when soft money was banned, as you will read shortly.

INDEPENDENT EXPENDITURES The campaign-financing laws did not prohibit corporations, labor unions, and special interest groups from making **independent expenditures** in an election campaign. Independent expenditures, as the term implies, are expenditures for activities that are independent of (not coordinated with) those of a candidate or a political party.

Decisions by the courts have distinguished two types of independent expenditures. In the first type, an interest group or other contributor wages an "issue campaign" without going so far as to say "Vote for Candidate X." An issue campaign might, however, go so far as to publish voter guides informing voters of candidates' positions. The courts have repeatedly upheld the right of groups to advocate their positions in this way.

Alternatively, a group might explicitly campaign for particular candidates. The Supreme Court has held that an issue-oriented group has a First Amendment right to advocate the election of its preferred candidates as long as it acts independently of the candidates' campaigns. In 1996, the Court held that these guidelines apply to expenditures by political parties as well.[12]

9-5d The Bipartisan Campaign Reform Act of 2002

The increasing use of soft money and independent expenditures led to a demand for further campaign-finance reform. In 2002, Congress passed, and the president signed, the Bipartisan Campaign Reform Act. The measure is also known as the McCain-Feingold Act after its chief sponsors, Senators John McCain (R., Ariz.) and Russell Feingold (D., Wisc.).

The new law banned soft money at the national level. It also regulated campaign ads paid for by interest groups and prohibited any such issue-advocacy commer-

---

soft money Campaign contributions not regulated by federal law, such as some contributions that are made to political parties instead of to particular candidates.

independent expenditure An expenditure for activities that are independent from (not coordinated with) those of a political candidate or a political party.

> **"A promising young man** should go into politics so that he can go on promising for the rest of his life."
>
> ~ **Robert Byrne,** American Author B. 1930

cials within thirty days of a primary election or sixty days of a general election.

The 2002 act set the amount that an individual could contribute to a federal candidate at $2,000 and the amount that an individual could give to all federal candidates at $95,000 over a two-year election cycle. (Under the law, some individual contribution limits are indexed for inflation and thus may change slightly with every election cycle.) Individuals could still contribute to state and local parties, so long as the contributions did not exceed $10,000 per year per individual. The new law went into effect the day after the 2002 general elections.

THE SUPREME COURT UPHOLDS McCAIN-FEINGOLD Several groups immediately filed lawsuits challenging the constitutionality of the new law. Supporters of the restrictions on campaign ads by special interest groups argued that the large amounts of funds spent on these ads create an appearance of corruption in the political process. In contrast, an attorney for the National Rifle Association (NRA) argued that because the NRA represents "millions of Americans speaking in unison . . . [it] is not a *corruption* of the democratic political process; it *is* the democratic political process."[13] In December 2003, the Supreme Court upheld nearly all of the clauses of the act in *McConnell v. Federal Election Commission.*[14]

THE SUPREME COURT CHANGES ITS MIND Beginning in 2007, however, the Supreme Court began to chip away at the limits on independent expenditures contained in McCain-Feingold. In that year, in *Federal Election Commission v. Wisconsin Right to Life, Inc.,* the Court invalidated a major part of the 2002 law and overruled a portion of its own 2003 decision upholding the act. In the four years since the earlier ruling, Chief Justice John Roberts, Jr., and Associate Justice Samuel Alito, Jr., had been appointed, and both were conservatives.

In a five-to-four decision, the Court held that issue ads could not be prohibited in the time period preceding elections (thirty days before primary elections and sixty

David Koch and Julia Koch (center) at the unveiling of the David H. Koch Plaza at the Metropolitan Museum of Art in New York City in 2014. While Koch is a patron of the arts, he is much better known for massive donations to conservative political causes. *Should such donations be limited?*

days before general elections) *unless* they were "susceptible of no reasonable interpretation other than as an appeal to vote for or against a specific candidate."[15] The Court concluded that restricting *all* television ads paid for by corporate or labor union treasuries in the weeks before an election amounted to censorship of political speech.

CITIZENS UNITED v. FEDERAL ELECTION COMMISSION (FEC)

A January 2010 Supreme Court ruling helped establish our current wide-open campaign-finance system. This decision, *Citizens United v. FEC,* was initially seen as fostering a vast new wave of corporate spending on elections. The actual results were somewhat different, as you will read shortly.

In the *Wisconsin Right to Life* case described earlier, the Court ruled out bans on issue ads placed by corporations and other organizations in the run-up to an election. In *Citizens United v. FEC,* the Court extended this protection to ads that attack or praise specific candidates, including ads that suggest voting for particular

candidates.[16] Two months later, in *Speechnow v. FEC,* a federal court of appeals held that it was not possible to limit contributions to independent-expenditure groups based on the size or source of the contribution.[17]

As a result of these two decisions, *Citizens United* and *Speechnow,* there is now no limit on the ability of corporations, unions, nonprofit groups, or individuals to fund advertising, provided that they do not contribute directly to a candidate's campaign. While Republican leaders applauded the *Citizens United* ruling as a victory for free speech, most Democratic leaders were appalled. They feared that the ruling would result in a massive tilting of the political landscape toward corporate wealth.

McCUTCHEON v. FEC

The most recent ruling by the Supreme Court to free up campaign-financing was handed down in April 2014. In *McCutcheon v. FEC,* the Court struck down a decades-old cap on the total amount that any individual can contribute to federal candidates in a two-year election cycle.[18] The overall limit had been $48,600. As a result of this ruling, to give one example, a wealthy individual could now make the maximum legal contribution to every single House candidate of a particular party.

9–5e The Current Campaign-Finance Environment

Because the *Citizens United* decision was issued less than a year before the 2010 elections, its impact in that year was modest. By 2012, however, the new rules had changed the shape of the campaign-finance environment. Individuals and PACs still faced limits on what they could contribute directly to candidates' campaigns and to the parties. Despite these limits, the cam-

paigns and parties were still able to raise huge sums. Meanwhile, independent organizations stood out as the wildcard in American politics. We list the largest independent expenditures in the 2014 election cycle in Table 9–1, which follows.

SUPER PACS A new type of organization came into existence to take advantage of the new rules. Known officially as "independent-expenditure only committees," the new bodies were soon dubbed super PACs.

The Myth of Independence. The super PACs' supposed independence from campaigns turned out to be a convenient fiction. By 2011, every major presidential candidate had one or more affiliated super PACs, usu-

TABLE 9–1 THE TWENTY TOP GROUPS MAKING INDEPENDENT EXPENDITURES DURING THE 2013–2014 CYCLE

This table lists independent expenditures only. Some groups, such as the party committees, have designated only a small part of their total fund-raising as independent expenditures.

Committee	Affiliation	Raised 2013–2014	Type	Disclosure of Contributors
National Republican Congressional Committee	Republican	$64,591,859	Party committee	full
Democratic Congressional Campaign Committee	Democratic	$55,037,623	Party committee	full
Democratic Senatorial Campaign Committee	Democratic	$47,150,656	Party committee	full
Crossroads GPS and American Crossroads	Karl Rove (Republican)	$46,876,858	501c, Super PAC	partial
Senate Majority PAC	Democratic	$42,611,228	Super PAC	full
US Chamber of Commerce	business	$33,554,401	501c	none
National Republican Senatorial Committee	Republican	$31,678,951	Party committee	full
House Majority PAC	Democratic	$21,598,144	Super PAC	full
National Rifle Association	gun rights	$19,927,656	PAC	full
Ending Spending Action Fund	conservative	$19,572,162	Super PAC	partial
NextGen Climate Action	Tom Snyder (environmental)	$19,313,475	Super PAC	full
Freedom Partners Action Fund	Koch brothers (conservative)	$18,997,147	Super PAC	partial
League of Conservation Voters	environmental	$17,389,444	501c, Super PAC	partial
National Association of Realtors	business	$10,306,180	Super PAC	none
Put Alaska First PAC	Senator Mark Begich (D)	$9,881,324	Super PAC	full
Patriot Majority USA	liberal/labor	$8,491,902	501c	none
Club for Growth	anti-tax	$8,448,353	501c, Super PAC	partial
Congressional Leadership Fund	House Republicans	$8,233,592	Super PAC	partial
Women Vote! (Emily's List)	Democratic women	$7,807,664	Super PAC	partial
American Action Network	Republican	$7,625,729	501c	none

Source: Center for Responsive Politics.

ally run by former members of the candidate's own campaign. Newt Gingrich, Ron Paul, Rick Perry, Mitt Romney, Rick Santorum—and Barack Obama—each had an associated super PAC. A division of labor soon developed. Super PACs would run negative ads to damage a candidate's opponents, while candidate committees accentuated the positive about the candidate.

The Role of the Individual Donor. When the *Citizens United* decision was handed down, a flood of corporate cash was expected to enter the political system. The ruling did result in more corporate (and union) spending, but far less than anticipated. Apparently, many companies were reluctant to take stands that might alienate a large number of customers. What caught everyone by surprise was the huge volume of finance poured into super PACs by individuals, notably individuals of great wealth.

For example, Charles and David Koch, two brothers with a long-standing commitment to conservative politics, set up their own independent committee, which soon became one of the largest. The Koch brothers were even more active in 2014 than they had been in 2012. In January 2012, Sheldon Adelson, a casino billionaire, contributed $5 million to Newt Gingrich's super PAC, and shortly thereafter Adelson's wife kicked in another $5 million. The Adelsons are credited with keeping Gingrich's campaign alive for an extra month. In June, Adelson donated $10 million to Mitt Romney's super PAC. Adelson's total donations to all candidates may have exceeded $100 million.

While conservative donors gained much attention, some billionaires also backed Democrats. As far back as 2004, for example, financier George Soros gave almost $24 million to independent groups dedicated to defeating Republican president George W. Bush. The largest Democratic donor in 2012 was Chicago businessman Fred Eychaner, who gave more than $8 million to Democratic super PACs and committees.

527 AND 501C COMMITTEES In addition to super PACs, another type of independent committee is the *527 committee,* named after the provision of the tax code that covers it. Spending by 527s rose rapidly after 2002, and in the 2004 election cycle, the committees spent about $612 million to "advocate positions," as they were not allowed to "expressly advocate" voting for specific candidates. By 2008, 527 committees began to decline in importance, and by 2012 they had been replaced almost completely by super PACS, which were allowed to campaign for and against candidates.

One reason for the decline of the 527 in 2008 was the creation of a new kind of body, the *501(c)4 organization,* known as the *501c.* Like the 527, this type of committee was named after a provision in the tax code. According to some lawyers, a 501c could make limited contributions directly to campaigns and—perhaps more importantly—could conceal the identities of its donors. So far, the FEC has refused to rule on the legality of this technique. Table 9–1 indicates which major independent committees are super PACs and which are 501c organizations. Some groups have organized both types.

The 501c's ability to hide its contributors created a new campaign-finance issue. Republicans argued that donors needed the right to remain anonymous so that they would not have to fear retribution. Democrats contended that anonymous contributions were simply a further corruption of the political process. Attempts to end donor anonymity through legislation failed. We discussed the issue of anonymous donations in the chapter-opening *America at Odds* feature.

CRITICAL THINKING

▶ Under what circumstances would you consider political contributions to be free speech—and under what circumstances would you see them as thinly veiled bribes to public officials?

AMERICA AT ODDS
Campaigns and Elections

Some observers believe that if the founders could see how presidential campaigns are conducted today, they would be shocked at how candidates "pander to the masses." Whether they would be shocked at the costliness of modern campaigns is not as clear. After all, the founders themselves were an elitist, wealthy group, as are many of today's successful candidates for high political office. In any event, Americans today are certainly stunned by how much it takes to win an election. Some of the specific controversies that divide Americans concerning campaigns are the following:

- *Is the electoral college a dangerous anachronism—or a force for stability within our political system?*

- *Should all voters be free to participate in any party primary—or does such a step make it too difficult for the parties to present a coherent group of candidates and policies?*

- *Should states retain their treasured right to set the dates of their presidential primaries—or should the national parties assume responsibility for establishing a rational primary schedule?*

- *Are campaign contributions a constitutionally protected form of free speech—or are they too often a source of corruption within the political system?*

- *Should all politically active groups be required to furnish the identities of their major contributors—or should we allow contributors to remain anonymous because they might suffer reprisals due to their contributions?*

Internet Resources

- For information about the 2016 delegate selection rules and the presidential primary calendar, visit the Web site of FrontloadingHQ at frontloading.blogspot.com.

- You can find out exactly what the laws are that govern campaign financing by accessing the Federal Election Commission's Web site. The commission provides documents and videos that explain what is and is not legal. You can also download actual data on campaign donations from the Campaign Finance Disclosure Portal. Go to www.fec.gov.

- For an ample collection of stories on political contributions, visit Political MoneyLine at www.politicalmoneyline.com.

- Another excellent source for information on campaign financing, including who's contributing what amounts to which candidates, is the Center for Responsive Politics. You can access its Web site at www.opensecrets.org.

- Common Cause offers additional information about campaign financing on its Web site at www.commoncause.org.

- Project Vote Smart offers information on campaign financing, as well as voting, on its Web site at www.votesmart.org.

STUDY TOOLS 9

READY TO STUDY?
- ☐ Review what you've read with the quiz below.
- ☐ Check your answers in Appendix D at the back of the book.
- ☐ For any questions you miss, read the corresponding Learning Outcome section again to prepare for class and your exam.
- ☐ Rip out and study the Chapter in Review card (at the back of the book).

VISIT WWW.CENGAGEBRAIN.COM:
- ☐ Interactive Quizzes
- ☐ Key Term Flashcards or Crossword Puzzles
- ☐ Audio Summaries
- ☐ Simulations, Animated Learning Modules, and Interactive Timelines
- ☐ Videos
- ☐ American Government NewsWatch

FILL-IN

LearningOutcome 9–1

1. The electoral college system is primarily a winner-take-all system, in which the candidate _____.

2. A candidate must win at least _____ electoral votes, cast by the electors, to become president through the electoral college system.

LearningOutcome 9–2

3. In a _____ primary, voters cast their ballots directly for candidates.

4. In the context of presidential primaries, the practice known as front-loading refers to _____.

LearningOutcome 9–3

5. The attempt to learn damaging information about an opponent in a political campaign is called _____ research.

LearningOutcome 9–4

6. A campaign technique known as microtargeting involves _____.

LearningOutcome 9–5

7. The Federal Election Campaign Act of 1971 and its amendments provided public financing for presidential primaries and general elections, funded by a checkoff on _____.

8. As a result of the Supreme Court's decision in *Citizens United v. Federal Election Commission* (2010), a new type of organization came into existence. Known officially as "independent-expenditure only committees," the new bodies were soon dubbed _____.

MULTIPLE CHOICE

LearningOutcome 9–1

9. The total number of electoral votes available is
   a. 538. **b.** 535. **c.** 435.

10. If no presidential candidate receives the required number of electoral votes,
   a. a runoff election is held in January.
   b. the House of Representatives votes on the candidates, with each state delegation casting only a single vote.
   c. the Senate votes on the candidates, with each senator casting one vote.

LearningOutcome 9–2

11. In a(n) _____ primary, only party members can vote to choose that party's candidates, and they may vote only in the primary of their own party.
   a. closed **b.** open **c.** indirect

12. In late summer of a presidential election year, _____ gather at their party's national convention to adopt the party platform and to nominate the party's presidential and vice-presidential candidates.
   a. poll watchers **b.** delegates **c.** electors

LearningOutcome 9–3

13. With the rise of candidate-centered campaigns in the past several decades, the role of the political party in managing campaigns has
   a. increased. **c.** declined.
   b. stayed about the same.

LearningOutcome 9–4

14. Barack Obama gained an edge on his rivals in part because of his superior use of
   a. radio. **c.** social media and the Internet.
   b. television.

LearningOutcome 9–5

15. The Federal Election Campaign Act allows corporations, labor unions, and interest groups to set up PACs to raise money for candidates. PACs can contribute up to _____ per candidate in each election, but there is no limit on the total amount of PAC contributions during an election cycle.
   a. $2,000 **b.** $5,000 **c.** $95,000

10 | Politics and the Media

LEARNING OUTCOMES After reading this chapter, you should be able to:

10–1 Explain the role of the media in a democracy.

10–2 Summarize how television influences the conduct of political campaigns.

10–3 Explain why talk radio has been described as the Wild West of the media.

10–4 Describe types of media bias and explain how such bias affects the political process.

10–5 Indicate the extent to which the Internet is reshaping news and political campaigns.

After finishing
this chapter go to
PAGE 235 for
STUDY TOOLS.

AMERICA AT ODDS

© Brian A Jackson/Shutterstock

Do We Still Need Newspapers?

The *New York Times*. The *Washington Post*. The *Wall Street Journal*. The *Christian Science Monitor*. These and hundreds of other major and minor newspapers have generated and disseminated the nation's news for more than one hundred years. But recent times have brought great changes to the newspaper industry. The Great Recession was hard on newspaper revenues. Some famous newspapers have filed for bankruptcy protection. Other newspapers have reduced their printing schedules or have gone completely online.

The online revolution has changed the newspaper business—and may destroy it. Classified advertising has always been a major revenue source for newspapers, but various Internet sites such as Craigslist have taken over this function in recent years. True, newspapers have gone online, but most have been unable to sell enough advertisements to pay for their online editions. The dean of the U.S. investing community, Warren Buffett, has said that the newspaper business faces "unending losses."

We Don't Need Newspapers—Free Content Is Everywhere

Those who do not mourn the loss of newspapers—particularly the younger generation—point out the obvious. Americans have more access to more news than ever before. Online news is available and updated day and night. An enormous number of citizen bloggers will help you find out what is happening anywhere in the world, at any time you want. So who needs newspapers?

In the past, local newspapers were monopolies. Today, journalists have to put up with competition just like everyone else, and that is for the best. Even if your hometown newspaper shuts down, "hyperlocal" Web sites are increasingly available to deliver local news.

In the past, most Americans had to put up with whatever point of view their local newspaper provided. That is no longer the case. You can find the news—presented in whatever way you like—on thousands of Internet news sites and millions of blogs. Newspapers are dead. Long live the news.

We Need Real Reporters, and Newspapers Offer Them

The reality of this world is that people have to be paid to do a good job, no matter what that job is. Journalists have families to feed. Where does all that free content on the Web come from? Most of it can ultimately be traced back to journalists working for the print media. This is true of hyperlocal sites as well. Even today, newspapers employ the overwhelming majority of all journalists. How many bloggers bother to attend city council meetings and report what happens? Precious few do.

A British reporter sums up the entire argument: "The real value that newspapers provide, whether in print or online, is organization, editing, and reputation." The issue is not the survival of the newspaper industry, but the survival of an informed citizenry.

We need to change the way newspapers work. We need to figure out ways in which online versions of publications can earn enough revenue to be self-supporting. If we do this, we can ensure that newspapers remain the mainstay of American news gathering and distribution.

Where do you stand?

1. Most young people rarely, if ever, read a newspaper. Does that mean they are not getting any news? Why or why not?

2. How much do you think the reputation of a news source really matters?

Explore this issue online

- Newspapers have been harder hit in Michigan than in any other state. Ann Arbor, home of the University of Michigan, is the largest urban area in the country to lose its only daily newspaper. For details of how the *Ann Arbor News* came to close its doors, search on "Ann Arbor News wiki." In 2013, the *News* was resurrected as primarily an online publication—see it at www.mlive.com/ann-arbor.

INTRODUCTION

The debate over whether we need newspapers, described in the chapter-opening *America at Odds* feature, is just one aspect of an important topic: the role of the media in American politics. Strictly defined, the term *media* means communication channels. It is the plural form of *medium,* as in a medium, or means, of communication. In this strict sense, any method used by people to communicate—including the telephone—is a communication medium.

In this chapter, though, we look at the **mass media**—channels through which people can communicate to large audiences. These channels include the **print media** (newspapers and magazines) and the **electronic media** (radio, television, and the Internet).

10–1 THE ROLE OF THE MEDIA IN A DEMOCRACY

LO Explain the role of the media in a democracy.

What the media say and do has an impact on what Americans think about political issues. But just as clearly, the media also *reflect* what Americans think about politics. Some scholars argue that the media are the fourth "check" in our political system—checking and balancing the power of the president, the Congress, and the courts. The power of the media today is enormous, but how the media use their power is an issue about which Americans are often at odds.

10–1a Media Characteristics

The media are a dominant presence in our lives largely because they provide entertainment. Americans today enjoy more leisure than at any time in history, and we fill it up with e-books, movies, Web surfing, texting, and television—a huge amount of television. But the media play a vital role in our political lives as well, particularly during

mass media Communication channels, such as newspapers and radio and television broadcasts, through which people can communicate to large audiences.

print media Communication channels that consist of printed materials, such as newspapers and magazines.

electronic media Communication channels that involve electronic transmissions, such as radio, television, and the Internet.

campaigns and elections. Politicians and political candidates have learned—often the hard way—that positive media exposure and news coverage are essential to winning votes.

As you read in Chapter 4, one of the most important civil liberties protected in the Bill of Rights is freedom of the press. Like free speech, a free press is considered a vital tool of the democratic process. If people are to cast informed votes, they must have access to a forum in which they can discuss public affairs fully and assess the conduct and competency of their officials. The media provide this forum.

In contrast, government censorship of the press is common in many nations around the globe. One example is China, where the Web is heavily censored, even though China now has more Internet users than any other country on earth.

10–1b The New Media and the Old

From the founding of the nation through the early years of the twentieth century, all media were print media—newspapers, magazines, and books. Beginning in the twentieth century, however, new media forms were introduced. Radio and motion pictures were the first new media, and they became important in the first half of the twentieth century.

Following World War II (1939–1945), broadcast television became the dominant form of communication. Cable television networks arrived in the 1970s. The Internet, including e-mail and the World Wide Web, came into widespread use by the general public in the 1990s.

THE DECLINE OF THE OLD MEDIA Film and radio did not displace print media in the early twentieth century. Television, though, had a much greater effect. Beginning about 1950, the number of adults reading a daily paper began to decline, although circulation remained steady due to population growth.

Later, the Internet proved to be even more devastating to newspapers. Newspaper circulation fell modestly in the 1990s. In 2006, however, circulation began to collapse, declining more than 5 percent each year. The *America at Odds* feature discussed some of the problems of the newspaper industry, and we will return to these problems later in the chapter.

YOUTH AND THE NEW MEDIA Today, millions of Americans have developed unprecedented habits of media consumption. Leaders of the revolution include the wealthy and "early adopters" of new technology. Above all, the new consumers include the young. As one might expect, the upcoming generation of media users

(Stewart): Carrie-Nelson/Shutterstock / (Colbert): Helga Esteb/Shutterstock

A surprisingly large number of young people get much of their news from Comedy Central's Jon Stewart (left) and Stephen Colbert (right). Colbert was set to take over the CBS *Late Show* in 2015. *Why do young people like these performers?*

Considering the electorate as a whole therefore, television remains a key medium in terms of political influence. Much of this chapter, therefore, deals with the impact of television.

10–1c The Media and the First Amendment

As noted earlier, freedom of the press is essential if the media are to play their role in supporting the democratic process. The concept of freedom of the press has been applied to print media since the adoption of the Bill of Rights. Such freedoms were not, however, immediately extended to other types of media as they came into existence.

rarely read newspapers. But even television is now of lesser importance.

True, young people still watch a variety of television programs. Many of them, however, primarily view such shows online, as streaming video. Even e-mail has been abandoned by many of today's youth. Instead, messages are transmitted via Facebook, Twitter, Tumblr, Google+, and the smartphone. For such persons, old-media personalities such as television news anchors and radio talk-show hosts are completely obsolete.

NEW MEDIA VERSUS OLD VOTERS   Yet radio, television, and print media remain important to American politics and government. Older Americans largely rely on these more traditional media outlets, and older voters outnumber the young. As of 2015, approximately 111 million Americans were age fifty or older. The number of U.S. residents age eighteen through twenty-nine was less than half that figure. Older voters are also much more likely to turn out to vote than younger ones. Finally, some of the most enthusiastic adopters of new media are not yet eighteen and cannot vote even if they want to.

To give an example, many young people may find radio host Rush Limbaugh—with his audience largely composed of middle-aged white men—to be irrelevant to their lives. Limbaugh is not irrelevant to American politics, however. His millions of listeners vote, and they can influence the outcome of Republican presidential primaries.

Film was one of the first types of new media to be considered under the First Amendment, and in 1915 the United States Supreme Court ruled that "as a matter of common sense," freedom of the press did not apply to the movies.[1] Radio received no protection upon its development, and neither did television. The Court did not extend First Amendment protections to the cinema until 1952.[2] Although the Court has stated that the First Amendment is relevant to broadcast media such as radio and television, to this day it has not granted these media complete protection.

In contrast, the Court extended First Amendment protections to the Internet in 1997, in its first opportunity to rule on the issue.[3] Cable TV received substantial protections in 2000.[4]

Although First Amendment protections now clearly prohibit the U.S. government from restricting speech on the Internet, other threats exist. We examine some of them in this chapter's *The Rest of the World* feature, which follows.

10–1d The Agenda-Setting Function of the Media

One of the criticisms often levied against the media is that they play too large a role in determining the issues, events, and personalities that are in the public eye. When

The Rest of the World

Worldwide Threats to the World Wide Web

The Internet was created by the U.S. military through the Defense Advanced Research Projects Agency—DARPA (formerly ARPA). Soon it was opened to university researchers and later to the public at large. Censoring it was almost impossible. "The Internet interprets censorship as damage," one early administrator exalted. "We will route around you!"

In time, the Internet, now mostly the World Wide Web, became an international—not just an American—institution. Every nation with a modern economy has embraced the Internet. Poorer countries that want to develop must do so as well. A worldwide Internet, however, means participation by unfree nations. Leaders of these nations have no interest in free speech. Given this, how can the Internet remain both free and worldwide?

Threats from Abroad

No other nation can prevent a country such as China from censoring the Internet within its own borders. Still, could unfree nations export their controls to the rest of the world? An Obama administration plan in 2014 fueled fear of such a development. Under the plan, the U.S. Commerce Department would give up control of the organization in charge of Internet names and addresses—the group that decided, say, that Google would own www.google.com. Many people feared that this function would pass to a United Nations body controlled by world governments.

That would bring in China, Iran, Russia, and other repressive regimes. Power over addresses could be leveraged to support censorship. New financial rules could be crippling. Russia has proposed, for example, that Facebook, Google, and other sites pay cable companies a fee every time someone accesses them. No one has the power to impose such rules on the United States, but the Internet could be fragmented between free and unfree systems. In response to widespread objections, the U.S. government announced that it would keep control of the Internet naming agency.

Threats from Ourselves

In 2013, the world learned that the U.S. National Security Agency (NSA), through its PRISM program, has been downloading massive amounts of data from Google, Microsoft, Yahoo, AOL, and other firms. While the exposure of PRISM touched off a debate over privacy in America, NSA snooping may have other consequences that the government never anticipated. President Obama has claimed that the NSA's actions do not violate the rights of U.S. citizens. But what about the rights of foreigners? Michael Hayden, a former NSA director, was blunt: the Fourth Amendment to the Constitution, which prohibits unreasonable searches, "is not an international treaty."

With the growth in *cloud computing,* more and more individuals and businesses now store important data on remote servers owned by such companies as Google and Microsoft. Europeans as well as Americans use cloud computing. But Europeans have just been informed that they have no privacy rights in data stored on American servers. The U.S. government can look at any data, at any time, for any reason, and U.S. high-tech firms will cooperate.

If you were a European concerned about your privacy, you might consider moving your data to your own country, where you would be protected by your own government. You might also support laws to restrict access to your country by firms that cooperate with foreign intelligence agencies such as the NSA.

CRITICAL ANALYSIS — **How might high-tech companies' cooperation with U.S. security agencies affect America's dominance of the high-tech sector?**

people take in the day's top news stories, they usually assume that these stories concern the most important issues facing the nation. In actuality, the media decide the relative importance of issues by publicizing some issues and ignoring others, and by giving some stories high priority and others low priority.

By helping to determine what people will talk and think about, the media set the *political agenda*—the issues that politicians will address. In other words, the media are engaged in **agenda setting.** To borrow from Bernard Cohen's classic statement on the media and public opinion, the press (media) may not be successful in telling people what to think, but it is "stunningly successful in telling its readers what to think about."[5]

For example, television played a significant role in shaping public opinion about the Vietnam War (1965–1975), which has been called the first "television war." Part of the public opposition to the war in the late 1960s came about as a result of the daily portrayal of the war's horrors on TV news programs. Film footage and narrative accounts of the destruction, death, and suffering in Vietnam brought the war into living rooms across the United States.

PRIMING AND FRAMING   Two additional concepts related to agenda setting are *priming* and *framing*.

Priming.   In **priming,** a television show or an Internet blogger publicizes facts or ideas that may influence how the public thinks about a particular issue. As an example of priming, if the public is informed that the general rate of taxation in the United States is lower than it has been at any time since the 1950s, people are likely to be more receptive to the idea of raising tax rates on upper-income individuals.

In contrast, if the media point out that compared with other wealthy nations, the United States collects a much larger share of its tax revenue from the upper classes, then popular responses to proposals to tax our richer citizens may be quite different.

Framing.   **Framing** an issue involves establishing the context in which it is understood. Frames are stories about how the world works. As an example, consider the different stories that can be told about someone who is experiencing poverty. A TV news show might cover a man whose condition was, to all appearances, due primarily to bad luck. Perhaps he suffered from a life-threatening disease, could not work, lost his job, and then became homeless. This description would set up a particular frame, encouraging viewers to take a positive attitude toward social spending that would provide aid to such an individual.

Another TV report might show a woman who became addicted to alcohol or drugs at an early age, dropped out of high school, and became pregnant without a partner to help support her. Such an account could lead to an entirely different frame, which could lead to a much more skeptical attitude toward spending that benefits the poor.

LIMITS OF AGENDA SETTING   The degree to which the media influence public opinion is not always that clear, however. As you read in Chapter 8, some studies show that people filter the information they receive from the media through their own preconceived ideas about

> "The press may not be successful much of the time in telling people what to think, but it is stunningly successful in telling its readers what to think about."
>
> ~ **Bernard C. Cohen,** American Political Scientist B. 1926

issues. People bring their own frames to political stories, in other words, and these frames can be very powerful.

Scholars who try to analyze the relationship between American politics and the media inevitably confront the chicken-and-egg conundrum: Do the media cause the public to hold certain views, or do the media merely reflect the public's views?

10–1e The Medium Does Affect the Message

Of all the media, television still has the greatest impact on most Americans, especially older ones. Television reaches almost every home in the United States. Even outside their homes, Americans can watch television—in airports, shopping malls, golf clubhouses, and medical offices. People can view television shows on their computers, and they can download TV programs to their smartphones and tablet devices and view the programs whenever and wherever they want.

THE NATURE OF TELEVISION COVERAGE   Today, Americans watch more television than ever, and it is the primary news source for more than 65 percent of the citizenry. As you will read shortly, politicians take maximum advantage of the power and influence of television. But does the television medium alter the presentation of political information in any way? Compare the coverage given to an important political issue by the print

- **agenda setting** The media's ability to determine which issues are considered important by the public and by politicians.
- **priming** An agenda setting technique in which a media outlet promotes specific facts or ideas that may affect the public's thinking on related topics.
- **framing** An agenda-setting technique that establishes the context of a media report. Framing can mean fitting events into a familiar story or filtering information through pre-conceived ideas.

of the Web manager, or Web strategist, is to create a well-designed, informative, and user-friendly campaign Web site to attract viewers, hold their attention, manage their e-mails, and track their credit-card contributions. The Web manager also hires bloggers to promote the candidate's views, arranges for podcasting of campaign information and updates to supporters, and hires staff to monitor the Web for news about the candidates and to track the online publications of *netroots groups*—online activists who support the candidate but are not controlled by the candidate's organization.

CONTROLLING THE NETROOTS

One of the challenges facing candidates today is delivering a consistent campaign message to voters. Netroots groups may make this task more difficult. Such a group may publish online promotional ads or other materials that do not represent a candidate's position, for example, or attack the candidate's opponent in ways that the candidate does not approve. Yet no candidate wants to alienate these groups, because they can raise significant sums of money and garner votes for the candidate.

CANDIDATES' 24/7 EXPOSURE

Just as citizen journalism has altered the news culture, so have citizen videos changed the traditional campaign. For example, a candidate can never know when a comment that she or he makes may be caught on camera by someone with a cell phone or digital camera and published on the Internet for all to see.

A candidate's opponents may post a compilation of video clips showing the candidate's inconsistent comments over time on a specific topic, such as abortion or the health-care reform legislation. The effect can be very damaging, because it makes the candidate's "flip-flopping" on the issue apparent.

GAFFES DURING THE 2012 CAMPAIGNS

Both major-party presidential candidates experienced the dangers of 24/7 exposure during the 2012 campaigns. Republican Mitt Romney became rather well known for *gaffes*—poorly chosen words. The most damaging of these was a video of Romney speaking to wealthy donors: "There are 47 percent of the people who will vote for the president no matter what . . . who believe that they are victims, who believe the government has a responsibility to care for them, who believe that they are entitled to health care, to food, to housing. . . . These are people who pay no income tax. . . . My job is not to worry about those people. I'll never convince them they should take personal responsibility and care for their lives." This comment reinforced the Democratic theme of Romney as a rich man out of touch with ordinary citizens. In fact, about half of the 47 percent who pay no income tax vote Republican.

Barack Obama occasionally put his foot in his mouth as well. Speaking to supporters, Obama tried to explain why the wealthy should pay more taxes: "If you were successful . . . somebody helped to create this unbelievable American system that we have that allowed you to thrive. Somebody invested in roads and bridges. If you've got a business—you didn't build that. Somebody else made that happen." In saying "you didn't build that," Obama was referring to infrastructure. A clumsy choice of words, however, made it sound as if he were referring to private businesses themselves. Republicans repeated the shorter version of the quote endlessly.

CRITICAL THINKING

▶ To what extent do the media—in particular, the new media—encourage political participation? To what extent might they discourage participation by providing apolitical entertainment?

AMERICA ⚑ AT ODDS
Politics and the Media

Americans love to hate the media, possibly because we spend so much time watching and reading them. Without a doubt, the media are undergoing a revolution today. With the loss of classified ads to the Internet, newspapers are in serious financial jeopardy. Online news sources, meanwhile, have yet to hit upon a reliable method of generating adequate income. In this changing environment, Americans are at odds over a number of media topics:

- *Do the difficulties faced by newspapers threaten the existence of competent journalism—or is this not an important problem?*

- *Is the media's agenda-setting function a vital contribution to the democratic process—or an improper attempt to manipulate viewers?*

- *Should protection of the First Amendment be extended to broadcast media without exception—or would such a move threaten the morals of the country and make it impossible for viewers to avoid sexual content?*

- *Are negative advertisements an inevitable and unremarkable aspect of political campaigns—or should the voters punish politicians who employ them?*

- *Does talk radio add to the vigor of our political discourse—or is it a corrupting influence that divides the nation?*

- *Do the mainstream media have a liberal bias—or do they merely publicize facts that do not square with conservative beliefs?*

Internet Resources

- Refdesk.com offers a huge collection of media resources. For a worldwide list of newspapers and other online news sources, go to refdesk.com/paper.html.

- Much material in the nation's smaller newspapers originates from the Associated Press (AP). Find AP stories for yourself at hosted.ap.org.

- The *Washington Post's* fact-checker, Glenn Kessler, is at www.washingtonpost.com/blogs/fact-checker. Similar services include factcheck.org, a project of the Annenberg Public Policy Center, and polifact.com of the *Tampa Bay Times.*

- A number of watchdog groups monitor the media in an attempt to expose bias, partisanship, or factual errors. Accuracy in Media is a conservative group. Find it at www.aim.org.

- Fairness and Accuracy in Reporting is a liberal watchdog group. Its Web site is at fair.org.

- With YouTube, historically important videos of all kinds are available. These include attack ads, videos of candidates making embarrassing statements, and presidential debates. The easiest way to find a video is to enter key words into a search engine. For example, to find the "daisy girl" ad mentioned in this chapter, search on "daisy girl youtube."

STUDY TOOLS 10

READY TO STUDY?

☐ Review what you've read with the quiz below.

☐ Check your answers in Appendix D at the back of the book.

☐ For any questions you miss, read the corresponding Learning Outcome section again to prepare for class and your exam.

☐ Rip out and study the Chapter in Review card (at the back of the book).

VISIT WWW.CENGAGEBRAIN.COM:

☐ Interactive Quizzes

☐ Key Term Flashcards or Crossword Puzzles

☐ Audio Summaries

☐ Simulations, Animated Learning Modules, and Interactive Timelines

☐ Videos

☐ American Government NewsWatch

FILL-IN

LearningOutcome 10–1

1. _____ is an agenda-setting technique in which a media outlet promotes specific facts or ideas that may affect the public's thinking on related topics.

2. Of all the media, _____ still has the greatest impact on most Americans.

3. A sound bite is _____.

4. Newspapers today are in financial difficulty because _____.

LearningOutcome 10–2

5. The first televised presidential debate, between _____, took place in 1960.

6. Spin doctors are _____.

LearningOutcome 10–3

7. The talk-radio audience is predominantly _____.

8. Talk radio is sometimes characterized as the Wild West of the media because _____.

LearningOutcome 10–4

9. It has been suggested that the media use the winner-loser framework to describe events throughout the campaigns, contributing to a bias against _____.

LearningOutcome 10–5

10. Citizen journalism refers to _____.

MULTIPLE CHOICE

LearningOutcome 10–1

11. In the news business, framing refers to
   a. fitting events into a familiar story or filtering information through preconceived ideas.
   b. news coverage that is managed by a political consultant to gain media exposure for a political candidate.
   c. narrowing the focus of news to the local area.

LearningOutcome 10–2

12. The 1964 "daisy girl" ad is an example of
   a. a personal attack ad.
   b. citizen journalism.
   c. a negative issue ad.

LearningOutcome 10–3

13. Modern talk radio took off in the United States during the
   a. 1930s, after Franklin Roosevelt's first "fireside chat."
   b. 1950s, after political advertising first appeared on television.
   c. 1990s, after the repeal of the fairness doctrine.

LearningOutcome 10–4

14. In a 2013 Gallup poll measuring the public's confidence in various institutions, _____ percent of the respondents stated that they had a "great deal" or "quite a lot" of confidence in television news.
   a. 67
   b. 42
   c. 18

LearningOutcome 10–5

15. _____ refers to the distribution of audio or video files to personal computers or mobile devices such as smartphones.
   a. Blogging
   b. Podcasting
   c. Narrowcasting

4LTR Press solutions are designed for today's learners through the continuous feedback of students like you. Tell us what you think about **GOVT7** and help us improve the learning experience for future students.

YOUR FEEDBACK MATTERS.

Complete the Speak Up survey in CourseMate at www.cengagebrain.com

 Follow us at www.facebook.com/4ltrpress

11 | The Congress

LEARNING OUTCOMES After reading this chapter, you should be able to:

11-1 Explain how seats in the House of Representatives are apportioned among the states.

11-2 Describe the power of incumbency.

11-3 Identify the key leadership positions in Congress, describe the committee system, and indicate some important differences between the House of Representatives and the Senate.

11-4 Summarize the specific steps in the lawmaking process.

11-5 Identify Congress's oversight functions and explain how Congress fulfills them.

11-6 Indicate what is involved in the congressional budgeting process.

After finishing this chapter go to
PAGE 261 for
STUDY TOOLS.

© Patsy Lynch/Retna Ltd./Corbis

AMERICA AT ODDS

© corgarashu/Shutterstock

Should It Take Sixty Senators to Pass Important Legislation?

The number of Senate votes required to force an end to a *filibuster* is sixty. A filibuster takes place when senators use the chamber's tradition of unlimited debate to block legislation. In years past, filibustering senators would speak for hours on a proposed bill. In recent decades, however, Senate rules have permitted filibusters in which actual continuous floor speeches are not required. Senators merely announce that they are filibustering.

The threat of a filibuster has created an *ad hoc* rule that important legislation needs the support of sixty senators. (There are exceptions. Budget bills can be handled using a special *reconciliation* rule that does not permit filibusters.) If one party can elect sixty or more U.S. senators, and if they all follow the party line, they can force through any legislation they want. The Democrats, in fact, enjoyed a supermajority in the Senate for seven months, from July 7, 2009, until February 4, 2010, when they lost a seat in a special election.

Are sixty votes an appropriate requirement for passing important legislation in the Senate?

Don't Let the Majority Trample on the Minority

In the course of our history, the filibuster in the U.S. Senate has served us well. Filibusters provide the minority with an effective means of preventing the majority from ramming legislation down the throats of American voters. Support for a measure can shift between forty-nine votes and fifty-one votes very quickly. Should such small changes be the basis for passing major legislation?

A simple majority does not signify an adequate degree of consensus. It takes two-thirds of both chambers of Congress to override a veto by the president. That's another supermajority. Changing the Constitution requires three-quarters of the state legislatures. If these supermajority rules were good enough for the founders, then the principle still is good enough for the Senate.

In the past, the American public has supported the filibuster in public opinion polls—for good reason. One of the most important characteristics of our political system is that it is not easy to create new laws. The existence of two chambers of Congress—and the president's veto power—ensures this. In particular, the Senate was always meant to be a body that could delay legislation.

Don't Let Obstructionists Determine Legislation

Supermajority rules allow a minority to block the preference of the majority. Even James Madison, who worried about the tyranny of the majority over the minority, recognized the opposite possibility. He said that "the fundamental principle of free government" might be reversed by requiring supermajorities. "It would be no longer majority that would rule: the power would be transferred to the minority."

Madison's warning has been amply justified. At one time, the filibuster was reserved for the defense of major principles. Not all of these principles were laudable—the filibuster was used to defend Jim Crow laws and to prevent African Americans from voting in much of the South. Still, the procedure was rare. Today, it is used for most legislation.

In recent years, the major parties have become politically unified and monolithic. Members of the minority are prepared to cast party-line votes to frustrate the will of the majority on most legislation. Such votes make governance almost impossible. Congress has never passed so few bills in each session as it does under current circumstances.

The Senate should reduce the votes required to end a filibuster to fifty-five or even fifty-one.

Where do you stand?

1. Why might it be appropriate to require supermajority voting for important legislation?

2. Under what circumstances do supermajority voting rules prevent democracy from being fully realized?

Explore this issue online

- You can find out more about the filibuster by entering "filibuster" into a search engine.

- For debates on the merits of the tradition, search on "filibuster pro con."

INTRODUCTION

Congress is the lawmaking branch of government. When someone says, "There ought to be a law," at the federal level it is Congress that will make that law. The framers had a strong mistrust of powerful executive authority. Consequently, they made Congress—not the executive branch (the presidency)—the central institution of American government. Yet, as noted in Chapter 2, the founders created a system of checks and balances to ensure that no branch of the federal government, including Congress, could exercise too much power.

Many Americans view Congress as a largely faceless, anonymous legislative body that is quite distant and removed from their everyday lives. Yet the people you elect to Congress represent and advocate for your interests at the very highest level of power.

Furthermore, the laws created by the men and women in the U.S. Congress affect the daily lives of every American in one way or another. Learning about your congressional representatives and how they are voting in Congress on issues that concern you is an important step toward becoming an informed voter. Even the details of how Congress makes law—such as the Senate rules described in the chapter-opening *America at Odds* feature—should be of interest to the savvy voter.

11–1 THE STRUCTURE AND MAKEUP OF CONGRESS

> **LO** Explain how seats in the House of Representatives are apportioned among the states.

The framers agreed that the Congress should be the "first branch of the government," as James Madison said, but they did not immediately agree on its organization. Ultimately, they decided on a *bicameral legislature*—a Congress consisting of two chambers. This was part of the Great Compromise, which you read about in Chapter 2.

The framers favored a bicameral legislature so that the two chambers, the House and the Senate, might serve as checks on each other's power and activity. The

apportionment The distribution of House seats among the states on the basis of their respective populations.

congressional district The geographic area that is served by one member in the House of Representatives.

House was to represent the people. The Senate was to represent the states and would protect the interests of small states by giving them the same number of senators (two per state) as the larger states.

11–1a Apportionment of House Seats

The Constitution provides for the **apportionment** (distribution) of House seats among the states on the basis of their respective populations. States with larger populations, such as California, have many more representatives than states with smaller populations, such as Wyoming. California, for example, currently has fifty-three representatives in the House. Wyoming has only one.

Every ten years, House seats are reapportioned based on the outcome of the decennial (ten-year) census conducted by the U.S. Census Bureau. Each state is guaranteed at least one House seat, no matter what its population. Today, seven states have only one representative.[1] The District of Columbia, American Samoa, Guam, the Northern Mariana Islands, and the U.S. Virgin Islands all send nonvoting delegates to the House. Puerto Rico, a self-governing possession of the United States, is represented by a nonvoting resident commissioner.

11–1b Congressional Districts

Whereas senators are elected to represent all of the people in a state, representatives are elected by the voters of a particular area known as a **congressional district.** The Constitution makes no provisions for congressional districts. In the early 1800s, each state was given the right to decide whether to have districts at all.

Most states set up single-member districts, in which voters in each district elected one of the state's representatives. In states that chose not to have districts, representatives were chosen at large, from the state as a whole. In 1842, however, Congress passed an act that required all states to send representatives to Congress from single-member districts.

THE SIZE OF THE HOUSE For many years, the number of House members increased as the population expanded. In 1929, however, a federal law fixed House membership at 435 members. Thus, today the 435 members of the House are chosen by the voters in 435 separate congressional districts across the country. If a state's population allows it to have only one representative, the entire state is one congressional district. In contrast, states with large populations have many districts. California, for example, because its population entitles it to send fifty-three representatives to the House, has fifty-three congressional districts. As a result of the rule limiting the size of the House to 435 members, U.S. congressional districts on average now have very substantial populations—about 730,000 people.

THE REQUIREMENT OF EQUAL REPRESENTATION

By default, the lines of the congressional districts are drawn by the state legislatures. Alternatively, the task may be handed off to a designated body such as an independent commission. States must meet certain requirements in drawing district boundaries. To ensure equal representation in the House, districts in a given state must contain, as nearly as possible, equal numbers of people. Additionally, each district must have contiguous boundaries and must be "geographically compact," although this last requirement is not enforced very strictly.

If congressional districts are not made up of equal populations, people's votes are not equally valuable. In the past, state legislators often used this fact to their advantage. For example, traditionally, many state legislatures were controlled by rural areas. By drawing districts that were not equal in population, rural leaders attempted to curb the number of representatives from growing urban centers. At one point in the 1960s, in many states the largest district had twice the population of the smallest district. In effect, this meant that a person's vote in the largest district had only half the value of a person's vote in the smallest district.

For some time, the United States Supreme Court refused to address this problem. In 1962, however, the Court ruled that the Tennessee state legislature's **malapportionment** was an issue that could be heard in the federal courts because it affected the constitutional requirement of equal protection under the law.[2] Two years later, the Supreme Court held that congressional districts must have equal populations.[3] This principle has come to be known as the **"one person, one vote" rule.** In other words, one person's vote has to count as much as another's vote.

GERRYMANDERING Although in the 1960s the Supreme Court ruled that congressional districts must be equal in population, it continued to be silent on the issue of gerrymandered districts. **Gerrymandering**

Martha McSally, a Republican congressional candidate in 2014, speaks with supporters in Tucson, Arizona. McSally is a former Air Force colonel. *Does a military background help in elections?*

© Bill Clark/Getty Images

occurs when a district's boundaries are drawn to maximize the influence of a certain group or political party.

Where a party's voters are scarce, the boundaries of a district can be drawn to include as many of the party's voters as possible. Where the party is strong, the lines are drawn so that the opponent's supporters are spread across two or more districts, thus diluting the opponent's strength. (The term *gerrymandering* was originally used to describe the district lines drawn to favor the party of Governor Elbridge Gerry of Massachusetts prior to the 1812 elections—see Figure 11–1, which follows.)

Although there have been constitutional challenges to political gerrymandering,[4] the practice continues. It was certainly evident following the 2010 census. Sophisticated computer programs were now able to analyze the partisan leanings of individual neighborhoods and city blocks. District lines were drawn to "pack" the opposing party's voters into the smallest number of districts or "crack" the opposing party's voters into several different districts. Packing and cracking make congressional races less competitive.

malapportionment A condition in which the voting power of citizens in one district is greater than the voting power of citizens in another district.

"one person, one vote" rule A rule, or principle, requiring that congressional districts have equal populations so that one person's vote counts as much as another's vote.

gerrymandering The drawing of a legislative district's boundaries in such a way as to maximize the influence of a certain group or political party.

FIGURE 11–1   THE FIRST "GERRYMANDER"

Prior to the 1812 elections, the Massachusetts legislature divided up Essex County in a way that favored Governor Elbridge Gerry's party. The result was a district that looked something like a salamander. A newspaper editor of the time referred to it as a "gerrymander," and the name stuck.

Source: *Congressional Quarterly's Guide to Congress*, 3d ed. (Washington, D.C.: Congressional Quarterly Press, 1982), p. 695.

How Gerrymandering Works.   For a better understanding of how gerrymandering works, look at the examples in Figure 11–2, which follows. In the examples, sixty-four voters must be distributed among four districts, each of which will have a population of sixteen. The two political parties are the O Party and the X Party.

In Example 1, each district contains only one kind of voter. This type of gerrymander is sometimes created when a state legislature is more interested in preserving the seats of incumbents than in benefiting a particular party. In this case, it would be almost impossible for a sitting member to lose in a general election.

In Example 2, every district is divided evenly between the parties. The slightest swing toward one of the parties could give that party all four seats. A legislature would almost never come up with these boundaries, but an independent redistricting board might do so.

Example 3 is a partisan gerrymander favoring the X Party. The district in the lower right is an example of pack-

minority-majority district   A district in which minority groups make up a majority of the population.

ing—the maximum possible number of O voters is packed into the district. In the other three districts, O Party supporters are cracked apart so that they do not have a majority in any of the districts. In these districts, the X Party has majorities of eleven to five, ten to six, and eleven to five.

Gerrymandering After the 2010 Census.   The 2010 elections were a Republican triumph, and the party won control of state legislatures across the country. These victories occurred just before the states were required to redraw the boundaries of congressional districts following the 2010 census. The result was a large number of Republican gerrymanders, which had a substantial effect on the 2012 elections. In these elections, Democratic candidates for the U.S. House actually collected more votes than Republican candidates. The Democrats picked up only eight seats, however. In the end, the partisan breakdown was 200 Democrats and 235 Republicans.

Consider Pennsylvania, which went for Barack Obama by 5.4 percentage points in 2012. Pennsylvania voters cast 2.72 million votes for Democratic House candidates and 2.65 million votes for Republicans. These votes elected five Democratic representatives and thirteen Republicans—even though more votes were cast for Democrats. The Republicans look set to enjoy the fruits of their 2010 redistricting for years to come.

Racial Gerrymandering.   Although political gerrymandering has a long history, gerrymandering to empower minority groups is a relatively new phenomenon. In the early 1990s, the U.S. Department of Justice instructed state legislatures to draw district lines to maximize the voting power of minority groups. As a result, several **minority-majority districts** were created. Many of these districts took on bizarre shapes. For example, North Carolina's newly drawn Twelfth Congressional District was 165 miles long—a narrow strip that, for the most part, followed Interstate 85.

Limits on Racial Gerrymandering.   The practice of racial gerrymandering has generated heated arguments on both sides of the issue. Some groups contend that minority-majority districts are necessary to ensure equal representation of minority groups, as mandated by the Voting Rights Act of 1965. They further contend that these districts have been instrumental in increasing the number of African Americans holding political office. Before 1990, redistricting plans in the South often created only white-majority districts.[5]

Opponents of racial gerrymandering argue that such race-based districting is unconstitutional because it violates the equal protection clause. In a series of cases in the 1990s, the Supreme Court agreed and held that when race is the dominant factor in the drawing of con-

FIGURE 11-2   EXAMPLES OF VOTER DISTRIBUTION

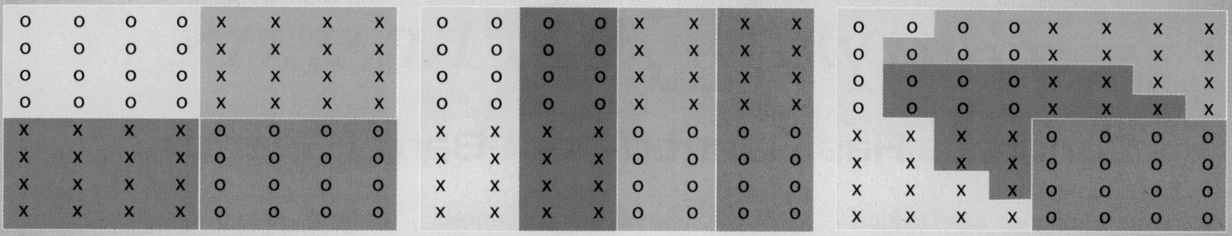

o o o o x x x x o o o o x x x x o o o o x x x x o o o o x x x x x x x x o o o o x x x x o o o o x x x x o o o o x x x x o o o o	o o o o x x x x o o o o x x x x o o o o x x x x o o o o x x x x x x x x o o o o x x x x o o o o x x x x o o o o x x x x o o o o	o o o o x x x x o o o o x x x x o o o o x x x x o o o o x x x x x x x x o o o o x x x x o o o o x x x x o o o o x x x x o o o o

Example 1: A bipartisan gerrymander that protects incumbents of both parties.

Example 2: An unstable system. All districts have the same number of voters from each party.

Example 3: A classic partisan gerrymander. The X Party should carry three districts.

gressional district lines, the districts are unconstitutional and must be redrawn.[6]

In 2001, however, the Supreme Court issued a ruling that seemed to suggest that it would not police racial gerrymandering very closely. North Carolina's Twelfth District, which had been redrawn in 1997, was again challenged in court as unconstitutional, and a lower court agreed. Yet when the case reached the Supreme Court, the justices concluded that there was insufficient evidence that race had been the dominant factor in redrawing the district's boundaries.[7]

11–1c The Representation Function of Congress

Of the three branches of government, Congress has the closest ties to the American people. Members of Congress represent the interests and wishes of the constituents in their home states. At the same time, they must also consider larger national issues, such as the economy and the environment. Often, legislators find that the interests of their constituents are at odds with the demands of national policy.

For example, limits on emissions of carbon dioxide may help reduce climate change, to the benefit of all Americans and the people of the world generally. Yet members of Congress who come from states where most electricity comes from coal-burning power plants may fear that new laws would hurt the local economy and cause companies to lay off workers.

All members of Congress face difficult votes that set representational interests against lawmaking realities. There are several views on how legislators should decide such issues.

THE TRUSTEE VIEW OF REPRESENTATION Some believe that representatives should act as **trustees** of the broad interests of the entire society, rather than serving only the narrow interests of their constituents. Under the trustee view, a legislator should act according to her or his conscience and perception of national needs. For example, a senator from North Carolina might support laws regulating the tobacco industry, even though the state's economy could be negatively affected.

THE INSTRUCTED-DELEGATE VIEW OF REPRESENTATION In contrast, others believe that members of Congress should behave as **instructed delegates.** The instructed-delegate view requires representatives to mirror the views of their constituents, regardless of their opinions. Under this view, a senator from Nebraska would strive to obtain subsidies for corn growers, and a representative from the Detroit area would seek to protect the automobile industry.

Legislators who are acting as instructed delegates are particularly likely to try to insert language into various bills that would benefit special interests back home. Such provisions are called **earmarks,** or pork-barrel legislation. We provide greater detail on earmarks in this chapter's *Perception versus Reality* feature, which follows.

THE PARTISAN VIEW OF REPRESENTATION Because the political parties often take different positions on legislative issues, there are times when members of Congress are very attentive to the wishes of the party leadership. Especially on matters that are controversial, the Democratic members of Congress will be more likely to vote in favor of policies endorsed by a

trustee A representative who tries to serve the broad interests of the entire society and not just the narrow interests of his or her constituents.

instructed delegate A representative who deliberately mirrors the views of the majority of his or her constituents.

earmark Spending provision inserted into legislation that benefits only a small number of people.

Perception vs. Reality

Congress Has Banned Pork-Barrel Spending

In recent years, Congress voted to fund a "bridge to nowhere" in Alaska, a program to combat wild hogs in Missouri, and payment of storage fees for Georgia peanut farmers. Such special interest spending is called *pork-barrel* spending—members of Congress "bring home the bacon" this way to benefit local businesses and workers.

Formally, an item of pork is called an *earmark*. The Congressional Research Service defines earmarks as spending provisions that apply to a very limited number of individuals or entities. The Office of Management and Budget defines earmarks as direct allocations of funds that bypass merit-based or competitive allocation processes of the executive branch. Those who defend earmarks often contend that Congress has a right to determine who benefits from government spending. After all, directing money to particular purposes is a core constitutional function of Congress.

The Perception

In 2010, immediately after the elections that gave them control of the U.S. House, Republicans announced that they would ban earmarks. It follows that pork must be history.

The Reality

First, realize that the Republican ban on pork applies only to earmarks that benefit private businesses. An earmark that benefits a local government is exempt. Still, the House Republican ban on earmarks has made it more difficult for members of Congress to do favors for the folks back home. Many members devote considerable ingenuity to creating end-runs around the rules, however. A simple method is just to deny that a particular funding request is an earmark. One senator identified more than one hundred such mislabeled provisions in a single House defense bill.

A common technique is to lobby executive agencies to place specific projects on their approved lists. If the appropriate agency endorses a project ostensibly on merit-based grounds, then, as if by magic, the project is no longer an earmark. For example, Republicans from Texas and Virginia who opposed a (non-earmarked) high-speed rail project in California were happy to submit letters from the Department of Transportation that endorsed high-speed rail projects—in Texas and Virginia.

One technique for benefiting specific corporations is to lower the tariff (import tax) on goods imported by that firm—and often imported by no one else. You might think that this kind of help would be an unusual procedure. You would be wrong. Congress regularly passes a Miscellaneous Tariff Bill that contains hundreds of such requests.

A final point: presidents are fond of inserting special funding requests into their budget proposals at the last minute, regardless of whether executive agencies signed off on these expenditures. The president, in short, is often the biggest "porkmeister" of all.

 BLOG ON You can visit the Web sites of two groups that oppose pork-barrel spending: Citizens Against Government Waste at cagw.org, and Taxpayers for Common Sense at www.taxpayer.net. Do the recommendations of these groups suggest that they have particular ideological leanings? If so, what are they?

Democratic president, while Republicans will be more likely to oppose them.

Typically, members of Congress combine these three approaches. Legislators may take a trustee approach on some issues, adhere to the instructed-delegate view on other matters, and follow the party line on still others.

CRITICAL THINKING

▶ Some states have tried to prevent gerrymandering by establishing independent redistricting commissions. What kinds of individuals should serve on such commissions? Why?

11-2 CONGRESSIONAL ELECTIONS

LO Describe the power of incumbency.

The U.S. Constitution requires that representatives to Congress be elected every second year by popular vote. Senators are elected every six years, also by popular vote (since the ratification of the Seventeenth Amendment). Under Article I, Section 4, of the Constitution, state legislatures control the "Times, Places and Manner of holding Elections for Senators and Representatives." Congress, however, "may at any time by Law make or alter such Regulations." You can see the results of the 2014 House elections in Figure 11–3, which follows.

11-2a Who Can Be a Member of Congress?

The Constitution sets forth only a few qualifications that those running for Congress must meet. To be a member of the House, a person must have been a citizen of the United States for at least seven years before his or her election, must be a legal resident of the state from which he or she is to be elected, and must be at least twenty-five years of age.

To be elected to the Senate, a person must have been a citizen for at least nine years, must be a legal resident of the state from which she or he is to be elected, and must be at least thirty years of age. The Supreme Court has ruled that neither the Congress nor the states can add to these three qualifications.[8]

Once elected to Congress, a senator or representative receives an annual salary from the government—$174,000 for rank-and-file members as of 2014. He or she also enjoys certain perks and privileges. Additionally, if a member of Congress wants to run for reelection in the next congressional elections, that person's chances are greatly enhanced by the power that incumbency brings to a reelection campaign.

FIGURE 11–3 MEMBERS OF THE U.S. HOUSE FOLLOWING THE 2014 ELECTIONS

Each dot represents one congressional district. Red dots show a Republican representative, and blue dots show a Democrat. In three metropolitan areas—Chicago, Los Angeles, and New York—the dots on the main map overlap so much that many of them are hidden. That is the reason for the three metro area close-ups.

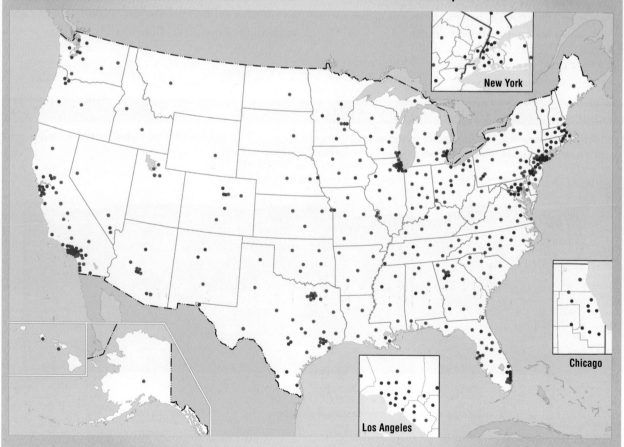

11–2b The Power of Incumbency

The power of incumbency has long been noted in American politics. Typically, incumbents win so often and by such large margins that some observers have claimed that our electoral system involves something similar to a hereditary entitlement. As you can see in Figure 11–4, which follows, most incumbents in Congress are reelected if they run.

Incumbent politicians enjoy several advantages over their opponents. A key advantage is their fund-raising ability. Most incumbent members of Congress have a much larger network of contacts, donors, and lobbyists than their opponents have. Incumbents raise, on average, twice as much in campaign funds as their challengers. Other advantages that incumbents can put to work to aid their reelection include:

▶ *Congressional franking privileges*—members of Congress can mail newsletters and other correspondence to their constituents at the taxpayers' expense. (In an era of e-mail and social networking, however, the franking privilege is much less valuable than it used to be.)

▶ *Professional staffs*—members have large administrative staffs both in Washington, D.C., and in their home districts.

▶ *Lawmaking power*—members can back legislation that will benefit their states or districts and then campaign on that legislative record in the next election.

▶ *Access to the media*—because they are elected officials, members have many opportunities to stage events for the press and thereby obtain free publicity.

▶ *Name recognition*—incumbent members are usually far better known to the voters than challengers are.

Critics argue that the advantages enjoyed by incumbents reduce the competition necessary for a healthy democracy. These incumbency advantages also serve to suppress voter turnout. Voters are less likely to turn out when an incumbent candidate is practically guaranteed reelection.

11–2c Congressional Terms

As noted earlier, members of the House of Representatives serve two-year terms, and senators serve six-year terms. This means that every two years we hold congressional elections: the entire House of Representatives and a third of the Senate are up for election. In January of every odd-numbered year, a "new" Congress convenes (of course, two-thirds of the senators are not new, and most House incumbents are reelected, so they are not new to Congress either). Each Congress has been numbered consecutively, dating back to 1789. The Congress that convened in 2015 was the 114th.

CONGRESSIONAL SESSIONS Each congressional term is divided into two regular sessions, one for each year. Until about 1940, Congress remained in session

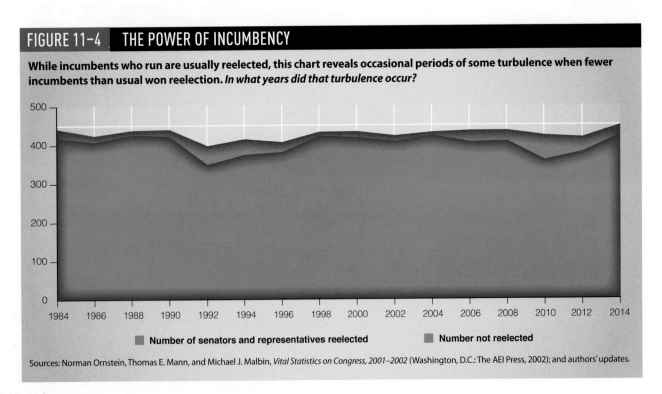

FIGURE 11–4   THE POWER OF INCUMBENCY

While incumbents who run are usually reelected, this chart reveals occasional periods of some turbulence when fewer incumbents than usual won reelection. *In what years did that turbulence occur?*

■ Number of senators and representatives reelected   ■ Number not reelected

Sources: Norman Ornstein, Thomas E. Mann, and Michael J. Malbin, *Vital Statistics on Congress, 2001–2002* (Washington, D.C.: The AEI Press, 2002); and authors' updates.

for only four or five months, but the complicated rush of legislation and the public's increased demand for services in recent years have forced Congress to remain in session through most of each year.[9] Both chambers, however, schedule short recesses, or breaks, for holidays and vacations. The president may call a *special session* during a recess, but because Congress now meets on nearly a year-round basis, such sessions are rare.

TERM LIMITS As you will read in Chapter 12, the president can serve for no more than two terms in office, due to the Twenty-second Amendment. There is no limit on the number of terms a senator or representative can serve, however. For example, Robert Byrd (D., W.V.) served more than fifty-two years in the U.S. Senate, from 1959 until he died in June 2010, at the age of ninety-two. Some observers favor term limits for members of Congress. The Supreme Court, however, has ruled that state-level attempts to impose term limits on members of the U.S. House or Senate are unconstitutional.[10]

CRITICAL THINKING

▶ What benefits could a state hope to gain from representation by a long-serving legislator?

11–3 CONGRESSIONAL LEADERSHIP, THE COMMITTEE SYSTEM, AND BICAMERALISM

LO Identify the key leadership positions in Congress, describe the committee system, and indicate some important differences between the House of Representatives and the Senate.

The Constitution provides for the presiding officers of both the House and the Senate, and each chamber has added other leadership positions as it has seen fit. Leadership and organization in both chambers are based on membership in the two major political parties. The majority party in each chamber chooses the major officers of that chamber, controls debate on the floor, selects all committee chairpersons, and has a majority on all committees.

11–3a House Leadership

The Constitution states that members of the House are to choose their Speaker and other officers but says nothing more about these positions. Today, important "other officers" include the majority and minority leaders and whips.

SPEAKER OF THE HOUSE Chief among the leaders in the House of Representatives is the **Speaker of the House.** This office is filled by a vote taken at the beginning of each congressional term. The Speaker has traditionally been a longtime member of the majority party who has risen in rank and influence through years of service in the House. The candidate for Speaker is selected by the majority-party caucus. The House as a whole then approves the selection.

As the presiding officer of the House and the leader of the majority party, the Speaker has a great deal of power. In the nineteenth century, the Speaker had even more authority. Speakers known by such names as "Uncle Joe Cannon" and "Czar Reed" ruled the House with a firm hand. A revolt in 1910 reduced the Speaker's powers and gave some of them to various committees. Nevertheless, the Speaker still has many important powers, including the following:

▶ The Speaker has substantial control over what bills are assigned to which committees.

▶ The Speaker may preside over the sessions of the House, recognizing or ignoring members who wish to speak.

▶ The Speaker votes in the event of a tie, interprets and applies House rules, rules on points of order (questions about procedures asked by members), puts questions to a vote, and interprets the outcome of most of the votes taken.

▶ The Speaker plays a major role in making important committee assignments

▶ The Speaker schedules bills for action.

The Speaker may choose whether to vote on any measure. If the Speaker chooses to vote, he or she appoints a temporary presiding officer (called a Speaker pro tempore), who then occupies the Speaker's chair. The Speaker does not often vote. Under the House rules, the only time the Speaker *must* vote is to break a tie. Otherwise, a tie automatically defeats a bill. On rare occasions, this rule creates an opportunity for the Speaker. If, by choosing to vote, the Speaker actually *creates* a tie, the proposal will be defeated.

MAJORITY LEADER The **majority leader** of the House is elected by the majority-party caucus to act as spokesperson for the party and to keep the party together.

Speaker of the House The presiding officer in the House of Representatives. The Speaker is a member of the majority party and is the most powerful member of the House.

majority leader The party leader elected by the majority party in the House or in the Senate.

When the Republicans took control of the House after the 2010 elections, former minority leader John Boehner (R., Ohio), left, was elected Speaker of the House. In 2014, Kevin McCarthy (R., Calif.), center, was elected House majority leader. Former Speaker Nancy Pelosi (D., Calif.), right, is the House minority leader. Pelosi had been the first woman to hold the Speaker position. *How much power do these individuals have?*

The majority leader's job is to help plan the party's legislative program, organize other party members to support legislation favored by the party, and make sure the chairpersons on the many committees finish work on bills that are important to the party. The majority leader makes speeches on important bills, stating the majority party's position.

MINORITY LEADER The House **minority leader** is the leader of the minority party. Although not as powerful as the majority leader, the minority leader has similar responsibilities. The primary duty of the minority leader is to maintain solidarity within the minority party. The minority leader persuades influential members of the party to follow the party's position and organizes fellow party members in criticism of the majority party's policies and programs.

WHIPS The leadership of each party includes assistants to the majority and minority leaders known as **whips.** Whips originated in the British House of Commons, where they were named after the "whipper in," the rider who keeps the hounds together in a fox hunt. The term is applied to assistant party leaders because of the pressure that they place on party members to uphold the party's positions.

---

minority leader The party leader elected by the minority party in the House or in the Senate.

whip A member of Congress who assists the majority or minority leader in the House or in the Senate in managing the party's legislative program.

Whips try to determine how each member is going to vote on an issue and then advise the party leaders on the strength of party support. Whips also try to see that members are present when important votes are to be taken and that they vote with the party leadership. For example, if the Republican Party strongly supports a tax-cut bill, the Republican Party whip might meet with other Republican Party members in the House to try to ensure that they will show up and vote with the party.

11–3b Senate Leadership

The Constitution makes the vice president of the United States the president of the Senate. As presiding officer, the vice president may call on members to speak and put questions to a vote. The vice president is not an elected member of the Senate, however, and may not take part in Senate debates. The vice president may cast a vote in the Senate only in the event of a tie.

PRESIDENT PRO TEMPORE Because vice presidents are rarely available—and do not often desire—to preside over the Senate, senators elect another presiding officer, the president pro tempore ("pro tem"), who serves in the absence of the vice president. The president pro tem is elected by the whole Senate and is ordinarily the member of the majority party with the longest continuous term of service in the Senate. The current president pro tem is Orrin Hatch (R., Utah). In the absence of both the president pro tem and the vice president, a temporary presiding officer is selected from the ranks of the Senate, usually a junior member of the majority party.

PARTY LEADERS The real power in the Senate is held by the majority leader, the minority leader, and

As a result of the 2014 elections, Republican senator Mitch McConnell of Kentucky, left, became the Senate majority leader, and Democratic senator Harry Reid of Nevada became the Senate minority leader. *How might a leadership position actually hurt a senator back home?*

their whips. The majority leader is the most powerful individual and chief spokesperson of the majority party. The majority leader directs the legislative program and party strategy. The minority leader commands the minority party's opposition to the policies of the majority party and directs the legislative strategy of the minority party.

11–3c Congressional Committees

Thousands of bills are introduced during every session of Congress, and no single member can possibly be adequately informed on all the issues that arise. The committee system is a way to provide for specialization, or a division of the legislative labor. Members of a committee concentrate on just one area or topic—such as agriculture or transportation—and develop sufficient expertise to draft appropriate legislation when needed. The flow of legislation through both the House and the Senate is determined largely by the speed with which these committees act on bills and resolutions.

STANDING COMMITTEES The permanent and most powerful committees of Congress are called **standing committees.** Their names are listed in Table 11–1, which follows. Normally, before any bill can be considered by the entire House or Senate, it must be approved by a majority vote in the standing committee to which it was assigned.

As mentioned, standing committees are controlled by the majority party in each chamber. Committee membership is generally divided between the parties according to the number of members in each chamber. In both the House and the Senate, committee *seniority*—the length of continuous service on a particular committee—typically plays a role in determining the committee chairpersons.

SUBCOMMITTEES AND OTHER COMMITTEES Most House and Senate committees also have **subcommittees** with limited areas of jurisdiction. Today, there are more than two hundred subcommittees.

Select Committees and Joint Committees. There are also other types of committees in Congress. Special, or select, committees are formed to study specific problems or issues. These committees may be either permanent or temporary.

Joint committees are created by the concurrent action of both chambers of Congress and consist of members from each chamber. Joint committees have dealt with the economy, taxation, and the Library of Congress.

Conference Committees. Conference committees, which also include members from both chambers, are formed for the purpose of achieving agreement between the House and the Senate on the exact wording of legislative acts when the two chambers pass legislative proposals in different forms. No bill can be sent to the White House to be signed into law unless it first passes both chambers in identical form.

If the leadership in either chamber believes that an acceptable compromise with the other chamber is impossible, it can block legislation simply by refusing to appoint members to a conference committee. In 2013,

---

standing committee A permanent committee in Congress that deals with legislation concerning a particular area, such as agriculture or foreign relations.

subcommittee A division of a larger committee that deals with a particular part of the committee's policy area. Most standing committees have several subcommittees.

TABLE 11-1 STANDING COMMITTEES IN THE 114TH CONGRESS, 2015–2017

House Committees	Senate Committees
Agriculture	Agriculture, Nutrition, and Forestry
Appropriations	Appropriations
Armed Services	Armed Services
Budget	Banking, Housing, and Urban Affairs
Education and the Workforce	Budget
Energy and Commerce	Commerce, Science, and Transportation
Financial Services	Energy and Natural Resources
Foreign Affairs	Environment and Public Works
Homeland Security	Finance
House Administration	Foreign Relations
Judiciary	Health, Education, Labor, and Pensions
Natural Resources	Homeland Security and Governmental Affairs
Oversight and Government Reform	Judiciary
Rules	Rules and Administration
Science and Technology	Small Business and Entrepreneurship
Small Business	Veterans' Affairs
Standards of Official Conduct	
Transportation and Infrastructure	
Veterans' Affairs	
Ways and Means	

the Republicans employed this technique on several bills, beginning with the 2014 federal budget resolution.

LITTLE LEGISLATURES   Most of the actual work of legislating is performed by the committees and subcommittees (the "little legislatures"[11]) within Congress. In creating or amending laws, committee members work closely with relevant interest groups and administrative agency personnel. For more details on the interaction among these groups, see the discussion of "issue networks" and "iron triangles" in Chapter 13.

11-3d The Differences between the House and the Senate

To understand what goes on in the chambers of Congress, we need to look at the effects of bicameralism. Each chamber has developed certain distinct features. The major differences between the House and the Senate are listed in Table 11–2, which follows.

SIZE MATTERS   Obviously, with 435 voting members, the House cannot operate the same way as the Senate, which has only 100 members. With its larger size, the House needs both more rules and more formality—otherwise, no work would ever get done. The most obvious formal rules have to do with debate on the floor.

The Senate normally permits extended debate on all issues that arise before it. In contrast, the House uses an elaborate system: The House **Rules Committee** normally proposes time limits on debate for any bill. The rules are then accepted or modified by the House. Despite its greater size, as a consequence of its stricter time limits on debate, the House is often able to act on legislation more quickly than the Senate.

THE "HASTERT RULE" IN THE HOUSE   One informal rule affecting only House Republicans can prevent consideration of legislation even if it has passed in the Senate. That is the *Hastert Rule*, named after a former Republican Speaker. Under the rule, when the Republicans have a majority in the House, the Speaker will not allow any measure to reach the floor unless it has the support of a majority of the Republican members of the House. Democratic Speakers also have the power to block legislation in this way, but they have not turned this procedure into an informal rule.

The Hastert Rule came under considerable pressure in late 2012 and 2013, when Republican Speaker John Boehner felt compelled to violate it repeatedly. Legislation in December 2012 prevented large-scale tax increases at the cost of allowing taxes to rise for the wealthiest citizens. It passed without the support of most Republicans. Boehner also lifted the rule to end the government shutdown that took place in October 2013. With more House Republicans after the 2014 elections, Boehner may find it easier to win majority support for legislation within his party.

Rules Committee   A standing committee in the House of Representatives that provides special rules governing how particular bills will be considered and debated by the House. The Rules Committee normally proposes time limits on debate for any bill.

TABLE 11-2 MAJOR DIFFERENCES BETWEEN THE HOUSE AND THE SENATE

House*	Senate*
Members chosen from local districts	Members chosen from entire state
Two-year term	Six-year term
Always elected by voters	Originally (until 1913) elected by state legislatures
May impeach (accuse, indict) federal officials	May convict federal officials of impeachable offenses
Larger (435 voting members)	Smaller (100 members)
More formal rules	Fewer rules and restrictions
Debate limited	Debate extended
Floor action controlled	Unanimous consent rules
Less prestige and less individual notice	More prestige and media attention
Originates bills for raising revenues	Has power of "advice and consent" on presidential appointments and treaties
Local or narrow leadership	National leadership

*Some of these differences, such as term of office, are provided for in the Constitution, while others, such as debate rules, are not.

IN THE SENATE, DEBATE CAN JUST KEEP GOING AND GOING At one time, both the House and the Senate allowed unlimited debate, but the House ended this practice in 1811. The use of unlimited debate in the Senate to obstruct legislation is called **filibustering** (as discussed in the chapter-opening *America at Odds* feature). Until 2013, the filibuster could also be used to hold up presidential nominations for judicial or executive positions, as we explain later in this chapter.

Today, under Senate Rule 22, filibusters may be ended by invoking **cloture**—a procedure for closing debate and bringing the matter under consideration to a vote in the Senate. Sixteen senators must sign a petition requesting cloture. Then, after two days have elapsed, three-fifths of the entire membership must vote for cloture. Normally, that means sixty senators. Once cloture is invoked, each senator may speak on a bill for no more than one hour before a vote is taken. Additionally, a final vote must take place within one hundred hours after cloture has been invoked.

THE SENATORIAL HOLD Senators have an additional tool they can use to delay legislation. Individual senators may place a *hold* on a particular bill. A senator simply informs the leader of his or her party of the hold. Party leaders do not announce who has placed a hold, so holds are often anonymous. Recent rule changes designed to curb anonymous holds have been ineffective. Cloture can be used to lift a hold.

Senators often place holds on nominees for executive or judicial positions in an attempt to win concessions from the executive branch. For example, in 2010, Senator Richard Shelby (R., Ala.) placed holds on at least seventy of President Obama's nominations in an attempt to force the administration to support two military spending programs in Alabama.

THE SENATE WINS THE PRESTIGE RACE, HANDS DOWN Because of the large number of representatives, few can garner the prestige that a senator enjoys. Senators have relatively little difficulty in gaining access to the media. Members of the House, who run for reelection every two years, have to survive many reelection campaigns before they can obtain such recognition. Usually, a representative must become an important committee leader to enjoy the consistent attention of the national news media.

One consequence of the prestige difference is that it has been very difficult for a member of the House to win a presidential nomination. In contrast, the parties have often nominated senators, and a number of senators have gone on to become president.

CRITICAL THINKING

▶ Vice presidents typically avoid presiding over the Senate, even though that is their chief constitutional responsibility. Why might they be so reluctant?

11-4 THE LEGISLATIVE PROCESS

LO Summarize the specific steps in the lawmaking process.

Look at Figure 11–5, which follows. It shows the basic process through which a bill becomes law at the national level. Not all of the complexities of the process are shown,

filibustering The Senate tradition of unlimited debate undertaken for the purpose of preventing action on a bill.

cloture A procedure for ending filibusters in the Senate and bringing the matter under consideration to a vote.

FIGURE 11–5   **HOW A BILL BECOMES A LAW**

This illustration shows the most typical way in which proposed legislation is enacted into law. It follows two hypothetical bills, House bill No. 100 (HR 100) and Senate bill No. 200 (S 200). The path of HR 100 is traced by an orange line, and that of S 200 by a purple line. In practice, most bills begin as similar proposals in both chambers. Bills must be passed by both chambers in identical form before they can be sent to the president.

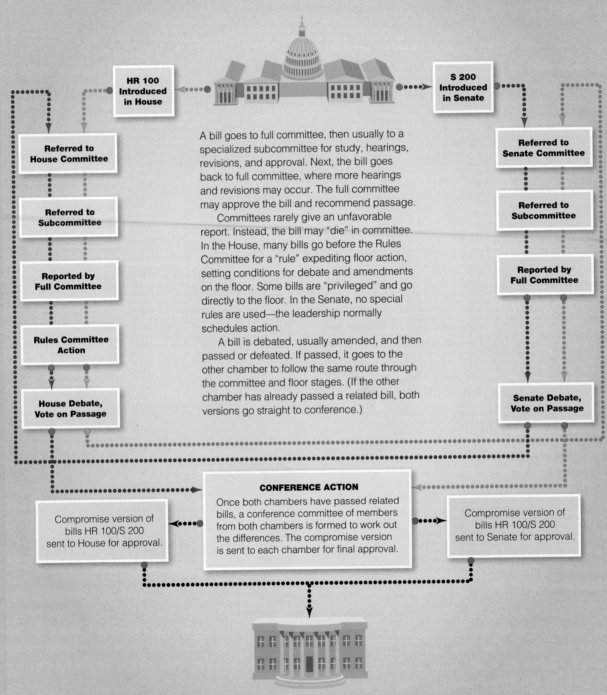

HR 100 Introduced in House

S 200 Introduced in Senate

Referred to House Committee

Referred to Subcommittee

Reported by Full Committee

Rules Committee Action

House Debate, Vote on Passage

Referred to Senate Committee

Referred to Subcommittee

Reported by Full Committee

Senate Debate, Vote on Passage

A bill goes to full committee, then usually to a specialized subcommittee for study, hearings, revisions, and approval. Next, the bill goes back to full committee, where more hearings and revisions may occur. The full committee may approve the bill and recommend passage.

Committees rarely give an unfavorable report. Instead, the bill may "die" in committee. In the House, many bills go before the Rules Committee for a "rule" expediting floor action, setting conditions for debate and amendments on the floor. Some bills are "privileged" and go directly to the floor. In the Senate, no special rules are used—the leadership normally schedules action.

A bill is debated, usually amended, and then passed or defeated. If passed, it goes to the other chamber to follow the same route through the committee and floor stages. (If the other chamber has already passed a related bill, both versions go straight to conference.)

CONFERENCE ACTION

Once both chambers have passed related bills, a conference committee of members from both chambers is formed to work out the differences. The compromise version is sent to each chamber for final approval.

Compromise version of bills HR 100/S 200 sent to House for approval.

Compromise version of bills HR 100/S 200 sent to Senate for approval.

A compromise bill approved by both chambers is sent to the president, who can sign it, veto it, or let it become law without a signature. Congress may override a veto by a two-thirds majority vote in each chamber.

to be sure. For example, the figure does not indicate the extensive lobbying and media politics that are often involved in the legislative process, nor does it mention the informal negotiations and "horse trading" that occur to get a bill passed.

The basic steps in the process are as follows:

1. **Introduction of legislation.** Although individual members of Congress or their staffs—as well as private citizens and lobbying groups—may come up with ideas for new legislation, most bills are proposed by the executive branch. Only a member of Congress can formally introduce legislation, however. In reality, many bills are proposed, developed, and even written by the White House or an executive agency. Then a "friendly" senator or representative introduces the bill in Congress. Such bills are rarely ignored entirely, although they are often amended or defeated.

To a degree not seen for some decades, the Obama administration during his first term let Congress take the lead on writing important new legislation dealing with issues such as health-care reform and financial regulation. Even under Obama, however, a majority of the legislation considered by Congress has come from the executive branch.

2. **Referral to committees.** As soon as a bill is introduced and assigned a number, it is sent to the appropriate standing committee. In the House, the Speaker assigns the bill to the committee. In the Senate, the presiding officer does so. For example, a farm bill in the House would be sent to the Agriculture Committee, and a gun control bill would be sent to the Judiciary Committee.

A committee chairperson will typically send the bill on to a subcommittee. For example, a Senate bill concerning NATO (the North Atlantic Treaty Organization) in Europe would be sent to the Senate Foreign Relations Subcommittee on European Affairs. Alternatively, the chairperson may decide to put the bill aside and ignore it. Most bills that are pigeonholed in this manner receive no further action.

Senator Elizabeth Warren (D., Mass.) and Senator Joe Manchin (D., W. Va.) at a Banking, Housing and Urban Affairs Committee hearing. Warren has been a strong critic of the banking industry. *Why might that position be popular?*

If a bill is not pigeonholed, committee staff members go to work researching it. The committee may hold public hearings during which people who support or oppose the bill can express their views. Committees also have the power to order witnesses to testify at public hearings. Witnesses may be executive agency officials, experts on the subject, or representatives of interest groups concerned about the bill.

The subcommittee must meet to approve the bill as it is, add new amendments, or draft a new bill. This meeting is known as the **markup session.** If members cannot reach a consensus on changes, a vote on the changes is taken.

When a subcommittee completes its work, the bill goes to the full standing committee, which then meets for its own markup session. The committee may hold its own hearings, amend the subcommittee's version, or simply approve the subcommittee's recommendations.

3. **Reports on a bill.** Finally, the committee will report the bill back to the full chamber. It can report the bill favorably, report the bill with amendments, or report a newly written bill. It can also report a bill unfavorably, but usually such a bill will have been pigeonholed earlier instead. Along with the bill, the committee will

markup session A meeting held by a congressional committee or subcommittee to approve, amend, or redraft a bill.

U.S. Republican Senator Rand Paul of Kentucky discusses the debt ceiling with a staff member at the Capitol in Washington, D.C. *Why does the debt ceiling matter?*

> "You've got to **work things out** in the cloakroom, and when you've got them worked out, you can debate a little before you vote."
>
> —Lyndon B. Johnson

on already-established obligations. Bankers and economists warned that such a default would result in disaster. In the end, the Republicans were at least partially successful. A deal with the Obama administration led to a variety of restraints on spending.

House Republicans attempted to repeat the tactic in 2013, with the added pressure of refusing to pass a continuing resolution to fund the government. Democrats, believing they had been taken advantage of in 2011, refused to budge. On October 1, the government began shutting down nonessential services. Essential staff members were required to work without pay. The House tactics were very unpopular with businesses and the public, and Republicans were forced to abandon them. For the time being, at least, the debt ceiling showdowns were off the agenda.

CRITICAL THINKING

▶ Why do you think Congress created entitlement programs that operate under open-ended authorizations instead of reauthorizing each of them every year?

AMERICA 🏴 AT ODDS
The Congress

The founders thought that Congress would be the branch of government that was closest to the people. Yet Congress is one of the least popular institutions in America. It seems that anything that Congress does annoys a substantial share of the electorate. Needless to say, Americans are at odds over Congress on a variety of issues:

- *Is the Senate's filibuster rule a legitimate safeguard of minority rights— or a disastrous handicap on Congress's ability to address the nation's problems?*

- *Is political gerrymandering just a normal part of the political game—or does it deprive voters of their rights?*

- *Does racial gerrymandering allow the voices of minority groups to be heard—or is it an unconstitutional violation of the equal protection clause?*

- *When voting on legislation, should members of Congress faithfully represent the views of their constituents—or should they stay true to their own beliefs about what is good for the nation?*

- *Should legislative earmarks, or "pork," be banned as a waste of taxpayers' resources—or is it appropriate for members of Congress to support specific projects in their own districts?*

Internet Resources

- If you are interested in Congress, consider investigating Politico, a political news blog, available at www.politico.com.

- Two newspapers that specifically cover Congress are *Roll Call*, located at www.rollcall.com, and *The Hill* at thehill.com.

- Congress.gov, maintained by the Library of Congress, provides a record of all bills introduced into Congress, information about each member of Congress and how he or she voted on specific bills, and other data.

- The U.S. Government Printing Office (GPO) Federal Digital System offers information on the Congress in session, bills pending and passed, and a history of the bills at www.gpo.gov/fdsys.

- You can find e-mail addresses and home pages for members of the House of Representatives at www.house.gov.

- For e-mail addresses and home pages for members of the Senate, go to www.senate.gov.

STUDY TOOLS 11

READY TO STUDY?
- ☐ Review what you've read with the quiz below.
- ☐ Check your answers in Appendix D at the back of the book.
- ☐ For any questions you miss, read the corresponding Learning Outcome section again to prepare for class and your exam.
- ☐ Rip out and study the Chapter in Review card (at the back of the book).

VISIT WWW.CENGAGEBRAIN.COM:
- ☐ Interactive Quizzes
- ☐ Key Term Flashcards or Crossword Puzzles
- ☐ Audio Summaries
- ☐ Simulations, Animated Learning Modules, and Interactive Timelines
- ☐ Videos
- ☐ American Government NewsWatch

FILL-IN

LearningOutcome 11–1

1. Every _____ years, seats in the House of Representatives are reapportioned based on the outcome of the census.

2. Under the trustee view of representation, a legislator should try to _____.

LearningOutcome 11–2

3. Incumbent members of Congress enjoy several advantages over their challengers in elections, including

   _____.

LearningOutcome 11–3

4. The Speaker of the House has the power to

   _____.

5. Filibusters may be ended by invoking _____.

LearningOutcome 11–4

6. A markup session is _____.

7. In the House, the _____ Committee plays a major role in the scheduling process and will also specify the amount of time to be spent on debate.

LearningOutcome 11–5

8. In practice, the Senate's power of "advice and consent" means that the Senate confirms or fails to confirm the president's nominees to _____.

LearningOutcome 11–6

9. The budgeting process is a two-part procedure that includes _____.

MULTIPLE CHOICE

LearningOutcome 11–1

10. To ensure equal representation in the House, districts in a given state must contain, as nea_ equal numbers of
    a. men and women.
    b. Republicans and Democrats.
    c. people.

LearningOutcome 11–2

11. The U.S. Constitution requires that members of Representatives be elected every
    a. second year by popular vote.
    b. six years by popular vote.
    c. second year by state legislatures.

LearningOutcome 11–3

12. In the Senate, the _____ is typically the most individual and directs the legislative program of his or her party.
    a. vice president
    b. majority leader
    c. president pro tempore

LearningOutcome 11–4

13. As soon as a bill is introduced in either the H Senate, it is sent to
    a. the floor of the chamber.
    b. the appropriate standing committee.
    c. a conference committee.

LearningOutcome 11–5

14. The Senate
    a. voted to impeach Richard Nixon.
    b. convicted Bill Clinton of impeachable offe thirds vote.
    c. tries officials who have been impeached i Representatives.

LearningOutcome 11–6

15. When Congress is unable to pass a complete beginning of the fiscal year, it usually passes _ enable the executive agencies to keep on do they were doing the previous year with the s_ of funding.
    a. continuing resolutions c. earmarks
    b. entitlement programs

WHY CHOOSE?

Every 4LTR Press solution comes complete with a visually engaging textbook in addition to an interactive eBook. Go to CourseMate for **GOVT7** to begin using the eBook. Access at **www.cengagebrain.com**

Complete the Speak Up survey in CourseMate at **www.cengagebrain.com**

 Follow us at **www.facebook.com/4ltrpress**

INTRODUCTION

President Lyndon B. Johnson (1963–1969) stated in his autobiography[1] that "of all the 1,886 nights I was President, there were not many when I got to sleep before 1 or 2 A.M., and there were few mornings when I didn't wake up by 6 or 6:30." President Harry Truman (1945–1953) once observed that no one can really understand what it is like to be president: there is no end to "the chain of responsibility that binds him," and he is "never allowed to forget that he is president." These responsibilities are, for the most part, unremitting. Unlike Congress, the president never adjourns.

At the apex of the political ladder, the presidency is the most powerful and influential political office that any one individual can hold. Presidents can help to shape not only domestic policy but also global developments.

Since the demise of the Soviet Union and the Communist-controlled governments in eastern Europe in the early 1990s, the president of the United States has been the leader of the most powerful nation on earth. The president heads the greatest military force anywhere. Presidents have more power to reach their political objectives than any other players in the American political system. (We discussed the president's ability to initiate military action with or without congressional consent in this chapter's opening *America at Odds* feature.) It is not surprising, therefore, that many Americans aspire to attain this office.

12–1 WHO CAN BECOME PRESIDENT?

LO List the constitutional requirements for becoming president.

The notion that anybody can become president of this country has always been a part of the American mythology. Certainly, the requirements for becoming president set forth in Article II, Section 1, of the Constitution are not difficult to meet:

> No Person except a natural born Citizen, or a Citizen of the United States, at the time of the Adoption of this Constitution, shall be eligible to the Office of President; neither shall any Person be eligible to that Office who shall not have attained to the Age of thirty-five Years, and been fourteen Years a Resident within the United States.

This language does make it impossible for a foreign-born naturalized citizen to become president, even if that person came to this country as an infant. For more on that issue, see this chapter's *Join the Debate* feature, which follows.

12–1a Perks of the President

Given the demands of the presidency, why would anyone seek the office? There are some very special perks associated with the presidency. The president enjoys, among other things, the use of the White House. The White House has 132 rooms located on 18.3 acres of land in the heart of the nation's capital. At the White House, the president in residence has a staff of more than eighty persons, including chefs, gardeners, maids, butlers, and a personal tailor.

Amenities also include a tennis court, a swimming pool, bowling lanes, and a private movie theater. Additionally, the president has at his or her disposal a fleet of automobiles, helicopters, and jets (including *Air Force*

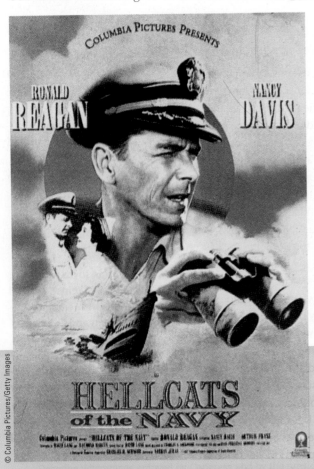

Promotional poster for the feature film *Hellcats of the Navy*, starring future president Ronald Reagan. *How might Reagan's career as an actor have helped him in politics?*

© Columbia Pictures/Getty Images

Join the Debate

A Foreign-Born President?

As you just read, Article II of the Constitution states that "[n]o Person except a natural born Citizen . . . shall be eligible to the Office of President." This restriction has long been controversial, for it has kept many otherwise qualified Americans from running for president. These persons have included former California governor Arnold Schwarzenegger, who was born in Austria, and former Michigan governor Jennifer M. Granholm, who was born in Canada. Both have been U.S. citizens for decades. In all, some 13 million Americans born outside the United States are excluded by this provision. The requirement of native birth has come up most recently because of claims by conspiracy theorists that President Obama was not born in the United States. These individuals claim that Obama's Hawaiian birth certificate was forged, and they are undeterred by the fact that Obama's birth was also announced in two Honolulu newspapers.

An Obsolete Provision

America is a nation of immigrants, so it strikes some as odd that a foreign-born person would be barred from aspiring to the presidency. Naturalized U.S. citizens are allowed to vote, to serve on juries, and to serve in the military. They are also allowed to serve as secretary of state and represent the nation in foreign affairs. Why can't they run for president? Critics of the Constitution's citizenship requirement think that the requirement should be abolished by a constitutional amendment. They point out that the clause was initially included in the Constitution to prevent European princes from attempting to force the young republic back under monarchical rule in the late 1700s. Clearly, the clause is now obsolete and should no longer apply.

A Requirement Still Valid Today

Other Americans believe that the constitutional ban should remain. They argue that national security could be compromised by a foreign-born president. With the immense power that the president wields, especially in foreign policy, loyalty is of the utmost concern.

In addition, the Constitution is difficult to amend, requiring support from two-thirds of both chambers of Congress and ratification by three-fourths of the states. The need for an amendment that would allow immigrants to run for president is hardly as pressing as the prior need for antidiscrimination amendments, such as the ones that abolished slavery and gave women the right to vote, opponents argue.

CRITICAL ANALYSIS **Do you see a problem with someone born in a foreign country serving as president? Why or why not?**

One, which costs about $180,000 an hour to run). For relaxation, the presidential family can go to Camp David, a resort hideaway in the Catoctin Mountains of Maryland. Other perks include free dental and medical care.

12–1b Presidential Age and Occupation

Modern presidents have included a haberdasher (Harry Truman), the owner of a peanut warehouse (Jimmy Carter), and an actor (Ronald Reagan), although all of these men also had significant political experience before assuming the presidency. The most common previous occupation of U.S. presidents, however, has been the legal profession. Out of forty-four presidents, twenty-seven have been lawyers. Many presidents have also been wealthy.

Although the Constitution states that anyone who is thirty-five years of age or older can become president, the average age at inauguration has been fifty-five. The youngest person elected president was John F. Kennedy (1961–1963), who assumed the presidency at the age of forty-three (the youngest person to hold the office was Theodore Roosevelt, who was forty-two when he became president after the assassination of William McKinley). The oldest was Ronald Reagan (1981–1989), who was sixty-nine years old when he became president.

12–1c Race, Gender, and Religion

For most of American history, all presidential candidates, even those of minor parties, were white, male, and of the Protestant religious tradition. In recent years, however, the pool of talent has expanded. In 1928, Democrat Al Smith became the first Roman Catholic to run for president on a major-party ticket, and in 1960 Democrat John F. Kennedy was elected as the first Catholic president. Among recent unsuccessful Democratic presidential candidates, Michael Dukakis was Greek Orthodox and John Kerry was Roman Catholic.

In 2008, the doors swung wide in the presidential primaries as the Democrats chose between a white woman, Hillary Clinton, and an African American man, Barack Obama. By that time, about 90 percent of Americans told pollsters that they would be willing to support an African American for president, and the same number would support a woman.

In 2012, none of the top three finishers in the Republican primaries was Protestant. Newt Gingrich and Rick Santorum were Catholic. Mitt Romney was a member of the Latter-Day Saints, commonly called the Mormons.

© National Photo Company Collection/Library of Congress

President Woodrow Wilson throwing out the first pitch on the opening day of the Major League Baseball season in 1916. *This action is an example of which of the president's roles?*

CRITICAL THINKING

▶ Why do some people believe so strongly that Barack Obama must have been born in a foreign country?

12–2 THE PRESIDENT'S MANY ROLES

LO Explain the roles that a president adopts while in office.

The president has the authority to exercise a variety of powers. Some of these are explicitly outlined in the Constitution, and some are simply required by the office—such as the power to persuade. In the course of exercising these powers, the president performs a variety of roles. For example, as commander in chief of the armed services, the president can exercise significant military powers.

Which roles a president executes successfully usually depends on what is happening domestically and internationally, as well as on the president's personality. Some presidents, including Bill Clinton (1993–2001) during his first term, have shown much more interest in domestic policy than in foreign policy. Others, such as George H. W. Bush (1989–1993), were more interested in foreign affairs than in domestic ones.

Table 12–1, which follows, summarizes the major roles of the president. An important role is, of course, that of chief executive. Other roles include those of commander in chief, head of state, chief diplomat, chief legislator, and political party leader.

12–2a Chief Executive

According to Article II of the Constitution,

The executive Power shall be vested in a President of the United States of America. . . . [H]e may require the Opinion, in writing, of the principal Officer in each of the executive Departments, upon any Subject relating to the Duties of their respective Offices . . . and he shall nominate, and by and with the Advice and Consent of the Senate, shall appoint . . . Officers of the United States . . . . [H]e shall take Care that the Laws be faithfully executed.

TABLE 12–1 ROLES OF THE PRESIDENT

	Role/Description	Examples
	**Chief executive** Enforces laws and federal court decisions, along with treaties approved by the United States	• Can appoint, with Senate approval, and remove high-ranking officers of the federal government • Can grant reprieves, pardons, and amnesties • Can handle national emergencies during peacetime, such as riots or natural disasters
	**Commander in chief** Leads the nation's armed forces	• Can commit troops for up to ninety days in response to a military threat (War Powers Resolution) • Can make secret agreements with other countries • Can set up military governments in conquered lands • Can end fighting by calling a cease-fire (armistice)
	**Head of state** Performs ceremonial activities as a personal symbol of the nation	• Decorates war heroes • Dedicates parks and museums • Throws out first pitch of baseball season • Lights national Christmas tree and pardons the national Thanksgiving turkey • Receives foreign heads of state
	**Chief diplomat** Directs U.S. foreign policy and is the nation's most important representative in dealing with foreign countries	• Can negotiate and sign treaties with other nations, which go into effect with Senate approval • Can make pacts (executive agreements) with other heads of state, without Senate approval • Can accept the legitimacy of another country's government (power of recognition)
	Chief legislator Informs Congress about the condition of the country and recommends legislative measures	• Proposes legislative program to Congress in traditional State of the Union address • Suggests budget to Congress and submits annual economic report • Can veto a bill passed by Congress • Can call special sessions of Congress
	Political party leader Heads political party	• Chooses a vice president • Makes several thousand top government appointments, often to party faithful (patronage) • Tries to execute the party's platform • Attends party fund-raisers • May help reelect party members running for office as mayors, governors, or members of Congress

This constitutional provision makes the president of the United States the nation's **chief executive,** or the head of the executive branch of the federal government.

When the framers created the office of the president, they created a uniquely American institution. Nowhere else in the world at that time was there a democratically elected chief executive. The executive branch is also unique among the branches of government because it is headed by a single individual—the president.

chief executive The head of the executive branch of government; in the United States, the president.

12–2b Commander in Chief

The Constitution states that the president "shall be Commander in Chief of the Army and Navy of the United States, and of the Militia of the several States, when called into the actual Service of the United States." As **commander in chief** of the nation's armed forces, the president exercises tremendous power.

Under the Constitution, war powers are divided between Congress and the president. Congress was given the power to declare war and the power to raise and maintain the country's armed forces. The president, as commander in chief, was given the power to deploy the armed forces. The president's role as commander in chief has evolved over the last century. We mentioned this shared power of the president and Congress in the chapter-opening *America at Odds* feature and will examine it in more detail later in this chapter.

Left to right, President Park Geun-hye of South Korea, President Obama, and Prime Minister Shinzo Abe of Japan. *How can the president benefit by meeting foreign leaders?*

© Official White House Photo by Pete Souza

12–2c Head of State

Traditionally, a country's monarch has performed the function of **head of state**—the country's representative to the rest of the world. The United States, of course, has no king or queen to act as head of state. Thus, the president of the United States fulfills this role.

The president engages in many symbolic or ceremonial activities, such as throwing out the first pitch to open the baseball season and turning on the lights of the national Christmas tree. The president also decorates war heroes, dedicates parks and museums, receives visiting heads of state at the White House, and goes on official state visits to other countries.

Some argue that presidents should not perform such ceremonial duties because they take time that the president should be spending on "real work." Most presidents, however, have found the role of head of state to be politically useful. (See this chapter's *The Rest of the World* feature, which follows, for more information on how one other country handles this issue.)

12–2d Chief Diplomat

A **diplomat** is a person who represents one country in dealing with representatives of another country. In the United States, the president is the nation's **chief diplomat.** The Constitution did not explicitly reserve this role to the president, but since the beginning of this nation, presidents have assumed the role based on their explicit constitutional powers to "receive [foreign] Ambassadors" and, with the advice and consent of the Senate, to appoint U.S. ambassadors and make treaties. As chief diplomat, the president directs the foreign policy of the United States and is our nation's most important representative.

12–2e Chief Legislator

Nowhere in the Constitution do the words *chief legislator* appear. The Constitution, however, does require that the president "from time to time give to the Congress

---

commander in chief The supreme commander of a nation's military force.

head of state The person who serves as the ceremonial head of a country's government and represents that country to the rest of the world.

diplomat A person who represents one country in dealing with representatives of another country.

chief diplomat The role of the president of the United States in recognizing and interacting with foreign governments.

The Unusual Role of the French President

Earlier in this text, you read about the parliamentary system used by many countries. In that system, the chief executive is chosen by the legislature, not the people. A few countries, however, have a hybrid system that is part parliamentary and part presidential. The best-known example of such a system is in France.

The Presidential-Parliamentary System

France has both a president, currently François Hollande, and a prime minister. Both represent the left-of-center party in France, the Socialists. In France, the president names the prime minister and the members of the cabinet. The prime minister and the cabinet, though, are responsible to the legislature, not the president.

The National Assembly, which is the lower house of Parliament, can force the entire cabinet to resign by passing a motion of no confidence. In other words, "the government"—the prime minister and the other cabinet members—cannot survive politically unless a majority in the National Assembly supports them, regardless of the president's preferences.

The Unique French Practice of Cohabitation

For much of the history of the modern French Republic, the legislature's ability to throw out the government was not important, because the president's party had a majority in the National Assembly. French legislators were willing to let the president—the head of the majority party—choose the government. In 1981, the French elected a Socialist president for the first time, and they also gave the Socialists a majority in the National Assembly. In the 1986 elections, however, France voted for a center-right Assembly major-ity. The Socialist president, François Mitterrand, still had two years left in his term of office. The French have a quaint term for the resulting situation: "cohabitation." During cohabitation, the prime minister and the rest of the cabinet are from one party and the president is from another.

Who Does What?

Nowhere in the French constitution is there an explicit statement of the division of powers between the president and the prime minister. The division of duties that exists today has evolved over time. Typically, the president is responsible for foreign policy and the prime minister for domestic policy. This distinction is most carefully observed during periods of cohabitation. When one party is in full control of the government, however, the president tends to take over completely.

CRITICAL ANALYSIS **Would our government work better if a prime minister served under the president?**

Information of the State of the Union, and recommend to their Consideration such Measures as he shall judge necessary and expedient." The president has, in fact, become a major player in shaping the congressional agenda—the set of measures that actually get discussed and acted on.

This was not always the case. In the nineteenth century, some presidents preferred to let Congress lead the way in proposing and implementing policy. Since the administration of Theodore Roosevelt (1901–1909), however, presidents have taken an activist approach. Presidents are now expected to develop a legislative program and propose a budget to Congress every year.

In the past, this shared power has often put Congress and the president at odds. President Bill Clinton's administration, for example, drew up a health-care reform package in 1993 and presented it to Congress almost on a take-it-or-leave-it basis. Congress left it. To avoid such confrontations, President Obama frequently let Congress determine much of the content of important new legislation, such as the health-care reform bills.

In the example of health-care reform, President Obama's deference to Congress had several negative consequences. These included an unusually large number of earmarks, a protracted and unpopular legislative process, and opportunities for conservatives to mobilize against the reforms. Still, in the end, Obama succeeded where Clinton had failed.

12–2f Political Party Leader

The president of the United States is also the *de facto* leader of his or her political party. The Constitution, of course, does not mention this role because, in the eyes of the founders, parties should have no place in the American political system.

As party leader, the president exercises substantial powers. For example, the president chooses the chairperson of the party's national committee. The president can also exert political power within the party by using presidential appointment and removal powers.

Naturally, presidents are beholden to the party members who put them in office. Thus, usually they indulge in the practice of **patronage**—appointing individuals to government or public jobs to reward those who helped them win the presidential contest.

The president may also reward party members with fund-raising assistance. (Campaign financing was discussed in Chapter 9.) The president is, in a sense, "fund-raiser in chief" for his or her party, and recent presidents, including Bill Clinton, George W. Bush, and Barack Obama, have proved themselves to be prodigious fund-raisers.

CRITICAL THINKING

▶ Does our president have too many roles to fill?

12–3 PRESIDENTIAL POWERS

LO Indicate the scope of presidential powers.

The president exercises numerous powers. Some of these powers are set forth in the Constitution. Others, known as *inherent powers,* are those that are necessary to carry out the president's constitutional duties. We look next at these powers, as well as at the expansion of presidential powers over time.

12–3a The President's Constitutional Powers

As you have read, the constitutional source for the president's authority is found in Article II of the Constitution, which states, "The executive Power shall be vested

patronage The practice by which elected officials give government jobs to individuals who helped them gain office.

treaty A formal agreement between the governments of two or more countries.

in a President of the United States of America." The Constitution then sets forth the president's relatively limited constitutional responsibilities.

THE SPECIFIED POWERS Article II grants the president broad but vaguely described powers. From the very beginning, there were different views as to what exactly the "executive Power" clause enabled the president to do. Nonetheless, Sections 2 and 3 of Article II list the following specific presidential powers. These powers parallel the roles of the president discussed in the previous section:

▶ To serve as commander in chief of the armed forces and the state militias.

▶ To appoint, with the Senate's consent, the heads of the executive departments, ambassadors, justices of the Supreme Court, and other top officials.

▶ To make treaties, with the advice and consent of the Senate.

▶ To grant reprieves and pardons, except in cases of impeachment.

▶ To deliver the annual State of the Union address to Congress and to send other messages to Congress from time to time.

▶ To call either house or both houses of Congress into special sessions.

▶ To receive ambassadors and other representatives from foreign countries.

▶ To commission all officers of the United States.

▶ To ensure that the laws passed by Congress "be faithfully executed."

In addition, Article I, Section 7, gives the president the power to veto legislation. We will now discuss some of these powers in more detail. As you will see, many of the president's powers are balanced by the powers of Congress. We return to the complex relationship between the president and Congress later in this chapter.

PROPOSAL AND RATIFICATION OF TREATIES A **treaty** is a formal agreement between two or more countries. The president has the sole power to negotiate and sign treaties with other countries. The Senate, however, must approve a treaty by a two-thirds vote of the members present before it becomes effective. If the treaty is approved by the Senate and signed by the president, it becomes law.

Presidents have not always succeeded in winning the Senate's approval for treaties. In 1999, Bill Clinton was unable to persuade the Senate to approve the Comprehensive Test Ban Treaty, which would have pro-

Lyndon B. Johnson came the closest of any presidential candidate ever to winning a majority of the votes of all citizens eligible to cast a ballot. We discussed his victory in Chapter 9. *Did he have a mandate? Why or why not?*

hibited all signers from testing nuclear weapons. Clinton argued that the United States no longer needed to test its nuclear weapons and that the treaty's restrictions on other countries would enhance our national security. The treaty was defeated largely on a party-line vote, with the Republicans opposed.

In contrast, Barack Obama convinced the Senate to approve the New Strategic Arms Reduction Treaty (New START) with Russia in December 2010. The treaty reduced by half the number of nuclear missiles in both countries and provided for inspections. New START was supported by all of the Democrats and by many Republicans.

THE POWER TO GRANT REPRIEVES AND PARDONS

The president's power to grant a pardon serves as a check on judicial power. A *pardon* is a release from punishment or the legal consequences of a crime. It restores a person to the full rights and privileges of citizenship.

In 1925, the United States Supreme Court upheld an expansive interpretation of the president's pardon power in a case involving an individual convicted for con-

tempt of court. The Court held that the power covers all offenses "either before trial, during trial, or after trial, by individuals, or by classes, conditionally or absolutely, and this without modification or regulation by Congress."[2] The president can grant a pardon for any federal offense, except in cases of impeachment.

One of the most controversial pardons was that granted by President Gerald Ford (1974–1977) to former president Richard Nixon (1969–1974) after the Watergate affair (to be discussed later in the chapter) before any formal charges were brought in court.

Sometimes pardons are granted to a class of individuals as a general amnesty. For example, President Jimmy Carter granted amnesty to tens of thousands of people who had resisted the draft during the Vietnam War by failing to register for the draft or by moving abroad.

THE PRESIDENT'S VETO POWER

As noted in Chapter 11, the president can **veto** a bill passed by Congress. Congress can override the veto with a two-thirds vote by the members present in each chamber. The result of a veto override is that the bill becomes law against the wishes of the president.

If the president does not send a bill back to Congress after ten congressional working days, the bill becomes law without the president's signature. If the president refuses to sign the bill and Congress adjourns within ten working days after the bill has been submitted to the president, however, the bill is killed for that session of Congress. As mentioned in Chapter 11, this is called a *pocket veto*.

Presidents used the veto power sparingly until the administration of Andrew Johnson (1865–1869). Johnson vetoed twenty-one bills. Franklin D. Roosevelt (1933–1945) vetoed more bills by far than any of his predecessors or successors in the presidency. During his administration, there were 372 regular vetoes, 9 of which were overridden by Congress, and 263 pocket vetoes.

THE VETO IN RECENT ADMINISTRATIONS

President George W. Bush (2001–2009) used his veto power very sparingly. Indeed, during the first six years of his presidency, Bush vetoed only one bill—a proposal to expand the scope of stem-cell research. Bush vetoed so few bills largely because the Republican-led Congress during those years strongly supported his agenda. After the Democrats took control of Congress in 2007, Bush vetoed eleven bills. Congress overrode four of the vetoes.

veto A Latin word meaning "I forbid"; the refusal by an official, such as the president of the United States or a state governor, to sign a bill into law.

With a Congress led by his own party during the first two years of his presidency, President Obama faced circumstances similar to those enjoyed by George W. Bush. Consequently, in his first two years in office, Obama exercised the veto power only twice. Surprisingly, Obama issued no vetoes during the next four years even though the Republicans were in control of the House. Apparently, no measure that Obama would have opposed was able to make its way through the Democratic-controlled Senate.

THE LINE-ITEM VETO

Many presidents have complained that they cannot control "pork-barrel" legislation—federal expenditures tacked onto bills to "bring home the bacon" to a particular congressional member's district. For example, expenditures on a specific sports stadium might be added to a bill involving crime. The reason is simple: the president would have to veto the entire bill to eliminate the pork—and that might not be feasible politically. Presidents have often argued in favor of a *line-item veto* that would enable them to veto just one (or several) items in a bill. In 1996, Congress passed and President Clinton signed a line-item veto bill. In 1998, though, the Supreme Court concluded that the bill was unconstitutional.[3]

12–3b The President's Inherent Powers

In addition to the powers explicitly granted by the Constitution, the president also has *inherent powers*—powers that are necessary to carry out the specific responsibilities of the president as set forth in the Constitution. The presidency is, of course, an institution of government, but it is also an institution that consists, at any one moment in time, of one individual. That means the lines between the presidential office and the person who holds that office often become blurred.

Certain presidential powers that are generally recognized today were simply assumed by strong presidents to be inherent powers of the presidency, and their successors then continued to exercise these powers.

© David Hume Kennerly/Getty Images

President Jimmy Carter (center) with Egyptian president Anwar Sadat (left) and Israeli prime minister Menachem Begin (right) at the signing of the Camp David Accords in 1978. Since then, Egypt and Israel have remained at peace with each other. *Would negotiating such agreements help a president politically? Why or why not?*

President Woodrow Wilson clearly indicated this interplay between presidential personality and presidential powers in the following observation:

> The President is at liberty, both in law and conscience, to be as big a man as he can. His capacity will set the limit; and if Congress be overborne by him, it will be no fault of the makers of the Constitution—it will be from no lack of constitutional powers on his part, but only because the President has the nation behind him, and Congress has not.[4]

In other words, because the Constitution is vague as to the actual carrying out of presidential powers, presidents are left to define the limits of their authority—subject, of course, to obstacles raised by the other branches of government.

12–3c The Expansion of Presidential Powers

The Constitution defines presidential powers in very general language, and even the founders were uncertain just how the president would perform the various functions. George Washington (1789–1797) set many of the precedents that have defined presidential power. For example, he removed officials from office, interpreting the constitutional power to appoint officials as implying power to remove them as well.[5]

Washington established the practice of meeting regularly with the heads of the three departments that then existed (plus the attorney general) and of turning to them for political advice. He set a precedent for the president to act as chief legislator by submitting proposed legislation to Congress.

EXPANSION UNDER LATER PRESIDENTS

Abraham Lincoln (1861–1865), confronting the problems of the Civil War during the 1860s, took several important actions while Congress was not in session. He suspended certain constitutional liberties, spent funds that Congress had not appropriated, blockaded southern ports, and banned "treasonable correspondence" from the U.S. mail. Lincoln carried out all of these actions in the name of his power as commander in chief and his constitutional responsibility to "take Care that the Laws be faithfully executed."[6]

Other presidents, including Thomas Jefferson, Andrew Jackson, Woodrow Wilson, Franklin D. Roosevelt, and George W. Bush, also greatly expanded the powers of the president. The power of the president continues to evolve, depending on the person holding the office, the relative power of Congress, and events at home and abroad.

THE PRESIDENT'S EXPANDED LEGISLATIVE POWERS
Congress has come to expect the president to develop a legislative program. From time to time, the president submits special messages on certain subjects. These messages call on Congress to enact laws that the

> "All the president is, is a
> # glorified
> # public
> # relations
> man who spends his
> time flattering, kissing,
> and kicking people to get
> them to do what they are
> supposed to do anyway."
>
> ~ **Harry Truman,** Thirty-Third president of the United States 1945–1953

president thinks are necessary. The president also works closely with members of Congress to persuade them to support particular programs. The president writes, telephones, and meets with various congressional leaders to discuss pending bills. The president also sends aides to lobby on Capitol Hill.

One study of the legislative process found that "no other single actor in the political system has quite the capability of the president to set agendas in given policy areas." As one lobbyist told a researcher, "Obviously, when a president sends up a bill [to Congress], it takes first place in the queue. All other bills take second place." As noted earlier, however, compared with some recent presidents, Barack Obama has showed a surprising willingness to let Congress determine the details of important legislation.

The Power to Persuade. The president's political skills and ability to persuade others play a large role in determining the administration's success. According to Richard Neustadt in his classic work *Presidential Power,* "Presidential power is the power to persuade."[7] For all of the resources at the president's disposal, the president still must rely on the cooperation of others if the administration's goals are to be accomplished. After three years in office, President Harry Truman made this remark about the powers of the president:

President Clinton signs a bill to restructure the Internal Revenue Service. *Why might such legislation be popular?*

RESPECTING AMERICAN TAXPAYERS AND THEIR VALUES

As chief diplomat, George Washington made foreign policy decisions without consulting Congress. This action laid the groundwork for an active presidential role in foreign policy.

By the time Abraham Lincoln gave his Inauguration Day speech, seven southern states had already seceded from the Union. Some scholars believe that Lincoln's skillful and vigorous handling of the Civil War increased the power and prestige of the presidency.

In its attempts to counter the effects of the Great Depression, Franklin D. Roosevelt's administration not only extended the role of the national government in regulating the nation's economic life, but also further increased the power of the president.

The president may have a great many powers given to him in the Constitution and may have certain powers under certain laws which are given to him by the Congress of the United States; but the principal power that the president has is to bring people in and try to persuade them to do what they ought to do without persuasion. That's what the powers of the president amount to.[8]

Persuasive powers are particularly important when divided government exists. If a president from one political party faces a Congress dominated by the other party, the president must overcome more opposition than usual to get legislation passed.

Going Public. The president may also use a strategy known as "going public"[9]—that is, using press conferences, public appearances, and televised events to arouse public opinion in favor of certain legislative programs. The public may then pressure legislators to support the administration's programs. A president who has the support of the public can wield significant persuasive power over Congress. Presidents who are voted into office through "landslide" elections have increased bargaining power because of their widespread popularity. Those with less popular support have less bargaining leverage.

The ability of the president to "go public" effectively is dependent on popular attitudes toward the president. It is also dependent on the political climate in Washington, D.C. In periods of severe political polarization—such as the last several years—going public can actually be counterproductive. Simply by endorsing a proposal that might have had bipartisan support, the president can turn the question into a partisan issue. Without support from at least some members of both parties, the proposal then fails to pass.

The Power to Influence the Economy. Some of the greatest expansions of presidential power occurred during Franklin Roosevelt's administration. Roosevelt claimed the presidential power to regulate the economy during the Great Depression in the 1930s. Since that time, Americans have expected the president to be actively involved in economic matters and social programs. That expectation becomes especially potent during a major economic downturn, such as the Great Recession that began in December 2007.

Each year, the president sends Congress a suggested budget and the *Economic Report of the President*. The budget message proposes what amounts of money the government will need for its programs. The *Economic Report of the President* presents the state of the nation's economy and recommends ways to improve it.

Perception VS. REALITY

Can the President Really Fix the Economy?

The economy has been in poor shape since the end of 2007. As political scientists know, a president running for reelection often won't be reelected if the state of the economy is not improving. There is clearly a public perception that the president can engage in numerous actions to "fix the economy." So, if the economy isn't growing, it's the president's fault.

The Perception

What the president wants, the president gets. If the president has the right ideas about how to improve the economy, he or she just has to make sure that those ideas become public policy. Therefore, when the economy is not adding jobs and the rate of economic growth is slow or nonexistent, clearly the president is responsible.

The Reality

What presidents say and what happens are not necessarily related.

When it comes to the economy, that statement is especially true. Consider *monetary policy*—changing the amount of money in circulation to warm up or cool down the economy. Presidents have almost no control over monetary policy because the independent Federal Reserve System (Fed) carries it out. Presidents can, to be sure, "jawbone" the current head of the Fed—try to exert influence—but that is about the extent of presidential power over monetary policy.

Fiscal policy—tax rates, subsidies, decreases and increases in government spending levels—is another policy lever. People often believe that the president can control such variables. The reality is often quite the opposite.

Only Congress can pass laws that change our tax code and that change the amount of taxpayer dollars spent. This is not to say that a president is incapable of influencing tax rates and the level of government spending, but such influence does not usually go very far if one or both chambers of Congress are in the hands of the other party. This is especially true today, given high levels of political polarization. President Ronald Reagan could dramatically lower tax rates when Democrats controlled Congress, but that was another era.

President Obama was able to get a stimulus bill passed in 2009 because the Democrats controlled both chambers of Congress. Since 2011, in contrast, the Republicans have controlled the House. Attempts by the Obama administration to negotiate with the House Republican leadership have proved to be extraordinarily difficult. As a result, the president has had little influence on taxing and spending decisions.

 BLOG ON To learn more about economic policy, try consulting two talented bloggers. Greg Mankiw, currently chair of the Harvard Economics Department, is a moderate Republican. Find him at gregmankiw.blogspot.com. Matt Yglesias is a pro-market progressive, and you can find his contributions to the Vox blog at www.vox.com/authors/matthew-yglesias.

Voters may rate a president based on the state of the economy. Experts have observed that the president's ability to control the level of economic activity is subject to severe limits. From the public's point of view, however, evaluating its leaders based on results makes good sense. If a president is under constant political pressure to improve the economy, he or she is likely to do whatever is possible to reach that goal. How much can a president actually do to affect the economy? We examine that question in this chapter's *Perception versus Reality* feature.

The Legislative Success of Various Presidents. Look at Figure 12–1, which follows. It shows the success records of presidents in getting their legislation passed. Success is defined as how often the president got his way on roll-call votes on which he took a clear position. As you can see, typically a president's success record was very high when he first took office and then gradually declined. This is sometimes attributed to the president's "honeymoon period," when Congress may be most likely to work with the president to achieve the president's legislative agenda.

FIGURE 12-1   PRESIDENTIAL SUCCESS RECORDS

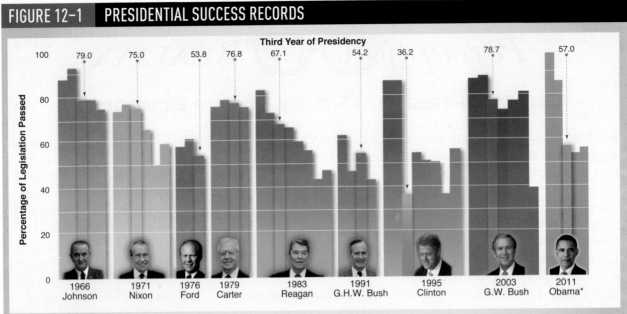

Obama's first-year success rate (2009), was 96 percent, the highest since the opening days of Franklin Roosevelt's presidency.
Source: *Congressional Quarterly Almanac.*

The media often put a great deal of emphasis on how successful a president is during the "first hundred days" in office. Ironically, this is also the period when the president is least experienced in the ways of the White House, particularly if the president was a Washington outsider, such as a state governor, before becoming president.

In 2009, President Obama had the most successful legislative year of any president in half a century. Large Democratic majorities in both chambers of Congress were surely important in explaining Obama's ability to obtain the legislation that he sought. Obama was also successful in 2010. After the Democrats lost control of the U.S. House in November 2010, however, Obama's success rate fell considerably.

THE INCREASING USE OF EXECUTIVE ORDERS

As the nation's chief executive, the president is considered to have the inherent power to issue **executive orders,** which are presidential orders to carry out policies described in laws that have been passed by Congress. These orders have the force of law.

Presidents have issued executive orders for a variety of purposes, including to establish procedures for appointing noncareer administrators, to restructure the White House bureaucracy, and to ration consumer goods and administer wage and price controls under emergency conditions. Other goals have included classifying government information as secret, implementing affirmative action policies, and regulating the export of certain items. Presidents issue executive orders frequently, sometimes as many as one hundred a year.

AN UNPRECEDENTED USE OF SIGNING STATEMENTS

A **signing statement** is a written statement issued by a president at the time he or she signs a bill into law. James Monroe (1817–1825) was the first president to issue such a statement. For many years, signing statements were rare—prior to the presidency of Ronald Reagan, only seventy-five were issued. Most were "rhetorical" in character. They might praise the legislation or the Congress that passed it, or criticize the opposition. On occasion, however, the statements noted constitutional problems with one or more clauses of a bill or provided details as to how the executive branch would interpret legislative language.

Reagan issued a grand total of 249 signing statements. For the first time, each statement was published in the *U.S. Code Congressional and Administrative News,* along with the text of the bill in question. A substantial share of the statements addressed constitutional issues. Reagan staff member Samuel Alito, Jr.—who now sits on the United States Supreme Court—issued a

executive order A presidential order to carry out a policy or policies described in a law passed by Congress.

signing statement A written statement, appended to a bill at the time the president signs it into law, indicating how the president interprets that legislation.

memo in favor of using signing statements to "increase the power of the Executive to shape the law."

SIGNING STATEMENTS UNDER BUSH President George W. Bush took the use of signing statements to an entirely new level. Bush's 161 statements challenged more than 1,100 clauses of federal law—more legal provisions than were challenged by all previous presidents put together.[10] The powers that the statements claimed for the president alarmed some people. One statement rejected Congress's authority to ban torture. Another affirmed that the president could have anyone's mail opened without a warrant.

As a presidential candidate, Barack Obama criticized Bush's use of signing statements and promised to limit his use of them. As president, he has reduced the number of signing statements substantially.

EVOLVING PRESIDENTIAL POWER IN FOREIGN AFFAIRS The precise extent of the president's power in foreign affairs is constantly evolving. The president is commander in chief and chief diplomat, but only Congress has the power to formally declare war, and the Senate must ratify any treaty that the president has negotiated with other nations. Nevertheless, from the beginning, our country has been led by the president in foreign affairs.

George Washington laid the groundwork for our long history of the president's active role in foreign policy. For

> "If one morning I walked on top of the water across the Potomac River, the headline that afternoon would read: 'President Can't Swim.'"
>
> ~ **Lyndon B. Johnson,** Thirty-Sixth President of the United States 1963–1969

example, when war broke out between Britain and France in 1793, Washington chose to disregard a treaty of alliance with France and to pursue a course of strict neutrality. Since that time, on many occasions presidents have taken military actions and made foreign policy without consulting Congress.

Executive Agreements. In foreign affairs, presidential power is enhanced by the ability to make **executive agreements,** which are pacts between the president and other heads of state. Executive agreements do not require Senate approval (even though Congress may refuse to appropriate the necessary money to carry out the agreements), but they have the same legal status as treaties.

Presidents form executive agreements for a wide range of purposes. Some involve routine matters, such as promises of assistance to other countries. Others concern matters of great importance. In 1940, for example, President Franklin Roosevelt formed an important executive agreement with British prime minister Winston Churchill. The agreement provided that the United States would lend American destroyers to Britain to help protect that nation and its shipping during World War II. In return, the British allowed the United States to use military and naval bases on British territories in the Western Hemisphere.

To prevent presidential abuse of the power to make executive agreements, Congress passed a law in 1972

© Jim Watson/Getty Images

President George W. Bush and Secretary of State Condoleezza Rice arrive at the White House. *What are some of the tools a president can use to carry out foreign policy?*

executive agreement A binding international agreement, or pact, that is made between the president and another head of state and that does not require Senate approval.

that requires the president to inform Congress within sixty days of making any executive agreement. The law did not limit the president's power to make executive agreements, however, and they continue to be used far more than treaties in making foreign policy.

Military Actions. As you read in the chapter opening *America at Odds* feature, the U.S. Constitution gives Congress the power to declare war. Consider however, that although Congress has declared war in only five different conflicts during our nation's history,[11] the United States has engaged in more than two hundred activities involving the armed services.

Without a congressional declaration of war, President Truman sent U.S. armed forces to Korea in 1950, thus involving American troops in the conflict between North and South Korea. The United States also entered the Vietnam War (1965–1975) without a declaration of war. President Nixon did not consult Congress when he made the decision to invade Cambodia in 1970. Neither did President Reagan when he sent troops to Lebanon and Grenada in 1983.

No congressional vote was taken before President George H. W. Bush sent troops into Panama in 1989. Bush did, however, obtain congressional approval to use American troops to force Iraq to withdraw from Kuwait in 1991. Without Congress, President Clinton made the decision to send troops to Haiti in 1994 and to Bosnia in 1995, as well as to bomb Iraq in 1998. In 1999, he also decided on his own authority to send U.S. forces under the command of NATO (the North Atlantic Treaty Organization) to bomb Yugoslavia.

President George H.W. Bush often seemed at ease during press conferences. *Why did he order U.S. forces into combat with Iraq in 1991?*

The War Powers Resolution. As commander in chief, the president can respond quickly to a military threat without waiting for congressional action. This power to involve the nation in a war upset many members of Congress as the undeclared war in Vietnam dragged on for years into the 1970s. Criticism of the president's role in the Vietnam conflict led to the passage of the War Powers Resolution of 1973.

The law, which was passed over President Nixon's veto, requires the president to notify Congress within forty-eight hours of deploying troops. It also prevents the president from keeping troops abroad for more than sixty days (or ninety days, if more time is needed for a successful withdrawal). If Congress does not authorize a longer period, the troops must be removed.

The War on Terrorism. President George W. Bush did not obtain a declaration of war from Congress for the war against terrorism that began on September 11, 2001. Instead, Congress passed a joint resolution authorizing the president to use "all necessary and appropriate force against those nations, organizations, or persons he determines planned, authorized, committed, or aided the terrorist attacks that occurred on September 11, 2001."

This resolution was the basis for America's subsequent involvement in Afghanistan. Also, in October 2002, Congress passed a joint resolution authorizing the use of U.S. armed forces against Iraq.

As a consequence of these resolutions, the president was able to invoke certain emergency wartime measures. For example, through executive order the president created military tribunals for trying terrorist suspects. The president also held some American citizens as "enemy combatants," denying them access to their attorneys.

Obama at War. President Obama inherited conflicts in Afghanistan and Iraq, and he was more interested in winding these conflicts down than expanding them. No requests for congressional authority were necessary. In 2011, however, Obama used air power in Libya without congressional authorization.

In 2013, with clear reluctance, Obama asked for authority to bomb the forces of dictator Bashar al-Assad in Syria. The reason was that Assad was using poison gas against his own

> # "As to the presidency, the two happiest days of my life were those of my entrance upon the office and my surrender of it."
>
> ~ **Martin Van Buren,** Eighth president of the United States 1837–1841

people. Assad then agreed to turn over his chemical weapons for destruction. This settlement was fortunate for Obama, in part because it appeared likely that Congress would refuse to give him support for military action.

As described in the chapter-opening *America at Odds* feature, Obama did not request authority to attack the terrorist group ISIS in Iraq and Syria in 2014. (He did ask for the power to arm nonextremist Syrian rebels, but given that such a step required spending money, he had little choice.) Some observers, contemplating Obama's request for a vote over Syria's chemical weapons and his failure to make such a request over Libya and ISIS, thought they saw a pattern. Obama was willing to seek authority for steps that he was not eager to take. For actions on which he was dead-set, he preferred to ignore Congress as much as possible.

Nuclear Weapons.   Since 1945, the president, as commander in chief, has been responsible for the most difficult of all military decisions—if and when to use nuclear weapons. In 1945, Harry Truman made the extraordinary decision to drop atomic bombs on the Japanese cities of Hiroshima and Nagasaki. "The final decision," he said, "on where and when to use the atomic bomb was up to me. Let there be no mistake about it." Today, the president travels at all times with the "football"—the briefcase containing the codes used to launch a nuclear attack.

CRITICAL THINKING

▸ Some observers believe that it is almost impossible for the president to change the nation's policies simply by delivering a speech, no matter how important the topic. Do you think this is true? Why or why not?

12–4 CONGRESSIONAL AND PRESIDENTIAL RELATIONS

> **LO** Describe advantages enjoyed by Congress and by the president in their institutional relationship.

Despite the seemingly immense powers at the president's disposal, the president is limited in what he or she can accomplish, or even attempt. In our system of checks and balances, the president must share some powers with the legislative and judicial branches of government. The president's power is checked not only by these institutions but also by the media, public opinion, and the voters. The founders hoped that this system of shared power would lessen the chance of tyranny.

Some scholars believe the relationship between Congress and the president is the most important one in the American system of government. Congress traditionally has had the upper hand in some areas, primarily in passing legislation. In some other areas, though, particularly in foreign affairs, the president can exert tremendous power that Congress has almost no ability to check.

12–4a Advantage: Congress

Congress has the advantage over the president in the areas of legislative authorization, the regulation of foreign and interstate commerce, and some budgetary matters. Of course, as you have already read, the president today proposes a legislative agenda and a budget to Congress every year. Nonetheless, only Congress has the power to pass the legislation and appropriate the money. The most the president can do constitutionally is veto an entire bill if it contains something that she or he does not like. (As noted, however, recent presidents have frequently used signing statements in an attempt to nullify portions of bills that they did not approve.)

Presidential popularity is a source of power for the president in dealings with Congress. Presidents spend a great deal of time courting public opinion, eyeing the "presidential approval ratings," and meeting with the press. Much of this activity is for the purpose of gaining leverage with Congress. Yet even when the president puts all of his or her persuasive powers to work in achieving a legislative agenda, Congress still retains the ultimate lawmaking authority.

DIVIDED GOVERNMENT   When government is divided—with at least one house of Congress controlled by a different party than the White House—the president can

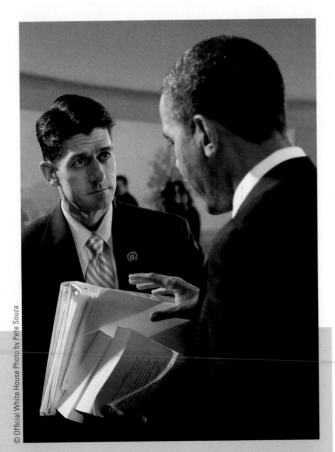

President Obama confers with Representative Paul Ryan (R., Wisc.) about health care. Ryan was the Republican candidate for vice president in 2012. *How much of a chance does Ryan have to be elected president in 2016?*

have difficulty even getting a legislative agenda to the floor for a vote. President Barack Obama faced such a problem in 2011, when the Republicans gained a majority in the House of Representatives. During his first two years as president, Obama had worked with a very cooperative Democrat-led Congress. After the Republicans became the majority party in the House, however, divided government existed again. Indeed, few people in public life could remember a time when partisan hostilities had been so intense.

DIFFERENT CONSTITUENCIES   Congress and the president have different constituencies, and this fact influences their relationship. Members of Congress represent a state or a local district, and this gives them a regional focus. As we discussed in Chapter 11, members of Congress like to have legislative successes of their own to bring home to their constituents—military bases that remain operative, public-works projects that create local jobs, or trade rules that benefit a big local employer. Ideally, the president's focus should be on the nation as a

whole: national defense, homeland security, the national economy. At times, this can put the president at odds even with members of his or her own party in Congress.

Furthermore, members of Congress and the president face different election cycles (every two years in the House, every six years in the Senate, and every four years for the president), and the president is limited to two terms in office. Consequently, the president and Congress sometimes feel a different sense of urgency about implementing legislation. For example, the president often senses the need to demonstrate legislative success during the first year in office, when the excitement over the elections is still fresh in the minds of politicians and the public.

12–4b Advantage: The President

The president has the advantage over Congress in dealing with a national crisis, in setting foreign policy, and in influencing public opinion. In times of crisis, the presidency is arguably the most crucial institution in government because, when necessary, the president can act quickly, speak with one voice, and represent the nation to the world.

Some scholars have argued that recent presidents have abused the powers of the presidency by taking advantage of crises. Others have argued that there is an unwritten "doctrine of necessity" under which presidential powers can and should be expanded during a crisis. When this has happened in the past, however, Congress has always retaken some control when the crisis was over, in a natural process of institutional give-and-take.

THE WAR ON TERRORISM   A problem faced during the George W. Bush administration was that the "war on terrorism" had no obvious end or conclusion. It was not clear when the crisis would be over and the nation could return to normal government relations and procedures. Many supporters of Barack Obama believed that upon election, he would restore civil liberties lost during Bush's war on terrorism. As it turned out, the Obama administration has kept most of Bush's policies in place. (You learned about this issue in greater detail in Chapter 4, in the section "Personal Privacy and National Security.")

EXECUTIVE PRIVILEGE   As you read in Chapter 11, Congress has the authority to investigate and oversee the activities of other branches of government. Nonetheless, both Congress and the public have accepted that a certain degree of secrecy by the executive branch is necessary to protect national security. Some presidents have claimed an inherent executive power to withhold information from, or to refuse to appear before, Congress or the courts. This is called **executive privilege,** and it has been invoked by presidents from the time of George Washington to the present.

ABUSES OF EXECUTIVE PRIVILEGE One of the problems with executive privilege is that it has been used for more purposes than simply to safeguard national security. President Nixon invoked executive privilege in an attempt to avoid handing over taped White House conversations to Congress during the **Watergate scandal.** President Clinton invoked the privilege in an attempt to keep details of his sexual relationship with White House intern Monica Lewinsky a secret.

After the Democrats took control of Congress in 2007 and began to investigate various actions undertaken by the Bush administration, they were frequently blocked in their attempts to obtain information by the claim of executive privilege. For example, during Congress's investigation of the Justice Department's firing of several U.S. attorneys for allegedly political reasons, the Bush administration raised the claim of executive privilege to prevent several people from testifying or submitting requested documents to Congress.

President Nixon with Chinese Prime Minister Zhou Enlai in Beijing in 1972. Nixon's opening to China was a foreign policy success, but his domestic abuses of presidential power led to his resignation in 1974. *What is the mechanism by which Congress can remove a sitting president?*

CRITICAL THINKING

▶ Would we be better off if executive privilege didn't exist, or are there some matters a president must be able to keep private? Discuss.

12–5 THE ORGANIZATION OF THE EXECUTIVE BRANCH

> **LO** Discuss the organization of the executive branch and the role of cabinet members in presidential administrations.

In the early days of this nation, presidents answered their own mail. Only in 1857 did Congress authorize a private secretary for the president, to be paid by the federal government. Even Woodrow Wilson typed most of his correspondence, although by that time several secretaries were assigned to the president. When Franklin Roosevelt became president in 1933, the entire staff consisted of thirty-seven employees. Not until Roosevelt's New Deal and World War II did the presidential staff become a sizable organization.

12–5a The President's Cabinet

The Constitution does not specifically mention presidential assistants and advisers. The Constitution states only that the president "may require the Opinion, in writing, of the principal Officer in each of the executive Departments." Since the time of our first president, however, presidents have had an advisory group, or **cabinet,** to turn to for counsel. Originally, the cabinet consisted of only four officials—the secretaries of state, treasury, and war and the attorney general.

Today, the cabinet includes fourteen department secretaries, the attorney general, and a number of other

executive privilege An inherent executive power claimed by presidents to withhold information from, or to refuse to appear before, Congress or the courts. The president can also accord the privilege to other executive officials.

Watergate scandal A scandal involving an illegal break-in at the Democratic National Committee offices in 1972 by members of President Richard Nixon's reelection campaign staff.

cabinet An advisory group selected by the president to assist with decision making. Traditionally, the cabinet has consisted of the heads of the executive departments and other officers whom the president may choose to appoint.

officials. (See Table 12–2, which follows, for the names of the major executive departments represented in the cabinet.) Additional cabinet members vary from one presidency to the next. Typically, the vice president is a member. President Clinton added ten officials to the cabinet, and George W. Bush added five. Barack Obama added the following members, in addition to the vice president:

▶ The administrator of the Environmental Protection Agency.

▶ The administrator of the Small Business Administration.

▶ The chair of the Council of Economic Advisers.

▶ The director of the Office of Management and Budget.

▶ The United States ambassador to the United Nations.

▶ The United States trade representative.

▶ The White House chief of staff.

USE OF THE CABINET Because the Constitution does not require the president to consult with the cabinet, the use of this body is purely discretionary. Some presidents have relied on the counsel of their cabinets more than others. After a cabinet meeting in which a vote was seven nays against his one aye, President Lincoln supposedly said, "Seven nays and one aye, the ayes have it."[12]

Still other presidents have sought counsel from so-called **kitchen cabinets,** informal groups of unofficial advisers. The term *kitchen cabinet* originated during the presidency of Andrew Jackson, who relied on the counsel of close friends who allegedly met with him in the kitchen of the White House.

In general, presidents usually don't rely heavily on the advice of the formal cabinet. They are aware that department heads are often more responsive to the wishes of their own staffs, to their own political ambitions, or to obtaining resources for their departments than they are to the presidents they serve.

OBAMA'S "CZARS" President Obama's response to the need to seek advice was to centralize the advisory function within the White House Office (discussed below) by appointing a large number of in-house "czars." Each of these White House czars has responsibility for a certain policy area.

kitchen cabinet The name given to a president's unofficial advisers. The term was coined during Andrew Jackson's presidency.

Executive Office of the President (EOP) A group of staff agencies that assist the president in carrying out major duties.

TABLE 12–2 THE MAJOR EXECUTIVE DEPARTMENTS

The heads of all of these departments are members of the president's cabinet.

Department	Year of First Establishment
Department of State	1789
Department of the Treasury	1789
Department of Defense*	1789
Department of Justice (headed by the attorney general)†	1789
Department of the Interior	1849
Department of Agriculture	1889
Department of Commerce‡	1903
Department of Labor‡	1903
Department of Health and Human Services§	1953
Department of Housing and Urban Development	1965
Department of Transportation	1967
Department of Energy	1977
Department of Education	1979
Department of Veterans Affairs	1989
Department of Homeland Security	2002

*Established in 1947 by merging the Department of War, created in 1789, and the Department of the Navy, created in 1798.
†Formerly the Office of the Attorney General; renamed and reorganized in 1870.
‡Formed in 1913 by splitting the Department of Commerce and Labor, which was created in 1903.
§Formerly the Department of Health, Education, and Welfare; renamed when the Department of Education was spun off in 1979.

Critics of the Obama administration believe that the czar system tends to undercut the authority of cabinet members. Congress also loses leverage, because cabinet members must be confirmed by the Senate, whereas czars are responsible only to the president.

12–5b The Executive Office of the President

In 1939, President Franklin Roosevelt set up the **Executive Office of the President (EOP)** to cope with the increased responsibilities brought on by the Great Depression. Since then, the EOP has grown significantly to accommodate the increasingly expansive role played by the national government, including the executive branch, in the nation's economic and social life.

The EOP is made up of the top advisers and assistants who help the president carry out major duties. Over the years, the EOP has changed according to the needs and leadership style of each president. It has become an increasingly influential and important part of the executive branch.

President Barack Obama, Vice President Joe Biden, then Secretary of State Hillary Clinton, and members of the national security team receive an update on the mission against Osama bin Laden in the Situation Room of the White House on May 1, 2011. *What happened to bin Laden?*

Table 12–3, which follows, lists various offices within the EOP as of 2014. Note that the organization of the EOP is subject to change. Presidents have frequently added new bodies to its membership and subtracted others. President Obama has made a number of changes to the EOP's table of organization during his years in office.

THE WHITE HOUSE OFFICE Of all of the executive staff agencies, the **White House Office** has the most direct contact with the president. The White House Office is headed by the **chief of staff,** who advises the president on important matters and directs the opera-

tions of the presidential staff. A number of other top officials, assistants, and special assistants to the president also provide aid in such areas as national security, the economy, and political affairs. The **press secretary** meets with reporters and makes public statements for the president. The counsel to the president serves as the White House lawyer and handles the president's legal matters.

The White House staff also includes speechwriters, researchers, the president's physician, and a correspondence secretary. Altogether, the White House Office has more than four hundred employees.

The White House staff has several duties. First, the staff investigates and analyzes problems that require the president's attention. Staff members who are specialists in certain areas, such as diplomatic relations or foreign trade, gather information for the president and suggest solutions. White House staff members also screen the questions, issues, and problems that people present to the president, so matters that can be handled by other officials do not reach the president's desk.

Additionally, the staff provides public relations support. For example, the press staff handles the president's relations with the White House press corps and schedules news conferences. Finally, the White House staff ensures that the president's initiatives are effectively transmitted to the relevant government personnel. Several staff members are usually assigned to work directly with members of Congress for this purpose.

THE FIRST LADY The White House Office also includes the staff of the president's spouse. First Ladies have at times taken important roles within the White House. For example, Franklin Roosevelt's wife, Eleanor, advocated the rights of women, labor, and African

TABLE 12–3	THE EXECUTIVE OFFICE OF THE PRESIDENT AS OF 2014
Agency	
Council of Economic Advisers	
Council on Environmental Quality	
Executive Residence	
National Security Staff	
Office of Administration	
Office of Management and Budget	
Office of National Drug Control Policy	
Office of Science and Technology Policy	
Office of the U.S. Trade Representative	
Office of the Vice President	
White House Office	

Source: www.whitehouse.gov.

White House Office The personal office of the president. White House Office personnel handle the president's political needs and manage the media, among other duties.

chief of staff The person who directs the operations of the White House Office and advises the president on important matters.

press secretary A member of the White House staff who holds news conferences for reporters and makes public statements for the president.

Americans. As First Lady, Hillary Clinton helped develop an unsuccessful plan for a national health-care system. In 2008, she was a leading contender for the Democratic presidential nomination. Had she won the presidency, Bill Clinton would have become the nation's First Gentleman.

THE OFFICE OF MANAGEMENT AND BUDGET The **Office of Management and Budget (OMB)** was originally the Bureau of the Budget. Under recent presidents, the OMB has become an important and influential unit of the Executive Office of the President. The main function of the OMB is to assist the president in preparing the proposed annual budget, which the president must submit to Congress in January of each year (see Chapter 11 for details).

The federal budget lists the revenues and expenditures expected for the coming year. It indicates which programs the federal government will pay for and how much they will cost. Thus, the budget is an annual statement of the public policies of the United States translated into dollars and cents. Making changes in the budget is a key way for presidents to influence the direction and policies of the federal government.

The president appoints the director of the OMB with the consent of the Senate. The director oversees the OMB's work and argues the administration's positions before Congress. The director also lobbies members of Congress to support the president's budget or to accept key features of it. Once the budget is approved by Congress, the OMB has the responsibility of putting it into practice. The OMB oversees the execution of the budget, checking on federal agencies to ensure that they use funds efficiently.

Beyond its budget duties, the OMB also reviews new bills prepared by the executive branch. It checks all legislative matters to be certain that they agree with the president's own positions.

THE NATIONAL SECURITY COUNCIL The **National Security Council (NSC)** was established in 1947 to manage the defense and foreign policy of the United States. Its members are the president, the vice president, and the secretaries of state and defense. It also includes several informal advisers. The NSC is the president's link to his or her key foreign and military advisers. The president's special assistant for national security affairs heads the NSC staff.

12–5c The Vice Presidency and Presidential Succession

As a rule, presidential nominees choose running mates who balance the ticket or whose appointment rewards or appeases party factions. For example, to balance the ticket geographically, a presidential candidate from the South may solicit a running mate from the West.

In 2008, Republican candidate John McCain chose as his running mate Alaska governor Sarah Palin. Palin shored up McCain's support among cultural conservatives. President Barack Obama picked Senator Joe Biden, who had thirty-five years of experience in Congress. Obama wished to counter detractors who claimed that he was too inexperienced.

In 2012, Republican presidential candidate Mitt Romney chose Representative Paul Ryan of Wisconsin to join his ticket. Ryan helped Romney appeal to the party's conservative wing. Ryan had gained recognition as chair of the House Budget Committee when he authored a series of proposed budgets that won near-universal Republican support.

© Official White House Photo

What powers does Vice President Joe Biden have under the Constitution?

Office of Management and Budget (OMB) An agency in the Executive Office of the President that has the primary duty of assisting the president in preparing and supervising the administration of the federal budget.

National Security Council (NSC) A council that advises the president on domestic and foreign matters concerning the safety and defense of the nation.

President Gerald Ford (right) confers with Vice President Nelson Rockefeller in 1974. For the first time in the history of the United States, neither leader had obtained office by winning a general election. *How did that situation come about?*

The Twenty-Fifth Amendment. The amendment states that when the president believes that he or she is incapable of performing the duties of the office, he or she must inform Congress in writing of this fact. When the president is unable to communicate, a majority of the cabinet, including the vice president, can declare that fact to Congress.

In either case, the vice president then serves as acting president until the president resumes normal duties. If a dispute arises over the return of the president's ability to discharge the normal functions of the presidential office, a two-thirds vote of both chambers of Congress is required if the vice president is to remain acting president. Otherwise, the president resumes these duties.

THE ROLE OF VICE PRESIDENTS For much of our history, the vice president has had almost no responsibilities. Still, the vice president is in a position to become the nation's chief executive should the president die, be impeached and convicted, or resign the presidential office. Nine vice presidents have become president because of the death or resignation of the president.

In recent years, the responsibilities of the vice president have grown immensely. The vice president has become one of the most—if not *the* most—important of the president's advisers. The first modern vice president to act as a major adviser was Walter Mondale, who served under Jimmy Carter. Later, Bill Clinton relied heavily on Vice President Al Gore, who shared many of Clinton's values and beliefs.

Without question, however, the most powerful vice president in American history was Dick Cheney, who served under George W. Bush. The unprecedented delegation of power that Cheney enjoyed would not have been possible without the president's agreement, and Bush clearly approved of it. Vice President Joe Biden has been one of President Barack Obama's most important advisers, but not at the level of Cheney.

PRESIDENTIAL SUCCESSION One of the questions left unanswered by the Constitution was what the vice president should do if the president becomes incapable of carrying out necessary duties while in office. The Twenty-fifth Amendment to the Constitution, ratified in 1967, filled this gap.

Vice-Presidential Vacancies. The Twenty-fifth Amendment also addresses the question of how the president should fill a vacant vice presidency. Section 2 of the amendment states, "Whenever there is a vacancy in the office of the Vice President, the President shall nominate a Vice President who shall take office upon confirmation by a majority vote of both Houses of Congress."

In 1973, Gerald Ford became the first appointed vice president of the United States after Spiro Agnew was forced to resign. One year later, President Richard Nixon resigned, and Ford advanced to the office of president. President Ford named Nelson Rockefeller as his vice president. For the first time in U.S. history, neither the president nor the vice president had been elected to his position.

What if both the president and the vice president die, resign, or are disabled? According to the Succession Act of 1947, the Speaker of the House of Representatives will then act as president on her or his resignation as Speaker and as representative. If the Speaker is unavailable, next in line is the president pro tem of the Senate, followed by the permanent members of the president's cabinet in the order of the creation of their departments (see Table 12–2 earlier in this chapter).

CRITICAL THINKING

▶ Members of the Washington political community often harbor a degree of resentment toward those who work in the White House Office. What might cause these feelings?

AMERICA AT ODDS
The Presidency

The president is the most conspicuous figure in our political system. Everyone has opinions about what the president should do—and in a presidential election year, who the president should be. To an extent not seen in regard to other offices, the public also has a serious interest in the president's personality and character. The president, after all, represents all of us. Americans are at odds over a variety of questions relating to the presidency. These include the following:

- *Should the president try, whenever possible, to compromise with other political players, such as the Congress—or should the president generally stand on principle?*

- *Should the president seek to expand his or her authority so as to deal more effectively with the nation's problems—or should the president try to adhere to a strict constitutional understanding of the powers of the office?*

- *Is it appropriate for the president to rely primarily on staff members within the White House Office when determining policy—or should the president offer the cabinet a substantial policymaking role?*

- *Should voters evaluate presidential candidates primarily on the positions they take on the issues—or are the president's character, personality, and decision-making style more important considerations?*

- *Should the president be the "moral leader" of the country in the sense of basing policies on religious values—or should the president avoid any intermingling of religion and policy?*

Internet Resources

- The White House home page offers links to many sources of information on the presidency. You can access this site at www.whitehouse.gov.

- If you are interested in reading the inaugural addresses of American presidents from George Washington to Barack Obama, go to www.bartleby.com/124.

- If you would like to research documents and academic resources concerning the presidency, a good Internet site to consult is provided by the University of Virginia's Miller Center of Public Affairs at millercenter.org/academic/americanpresident.

- To access material on the various presidential libraries, visit the National Archives site at www.archives.gov/presidential-libraries.

- The Gallup poll lets you follow daily reports about the president's popularity and other topics. Find the Gallup home page at www.gallup.com. Then, under "Gallup Daily" in the rightmost column, click on "Obama Approval."

- In no field is the president more powerful than in foreign policy. If you have an interest in that topic, check out the Foreign Policy Web site at www.foreignpolicy.com.

STUDY TOOLS 12

READY TO STUDY?

- ☐ Review what you've read with the quiz below.
- ☐ Check your answers in Appendix D at the back of the book.
- ☐ For any questions you miss, read the corresponding Learning Outcome section again to prepare for class and your exam.
- ☐ Rip out and study the Chapter in Review card (at the back of the book).

VISIT WWW.CENGAGEBRAIN.COM:

- ☐ Interactive Quizzes
- ☐ Key Term Flashcards or Crossword Puzzles
- ☐ Audio Summaries
- ☐ Simulations, Animated Learning Modules, and Interactive Timelines
- ☐ Videos
- ☐ American Government NewsWatch

FILL-IN

LearningOutcome 12–1

1. The most common previous occupation of U.S. presidents has been _____.

LearningOutcome 12–2

2. The president leads the nation's armed forces in his or her role as _____.

3. In his or her role as _____, the president delivers the traditional State of the Union address and has the power to veto bills passed by Congress.

LearningOutcome 12–3

4. The president has the power to issue executive orders, which are _____.

5. The _____ requires the president to notify Congress within forty-eight hours of deploying troops.

LearningOutcome 12–4

6. Executive privilege is _____.

LearningOutcome 12–5

7. Traditionally, the cabinet has consisted of _____.

8. The Executive Office of the President (EOP) is made up of a number of executive staff agencies, including the _____.

MULTIPLE CHOICE

LearningOutcome 12–1

9. Which of the following is a constitutional requirement for becoming president of the United States?
   a. Must be at least thirty years old.
   b. Must be of sound moral character.
   c. Must be a natural born citizen of the United States.

LearningOutcome 12–2

10. When the president ____, he or she is performing the role of head of state.
    a. attends party fund-raisers
    b. makes executive agreements
    c. receives foreign dignitaries

11. When the president negotiates and signs treaties with other nations, he or she is performing the role of
    a. chief diplomat.
    b. chief executive.
    c. commander in chief.

LearningOutcome 12–3

12. The presidential strategy known as "going public" refers to
    a. using press conferences, public appearances, and televised events to arouse public opinion in favor of certain legislative programs.
    b. publicly acknowledging mistakes or misconduct.
    c. appearing on talk shows.

13. Legislative success for presidents is defined as how often they
    a. got their way on roll-call votes on which they took a clear position.
    b. were able to get presidential legislative proposals introduced in Congress.
    c. were able to veto legislation.

LearningOutcome 12–4

14. The term *divided government* refers to the
    a. cultural and political differences between the red states and the blue states.
    b. case when at least one chamber of Congress is held by a different party than the White House.
    c. separation of powers.

LearningOutcome 12–5

15. If a vacancy occurs in the vice presidency,
    a. there is currently no provision for filling the office.
    b. the Speaker of the House acts as vice president.
    c. a vice president is nominated by the president and confirmed by a majority vote in both chambers of Congress.

13 | The Bureaucracy

© Bill Clark/CQ-Roll Call Group/Getty Images

LEARNING OUTCOMES After reading this chapter, you should be able to:

13-1 Describe the size and functions of the U.S. bureaucracy and the major components of federal spending.

13-2 Discuss the structure and basic components of the federal bureaucracy.

13-3 Describe how the federal civil service was established and how bureaucrats get their jobs.

13-4 Explain how regulatory agencies make rules and how issue networks affect policymaking in government.

13-5 Identify some of the ways in which the government has attempted to curb waste and improve efficiency in the bureaucracy.

After finishing this chapter go to
PAGE 310 for
STUDY TOOLS.

AMERICA AT ODDS

WARNING:
This is not a toy
Unsuitable for children
under 3 years of age
due to small detachable parts.

0-3

© Peter Baxter/Shutterstock

Is Federal Regulation Excessive?

Many people believe that the financial crisis of 2008 and 2009 was caused by inadequate regulation of financial enterprises. As a result, these businesses took on far too much risk. It's not surprising, therefore, that Congress later imposed a large number of new regulations on the financial industry. Compliance will be costly.

In the distant past, there was very little government regulation of American business. Take the health-care industry, for example. A hundred years ago, drugs were not tested before they were put on the market. Physicians were licensed by the states, but that was about it.

Today, regulation is widespread. Estimates of its costs vary dramatically. According to the Office of Management and Budget (OMB), the annual cost of federal regulations lies between $60 billion and $85 billion, with total benefits of $229 billion to $982 billion. Others argue that the OMB's sums are not comprehensive. One study quoted by conservatives puts total costs at $1.75 trillion per year. Liberals do not find this figure credible—it puts the costs at 10 percent of the entire economy. Whatever the true costs are, the question remains: Are current levels of regulation appropriate?

Unbridled Capitalism Is Dead

The law of the capitalist jungle is what got us into the biggest financial crisis since the Great Depression. Investment banking firms created ever-riskier financial assets, which they sold to unsuspecting individuals and even to local governments as solid, gold-plated investments. In the mortgage industry, unscrupulous salespeople who earned big commissions tricked unsuspecting families into buying homes that were too expensive for their modest means. These problems were largely due to an absence of proper regulation.

Even with something as important as the prescription drugs that we take, the government is not giving us enough protection. Recently, despite its staff members' misgivings, the Food and Drug Administration allowed a drug named Avandia to hit the market. That drug turned out to have potential cardiac side effects, and no safety statement on the drug's label warned of them. We need more regulation to protect our lives and our pocketbooks.

Too Much of Anything Is Bad

While no one proposes that all regulation should be eliminated, many believe that the amount of regulation in effect today is too costly relative to the benefits received. We all want safer products, but the Consumer Product Safety Commission now requires that warning labels appear on even common products. A standard ladder has six hundred words of warning pasted on it, including a warning not to place it in front of a swinging door. What are we, idiots? Every toy has a warning that says, "Small parts may cause a choking risk." Parents don't know this?

Studies indicate that virtually no one reads warning labels anymore because the warnings are either too obvious or too long. And besides, what happened to personal responsibility in America? The average American is no longer expected to use common sense about any of her or his purchases or activities. Regulation has its place, but it shouldn't control the entire life of a nation.

Where do you stand?

1. How much do you think you benefit from regulation in our economy? Give some examples.

2. Are there any circumstances under which warning labels on consumer products could help you? Give some examples.

Explore this issue online

- Type "approving drugs quickly" into any search engine. The results will include arguments for and against the FDA's new "Expedited Drug Development Pathway."

- ProcCon.org provides arguments on both sides of many issues, including regulatory questions. The section "Health and Medicine" is especially relevant to regulation.

INTRODUCTION

Did you eat breakfast this morning? If you did, **bureaucrats**—individuals who work in the offices of the government bureaucracy—had a lot to do with that breakfast.

If you had bacon, the meat was inspected by federal agents. If you drank milk, the price was affected by rules and regulations of the Department of Agriculture. If you looked at a cereal box, you saw fine print about fat and vitamins, which was the result of regulations made by several other federal agencies, including the Food and Drug Administration. If you ate leftover pizza for breakfast, state or local inspectors made sure that the kitchen of the pizza eatery was sanitary and safe. Other bureaucrats ensured that the employees who put together (and perhaps delivered) the pizza were protected against discrimination in the workplace.

Government bureaucrats deliver our mail, clean our streets, teach in our public schools, run our national parks, and attempt to ensure the safety of our food and the prescription drugs that we take. Life as we know it would be quite different without the bureaucrats who keep our governments—federal, state, and local—in operation. Still, Americans differ about the positive and negative aspects of various federal bureaucracies, as discussed in the chapter-opening *America at Odds* feature.

13–1 THE NATURE AND SIZE OF THE BUREAUCRACY

LO Describe the size and functions of the U.S. bureaucracy and the major components of federal spending.

Today, the word *bureaucracy* often evokes a negative reaction. For some, it conjures up visions of depersonalized automatons performing chores without any sensitivity toward the needs of those they serve. For others, it is synonymous with government "red tape." A **bureaucracy,** however, is simply a large, complex administrative organization that is structured hierarchically in a pyramid-like fashion.[1] Government bureau-

crats carry out the policies of elected government officials.

The concept of a bureaucracy is not confined to the federal government. Any large organization must have a bureaucracy. In each bureaucracy, everybody (except the head of the bureaucracy) reports to at least one other person. In the federal government, the head of the bureaucracy is the president of the United States, and the bureaucracy is part of the executive branch.[2]

13–1a The Uses of Bureaucracy

A bureaucratic form of organization allows each person to concentrate on her or his area of knowledge and expertise. In your college or university, for example, you do not expect the basketball coach to solve the problems of the finance office. The reason the federal government bureaucracy exists is that Congress, over time, has delegated certain tasks to specialists.

For example, in 1914 Congress passed the Federal Trade Commission Act, which established the Federal Trade Commission to regulate deceptive and unfair trade practices. Those appointed to the commission were specialists in that area. Similarly, Congress passed the Consumer Product Safety Act in 1972, which established the Consumer Product Safety Commission to investigate the safety of consumer products. The commission is one of many federal administrative agencies.

Another key aspect of any bureaucracy is that the power to act resides in the *position* rather than in the *person*. In your college or university, the person who is president now has more or less the same authority as any previous president. Additionally, bureaucracies usually entail *standard operating procedures*—directives on what procedures should be followed in specific circumstances. Bureaucracies normally also have a merit system, meaning that people are hired and promoted on the basis of demonstrated skills and achievements.

13–1b The Growth of Bureaucracy

The federal government that existed in 1789 was small. It had three departments, each with only a few employees: (1) the Department of State (nine employees), (2) the Department of War (two employees), and (3) the Department of the Treasury (thirty-nine employees). By 1798, nine years later, the federal bureaucracy was still quite small. The secretary of state had seven clerks. His total expenditures on stationery and printing amounted to $500, or about $10,250 in 2015 dollars. The Department of War spent, on average, a grand total of $1.4 million each year, or about $28.8 million in 2015 dollars.

bureaucrat An individual who works in a bureaucracy. As generally used, the term refers to a government employee.

bureaucracy A large, complex, hierarchically structured administrative organization that carries out specific functions.

GROWING GOVERNMENT EMPLOYMENT Times have changed. Figure 13–1, which follows, shows the number of government employees at the local, state, and national levels from 1959 to 2014 as a percentage of the total U.S. population. Most growth has been at the state and local levels. All in all, the three levels of government employ about 16 percent of the civilian labor force. Today, more Americans are employed by government (at all three levels) than by the entire manufacturing sector of the U.S. economy.

As you examine Figure 13–1, you will notice a substantial increase in government employment relative to the population from 1959 up to about 1980. During those years, the absolute number of government workers nearly doubled. Government employment has been more stable since 1980, when Republican Ronald Reagan was elected president.

THE IMPACT OF PRESIDENT REAGAN Indeed, during Reagan's first four years in office, government employment fell. Most of this decrease was at the local level. The drop was caused in part by the recession of 1980–1982 and in part by the elimination of revenue shar-

ing. This program had transferred large sums from the federal government to state and especially local governments. The loss of government jobs was made up in Reagan's second term, but the rapid rise in government employment relative to population seen before 1980 did not return.

Recently, government employment has once again dropped, in absolute as well as relative terms. President Obama's 2009 stimulus program, which transferred large sums to local governments, helped stabilize government employment through 2010. By 2014, however, almost 750,000 fewer people worked for the various levels of government. Most of those who lost their jobs had worked at the local level. It is also notable that the United States Postal Service shed almost 200,000 jobs between 2006 and 2014.

13–1c The Costs of Maintaining the Government

The costs of maintaining the government are high and growing. In 1929, government at all levels accounted for about 11 percent of the nation's gross domestic product

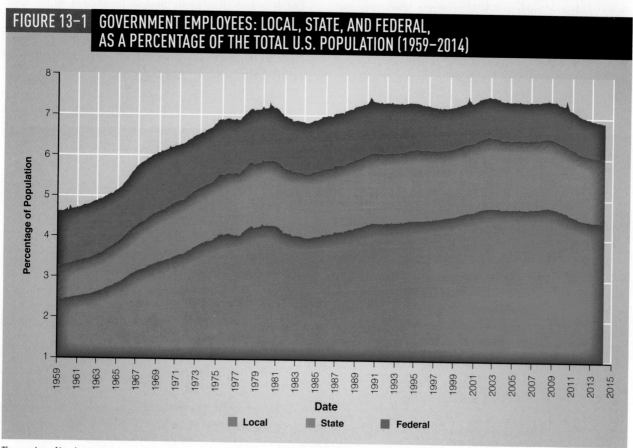

FIGURE 13–1 GOVERNMENT EMPLOYEES: LOCAL, STATE, AND FEDERAL, AS A PERCENTAGE OF THE TOTAL U.S. POPULATION (1959–2014)

The number of local government employees has the greatest effect on total government employment. The brief spikes in 1980, 1990, 2000, and 2010 represent temporary federal census workers.

Source: The Federal Reserve Economic Data (FRED) service of the St. Louis Federal Reserve.

(GDP). Today, that figure is about 36 percent. Average citizens pay a significant portion of their income to federal, state, and local governments. They do this by paying income taxes, sales taxes, property taxes, and many other types of taxes and fees.

The government is costly, to be sure, but it also provides numerous services for Americans. Cutting back on the size of government inevitably means a reduction in those services. The trade-off between government spending and popular services has been central to American politics throughout our history.

13-1d Where Does All the Money Go?

It is worth examining where federal spending actually goes. If you ask people on the street, you will get varied responses—from too much spent on welfare to too much spent on foreign aid. As it turns out, neither of those categories makes up a very large percentage of federal government spending. Consider Figure 13–2, which follows.

SOCIAL SPENDING　As you can see in Figure 13–2, over half of the federal budget consists of various social programs, shown in shades of blue and green. Some of these programs, such as Social Security, Medicare, and unemployment compensation, are funded by payroll taxes and paid out to all qualifying persons, regardless of income. Together, these three programs make up 36 percent of the federal budget.

Other programs, including Medicaid and the Supplemental Nutrition Assistance Program (SNAP, formerly "food stamps"), are available only to low-income individuals. The three "low-income" pie slices make up 24 percent of spending, or more than $900 billion in Fiscal Year 2015. Temporary Assistance for Needy Families (TANF)—traditional cash welfare—is hiding in the "miscellaneous low-income" slice. It accounts for only 0.5 percent of the federal budget—$17 billion. It is completely overshadowed within its pie slice by disability payments, low-income housing programs, and tax refunds.

DEFENSE　Defense spending is a big number—with veterans' benefits, it amounts to almost a quarter of the whole. The wars in Iraq and Afghanistan were obviously expensive. One recent estimate of their cost was $170 billion a year, or 4.6 percent of the total. That is serious money, but it's not really "busting the bank." Furthermore, spending on wars has fallen.

EVERYTHING ELSE　At 7 percent of the total, "everything else" includes a vast range of programs. One example is military and economic foreign aid, at 1.2 percent of the total, or $49 billion. That's a substantial sum, but it is less than many people imagine it to be. One item that bears watching is the interest on the national debt, which currently is about $250 billion per year. Federal budget deficits will cause this figure to grow in future years.

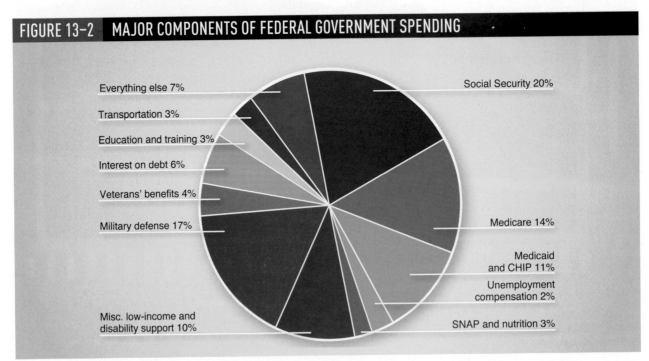

FIGURE 13–2　MAJOR COMPONENTS OF FEDERAL GOVERNMENT SPENDING

Everything else 7%
Transportation 3%
Education and training 3%
Interest on debt 6%
Veterans' benefits 4%
Military defense 17%
Misc. low-income and disability support 10%
Social Security 20%
Medicare 14%
Medicaid and CHIP 11%
Unemployment compensation 2%
SNAP and nutrition 3%

Source: Office of Management and Budget.

13–2 HOW THE FEDERAL BUREAUCRACY IS ORGANIZED

LO Discuss the structure and basic components of the federal bureaucracy.

A complete organization chart of the federal government would cover an entire wall. A simplified version is provided in Figure 13–3, which follows. The executive branch consists of a number of bureaucracies that provide services to Congress, to the federal courts, and to the president directly.

The executive branch of the federal government includes four major types of structures:

▶ **Executive departments.**

▶ **Independent executive agencies.**

▶ **Independent regulatory agencies.**

▶ **Government corporations.**

Each type of structure has its own relationship to the president and its own internal workings.

13–2a The Executive Departments

You were introduced to the various executive departments in Chapter 12, when you read about how the president works with the cabinet and other close advisers. The fifteen executive departments, which are directly accountable to the president, are the major service organizations of the federal government. They are responsible for performing government functions such as training troops (Department of Defense), printing currency (Department of the Treasury), and enforcing federal laws setting minimum safety and health standards for workers (Department of Labor).

Table 13–1, which follows, provides an overview of each of the departments within the executive branch. The table lists a few of the many activities undertaken by each department. Because the president appoints the department heads, they are expected to help carry out the president's policy objectives. Often, they attempt to maximize the president's political successes as well.

Each executive department was created by Congress as the perceived need for it arose, and each department manages a specific policy area. In 2002, for example, Congress created the Department of Homeland Security to deal with terrorism and other threats. The head of each department is known as the secretary, except for the Department of Justice, which is headed by the attorney general. Each department head is appointed by the president and confirmed by the Senate.

13–2b A Typical Departmental Structure

Each cabinet department consists of the department's top administrators (the secretary of the department, deputy secretary, undersecretaries, and the like), plus a number of agencies. For example, the National Park Service is an agency within the Department of the Interior. The Drug Enforcement Administration is an agency within the Department of Justice.

Although there are organizational differences among the departments, each department generally follows a typical bureaucratic structure. The Department of Agriculture provides a model for how an executive department is organized (see Figure 13–4, which follows).

One aspect of the secretary of agriculture's job is to carry out the president's agricultural policies. Another aspect is to promote and protect the department. The secretary spends time ensuring that Congress allocates enough money for the department to work effectively. The secretary also makes sure that constituents, or the people the department serves—farmers and major agricultural corporations—are happy. In general, the secretary tries to maintain or improve the status of the department with respect to all of the other departments and units of the federal bureaucracy.

The secretary of agriculture is assisted by a deputy secretary and several assistant secretaries and undersecretaries, all of whom are nominated by the president and put into office with Senate approval. The secretary and assistant secretaries have staffs that help with all sorts of jobs, such as hiring new people and generating positive public relations for the Department of Agriculture.

13–2c Independent Executive Agencies

Independent executive agencies are federal bureaucratic organizations that have a single function. They are independent in the sense that they are not

independent executive agency A federal agency that is not located within a cabinet department.

FIGURE 13-3 THE ORGANIZATION OF THE FEDERAL GOVERNMENT

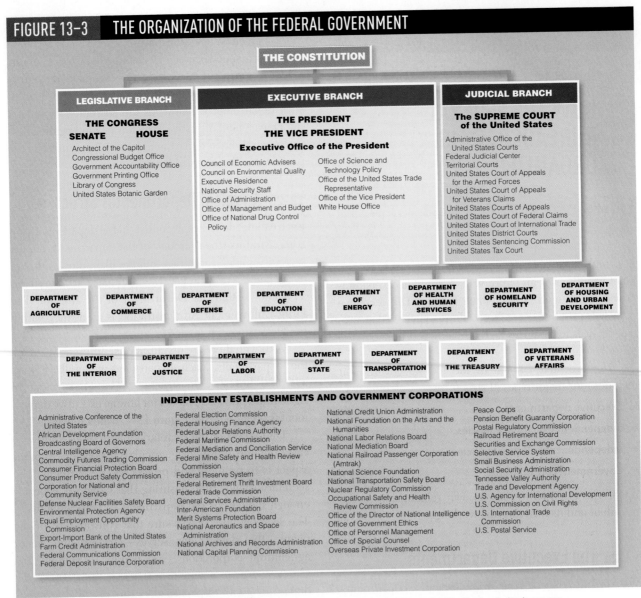

THE CONSTITUTION

LEGISLATIVE BRANCH

THE CONGRESS
SENATE   HOUSE

Architect of the Capitol
Congressional Budget Office
Government Accountability Office
Government Printing Office
Library of Congress
United States Botanic Garden

EXECUTIVE BRANCH

THE PRESIDENT
THE VICE PRESIDENT

Executive Office of the President

Council of Economic Advisers
Council on Environmental Quality
Executive Residence
National Security Staff
Office of Administration
Office of Management and Budget
Office of National Drug Control
  Policy

Office of Science and
  Technology Policy
Office of the United States Trade
  Representative
Office of the Vice President
White House Office

JUDICIAL BRANCH

The SUPREME COURT
of the United States

Administrative Office of the
  United States Courts
Federal Judicial Center
Territorial Courts
United States Court of Appeals
  for the Armed Forces
United States Court of Appeals
  for Veterans Claims
United States Courts of Appeals
United States Court of Federal Claims
United States Court of International Trade
United States District Courts
United States Sentencing Commission
United States Tax Court

DEPARTMENT OF AGRICULTURE | DEPARTMENT OF COMMERCE | DEPARTMENT OF DEFENSE | DEPARTMENT OF EDUCATION | DEPARTMENT OF ENERGY | DEPARTMENT OF HEALTH AND HUMAN SERVICES | DEPARTMENT OF HOMELAND SECURITY | DEPARTMENT OF HOUSING AND URBAN DEVELOPMENT

DEPARTMENT OF THE INTERIOR | DEPARTMENT OF JUSTICE | DEPARTMENT OF LABOR | DEPARTMENT OF STATE | DEPARTMENT OF TRANSPORTATION | DEPARTMENT OF THE TREASURY | DEPARTMENT OF VETERANS AFFAIRS

INDEPENDENT ESTABLISHMENTS AND GOVERNMENT CORPORATIONS

Administrative Conference of the
  United States
African Development Foundation
Broadcasting Board of Governors
Central Intelligence Agency
Commodity Futures Trading Commission
Consumer Financial Protection Board
Consumer Product Safety Commission
Corporation for National and
  Community Service
Defense Nuclear Facilities Safety Board
Environmental Protection Agency
Equal Employment Opportunity
  Commission
Export-Import Bank of the United States
Farm Credit Administration
Federal Communications Commission
Federal Deposit Insurance Corporation

Federal Election Commission
Federal Housing Finance Agency
Federal Labor Relations Authority
Federal Maritime Commission
Federal Mediation and Conciliation Service
Federal Mine Safety and Health Review
  Commission
Federal Reserve System
Federal Retirement Thrift Investment Board
Federal Trade Commission
General Services Administration
Inter-American Foundation
Merit Systems Protection Board
National Aeronautics and Space
  Administration
National Archives and Records Administration
National Capital Planning Commission

National Credit Union Administration
National Foundation on the Arts and the
  Humanities
National Labor Relations Board
National Mediation Board
National Railroad Passenger Corporation
  (Amtrak)
National Science Foundation
National Transportation Safety Board
Nuclear Regulatory Commission
Occupational Safety and Health
  Review Commission
Office of the Director of National Intelligence
Office of Government Ethics
Office of Personnel Management
Office of Special Counsel
Overseas Private Investment Corporation

Peace Corps
Pension Benefit Guaranty Corporation
Postal Regulatory Commission
Railroad Retirement Board
Securities and Exchange Commission
Selective Service System
Small Business Administration
Social Security Administration
Tennessee Valley Authority
Trade and Development Agency
U.S. Agency for International Development
U.S. Commission on Civil Rights
U.S. International Trade
  Commission
U.S. Postal Service

Sources: *United States Government Manual 2014* (National Archives and Records Administration, Office of the Federal Register) and whitehouse.gov.

located within a cabinet department. Rather, independent executive agency heads report directly to the president. A new federal independent executive agency can be created only through cooperation between the president and Congress.

THE CREATION OF INDEPENDENT AGENCIES

Prior to the twentieth century, the federal government did almost all of its work through the executive departments. In the twentieth century, in contrast, presidents began to ask for certain executive agencies to be kept separate, or

partisan politics Political actions or decisions that benefit a particular party.

independent, from existing departments. Today, there are more than two hundred independent executive agencies.

THE DANGER OF PARTISAN POLITICS Sometimes, agencies are kept independent because of the sensitive nature of their functions. But at other times, Congress creates independent agencies to protect them from **partisan politics**—politics in support of a particular party. The U.S. Commission on Civil Rights, which was created in 1957, is a case in point. Congress wanted to protect the work of the commission from the influences not only of Congress's own political interests but also of the president.

The Central Intelligence Agency (CIA), which was formed in 1947, is another good example. Both Congress and the president know that the intelligence activities

TABLE 13-1 EXECUTIVE DEPARTMENTS

Department (Year of Original Establishment)	Principal Duties	Selected Subagencies
State (1789)	Negotiates treaties; develops our foreign policy; protects citizens abroad.	Bureau of Consular Affairs (passports).
Treasury (1789)	Pays all federal bills; borrows money; collects federal taxes; mints coins and prints paper currency; supervises national banks.	Internal Revenue Service; U.S. Mint.
Defense (1789)*	Manages the armed forces (Army, Navy, Air Force, Marines); operates military bases.	National Security Agency; Departments of the Air Force, Navy, Army; Defense Intelligence Agency; the service academies.
Justice (1789)†	Furnishes legal advice to the president; enforces federal criminal laws; supervises the federal corrections system (prisons).	Federal Bureau of Investigation; Drug Enforcement Administration; Bureau of Prisons; U.S. Marshals Service.
Interior (1849)	Supervises federally owned lands and parks; operates federal hydroelectric power facilities; supervises Native American affairs.	U.S. Fish and Wildlife Service; National Park Service; Bureau of Indian Affairs; Bureau of Land Management.
Agriculture (1889)	Provides assistance to farmers and ranchers; conducts research to improve agriculture; works to protect forests.	Agricultural Research Service; Food Safety and Inspection Service; Federal Crop Insurance Corporation; Forest Service.
Commerce (1903)‡	Grants patents and trademarks; conducts national census; monitors the weather; protects the interests of businesses.	Bureau of the Census; Bureau of Economic Analysis; Patent and Trademark Office; National Oceanic and Atmospheric Administration.
Labor (1903)‡	Administers federal labor laws; promotes the interests of workers.	Occupational Safety and Health Administration; Bureau of Labor Statistics; Wage and Hour Division.
Health and Human Services (1953)§	Promotes public health; enforces pure food and drug laws; sponsors health-related research.	Food and Drug Administration; Centers for Disease Control and Prevention; National Institutes of Health; Centers for Medicare and Medicaid Services.
Housing and Urban Development (1965)	Deals with the nation's housing needs; develops and rehabilitates urban communities; oversees resale of mortgages.	Government National Mortgage Association; Office of Fair Housing and Equal Opportunity.
Transportation (1967)	Finances improvements in mass transit; develops and administers programs for highways, railroads, and aviation.	Federal Aviation Administration; Federal Highway Administration; National Highway Traffic Safety Administration.
Energy (1977)	Promotes the conservation of energy and resources; analyzes energy data; conducts research and development.	Office of Civilian Radioactive Waste Management; National Nuclear Security Administration.
Education (1979)	Coordinates federal programs and policies for education; administers aid to education; promotes educational research.	Office of Special Education and Rehabilitation Services; Office of Elementary and Secondary Education; Office of Postsecondary Education.
Veterans Affairs (1989)	Promotes the welfare of veterans of the U.S. armed forces.	Veterans Health Administration; Veterans Benefits Administration.
Homeland Security (2002)	Works to prevent terrorist attacks within the United States, control America's borders, and minimize the damage from potential attacks and natural disasters.	U.S. Customs and Border Protection; U.S. Bureau of Citizenship and Immigration Services; U.S. Coast Guard; Secret Service; Federal Emergency Management Agency.

*Established in 1947 by merging the Department of War, created in 1789, and the Department of the Navy, created in 1798.
†Formerly the Office of the Attorney General; renamed and reorganized in 1870.
‡Formed in 1913 by splitting the Department of Commerce and Labor, which was created in 1903.
§Formerly the Department of Health, Education, and Welfare; renamed when the Department of Education was spun off in 1979.

FIGURE 13-4 THE ORGANIZATION OF THE DEPARTMENT OF AGRICULTURE

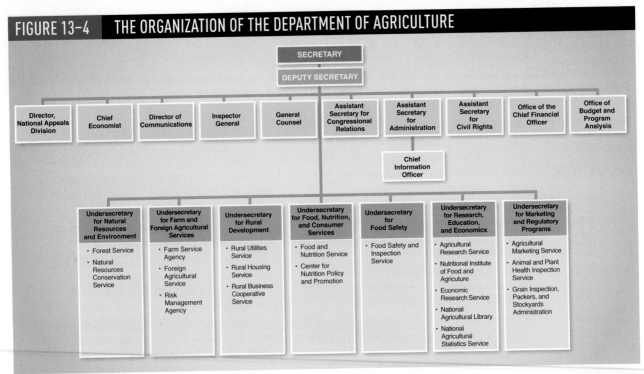

Source: *United States Government Manual 2014* (National Archives and Records Administration, Office of the Federal Register).

of the CIA could be abused if it were not independent. Finally, the General Services Administration (GSA) was created as an independent executive agency in 1949 to provide services and office space for most federal agencies. To serve all parts of the government, the GSA has to be an independent agency.

Among the more than two hundred independent executive agencies, a few stand out in importance either because of the mission they were established to accomplish or because of their large size. We list selected independent executive agencies in Table 13–2, which follows.

13–2d Independent Regulatory Agencies

An **independent regulatory agency** is responsible for a specific type of public policy. Its function is to create and implement rules that regulate private activity and protect the public interest in a particular sector of the economy.

independent regulatory agency A federal organization that is responsible for creating and implementing rules that regulate private activity and protect the public interest in a particular sector of the economy.

government corporation An agency of the government that is run as a business enterprise. Such agencies engage primarily in commercial activities, produce revenues, and require greater flexibility than most government agencies have.

One of the earliest independent regulatory agencies was the Interstate Commerce Commission (ICC), established in 1887. (This agency was abolished in 1995.) After the ICC was formed, other agencies were created to regulate aviation (the Civil Aeronautics Board, or CAB, which was abolished in 1985), communications (the Federal Communications Commission, or FCC), the stock market (the Securities and Exchange Commission, or SEC), and many other areas of business. Table 13–3, which follows, lists some major independent regulatory agencies.

13–2e Government Corporations

Another form of federal bureaucratic organization is the **government corporation,** a business that is owned by the government. Government corporations are not exactly like corporations in which you buy stock and become a shareholder. The U.S. Postal Service (USPS) is a government corporation, for example, but it does not sell shares.

Government corporations are like private corporations in that they provide a service that could be handled by the private sector. They are also like private corporations in that they charge for their services, though sometimes they charge less than private-sector corporations do for similar services. Table 13–4, which follows, lists selected government corporations.

TABLE 13–2 SELECTED INDEPENDENT EXECUTIVE AGENCIES

Name	Date Formed	Principal Duties
Central Intelligence Agency (CIA)	1947	Gathers and analyzes political and military information about foreign countries; conducts covert operations outside the United States.
General Services Administration (GSA)	1949	Purchases and manages property of the federal government; oversees federal government spending projects; discovers overcharges in government programs.
Small Business Administration (SBA)	1953	Promotes the interests of small businesses; provides low-cost loans to small businesses.
National Aeronautics and Space Administration (NASA)	1958	Is responsible for the U.S. space program, including building, testing, and operating space vehicles.
Environmental Protection Agency (EPA)	1970	Undertakes programs aimed at reducing air and water pollution; works with state and local agencies to fight environmental hazards.
Social Security Administration (SSA)*	1994	Manages the government's Social Security programs, including Retirement and Survivors Insurance, Disability Insurance, and Supplemental Security Income.

*Separated from the Department of Health and Human Services in 1994; originally established in 1946.

FACING LOSSES   When a private business fails to make a profit, its shareholders have a problem. The value of the company may drop, in some instances to zero. If a small business loses money, its owners must either raise more capital or shut down the firm. If a government corporation runs at a loss, taxpayers may be forced to foot the bill.

The U.S. Postal Service is an example of this problem. In recent years, as Americans have increasingly relied on the Internet for communications, the volume of first-class mail had dropped considerably. As a result, the USPS has been losing money. (This in spite of the fact that parcel deliveries have gone up, also because of the Internet—specifically, as a result of online shop-

ping.) Losses in 2012 amounted to $16 billion. In August 2012, the service defaulted on a monthly $5.5 billion payment due to the U.S. Treasury to finance retirees' health-care expenses. It has defaulted on this payment every year since. The USPS has cut costs dramatically, spending $4 billion less in 2013 than it did in 2012. Still, it lost $5 billion in 2013. In the first three quarters of 2014, it lost $4.25 billion. Some observers claim that the service's real problem is that Congress has forced it to pre-fund retiree benefits in a way that no other business or government agency must do.

To solve the problem permanently, the USPS proposed to lay off additional employees, close rural post

TABLE 13–3 SELECTED INDEPENDENT REGULATORY AGENCIES

Name	Date Formed	Principal Duties
Federal Reserve System (Fed)	1913	Determines policy on interest rates, credit availability, and the money supply.
Federal Trade Commission (FTC)	1914	Works to prevent businesses from engaging in unfair trade practices and forming business monopolies.
Securities and Exchange Commission (SEC)	1934	Regulates the nation's stock exchanges; requires financial disclosure by companies that wish to sell stocks and bonds to the public.
Federal Communications Commission (FCC)	1934	Regulates interstate and international communications by radio, television, wire, satellite, and cable.
National Labor Relations Board (NLRB)	1935	Protects employees' rights to join unions and to bargain collectively with employers; attempts to prevent unfair labor practices by both employers and unions.
Equal Employment Opportunity Commission (EEOC)	1964	Works to eliminate discrimination that is based on religion, gender, race, color, national origin, age, or disability; examines claims of discrimination.

TABLE 13-4 SELECTED GOVERNMENT CORPORATIONS

Name	Date Formed	Principal Duties
Tennessee Valley Authority (TVA)	1933	Operates a Tennessee River control system and generates power for a seven-state region; controls floods and promotes the navigability of the Tennessee River.
Federal Deposit Insurance Corporation (FDIC)	1933	Insures individuals' bank deposits up to $250,000 and oversees the business activities of banks.
National Railroad Passenger Corporation (Amtrak)	1970	Provides a national and intercity rail passenger service network; controls more than 23,000 miles of track with about 505 stations.
U.S. Postal Service (formed from the old U.S. Post Office department—the Post Office itself is older than the Constitution)	1971	Delivers mail throughout the United States and its territories. Is the largest government corporation.

offices, reduce pension benefits, and even end Saturday delivery. Many of these steps require congressional approval, which was not forthcoming. The alternative would be direct federal subsidies to the service, which has been self-supporting since the early 1980s.

INTERMEDIATE FORMS OF ORGANIZATION A number of intermediate forms of organization exist that fall between a government corporation and a private one. In some circumstances, the government can take control of a private corporation. When a company goes bankrupt, for example, it is subject to the supervision of a federal judge until it exits from bankruptcy or is liquidated. The government can also purchase stock in a private corporation. The government used this technique to funnel funds into major banks during the financial crisis that began in September 2008. In addition, the government can set up a corporation and sell stock to the public.

The Federal Home Loan Mortgage Corporation (Freddie Mac) and the Federal National Mortgage Association (Fannie Mae) are examples of stockholder-owned government-sponsored enterprises. Fannie Mae (founded in 1938) and Freddie Mac (created in 1970) buy, resell, and guarantee home mortgages. In September 2008, the government placed the two businesses into a conservatorship—effectively a bankruptcy overseen by the Federal Housing Finance Agency instead of a federal judge. The government also took an 80 percent share of the stock of each firm. Fannie Mae and Freddie Mac became examples of almost every possible way that the government can intervene in a private company.

civil service Nonmilitary government employees.

CRITICAL THINKING

▶ Some people have advocated selling off government corporations, such as the U.S. Postal Service, and turning them into truly private enterprises. Would it be a good idea to "privatize" the U.S. Postal Service? Why or why not?

13-3 HOW BUREAUCRATS GET THEIR JOBS

LO Describe how the federal civil service was established and how bureaucrats get their jobs.

As already noted, federal bureaucrats holding top-level positions are appointed by the president and confirmed by the Senate. These bureaucrats include department and agency heads, their deputy and assistant secretaries, and the like. The list of positions that are filled by appointments is published after each presidential election in a document called *Policy and Supporting Positions*. The volume is more commonly known as the *Plum Book*, because the eight thousand jobs it summarizes are known as "political plums." Normally, these jobs go to those who supported the winning presidential candidate.

13-3a The Civil Service

The rank-and-file bureaucrats—the rest of the federal bureaucracy—are part of the **civil service** (nonmilitary employees of the government). They obtain their jobs through the Office of Personnel Management (OPM), an agency established by the Civil Service Reform Act of 1978. The OPM recruits, interviews, and tests potential government workers and determines who should be hired. The OPM makes recommendations to individual agencies as to which

A U.S. Postal Service letter carrier. *How do postal employees get their jobs?*

persons meet relevant standards (typically, the top three applicants for a position), and the agencies then generally decide which of the recommended individuals they will hire.

The 1978 act also created the Merit Systems Protection Board (MSPB) to oversee promotions, employees' rights, and other employment matters. The MSPB evaluates charges of wrongdoing, hears employee appeals from agency decisions, and can order corrective action against agencies and employees.

13–3b Origins of the Merit System

The idea that the civil service should be based on a merit system dates back more than a century. The Civil Service Reform Act of 1883 established the principle of government employment on the basis of merit through open, competitive examinations.

Initially, only about 10 percent of federal employees were covered by the merit system. Today, more than 90 percent of the federal civil service is recruited on the basis of merit. Are public employees paid too much? For a discussion of this question, see this chapter's *Join the Debate* feature, which follows.

CRITICAL THINKING

▶ When most private companies hire new employees, they don't use systems similar to those of the civil service. Why is this so?

13–4 REGULATORY AGENCIES: ARE THEY THE FOURTH BRANCH OF GOVERNMENT?

LO Explain how regulatory agencies make rules and how issue networks affect policymaking in government.

In Chapter 2, we considered the system of checks and balances among the three branches of the U.S. government—executive, legislative, and judicial. Recent history, however, shows that it may be time to regard the regulatory agencies as a fourth branch of the government. Although the U.S. Constitution does not mention regulatory agencies, these agencies can and do make **legislative rules** that are as legally binding as laws passed by Congress. With such powers, regulatory agencies have an influence that rivals that of the president, Congress, and the courts. Indeed, most Americans do not realize how much of our "law" is created by regulatory agencies.

Regulatory agencies have been on the American political scene since the nineteenth century, but their golden age came during the regulatory explosion of the 1960s and 1970s. Congress itself could not have overseen the actual implementation of all of the laws that it was enacting at that time to control pollution and deal with other social problems. It therefore chose (and still chooses) to delegate to administrative agencies the tasks involved in implementing its laws. By delegating some of its authority to an administrative agency, Congress can indirectly monitor a particular area in which it has passed legislation without becoming bogged down in the details relating to the enforcement of that legislation—details that are often best left to specialists.

13–4a Agency Creation

To create a federal administrative agency, Congress passes **enabling legislation,** which specifies the name, purpose, composition, and powers of the agency being created.

AN EXAMPLE: THE FTC The Federal Trade Commission (FTC), for example, was created in 1914 by the Federal Trade Commission Act, as mentioned earlier.

legislative rule An administrative agency rule that carries the same weight as a statute enacted by a legislature.

enabling legislation A law enacted by a legislature to establish an administrative agency. Enabling legislation normally specifies the name, purpose, composition, and powers of the agency being created.

Join the Debate

Are Government Workers Paid Too Much?

Popular beliefs about the pay of government workers vary dramatically. Many people believe that only individuals working in private business can hope to receive large paychecks. Others, however, see government workers as an elite group whose members enjoy secure and high-paid jobs, unlike average American workers who are competing in the global economy.

Are government workers paid too much? That can be a difficult question to answer. Those arguing about this issue do not even agree on how public sector pay compares with pay in the private sector.

Yes, They're Overpaid

Conservatives who believe that government workers are a new elite point to generous retirement benefits. Government workers typically have "defined benefit" plans that guarantee their retirement income. Private-sector employees who are lucky enough to have any kind of pension now generally have "defined contribution" plans under which benefits rise and fall with the stock market.

Government wages aren't bad, either. An article by two U.S. Bureau of Labor Statistics (BLS) economists found that, on average, workers in state government have total compensation 3 to 10 percent greater than workers in the private sector, while in local government the gap is 10 to 19 percent.[3] A 2012 study showed federal government workers earning an average of $123,049 in wages and benefits, about twice the $61,051 in total compensation for the average private-sector worker. In fairness, FactCheck.org determined that due to an error, the federal pay number should have been about $113,000.[4] That's still a lot. It's not fair that government workers get a better deal than the rest of us.

No, They're Not

Other studies yield different results. A paper by a Boston College team concluded that state and local workers are paid 9.5 percent less than comparable workers in the private sector, although generous benefits reduce the gap to 4 percent.[5] It's worth remembering that many government workers don't do the same kind of work as employees in the private sector. On average, federal workers are much better educated and more likely to be employed in jobs that are also well paid in the private sector. At the local level, for example, teachers and police officers need to be well educated. At the state level, the same is true for college professors and judges, among others. Most teachers could make more money if they did something else.

At the federal level, the real point may not be that pay is high, but that pay scales are more egalitarian than in private business. The Congressional Budget Office has found that federal workers with only a high-school education are paid 36 percent more than in the private sector. Employees with professional degrees, however, earn 18 percent less.[6]

 CRITICAL ANALYSIS ── Is it important for government to try to attract high-quality employees? Why or why not?

The act prohibits unfair and deceptive trade practices. The act also describes the procedures that the agency must follow to charge persons or organizations with violations of the act, and it provides for judicial review of agency orders.

Other portions of the act grant the agency powers to "make rules and regulations for the purpose of carrying out the Act," to conduct investigations of business practices, to obtain reports on business practices from interstate corporations, to investigate possible violations of federal antitrust statutes, to publish findings of its investigations, and to recommend new legislation.

Finally, the act empowers the FTC to hold trial-like hearings and to **adjudicate** (formally resolve) certain kinds of disputes that involve FTC regulations or federal antitrust laws. When adjudication takes place, within the FTC or any other regulatory agency, an administrative law judge (ALJ) conducts the hearing and, after weighing the evidence presented, issues an *order*. Unless it is overturned on appeal, the ALJ's order becomes final.

adjudicate To render a judicial decision. In administrative law, it is the process in which an administrative law judge hears and decides issues that arise when an agency charges a person or firm with violating a law or regulation enforced by the agency.

THE POWER OF REGULATORY AGENCIES Enabling legislation makes the regulatory agency a potent organization. For example, the Securities and Exchange Commission (SEC) imposes rules regarding the disclosures a company must make to those who purchase its new stock. Under its enforcement authority, the SEC also investigates and prosecutes alleged violations of these regulations. Finally, SEC judges decide whether its rules have been violated and, if so, what punishment should be imposed on the offender (although the judgment may be appealed to a federal court).

A young farmer in Colorado. *What interest groups represent her?*

13-4b Rulemaking

A major function of a regulatory agency is **rulemaking**—the formulation of new regulations. The power that an agency has to make rules is conferred on it by Congress in the agency's enabling legislation.

For example, the Occupational Safety and Health Administration (OSHA) was authorized by the Occupational Safety and Health Act of 1970 to develop and issue rules governing safety in the workplace. Under this authority, OSHA has issued various safety standards, including rules to prevent the spread of certain diseases, such as acquired immune deficiency syndrome (AIDS). The rules specify various standards—on how contaminated instruments should be handled, for instance—with which health-care workers must comply.

REQUIREMENTS FOR MAKING RULES Agencies cannot just make a rule whenever they wish. Rather, they must follow certain procedural requirements, particularly those set forth in the Administrative Procedure Act of 1946. Agencies must also make sure that their rules are based on substantial evidence and are not "arbitrary and capricious." Therefore, before proposing a new rule, an agency may engage in extensive investigation to obtain data on the problem to be addressed by the rule. Based on this information, the agency may undertake a cost-benefit analysis of a new rule to determine whether its benefits outweigh its costs.

A COST-BENEFIT ANALYSIS As an example of cost-benefit analysis in rulemaking, consider the Clean Air Fine Particle Implementation Rule, issued by the Environmental Protection Agency (EPA) in 2007. The EPA estimated the costs of the regulation as $7.3 billion per year, with benefits ranging from $19 billion to $167 billion per year. The benefits largely consist of reductions in health-care costs and premature deaths—and, as these figures suggest, such calculations can be highly uncertain. Does the United States suffer from excessive regulation, as some have claimed? We examined that question in the chapter-opening *America at Odds* feature. An additional question is whether state and local regulations may be even more burdensome than federal ones. We look at that issue in the *Perception versus Reality* feature, which follows.

13-4c Policymaking

Bureaucrats in federal agencies are expected to exhibit **neutral competency,** which means that they are supposed to apply their technical skills to their jobs without regard to political issues. In principle, they should not be swayed by the thought of personal or political gain. In reality, each independent agency and each executive department is interested in its own survival and expansion. All agencies and departments wish to retain or expand their functions and staffs. To do this, they must gain the goodwill of both the White House and Congress.

SUPPORT FROM CONGRESS While the administrative agencies of the federal government are prohibited from directly lobbying Congress, departments and agencies have developed techniques to help them gain congressional support. Each organization maintains a

rulemaking The process undertaken by an administrative agency when formally proposing, evaluating, and adopting a new regulation.

neutral competency The application of technical skills to jobs without regard to political issues.

Perception vs. Reality

State and Local Regulations Aren't a Problem

Our government has certainly grown in size since World War II. Many Americans complain about "big government." These people contend that government does too much. Taxes are too high. Regulations take away our freedom. The "government" in question is the one in Washington, D.C.

The Perception

Big government is the problem, and big government means the federal government. Government closest to the people governs best. Therefore, state and local governments should have more power, and the federal government should have less.

The Reality

In recent years, more and more commentators have begun arguing that regulations imposed by state and local governments are even more costly than the ones imposed by the feds. Consider housing policies. The zoning regulations that control hous-ing construction are almost entirely local. Typically, zoning restricts development to ensure low population densities in our major urban areas. City dwellers want to keep out new high rises. Suburbanites want to stop the construction of townhouses and apartment buildings. As a result, cities with highly productive industries, such as Boston, New York, Los Angeles, San Francisco, and Seattle, don't have enough housing for all the people who would like to live there.

The law of supply and demand takes its course: the cost of the housing that does exist rises astronomically. Americans willing to move in search of economic opportunity are priced out. Instead, they go to places where the cost of housing is tolerable—places such as Houston, which has no zoning code. But jobs don't pay as well in Houston as they do in San Francisco. The national cost of excessive resi-dential zoning may run into hundreds of billions of dollars.

As another example, look at state (and sometimes local) occupational licensing requirements. Of course, it's generally agreed that not everyone who wants to should be a surgeon or a lawyer. We need to be sure that people who handle matters of life and death know what they are doing. But do we really need to license interior designers, as is done in Florida? Do barbers really have to be licensed? Should dental hygienists be required to work for dentists, who then get a cut of their income? Some 29 percent of American workers need a state-issued license to do their jobs legally. Excessive licensing not only makes the services we buy more expensive, but also restricts job opportunities. These restrictions simply serve the interests of those already in particular trades by reducing the number of competitors.

BLOG ON *New York Magazine* columnist Jonathan Chait is best known for his aggressive criticism of conservatives. In "The Worst Governments in America Are Local," however, he takes on both political parties. Find this article by searching on "chait worst governments."

---

congressional information office, which specializes in helping members of Congress by supplying any requested information and solving casework problems.

For example, if a member of the House of Representatives receives a complaint from a constituent that his Social Security payments are not arriving on time, that member of Congress may go to the Social Security Administration and ask that something be done.

Typically, requests from members of Congress receive immediate attention.

IRON TRIANGLES   Analysts have determined that one way to understand the bureaucracy's role in policy-making is to examine the **iron triangle,** which is a three-way alliance among legislators (members of Congress), bureaucrats, and interest groups. Presumably, the laws that are passed and the policies that are established benefit the interests of all three corners of the iron triangle, as shown in Figure 13–5, which follows. Iron triangles are well established in almost every part of the bureaucracy.

iron triangle   A three-way alliance among legislators, bureaucrats, and interest groups to make or preserve policies that benefit their respective interests.

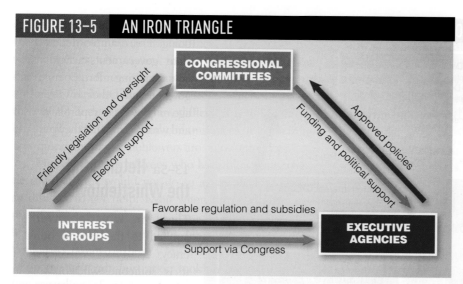

FIGURE 13–5   AN IRON TRIANGLE

CONGRESSIONAL COMMITTEES

Friendly legislation and oversight

Electoral support

Funding and political support

Approved policies

INTEREST GROUPS

Favorable regulation and subsidies

Support via Congress

EXECUTIVE AGENCIES

have been around a long time and have their own ideas about what is appropriate for the Agriculture Department's budget. They carefully scrutinize the ideas of the president and the secretary of agriculture.

The Influence of Interest Groups. The various interest groups—including producers of farm chemicals and farm machinery, agricultural cooperatives, grain dealers, and exporters—have vested interests in what the Department of Agriculture does and in what Congress lets the department do. Those interests are well represented by the lobbyists who crowd the halls of Congress. Many lobbyists have been working for agricultural interest groups for decades. They know the congressional committee members and Agriculture Department staff very well and meet with them routinely.

ISSUE NETWORKS The iron triangle relationship does not apply to all policy domains. When making policy decisions on environmental and welfare issues, for example, many members of Congress and agency officials rely heavily on "experts." Legislators and agency heads tend to depend on their staff members for specialized knowledge of rules, regulations, and legislation.

These experts have frequently served variously as interest group lobbyists and as public-sector staff members during their careers, creating a revolving-door effect. They often have strong opinions and interests regarding the direction of policy and are thus able to exert a great deal of influence on legislators and bureaucratic agencies.

The relationships among these experts, which are less structured than iron triangles, are often referred to as **issue networks.** Like iron triangles, issue networks are made up of people with similar policy concerns. Issue networks are less interdependent and unified than iron triangles, however, and often include more players, such as media outlets.[7] (See Figure 13–6, which follows.)

Who Belongs to an Iron Triangle? As an example, consider agricultural policy. The Department of Agriculture consists of about 100,000 individuals working directly for the federal government and thousands of other individuals who work indirectly for the department as contractors, subcontractors, or consultants. Now think about the various interest groups and client groups that are concerned with what the bureaus and agencies in the Agriculture Department can do for them. These groups include the American Farm Bureau Federation, the National Milk Producers Federation, various regional citrus growers associations, and many others. Finally, in Congress two major committees are concerned with agriculture: the House Committee on Agriculture and the Senate Committee on Agriculture, Nutrition, and Forestry.

The bureaucrats, interest groups, and legislators who make up this iron triangle cooperate to create mutually beneficial regulations and legislation. Because of the connections between agricultural interest groups and policymakers within the government, the agricultural industry has benefited greatly over the years from significant farm subsidies.

Congress's Role. The Department of Agriculture is headed by the secretary of agriculture, who is nominated by the president (and confirmed by the Senate). But that secretary cannot even buy a desk lamp if Congress does not approve the appropriations for the department's budget.

Within Congress, the responsibility for considering the Department of Agriculture's request for funding belongs first to the House and Senate appropriations committees and then to the agriculture subcommittees of the appropiations committees. The members of those committees, most of whom represent agricultural states,

"The only thing that saves us from the bureaucracy is its inefficiency."

~ Eugene J. McCarthy, U.S. Senator from Minnesota 1959–1971

productivity and efficiency. About one-third of the major firms in this country use some kind of alternative pay system, such as team-based pay, skill-based pay, profit-sharing plans, or individual bonuses. In contrast, workers for the federal government traditionally have received fixed salaries. Promotions and salary increases are given on the basis of seniority, not output.

The federal government has been experimenting with pay-for-performance systems. For example, the U.S. Postal Service has implemented the Economic Value Added Variable Pay Program, which ties bonuses to performance. As part of a five-year test of a new pay system, three thousand scientists working in Air Force laboratories received salaries based on results.

13–5d Privatization

Another idea for reforming government bureaucracies is **privatization,** which means turning over certain types of government work to the private sector. Privatization can take place by contracting out (outsourcing) work to the private sector or by *managed competition,* in which the task of providing public services is opened up to competition. In managed competition, both the relevant government agency and private firms can compete for the work.

State and local governments have been experimenting with privatization for some time. Almost all of the states have privatized at least a few of their services, and some states, including California, Colorado, and Florida, have privatized more than one hundred activities formerly undertaken by government. In Scottsdale, Arizona, the city contracts for fire protection. In Baltimore, Maryland, nine of the city's schools are outsourced to private entities.

privatization The transfer of the task of providing services traditionally provided by government to the private sector.

13–5e Government in the Sunshine

The last four decades of the twentieth century saw a trend toward more openness in government. The theory was that because Americans pay for the government, they own it—and they have a right to know what the government is doing with the taxpayers' dollars.

In response to pressure for more government openness and disclosure, Congress passed the Freedom of Information Act in 1966. This act requires federal agencies to disclose any information in agency files, with some exceptions, to any persons requesting it. Since the 1970s, *sunshine laws,* which require government meetings to be open to the public, have been enacted at all levels of American government.

The trend toward greater openness in government came to an abrupt halt on September 11, 2001. In the wake of the terrorist attacks on the World Trade Center and the Pentagon, the government began tightening its grip on information. In the months following the attacks, hundreds of thousands of documents were removed from government Web sites. No longer can the public access plans of nuclear power plants, descriptions of airline security violations, or maps of pipeline routes. Agencies were instructed to be more cautious about releasing information in their files and were given new guidelines on what should be considered public information.

13–5f Government Online

Increasingly, government agencies have attempted to improve their effectiveness and efficiency by making use of the Internet. One method has been to make information available to the public online. This may appear to run counter to the information restrictions imposed following 9/11, but much government information is not relevant to national security issues.

Under the Obama administration, for example, it is possible to get annual data on immigration, on airline flight delays, and on job-related deaths that name the employer of the deceased. The *Federal Register,* a record of government notices, can now be read online.

Local governments have posted such information as real estate records, restaurant health inspection scores, and the geographic locations of crimes. Some parts of the government have resisted the trend toward openness, however. Lawyers and other interested parties must often pay to obtain information held by the courts.

FILING FORMS ONLINE Another way that government agencies are using the Internet to improve services is to let citizens file forms and apply for services online.

The home page of USA.gov, the federal government's online "front door." *In what ways have you personally interacted with the federal government?*

For example, if you change your address, you may be able to request an update sticker for your driver's license by visiting a state Web site. Also, you may be able to apply for unemployment benefits without visiting an unemployment office, and receive payments through a government-issued debit card. The federal government distributes payments for Medicare, tax refunds, and a variety of other programs automatically and electronically.

E-FRAUD One danger of automatic payments is the possibility of fraud. This problem is not new. Criminals have long attempted to defraud the government—and the taxpayer—by filing false income tax forms or by making improper claims following natural disasters. The Internet,

however, has made it possible for crooks to "game the system" more easily. Claims can be processed without examination by an actual person. Such faulty payment systems demonstrate that bureaucrats still have a role to play, even in the high-tech era.

CRITICAL THINKING
▶ In the name of security, some states have gone so far as to bar access to emergency evacuation plans. Why might these states have done this? What problems could result if citizens lack access to this information?

AMERICA ⊞ AT ODDS
The Bureaucracy

Although the story is often told about red tape and wasteful spending generated by our bureaucracy, all in all, the U.S. bureaucracy compares favorably with bureaucracies in other countries. Citizens typically overestimate the amount of "government waste" by very large margins. Still, the U.S. government faces the same problems with its bureaucracy—sluggishness, inefficiency, and even incompetence—that large businesses and organizations throughout the country face. Americans are at odds over a number of issues relating to the bureaucracy, including the following:

- *Can new financial regulations eliminate the danger of a catastrophe such as the one we experienced in September 2008—or will clever financiers find ways around any new regulations?*

- *Do the recent health-care reforms provide vital protection to the citizenry—or are they an example of excessive government meddling in the private sector?*

- *Are government employees overpaid—or is their pay appropriate, given their responsibilities?*

- *Is the outsourcing of government services a way to improve efficiency—or does it mostly serve to hide the true cost and scope of government?*

- *Should our leaders focus on openness and transparency in government—or are such measures dangerous during the war on terrorism?*

Internet Resources

- The National Aeronautics and Space Administration Web site is one of the most popular sites sponsored by a federal agency. Find it at www.nasa.gov.

- One of the best federal sites is that of the Centers for Disease Control. For advice on what to do in case of a natural disaster, see the comic book *Preparedness 101: Zombie Pandemic* at www.cdc.gov/phpr/documents /Zombie_GN_Final.pdf.

- To see another example of a federal Web site with vast amounts of interesting information, visit the U.S. Bureau of the Census at www.census.gov.

- The Web site of the Office of Management and Budget offers information on increasing the government's efficiency—and, of course, on the federal budget. You can access the site at www.whitehouse.gov/omb.

- The *United States Government Manual* contains information on the functions, organization, and administrators of every federal department. You can access the most recent edition of the manual online at www.usgovernmentmanual.gov.

- To learn more about the mission of the General Services Administration and its role in managing the federal bureaucracy, go to www.gsa.gov.

STUDY TOOLS 13

READY TO STUDY?

- ☐ Review what you've read with the quiz below.
- ☐ Check your answers in Appendix D at the back of the book.
- ☐ For any questions you miss, read the corresponding Learning Outcome section again to prepare for class and your exam.
- ☐ Rip out and study the Chapter in Review card (at the back of the book).

VISIT WWW.CENGAGEBRAIN.COM:

- ☐ Interactive Quizzes
- ☐ Key Term Flashcards or Crossword Puzzles
- ☐ Audio Summaries
- ☐ Simulations, Animated Learning Modules, and Interactive Timelines
- ☐ Videos
- ☐ American Government NewsWatch

FILL-IN

LearningOutcome 13–1

1. All in all, the three levels of government employ about _____ percent of the civilian labor force.

LearningOutcome 13–2

2. The head of each executive department is known as the _____, except for the Department of Justice, which is headed by the attorney general.

3. The _____ Department grants patents and trademarks, conducts the national census, and monitors the weather.

LearningOutcome 13–3

4. Federal bureaucrats holding top-level positions are appointed by the _____ and confirmed by the _____.

5. The Civil Service Reform Act of 1883 established the principle of government employment on the basis of _____.

LearningOutcome 13–4

6. To create a federal administrative agency, Congress passes _____, which specifies the name, purpose, composition, and powers of the agency being created.

7. An iron triangle is _____.

LearningOutcome 13–5

8. A whistleblower is someone who _____.

MULTIPLE CHOICE

LearningOutcome 13–1

9. The amount spent on defense, together with veterans' benefits, accounts for about ____ percent of federal spending.
   a. 5   **b.** 21   **c.** 49

LearningOutcome 13–2

10. The principal duties of the ____ Department include negotiating treaties, developing foreign policy, and protecting citizens abroad.
    a. State   **c.** Defense
    b. Homeland Security

11. The independent executive agencies
    a. are businesses owned by the government.
    b. create and implement rules that regulate private activity and protect the public interest in a particular sector of the economy.
    c. are federal bureaucratic organizations that have a single function.

12. The ____ is a government corporation.
    a. General Services Administration
    b. U.S. Postal Service
    c. Securities and Exchange Commission

LearningOutcome 13–3

13. The document called *Policy and Supporting Positions* (the *Plum Book*) summarizes about ____ jobs that are filled by appointments after each presidential election.
    a. six hundred
    b. one thousand
    c. eight thousand

LearningOutcome 13–4

14. The process undertaken by an administrative agency when formally proposing, evaluating, and adopting a new regulation is called
    a. adjudication.
    b. rulemaking.
    c. neutral competency.

LearningOutcome 13–5

15. "Sunshine laws" require government
    a. meetings to be open to the public.
    b. agencies to outsource work to the private sector.
    c. agencies to let citizens file forms and apply for services online.

14 | The Judiciary

© Chip Somodevilla/Getty Images New /Getty Image.

LEARNING OUTCOMES After reading this chapter, you should be able to:

14–1 Summarize the origins of the American legal system and the basic sources of American law.

14–2 Delineate the structure of the federal court system.

14–3 Say how federal judges are appointed.

14–4 Explain how the federal courts make policy, and describe the role of ideology and judicial philosophies in judicial decision making.

14–5 Identify some of the criticisms of the federal courts and some of the checks on the power of the courts.

After finishing
this chapter go to
PAGE 332 for
STUDY TOOLS.

AMERICA AT ODDS

© Ruslan Grumble/Shutterstock

Should the People Elect Judges?

The founders of the American republic were concerned that too great a degree of popular control over the government could lead to "mob rule," and so they sought to insulate various institutions from direct popular elections. Federal judges, in particular, were to be appointed and serve for life. In contrast, in many states, all judges are popularly elected.

From time to time, judges are defeated at the polls. The most common way to defeat a judge is to accuse that official of being "soft on crime." Some people believe that despite the long prison sentences common in recent years, the judicial system is still too friendly to criminals. Others believe that elections tempt judges to cut corners on civil liberties. Should state judges be named through appointment? Or should the states rely on popular election?

The People Should Rule

Those who favor electing judges do not believe that judges can be insulated from politics. Governors, who often do the appointing when judges aren't elected, are highly political creatures. They tend to appoint supporters of their own party. If politics is going to play a role in judicial selection, then the people ought to have their say directly. Let the voters decide whether a judge is tough enough on crime or too tough on business. We admit ordinary people into the judicial process through juries, and judges should respond to public opinion as well. Officials who do not have to win a popular election may become remote from the people. Living in upscale neighborhoods, they will never experience what it is like to walk home at night fearing for their safety. Instead, they can end up living in a legal never-never land where abstractions matter more than the real world. It takes elections to give us the kinds of judges that we really want.

The Courts Must Be Insulated From Popular Pressure

Many opponents of judicial elections believe that they allow too much opportunity for popular panics and prejudices to influence the process. Popular "lock 'em up" attitudes toward criminals do not lead to an optimum strategy for crime reduction. Rather, we need to study what works and what doesn't. In some states, "get tough" policies have led to absurd cases of individuals serving life sentences for trivial offenses. The last thing we need is to place additional pressure on judges by threatening them with removal.

Any move toward greater use of elections would bring with it a further problem—the corrupting influence of campaign contributions. Several states that use judicial elections are famous for their harsh sentences and enthusiasm for the death penalty. Judges in these states are also conspicuously friendly toward the moneyed interests that helped get them elected.

Where do you stand?

1. How much information do voters typically have about judicial candidates?

2. If judges had to raise campaign contributions, what kinds of people would be most likely to contribute? Why?

Explore this issue online

- Justice at Stake is a national organization that supports appointing, not electing, judges. Its Web site is at www.justiceat-stake.org.

- Randolph Hammock, a Los Angeles County Superior Court judge, has written an article defending the election of judges. Find it by searching on "hammock judicial elections."

INTRODUCTION

As you read in this chapter's opening *America at Odds* feature, the question of whether judges should be elected has elicited controversy. Also controversial is the policy-making function of the United States Supreme Court. After all, when the Court renders an opinion on how the Constitution is to be interpreted, it is, necessarily, making policy on a national level.

To examine the nature of this controversy, we first need to explain how the **judiciary** (the courts) functions in this country. We begin by looking at the origins and sources of American law. We then describe the federal court system, at the apex of which is the United States Supreme Court, and consider various issues relating to the courts.

> ## "It is confidence
> in the men and women who administer the judicial system, ## that is the true backbone of the rule of law."
>
> ~ **John Paul Stevens,** Associate Justice of the United States Supreme Court 1975–2010

14-1 THE ORIGINS AND SOURCES OF AMERICAN LAW

LO Summarize the origins of the American legal system and the basic sources of American law.

The American colonists brought with them the legal system that had developed in England over hundreds of years. Thus, to understand how the American legal system operates, we need to go back in time to the early English courts and the traditions they established.

14-1a The Common Law Tradition

After the Normans conquered England in 1066, William the Conqueror and his successors began the process of unifying the country under their rule. One of the methods they used was the establishment of the "king's courts," or *curiae regis*. Before the Norman Conquest, disputes had been settled according to the local legal customs in various regions of the country. The law developed in the king's courts, however, applied to the country as a whole. What evolved in these courts was the beginning of the **common law**—the body of general rules that was applied throughout the entire English realm.

THE RULE OF PRECEDENT The early English courts developed the common law rules from the principles underlying judges' decisions in actual legal controversies. Judges attempted to be consistent, and whenever possible, they based their decisions on the principles applied in earlier cases. They also considered new kinds of cases with the awareness that their decisions would make new law. Each interpretation became part of the law on the subject and served as a legal **precedent**—that is, a decision that furnished an example or authority for deciding subsequent cases involving identical or similar legal issues and facts.

Stare Decisis.   The practice of deciding new cases with reference to former decisions, or precedents, eventually became a cornerstone of the English and American judicial systems. The practice formed a doctrine called *stare decisis* ("to stand on decided cases").

Under this doctrine, judges are obligated to follow the precedents established in their jurisdictions. For example, if the Supreme Court of Georgia holds that a state law requiring candidates for state office to pass drug tests is unconstitutional, that decision will control the outcome of future cases on that issue brought before the state courts in Georgia.

Similarly, a decision made on a given issue by the United States Supreme Court (the nation's highest court) is binding on all inferior (lower) courts. For exam-

---

judiciary The courts; one of the three branches of government in the United States.

common law The body of law developed from judicial decisions in English and U.S. courts, not attributable to a legislature.

precedent A court decision that furnishes an example or authority for deciding subsequent cases involving identical or similar facts and legal issues.

stare decisis A common law doctrine under which judges normally are obligated to follow the precedents established by prior court decisions. Pronounced *ster-*ay dih-*si*-sis.

ple, if the Georgia case on drug testing is appealed to the United States Supreme Court and the Court agrees that the Georgia law is unconstitutional, the high court's ruling will be binding on *all* courts in the United States. In other words, similar drug-testing laws in other states will be invalid and unenforceable.

DEPARTURES FROM PRECEDENT Sometimes a court will depart from the rule of precedent if it decides that a precedent is simply incorrect or that technological or social changes have rendered the precedent inapplicable. Cases that overturn precedent often receive a great deal of publicity.

An Example: *Brown v. Board of Education.* For example, in 1954, in *Brown v. Board of Education of Topeka,*[1] the United States Supreme Court expressly overturned precedent when it concluded that separate educational facilities for African Americans, which had been upheld as constitutional in many earlier cases under the "separate-but-equal" doctrine[2] (see Chapter 5), were inherently unequal and violated the equal protection clause. The Supreme Court's departure from precedent in *Brown* received a tremendous amount of publicity as people began to realize the political and social ramifications of this change in the law.

Another Example: *Citizens United v. FEC.* More recently, the Supreme Court departed from precedent in its 2010 ruling *Citizens United v. Federal Election Commission.*[3] In this decision, the Court determined that the government may not ban political spending by corporations in elections when the spending is undertaken independently of the campaigns of individual candidates. (The ruling implicitly covers unions and nonprofit groups as well.) The Court's verdict overturned two precedents that had upheld restrictions on corporate spending: *Austin v. Michigan Chamber of Commerce* (1990)[4] and *McConnell v. Federal Election Commission* (2003).[5]

14–1b Primary Sources of American Law

In any governmental system, the primary function of the courts is to interpret and apply the law. In the United States, the courts interpret and apply several sources of law when deciding cases. We look here only at the **primary sources of law**—that is, sources that *establish* the law—and the relative priority of these sources when particular laws come into conflict.

CONSTITUTIONAL LAW The U.S. government and each of the fifty states have separate written constitutions that set forth the general organization, powers, and

> # "It is better, so the Fourth Amendment teaches, that the guilty sometimes go free than that citizens be subject to easy arrest."
>
> ~ **William O. Douglas,** Associate Justice of the United States Supreme Court 1939–1975

limits of their respective governments. **Constitutional law** consists of the rights and duties set forth in these constitutions.

The U.S. Constitution is the supreme law of the land. As such, it is the basis of all law in the United States. Any law that violates the Constitution is invalid and unenforceable. Because of the paramount importance of the U.S. Constitution in the American legal system, the complete text of the Constitution is found in Appendix B.

The Tenth Amendment to the U.S. Constitution reserves to the states and to the people all powers not granted to the federal government. Each state in the union has its own constitution. Unless they conflict with the U.S. Constitution or a federal law, state constitutions are supreme within the borders of their respective states.

STATUTORY LAW Statutes enacted by legislative bodies at any level of government make up another source of law, which is generally referred to as **statutory law.** Federal statutes—laws enacted by the U.S. Congress—apply to all of the states. State statutes—laws enacted by state legislatures—apply only within the state that enacted the laws. Any state statute that conflicts with the U.S. Constitution, with federal laws enacted by Congress, or with the state's constitution will be deemed invalid if challenged in court and will not be enforced.

---

primary source of law A source of law that establishes the law. Primary sources of law include constitutions, statutes, administrative agency rules and regulations, and decisions rendered by the courts.

constitutional law Law based on the U.S. Constitution and the constitutions of the various states.

statutory law The body of law enacted by legislatures (as opposed to constitutional law, administrative law, or case law).

Statutory law also includes the ordinances (such as local zoning or housing-construction laws) passed by cities and counties. None of these may violate the U.S. Constitution, the relevant state constitution, or any existing federal or state laws.

ADMINISTRATIVE LAW Another important source of American law consists of **administrative law**—the rules, regulations, orders, and decisions of administrative agencies. As you read in Chapter 13, at the federal level Congress creates executive agencies, such as the Food and Drug Administration and the Environmental Protection Agency, to perform specific functions. Typically, when Congress establishes an agency, it authorizes the agency to create rules that have the force of law and to enforce those rules by bringing legal actions against violators.

Rules issued by various government agencies now affect nearly every aspect of our lives. For example, almost all of a business's operations, including the firm's capital structure and financing, its hiring and firing procedures, its relations with employees and unions, and the way it manufactures and markets its products, are subject to government regulation.

Government agencies exist at the state and local levels as well. States commonly create agencies that parallel federal agencies. Just as federal statutes take precedence over conflicting state statutes, federal agency regulations take precedence over conflicting state regulations.

CASE LAW As is evident from the earlier discussion of the common law tradition, another basic source of American law consists of the rules of law announced in court decisions, or **case law.** These rules of law include interpretations of constitutional provisions, of statutes enacted by legislatures, and of regulations issued by administrative agencies.

Thus, even though a legislature passes a law to govern a certain area, how that law is interpreted and

> # "Our Constitution is colorblind, and neither knows nor tolerates classes among citizens."
>
> ~ **John Marshall Harlan,** Associate Justice of the United States Supreme Court 1877–1911

applied depends on the courts. The importance of case law, or *judge-made law*, is one of the distinguishing characteristics of the common law tradition.

14–1c Civil Law and Criminal Law

All of the sources of law just discussed can be classified in other ways as well. One of the most significant classification systems divides all law into two categories: civil law and criminal law.

Civil law spells out the duties that individuals in society owe to other persons or to their governments, excluding the duty not to commit crimes. Typically, in a civil case, a private party sues another private party (although the government can also sue a party for a civil law violation). The object of a civil lawsuit is to make the defendant—the person being sued—comply with a legal duty (such as a contractual promise) or pay money damages for failing to comply with that duty.

Criminal law, in contrast, has to do with wrongs committed against the public as a whole. Criminal acts are prohibited by local, state, or federal government statutes. Thus, criminal defendants are prosecuted by public officials, such as a district attorney (D.A.), on behalf of the government, not by their victims or other private parties.

In a criminal case, the government seeks to impose a penalty (usually a fine and/or imprisonment) on a person who has violated a criminal law. For example, when someone robs a convenience store, that person has committed a crime and, if caught and proved guilty, will usually spend time in prison.

14–1d Basic Judicial Requirements

A court cannot decide just any issue at any time. Before a court can hear and decide a case, specific requirements must be met. To a certain extent, these requirements act as restraints on the judiciary because they limit the types of cases that courts can hear and decide. Courts also have procedural requirements that judges must follow.

---

administrative law The body of law created by administrative agencies (in the form of rules, regulations, orders, and decisions) in order to carry out their duties and responsibilities.

case law The rules of law announced in court decisions. Case law includes the aggregate of reported cases that interpret judicial precedents, statutes, regulations, and constitutional provisions.

civil law The branch of law that spells out the duties that individuals in society owe to other persons or to their governments, excluding the duty not to commit crimes.

criminal law The branch of law that defines and governs actions that constitute crimes. Generally, criminal law has to do with wrongful actions committed against society for which society demands redress.

JURISDICTION In Latin, *juris* means "law," and *diction* means "to speak." Therefore, **jurisdiction** literally refers to the power "to speak the law." Jurisdiction applies either to the geographic area in which a court has the right and power to decide cases, or to the right and power of a court to decide matters concerning certain persons, types of property, or subjects. Before any court can hear a case, it must have jurisdiction over the person against whom the suit is brought, the property involved in the suit, and the subject matter.

The Jurisdiction of State Courts. A state trial court usually has jurisdictional authority over the residents of a particular area of the state, such as a county or district. (A **trial court** is, as the term implies, a court in which trials are held and testimony is taken.) A state's highest court (often called the *state supreme court*)[6] has jurisdictional authority over all residents within the state. In some cases, if an individual has committed an offense such as injuring someone in an automobile accident or selling defective goods within the state, the court can exercise jurisdiction even if the individual is a resident of another state.

State courts can also exercise jurisdiction over those who do business within the state. A New York company that distributes its products in California, for example, can be sued by a California resident in a California state court.

Federal Court Jurisdiction. Because the federal government is a government of limited powers, the jurisdiction of the federal courts is limited. Article III, Section 2, of the Constitution states that the federal courts can exercise jurisdiction over all cases "arising under this Constitution, the Laws of the United States, and Treaties made, or which shall be made, under their Authority." Whenever a case involves a claim based, at least in part, on the U.S. Constitution, a treaty, or a federal law, a **federal question** arises. Any lawsuit involving a federal question can originate in a federal court.

Federal courts can also exercise jurisdiction over cases involving **diversity of citizenship.** Such cases may arise when the parties in a lawsuit live in different states or when one of the parties is a foreign government or a foreign citizen. Before a federal court can take jurisdiction in a diversity case, the amount in controversy

Four alleged members of the Bonanno crime family appear in a Manhattan court. They were charged with running gambling operations, loansharking, extortion, and selling fake Viagra. *What kind of law applies in these cases?*

must be more than $75,000. (Congress raised the limit to $75,000 in 1996. In 1789, the sum was $500, which is just under $14,000 in 2015 dollars.)

STANDING TO SUE To bring a lawsuit before a court, a person must have **standing to sue,** or a sufficient "stake" in the matter to justify bringing a suit. Thus, the party bringing the suit must have suffered a harm or been threatened with a harm by the action at issue, and the issue must be justiciable. A **justiciable controversy** is one that is real and substantial, as opposed to hypothetical or academic.

jurisdiction The authority of a court to hear and decide a particular case.

trial court A court in which trials are held and testimony is taken.

federal question A question that pertains to the U.S. Constitution, acts of Congress, or treaties. A federal question provides a basis for federal court jurisdiction.

diversity of citizenship A basis for federal court jurisdiction over a lawsuit that arises when (1) the parties in the lawsuit live in different states or when one of the parties is a foreign government or a foreign citizen, and (2) the amount in controversy is more than $75,000.

standing to sue The requirement that an individual must have a sufficient stake in a controversy before he or she can bring a lawsuit. The party bringing the suit must demonstrate that he or she has either been harmed or been threatened with a harm.

justiciable controversy A controversy that is not hypothetical or academic but real and substantial; a requirement that must be satisfied before a court will hear a case. *Justiciable* is pronounced jus-*tish*-a-bul.

The requirement of standing to sue clearly limits the issues that can be decided by the courts. Furthermore, both state and federal governments can specify by law when an individual or group has standing to sue. For example, the federal government will not allow a taxpayer to sue the Department of Defense for spending tax dollars wastefully.

COURT PROCEDURES Both the federal and the state courts have established procedural rules that apply in all cases. These procedures are designed to protect the rights and interests of the parties, ensure that the litigation proceeds in a fair and orderly manner, and identify the issues that must be decided by the court—thus saving court time and costs. Different procedural rules apply in criminal and civil cases. Generally, criminal procedural rules attempt to ensure that defendants are not deprived of their constitutional rights.

Parties involved in civil or criminal cases must comply with court procedural rules or risk being held in **contempt of court.** A party who is held in contempt of court can be fined, taken into custody, or both. A court must take care to ensure that the parties—and the court itself—comply with procedural requirements. Procedural errors often serve as grounds for a mistrial or for appealing the court's decision to a higher tribunal.

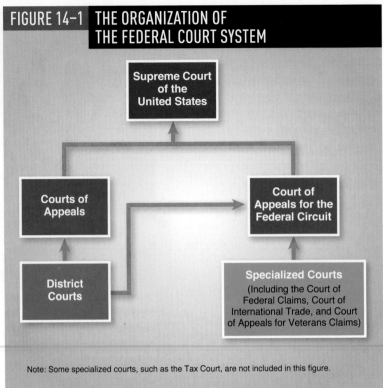

FIGURE 14-1 THE ORGANIZATION OF THE FEDERAL COURT SYSTEM

Note: Some specialized courts, such as the Tax Court, are not included in this figure.

CRITICAL THINKING

▶ Why does national law—even administrative law established by a federal agency—overrule conflicting law that the people of a state have written into their state constitution?

14–2 THE FEDERAL COURT SYSTEM

LO Delineate the structure of the federal court system.

The federal court system is a three-tiered model consisting of U.S. district courts (trial courts), U.S. courts of appeals, and the United States Supreme Court. Figure 14–1 shows the organization of the federal court system.

contempt of court A ruling that a person has disobeyed a court order or has shown disrespect to the court or to a judicial proceeding.

Bear in mind that the federal courts constitute only one of the fifty-two court systems in the United States. Each of the fifty states has its own court system, as does the District of Columbia. No two state court systems are exactly the same. In general, though, the states have different levels, or tiers, of courts, just as the federal system does.

Normally, state courts deal with questions of state law, and the decisions of a state's highest court on matters of state law are normally final. If a federal question is involved, however, a decision of a state supreme court may be appealed within the federal court system. We will discuss the federal court system in the pages that follow.

14–2a U.S. District and Specialized Courts

On the lowest tier of the federal court system are the U.S. district courts, or federal trial courts—the courts in which cases involving federal laws begin. The cases in these courts are decided by a judge or a jury. There is at least one federal district court in every state, and there is one in the District of Columbia. The number of judicial districts varies over time, primarily owing to population changes and corresponding caseloads. Currently, there are ninety-four judicial districts. Figure 14–2, which follows, shows their geographic boundaries.

FIGURE 14-2 U.S. COURTS OF APPEALS AND U.S. DISTRICT COURTS

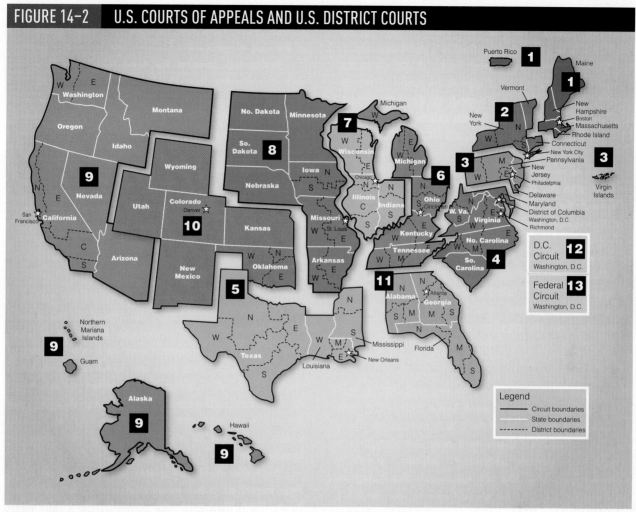

Source: Administrative Office of the United States Courts.

The federal system also includes other trial courts, such as the Court of International Trade and others shown in Figure 14–1. These courts have limited, or specialized, subject-matter jurisdiction—that is, they can exercise authority over only certain kinds of cases.

One specialized court has recently received exceptional scrutiny—the Foreign Intelligence Surveillance Court (FISC). This court was initially created to issue search warrants against suspected foreign spies inside the United States. The Patriot Act of 2001 greatly expanded its powers. The FISC almost never rejects a warrant request. It meets in secret and releases no information on individual cases.

More controversially, the court does not report the legal interpretations under which it issues its rulings. In 2013, revelations of large-scale surveillance by the National Security Agency (NSA) raised questions about the FISC's practices. (NSA actions must be approved by the FISC.) Some legal experts doubted that the FISC's decisions could be squared with the Fourth Amendment to the U.S. Constitution, which bars unreasonable searches.

14-2b U.S. Courts of Appeals

On the middle tier of the federal court system are the U.S. courts of appeals. Courts of appeals, or **appellate courts,** do not hear evidence or testimony. Rather, an appellate court reviews the transcript of the trial court's proceedings, other records relating to the case, and attorneys' arguments as to why the trial court's decision should or should not stand.

In contrast to a trial court, where normally a single judge presides, an appellate court consists of a panel of

> **appellate court** A court having appellate jurisdiction. An appellate court normally does not hear evidence or testimony but reviews the transcript of the trial court's proceedings, other records relating to the case, and attorneys' arguments as to why the trial court's decision should or should not stand.

three or more judges. The task of the appellate court is to determine whether the trial court erred in applying the law to the facts and issues involved in a particular case.

There are thirteen federal courts of appeals in the United States. The courts of appeals for twelve of the circuits, including the Court of Appeals for the D.C. Circuit, hear appeals from the U.S. district courts located within their respective judicial circuits (see Figure 14–2).

Decisions made by federal administrative agencies may be reviewed by either a district court or the court of appeals, depending on the agency. The Court of Appeals for the Federal Circuit has national jurisdiction over certain types of cases, such as those concerning patent law and some claims against the national (federal) government.

The decisions of the federal appellate courts may be appealed to the United States Supreme Court. If a decision is not appealed, or if the high court declines to review the case, the appellate court's decision is final.

14–2c The United States Supreme Court

The highest level of the three-tiered model of the federal court system is the United States Supreme Court. According to Article III of the U.S. Constitution, there is only one national Supreme Court, but Congress is empowered to create additional ("inferior") courts as it deems necessary. The inferior courts that Congress has created include the second tier in our model—the U.S. courts of appeals—as well as the district courts and any other courts of limited, or specialized, jurisdiction.

The United States Supreme Court consists of nine justices—a chief justice and eight associate justices—although that number is not mandated by the Constitution. The Supreme Court has original, or trial, jurisdiction only in unusual instances (set forth in Article III, Section 2). In other words, only rarely does a case originate at the Supreme Court level. Most of the Court's work is as an appellate court. The Supreme Court has appellate authority over cases decided by the U.S. courts of appeals, as well as over some cases decided in the state courts when federal questions are at issue.

THE WRIT OF *CERTIORARI* To bring a case before the Supreme Court, a party may request that the Court issue a **writ of *certiorari,*** often called "cert." The writ

writ of *certiorari* An order from a higher court asking a lower court for the record of a case. *Certiorari* is pronounced sur-shee-uh-*rah*-ree.

of *certiorari* is an order that the Supreme Court issues to a lower court requesting the latter to send it the record of the case in question.

Parties can petition the Supreme Court to issue a writ of *certiorari,* but whether the Court will do so is entirely within its discretion. The Court will not issue a writ unless at least four of the nine justices approve. In no instance is the Court required to issue a writ of *certiorari.*[7]

Most petitions for writs of *certiorari* are denied. A denial is not a decision on the merits of a case, nor does it indicate that the Court agrees with a lower court's opinion. The denial of a writ has no value as a precedent. A denial simply means that the decision of the lower court remains the law within that court's jurisdiction.

WHICH CASES REACH THE SUPREME COURT?

There is no absolute right to appeal to the United States Supreme Court. Although thousands of cases are filed with the Supreme Court each year, on average the Court hears fewer than one hundred. As shown in Figure 14–3, which follows, the number of cases heard by the Court each year has declined significantly since the 1980s. In large part, this has occurred because the Court has raised its standards for accepting cases in recent years.

Typically, the Court grants petitions for cases that raise important policy issues that need to be addressed. In its 2013–2014 term, for example, the Court heard cases involving such issues as the following:

▶ Is it constitutional to limit the total amount of money that an individual can donate to candidates for office? (The Court ruled that the donations cannot be limited.)[8]

▶ Can municipal governments begin legislative sessions with prayers even when almost all of the prayers are from one religion—in this case, Christianity? (The Court found that such prayers were acceptable.)[9]

▶ Could Massachusetts establish a thirty-five-foot buffer zone to limit the access of anti-abortion protestors to abortion clinics? (The Court held that this zone was too large.)[10]

▶ Do closely held corporations have the right to deny their employees certain types of birth control benefits in insurance plans that conform to the Affordable Care Act—health-care reform legislation enacted in 2010? (In *Burwell v. Hobby Lobby,* the Court ruled that such corporations have that right.)[11]

If the lower courts have rendered conflicting opinions on an important issue, the Supreme Court may review one or more cases involving that issue to

FIGURE 14–3 THE NUMBER OF SUPREME COURT OPINIONS

The number of Supreme Court opinions peaked at 151 in the Court's 1982 term, declined more or less steadily through 1995, and then leveled off. During the 2013 term (ending in June 2014), the Court issued 77 opinions.

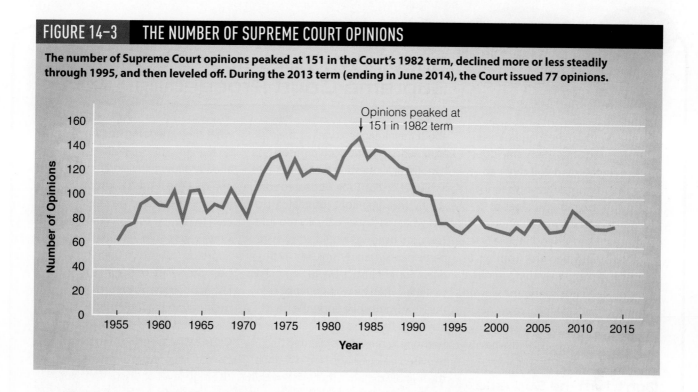

define the law on the matter. For example, in 2010 and 2011, various federal appellate courts issued conflicting opinions as to whether it is constitutional to require citizens to purchase health-care insurance, as provided by the health-care reforms enacted in 2010. The conflicting rulings were eventually resolved by the Court in *National Federation of Independent Business v. Sebelius*.[12]

SUPREME COURT OPINIONS Like other appellate courts, the United States Supreme Court normally does not hear any evidence. The Court's decision in a particular case is based on the written record of the case and the written arguments (legal briefs) that the attorneys submit. The attorneys also present **oral arguments**—spoken arguments presented in person rather than on paper—to the Court. Some observers of the Court have advocated that the oral arguments be video-recorded and provided to the public through C-SPAN. We discuss that question in this chapter's *Join the Debate* feature, which follows.

Reaching an Opinion. After considering all this information, the justices discuss the case in **conference.** The conference is strictly private—only the justices are allowed in the room.

When the Court has reached a decision, the chief justice, if in the majority, assigns the task of writing the Court's **opinion** to one of the justices. When the chief justice is not in the majority, the most senior jus-

tice voting with the majority assigns the writing of the Court's opinion. The opinion outlines the reasons for the Court's decision, the rules of law that apply, and the judgment.

Concurring and Dissenting Opinions. Often, one or more justices who agree with the Court's decision do so for reasons different from those outlined in the majority opinion. These justices may write **concurring opinions,** setting forth their own legal reasoning on the issue. Frequently, one or more justices disagree with the Court's conclusion. These justices may write **dissenting opinions,** outlining the reasons they feel the majority erred in arriving at its decision.

Although a dissenting opinion does not affect the outcome of the case before the Court, it may be

oral argument A spoken argument presented to a judge in person by an attorney on behalf of her or his client.

conference In regard to the Supreme Court, a private meeting of the justices in which they present their arguments concerning a case under consideration.

opinion A written statement by a court expressing the reasons for its decision in a case.

concurring opinion A statement written by a judge or justice who agrees (concurs) with the court's decision, but for reasons different from those in the majority opinion.

dissenting opinion A statement written by a judge or justice who disagrees with the majority opinion.

Should We Televise Supreme Court Proceedings?

Currently, you can hear audio recordings of United States Supreme Court oral arguments, and you can read written transcripts. But you cannot see any photographic images of what takes place—no still photos and certainly no video. In these days of instant video gratification, it seems like an anomaly that Supreme Court proceedings cannot be viewed on, say, YouTube. Still, there are arguments for and against allowing television cameras inside the Supreme Court.

Don't Turn the Supreme Court Into a Video Circus

Audio and written records of Supreme Court proceedings are fine. If we televise oral arguments to millions throughout the world, however, the Court's justices will be more guarded in their comments. They will worry about their images as well as their arguments. A justice could pose a hypothetical question that ends up as a snippet on YouTube. Repeated constantly, this clip might completely distort what the justice actually thought. Televised hearings would emphasize participants' mannerisms and even dress. Former justice David Souter has said that when he was a member of the New Hampshire Supreme Court, cameras altered his behavior. Justice Anthony Kennedy has claimed that televised proceedings would change the friendly dynamic that exists within the Supreme Court. Let's keep the cameras out.

We Pay Their Salaries— Let's See What They Do

The nine Supreme Court justices are taxpayer-financed government officials. Voters should be able to see what they are doing and how they do it. Many state appellate courts already allow television cameras, and it's time for the Supreme Court to join in. Televised proceedings lead to greater transparency. If Americans could actually see the Supreme Court in action, they would be more aware of the importance of law in our system. We would have a greater understanding of key Court cases. Those who have attended the Court's oral arguments in person have walked away impressed with the high level of discussion. Not everyone can visit the Supreme Court building personally, however. Video would allow everyone the opportunity to experience the Court's work. Let the cameras in.

 CRITICAL ANALYSIS — If there were a C-SPAN channel devoted to Supreme Court proceedings, would you ever watch it? Why or why not?

important later. In a subsequent case concerning the same issue, a jurist or attorney may use the legal reasoning in the dissenting opinion as the basis for an argument to reverse the previous decision and establish a new precedent.

> ### CRITICAL THINKING
>
> ▶ Some people believe that the Supreme Court should accept more cases and thereby resolve more issues. Others contend that such a move would result in less well-thought-out opinions. Who do you think has the better argument, and why?

14-3 FEDERAL JUDICIAL APPOINTMENTS

LO Say how federal judges are appointed.

Unlike state court judges, who are often elected, all federal judges are appointed. Article II, Section 2, of the Constitution authorizes the president to appoint the justices of the Supreme Court with the advice and consent of the Senate. Laws enacted by Congress provide that the same procedure is to be used for appointing judges to the lower federal courts as well.

> **"As nightfall doesn't come at once, neither does oppression.** In both instances, . . . we must be aware of change in the air, however slight, lest we become unwitting victims of the darkness."
>
> ~ **William O. Douglas,** Associate Justice of the United States Supreme Court
> 1939–1975

Federal judges receive lifetime appointments (because under Article III of the Constitution they "hold their Offices during good Behaviour"). Federal judges may be removed from office through the impeachment process, but such proceedings are extremely rare and are usually undertaken only if a judge engages in blatantly illegal conduct, such as bribery. In the history of this nation, only fifteen federal judges have been impeached, and only eleven left office due to a conviction or resignation. Normally, federal judges serve until they resign, retire, or die.

Although the Constitution sets no specific qualifications for those who serve on the Supreme Court, those who have done so share one characteristic: all have been attorneys. The backgrounds of the Supreme Court justices have been far from typical of the characteristics of the American public as a whole. Table 14–1 summarizes the backgrounds of all of the 112 United States Supreme Court justices to 2015.

14–3a The Nomination Process

The president receives suggestions and recommendations as to potential nominees for judicial positions from various sources, including the Justice Department, senators, other judges, the candidates themselves, state political leaders, bar associations, and other interest groups. After selecting a nominee, the president submits her or his name to the Senate for approval. The Senate Judiciary Committee then holds hearings and makes its recommendation to the Senate, where it takes a majority vote to confirm the nomination.

TABLE 14–1 BACKGROUNDS OF UNITED STATES SUPREME COURT JUSTICES TO 2015	Number of Justices (112 = Total)
Occupational Position before Appointment	
Private legal practice	25
State judgeship	21
Federal judgeship	31
U.S. attorney general	7
Deputy or assistant U.S. attorney general	2
U.S. solicitor general	3
U.S. senator	6
U.S. representative	2
State governor	3
Federal executive post	9
Other	3
Religious Affiliation	
Protestant	83
Roman Catholic	14
Jewish	7
Unitarian	7
No religious affiliation	1
Age on Appointment	
Under 40	5
41–50	33
51–60	60
61–70	14
Political Party Affiliation	
Federalist (to 1835)	13
Jeffersonian Republican (to 1828)	7
Whig (to 1861)	1
Democrat	46
Republican	44
Independent	1
Education	
College graduate	96
Not a college graduate	16
Gender	
Male	108
Female	4
Race	
White (non-Hispanic)	109
African American	2
Hispanic	1

Sources: *Congressional Quarterly's Guide to the U.S. Supreme Court* (Washington, D.C.: Congressional Quarterly Press, 1997); and authors' updates.

SENATORIAL COURTESY When judges are nominated to the district courts (and, to a lesser extent, the U.S. courts of appeals), a senator of the president's political party from the state where there is a vacancy traditionally has been allowed to veto the president's choice. This practice is known as **senatorial courtesy.** At times, senatorial courtesy even permits senators from the opposing party to veto presidential choices. Because of senatorial courtesy, home-state senators of the president's party may be able to influence the choice of the nominee.

PARTISANSHIP It should come as no surprise that partisanship plays a significant role in the president's selection of nominees to the federal bench, particularly to the Supreme Court, the crown jewel of the federal judiciary. Traditionally, presidents have attempted to strengthen their legacies by appointing federal judges with political and philosophical views similar to their own. In the history of the Supreme Court, fewer than 13 percent of the justices nominated by a president have been from an opposing political party.

That said, presidents have often discovered that the justices they appointed took very different positions than expected. President Dwight D. Eisenhower (1953–1961), for example, had no idea when he appointed Chief Justice Earl Warren that Warren would seek to overturn the system of racial segregation. The Court accomplished this goal through rulings such as *Brown v. Board of Education* (see Chapter 5).[13]

COURTS OF APPEALS Appointments to the U.S. courts of appeals can also have a lasting impact. Recall that these courts occupy the level just below the Supreme Court in the federal court system. Also recall that the decisions rendered by these courts—about 60,000 per year—are final unless overturned by the Supreme Court. Given that the Supreme Court renders opinions in fewer than one hundred cases a year, the decisions of the federal appellate courts have a wide-reaching effect on American society.

For example, consider a decision interpreting the federal Constitution by the U.S. Court of Appeals for the Ninth Circuit. If not overruled by the Supreme Court, it establishes a precedent that will be followed in the states of Alaska, Arizona, California, Hawaii, Idaho, Montana, Nevada, Oregon, and Washington.

> **senatorial courtesy** A practice that allows a senator of the president's party to veto the president's nominee to a federal court judgeship within the senator's state.

© Jose Cabezas/AFP/Getty Images

Sonia Sotomayor became the first Latina on the Supreme Court when she was confirmed by the Senate in 2009. *Why might President Obama have chosen her?*

14–3b Confirmation or Rejection by the Senate

The president's nominations are not always confirmed. In fact, almost 20 percent of presidential nominations for the Supreme Court have been either rejected or not acted on by the Senate. The process of nominating and confirming federal judges, especially Supreme Court justices, often involves political debate and controversy. Many bitter battles over Supreme Court appointments have ensued when the Senate and the president have disagreed on political issues.

From 1893 until 1968, the Senate rejected only three Court nominees. From 1968 through 1986, however, two presidential nominees to the highest court were rejected, and two more nominations, both by President Ronald Reagan, failed in 1987. The most significant of these nominees was Robert Bork, who faced hostile questioning about his views on the Constitution during the confirmation hearings. The Bork hearings are often considered to be a turning point after which confirmation hearings became much more contentious.

One of President George H. W. Bush's nominees to the Supreme Court—Clarence Thomas—was also the subject of considerable controversy. The nation watched on television as Anita Hill, a former aide, leveled charges of sexual harassment at Thomas, who nevertheless was confirmed.

GEORGE W. BUSH'S APPOINTMENTS During George W. Bush's second term, Chief Justice William Rehnquist died, and Sandra Day O'Connor, the Court's first woman justice, retired. These events allowed Bush to nominate John G. Roberts, Jr., to replace Rehnquist and Samuel A. Alito, Jr., to replace O'Connor. Both nominations were confirmed by the Senate with relatively little difficulty. The appointment of Alito, in particular, changed the character of the Court, because he was distinctly more conservative than O'Connor.

OBAMA'S NOMINEES In May 2009, as a result of a judicial retirement, President Barack Obama named Sonia Sotomayor to the Court. Sotomayor had served for more than a decade as a judge of the U.S. Court of Appeals for the Second Circuit and was the first Hispanic American ever nominated to the Supreme Court.

A second retirement gave Obama an additional chance to pick a nominee, in May 2010. He chose Elena Kagan, his solicitor general. At her confirmation hearings, several Republicans seized on an incident that had occurred when Kagan was dean of Harvard Law School. In line with Harvard policy, Kagan placed restrictions on military recruiters. The restrictions were in response to the military's "don't ask, don't tell" policy, which prevented lesbians and gay men from serving openly. Still, Kagan was confirmed. It was a sign of the increased political polarization in the Senate that neither Sotomayor nor Kagan received more than a handful of votes from Republican senators.

© Chip Somodevilla/Getty Images

Justice Elena Kagan attends the State of the Union speech. Some of the Court's more conservative members avoid this function. *Why might that be so?*

CRITICAL THINKING

▶ In recent years, senators have increasingly made use of the filibuster to delay or prevent the approval of judicial nominees. Is this a legitimate tactic or an example of partisan excess? Explain.

14–4 THE COURTS AS POLICYMAKERS

LO Explain how the federal courts make policy, and describe the role of ideology and judicial philosophies in judicial decision making.

In the United States, judges and justices play a major role in government. Unlike judges in some other countries, U.S. judges have the power to decide on the constitutionality of laws or actions undertaken by the other branches of government.

Clearly, the function of the courts is to interpret and apply the law, not to make law—that is the function of the legislative branch of government. Yet judges can and do "make law." Indeed, they cannot avoid making law in some cases, because the law does not always provide clear answers to questions that come before the courts.

14–4a The Issue of Broad Language

The text of the U.S. Constitution is set forth in broad terms. When a court interprets a constitutional provision and applies that interpretation to a specific set of circumstances, the court is essentially "making the law" on that issue. Examples of how the courts, and especially the United States Supreme Court, make law abound.

Consider privacy rights, which we discussed in Chapter 4. Nothing in the Constitution or its amendments specifically states that we have a right to privacy. Yet the Supreme Court, through various decisions, has established such a right by deciding that it is implied by several constitutional amendments. The Court has also held that this right to privacy includes a number of specific rights, such as the right to have an abortion.

Statutory provisions and other legal rules also tend to be expressed in general terms, and the courts must decide how those general provisions and rules apply to specific cases. The Americans with Disabilities Act of 1990 is an example. The act requires employers to reasonably accommodate the needs of employees with disabilities.

But the act does not say exactly what employers must do to "reasonably accommodate" such persons. Thus, the courts must decide, on a case-by-case basis, what this phrase means.

Additionally, in some cases there is no relevant law or precedent to follow. In recent years, for example, courts have been struggling with new kinds of legal issues stemming from new communications technologies, including the Internet. Until legislative bodies enact laws governing these issues, it is up to the courts to fashion the law that will apply—and thus make policy.

14–4b The Power of Judicial Review

Recall from Chapter 2 that the U.S. Constitution divides government powers among the executive, legislative, and judicial branches. This division of powers is part of our system of checks and balances. Essentially, the founders gave each branch of government the constitutional authority to check the other two branches. The federal judiciary can exercise a check on the actions of either of the other branches through its power of **judicial review.**

The Constitution does not actually mention judicial review. Rather, the Supreme Court claimed the power for itself in *Marbury v. Madison.*[14] In that case, which was decided by the Court in 1803, Chief Justice John Marshall held that a provision of a 1789 law affecting the Supreme Court's jurisdiction violated the Constitution and was thus void. Marshall declared, "It is emphatically the province and duty of the judicial department [the courts] to say what the law is. . . . If two laws conflict with each other, the courts must decide on the operation of each. . . . [I]f a law be in opposition to the constitution . . . the court must determine which of these conflicting rules governs the case. This is the very essence of judicial duty."

Most constitutional scholars believe that the framers intended that the federal courts should have the power of judicial review. In *Federalist Paper* No. 78, Alexander Hamilton clearly espoused the doctrine. Hamilton stressed the importance of the "complete independence" of federal judges and their special duty to "invalidate all acts contrary to the manifest tenor of the Constitution." Without judicial review by impartial courts, there would be nothing to ensure that the other branches of government stayed within constitutional limits when exercising their powers, and "all the reservations of particular rights or privileges would amount to nothing." Chief Justice Marshall shared Hamilton's views and adopted Hamilton's reasoning in *Marbury v. Madison.*

14–4c Judicial Activism versus Judicial Restraint

As already noted, making policy is not the primary function of the federal courts. Yet it is unavoidable that courts do, in fact, influence or even establish policy when they interpret and apply the law. Further, the power of judicial review gives the courts, and particularly the Supreme Court, an important policymaking tool. When the Supreme Court upholds or invalidates a state or federal statute, the consequences for the nation can be profound.

One issue that is often debated is how the federal courts should wield their policymaking power, particularly the power of judicial review. Often, this debate is couched in terms of judicial activism versus judicial restraint.

ACTIVIST VERSUS RESTRAINTIST JUSTICES The terms *judicial activism* and *judicial restraint* do not have precise meanings. Generally, however, an activist judge or justice believes that the courts should actively use their powers to check the legislative and executive branches to ensure that they do not exceed their authority. A restraintist judge or justice, in contrast, generally assumes that the courts should defer to the decisions of the legislative and executive branches. After all, members of Congress and the president are elected by the people, whereas federal court judges are not. In other words, the courts should not thwart the implementation of legislative acts unless those acts are clearly unconstitutional.

POLITICAL IDEOLOGY AND JUDICIAL ACTIVISM/RESTRAINT One of the Supreme Court's most activist eras occurred during the period from 1953 to 1969 under the leadership of Chief Justice Earl Warren. The Warren Court propelled the civil rights movement forward by holding, among other things, that laws permitting racial segregation violated the equal protection clause (see Chapter 5).

Because of the activism of the Warren Court, the term *judicial activism* has often been linked with liberalism. Indeed, many liberals are in favor of an activist federal judiciary because they believe that the judiciary can "right" the "wrongs" that result from unfair laws or from "antiquated" legislation at the state and local levels. Neither judicial activism nor judicial restraint is neces-

judicial review The power of the courts to decide on the constitutionality of legislative enactments and of actions taken by the executive branch.

sarily linked to a particular political ideology, however. In fact, many observers claim that today's Supreme Court is often activist on behalf of a conservative agenda.

14-4d Ideology and the Courts

The policymaking role of the courts gives rise to an important question: To what extent do ideology and personal policy preferences affect judicial decision making? Numerous scholars have attempted to answer this question, especially with respect to Supreme Court justices.

Few doubt that ideology affects judicial decision making, although, of course, other factors play a role as well. Certainly, there are numerous examples of ideology affecting Supreme Court decisions. As new justices replace old ones and new ideological alignments are formed, the Court's decisions are affected. Yet many scholars argue that there is no real evidence that personal preferences influence Supreme Court decisions to an *unacceptable* extent.

Keep in mind that judicial decision making, particularly at the Supreme Court level, can be very complex. When deciding cases, the Supreme Court often must consider any number of sources of law, including constitutions, statutes, and administrative agency regulations—as well as cases interpreting relevant portions of those sources. At times, the Court may also take demographic data, public opinion, foreign laws, and other factors into account. How much weight is given to each of these sources or factors will vary from justice to justice. After all, reasoning of any kind, including judicial reasoning, does not take place in a vacuum.

It is only natural that a justice's life experiences, personal biases, and intellectual abilities and predispositions will touch on the reasoning process. Nevertheless, it is expected that when reviewing a case, a Supreme Court justice does not start out with a conclusion (such as "I don't like this particular law that Congress passed") and then look for legal sources to support that conclusion.

14-4e Ideology and Today's Supreme Court

In contrast to the liberal Supreme Court under Earl Warren, today's Court is generally conservative. The Court began its rightward shift after President Ronald Reagan (1981–1989) appointed conservative William Rehnquist as chief justice in 1986, and the Court moved further to the right as other conservative appointments to the bench were made by Reagan and George H. W. Bush (1989–1993).

THE ROBERTS COURT Many Supreme Court scholars believe that the appointments of John Roberts (as chief justice) and especially Samuel Alito (as associate justice) caused the Court to drift even further to the right. Certainly, the five conservative justices on the bench during the Roberts Court's first five terms voted together and cast the deciding votes in numerous cases. The remaining justices held liberal to moderate views and often formed an opposing bloc.

A notable change in the Court occurred when Alito replaced retiring justice Sandra Day O'Connor. O'Connor had often been the "swing" vote on the Court, sometimes voting with the liberal bloc and at other times siding with the conservatives.

On the Roberts Court, the swing voter is usually Justice Anthony Kennedy, who is generally more conservative in his views than O'Connor was. Although Justice Kennedy dislikes being described as a swing voter, he often decides the outcome of a case. In the 2013–2014 term, for example, Kennedy was the only justice to be on the winning side in all eleven cases that were decided by a narrow five-to-four vote.

President Obama's naming of Justices Elena Kagan and Sonia Sotomayor to the Court did not change its ideological balance. Both women joined the liberal bloc, but the men they replaced had been liberal as well.

Chief Justice John Roberts, Jr., and Justice Samuel Alito, Jr. *How did the appointment of these two justices change the Court?*

THE COURT'S CONSERVATISM In recent years, the nature of the Court's conservatism has come into sharper focus. It is a mistake to equate the ideology of the Court's majority with the conservatism, say, of the Republicans in Congress or with the ideology of the conservative movement. To be sure, there are members of the Court who are unmistakably *movement conservatives*—that is, members in good standing of the conservative movement. Justices Antonin Scalia and Clarence Thomas are in this camp.

Yet Justice Kennedy and Chief Justice Roberts—and even Justice Alito—often "march to their own drummer." A leading example was Chief Justice Roberts's ruling on Obamacare, in which he found that incentives to obtain health-care insurance could be written into the tax code. Any conservative hostility that Roberts may have felt toward the health-care reform legislation was clearly checked by his commitment to judicial restraint. In contrast to this position, the four other conservative justices contended that the Affordable Care Act was unconstitutional as a whole. The four liberal justices believed that the *individual mandate* to obtain insurance followed from the Constitution's commerce clause.

Another area in which Court conservatives have frequently parted from the conservative movement is

Although often considered a conservative when he served on the Rehnquist Court, Justice Anthony Kennedy has typically held the "swing" vote on the closely divided Roberts Court. *On what kinds of cases did Kennedy break with the conservative movement?*

> # "The Constitution itself should be our guide, not our own concept of what is fair, decent, and right."
>
> ~ **Hugo L. Black,** Associate Justice of the United States Supreme Court 1937–1971

that of gay rights. Justice Kennedy, in particular, has favored gay rights ever since *Lawrence v. Texas*, a 2003 ruling that abolished laws against homosexual acts.[15] Justice Kennedy joined the Court's liberals in this case, providing the fifth vote that decided the issue. Kennedy's vote was also decisive in later gay rights cases, such as *United States v. Windsor*.[16] In that 2013 case, the Court found that the federal government is required to accept same-sex marriages that are legal under state law. (In contrast, Kennedy's views on the Affordable Care Act were more conventionally conservative. During oral arguments, Kennedy made his opposition to the health reform legislation very clear.)

14–4f Approaches to Legal Interpretation

It would be a mistake to look at the judicial philosophy of today's Supreme Court solely in terms of the political ideologies of liberalism and conservatism. In fact, some Supreme Court scholars have suggested that other factors are as important as, or more important than, the justices' political philosophies in determining why they decide as they do. These factors include the justices' attitudes toward legal interpretation and their perceptions of the Supreme Court's role in the federal judiciary. Two important judicial philosophies, both of which are often associated with conservative principles, are *strict construction* and *originalism*.

STRICT CONSTRUCTION The term *strict construction* is widely used in the press and by politicians. Republican presidential candidates routinely promise to appoint justices who will interpret the Constitution strictly and not "legislate from the bench." The opposite of strict construction is *broad construction*. Advocates of strict construction often contend that the government should do nothing that is not specifically mentioned in the Constitution. In 1803, for example,

Justice Stephen Breyer and Justice Ruth Bader Ginsburg are generally considered to be members of the Court's so-called liberal wing. *How might they tend to interpret the law?*

construed strictly, and it should not be construed leniently; it should be construed reasonably, to contain all that it fairly means."[17]

What Scalia means by textualism is that when determining the meaning of legislation, he refuses to consider the legislative debates that took place when the measure was passed, the nature of the problem the legislation was meant to address, or anything other than the actual text of the law.

ORIGINAL INTENT A second conservative philosophy is called *originalism.* Justice Thomas is a well-known advocate of this approach. Originalists believe that to determine the meaning of a particular constitutional phrase, the Court should look to the intentions of the founders. What did the framers of the Constitution themselves intend when they included the phrase in the document? To discern the intent of the founders, justices might look to sources that shed light on the founders' views. These sources could include writings by the founders, newspaper articles from that period, the *Federalist Papers,* and notes taken during the Constitutional Convention.

some strict constructionists argued that the national government had no power to double the size of the country by purchasing the Louisiana Territory. Such radical strict constructionism had little support in 1803 and is accepted by few people today.

Despite the wide popularity of strict construction as a concept, members of the Supreme Court generally reject the description. Justice Scalia, for example, who is normally considered one of the purest examples of a strict constructionist on the Court, prefers to call himself a *textualist* instead. Scalia writes, "I am not a strict constructionist, and no one ought to be. . . . A text should not be

ORIGINALISM, TEXTUALISM, AND MODERNISM
Such analysis is precisely what textualists wish to avoid when it comes to assessing modern-day statutory law. Nevertheless, Justice Scalia considers himself an originalist as well as a textualist. In the 2013–2014 term, Scalia was in agreement with Justice Thomas 91 percent of the time.

Originalism can be contrasted with what has been called *modernism.* Modernists seek to examine the Constitution in the context of today's society and to consider how modern life affects the words in the document. For an example of how originalism and modernism contrast, consider *Lawrence v. Texas,* a case mentioned earlier.

Justice Kennedy's majority opinion in the case held that laws that criminalize same-sex intimate relations are unconstitutional under the Fourteenth Amendment. An originalist could object to this judgment because the legislators who adopted the amendment never considered that it might apply to gay men and

Justice Clarence Thomas and Justice Antonin Scalia are widely seen as conservatives. *How might they approach the text of legislation?*

lesbians. In fact, both Scalia and Thomas opposed the ruling. In contrast, modernists might argue that discrimination against gays and lesbians is exactly the type of evil that the amendment sought to prevent, even though such an application never occurred to those who wrote it.

CRITICAL THINKING

▶ If President Obama is able to replace one of the justices on the Supreme Court because of death or retirement, how might the new Court rule on abortion? On affirmative action?

14–5 ASSESSING THE ROLE OF THE FEDERAL COURTS

LO Identify some of the criticisms of the federal courts and some of the checks on the power of the courts.

The federal courts have often come under attack, particularly in the last decade or so, for many reasons. This should come as no surprise in view of the policymaking power of the courts. After all, a Supreme Court decision can establish national policy on such issues as abortion, racial segregation, and gay rights. Critics, especially on the political right, frequently accuse the judiciary of "legislating from the bench." We discuss these criticisms in this chapter's *Perception versus Reality* feature, which follows.

14–5a Criticisms of the Federal Courts

Certainly, policymaking by unelected judges and justices in the federal courts has serious implications in a democracy. Some Americans, including many conservatives, contend that making policy from the bench has upset the balance of powers envisioned by the framers of the Constitution. They cite Thomas Jefferson, who once said, "To consider the judges as the ultimate arbiters of all constitutional questions [is] a very dangerous doctrine indeed, and one which would place us under the despotism of an oligarchy."[18] This group believes that we should rein in the power of the federal courts, and particularly judicial activism.

14–5b The Case for the Courts

On the other side of the debate over the courts are those who argue in favor of leaving the courts alone. Several federal court judges have sharply criticized congressional efforts to interfere with their authority. They claim that such efforts violate the Constitution's separation of powers. James M. Jeffords, a former independent senator from Vermont, likened the federal court system to a referee: "The first lesson we teach children when they enter competitive sports is to respect the referee, even if we think he [or she] might have made the wrong call. If our children can understand this, why can't our political leaders?"[19]

Others argue that there are already sufficient checks on the courts. We look at some of those next.

JUDICIAL TRADITIONS AND DOCTRINES One check on the courts is judicial restraint. Supreme Court justices traditionally have exercised a great deal of self-restraint. Justices sometimes admit to making decisions that fly in the face of their personal values and policy preferences, simply because they feel obligated to do so in view of existing law.

Self-restraint is also mandated by various established judicial traditions and doctrines, including the doctrine of *stare decisis,* which theoretically obligates the Supreme Court to follow its own precedents. Furthermore, the Supreme Court will not hear a meritless appeal just so it can rule on the issue.

Finally, more often than not, the justices narrow their rulings to focus on just one aspect of an issue, even though there may be nothing to stop them from broadening their focus and thus widening the impact of their decisions.

OTHER CHECKS The judiciary is subject to other checks as well. Courts may make rulings, but they cannot force federal and state legislatures to appropriate the funds necessary to carry out those rulings. For example, if a state supreme court decides that prison conditions must be improved, the state legislature has to find the funds to carry out the ruling or the improvements will not take place.

Additionally, legislatures can revise old laws or pass new ones in an attempt to negate a court's ruling. This may happen when a court interprets a statute in a way that Congress did not intend. Congress may also propose amendments to the Constitution to reverse Supreme Court rulings, and Congress has the authority to limit or otherwise alter the jurisdiction of the lower federal courts. Finally, although it is most unlikely, Congress could even change the number of justices on the Supreme Court, in an attempt to change the ideological balance on the Court. (President Franklin D. Roosevelt proposed such a plan in 1937—without success.)

Perception vs. REALITY

The Supreme Court Legislates from the Bench

Our Constitution gives legislative powers to the Congress exclusively. All executive powers are granted to the president. And all judicial powers are given to the judiciary. The United States Supreme Court is the final arbiter and interpreter of what is and is not constitutional. Because of its power of judicial review, it has the ability to "make law," or so it seems.

The Perception

Using the power of judicial review, the Supreme Court creates new laws. In 1954, the Court determined that racial segregation is illegal, a position that is universally accepted today but was hugely controversial back in the 1950s. The Court has also legalized sexual acts between same-sex adults and, of course, abortion. These decisions, especially the legalization of abortion, remain very divisive today.

Such decisions have had a major impact on the nature of American society. Because citizens elect members of Congress and the president only—and not members of the Supreme Court—it is undemocratic to allow these nine justices to determine laws for our nation.

The Reality

The Supreme Court cannot actually write new laws. It can only eliminate old ones. When the Court threw out laws that criminalized adult sexual activity by gay men and lesbians, it was abolishing laws, not creating them. The Court does not have the power to legislate—to create new laws.

Consider what would happen if the Court decided that some basic level of health care is a constitutional right—a highly unlikely event. Could the Court establish mechanisms by which such a right could be enforced? It could not. It takes members of Congress months of hard work to craft bills that affect our health-care system. Such legislation fills thousands of pages and can be developed only with the assistance of large numbers of experts and lobbyists. The federal courts could not undertake such projects even if they wanted to.

The courts must decide how they will handle the cases that are brought before them. To do so establishes judicial policy. It does not constitute lawmaking. In any event, we have no alternative to judicial review when it comes to determining what is or is not constitutional. Without the Supreme Court, Congress and the president could make all sorts of laws that violate our Constitution and infringe on our rights, and there would be nothing to stop them. As Chief Justice John Roberts said during his confirmation hearings, "Judges are like umpires. Umpires don't make the rules; they apply them."

 Plenty of bloggers follow the activities of the Supreme Court. One of the best is SCOTUSblog, at www.scotusblog.com, sponsored by Bloomberg Law. Another is the U.S. Supreme Court Blog, written by Paul M. Rashkind, a Florida lawyer. Find it at ussc.blogspot.com.

THE PUBLIC'S REGARD FOR THE SUPREME COURT Some have proposed that Congress, not the Supreme Court, be the final arbiter of the Constitution. In debates on this topic, one factor is often overlooked: the American public's high regard for the Supreme Court and the federal courts generally. The Court continues to be respected as a fair arbiter of conflicting interests and the protector of constitutional rights and liberties.

Even when the Court issued its decision to halt the manual recount of votes in Florida following the 2000 elections, which effectively handed the presidency to George W. Bush, Americans respected the Court's decision-making authority—although many disagreed with the Court's decision. Polls continue to show that Americans have much more trust and confidence in the Supreme Court than they do in Congress.

CRITICAL THINKING
▸ Why do you think that Americans trust the Supreme Court much more than they do Congress?

A Supreme Court decision can affect the lives of millions of Americans. For example, in 1973 the Supreme Court, in *Roe v. Wade*, held that the constitutional right to privacy included the right to have an abortion. The influence wielded by the Court today is a far cry from the Court's relative obscurity at the founding of this nation. Initially, the Supreme Court was not even included in the plans for government buildings in the national capital. It did not have its own building until 1935. Over time, however, the Court has established a reputation with the public for dispensing justice in a fair and reasonable manner. Still, Americans are at odds over a number of judicial issues:

- *Should state judges be elected—or does selection by appointment lead to a better court system?*

- *Should the United States Supreme Court accept more cases to provide a greater number of definitive rulings—or should it take on relatively few cases so that it can treat each one thoroughly?*

- *Should senators accept a Supreme Court nomination by a president of the opposing party whenever the nominee appears to have sound judicial temperament—or should senators vote only for those nominees who share their political philosophies?*

- *Should judges defer to the decisions of legislatures and administrative agencies whenever possible—or should they strictly police the constitutionality of legislative and executive decisions?*

- *Is it crucial that the Constitution be interpreted in terms of the beliefs of the founders—or should justices take account of modern circumstances that the founders could not have envisioned?*

Internet Resources

- An excellent Web site for information on the justices of the United States Supreme Court is www.oyez.org. This site offers biographies of the justices, links to opinions they have written, and, for justices who have served after 1920, video and audio materials.

- Another helpful Web site is www.law.cornell.edu/supct. This collection of United States Supreme Court cases includes recent Court decisions, as well as selected historic decisions rendered by the Court.

- The Supreme Court makes its opinions available online at its official Web site. Go to www.supremecourt.gov.

- Increasingly, decisions of the state courts are available online. You can find texts of state cases, information about state agencies and courts, and the laws of other countries by accessing Washburn University's WashLaw at www.washlaw.edu.

- To learn more about the federal court system, go to www.uscourts.gov.

STUDY TOOLS 14

READY TO STUDY?

- ☐ Review what you've read with the quiz below.
- ☐ Check your answers in Appendix D at the back of the book.
- ☐ For any questions you miss, read the corresponding Learning Outcome section again to prepare for class and your exam.
- ☐ Rip out and study the Chapter in Review card (at the back of the book).

VISIT WWW.CENGAGEBRAIN.COM:

- ☐ Interactive Quizzes
- ☐ Key Term Flashcards or Crossword Puzzles
- ☐ Audio Summaries
- ☐ Simulations, Animated Learning Modules, and Interactive Timelines
- ☐ Videos
- ☐ American Government NewsWatch

FILL-IN

LearningOutcome 14–1

1. Primary sources of American law include _____.

LearningOutcome 14–2

2. To bring a case before the Supreme Court, a party may request a _____, which is an order that the Court issues to a lower court requesting that court to send it the record of the case in question.

3. The attorneys involved with a case will present _____ to the Supreme Court, after which the justices discuss the case in conference.

4. A _____ opinion is a statement written by a justice who agrees with the Court's decision, but for reasons different from those outlined by the majority.

LearningOutcome 14–3

5. Because of a practice known as _____, home-state senators of the president's political party may be able to influence the choice of a nominee for the U.S. district court in that state.

LearningOutcome 14–4

6. Two important judicial philosophies that describe justices' attitudes toward legal interpretation, both of which are often associated with conservative principles, are _____.

LearningOutcome 14–5

7. Congress can check the power of the courts in several ways, including _____.

MULTIPLE CHOICE

LearningOutcome 14–1

8. A precedent is best defined as a
   a. controversy that is real and substantial.
   b. court decision that furnishes an example or authority for deciding subsequent cases.
   c. ruling that a person has disobeyed a court order.

LearningOutcome 14–2

9. The U.S. courts of appeals
   a. are the courts in which cases involving federal law begin.
   b. hear appeals from the U.S. district courts located within their respective judicial circuits.
   c. hear testimony and evidence before they make decisions in cases.

LearningOutcome 14–3

10. A nominee for the Supreme Court must be confirmed by a
    a. majority vote in the Senate.
    b. two-thirds vote in the Senate.
    c. majority vote in the House Judiciary Committee.

LearningOutcome 14–4

11. The power of the courts to decide on the constitutionality of legislative enactments and of actions taken by the executive branch is called
    a. judicial review.   b. *stare decisis.*   c. jurisdiction.

LearningOutcome 14–5

12. Judicial self-restraint is mandated by various judicial traditions and doctrines, such as _____, which theoretically obligates the Supreme Court to follow its own precedents.
    a. *curiae regis*   c. justiciable controversy
    b. *stare decisis*

15 | Domestic Policy

© Edward Le Poulin/Corbis

LEARNING OUTCOMES   After reading this chapter, you should be able to:

15–1 Explain what domestic policy is, and summarize the steps in the policymaking process.

15–2 Discuss the issue of health-care funding and recent legislation on universal health insurance.

15–3 Summarize the issues of energy independence, climate change, and alternative energy sources.

15–4 Describe the two major areas of economic policymaking, and discuss the issue of the public debt.

After finishing
this chapter go to
PAGE 353 for
STUDY TOOLS.

AMERICA AT ODDS

© Sakhorn/Shutterstock

Do We Send Too Many People to Prison?

Currently, there are about 2.2 million U.S. residents in prison or jail. That's roughly one in every one hundred adults. We are setting records—the share of our population in prison is thirteen times more than in Japan, nine times more than in Germany, and five times more than in Britain.

In 1970, the proportion of Americans behind bars—the *incarceration rate*—was only one-fourth of what it is today. Not surprisingly, the number of drug offenders in prison is responsible for much of this increase. Such lockups have multiplied thirteenfold since 1980.

Defense attorney Jim Felman of Tampa, Florida, said that America is conducting "an experiment in imprisoning first-time nonviolent offenders for periods of time previously reserved only for those who had killed someone." Holding that many prisoners is not cheap. It costs about $50,000 a year to house a convicted criminal in a state prison. Because of these costs, a number of conservative governors have begun to rethink their commitment to high rates of incarceration. Indeed, the massive growth in prison populations that marked the last few decades appears to have come to an end, and the incarceration rate is no longer growing. Given all this, do we still send too many Americans to prison?

Keep Criminals behind Bars—It Works

Supporters of aggressive incarceration policies argue that still more criminals should be behind bars. Putting more people in prison reduces crime rates. After all, incentives matter. If potential criminals know that they will be thrown in jail more readily and stay there longer, they will have less incentive to engage in illegal activities.

Also, the crime rate is strongly determined by the number of criminals at large. When we remove a criminal from the streets and put that person in prison, the prisoner can no longer commit crimes that harm the public. This effect of removal is called *incapacitation*. The evidence shows that during the 1960s, when incarceration rates fell, the crime rate more than doubled. As incarceration rates rose sharply in the 1990s, the crime rate went steadily down. As a comparison, the risk of criminal punishment in England has been falling. In consequence, crime rates have risen in England while they have fallen in the United States.

Tough sentencing is effective. We should not turn career criminals loose on the streets.

Too Many Laws and Too Many Prisoners

Those who argue against our high rates of incarceration point out that many individuals are convicted of nonviolent crimes. The government should not be spending $50,000 a year or more to keep such people in prison.

Too many acts have been criminalized, particularly at the federal level. Many crimes are so vaguely defined that most Americans would not know if they were breaking the law. Granted, hardcore criminals should be behind bars. But what about the casual pot smoker? (In 2013, about 700,000 people were arrested for possession of marijuana.) Or someone convicted under a federal statute designed to protect the environment? Lying to a federal official is a felony. Who can say how many people might be imprisoned based on such an act?

Many states have "habitual-offender" laws. In California, for example, more than 4,000 individuals are serving life sentences because they were convicted of a third offense—one that was neither violent nor serious. The cost to society of putting drug users behind bars is much greater than the benefits. Wouldn't that money be better spent on rehabilitation?

Where do you stand?

1. Could factors other than high incarceration rates be causing our current low crime rates? What might they be?

2. Why do you think federal, state, and local governments arrest so many drug-law violators?

Explore this issue online

- You can find several articles in the *Economist*, a British magazine, arguing that the United States imprisons too many people. Search on "economist us prison."

- The Criminal Justice Legal Foundation is among the few groups that advocate increased rates of incarceration. See its arguments at www.cjlf.org.

INTRODUCTION

Whether we send too many people to prison is just one of the issues that confront our nation's policymakers today. How are questions of national importance, such as this one, decided? Who are the major participants in the decision-making process?

To learn the answers to these questions, we need to delve into the politics of policymaking. *Policy,* or *public policy,* can be defined as a plan or course of action taken by the government to respond to a political issue or to enhance the social or political well-being of society. Public policy is the end result of the policymaking process, which will be described shortly.

In this chapter, after discussing how policy is made through the policymaking process, we look at several aspects of **domestic policy,** which consists of public policy concerning issues *within* a national unit. Specifically, we examine health-care policy, energy policy, and economic policy. We focus on these policy areas because they have been among the Obama administration's top priorities.

Bear in mind that although the focus here is on policy and policymaking at the national level, state and local governments also engage in policymaking. These governments establish policies to achieve goals relating to activities within their boundaries. This process is clearly at work in the criminal justice issues discussed in this chapter's opening *America at Odds* feature.

15–1 THE POLICYMAKING PROCESS

> **LO** Explain what domestic policy is, and summarize the steps in the policymaking process.

A new law does not appear out of nowhere. First, the problem addressed by the new law has to become part of the political agenda—that is, the problem must be defined as a political issue to be resolved by government action. Furthermore, once the issue gets on the political agenda, proposed solutions to the problem have to be formulated and then adopted. Issue identification and agenda setting, policy formulation, and policy adoption are all parts of the **policymaking process,** illustrated in Figure 15–1, which follows. The process does not end there, however. Once the law is passed, it has to be implemented and then evaluated.

Each phase of the policymaking process involves interactions among various individuals and groups. The president and members of Congress are obviously important participants in the process. Remember from Chapter 6 that interest groups also play a key role. Groups that may be affected adversely by a new policy will try to convince Congress not to adopt the policy. Groups that will benefit from the policy will exert whatever influence they can on Congress to do the opposite. Congressional committees and subcommittees may investigate the problem to be addressed by the policy and, in so doing, solicit input from members of various groups or industries.

The participants in policymaking and the nature of the debates involved depend on the particular policy being proposed, formed, or implemented. Whatever the policy, however, debate over its pros and cons occurs during each stage of the policymaking process. Additionally, making policy decisions inevitably involves *trade-offs,* in which policymakers must sacrifice one goal to achieve another because of budget constraints and other factors.

15–1a Issue Identification and Agenda Setting

If no one recognizes a problem, then no matter how important the problem may be, politically it does not yet really exist. Thus, *issue identification* is part of the first stage of the policymaking process. Some group—whether it be the media, the public, politicians, or even foreign commentators—must identify a problem that can be solved politically. The second part of this stage of the policymaking process involves getting the issue on the political agenda to be addressed by Congress. This is called **agenda setting,** or *agenda building.*

A problem in society may be identified as an issue and included on the political agenda when an event or series of events leads to a call for action. For example, the failure of a major bank may lead to the conclusion that the financial industry is in trouble and that the government should take action to rectify the problem. Dramatic increases in health-care costs may cause the media or other groups to consider health care a priority that should be on the national political agenda. Sometimes, the social or economic effects of a national

domestic policy Public policy concerning issues within a national unit, such as national policy concerning health care or the economy.

policymaking process The procedures involved in getting an issue on the political agenda; formulating, adopting, and implementing a policy with regard to the issue; and then evaluating the results of the policy.

agenda setting Getting an issue on the political agenda to be addressed by Congress; part of the first stage of the policymaking process.

FIGURE 15-1 THE POLICYMAKING PROCESS

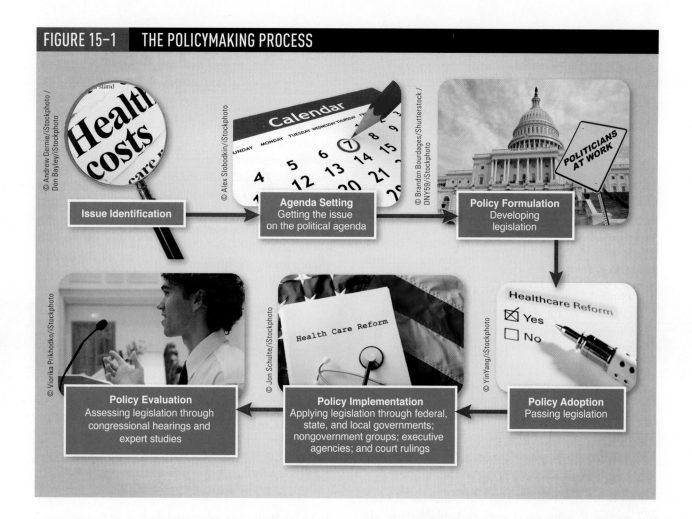

Issue Identification

Agenda Setting
Getting the issue
on the political agenda

Policy Formulation
Developing
legislation

Policy Evaluation
Assessing legislation through
congressional hearings and
expert studies

Policy Implementation
Applying legislation through federal,
state, and local governments;
nongovernment groups; executive
agencies; and court rulings

Policy Adoption
Passing legislation

Healthcare Reform
☒ Yes
☐ No

POLITICIANS AT WORK

Health Care Reform

calamity, such as the Great Depression of the 1930s or the terrorist attacks of September 11, 2001, create a pressing need for government action.

15–1b Policy Formulation and Adoption

The second stage in the policymaking process involves the formulation and adoption of specific plans for achieving a particular goal, such as health-care reform. The president, members of Congress, administrative agencies, and interest group leaders typically are the key participants in developing proposed legislation. Remember from Chapter 13 that iron triangles and issue networks work together in forming mutually beneficial policies. To a certain extent, the courts also establish policies when they interpret statutes passed by legislative bodies or make decisions concerning disputes not yet addressed by any law, such as disputes involving new technology.

Note that some issues may become a part of the political agenda but never proceed beyond that stage of the policymaking process. Usually, this happens when it is impossible to achieve a consensus on what policy should be adopted.

15–1c Policy Implementation

Because of our federal system, the implementation of national policies necessarily requires the cooperation of the federal government and the various state and local governments. A case in point is the Obama administration's Race to the Top program, which was included in the February 2009 stimulus package. Race to the Top was a competition among state governments to win up to $4.35 billion in federal education grants. The states competed by undertaking reforms to their kindergarten–through–high school educational systems. Reforms included performance-based standards for teachers and promotion of charter schools. All but four states entered the competition.

Successful implementation usually requires the support of groups outside the government. For example, the first-round Race to the Top winners—Delaware and Tennessee—were able to persuade their teachers' unions to support the reforms.

Policy implementation also involves agencies in the executive branch (see Chapter 13). Once Congress establishes a policy by enacting legislation, the executive branch, through its agencies, enforces the new policy.

Furthermore, the courts are involved in policy implementation, because the legislation and administrative regulations enunciating the new policy must be interpreted and applied to specific situations by the courts.

15–1d Policy Evaluation

The final stage of policymaking involves evaluating the success of a policy during and following its implementation. Groups both inside and outside the government participate in the evaluation process.

Congress may hold hearings to obtain feedback from different groups on how a statute or regulation has affected them. Scholars and scientists may conduct studies to determine whether a particular law, such as an environmental law designed to reduce air pollution, has actually achieved the desired result—less air pollution. Sometimes, feedback obtained in these or other ways indicates that a policy has failed, and a new policymaking process may be undertaken to modify the policy or create a more effective one.

15–1e Policymaking and Special Interests

The policymaking steps just discussed may seem straightforward, but they are not. Every bill that passes through Congress is a compromise. Every bill that passes through Congress is also an opportunity for individual members of Congress to help constituents, particularly those who were kind enough to contribute financially to the members' reelection campaigns.

THE FARM BILL Consider the Agricultural Act of 2014, commonly known as the 2014 farm bill. The act authorizes about $95 billion per year over the next decade. About $75 billion is actually for the Special Nutrition Assistance Program (SNAP), or food stamps. As we observed in the *America at Odds* feature in Chapter 6, combining food stamp authorization with agricultural subsidies has been a way to get urban liberals to vote for the legislation.

The centerpiece of the farm bill was the abolition of *direct payments* for certain crops—payments made regardless of whether the recipient actually planted the crops in question. Most of the funds saved were transferred to a much-enlarged crop insurance program. Supporters claimed that the new bill would reduce federal expenditures. Critics, pointing to falling prices for corn, soybeans, and wheat, argued that it would in fact be more expensive.

SPECIAL PROVISIONS TO HELP THE BILL ALONG A polarized Congress meant that the bill would be hard to pass—indeed, it was two years late.

Special provisions, not requested by the Department of Agriculture, helped the bill along. A pilot program for industrial hemp production helped secure the support of members from Kentucky. Profit-margin insurance for catfish helped sew up the Mississippi delegation. Newly insured products include biofuels, lamb, peanuts, poultry, sesame, sushi rice, and swine. Various GMO (genetically modified organism) crops now receive special insurance treatment. The bill included livestock disaster relief and funds to combat a disease called citrus greening in Florida.

Some provisions had little to do with agriculture or nutrition. The EPA was prohibited from proceeding with a program against overfishing. Central State University in Ohio, a historically black college, received additional federal aid. Clearly, policymaking is a complicated process.

15–2 HEALTH-CARE POLICY

LO Discuss the issue of health-care funding and recent legislation on universal health insurance.

In March 2010, Congress passed the Patient Protection and Affordable Care Act and a companion bill. The two bills, which President Barack Obama immediately signed, contained health-care reforms that were among the most consequential government initiatives in many years.

Even before the new legislation was adopted, the federal government was paying the health-care costs of more than 100 million Americans. When President Obama took office, the government was picking up the tab for about 50 percent of the nation's health-care costs. Private insurance was responsible for about a third of all health-care payments, and the rest was met either by patients themselves or by charity. Paying for health-care expenses, in other words, was already a major federal responsibility, and questions about how the government should carry out that function in the future were unavoidable.

15–2a Two Problems with U.S. Health Care

Our system for funding health care has suffered from two major problems. One is that health care is expensive. About 18 percent of national spending in the United States goes to health care, compared with 12 percent in France, 11 percent in Canada, and 9 percent in Australia.

> "It helps to think of the government as **an insurance company with an army.**"
>
> ~ **Mike Holland,** Office of Science and Technology Policy under President George W. Bush

U.S. health-care costs have been rising for years, as you can see in Figure 15–2, which follows.

Also, 50 million Americans—close to 16 percent of the population—still had no health-care insurance as of 2013, before the Affordable Care Act was fully implemented. Lack of coverage means that people may put off seeing a physician until it is too late for effective treatment or may be forced into bankruptcy due to large medical bills. One study has estimated that 20,000 people each year die prematurely because they lack health insurance.[1] (Others dispute these findings.) All other economically advanced nations provide health insurance to everyone, typically through a government program similar to Social Security or Medicare in the United States.

Before discussing the recently passed health-care reforms, let's first look at the programs that were already in place. The most important of these is **Medicare,** which provides health-care insurance to Americans aged sixty-five and over, and **Medicaid,** which funds health-care coverage for low-income persons.

15–2b Medicaid and Medicare

The federal government pays for health care in a variety of ways. Like many major employers, it buys health-care insurance for its employees. Members of the armed forces, veterans, and Native Americans receive medical services provided directly by the government. Most federal spending on health care, however, is accounted for by Medicare and Medicaid. Both are costly, and each in its own way poses a serious financial problem for the government.

MEDICAID A joint federal-state program, Medicaid provides health-care subsidies to low-income persons. The federal government provides about 60 percent of the Medicaid budget, and the states provide the rest. More than 60 million people are in the program. Many Medicaid recipients are elderly residents of nursing homes—the Medicare program does not pay for nursing home expenses.

Although recent cost-containment measures have slowed the growth of Medicaid spending, the cost of Medicaid has doubled in the last decade. This increase has put a considerable strain on the budgets of many states. About 17 percent of the average state general fund budget now goes to Medicaid. Another program, the **Children's Health Insurance Program (CHIP),** covers children in families with incomes that are modest but too high to qualify for Medicaid. By fiscal year 2015, the total cost of Medicaid and CHIP for all levels of government was about $535 billion.

The Great Recession put a considerable strain on the states' ability to pick up their share of Medicaid payments. The Obama administration's February 2009 stimulus package, therefore, included $87 billion to reduce temporarily the Medicaid burden on the states. Congressional Democrats also substantially increased the size of CHIP within weeks of Obama's inauguration.

MEDICARE Medicare is the federal government's health-care program for persons sixty-five years of age and older. Medicare is now the

Medicare A federal government program that pays for health-care insurance for Americans aged sixty-five years and over.

Medicaid A joint federal-state program that pays for health-care services for low-income persons.

Children's Health Insurance Program (CHIP) A joint federal-state program that provides health-care insurance for low-income children.

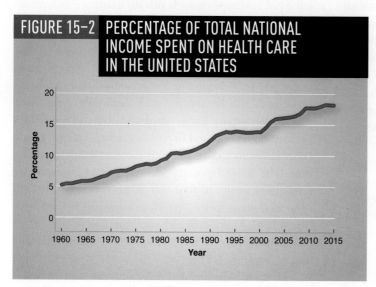

FIGURE 15–2 PERCENTAGE OF TOTAL NATIONAL INCOME SPENT ON HEALTH CARE IN THE UNITED STATES

Source: National Health Expenditure Accounts, Centers for Medicare & Medicaid Services.

government's second-largest domestic spending program, after Social Security. In 1970, Medicare accounted for only 0.7 percent of total annual U.S. national income (gross domestic product, or GDP). It currently accounts for about 3 percent of GDP, and costs are expected to rise as millions of "baby boomers" retire over the next two decades.

By 2030, the sixty-five-and-older population is expected to double. Further, technological developments in health care and the advancement of medical science are driving medical costs up every year. There are simply more actions that medical science can take to keep people alive—and Americans naturally want to take advantage of these services.

ENTITLEMENT PROGRAMS Medicare and Medicaid are examples of federal **entitlement programs.** Social Security and unemployment compensation are two other examples. Entitlement programs pay out benefits to persons who meet specified requirements. In the case of Social Security, for example, the government issues payments based on a recipient's age at retirement and past wage or salary income.

Characteristics of Entitlements.   A special characteristic of entitlement programs is that they continue from year to year, regardless of whether Congress passes an annual funding measure. An entitlement continues until the government explicitly adopts a new law to change the benefits or otherwise alter the program. Further, Congress has no direct control over how much an entitlement program will cost in any particular year. It is usually possible to estimate the costs, but the actual amount of spending depends on how many eligible persons sign up for the benefits.

In this way, entitlements are different from *discretionary spending.* In a discretionary program, Congress establishes a binding annual budget for a government agency that the agency cannot exceed. Note that "discretionary" does not mean "unimportant." As an exam-

"Nature provides a free lunch, but only if we control our appetites."

~ William Doyle Ruckelshaus,
First Head of the Environmental Protection Agency 1970–1973

ple, the nation's armed forces are funded through discretionary spending.

Entitlements and Politics. Entitlements lie at the heart of the political differences between liberals and conservatives. For liberals, entitlements are an essential part of the social compact that binds us together. For conservatives, entitlements breed a dangerous dependency on the government. In understanding the 2010 Affordable Care Act—commonly called Obamacare—it is important to realize that the program was primarily designed as an entitlement.

15–2c The Democrats Propose Universal Coverage

As noted earlier, the United States has been the only economically advanced nation that did not provide universal health-insurance coverage to its citizens. Democratic president Bill Clinton (1993–2001) and first lady Hillary Clinton made a serious push for a universal plan during President Clinton's first term, but the project failed to pass Congress.

Many universal health-insurance plans—for example, the systems in Canada and France—involve government monopolies. In these nations, the government is responsible for providing basic health-care insurance to everyone through **national health insurance.** Some wealthy nations, such as the Netherlands and Switzerland, provide universal coverage through private insurance companies instead. The plan that the United States has adopted also provides a large role for the private sector.

CONGRESS ADDRESSES THE ISSUE   The program developed by Congress in 2009 assumed that employer-provided health insurance would continue to be a major part of the system. Large employers that did not offer a plan would be required to pay a penalty. Medicaid would be available to individuals with incomes up to about 1.5 times the federal poverty level. (In 2014, the poverty level for a family of four was $23,850.) A new health-insurance marketplace, the Health Insurance Exchange, would allow individuals and small employers to shop for plans. Insurance companies would not be allowed to deny anyone coverage.

Most individuals would be required to obtain coverage or pay an income tax penalty. This requirement is

entitlement program A government program that provides benefits to all persons who meet specified requirements.

national health insurance A program, found in many of the world's economically advanced nations, under which the central government provides basic health-care insurance coverage to everyone in the country.

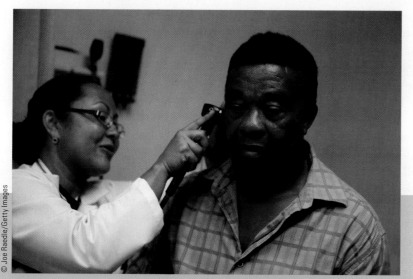

A patient receives a checkup from a physician in April 2014 in Hollywood, Florida. He is newly insured under the Affordable Care Act. *Are patients without insurance likely to receive regular checkups? Why or why not?*

known as the **individual mandate** or the *personal mandate.* Those with low-to-middle incomes would receive help in paying their premiums. Subsidies would be phased out for those earning more than four times the federal poverty level.

To fund the program, Congress adopted various new taxes and fees, such as a new tax on investments for high-income persons, an increased Medicare tax rate, and a new tax on high-end ("Cadillac") health policies that cost more than a specified amount.

EXPECTED RESULTS The bills passed by Congress and signed by President Obama were to become effective over a period of several years. One immediate change was that young people could remain covered by their parents' insurance until they turned twenty-six. Another immediate result was subsidies to small employers that obtained insurance plans for their employees.

The most important provisions, however, would not take effect until January 1, 2014. From that day on, subsidies would help citizens purchase health-care insurance if they were not covered by Medicare, Medicaid, or an employer's plan. Insurance could be purchased through online insurance exchanges run either by the states or by the federal government.

THE CONSERVATIVE REACTION In 2009, the Democrats were able to win the support—or at least the acquiescence—of groups that had opposed universal health-care plans in the past. That included the American Medical Association, hospitals, insurance companies,

and pharmaceutical firms. Nevertheless, opposition to the reforms was widespread and strong. Conservatives saw the Affordable Care Act as a "big government takeover" of health care and a threat to popular freedoms. The individual mandate was at the heart of much of the opposition. After all, it was a way of pressuring people to do something that they might not otherwise do. Supporters of reform could point out that the system would face financial collapse unless everyone, healthy or unhealthy, bought insurance. This fact did nothing to make the reforms, dubbed Obamacare by opponents, more palatable.

Attempts to Repeal the Legislation. As we explained in Chapter 3, attempts to challenge the constitutionality of the reforms failed, although the Supreme Court did allow state governments to opt out of expanding the Medicaid program.[2] Repeated attempts by Republicans in the House to repeal or delay Obamacare were ineffectual. Because most of the program took the form of an entitlement, the Republicans would need control of both chambers of Congress and the presidency to abolish it. In 2012, however, Obama was reelected and the Democrats retained control of the Senate. Repeal of Obamacare was one of the Republican demands during the government shutdown of October 2013, but that campaign eventually collapsed.

Halbig v. Burwell. Opponents of the Affordable Care Act were heartened in July 2013 by a ruling of the D.C. Court of Appeals. In *Halbig v. Burwell,* a three-judge panel voted 2–1 that the act did not in fact allow the federal government to subsidize participants in the federal insurance exchanges.[3] Most legal experts, however, doubted that this ruling would survive further appeals.

IMPLEMENTATION BEGINS On October 1, 2013, Americans who were eligible to buy health-care insurance through a state or federal exchange had their first chance to do so. It was expected, though not required, that most of the signups would take place online. Many of the state online exchanges functioned effectively.

individual mandate In the context of health-care reform, a requirement that all persons obtain health-care insurance from one source or another. Those failing to do so must pay a penalty.

A few never worked properly, forcing signups to take place off-line. The federal site turned out to be almost completely nonfunctional. Some signups were processed by Thanksgiving, but the site was not fully operational until the end of the year. Obamacare's disastrous roll-out was a major political blow to the Democrats, and it completely reversed the popularity advantage they derived from the government shutdown that same month.

By the end of the signup period in April 2014, however, 8 million Americans had obtained insurance policies through the state and federal exchanges. This was 2 million more than predicted by the Congressional Budget Office. (It was also millions less than the number of people who were actually eligible, but new programs of this type have always experienced slow initial signups.) Obamacare remained highly unpopular among Republicans, but its importance as a political issue had begun to decline.

CRITICAL THINKING

▶ Is it reasonable for health care to continue to absorb increasingly larger shares of the nation's budget—or will that interfere too much with our country's ability to purchase other goods and services? Explain your reasoning.

15–3 ENERGY POLICY

LO Summarize the issues of energy independence, climate change, and alternative energy sources.

Energy policy was a second major priority for the Obama administration, but its accomplishments in this area have been relatively modest. The Democrats did move a major energy bill through the House in 2009, but it died in the Senate. Energy policy is important because of two problems: (1) our reliance on imported oil, and (2) the possibility of global climate change.

Corporate Average Fuel Economy (CAFE) standards
A set of federal standards under which each vehicle manufacturer (or the industry as a whole) must meet a miles-per-gallon benchmark averaged across all new cars or trucks.

global warming An increase in the average temperature of the Earth's surface over the last half century and its projected continuation; referred to more generally as *climate change*.

15–3a The Problem of Imported Oil

It is estimated that in 2016, our nation will import 25 percent of its petroleum supply. This figure has fallen substantially in recent years. In 2005, imports were more than 60 percent of consumption. Still, oil imports are a potential problem largely because many of the nations that export oil are not particularly friendly to the United States. Some, such as Iran, are outright adversaries. Other oil exporters that could pose difficulties include Iraq, Libya, Nigeria, Russia, and Venezuela.

Fortunately for the United States, the sources of our imported oil are highly diversified, and we are not excessively dependent on any one nation. Canada and Mexico, friendly neighbors, supply 45 percent of our imports. Many of our European and Asian allies, however, are dependent on imports from questionable regimes.

THE PRICE OF OIL   Until fairly recently, the price of oil was low, and the U.S. government was under little pressure to address our dependence on imports. In 1998, the price per barrel fell below $12. In July 2008, however, the price of oil spiked to more than $125 a barrel, forcing U.S. gasoline prices above $4 per gallon. Thereafter, oil prices fell dramatically when demand collapsed due to the global economic panic of that period. Oil prices then rose again along with the economic recovery—the price of gasoline reached $4 per gallon in some states in 2011 and 2012.

FUEL EFFICIENCY STANDARDS   In the 1970s, the federal government responded to an earlier spurt in oil prices by imposing fuel-mileage standards on cars and trucks sold in this country. Under the **Corporate Average Fuel Economy (CAFE) standards,** each vehicle manufacturer had to meet a miles-per-gallon benchmark, which was averaged across all cars and trucks that it sold.

With the steep rise in oil prices in 2007 and 2008, measures to restrain U.S. fuel consumption were on the agenda again. In 2009, President Obama issued higher fuel efficiency standards for cars and trucks. In August 2012, the Obama administration raised fuel efficiency standards even higher. By 2025, the nation's combined fleet of new cars and light trucks must have an average fuel efficiency of about 49 miles per gallon.

15–3b Climate Change

Observations collected by agencies such as the National Aeronautics and Space Administration (NASA) suggest that during the last half century, average global temperatures increased by about 0.74 degrees Celsius (1.33 degrees Fahrenheit). Most climatologists believe that this **global warming** is the result of human activities, especially the release of **green-house gases** such as CO_2 into the atmosphere.

A United Nations body, the Intergovernmental Panel on Climate Change (IPCC), estimated in 2013 that during the twenty-first century, global temperatures could rise an additional 1.0 to 4.8 degrees Celsius (1.8 to 8.6 degrees Fahrenheit). Warming may continue in subsequent centuries.

The predicted outcomes of climate change vary, depending on the climate models on which they are based. If the oceans grow warmer, seawater will expand, and polar ice will melt. (This last event is already underway.) These two developments will cause sea levels to rise, possibly negatively affecting coastal areas. Rainfall patterns are expected to change, turning some areas into deserts but allowing agriculture to expand elsewhere. Other likely effects could include increases in extreme weather.

Fuel-efficient automobiles such as this Honda hybrid are a major way in which the United States is curbing its consumption of petroleum. Another is a reduction in the number of miles driven. *Why are young people driving less than previous generations did?*

THE CLIMATE CHANGE DEBATE Some scientists dispute the consensus view of climate change. They argue that any observed warming is due largely to natural causes and may not continue into the future. Although this position is rare among scientists, it has been common in the broader community of Americans. Some public opinion polls taken in 2010, for example, revealed that only a third of Americans believed that climate change is the result of human activities. By 2013, however, belief that human activities were responsible for global warming had risen from one-third to about half of all respondents in some polls. Hot summers, widespread drought, and severe storms may have contributed to these results.

Attitudes toward climate change have become highly politicized. Some commentators on the political right contend that global warming is a giant liberal hoax designed to clear the way for increased government control of the economy and society. At the same time, many on the political left believe that the right-wing refusal to accept the existence of climate change threatens the very future of the human race.

Members of Congress are influenced by these attitudes even if they do not necessarily share them. As a result, congressional Republicans and Democrats have almost no common ground on questions of how

potential climate change might be reduced or its effects mitigated.

15–3c New Energy Sources

The issues of U.S. energy security and climate change raise the question of whether we can develop new energy sources. Energy security means finding energy sources that are produced either in this country or by friendly neighbors such as Canada. A reduction in global warming means deploying energy sources that do not release CO_2 and other greenhouse gases into the atmosphere. As explained next, however, new energy sources may be accompanied by problems.

EXPANDED SUPPLIES OF OIL AND NATURAL GAS By 2012, many Americans had begun to realize that they were entering a new era of energy production. U.S. oil production, which declined rapidly after 1985, began to grow again in 2009. As noted earlier, it is expected that crude oil imports will soon drop to 25 percent of consumption, down from more than 60 percent. In 2011, U.S. exports of petroleum *products*—refined goods such as gasoline—exceeded imports for the first time since 1949.

greenhouse gas A gas that, when released into the atmosphere, traps the sun's heat and slows its release into outer space. Carbon dioxide (CO_2) is a major example.

UNEMPLOYMENT The most important sign that the economy is still troubled is the high rate of **unemployment.** The rate of unemployment is measured by a government survey. People are defined as unemployed if they are without a job and are actively looking for one. An unemployment rate of 7 percent means that there are seven people looking for work for every ninety-three people who have a job. If "discouraged workers," who have given up looking for work, are also counted, the unemployment rate is substantially higher.

Even in the best of times, there is always a degree of unemployment, because some people are between jobs. Unemployment rates of 8 or 9 percent, however, are clear signs of economic and social distress. Few experiences are more psychologically damaging than extended unemployment. Reducing unemployment is a major policy objective.

INFLATION Unemployment and recession go hand in hand. A second economic problem that the government must occasionally address is associated with economic booms. That problem is **inflation,** a sustained rise in average prices. A rise in prices is equivalent to a decline in the value of the dollar. High rates of inflation were a serious problem in the 1970s, but rates have fallen since. Even though the rate of inflation is now relatively low, many people are fearful that high rates could return at some point in the future.

The national government has two main tools to smooth the business cycle and to reduce unemployment and inflation. These tools are monetary policy and fiscal policy, and we describe them in the following sections.

President Obama picked Janet Yellen, vice chair of the U.S. Federal Reserve, to replace Ben Bernanke as chair of the Fed. Bernanke retired in January 2014. Yellen is the first woman to lead the Fed. *What does the Fed do?*

15–4b Monetary Policy

One of the tools used in managing the economy is **monetary policy,** which involves changing the amount of money in circulation to affect interest rates, credit markets, the rate of inflation, the rate of economic growth, and the rate of unemployment. Monetary policy is under the control of the Federal Reserve System, an independent regulatory agency that is one of the government's most important sources of economic power.

The Federal Reserve System (the Fed) was established by Congress as the nation's central banking system in 1913. The Fed is governed by a board of seven governors, including the very influential chairperson. The president appoints the members of the board of governors, and the Senate must approve the nominations. Members of the board serve for fourteen-year terms. In addition to controlling the money supply, the Fed has a number of responsibilities in supervising and regulating the nation's banking system.

EASY MONEY, TIGHT MONEY The Fed and its **Federal Open Market Committee (FOMC)** make decisions about monetary policy several times each year. In theory, monetary policy is relatively straightforward. In periods of recession and high unemployment, the Fed pursues an **easy-money policy** to stimulate the economy by expanding the rate of growth of the money sup-

---

unemployment The state of not having a job even when actively seeking one.

inflation A sustained rise in average prices; equivalent to a decline in the value of the dollar.

monetary policy Actions taken by the Federal Reserve Board to change the amount of money in circulation to affect interest rates, credit markets, the rate of inflation, the rate of economic growth, and the rate of unemployment.

Federal Open Market Committee (FOMC) The most important body within the Federal Reserve System; decides how monetary policy should be carried out.

easy-money policy A monetary policy that involves stimulating the economy by expanding the rate of growth of the money supply.

ply. An easy-money policy supposedly will lead to lower interest rates and induce consumers to spend more and producers to invest more.

In periods of rising inflation, the Fed does the reverse: it reduces the rate of growth in the amount of money in circulation—this is called a *tight-money policy*. This policy should cause interest rates to rise, thus inducing consumers to spend less and businesses to invest less.

"PUSHING ON A STRING" Although an easy-money policy may sound simple, the reality is not simple at all. To give one example, if times are hard enough, people and businesses may not want to borrow even if interest rates go down to zero. The government cannot force anyone to borrow, after all.

This state of affairs is not hypothetical—it has characterized the economy since 2008. The Fed has managed to keep the interest rate for short-term federal debt almost at zero, but rates of borrowing remain depressed. Instead of percolating into the actual economy, much of the extra money created by the Fed has piled up in excess bank reserves. With some reason, the failure of easy-money policy to spur the economy has been described as "pushing on a string."

The Fed has responded to the failure of its easy-money policy by adopting some unorthodox tactics. Ordinarily, the Fed expands the money supply by using the newly created money to purchase short-term federal government debt. Since 2010, however, it has undertaken programs of buying long-term federal debt in the hope that long-term purchases will be more effective than short-term ones. In addition, the Fed has begun purchasing private-sector debt obligations, such as securities based on residential mortgages.

CONSERVATIVE CRITICISMS The Fed's recent policies have alarmed some conservatives. A number of economists fear that at some point in the future the extra money created by the Fed—which is currently just sitting there—could pass into the real economy with explosive speed. The result would be increased inflation. In 2011, the Republican leadership in Congress sent a joint letter to the Fed demanding that it halt its activist policies. Texas governor Rick Perry, a candidate for president, went so far as to call the Fed's actions "treasonous."

A second response to the Fed's actions has been the growth in the philosophy of "hard money" among radical conservatives. Hard-money advocates believe that the government should not be in the business of creating money at all, but should tie the value of the dollar to commodities such as gold. Mainstream economists, both liberal and conservative, believe that such a policy would

lead to a dramatic contraction in the money supply and a recession of unprecedented severity.

15–4c Fiscal Policy

Prior to the onset of the Great Recession, mainstream economists agreed on one point: under ordinary circumstances, monetary policy would be sufficient to steer the economy. If monetary policy proved to be inadequate, however, many economists also recommended use of a second tool—fiscal policy.

The principle underlying **fiscal policy,** like the one that underlies monetary policy, is relatively simple: when unemployment is rising and the economy is going into a recession, fiscal policy should stimulate economic activity by decreasing taxes, increasing government spending, or both. When unemployment is decreasing and prices are rising (that is, when we have inflation), fiscal policy should curb economic activity by reducing government spending, increasing taxes, or both.

In the past, fiscal policy meant raising or lowering rates of taxation. Such changes could be accomplished quickly and would not trigger disputes about government spending. The severity of the Great Recession, however, led some economists to recommend increases in government spending as well.

U.S. fiscal policy is associated with the economic theories of the British economist John Maynard Keynes (1883–1946). Keynes's theories, which we address next, were the result of his study of the Great Depression of the 1930s.

KEYNES AND THE GREAT DEPRESSION According to **Keynesian economics,** the nation cannot automatically recover from a disaster such as the Great Depression—or for that matter, the Great Recession. In both cases, the shock that initiates the crisis frightens consumers and businesses so much that they, in great numbers, begin to reduce their borrowing and spending.

Unfortunately, if everyone in the economy tries to cut spending at the same time, demand for goods and services drops sharply. That, in turn, reduces the income of everyone selling these goods and services. People become even more reluctant to borrow and spend. The cycle feeds on itself.

---

fiscal policy The use of changes in government expenditures and taxes to alter national economic variables.

Keynesian economics An economic theory proposed by British economist John Maynard Keynes that is typically associated with the use of fiscal policy to alter national economic variables.

British economist John Maynard Keynes developed theories of how to pull the world out of the Great Depression in the 1930s. *What policies did Keynes advocate to end a depression?*

The Keynesian solution to this type of impasse is for the government to provide the demand by a huge, if temporary, spending program. The spending has to be financed by borrowing. The government, in other words, begins borrowing when the private sector stops. Some economists believe that just such a spending program broke the back of the Great Depression—that is, the "spending program" known as World War II (1939–1945).

KEYNES AND THE GREAT RECESSION Until recently, support for Keynesianism was relatively bipartisan. Republican president Richard Nixon once said, "I am now a Keynesian." Even President George W. Bush justified his tax cuts with Keynesian rhetoric. From the years after World War II until the first years of the twenty-first century, it was relatively easy to be a Keynesian. After all, Keynesian solutions could be implemented through relatively small changes to rates of taxation. The Bush administration sponsored just such a tax-based stimulus in early 2008, when the Great Recession had already begun but was not yet a major disaster.

Obama versus the Republicans. In February 2009, with the full scope of the recession evident, Obama proposed and Congress passed a stimulus package of roughly $800 billion, made up mostly of spending, not tax cuts. This was a classical Keynesian response to the recession,

but it turned out to be a one-time measure. From 2009 on, Republicans in Congress strongly rejected Keynesianism. An important group of economists had long opposed Keynesian theories. They argued that it is not possible to stimulate the economy through federal borrowing. The borrowing just drains funds from some other part of the economy. A few members of Congress turned to these thinkers. Most of the Republicans, however, simply objected to the use of budget deficits as a recession-fighting tool.

The Eclipse of Keynesianism. If it took World War II to eliminate unemployment in the 1940s, Keynesian economics faced a problem in 2009. The increase in the federal budget deficit necessary to end the economic crisis could be very large. Some Keynesians outside the Obama administration calculated that, to have a real impact, stimulus spending would have to be three times the $800 billion already committed.[5] That type of program was politically impossible. Few Americans would accept new government spending programs amounting to trillions of dollars. By the time of his State of the Union address in 2010, Obama himself was employing rhetoric that was substantially anti-Keynesian.

State and local government spending dropped sharply after the expiration of the 2009 stimulus, and more than half a million state and local workers lost their jobs. At the federal level, even though explicitly Keynesian fiscal policies were off the table, the government continued to run trillion-dollar budget deficits through 2012. The size of these deficits became a major political issue. By 2013, however, the deficit had begun to decline noticeably.

15–4d The Federal Tax System

The government raises money to pay its expenses in two ways: through taxes levied on business and personal income and through borrowing. The American income tax system is progressive—meaning that as you earn more income, you pay a higher tax rate on the additional income earned.

The 2014 tax rates are shown in Table 15–1, which follows. More than 40 percent of American families earn so little that they have no income tax liability at all, and this figure temporarily hit 47 percent at the height of the recession. (For a discussion of the amount of taxes paid by the rich versus other groups in American society, see this chapter's *Perception versus Reality* feature, which follows.)

THE ACTION-REACTION SYNDROME The Internal Revenue Code consists of thousands of pages, thousands of sections, and thousands of subsections. In other words, our tax system is not simple. Part of the reason for this complexity is that tax policy has always been plagued by the **action-reaction syndrome,** a term describing the following phenomenon: *for every government action, there will be a reaction by the public.*

Often, the government will react with another action, and the public will follow with further reaction. The ongoing action-reaction cycle is clearly operative in policymaking on taxes.

TAX LOOPHOLES   Generally, the action-reaction syndrome means that the higher the tax rate—the action on the part of the government—the greater the public's reaction to that tax rate. Individuals and corporations facing high tax rates will react by making concerted attempts to

get Congress to add various loopholes to the tax law that will allow them to reduce their taxable incomes.

Years ago, when Congress imposed very high tax rates on high incomes, it also provided for more loopholes. These loopholes enabled many wealthy individuals to decrease their tax bills significantly. For example, special tax provisions allowed investors in oil and gas wells to reduce their taxable income. Additional loopholes permitted individuals to shift income from one year to the next—which meant that they could postpone the

> **action-reaction syndrome**   The principle that for every government action, there will be a reaction by the public.

Perception vs. REALITY

Tax-Rate Cuts Allow the Rich to Pay Lower Taxes

As the saying goes, only two things are certain—death and taxes. In recent years, though, different presidents have instituted a number of tax-rate cuts. A major reduction occurred in 2003 under the administration of George W. Bush.

The Perception

You often hear or read that the Bush tax-rate cuts favored the rich. After all, it's the rich who received the lion's share of the benefits from these tax-rate cuts.

The Reality

First, we must distinguish between tax rates and taxes paid. It is true that the Bush tax cuts lowered the top marginal income tax rate from 39.6 percent to 35 percent and that the long-term capital gains tax rate dropped from 20 percent to 15 percent. Also, the rate applied to dividends fell. Therefore, the tax rates on the highest-income individuals did indeed fall after the tax cuts of 2003 were enacted.

At the same time, though, the percentage of taxes paid by the rich went up, not down. Indeed, the share of individual income taxes paid by the top 1 percent of income earners rose steadily from about 1981 to 2000, dropped off a bit from 2000 to 2003, and has risen ever since.

According to the nonpartisan Congressional Budget Office, the top 40 percent of income earners in the United States pay 99.1 percent of all income taxes. The top 10 percent pay more than 70 percent of all income taxes. At the bottom end of the scale, more than 40 percent of this nation's households pay no income taxes at all (though they do pay Social Security and Medicare contributions). Finally, it is true that the rich have been getting richer in the United States. Nevertheless, their individual tax liabilities have gone up more quickly than their share of income.

These data give us some indication of what may happen now that Congress has failed to extend the Bush tax cuts on the upper tax brackets. As a result of changes made in December 2012, the top long-term capital gains tax rate rose to 23.8 percent. The marginal income tax rate for a couple making more than $450,000 per year went up from 35 percent to 39.6 percent. Wealthy individuals are likely to respond to these higher tax rates by adjusting their behavior. The higher rates could actually result in the rich paying less in taxes, not more.

 BLOG ⏻   **Scott Adams, creator of the Dilbert comic strip, makes hilarious and fresh observations about all sorts of things on his blog. Taxing the rich is just one of his topics—try searching on "dilbert blog tax 2007."**

Single Persons		Married Filing Jointly	
Marginal Tax Bracket	Marginal Tax Rate	Marginal Tax Bracket	Marginal Tax Rate
Up to $9,075	10%	Up to $18,150	10%
$9,076–$36,900	15%	$18,151–$73,800	15%
$36,901–$89,350	25%	$73,801–$148,850	25%
$89,351–$186,350	28%	$148,851–$226,850	28%
$186,351–$405,100	33%	$226,851–$405,100	33%
$405,101–$406,750	35%	$405,101–$457,600	35%
$406,751 or more	39.6%	$457,601 or more	39.6%

Source: Internal Revenue Service.

payment of their taxes for one year. Still more loopholes let U.S. citizens form corporations outside the United States in order to avoid some taxes completely.

WILL WE EVER HAVE A TRULY SIMPLE TAX SYSTEM? The Tax Reform Act of 1986 was intended to lower taxes and simplify the tax code—and it did just that for most taxpayers. A few years later, however, large federal deficits forced Congress to choose between cutting spending and raising taxes, and Congress opted to do the latter. Tax increases occurred under the administrations of both George H. W. Bush (1989–1993) and Bill Clinton (1993–2001). In fact, the tax rate for the highest income bracket rose from 28 percent in 1986 to 39.6 percent in 1993. Thus, the effective highest marginal tax rate increased significantly.

In response to this sharp increase in taxes, those who were affected lobbied Congress to legislate special exceptions and loopholes so that the full impact of the rate increase would not be felt by the wealthiest Americans. As a result, the tax code is more complicated than it was before the 1986 Tax Reform Act.

While in principle everyone is for a simpler tax code, in practice Congress rarely is able to pass tax-reform legislation. Why? The reason is that those who now benefit from our complicated tax code will not give up their tax breaks without a fight.

public debt The total amount of money that the national government owes as a result of borrowing; also called the *national debt*.

These groups include homeowners who deduct interest on their mortgages (and therefore the home-building industry as well), charities that receive tax-deductible contributions, and businesses that get tax breaks for research and development. Two other groups also benefit greatly from the current complicated tax code: tax accountants and tax lawyers.

15–4e The Public Debt

When the government spends more than it receives, it has to finance this shortfall. Typically, it borrows. The U.S. Treasury sells IOUs on behalf of the U.S. government. They are called U.S. Treasury bills, notes, or bonds, depending on how long the funds are borrowed. All are commonly called *treasuries*.

The sale of these obligations to corporations, private individuals, pension plans, foreign governments, foreign companies, and foreign individuals is big business. After all, except for a few years in the late 1990s and early 2000s, federal government expenditures have always exceeded federal government revenues. Does the fact that foreign governments own large quantities of treasuries pose a problem? We look at that question in this chapter's *Join the Debate* feature, which follows.

Every time there is a federal government deficit, there is an increase in the total accumulated **public debt** (also called the *national debt*), which is defined as the total value of all outstanding federal government

Every time Congress must raise the national debt ceiling, there are protesters who want the federal government to "Hold the Line."

Is it a Problem That We Owe Trillions of Dollars to Foreigners?

One issue with a growing federal debt involves how much is owned by foreign interests. Today, almost half of the U.S. net public debt is owned by foreign individuals, foreign businesses, and foreign central banks. The largest debt holder is the People's Republic of China. The federal government owes China about $1.27 trillion. Japan is in second place, with $1.22 trillion.

As long as China exports more to the United States than it imports from us, it accumulates dollars. China (and Japan) have chosen to use those dollars to buy U.S. government treasuries rather than to import more American-made goods. One consequence of these purchases is to keep the Chinese currency cheap and the U.S. dollar expensive. This currency manipulation makes Chinese exports cheaper, to the benefit of Chinese exporters.

If You Owe Someone Trillions, They Have Leverage

China alone owns more of the U.S. debt than all American households put together. Some people argue that these holdings constitute a national security threat. China has made no bones about its desire to replace the United States as the dominant power in East Asia. Owning so much U.S. debt could give China a weapon if it ever chose to use it. A senior editor of the *People's Daily,* a leading Chinese newspaper, has written: "Now is the time for China to use its 'financial weapon' to teach the United States a lesson if it moves forward with a plan to [sell] arms to Taiwan."[6]

If China were to dump its holdings of U.S. treasuries, the result could be a collapse in the markets for treasuries in this country. The price of treasuries could fall greatly. The result could be much higher interest rates and a recession. To be sure, China would also lose vast sums due to the collapse in value of one of its largest financial assets. Many suggest that no rational government would do such a thing. But what if the Chinese were not rational? Throughout history, nations have been willing to make great sacrifices in times of war.

China Would Do Us a *Favor* If It Dumped Its Treasuries

Experts on China contend that its government is highly rational. Its leaders are also very good at bluff-ing. So far, there have been no signs that foreign investors are losing their appetite for treasuries. Indeed, during the recent economic crises, frightened investors bought more treasuries in the belief that they were the safest possible investment. As a result, the government has been able to borrow at very low interest rates. For example, the September 2014 rate for four-week bills, the shortest-term obligations, was 0.01 percent. After inflation, investors buying these bills were actually losing money on the deal.

Further, recent studies suggest that if China were to dump its treasuries, the main effect would not be higher interest rates. Rather, the value of the dollar relative to the Chinese yuan would fall. After all, the Chinese bought all these treasuries to keep the yuan cheap and the dollar expensive. If the value of the dollar fell, it would be cheaper to manufacture goods in America, and U.S. exports would rise. The cost of toys and shoes made in China might go up, but more Americans would have jobs.[7]

CRITICAL ANALYSIS — **Why would anyone make an almost-no-interest loan to the federal government?**

borrowing. If the existing public debt is $5 trillion and the government runs a deficit of $100 billion, then at the end of the year the public debt is $5.1 trillion. Figure 15–3, which follows, shows what has happened to the *net* public debt over time, in comparison with the overall size of the economy. (The net public debt doesn't count sums that the government owes to itself, although it does include funds held by the Fed.)

THE BURDEN OF THE PUBLIC DEBT We often hear about the burden of the public debt. Some even maintain that the government will eventually go bankrupt. As long as the government can collect taxes to pay interest on its public debt, however, that will never happen. What happens instead is that when treasuries come due, they are simply "rolled over," or refinanced. That is, if a $1 million Treasury bond

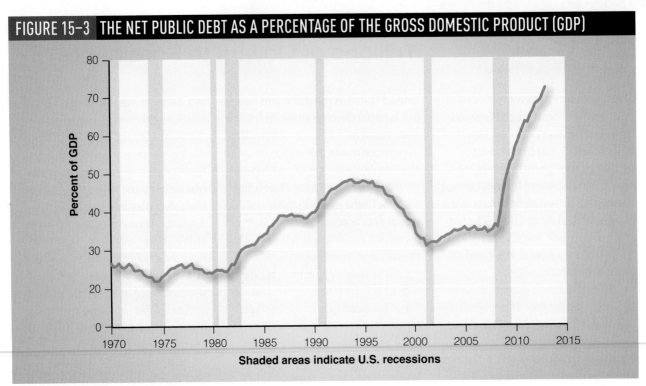

Shaded areas indicate U.S. recessions

Source: research.stlouisfed.org.

comes due today and is cashed in, the U.S. Treasury pays it off with the money it gets from selling another $1 million bond.

The interest on treasuries is paid by federal taxes. Even though much of the interest is being paid to American citizens, the more the federal government borrows to meet these payments, the greater the percentage of its budget that is committed to making interest payments. This reduces the government's ability to supply funds for anything else, including transportation, education, housing programs, and the military.

BUDGET DEFICIT EXPLOSION, 2009–2012   As discussed earlier, the initial response of the federal government to the Great Recession was to increase spending. At the same time, the economy was shrinking, so tax revenues were shrinking, too. Between increased spending and lower revenues, the federal budget deficit shot up. The deficit for 2011 was $1.3 trillion. That was about

8.6 percent of the entire economy. If we look at all levels of government together, for every five dollars of spending, three were backed up by tax receipts. The other two were borrowed.

By 2015, however, the federal budget deficit was down to $564 billion. Given current policies, the deficit should bottom out at $413 billion in 2018 and not rise significantly until the 2020s. Some economists contend that so long as the deficit does not cause the public debt to grow faster than the economy as a whole, we have no problem. To meet that standard, however, the deficit would need to fall below $350 billion and stay low thereafter. We discussed the deficit issue in the *Join the Debate* feature in Chapter 11.

CRITICAL THINKING

▶ Does your family benefit from any tax breaks that you know of? If so, what are they?

AMERICA ⚑ AT ODDS
Domestic Policy

The Preamble to the U.S. Constitution states that one of the goals of the new government was to "promote the general Welfare." Domestic policy is certainly the main way in which our government seeks to promote the general welfare. But how should this be done? Americans are at odds over many domestic issues. A few of them are listed here:

- *Do we send too many people to prison—or do our current incarceration policies protect the public?*

- *Should health-care insurance be a right of all citizens—or does such a program sap individual initiative and lead to an over-mighty government?*

- *Is climate change a serious problem that must be addressed now—or are the risks overblown and the proposed solutions a danger to our economy?*

- *Is new offshore drilling essential to our energy independence—or is it an unacceptable threat to the environment?*

- *Is a budgetary stimulus a necessary tool to fight recessions—or does it simply worsen the long-term budget deficit?*

Internet Resources

- To learn what the natural gas industry has to say about fracking and other topics, visit America's Natural Gas Alliance at anga.us. For Artists against Fracking, a major anti-fracking group, go to www.facebook.com/ArtistsAgainstFracking.

- The U.S. Census Bureau provides fast and easy access to data at quickfacts.census.gov.

- For a conservative view of domestic policy issues, including economic policy, see the Heritage Foundation site at www.heritage.org.

- Economist Paul Krugman is one of the most readable and entertaining advocates of Keynesian economics and other liberal domestic policies. You can access his blog through twitter.com/NYTimeskrugman.

- The size of the national debt is a hot topic. You can find out more about the size of the national debt and other subjects at www.treasurydirect.gov.

- If you are interested in reading the *Economic Report of the President*, go to www.whitehouse.gov/administration/eop/cea/economic-report-of-the-president.

STUDY TOOLS 15

READY TO STUDY?

- ☐ Review what you've read with the quiz below.
- ☐ Check your answers in Appendix D at the back of the book.
- ☐ For any questions you miss, read the corresponding Learning Outcome section again to prepare for class and your exam.
- ☐ Rip out and study the Chapter in Review card (at the back of the book).

VISIT WWW.CENGAGEBRAIN.COM:

- ☐ Interactive Quizzes
- ☐ Key Term Flashcards or Crossword Puzzles
- ☐ Audio Summaries
- ☐ Simulations, Animated Learning Modules, and Interactive Timelines
- ☐ Videos
- ☐ American Government NewsWatch

FILL-IN

LearningOutcome 15–1

1. The stages of the policymaking process are
   _____.

LearningOutcome 15–2

2. _____ is now the federal government's second-largest domestic spending program, after Social Security.

3. The individual mandate in the 2010 health-care reform legislation is a requirement that _____.

LearningOutcome 15–3

4. The nations of _____ supply 45 percent of our oil imports.

5. The predicted outcomes of climate change include
   _____.

6. Renewable energy technologies include _____.

LearningOutcome 15–4

7. A period in which the economy stops growing altogether and undergoes a contraction is called a _____.

8. Monetary policy is under the control of the _____, an independent regulatory agency.

9. Today, about half of the U.S. net public debt is owned by foreign individuals, foreign businesses, and foreign central banks. The largest debt holder is _____.

MULTIPLE CHOICE

LearningOutcome 15–1

10. A discussion in the media about a problem that might have a political solution is an example of
    a. policy adoption.
    b. policy implementation.
    c. issue identification.

LearningOutcome 15–2

11. About _____ percent of national spending in the United States goes to health care.
    a. 4
    b. 18
    c. 29.5

12. One immediate change brought about by the health-care reform bills that passed in 2010 was that young people can remain covered by their parents' insurance until they turn
    a. 26.
    b. 21.
    c. 18.

LearningOutcome 15–3

13. The CAFE standards
    a. regulate offshore drilling.
    b. measure the effect of greenhouse gases.
    c. are designed to force auto and truck manufacturers to increase the fuel efficiency of their vehicles.

LearningOutcome 15–4

14. _____ policy uses changes in government expenditures and taxes to alter national economic variables.
    a. Monetary
    b. Fiscal
    c. Domestic

15. According to the nonpartisan Congressional Budget Office, more than _____ percent of this nation's households pay no income taxes at all.
    a. 10
    b. 23
    c. 40

USE THE TOOLS.

16 | Foreign Policy

©AP-Photo/Evgeniy Maloletka

LEARNING OUTCOMES After reading this chapter, you should be able to:

16–1 Discuss how foreign policy is made, and identify the key players in this process.

16–2 Summarize the history of American foreign policy through the years.

16–3 Identify the foreign policy challenges presented by terrorism.

16–4 Explain the principal issues dividing the Israelis and the Palestinians and the solutions proposed by the international community.

16–5 Outline some of the actions taken by the United States to curb the threat of nuclear weapons.

16–6 Describe China's emerging role as a world power.

After finishing this chapter go to
PAGE 377 for
STUDY TOOLS.

AMERICA AT ODDS

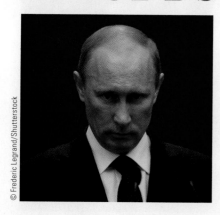

© Frederic Legrand/Shutterstock

Are We Facing a New Cold War?

Most students today are too young to remember the Union of Soviet Socialist Republics—the Soviet Union. That country broke up into fifteen independent republics in 1991. From the end of World War II until the late 1980s, America and its allies were pitted against the Soviet Union in what was called the "Cold War." (You'll read more about the Cold War in this chapter.)

Millions of Soviet soldiers were under arms during the Cold War. The U.S.S.R. had a world-class navy and a vast arsenal of nuclear weapons. The heart of the old Soviet Union was the Russian Republic, which contained about half the U.S.S.R.'s population. Today's Russia is much weaker than the Soviet Union. Yet in recent years, Russia's president, Vladimir Putin, has begun to demonstrate an alarming degree of aggressiveness. Does this mean we have entered a new Cold War?

Like It or Not, We've Entered a New Cold War

Consider what Putin has done. He has threatened Europe by cutting off natural gas supplies. He has waged war on the small nation of Georgia, detaching portions of Georgian territory. Because Putin opposed Ukraine's new Europe-friendly government, he invaded and annexed Ukraine's Crimean peninsula. He then sponsored an insurrection in Russian-speaking areas of eastern Ukraine. When it seemed that the Ukrainian government would put down the rebellion, Russia moved its own troops into Ukraine to prevent such a result. Recently, Putin has initiated a series of provocations aimed at the small Baltic nations. Unlike Ukraine, however, the Baltic states are members of the North Atlantic Treaty Organization (NATO). That means that America and most of Europe are sworn to defend their territory as if it were our own.

Putin has said that the biggest geopolitical disaster of the twentieth century was the fall of the Soviet Union. He wants to restore its former glory. His speeches not only are anti-American, but he calls his enemies fascists who want to oppress their Russian neighbors. If all this doesn't amount to a new Cold War, what would?

An Aggressive Leader Does Not Make a Cold War

There is no question that Putin has begun making trouble for the world. Yet consider the balance of forces. Add the European Union to the United States and you have an economy sixteen times the size of Russia's. The U.S. defense budget is seven times that of Russia's. The old Soviet Union drew strength from the ideology of communism, which had supporters around the world. Today's Russia has no ideology that can match the attractions of the West. Indeed, the crisis in Ukraine began because that nation wanted to draw closer to the European Union—an organization that is truly attractive to the peoples of Eastern Europe.

President Obama had it right in 2014, when he said: "This is not another Cold War that we're entering into. Unlike the Soviet Union, Russia leads no block of nations and has no global ideology." Russia is a regional power threatening its immediate neighbors—"Not out of strength, but out of weakness." Containing the ambitions of a single rogue power is not a worldwide struggle, and it does not amount to a new Cold War.

Where do we stand?

1. Does it matter that the nations Putin has threatened militarily are all former members of the Soviet Union? Why or why not?

2. Why don't people refer to the war on terrorism as a Cold War?

Explore this issue online

- For an insightful article in the magazine *National Interest,* search on "Seven Ways a New Cold War Will Be Different."

- The Vox Web site has a card stack titled "Everything You Need to Know about Ukraine." Find it by searching on "vox Ukraine."

INTRODUCTION

What we call **foreign policy** is a systematic and general plan that guides a country's attitudes and actions toward the rest of the world. Foreign policy includes all of the economic, military, commercial, and diplomatic positions and actions that a nation takes in its relationships with other countries. Although foreign policy may seem quite removed from the concerns of everyday life, it can and does have a significant impact on the day-to-day lives of Americans.

American foreign policy has been shaped by two principles that are often seen as contradicting each other. One is **moral idealism,** the belief that the most important goal in foreign policy is to do what is right. Moral idealists think that it is possible for nations to relate to each other as part of a rule-based community. Moral idealism appeals to the often-held American belief that our nation is special and should provide an example to the rest of the world.

A contrasting view is **political realism,** the belief that nations are inevitably selfish. In this view, foreign countries therefore, are by definition dangerous. The chapter-opening *America at Odds* feature, for example, discusses the dangers posed by Russia. Foreign policy must therefore be based on protecting our national security, regardless of moral arguments. Although there have been times when one or the other of these two principles has dominated, U.S. foreign policy has usually been a mixture of both.

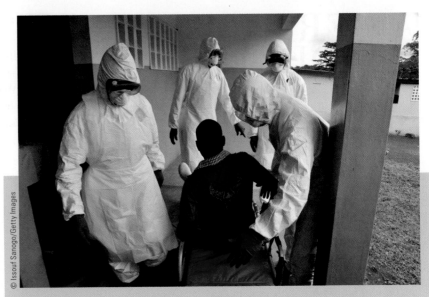

© Issouf Sanogo/Getty Images

African health-care workers train to deal with the deadly Ebola virus, which has killed thousands in the nations of Guinea, Liberia, and Sierra Leone. In September 2014, President Obama announced that America would send up to 3,000 military personnel to fight the disease. *How does this action exemplify the principle of moral idealism in foreign policy?*

16–1 WHO MAKES U.S. FOREIGN POLICY?

LO Discuss how foreign policy is made, and identify the key players in this process.

The framers of the Constitution envisioned that the president and Congress would cooperate in developing American foreign policy. The Constitution did not spell out exactly how this was to be done, though. As commander in chief, the president has assumed much of the decision-making power in the area of foreign policy. Nonetheless, members of Congress, a number of officials, and a vast national security bureaucracy help to shape the president's decisions and to limit the president's powers.

16–1a The President's Role

Article II, Section 2, of the Constitution names the president commander in chief of the armed forces. As commander in chief, the president oversees the military and guides defense policies. Presidents have interpreted this role broadly, sending American troops, ships, and weapons to trouble spots at home and around the world.

The Constitution authorizes the president to make treaties, which must be approved by two-thirds of the Senate. In addition, the president is empowered to form

foreign policy A systematic and general plan that guides a country's attitudes and actions toward the rest of the world. Foreign policy includes all of the economic, military, commercial, and diplomatic positions and actions that a nation takes in its relationships with other countries.

moral idealism In foreign policy, the belief that the most important goal is to do what is right. Moral idealists think that it is possible for nations to cooperate as part of a rule-based community.

political realism In foreign policy, the belief that nations are inevitably selfish and that we should seek to protect our national security, regardless of moral arguments.

> # "To be prepared for war
> is one of the most
> effectual means of
> preserving peace."
>
> ~ **George Washington,** Commander of the Continental Army and
> First President of the United States 1789–1797

executive agreements—pacts between the president and the heads of other nations. These executive agreements do not require Senate approval.

The president's foreign policy responsibilities have special significance in that the president has ultimate control over the use of nuclear weapons. The president also influences foreign policymaking in the role of head of state. As the symbolic head of our government, the president represents the United States to the rest of the world. When a serious foreign policy issue or international question arises, the nation expects the president to make a formal statement on the matter.

16–1b The Cabinet

Many members of the president's cabinet concern themselves with international problems and recommend policies to deal with them. As U.S. power in the world has grown and as economic factors have become increasingly important, the departments of Agriculture, Commerce, Energy, and Treasury have become more involved in foreign policy decisions. The secretary of state and the secretary of defense, however, are the only cabinet members who concern themselves with foreign policy matters on a full-time basis.

THE DEPARTMENT OF STATE
The Department of State is, in principle, the government agency most directly involved in foreign policy. The department is responsible for diplomatic relations with nearly two hundred independent nations around the globe, as well as with the United Nations and other multilateral organizations, such as the Organization of American States. Most U.S. relations with other countries are maintained through embassies, consulates, and other U.S. offices around the world.

As the head of the State Department, the secretary of state has traditionally played a key role in foreign policymaking, and many presidents have relied heavily on the advice of their secretaries of state. Under many presidents since the end of World War II, however, the State Department has taken a back seat in foreign policy to the president's National Security Council, described below. The Obama administration has been an exception to this trend—secretaries of state Hillary Clinton and John Kerry have played the leading role in foreign policy.

THE DEPARTMENT OF DEFENSE The Department of Defense is the principal executive department that establishes and carries out defense policy and protects our national security. The secretary of defense advises the president on all aspects of U.S. military and defense policy, supervises all of the military activities of the U.S. government, and works to see that the decisions of the president as commander in chief are carried out. The secretary advises and informs the president on the nation's military forces, weapons, and bases and works closely with the U.S. military, especially the Joint Chiefs of Staff, in gathering and studying defense information.

The Joint Chiefs of Staff (JCS) include the chair and vice chair of the JCS; the military service chiefs of the Army, Navy, Air Force, and Marines; and the chief of the National Guard. All are appointed by the president and confirmed by the Senate.

© Jacquelyn Martin/Pool/Getty Images

U.S. Secretary of Defense Chuck Hagel visits a U.S. naval base in Japan in 2013. *Why does the United States continue to station troops in Japan and South Korea?*

The joint chiefs regularly serve as the key military advisers to the president, the secretary of defense, and the National Security Council. They are responsible for handing down the president's orders to the nation's military units, preparing strategic plans, and recommending military actions. They also propose military budgets, new weapons systems, and military regulations.

16–1c Other Agencies

Several other government agencies are also involved in the foreign relations of the United States. Two key agencies in the area of foreign policy are the National Security Council and the Central Intelligence Agency.

THE NATIONAL SECURITY COUNCIL The National Security Council (NSC) was established by the National Security Act of 1947. The formal members of the NSC include the president, the vice president, the secretary of state, and the secretary of defense. Meetings are often attended by the chairperson of the Joint Chiefs of Staff, the director of the Central Intelligence Agency, and representatives from other departments.

The national security adviser, who is a member of the president's White House staff, is the director of the NSC. The adviser informs the president, coordinates advice and information on foreign policy, and serves as a liaison with other officials.

The NSC and its members can be as important and powerful as the president wants them to be. Some presidents have made frequent use of the NSC, whereas others have convened it infrequently. Similarly, the importance of the role played by the national security adviser in shaping foreign policy can vary significantly, depending on the administration and the adviser's identity.

THE CENTRAL INTELLIGENCE AGENCY The Central Intelligence Agency (CIA) was created after World War II to coordinate American intelligence activities abroad. The CIA provides the president and his or her advisers with up-to-date information about the political, military, and economic activities of foreign governments.

The CIA gathers much of its intelligence from overt sources, such as foreign radio broadcasts and newspapers, people who travel abroad, the Internet, and satellite photographs. Other information is gathered from covert activities, such as the CIA's own secret investigations into the economic or political affairs of other nations. Covert operations may involve secretly supplying weapons to a force rebelling against an unfriendly government or seizing suspected terrorists in a clandestine operation and holding them for questioning.

The CIA has tended to operate autonomously, and the details of its work, methods, and operating funds have been kept secret. Intelligence reform passed by Congress in 2004, however, makes the CIA accountable to a national intelligence director. The CIA is now required to cooperate more with other U.S. intelligence agencies and has lost a degree of the autonomy it once enjoyed.

16–1d Powers of Congress

Although the executive branch takes the lead in foreign policy matters, Congress also has some power over foreign policy. Remember that Congress alone has the power to declare war. It also has the power to appropriate funds to build new weapons systems, equip the U.S. armed forces, and provide for foreign aid. The Senate has the power to approve or reject the implementation of treaties and the appointment of ambassadors.

In 1973, Congress passed the War Powers Resolution, which limits the president's use of troops in military action without congressional approval. Presidents since then, however, have not interpreted the resolution to mean that Congress must be consulted before military action is taken. On several occasions, presidents have ordered military action and then informed Congress after the fact.

A few congressional committees are directly concerned with foreign affairs. The most important are the Armed Services Committee and the Committee on Foreign Affairs in the House, and the Armed Services Committee and the Foreign Relations Committee in the Senate. Other congressional committees deal with matters that indirectly influence foreign policy, such as oil, agriculture, and imports.

CRITICAL THINKING

▶ Should American citizens know more about what the CIA does, or would such knowledge merely benefit our opponents? In either case, why?

16–2 A SHORT HISTORY OF AMERICAN FOREIGN POLICY

LO Summarize the history of American foreign policy through the years.

Many U.S. foreign policy initiatives have been rooted in moral idealism. A primary consideration in U.S. foreign policy, though, has always been *national security*—the protection of the independence and political integrity of the nation.

President James Monroe (1817–1825) said that the United States would not accept foreign intervention in the Western Hemisphere. *What position did Monroe take on U.S. intervention in Europe?*

Over the years, the United States has attempted to preserve its national security in many ways. These ways have changed over time and are not always internally consistent. This inconsistency results from the fact that foreign policymaking, like domestic policymaking, reflects the influence of various political groups in the United States. These groups—including the voting public, interest groups, Congress, and the president and relevant agencies of the executive branch—are often at odds over what the U.S. position should be on particular foreign policy issues.

16–2a Isolationism

The nation's founders and the early presidents believed that **isolationism**—avoiding political involvement with other nations—was the best way to protect American interests. The United States was certainly not yet strong enough to directly influence European developments. As president of the new nation, George Washington did little in terms of foreign policy. Indeed, in his Farewell Address in 1797, he urged Americans to "steer clear of permanent alliances with any portion of the foreign world." During the 1700s and 1800s, the United States generally attempted to avoid conflicts and political engagements elsewhere.

In accordance with this isolationist philosophy, President James Monroe in 1823 proclaimed what became known as the **Monroe Doctrine.** In his message to Congress in December 1823, Monroe stated that the United States would not tolerate foreign intervention in the Western Hemisphere. In return, promised Monroe, the United States would stay out of European affairs. The Monroe Doctrine buttressed the policy of isolationism toward Europe.

16–2b The Beginning of Interventionism

Isolationism gradually gave way to **interventionism** (direct involvement in foreign affairs). The first true step toward interventionism occurred with the Spanish-American War of 1898. The United States fought this war to free Cuba from Spanish rule. Spain lost and subsequently ceded control of several of its possessions, including Guam, Puerto Rico, and the Philippines, to the United States. The United States thus acquired a **colonial empire** and was acknowledged as a world power.

The growth of the United States as an industrial economy also confirmed the nation's position as a world power. For example, in the early 1900s, President Theodore Roosevelt proposed that the United States could invade Latin American countries when it was necessary to guarantee political or economic stability.

16–2c The World Wars

When World War I broke out in 1914, President Woodrow Wilson initially proclaimed a policy of **neutrality**—the United States would not take sides in the conflict. The United States did not enter the war until 1917, after U.S. ships in international waters were attacked by German submarines that were blockading Britain.

Wilson called the war a way to "make the world safe for democracy." In his eyes, Germany was not merely dangerous but evil. Wilson, in short, was our most famous presidential advocate of *moral idealism.*

isolationism A political policy of noninvolvement in world affairs.

Monroe Doctrine A U.S. policy, announced in 1823 by President James Monroe, that the United States would not tolerate foreign intervention in the Western Hemisphere, and in return, the United States would stay out of European affairs.

interventionism Direct involvement by one country in another country's affairs.

colonial empire A group of dependent nations that are under the rule of an imperial power.

neutrality The position of not being aligned with either side in a dispute or conflict, such as a war.

The United States entered World War II after the surprise Japanese attack on Pearl Harbor, Hawaii, on December 7, 1941. *Which nations were our allies in this conflict?*

16–2d The Cold War

After World War II ended in 1945, the wartime alliance between the United States and the Soviet Union began to deteriorate quickly. The Soviet Union opposed America's political and economic systems. Many Americans considered Soviet attempts to spread Communist systems to other countries a major threat to democracy. After the war ended, countries in Eastern Europe—Bulgaria, Czechoslovakia, East Germany, Hungary, Poland, and Romania—fell under Soviet domination, forming what became known as the **Soviet bloc.**

THE IRON CURTAIN Britain's wartime prime minister, Winston Churchill, established the tone for a new relationship between the Soviet Union and the Western allies in a famous speech in 1946:

After World War I ended in 1918, the United States returned to a policy of isolationism. Consequently, we refused to join the League of Nations, an international body intended to resolve peacefully any future conflicts between nations.

But the U.S. policy of isolationism ended when the Japanese attacked Pearl Harbor in 1941. We joined the Allies—Australia, Britain, Canada, China, France, and the Soviet Union—to fight the Axis nations of Germany, Italy, and Japan. One of the most significant foreign policy actions during World War II was the dropping of atomic bombs on the Japanese cities of Hiroshima and Nagasaki in August 1945 in a successful attempt to force Japan to surrender.

An iron curtain has descended across the Continent. Behind that line all are subject in one form or another, not only to Soviet influence but to a very high . . . measure of control from Moscow.

The reference to an **iron curtain** described the political boundaries between the democratic countries in Western Europe and the Soviet-controlled Communist countries in Eastern Europe.

THE MARSHALL PLAN AND THE POLICY OF CONTAINMENT In 1947, when it appeared that local Communists, backed by the Soviets, would take over Greece and Turkey, President Harry Truman took action. He convinced Congress to appropriate $400 million ($4.34 billion in 2015 dollars) in aid for those countries to prevent the spread of communism.

The Truman Doctrine and the Marshall Plan. The president also proclaimed what became known as the *Truman Doctrine.* It would be "the policy of the United States to support free peoples who are resisting attempted subjugation by armed minorities or by outside pressures."[1]

The Truman administration also instituted a policy of economic assistance to war-torn Europe, called the **Marshall Plan** after George Marshall, who was then the U.S. secretary of state. During the next five years,

Soviet bloc The group of Eastern European nations that fell under the control of the Soviet Union following World War II.

iron curtain A phrase coined by Winston Churchill to describe the political boundaries between the democratic countries in Western Europe and the Soviet-controlled Communist countries in Eastern Europe.

Marshall Plan A plan providing for U.S. economic assistance to European nations following World War II to help those nations recover from the war. The plan was named after George C. Marshall, secretary of state from 1947 to 1949.

Britain's Winston Churchill was a valuable friend of the United States during World War II. *What did Churchill mean when he referred to the "iron curtain"?*

THE ARMS RACE AND DETERRENCE The tensions induced by the Cold War led both the Soviet Union and the United States to try to surpass each other militarily. They began competing for more and better weapons, particularly nuclear weapons, with greater destructive power.

This phenomenon, known as the *arms race*, was supported by a policy of **deterrence**—of rendering ourselves and our allies so strong militarily that our very strength would deter (stop or discourage) any attack on us. Out of deterrence came the theory of **mutually assured destruction (MAD),** which held that if the forces of two nations were capable of destroying each other, neither nation would take a chance on war.

THE CUBAN MISSILE CRISIS In 1962, the United States and the Soviet Union came close to a nuclear confrontation in what became known as the **Cuban missile crisis.** The United States learned that the Soviet Union had placed nuclear weapons on the island of Cuba, ninety miles from the coast of Florida.

The crisis was defused diplomatically. A U.S. naval blockade of Cuba convinced the Soviet Union to agree to remove the missiles. The United States also agreed to remove some of its missiles near the Soviet border in Turkey. Both sides recognized that a nuclear war between the two superpowers was unthinkable.

DÉTENTE AND ARMS CONTROL In 1969, the United States and the Soviet Union began negotiations on a treaty to limit the number of antiballistic missiles (ABMs) and offensive missiles that each country could develop and deploy. In 1972, both sides signed the Strategic Arms Limitation Treaty (SALT I). This

Congress appropriated $17 billion (about $184 billion in 2015 dollars) for aid to sixteen European countries. By 1952, the nations of Western Europe, with U.S. help, had recovered and were again prospering.

The Containment Policy and NATO. These actions marked the beginning of a policy of **containment** designed to contain (prevent) the spread of communism by offering threatened nations U.S. military and economic aid.[2] To make the policy of containment effective, the United States initiated a program of collective security involving the formation of mutual defense alliances with other nations.

In 1949, through the North Atlantic Treaty, the United States, Canada, and ten European nations formed a military alliance—the North Atlantic Treaty Organization (NATO). The treaty declared that an attack on any member of the alliance would be considered an attack against all members.

THE COLD WAR BEGINS Thus, by 1949, almost all illusions of friendship between the Soviet Union and the Western allies had disappeared. The United States became the leader of a bloc of democratic nations in Western Europe, the Pacific, and elsewhere.

The tensions between the Soviet Union and the United States became known as the **Cold War**—a war of words, warnings, and ideologies that lasted from the late 1940s through the late 1980s. Although the Cold War was mainly a war of words and belief systems, "hot" wars in Korea (1950–1953) and Vietnam (1965–1975) grew out of the efforts to contain communism.

containment A U.S. policy designed to contain the spread of communism by offering military and economic aid to threatened nations.

Cold War The war of words, warnings, and ideologies between the Soviet Union and the United States that lasted from the late 1940s through the late 1980s.

deterrence A policy of building up military strength for the purpose of discouraging (deterring) military attacks by other nations; the policy that supported the arms race between the United States and the Soviet Union during the Cold War.

mutually assured destruction (MAD) A phrase referring to the assumption that if the forces of two nations are capable of destroying each other, neither nation will take a chance on war.

Cuban missile crisis A nuclear standoff that occurred in 1962 when the United States learned that the Soviet Union had placed nuclear warheads in Cuba.

event marked the beginning of a period of **détente,** a French word that means a "relaxation of tensions."

In 1983, President Ronald Reagan (1981–1989) nearly reignited the arms race by proposing a missile defense system known as the strategic defense initiative (SDI, or "Star Wars"). Nonetheless, Reagan pursued arms control agreements with Soviet leaders, as did Reagan's successor, President George H. W. Bush (1989–1993).

THE DISSOLUTION OF THE SOVIET UNION In the late 1980s, the political situation inside the Soviet Union began to change rapidly. Mikhail Gorbachev, the new leader, had initiated an effort to democratize the Soviet political system and decentralize the economy. The reforms quickly spread to other countries in the Soviet bloc. In 1989, the Berlin Wall, constructed nearly thirty years earlier to separate Soviet-dominated East Berlin from West Berlin, was torn down. East Germany and West Germany were reunited in 1990.

In August 1991, a number of disgruntled Communist Party leaders who wanted to reverse the reforms briefly seized control of the Soviet central government. Russian citizens rose up in revolt and defied those leaders. The democratically elected president of the Russian republic (the largest republic in the Soviet Union), Boris Yeltsin, confronted troops in Moscow that were under the control of the conspirators. The attempted coup collapsed after three days. The Communist Party in the Soviet Union lost almost all of its power.

The fifteen republics constituting the Soviet Union—including the Russian republic—declared their independence. By the end of the year, the Union of Soviet Socialist Republics (USSR) no longer existed. For years following the collapse of the Soviet Union, Russia—the main successor state—posed little or no threat to world peace. Under President Vladimir Putin, however, Russian policy has been much more aggressive. We discussed these developments in the chapter-opening *America at Odds* feature. We provide additional detail in this chapter's *Perception versus Reality* feature, which follows.

> **"Soviet Union foreign policy is a puzzle, inside a riddle wrapped in an enigma."**
>
> ~ Winston Churchill,
> British prime minister during World War II
> 1874–1965

16–2e Post–Cold War Foreign Policy

The demise of the Soviet Union altered the framework and goals of U.S. foreign policy. During the Cold War, the moral underpinnings of American foreign policy were clear to all—the United States was the defender of the "free world" against the Soviet aggressor.

When the Cold War ended, U.S. foreign policymakers were forced, for the first time in decades, to rethink the nation's foreign policy goals and adapt them to a world arena in which, at least for a while, the United States was the only superpower.

U.S. foreign policymakers have struggled since the end of the Cold War to determine the degree of intervention that is appropriate and prudent for the U.S. military. Should we intervene in a humanitarian crisis, such as a famine? Should the U.S. military participate in peacekeeping missions, such as those instituted after civil or ethnic strife in other countries? Americans have faced these questions in Bosnia, Kosovo, Rwanda, Somalia, and Sudan.

Yet no overriding framework emerged in U.S. foreign policy until September 11, 2001. Since that date, our goal has been to capture and punish the terrorists who planned and perpetrated the events of that day and to prevent future terrorist attacks against Americans. Sometimes, that goal has involved "regime change," one of the objectives of the war against Iraq in 2003.

CRITICAL THINKING

▶ The Cold War between the United States and the Soviet Union never turned into a shooting war. Why not?

16–3 THE WAR ON TERRORISM

LO Identify the foreign policy challenges presented by terrorism.

One of the most difficult challenges faced by governments around the world is how to control terrorism. *Terrorism* is defined as the use of staged violence, often against civilians, to achieve political goals. Terrorism has occurred in almost every region of the world.

The most devastating terrorist attack in U.S. history occurred on September 11, 2001, when radical Islamist terrorists used hijacked airliners as missiles to bring down the World Trade Center towers in New York City and

détente A French word meaning a "relaxation of tensions." Détente characterized the relationship between the United States and the Soviet Union in the 1970s as they attempted to pursue cooperative dealings and arms control.

Perception vs. Reality

Russia Is Just Doing What Great Powers Always Do

In the wake of Russia's annexation of Ukraine's Crimean peninsula, some experts defended the actions of Russia's Vladimir Putin. They argued that Ukraine was part of Russia's natural *sphere of influence*. That is, Russia has interests in Ukraine that exceed those of any other world power. Other nations should respect Russia's interests.

The Perception

In attempting to control nations that lie within its sphere of influence, Russia is only doing what great powers have always done. How would the United States like it if Canada tried to ally with Russia or China? Strong nations always make their own rules. To ensure peace, we should respect Russian influence over nations that were formerly part of the Soviet Union.

The Reality

We no longer live in the nineteenth century. Since the end of World War II, the nations of the world have gone beyond the "laws of war" to a true system of international law. Key principles of international law seek to keep nations from doing "what great powers have always done." One major principle is that national boundaries must not be altered without the consent of the people affected. No longer would it be it legitimate for Germany to annex Alsace-Lorraine from France as it did in 1871, for example. A second principle is respect for the sovereign rights of all nations.

Like any legal system, international law has been violated frequently. Nations have invaded other nations and replaced their governments. Yet none of the world's great powers have gone to war with each other since 1950.[3] Likewise, the inviolability of international borders has received remarkable respect. Since 1950, it has been hard to identify cases in which national borders have been altered unilaterally. True, scores of new nations have become independent, but these countries have respected the territorial lines drawn when they were still colonies or provinces.

This respect ends with Putin. He has not merely annexed Crimea. He has also established a breakaway region in eastern Ukraine that consists of two of the nation's most important industrial cities, plus surrounding territory. Putin intends to use his control of this region to subvert Ukraine's independence. Ukraine is not to grow any closer to the West. It will be pressured to align its economy with that of Russia.

It is not true that Putin has only behaved as other great powers do. Communist Cuba lies within America's sphere of interest, militarily unmolested. The United States may have briefly conquered Iraq, but today that nation is free to ally with Iran. Putin's contempt for international law is unique, and the rest of the world will have to confront this issue.

BLOG ON An obvious place to learn about international law is the United Nations page at www.un.org/en/law. Singapore's Centre for International Law is also worth a look—go to cil.nus.edu.sg. Also see Cornell University's www.law.cornell.edu/wex/international_law.

---

to destroy part of the Pentagon building in Washington, D.C. A fourth airplane crashed in a Pennsylvania field after passengers fought back against the hijackers. In all, almost three thousand innocent civilians were killed as a result of these terrorist acts.

Other examples of terrorist acts include the Palestinian attacks on Israeli Olympic athletes in Munich, Germany in 1972; the Libyan suitcase bombing of an American airliner over Lockerbie, Scotland, in 1988; the bombing of two U.S. embassies in Africa in 1998; the bombing of the Navy ship USS *Cole* in a Yemeni port in 2000; and coordinated bomb attacks on London's transportation system in 2005.

16–3a Varieties of Terrorism

Terrorists are willing to destroy others' lives and property, and often sacrifice their own lives, for a variety of reasons. Terrorist acts generally fall into one of the three broad categories discussed next.

With the insurgency fatally undermined, the United States planned its withdrawal. President Barack Obama announced that U.S. combat forces would leave Iraq by the end of August 2010, and the rest of the troops would be out by the end of 2011. In fact, U.S. forces departed slightly ahead of schedule.

16-3d Again, Afghanistan

The war in Iraq tended to draw the Bush administration's attention away from Afghanistan, which was never completely at peace even after the Taliban had been ousted from Kabul, the capital. By 2006, the Taliban had regrouped and were waging a war of insurgency against the new government. The United States and its NATO allies were now the new government's principal military defenders.

THE AFGHAN-PAKISTANI BORDER A problem for the coalition forces was that the Taliban were able to take shelter on the far side of the Afghan-Pakistani border, in Pakistan's Federally Administered Tribal Areas. These districts are largely free from central government control.

In 2009, Taliban forces began to take complete control of districts in the Tribal Areas and adjacent districts in the Northwest Frontier Province. Facing a direct challenge to Pakistan's sovereignty, the Pakistani military began to engage the Taliban forces in what soon became a major struggle.

U.S. ATTACKS IN PAKISTAN Under the George W. Bush administration, the CIA began operating remote-controlled aircraft (drones) known as Predators over Pakistan. Predators are equipped with small missiles, which were used to kill a number of Taliban and al Qaeda leaders. President Obama ramped up the Predator program significantly.

One result was increasing tensions with Pakistan, which could not openly support the Predator campaign. Pakistan's role in Afghanistan, in fact, has been quite complicated. The nation has been nominally allied with the United States. At the same time, Pakistan's intelligence agency, Inter-Services Intelligence, has funded a variety of Islamist militant groups, including units that have engaged in terrorist attacks on the government of Afghanistan and U.S. forces in that country.

THE DEATH OF BIN LADEN During the winter of 2010–2011, U.S. intelligence agencies learned that al Qaeda leader Osama bin Laden might be hiding in the Pakistani city of Abbottabad. On May 1, 2011, U.S. Navy Seals entered bin Laden's residential compound and killed him.

The reaction in America was one of relief and satisfaction. The reaction in Pakistan was quite different.

Many Pakistanis considered the incident a violation of their country's sovereignty. American commentators speculated that bin Laden could not have hidden in Abbottabad without support from elements of the military, as that city is home to the Pakistan Military Academy.

OBAMA AND AFGHANISTAN In 2009, President Obama increased the number of U.S. troops in Afghanistan by 47,000. At the same time, he indicated that he hoped to withdraw some U.S. forces as early as 2011. In fact, only 10,000 U.S. soldiers left Afghanistan that year. Withdrawals picked up speed in 2012, however, and almost all U.S. troops were out of Afghanistan by the end of 2014.

16-3e The Civil War in Syria and the Growth of ISIS

In September 2014, the air forces of the United States and five Arab states began a campaign of bombing in Iraq and Syria. The campaign was directed at an organization known as ISIS. France and several other nations participated in air strikes limited to Iraq. President Obama had spent much of his administration in an attempt to reduce and eventually end United States interventions in Middle Eastern nations, but now we were back at war. What happened?

THE LEGACY OF THE "ARAB SPRING" Beginning in December 2010, the Arab world was swept by a wave of protests against autocratic rulers. With the sole exception of Tunisia, the protesters failed to win their democratic objectives. In Egypt, the dictator Hosni Mubarak was ousted, but a democratic regime was overthrown by the nation's military. A civil war in Libya dislodged the dictator Muammar Gaddafi, but Libyans thereafter were unable to establish an effective national government. (The rebels were greatly aided by international air support organized by President Obama, who received criticism for not obtaining congressional approval of the air strikes.)

CIVIL WAR IN SYRIA Protests in Syria developed into a civil war, as rebels attempted to forcibly overthrow the regime of Bashar al-Assad. By 2014, the fighting had killed more than 200,000 Syrians. Almost 10 million out of a total population of 23 million had been driven from their homes. Many people around the world called for Western intervention to assist the rebels, but the limited aid that was provided came from several Arab states. A problem for the United States and its allies was that only a minority of the rebels could be called pro-democratic. Others were Islamists of varying levels of radicalism.

The United States and other powers did force al-Assad to give up his chemical weapons, however, as discussed later in this chapter.

THE RISE OF ISIS The most radical faction fighting in Syria was called **ISIS,** short for the "Islamic State in Iraq and Greater Syria." An alternative transliteration of the Arabic is ISIL, the "Islamic State in Iraq and the Levant." (Both "Greater Syria" and "the Levant" refer to the lands on the eastern shore of the Mediterranean from the Gaza Strip north to Syria proper.) As the name indicates, ISIS was active in both Syria and Iraq. In fact, ISIS is a reorganized version of the group once known as al Qaeda in Iraq. In February 2014, however, al Qaeda expelled ISIS, citing the group's brutality and "notorious intractability."

ISIS Attacks Iraq. As mentioned in the *America at Odds* feature in Chapter 12, in June 2014 ISIS swept through northern Iraq, almost to Baghdad. The Iraqi army fled, despite outnumbering ISIS forces greatly. ISIS changed its name to simply "the Islamic State" and set up a government in the Iraqi city of Mosul. When its forces threatened to overrun the autonomous Kurdish region in Northern Iraq, President Obama provided air support to the Kurds. When ISIS attempted to kill the entire population of a religious minority called the Yezidis, U.S. air cover helped the Kurds rescue members of this group.

Obama and the Iraqi Government. The advance of ISIS through Iraq was aided by the hostility felt by Sunnis toward the government of Iraq, which had mistreated them. Initially, Obama held off on direct support for the Iraqi government because he did not want America to provide a "Shiite air force" that protected sectarian interests within Iraq. After the Iraqi government was reorganized in an attempt to conciliate the Sunnis, however, the United States agreed to provide it air support. Obama promised the American people that the United States would not provide "boots on the ground"—infantry forces would need to be organized by the Iraqis themselves.

> **CRITICAL THINKING**

▸ Sometimes, it is possible to negotiate with certain terrorist groups, such as the Irish Republican Army, and "bring them in from the cold." Why might such a strategy be impossible with al Qaeda?

16-4 THE ISRAELI-PALESTINIAN CONFLICT

LO Explain the principal issues dividing the Israelis and the Palestinians and the solutions proposed by the international community.

The long-running conflict between Israel and its Arab neighbors has poisoned the atmosphere in the Middle East for more than half a century. American presidents dating back at least to Richard Nixon (1969–1974) have attempted to persuade the parties to reach a settlement. Barack Obama is only the latest American leader to address the problem.

16-4a The Arab-Israeli Wars

For many years after Israel was founded in 1948, the neighboring Arab states did not accept its legitimacy as a nation. The result was a series of wars between Israel and neighboring states, including Egypt,

© AFP/Getty Images

An emergency response worker carries a wounded child following an air attack by government forces on the northern Syrian city of Aleppo in February 2014. *Why has the United States been reluctant to intervene in this civil war?*

ISIS The Islamic State in Iraq and Greater Syria; a terrorist organization that by 2014 had taken over substantial portions of Iraq and Syria. Also known as *ISIL* (the Islamic State in Iraq and the Levant) or the Islamic State.

ISIS supporters display its black flag during a march in Mosul, Iraq, in June 2014. *Why might it be that ISIS fighters have been so successful?*

incursions across the Israeli-Lebanon border. Israel and Jordan eventually signed a peace treaty in 1994, but no peace treaty between Israel and Syria has yet been negotiated, and the conflict between Israel and the Palestinians has remained.

16–4b The Israeli-Palestinian Dispute

Resolving the Israeli-Palestinian dispute has always presented more difficulties than achieving peace between Israel and neighbors such as Egypt. One problem is that the hostilities between the two parties run deeper. On the Palestinian side, many families lost their homes after the 1948 war. Then, after the 1967 war, the West Bank of the Jordan River and the Gaza Strip fell under Israeli control, and the Palestinians living in these areas became an occupied people.

On the Israeli side, the sheer viciousness of the Palestinian terrorist attacks—which frequently resulted in the deaths of civilians, including children—made negotiations with those responsible hard to imagine. A further complication was the Israeli settlements on the West Bank and the Gaza Strip, which the Palestinians considered their own. Israeli settlers living on the West Bank had an obvious interest in opposing any peace deal that required them to move.

Despite the difficulties, the international community, including the United States, was in agreement on several principles for settling the conflict. Lands seized by Israel in the 1967 war should be restored to the Palestinians, who could organize their own independent nation-state there. In turn, the Palestinians would have to recognize Israel's right to exist and take concrete steps to guarantee Israel's security.

The international consensus did not address some important issues. These include what compensation, if any, should go to Palestinians who lost homes in what is now Israel. (In fact, the Palestinian leadership has never abandoned its demand that the descendants of Palestinians forced out of Israel be allowed to return, even though it is generally recognized that this demand must be given up as part of a final deal.) A second issue is whether Israel could adjust its borders to incorporate some of the Israeli settlement areas, plus part or all of eastern Jerusalem, which had been under Arab control before 1967.

Jordan, and Syria, waged in 1948, 1956, 1967, and 1973. Following the 1948 Arab-Israeli War, a large number of Palestinians—Arab residents of the area, known as Palestine until 1948—were forced into exile, adding to Arab grievances.

The failure of the Arab states in the 1967 war led to additional Palestinian refugees and the rise of the **Palestine Liberation Organization (PLO),** a nonstate body committed to armed struggle against Israel. In the late 1960s and early 1970s, Palestinian groups launched a wave of terrorist attacks against Israeli targets around the world.

Following the 1973 Yom Kippur War, Egyptian president Anwar el-Sadat launched a major peace initiative. He traveled to Israel in 1977 and addressed the Israeli parliament, a major turning point. U.S. president Jimmy Carter (1977–1981) then sponsored intensive negotiations.

Egypt and Israel signed a peace treaty in 1979 that marked the end to an era of major wars between Israel and other states. Lower-level conflicts continued, however. On several occasions, Israel launched attacks against nonstate militias in Lebanon in response to

Palestine Liberation Organization (PLO) An organization formed in 1964 to represent the Palestinian people. The PLO has a long history of terrorism but for some years has functioned primarily as a political party.

> # "The purpose of foreign policy
> is not to provide an outlet
> for our own sentiments of
> hope or indignation; it
> ## is to shape real events in a real world."
>
> ~ **John F. Kennedy,** Thirty-Fifth President of the United States 1961–1963

16–4c Negotiations

In 1993 in Oslo, Norway, Israel and the PLO met officially for the first time. The resulting **Oslo Accords** were signed in Washington under the watchful eye of President Bill Clinton. A major result was the establishment of a Palestinian Authority, under Israeli control, on the West Bank and the Gaza Strip.

NEGOTIATIONS COLLAPSE In 2000, talks between Israel and the Palestinian Authority collapsed in acrimony. After the failure of these talks, an uprising by Palestinian militants led to Israeli military incursions into the West Bank and the almost complete collapse of the Palestinian Authority. In 2005, Israeli prime minister Ariel Sharon, concluding that he had no credible peace partner, carried out a plan to unilaterally withdraw from the Gaza Strip and to build an enormous security fence between Israel and the West Bank. The fence came under strong international criticism because it incorporated parts of the West Bank into Israel.

A DIVIDED PALESTINE Gaza was taken over in 2007 by Hamas, a radical Islamist party that refuses to recognize Israel. After the imposition of an Israeli blockade, Hamas launched missile attacks on Israel, which in turn briefly occupied the strip in December 2008. The West Bank remained under the control of the PLO-led Palestinian Authority, and so the Palestinians, now politically divided, were in an even worse bargaining position than before.

On the West Bank, the Palestinian Authority succeeded in reestablishing itself as an effective government, and the territory entered a period of relative stability and economic growth.

OBAMA AND THE NEGOTIATIONS In 2009, Israel chose Benjamin Netanyahu, a staunch conservative, as its new prime minister. Attempts by the Obama administration to restart Israeli-Palestinian talks were frustrated by disagreements about Israeli settlements on the West Bank—Netanyahu strongly supported the settlers. In 2013, Netanyahu and Palestinian leader Mahmoud Abbas formally reopened negotiations with U.S. assistance. The talks collapsed in April 2014, however. Israeli settlements on the West Bank were one reason. Another was an attempt by the Palestinians to establish a unity government representing both the PLO and Hamas. Because Hamas refuses to recognize Israel's legitimacy, Israel and many Western nations will not deal with it.

THE 2014 GAZA STRIP WAR In June 2014, three Israeli teenagers were abducted and murdered. The Israeli government blamed Hamas for this crime. It arrested several hundred Palestinians, including

Israeli tanks returning from the Hamas-controlled Gaza Strip in August 2014 following the first of a series of cease-fires. *Why do Israel and the United States refuse to talk to Hamas?*

Oslo Accords The first agreement signed between Israel and the PLO; led to the establishment of the Palestinian Authority in the occupied territories.

almost the entire Hamas West Bank leadership. Hamas in the Gaza Strip launched a rocket campaign against Israel, which responded with heavy bombing. By the time a cease-fire was established in August, almost 2,200 Palestinians had been killed. Israel had suffered 72 fatalities. Much of the Gaza Strip's housing and infrastructure had been damaged or destroyed. Almost all Israelis and Americans supported the bombing as a necessary act of defense, but much of the rest of the world criticized it as disproportionate.

CRITICAL THINKING
▶ **Why do you think that Americans support Israel so strongly?**

16–5 WEAPONS PROLIFERATION IN AN UNSTABLE WORLD

LO Outline some of the actions taken by the United States to curb the threat of nuclear weapons.

The Cold War may be over, but the threat of nuclear warfare—which formed the backdrop of foreign policy during the Cold War—has by no means disappeared. The existence of nuclear weapons in Russia and in other countries around the world continues to challenge U.S. foreign policymakers.

Concerns about nuclear proliferation mounted in 1998 when India and Pakistan detonated nuclear devices within a few weeks of each other—events that took U.S. intelligence agencies by surprise. Increasingly, American officials have focused on the threat of an attack by a rogue nation or a terrorist group that possesses weapons of mass destruction. Of most concern today are attempts by North Korea and Iran to develop nuclear capabilities and the recent use of chemical weapons by the Assad regime in Syria.

16–5a North Korea's Nuclear Program

North Korea signed the Treaty on the Non-Proliferation of Nuclear Weapons in 1985 and submitted to weapons inspections by the International Atomic Energy Agency (IAEA) in 1992. Throughout the 1990s, however, there were discrepancies between North Korean declarations and IAEA inspection findings. In 2002, North Korea expelled the IAEA inspectors.

OPENING NEGOTIATIONS The administration of George W. Bush had been reluctant to engage in diplomatic relations with North Korea. Bush insisted that any talks with North Korea must also include all of North Korea's neighbors—China, Japan, Russia, and South Korea. In 2003, North Korea finally agreed to such talks.

Since that time, it has proved quite difficult to keep North Korea at the bargaining table—its representatives have stormed out of the talks repeatedly, for the most trivial reasons. China is the one power with substantial economic leverage over North Korea, and typically, Chinese leaders have been the ones to lead the North Koreans back to the table.

Tensions heightened in October 2006, when North Korea conducted its first nuclear test. Nevertheless, the Bush administration continued to participate with North Korea's neighbors in multilateral negotiations. In the spring of 2007, North Korea agreed that it would begin to dismantle its nuclear facilities and would allow inspectors from the United Nations (UN) into the country.

In return, the other nations agreed to provide various kinds of aid, and the United States would begin to discuss normalization of relations with North Korea. By mid-2007, North Korea had shut down one of its nuclear

North Korean leader Kim Jong Un, accompanied by his wife Ri Sol Ju, attends a concert in Pyongyang. *Why do you think that North Korea wants nuclear weapons?*

reactors and had admitted a permanent UN inspection team into the country.

THE COLLAPSE OF NEGOTIATIONS   In April 2009, North Korea tested a long-range missile under the guise of attempting to launch a satellite. The UN Security Council voted unanimously to condemn the test. This vote demonstrated that the Chinese, who have a permanent Security Council seat, were annoyed as well. North Korea then pulled out of the six-party talks and expelled all nuclear inspectors from the country. In May 2009, North Korea tested another nuclear device, to universal disapproval.

After a third test in 2013, China for the first time imposed significant economic penalties—or *sanctions*—on North Korea. The UN Security Council imposed its own sanctions, which led to an explosion of violent rhetoric from the northern regime directed at South Korea and the United States.

North Korea's aggressive behavior may have been linked to a succession crisis. In 2011, the dictator Kim Jong Il died and was succeeded by his youngest son, Kim Jong Un. Kim Jong Il himself was the son of North Korea's first Communist dictator. North Korea, therefore, is unique in that it is effectively a Communist monarchy.

16–5b Iran: An Emerging Nuclear Threat?

In November 1979, militant students in Tehran, Iran, seized the U.S. embassy and took fifty-two American citizens hostage. The crisis lasted 444 days. Ever since, Iran and the United States have been at odds with each other.

In the years that followed, the rest of the world discovered that Iran was engaged in a covert nuclear program. Investigators for the International Atomic Energy Agency reported that Iran was enriching uranium that could be used in the fabrication of a nuclear bomb.

In spite of numerous UN resolutions, Iran is still producing uranium, and at a faster rate. The existence of a second uranium enrichment plant was made public in the fall of 2009. Simultaneously, Iran has been developing missiles that eventually could be capable of carrying a nuclear payload.

Iranian leaders have publicly stated that they have no intention of using their nuclear program for destructive purposes. They claim that they are seeking only to develop nuclear energy plants.

IRAN AS A SECURITY THREAT   Like North Korea, Iran has been openly hostile to the United States. In addition, Mahmoud Ahmadinejad, president of Iran from 2005 to 2013, repeatedly called for the complete destruction of Israel. It is no surprise, therefore, that Israel considers Iranian nuclear weapons to be a threat to its existence.

© Majid Saeedi/Getty Images News/Getty Images

Hassan Rouhani during his campaign to be elected Iran's new president in 2013. *What might follow from the fact that the United States and Iran are both enemies of ISIS?*

Perhaps more surprising is that Iran's Arab neighbors consider these weapons a threat as well. Leaked U.S. diplomatic cables reveal that Arab leaders have urged the United States to take out the Iranian nuclear program by force.

DIPLOMATIC EFFORTS   The George W. Bush administration refused to negotiate directly with the Iranians. Therefore, Britain, France, and Germany took the lead in diplomatic efforts to encourage Iran to abandon its nuclear program. The United Nations has imposed sanctions on Iran, as has the United States. Past attempts to strengthen UN sanctions, however, have been frustrated by the opposition of China and Russia.

The Obama administration was open to negotiations with Iran. Accordingly, when talks resumed in 2009, the United States was also at the table, as was Russia.

WAR OR PEACE?   Because negotiations with Iran appeared to be going nowhere, the United States and its allies increasingly turned to coercive measures. The United States was able to persuade or pressure a majority of the world's nations not to buy Iran's oil. The United States was also able to cut Iran off from the international banking system. This step made it extremely difficult for Iran to finance imports and exports. By 2013, the Iranian economy was in serious trouble.

Another coercive measure would be to bomb Iran's nuclear sites. In 2008, Israel began preparations that would allow it to launch such a strike if necessary. After Benjamin Netanyahu became prime minister of Israel in 2009, he called for air strikes with increasing urgency. One type of attack, in fact, was launched immediately. In 2010, a sophisticated U.S. computer "worm" took down about a thousand of the five thousand centrifuges used in Iran's uranium enrichment program. Many were completely destroyed.

AGAIN, NEGOTIATIONS   In 2013, Iran elected a new president, Hassan Rouhani. In short order, Rouhani initiated a charm offensive aimed at re-establishing diplomatic negotiations. The new leader repudiated the anti-Israel rhetoric of previous Iranian president Ahmadinejad.

At the United Nations, Rouhani called for a diplomatic resolution of the nuclear issue. Shortly thereafter, serious negotiations resumed between Iran and six other nations, including the United States. In November 2013, Iran and the multinational team announced a six-month interim deal. Iran would freeze parts of its nuclear program in return for the lifting of some sanctions. The deadline for an agreement was later extended to November 2014.

16–5c Use of Chemical Weapons by Syria

Most nations have signed treaties banning the use of chemical weapons—they were, in fact, one of the few instruments of horror that were never used on the battlefield in World War II. Only a handful of nations have refused to sign, including North Korea, Iraq (under Saddam Hussein), and Syria. In August 2013, the government of Syria used the nerve gas sarin against suburbs of Damascus that were under the control of antiregime rebels. The attack killed more than a thousand civilians. Syrian dictator Bashar al-Assad may have used chemical weapons earlier, but this incident was so conspicuous that it could not be ignored.

President Obama proposed to punish the Assad regime for its use of poison gas by launching air strikes. Obama took the unusual step of asking Congress for its approval of the strikes. It seemed quite possible that Congress would vote down such a resolution. In September, however, the government of Russia announced that Syria was willing to sign the Chemical Weapons Convention, a treaty governing chemical weap-

ons, and place its weapons under international control. This initiative was a diplomatic triumph for Russian president Vladimir Putin. The U.S. Senate postponed the vote on the bombing resolution indefinitely.

By October 2013, to the surprise of many, the Assad regime was cooperating with international inspectors. The chemical weapons were removed from Syria to a U.S. ship equipped with special decontamination systems. In August 2014, President Obama announced that the destruction of the weapons was complete.

16–6 CHINA—THE NEXT SUPERPOWER?

LO Describe China's emerging role as a world power.

Some of the foreign policy challenges faced by the United States do not necessarily involve issues of war and peace. Economic matters, including international trade and currency problems, can be very important. One example is the recent European economic crisis, which at times has affected the U.S. economy as well. We discuss that problem in this chapter's *Join the Debate* feature, which follows.

An even greater challenge may be the growing importance of China. Following President Richard Nixon's historic visit to China in 1972, American diplomatic and economic relations with the Chinese gradually improved. Diplomacy with China focused on cultivating a more pro-Western disposition in the formerly isolationist nation. Relations with China are important in part because that nation has enjoyed economic growth averaging almost 10 percent a year for more than thirty years in a row. Such growth has turned China into a great power.

16–6a Chinese-American Trade Relations

The rapid growth of the Chinese economy and increasingly close trade ties between the United States and China have helped bring about a policy of diplomatic outreach. Many Americans protested, however, when the U.S. government extended **normal trade relations (NTR) status** to China on a year-to-year basis. Labor groups objected because they feared that American workers would lose jobs that could be performed at lower

normal trade relations (NTR) status   A trade status granted through an international treaty by which each member nation must treat other members at least as well as it treats the country that receives its most favorable treatment. This status was formerly known as *most-favored-nation status.*

Join the Debate

Is the Euro Doomed?

Decades ago, European leaders had a dream of forging a European union of nations so that world war could never happen again. They created the Common Market and then the European Union (EU). In 2000, sixteen EU countries adopted a common currency called the *euro*. Today, out of the twenty-eight European Union countries, eighteen use the euro. This group of nations is often referred to as the *euro zone*. Since the Great Recession, the euro zone has suffered serious debt crises. As a result, some people wonder whether the euro can survive.

Adopting the euro allowed poorer nations on the periphery of Europe to borrow as cheaply as the richer core nations, such as France and Germany. Investors from the core nations—including large European banks—lent huge sums of money to the periphery countries. When the Great Recession struck, it became clear that people in Greece, Ireland, Portugal, and Spain had borrowed too many euros and would have trouble paying them back. The problem was especially bad in Greece, where the government had shown exceptional irresponsibility. A system of bailouts from richer euro-zone countries to poorer ones began. The process is still ongoing.

The question remains: Can the euro survive? The United States has a stake in what happens in Europe, because trouble there can drag down our economy as well.

The Euro Is Here to Stay

The euro's defenders say that reports of the euro's demise are premature and, indeed, misguided. Germany, in particular, will not let the euro zone break apart. Germany has benefited greatly from the euro zone and especially from the way that the euro has kept Germany's exports cheap and competitive. True, a monetary union without a political union can lead to problems. It will take time to establish agreements that allow the eighteen different economies in the euro zone to be guided by a set of binding rules that cover government spending and financing.

Also, the European Central Bank (ECB) established by the EU can, if necessary, buy the debt of countries that are in trouble. It has done so already. As long as the ECB helps poorer countries to avoid defaulting on their debts, you can bet that the euro will be around for a long time.

The Euro Cannot Last

Pessimists contend that, although the euro may not be doomed immediately, it cannot last much longer. The euro is forcing the nations of the periphery into endless economic depression, with staggering unemployment levels. Eventually, these countries will rebel. True, these nations tend to have excessive regulation and rules making it hard to fire and hire workers. Germany and other northern nations claim that if the nations in the periphery would only reform, everything would be fine.

Yet such reforms wouldn't change the fact that the Mediterranean nations are stuck with a currency that is priced too high, making their exports too expensive. Because these countries do not have their own currencies, they cannot devalue their currency and become competitive. If Germany and other countries were to pursue expansionary policies, countries in the periphery might have someplace to which they could export. But Germany is too afraid of inflation to follow such a strategy. So don't bet that the euro will last.

CRITICAL ANALYSIS **What might happen to the value of the dollar in international trade if the euro disappeared?**

wages in Chinese factories. Human rights organizations denounced the Chinese government's well-documented mistreatment of its people.

Despite this heavy opposition, Congress granted China permanent NTR status in 2000 and endorsed China's application to join the World Trade Organization in 2001.

16–6b A Future Challenger to American Dominance?

Many U.S. observers have warned that China is destined to challenge American global supremacy. China has one of the fastest-growing economies in the world, along with a population of 1.3 billion, and its gross domestic product

Chinese workers on the assembly line at a joint venture with French automaker Peugeot-Citroën in the city of Wuhan. *If China begins offering cars for sale in the United States, do you think many people will buy them?*

(GDP) is expected to surpass that of the United States by 2020. Measured in its own currency, China's GDP is more than *two hundred times* what it was in 1978, when China implemented reforms to make the economy more market oriented. Never in the history of the world have so many people been lifted out of poverty so quickly.

THE ISSUE OF TAIWAN   Although China has not demonstrated any ambition to acquire non-Chinese territory, it has a rather expansive definition of what Chinese territory is. China considers Taiwan, a former Chinese province, to be a legal part of China. In practice, however, since 1949 the island has functioned as an independent nation. The United States has historically supported a free and separate Taiwan and has reiterated that any reunion of China and Taiwan must come about by peaceful means.

RECENT CHINESE NATIONALISM   In recent years, China has exhibited nationalist tendencies that have alarmed some of its neighbors. China is engaged in a territorial dispute with Japan over uninhabited islands in the East China Sea. China has also claimed almost all of the uninhabited islands located in the South China Sea, even ones that are a considerable distance from the Chinese mainland. These claims have resulted in diplo-

matic disputes with Brunei and Malaysia—and military confrontations with the Philippines and Vietnam.

In 2012, President Obama announced a "pivot" to East Asia. The pivot involves shifting naval resources into the region and negotiating enhanced security relationships with area nations. China's response was to accuse the United States of attempting to "contain" China.

REGIONAL ISSUES   Within China itself, nationalism has often taken the form of discrimination against minority nationalities. These include the people of Tibet and also the Uighurs, a Muslim people in the western region of Xinjiang. Both Tibet and Xinjiang have experienced very large inflows of the majority Chinese group, known as *Han Chinese.* Many Tibetans and Uighurs believe that they are becoming oppressed minorities within their own countries. As a result, disturbances have been common.

An additional regional problem was the status of Hong Kong. That city-state has enjoyed substantial autonomy as a 'special administrative region' since China took it over from Britain in 1997. At that time, China promised that Hong Kong citizens would be allowed to vote in free elections at some point in the future. In 2014, the Chinese government published a plan to supposedly do just that. The plan, however, gave the national government veto power over nominations. The result was a massive wave of pro-democracy protests, the largest in Hong Kong's history. Despite the demonstrations, it seemed unlikely that the Chinese government would back down on its demand to control nominations.

> **CRITICAL THINKING**
> ▶ If we have strong trade relations with a country, does that make it less likely that we would ever go to war with that country? Why or why not?

AMERICA ⚐ AT ODDS
Foreign Policy

In 1947, Republican senator Arthur Vandenberg of Michigan announced, "Politics stops at the water's edge." By this, Vandenberg, formerly a fierce isolationist, meant that Republicans and Democrats should cooperate in dealing with such foreign policy issues as the Cold War with the Soviet Union.

Bipartisanship was never complete even in Vandenberg's day, however, and it is much less common today. True, the two major parties are more likely to cooperate over a foreign policy issue than over domestic policy. Nevertheless, Americans are at odds over many foreign policy issues, as reflected in Congress. The following are a few of these issues:

- *In foreign policy, is it best to ally with other nations whenever possible—or should America carefully guard its ability to act alone?*

- *Should the president take complete charge of the foreign policy process, including the use of armed force—or should the president collaborate closely with Congress?*

- *Should the war on terrorism be the central focus of U.S. foreign policy—or should we devote equal energy to managing our relations with rising powers such as China?*

- *Should the United States take a firm line with Russia over Ukraine, or is it more important to head off a new Cold War?*

- *In attempting to promote peace between Israelis and Palestinians, should the United States put most of its pressure on the Palestinians—or should it also pressure the Israelis to, for example, suspend the construction of new Jewish settlements on the West Bank?*

Internet Resources

- One of the best resources on the Web for learning about foreign countries is the *CIA's World Factbook*. You can find it at www.cia.gov/library/publications/the-world-factbook.

- The English-language Web site of the United Nations is at www.un.org/en.

- Several international organizations focus on economics, including development issues and world statistics. For the Web site of the International Monetary Fund (IMF), go to www.imf.org. The World Bank is at www.worldbank.org.

- The Organization for Economic Cooperation and Development (OECD) provides statistics that compare economically advanced nations. It is at www.oecd.org.

- You can find news about international events at an interesting Web site sponsored by the Peterson Institute for International Economics at www.iie.com.

- For national security issues, visit the U.S. Department of Defense at www.defense.gov and the North Atlantic Treaty Organization (NATO) at www.nato.int.

STUDY TOOLS 16

READY TO STUDY?

- ☐ Review what you've read with the quiz below.
- ☐ Check your answers in Appendix D at the back of the book.
- ☐ For any questions you miss, read the corresponding Learning Outcome section again to prepare for class and your exam.
- ☐ Rip out and study the Chapter in Review card (at the back of the book).

VISIT WWW.CENGAGEBRAIN.COM:

- ☐ Interactive Quizzes
- ☐ Key Term Flashcards or Crossword Puzzles
- ☐ Audio Summaries
- ☐ Simulations, Animated Learning Modules, and Interactive Timelines
- ☐ Videos
- ☐ American Government NewsWatch

He has combined with others to subject us to a Jurisdiction foreign to our Constitution, and unacknowledged by our Laws; giving his Assent to their Acts of pretended Legislation:

For quartering large Bodies of Armed Troops among us:

For protecting them, by a mock Trial, from Punishment for any Murders which they should commit on the Inhabitants of these States:

For cutting off our Trade with all Parts of the World:

For imposing Taxes on us without our Consent:

For depriving us, in many cases, of the Benefits of Trial by Jury:

For transporting us beyond Seas to be tried for pretended Offences:

For abolishing the free System of English Laws in a neighbouring Province, establishing therein an arbitrary Government, and enlarging its Boundaries, so as to render it at once an Example and fit Instrument for introducing the same absolute Rule into these Colonies:

For taking away our Charters, abolishing our most valuable Laws, and altering fundamentally the Forms of our Governments:

For suspending our own Legislatures, and declaring themselves invested with Power to legislate for us in all Cases whatsoever.

He has abdicated Government here, by declaring us out of his Protection and waging War against us.

He has plundered our Seas, ravaged our Coasts, burnt our towns, and destroyed the Lives of our People.

He is, at this Time, transporting large Armies of foreign Mercenaries to compleat the works of Death, Desolation, and Tyranny, already begun with circumstances of Cruelty and Perfidy, scarcely paralleled in the most barbarous Ages, and totally unworthy the Head of a civilized Nation.

He has constrained our fellow Citizens taken Captive on the high Seas to bear Arms against their Country, to become the Executioners of their Friends and Brethren, or to fall themselves by their Hands.

He has excited domestic Insurrections amongst us, and has endeavoured to bring on the Inhabitants of our Frontiers, the merciless Indian Savages, whose known Rule of Warfare, is an undistinguished Destruction, of all Ages, Sexes and Conditions.

In every state of these Oppressions we have Petitioned for Redress in the most humble Terms: Our repeated Petitions have been answered only by repeated Injury. A Prince, whose Character is thus marked by every act which may define a Tyrant, is unfit to be the Ruler of a free People.

Nor have we been wanting in Attentions to our British Brethren. We have warned them from Time to Time of Attempts by their Legislature to extend an unwarrantable Jurisdiction over us. We have reminded them of the Circumstances of our Emigration and Settlement here. We have appealed to their native Justice and Magnanimity, and we have conjured them by the Ties of our common Kindred to disavow these Usurpations, which, would inevitably interrupt our Connections and Correspondence. They too have been deaf to the Voice of Justice and of Consanguinity. We must, therefore, acquiesce in the Necessity, which denounces our Separation, and hold them, as we hold the rest of Mankind, Enemies in War, in Peace, Friends.

We, therefore, the Representatives of the UNITED STATES OF AMERICA, in General Congress Assembled, appealing to the Supreme Judge of the World for the Rectitude of our Intentions, do, in the Name, and by the Authority of the good People of these Colonies, solemnly Publish and Declare, That these United Colonies are, and of Right ought to be, Free and Independent States; that they are absolved from all Allegiance to the British Crown, and that all political Connection between them and the State of Great-Britain, is and ought to be totally dissolved; and that as Free and Independent States, they have full Power to levy War, conclude Peace, contract Alliances, establish Commerce, and to do all other Acts and Things which Independent States may of right do. And for the support of this declaration, with a firm Reliance on the Protection of divine Providence, we mutually pledge to each other our lives, our Fortunes, and our sacred Honor.

THE CONSTITUTION OF THE UNITED STATES

PREAMBLE

We the People of the United States, in Order to form a more perfect Union, establish Justice, insure domestic Tranquility, provide for the common defence, promote the general Welfare, and secure the Blessings of Liberty to ourselves and our Posterity, do ordain and establish this Constitution for the United States of America.

ARTICLE I

Section 1. All legislative Powers herein granted shall be vested in a Congress of the United States, which shall consist of a Senate and House of Representatives.

Section 2. The House of Representatives shall be composed of Members chosen every second Year by the People of the several States, and the Electors in each State shall have the Qualifications requisite for Electors of the most numerous Branch of the State Legislature.

No Person shall be a Representative who shall not have attained to the Age of twenty five Years, and been seven Years a Citizen of the United States, and who shall not, when elected, be an Inhabitant of that State in which he shall be chosen.

Representatives and direct Taxes shall be apportioned among the several States which may be included within this Union, according to their respective Numbers, which shall be determined by adding to the whole Number of free Persons, including those bound to Service for a Term of Years, and excluding Indians not taxed, three fifths of all other Persons. The actual Enumeration shall be made within three Years after the first Meeting of the Congress of the United States, and within every subsequent Term of ten Years, in such Manner as they shall by Law direct. The Number of Representatives shall not exceed one for every thirty Thousand, but each State shall have at Least one Representative; and until such enumeration shall be made, the State of New Hampshire shall be entitled to chuse three, Massachusetts eight, Rhode Island and Providence Plantations one, Connecticut five, New York six, New Jersey four, Pennsylvania eight, Delaware one, Maryland six, Virginia ten, North Carolina five, South Carolina five, and Georgia three.

When vacancies happen in the Representation from any State, the Executive Authority thereof shall issue Writs of Election to fill such Vacancies.

The House of Representatives shall chuse their Speaker and other Officers; and shall have the sole Power of Impeachment.

Section 3. The Senate of the United States shall be composed of two Senators from each State, chosen by the Legislature thereof, for six Years; and each Senator shall have one Vote.

Immediately after they shall be assembled in Consequence of the first Election, they shall be divided as equally as may be into three Classes. The Seats of the Senators of the first Class shall be vacated at the Expiration of the second Year, of the second Class at the Expiration of the fourth Year, and of the third Class at the Expiration of the sixth Year, so that one third may be chosen every second Year; and if Vacancies happen by Resignation, or otherwise, during the Recess of the Legislature of any State, the Executive thereof may make temporary Appointments until the next Meeting of the Legislature, which shall then fill such Vacancies.

No Person shall be a Senator who shall not have attained to the Age of thirty Years, and been nine Years a Citizen of the United States, and who shall not, when elected, be an Inhabitant of that State for which he shall be chosen.

The Vice President of the United States shall be President of the Senate, but shall have no Vote, unless they be equally divided.

The Senate shall chuse their other Officers, and also a President pro tempore, in the Absence of the Vice President, or when he shall exercise the Office of President of the United States.

The Senate shall have the sole Power to try all Impeachments. When sitting for that Purpose, they shall be on Oath or Affirmation. When the President of the United States is tried, the Chief Justice shall preside: And no Person shall be convicted without the Concurrence of two thirds of the Members present.

Judgment in Cases of Impeachment shall not extend further than to removal from Office, and disqualification to hold and enjoy any Office of honor, Trust, or Profit under the United States: but the Party convicted shall nevertheless be liable and subject to Indictment, Trial, Judgment, and Punishment, according to Law.

Section 4. The Times, Places and Manner of holding Elections for Senators and Representatives, shall be prescribed in each State by the Legislature thereof; but the Congress may at any time by Law make or alter such Regulations, except as to the Places of chusing Senators.

The Congress shall assemble at least once in every Year, and such Meeting shall be on the first Monday in December, unless they shall by Law appoint a different Day.

Section 5. Each House shall be the Judge of the Elections, Returns, and Qualifications of its own Members, and a Majority of each shall constitute a Quorum to do Business; but a smaller Number may adjourn from day to day, and may be authorized to compel the Attendance of absent Members, in such Manner, and under such Penalties as each House may provide.

Each House may determine the Rules of its Proceedings, punish its Members for disorderly Behavior, and, with the Concurrence of two thirds, expel a Member.

Each House shall keep a Journal of its Proceedings, and from time to time publish the same, excepting such Parts as may in their Judgment require Secrecy; and the Yeas and Nays of the Members of either House on any question shall, at the Desire of one fifth of those Present, be entered on the Journal.

Neither House, during the Session of Congress, shall, without the Consent of the other, adjourn for more than three days, nor to any other Place than that in which the two Houses shall be sitting.

Section 6. The Senators and Representatives shall receive a Compensation for their Services, to be ascertained by Law, and paid out of the Treasury of the United States. They shall in all Cases, except Treason, Felony and Breach of the Peace, be privileged from Arrest during their Attendance at the Session of their respective Houses, and in going to and returning from the same; and for any Speech or Debate in either House, they shall not be questioned in any other Place.

No Senator or Representative shall, during the Time for which he was elected, be appointed to any civil Office under the Authority of the United States, which shall have been created, or the Emoluments whereof shall have been increased during such time; and no Person holding any Office under the United States, shall be a Member of either House during his Continuance in Office.

Section 7. All Bills for raising Revenue shall originate in the House of Representatives; but the Senate may propose or concur with Amendments as on other Bills.

Every Bill which shall have passed the House of Representatives and the Senate, shall, before it become a Law, be presented to the President of the United States; If he approve he shall sign it, but if not he shall return it, with his Objections to the House in which it shall have originated, who shall enter the Objections at large on their Journal, and proceed to reconsider it. If after such Reconsideration two thirds of that House shall agree to pass the Bill, it shall be sent together with the Objections, to the other House, by which it shall likewise be reconsidered, and if approved by two thirds of that House, it shall become a Law. But in all such Cases the Votes of both Houses shall be determined by Yeas and Nays, and the Names of the Persons voting for and against the Bill shall be entered on the Journal of each House respectively. If any Bill shall not be returned by the President within ten Days (Sundays excepted) after it shall have been presented to him, the Same shall be a Law, in like Manner as if he had signed it, unless the Congress by their Adjournment prevent its Return in which Case it shall not be a Law.

Every Order, Resolution, or Vote, to which the Concurrence of the Senate and House of Representatives may be necessary (except on a question of Adjournment) shall be presented to the President of the United States; and before the Same shall take Effect, shall be approved by him, or being disapproved by him, shall be repassed by two thirds of the Senate and House of Representatives, according to the Rules and Limitations prescribed in the Case of a Bill.

Section 8. The Congress shall have Power To lay and collect Taxes, Duties, Imposts and Excises, to pay the Debts and provide for the common Defence and general Welfare of the United States; but all Duties, Imposts and Excises shall be uniform throughout the United States;

To borrow Money on the credit of the United States;

To regulate Commerce with foreign Nations, and among the several States, and with the Indian Tribes;

To establish an uniform Rule of Naturalization, and uniform Laws on the subject of Bankruptcies throughout the United States;

To coin Money, regulate the Value thereof, and of foreign Coin, and fix the Standard of Weights and Measures;

To provide for the Punishment of counterfeiting the Securities and current Coin of the United States;

To establish Post Offices and post Roads;

To promote the Progress of Science and useful Arts, by securing for limited Times to Authors and Inventors the exclusive Right to their respective Writings and Discoveries;

To constitute Tribunals inferior to the supreme Court;

To define and punish Piracies and Felonies committed on the high Seas, and Offenses against the Law of Nations;

To declare War, grant Letters of Marque and Reprisal, and make Rules concerning Captures on Land and Water;

To raise and support Armies, but no Appropriation of Money to that Use shall be for a longer Term than two Years;

To provide and maintain a Navy;

To make Rules for the Government and Regulation of the land and naval Forces;

To provide for calling forth the Militia to execute the Laws of the Union, suppress Insurrections and repel Invasions;

To provide for organizing, arming, and disciplining, the Militia, and for governing such Part of them as may be employed in the Service of the United States, reserving to the States respectively, the Appointment of the Officers, and the Authority of training the Militia according to the discipline prescribed by Congress;

To exercise exclusive Legislation in all Cases whatsoever, over such District (not exceeding ten Miles square) as may, by Cession of particular States, and the Acceptance of Congress, become the Seat of the Government of the United States, and to exercise like Authority over all Places purchased by the Consent of the Legislature of the State in which the Same shall be, for the Erection of Forts, Magazines, Arsenals, dock-Yards, and other needful Buildings;—And

To make all Laws which shall be necessary and proper for carrying into Execution the foregoing Powers, and all other Powers vested by this Constitution in the Government of the United States, or in any Department or Officer thereof.

Section 9. The Migration or Importation of such Persons as any of the States now existing shall think proper to admit, shall not be prohibited by the Congress prior to the Year one thousand eight hundred and eight, but a Tax or duty may be imposed on such Importation, not exceeding ten dollars for each Person.

The privilege of the Writ of Habeas Corpus shall not be suspended, unless when in Cases of Rebellion or Invasion the public Safety may require it.

No Bill of Attainder or ex post facto Law shall be passed.

No Capitation, or other direct, Tax shall be laid, unless in Proportion to the Census or Enumeration herein before directed to be taken.

No Tax or Duty shall be laid on Articles exported from any State.

No Preference shall be given by any Regulation of Commerce or Revenue to the Ports of one State over those of another: nor shall Vessels bound to, or from, one State be obliged to enter, clear, or pay Duties in another.

No Money shall be drawn from the Treasury, but in Consequence of Appropriations made by Law; and a regular Statement and Account of the Receipts and Expenditures of all public Money shall be published from time to time.

No Title of Nobility shall be granted by the United States: And no Person holding any Office of Profit or Trust under them, shall, without the Consent of the Congress, accept of any present, Emolument, Office, or Title, of any kind whatever, from any King, Prince, or foreign State.

Section 10. No State shall enter into any Treaty, Alliance, or Confederation; grant Letters of Marque and Reprisal; coin Money; emit Bills of Credit; make any Thing but gold and silver Coin a Tender in Payment of Debts; pass any Bill of Attainder, ex post facto Law, or Law impairing the Obligation of Contracts, or grant any Title of Nobility.

No State shall, without the Consent of the Congress, lay any Imposts or Duties on Imports or Exports, except what may be absolutely necessary for executing its inspection Laws: and the net Produce of all Duties and Imposts, laid by any State on Imports or Exports, shall be for the Use of the Treasury of the United States; and all such Laws shall be subject to the Revision and Controul of the Congress.

No State shall, without the Consent of Congress, lay any Duty of Tonnage, keep Troops, or Ships of War in time of Peace, enter into any Agreement or Compact with another State, or with a foreign Power, or engage in War, unless actually invaded, or in such imminent Danger as will not admit of delay.

ARTICLE II

Section 1. The executive Power shall be vested in a President of the United States of America. He shall hold his Office during the Term of four Years, and, together with the Vice President, chosen for the same Term, be elected, as follows:

Each State shall appoint, in such Manner as the Legislature thereof may direct, a Number of

Electors, equal to the whole Number of Senators and Representatives to which the State may be entitled in the Congress; but no Senator or Representative, or Person holding an Office of Trust or Profit under the United States, shall be appointed an Elector.

The Electors shall meet in their respective States, and vote by Ballot for two Persons, of whom one at least shall not be an Inhabitant of the same State with themselves. And they shall make a List of all the Persons voted for, and of the Number of Votes for each; which List they shall sign and certify, and transmit sealed to the Seat of the Government of the United States, directed to the President of the Senate. The President of the Senate shall, in the Presence of the Senate and House of Representatives, open all the Certificates, and the Votes shall then be counted. The Person having the greatest Number of Votes shall be the President, if such Number be a Majority of the whole Number of Electors appointed; and if there be more than one who have such Majority, and have an equal Number of Votes, then the House of Representatives shall immediately chuse by Ballot one of them for President; and if no Person have a Majority, then from the five highest on the List the said House shall in like Manner chuse the President. But in chusing the President, the Votes shall be taken by States, the Representation from each State having one Vote; A quorum for this Purpose shall consist of a Member or Members from two thirds of the States, and a Majority of all the States shall be necessary to a Choice. In every Case, after the Choice of the President, the Person having the greater Number of Votes of the Electors shall be the Vice President. But if there should remain two or more who have equal Votes, the Senate shall chuse from them by Ballot the Vice President.

The Congress may determine the Time of chusing the Electors, and the Day on which they shall give their Votes; which Day shall be the same throughout the United States.

No person except a natural born Citizen, or a Citizen of the United States, at the time of the Adoption of this Constitution, shall be eligible to the Office of President; neither shall any Person be eligible to that Office who shall not have attained to the Age of thirty five Years, and been fourteen Years a Resident within the United States.

In Case of the Removal of the President from Office, or of his Death, Resignation or Inability to discharge the Powers and Duties of the said Office, the same shall devolve on the Vice President, and the Congress may by Law provide for the Case of Removal, Death, Resignation or Inability, both of the President and Vice President, declaring what Officer shall then act as President, and such Officer shall act accordingly, until the Disability be removed, or a President shall be elected.

The President shall, at stated Times, receive for his Services, a Compensation, which shall neither be increased nor diminished during the Period for which he shall have been elected, and he shall not receive within that Period any other Emolument from the United States, or any of them.

Before he enter on the Execution of his Office, he shall take the following Oath or Affirmation: "I do solemnly swear (or affirm) that I will faithfully execute the Office of President of the United States, and will to the best of my Ability, preserve, protect and defend the Constitution of the United States."

Section 2.   The President shall be Commander in Chief of the Army and Navy of the United States, and of the Militia of the several States, when called into the actual Service of the United States; he may require the Opinion, in writing, of the principal Officer in each of the executive Departments, upon any Subject relating to the Duties of their respective Offices, and he shall have Power to grant Reprieves and Pardons for Offenses against the United States, except in Cases of Impeachment.

He shall have Power, by and with the Advice and Consent of the Senate to make Treaties, provided two thirds of the Senators present concur; and he shall nominate, and by and with the Advice and Consent of the Senate, shall appoint Ambassadors, other public Ministers and Consuls, Judges of the supreme Court, and all other Officers of the United States, whose Appointments are not herein otherwise provided for, and which shall be established by Law; but the Congress may by Law vest the Appointment of such inferior Officers, as they think proper, in the President alone, in the Courts of Law, or in the Heads of Departments.

The President shall have Power to fill up all Vacancies that may happen during the Recess of the Senate, by granting Commissions which shall expire at the End of their next Session.

Section 3.   He shall from time to time give to the Congress Information of the State of the Union, and recommend to their Consideration such Measures as he shall judge necessary and expedient; he may, on extraordinary Occasions, convene both Houses, or either of them, and in Case of Disagreement between them, with Respect to the Time of Adjournment, he may adjourn them to such Time as he shall think proper; he shall receive Ambassadors and other public Ministers; he shall take Care that the Laws be faithfully executed, and shall Commission all the Officers of the United States.

Section 4. The President, Vice President and all civil Officers of the United States, shall be removed from Office on Impeachment for, and Conviction of, Treason, Bribery, or other high Crimes and Misdemeanors.

ARTICLE III

Section 1. The judicial Power of the United States, shall be vested in one supreme Court, and in such inferior Courts as the Congress may from time to time ordain and establish. The Judges, both of the supreme and inferior Courts, shall hold their Offices during good Behaviour, and shall, at stated Times, receive for their Services a Compensation, which shall not be diminished during their Continuance in Office.

Section 2. The judicial Power shall extend to all Cases, in Law and Equity, arising under this Constitution, the Laws of the United States, and Treaties made, or which shall be made, under their Authority;—to all Cases affecting Ambassadors, other public Ministers and Consuls;—to all Cases of admiralty and maritime Jurisdiction;—to Controversies to which the United States shall be a Party;—to Controversies between two or more States;—between a State and Citizens of another State;—between Citizens of different States;—between Citizens of the same State claiming Lands under Grants of different States, and between a State, or the Citizens thereof, and foreign States, Citizens or Subjects.

In all Cases affecting Ambassadors, other public Ministers and Consuls, and those in which a State shall be a Party, the supreme Court shall have original Jurisdiction. In all the other Cases before mentioned, the supreme Court shall have appellate Jurisdiction, both as to Law and Fact, with such Exceptions, and under such Regulations as the Congress shall make.

The Trial of all Crimes, except in Cases of Impeachment, shall be by Jury; and such Trial shall be held in the State where the said Crimes shall have been committed; but when not committed within any State, the Trial shall be at such Place or Places as the Congress may by Law have directed.

Section 3. Treason against the United States, shall consist only in levying War against them, or, in adhering to their Enemies, giving them Aid and Comfort. No Person shall be convicted of Treason unless on the Testimony of two Witnesses to the same overt Act, or on Confession in open Court.

The Congress shall have Power to declare the Punishment of Treason, but no Attainder of Treason shall work Corruption of Blood, or Forfeiture except during the Life of the Person attainted.

ARTICLE IV

Section 1. Full Faith and Credit shall be given in each State to the public Acts, Records, and judicial Proceedings of every other State. And the Congress may by general Laws prescribe the Manner in which such Acts, Records and Proceedings shall be proved, and the Effect thereof.

Section 2. The Citizens of each State shall be entitled to all Privileges and Immunities of Citizens in the several States.

A Person charged in any State with Treason, Felony, or other Crime, who shall flee from Justice, and be found in another State, shall on Demand of the executive Authority of the State from which he fled, be delivered up, to be removed to the State having Jurisdiction of the Crime.

No Person held to Service or Labour in one State, under the Laws thereof, escaping into another, shall, in Consequence of any Law or Regulation therein, be discharged from such Service or Labour, but shall be delivered up on Claim of the Party to whom such Service or Labour may be due.

Section 3. New States may be admitted by the Congress into this Union; but no new State shall be formed or erected within the Jurisdiction of any other State; nor any State be formed by the Junction of two or more States, or Parts of States, without the Consent of the Legislatures of the States concerned as well as of the Congress.

The Congress shall have Power to dispose of and make all needful Rules and Regulations respecting the Territory or other Property belonging to the United States; and nothing in this Constitution shall be so construed as to Prejudice any Claims of the United States, or of any particular State.

Section 4. The United States shall guarantee to every State in this Union a Republican Form of Government, and shall protect each of them against Invasion; and on Application of the Legislature, or of the Executive (when the Legislature cannot be convened) against domestic Violence.

ARTICLE V

The Congress, whenever two thirds of both Houses shall deem it necessary, shall propose Amendments to this Constitution, or, on the Application of the Legislatures of two thirds of the several States, shall call a Convention for proposing Amendments, which, in either Case, shall be valid to all Intents and Purposes, as part of this Constitution, when ratified by the Legislatures of three fourths of the several States, or by Conventions in three fourths thereof, as the one or the other Mode of Ratification may be proposed by the Congress; Provided that no Amendment which may be made prior to the Year One thousand eight hundred and eight shall in any Manner affect the first and fourth Clauses in the Ninth Section of the first Article; and that no State, without its Consent, shall be deprived of its equal Suffrage in the Senate.

ARTICLE VI

All Debts contracted and Engagements entered into, before the Adoption of this Constitution shall be as valid against the United States under this Constitution, as under the Confederation.

This Constitution, and the Laws of the United States which shall be made in Pursuance thereof; and all Treaties made, or which shall be made, under the Authority of the United States, shall be the supreme Law of the Land; and the Judges in every State shall be bound thereby, any Thing in the Constitution or Laws of any State to the Contrary notwithstanding.

The Senators and Representatives before mentioned, and the Members of the several State Legislatures, and all executive and judicial Officers, both of the United States and of the several States, shall be bound by Oath or Affirmation, to support this Constitution; but no religious Test shall ever be required as a Qualification to any Office or public Trust under the United States.

ARTICLE VII

The Ratification of the Conventions of nine States shall be sufficient for the Establishment of this Constitution between the States so ratifying the Same.

AMENDMENT I [1791]

Congress shall make no law respecting an establishment of religion, or prohibiting the free exercise thereof; or abridging the freedom of speech, or of the press; or the right of the people peaceably to assemble, and to petition the Government for a redress of grievances.

AMENDMENT II [1791]

A well regulated Militia, being necessary to the security of a free State, the right of the people to keep and bear Arms, shall not be infringed.

AMENDMENT III [1791]

No Soldier shall, in time of peace be quartered in any house, without the consent of the Owner, nor in time of war, but in a manner to be prescribed by law.

AMENDMENT IV [1791]

The right of the people to be secure in their persons, houses, papers, and effects, against unreasonable searches and seizures, shall not be violated, and no Warrants shall issue, but upon probable cause, supported by Oath or affirmation, and particularly describing the place to be searched, and the persons or things to be seized.

AMENDMENT V [1791]

No person shall be held to answer for a capital, or otherwise infamous crime, unless on a presentment or indictment of a Grand Jury, except in cases arising in the land or naval forces, or in the Militia, when in actual service in time of War or public danger; nor shall any person be subject for the same offense to be twice put in jeopardy of life or limb; nor shall be compelled in any criminal case to be a witness against himself, nor be deprived of life, liberty, or property, without due process of law; nor shall private property be taken for public use, without just compensation.

AMENDMENT VI [1791]

In all criminal prosecutions, the accused shall enjoy the right to a speedy and public trial, by an impartial jury of the State and district wherein the crime shall have been committed, which district shall have been previously ascertained by law, and to be informed of the nature and cause of the accusation; to be confronted with the witnesses against him; to have compulsory process for obtaining witnesses in his favor, and to have the Assistance of Counsel for his defence.

AMENDMENT VII [1791]

In Suits at common law, where the value in controversy shall exceed twenty dollars, the right of trial by jury shall be preserved, and no fact tried by a jury, shall be otherwise re-examined in any Court of the United States, than according to the rules of the common law.

AMENDMENT VIII [1791]

Excessive bail shall not be required, nor excessive fines imposed, nor cruel and unusual punishments inflicted.

AMENDMENT IX [1791]

The enumeration in the Constitution, of certain rights, shall not be construed to deny or disparage others retained by the people.

AMENDMENT X [1791]

The powers not delegated to the United States by the Constitution, nor prohibited by it to the States, are reserved to the States respectively, or to the people.

AMENDMENT XI [1795]

The Judicial power of the United States shall not be construed to extend to any suit in law or equity, commenced or prosecuted against one of the United States by Citizens of another State, or by Citizens or Subjects of any Foreign State.

AMENDMENT XII [1804]

The Electors shall meet in their respective states, and vote by ballot for President and Vice-President, one of whom, at least, shall not be an inhabitant of the same state with themselves; they shall name in their ballots the person voted for as President, and in distinct ballots the person voted for as Vice-President, and they shall make distinct lists of all persons voted for as President, and of all persons voted for as Vice-President, and of the number of votes for each, which lists they shall sign and certify, and transmit sealed to the seat of the government of the United States, directed to the President of the Senate;—The President of the Senate shall, in the presence of the Senate and House of Representatives, open all the certificates and the votes shall then be counted;—The person having the greatest number of votes for President, shall be the President, if such number be a majority of the whole number of Electors appointed; and if no person have such majority, then from the persons having the highest numbers not exceeding three on the list of those voted for as President, the House of Representatives shall choose immediately, by ballot, the President. But in choosing the President, the votes shall be taken by states, the representation from each state having one vote; a quorum for this purpose shall consist of a member or members from two-thirds of the states, and a majority of all states shall be necessary to a choice. And if the House of Representatives shall not choose a President whenever the right of choice shall devolve upon them, before the fourth day of March next following, then the Vice-President shall act as President, as in the case of the death or other constitutional disability of the President.—The person having the greatest number of votes as Vice-President, shall be the Vice-President, if such number be a majority of the whole number of Electors appointed, and if no person have a majority, then from the two highest numbers on the list, the Senate shall choose the Vice-President; a quorum for the purpose shall consist of two-thirds of the whole number of Senators, and a majority of the whole number shall be necessary to a choice. But no person constitutionally ineligible to the office of President shall be eligible to that of Vice-President of the United States.

AMENDMENT XIII [1865]

Section 1. Neither slavery nor involuntary servitude, except as a punishment for crime whereof the party shall have been duly convicted, shall exist within the United States, or any place subject to their jurisdiction.

Section 2. Congress shall have power to enforce this article by appropriate legislation.

AMENDMENT XIV [1868]

Section 1. All persons born or naturalized in the United States, and subject to the jurisdiction thereof, are citizens of the United States and of the State wherein they reside. No State shall make or enforce any law which shall abridge the privileges or immunities of citizens of the United States; nor shall any State deprive any person of life, liberty, or property, without due process of law; nor deny to any person within its jurisdiction the equal protection of the laws.

Section 2. Representatives shall be apportioned among the several States according to their respective numbers, counting the whole number of persons in each State, excluding Indians not taxed. But when the right to vote at any election for the choice of electors for President and Vice President of the United States, Representatives in Congress, the Executive and Judicial officers of a State, or the members of the Legislature thereof, is denied to any of the male inhabitants of such State, being twenty-one years of age, and citizens of the United States, or in any way abridged, except for participation in rebellion, or other crime, the basis of representation therein shall be reduced in the proportion which the number of such male citizens shall bear to the whole number of male citizens twenty-one years of age in such State.

Section 3. No person shall be a Senator or Representative in Congress, or elector of President and Vice President, or hold any office, civil or military, under the United States, or under any State, who having previously taken an oath, as a member of Congress, or as an officer of the United States, or as a member of any State legislature, or as an executive or judicial officer of any State, to support the Constitution of the United States, shall have engaged in insurrection or rebellion against the same, or given aid or comfort to the enemies thereof. But Congress may by a vote of two-thirds of each House, remove such disability.

Section 4. The validity of the public debt of the United States, authorized by law, including debts incurred for payment of pensions and bounties for services in suppressing insurrection or rebellion, shall not be questioned. But neither the United States nor any State shall assume or pay any debt or obligation incurred in aid of insurrection or rebellion against the United States, or any claim for the loss or emancipation of any slave; but all such debts, obligations and claims shall be held illegal and void.

Section 5. The Congress shall have power to enforce, by appropriate legislation, the provisions of this article.

AMENDMENT XV [1870]

Section 1. The right of citizens of the United States to vote shall not be denied or abridged by the United States or by any State on account of race, color, or previous condition of servitude.

Section 2. The Congress shall have power to enforce this article by appropriate legislation.

AMENDMENT XVI [1913]

The Congress shall have power to lay and collect taxes on incomes, from whatever source derived, without apportionment among the several States, and without regard to any census or enumeration.

AMENDMENT XVII [1913]

Section 1. The Senate of the United States shall be composed of two Senators from each State, elected by the people thereof, for six years; and each Senator shall have one vote. The electors in each State shall have the qualifications requisite for electors of the most numerous branch of the State legislatures.

Section 2. When vacancies happen in the representation of any State in the Senate, the executive authority of such State shall issue writs of election to fill such vacancies: Provided, That the legislature of any State may empower the executive thereof to make temporary appointments until the people fill the vacancies by election as the legislature may direct.

Section 3. This amendment shall not be so construed as to affect the election or term of any Senator chosen before it becomes valid as part of the Constitution.

AMENDMENT XVIII [1919]

Section 1. After one year from the ratification of this article the manufacture, sale, or transportation of intoxicating liquors within, the importation thereof into, or the exportation thereof from the United States and all territory subject to the jurisdiction thereof for beverage purposes is hereby prohibited.

Section 2. The Congress and the several States shall have concurrent power to enforce this article by appropriate legislation.

Section 3. This article shall be inoperative unless it shall have been ratified as an amendment to the Constitution by the legislatures of the several States, as provided in the Constitution, within seven years from the date of the submission hereof to the States by the Congress.

AMENDMENT XIX [1920]

Section 1. The right of citizens of the United States to vote shall not be denied or abridged by the United States or by any State on account of sex.

Section 2. Congress shall have power to enforce this article by appropriate legislation.

AMENDMENT XX [1933]

Section 1. The terms of the President and Vice President shall end at noon on the 20th day of January, and the terms of Senators and Representatives at noon on the 3d day of January, of the years in which such terms would have ended if this article had not been ratified; and the terms of their successors shall then begin.

Section 2. The Congress shall assemble at least once in every year, and such meeting shall begin at noon on the 3d day of January, unless they shall by law appoint a different day.

Section 3. If, at the time fixed for the beginning of the term of the President, the President elect shall have died, the Vice President elect shall become President. If the President shall not have been chosen before the time fixed for the beginning of his term, or if the President elect shall have failed to qualify, then the Vice President elect shall act as President until a President shall have qualified; and the Congress may by law provide for the case wherein neither a President elect nor a Vice President elect shall have qualified, declaring who shall then act as President, or the manner in which one who is to act shall be selected, and such person shall act accordingly until a President or Vice President shall have qualified.

Section 4. The Congress may by law provide for the case of the death of any of the persons from whom the House of Representatives may choose a President whenever the right of choice shall have devolved upon them, and for the case of the death of any of the persons from whom the Senate may choose a Vice President whenever the right of choice shall have devolved upon them.

Section 5. Sections 1 and 2 shall take effect on the 15th day of October following the ratification of this article.

Section 6. This article shall be inoperative unless it shall have been ratified as an amendment to the Constitution by the legislatures of three-fourths of the several States within seven years from the date of its submission.

AMENDMENT XXI [1933]

Section 1. The eighteenth article of amendment to the Constitution of the United States is hereby repealed.

Section 2. The transportation or importation into any State, Territory, or possession of the United States for delivery or use therein of intoxicating liquors, in violation of the laws thereof, is hereby prohibited.

Section 3. This article shall be inoperative unless it shall have been ratified as an amendment to the Constitution by conventions in the several States, as provided in the Constitution, within seven years from the date of the submission hereof to the States by the Congress.

AMENDMENT XXII [1951]

Section 1. No person shall be elected to the office of the President more than twice, and no person who has held the office of President, or acted as President, for more than two years of a term to which some other person was elected President shall be elected to the office of President more than once. But this Article shall not apply to any person holding the office of President when this Article was proposed by the Congress, and shall not prevent any person who may be holding the office of President, or acting as President, during the term within which this Article becomes operative from holding the office of President or acting as President during the remainder of such term.

Section 2. This article shall be inoperative unless it shall have been ratified as an amendment to the Constitution by the legislatures of three-fourths of the several States within seven years from the date of its submission to the States by the Congress.

AMENDMENT XXIII [1961]

Section 1. The District constituting the seat of Government of the United States shall appoint in such manner as the Congress may direct:

A number of electors of President and Vice President equal to the whole number of Senators and Representatives in Congress to which the District would be entitled if it were a State, but in no event more than the least populous state; they shall be in addition to those appointed by the states, but they shall be considered, for the purposes of the election of President and Vice President, to be electors appointed by a state; and they shall meet in the District and perform such duties as provided by the twelfth article of amendment.

Section 2. The Congress shall have power to enforce this article by appropriate legislation.

AMENDMENT XXIV [1964]

Section 1. The right of citizens of the United States to vote in any primary or other election for President or Vice President, for electors for President or Vice President, or for Senator or Representative in Congress, shall not be denied or abridged by the United States, or any State by reason of failure to pay any poll tax or other tax.

Section 2. The Congress shall have power to enforce this article by appropriate legislation.

AMENDMENT XXV [1967]

Section 1. In case of the removal of the President from office or of his death or resignation, the Vice President shall become President.

Section 2. Whenever there is a vacancy in the office of the Vice President, the President shall nominate a Vice President who shall take office upon confirmation by a majority vote of both Houses of Congress.

Section 3. Whenever the President transmits to the President pro tempore of the Senate and the Speaker of the House of Representatives his written declaration that he is unable to discharge the powers and duties of his office, and until he transmits to them a written declaration to the contrary, such powers and duties shall be discharged by the Vice President as Acting President.

Section 4. Whenever the Vice President and a majority of either the principal officers of the executive departments or of such other body as Congress may by law provide, transmit to the President pro tempore of the Senate and the Speaker of the House of Representatives their written declaration that the President is unable to discharge the powers and duties of his office, the Vice President shall immediately assume the powers and duties of the office as Acting President.

Thereafter, when the President transmits to the President pro tempore of the Senate and the Speaker of the House of Representatives his written declaration that no inability exists, he shall resume the powers and duties of his office unless the Vice President and a majority of either the principal officers of the executive department or of such other body as Congress may by law provide, transmit within four days to the President pro tempore of the Senate and the Speaker of the House of Representatives their written declaration that the President is unable to discharge the powers and duties of his office. Thereupon Congress shall decide the issue, assembling within forty-eight hours for that purpose if not in session. If the Congress, within twenty-one days after receipt of the latter written declaration, or, if Congress is not in session, within twenty-one days after Congress is required to assemble, determines by two-thirds vote of both Houses that the President is unable to discharge the powers and duties of his office, the Vice President shall continue to discharge the same as Acting President; otherwise, the President shall resume the powers and duties of his office.

AMENDMENT XXVI [1971]

Section 1. The right of citizens of the United States, who are eighteen years of age or older, to vote shall not be denied or abridged by the United States or by any State on account of age.

Section 2. The Congress shall have power to enforce this article by appropriate legislation.

AMENDMENT XXVII [1992]

No law, varying the compensation for the services of the Senators and Representatives, shall take effect, until an election of Representatives shall have intervened.

FEDERALIST PAPERS NO. 10 AND NO. 51

The founders completed drafting the U.S. Constitution in 1787. It was then submitted to the thirteen states for ratification, and a major debate ensued. As you read in Chapter 2, on the one side of this debate were the Federalists, who urged that the new Constitution be adopted. On the other side of the debate were the Anti-Federalists, who argued against ratification.

During the course of this debate, three men well known for their Federalist views—Alexander Hamilton, James Madison, and John Jay—wrote a series of essays in which they argued for immediate ratifcation of the Constitution. The essays appeared in the New York City Independent Journal *in October 1787, just a little over a month after the Constitutional Convention adjourned. Later, Hamilton arranged to have the essays collected and published in book form. The articles filled two volumes, both of which were published by May 1788. The essays are often referred to collectively as the* Federalist Papers.

Scholars disagree as to whether the Federalist Papers *had a significant impact on the decision of the states to ratify the Constitution. Nonetheless, many of the essays are masterpieces of political reasoning and have left a lasting imprint on American politics and government. Above all, the* Federalist Papers *shed an important light on what the founders intended when they drafted various constitutional provisions.*

Here we present just two of these essays, Federalist Paper No. 10 *and* Federalist Paper No. 51. *Each essay was written by James Madison, who referred to himself as "Publius." We have annotated each document to clarify the meaning of particular passages. The annotations are set in italics to distinguish them from the original text of the documents.*

#10

Federalist Paper No. 10 is a classic document that is often referred to by teachers of American government. Authored by James Madison, it sets forth Madison's views on factions in politics. The essay was written, in large part, to counter the arguments put forth by the Anti-Federalists that small factions might take control of the government, thus destroying the representative nature of the republican form of government established by the Constitution. The essay opens with a discussion of the "dangerous vice" of factions and the importance of devising a form of government in which this vice will be controlled.

Among the numerous advantages promised by a well-constructed Union, none deserves to be more accurately developed than its tendency to break and control the violence of faction. The friend of popular governments never finds himself so much alarmed for their character and fate as when he contemplates their propensity to this dangerous vice. He will not fail, therefore, to set a due value on any plan which, without violating the principles to which he is attached, provides a proper cure for it. The instability, injustice, and confusion introduced into the public councils have, in truth, been the mortal diseases under which popular governments have everywhere perished, as they continue to be the favorite and fruitful topics from which the adversaries to liberty derive their most specious declamations. The valuable improvements made by the American constitutions on the popular models, both ancient and modern, cannot certainly be too much admired; but it would be an unwarrantable partiality to contend that they have as effectually obviated the danger on this side, as was wished and expected. Complaints are everywhere heard from our most considerate and virtuous citizens, equally the friends of public and private faith and of public and personal liberty, that our governments are too unstable, that the public good is disregarded in the conflicts of rival parties, and that measures are too often decided, not according to the rules of justice and the rights of the minor party, but by the superior force of an interested and overbearing majority. However anxiously we may wish that these complaints had no foundation, the evidence of known facts will not permit us to deny that they are in some degree true. It will be found, indeed, on a candid review of our situation, that some of the distresses under which we labor have been erroneously charged on the operation of our governments; but it will be found, at the same time, that other causes will not alone account for many of our heaviest misfortunes;

and, particularly, for that prevailing and increasing distrust of public engagements and alarm for private rights which are echoed from one end of the continent to the other. These must be chiefly, if not wholly, effects of the unsteadiness and injustice with which a factious spirit has tainted our public administration.

In the following paragraph, Madison clarifies for his readers his understanding of what the term faction means.

By a faction I understand a number of citizens, whether amounting to a majority or minority of the whole, who are united and actuated by some common impulse of passion, or of interest, adverse to the rights of other citizens, or the permanent and aggregate interests of the community.

In the following passages, Madison looks at the two methods of curing the "mischiefs of factions." One of these methods is removing the causes of faction. The other is to control the effects of factions.

There are two methods of curing the mischiefs of faction: the one, by removing its causes; the other, by controlling its effects.

There are again two methods of removing the causes of faction: the one, by destroying the liberty which is essential to its existence; the other, by giving to every citizen the same opinions, the same passions, and the same interests.

It could never be more truly said than of the first remedy that it was worse than the disease. Liberty is to faction what air is to fire, an aliment without which it instantly expires. But it could not be a less folly to abolish liberty, which is essential to political life, because it nourishes faction than it would be to wish the annihilation of air, which is essential to animal life, because it imparts to fire its destructive agency.

The second expedient is as impracticable as the first would be unwise. As long as the reason of man continues fallible, and his is at liberty to exercise it, different opinions will be formed. As long as the connection subsists between his reason and his self-love, his opinions and his passions will have a reciprocal influence on each other; and the former will be objects to which the latter will attach themselves. The diversity in the faculties of men, from which the rights of property originate, is not less an insuperable obstacle to a uniformity of interests. The protection of these faculties is the first object of government. From the protection of different and unequal faculties of acquiring property, the possession of different degrees and kinds of property immediately results; and from the influence of these on the sentiments and views of the respective proprietors ensues a division of the society into different interests and parties.

The latent causes of faction are thus sown in the nature of man; and we see them everywhere brought into different degrees of activity, according to the different circumstances of civil society. A zeal for different opinions concerning religion, concerning government, and many other points, as well of speculation as of practice; an attachment to different leaders ambitiously contending for pre-eminence and power; or to persons of other descriptions whose fortunes have been interesting to the human passions, have, in turn, divided mankind into parties, inflamed them with mutual animosity, and rendered them much more disposed to vex and oppress each other than to co-operate for their common good. So strong is this propensity of mankind to fall into mutual animosities that where no substantial occasion presents itself the most frivolous and fanciful distinctions have been sufficient to kindle their unfriendly passions and excite their most violent conflicts. But the most common and durable source of factions has been the various and unequal distribution of property. Those who hold and those who are without property have ever formed distinct interests in society. Those who are creditors, and those who are debtors, fall under a like discrimination. A landed interest, a manufacturing interest, a mercantile interest, a moneyed interest, with many lesser interests, grow up of necessity in civilized nations, and divide them into different classes, actuated by different sentiments and views. The regulation of these various and interfering interests forms the principal task of modern legislation and involves the spirit of party and faction in the necessary and ordinary operations of government.

No man is allowed to be a judge in his own cause, because his interest would certainly bias his judgment, and, not improbably, corrupt his integrity. With equal, nay with greater reason, a body of men are unfit to be both judges and parties at the same time; yet what are many of the most important acts of legislation but so many judicial determinations, not indeed concerning the rights of single persons, but concerning the rights of large bodies of citizens? And what are the different classes of legislators but advocates and parties to the causes which they determine? Is a law proposed concerning private debts? It is a question to which the creditors are parties on one side and the debtors on the other. Justice ought to hold the balance between them. Yet the parties are, and must be, themselves the judges; and the most numerous party, or in other words, the most powerful faction must be expected to prevail. Shall domestic manufacturers be encouraged, and in what degree, by restrictions on foreign manufacturers? Are questions which would be differently decided by the landed and the manufacturing classes, and probably by neither with a sole regard to justice and the public good. The apportionment of taxes on the various descriptions of property is an act which seems to require the most exact impartiality; yet there is, perhaps, no legislative act in which greater opportunity and temptation are given to a predominant party to trample on the rules of justice. Every shilling with which they overburden the inferior number is a shilling saved to their own pockets.

It is in vain to say that enlightened statesmen will be able to adjust these clashing interests and render them all subservient to the public good. Enlightened statesmen will not always be at the helm. Nor, in many cases, can such an adjustment be made at all without taking into view indirect and remote considerations, which will rarely prevail over the immediate interest which one party may find in disregarding the rights of another or the good of the whole.

The inference to which we are brought is that the causes of faction cannot be removed and that relief is only to be sought in the means of controlling its effects.

In the preceding passages, Madison has explored the causes of factions and has concluded that they cannot "be removed" without removing liberty itself, which is one of the causes, or altering human nature. He now turns to a discussion of how the effects of factions might be controlled.

If a faction consists of less than a majority, relief is supplied by the republican principle, which enables the majority to defeat its sinister views by regular vote. It may clog the administration, it may convulse the society; but it will be unable to execute and mask its violence under the forms of the Constitution. When a majority is included in a faction, the form of popular government, on the other hand, enables it to sacrifice to its ruling passion or interest both the public good and the rights of other citizens. To secure the public good and private rights against the danger of such a faction, and at the same time to preserve the spirit and the form of popular government, is then the great object to which our inquiries are directed. Let me add that it is the great desideratum by which alone this form of government can be rescued from the opprobrium under which it has so long labored and be recommended to the esteem and adoption of mankind.

According to Madison, one way of controlling the effects of factions is to make sure that the majority is not able to act in "concert," or jointly, to "carry into effect schemes of oppression."

By what means is this object attainable? Evidently by one of two only. Either the existence of the same passion or interest in a majority at the same time must be prevented, or the majority, having such coexistent passion or interest, must be rendered, by their number and local situation, unable to concert and carry into effect schemes of oppression. If the impulse and the opportunity be suffered to coincide, we well know that neither moral nor religious motives can be relied on as an adequate control. They are not found to be such on the injustice and violence of individuals, and lose their efficacy in proportion to the number combined together, that is, in proportion as their efficacy becomes needful.

From this view of the subject it may be concluded that a pure democracy, by which I mean a society consisting of a small number of citizens, who assemble and administer the government in person, can admit of no cure for the mischiefs of faction. A common passion or interest will, in almost every case, be felt by a majority of the whole; a communication and concert results from the form of government itself; and there is nothing to check the inducements to sacrifice the weaker party or an obnoxious individual. Hence it is that such democracies have ever been spectacles of turbulence and contention; have ever been found incompatible with personal security or the rights of property; and have in general been as short in their lives as they have been violent in their deaths. Theoretic politicians, who have patronized this species of government, have erroneously supposed that by reducing mankind to a perfect equality in their political rights, they would at the same time be perfectly equalized and assimilated in their possessions, their opinions, and their passions.

In the following six paragraphs, Madison sets forth some of the reasons why a republican form of government promises a "cure" for the mischiefs of factions. He begins by clarifying the difference between a republic and a democracy. He then describes how in a large republic, the elected representatives of the people will be large enough in number to guard against factions— the "cabals," or concerted actions, of "a few." On the one hand, representatives will not be so removed from their local districts as to be unacquainted with their constituents' needs. On the other hand, they will not be "unduly attached" to local interests and unfit to understand "great and national objects." Madison concludes that the Constitution "forms a happy combination in this respect."

A republic, by which I mean a government in which the scheme of representation takes place, opens a different prospect and promises the cure for which we are seeking. Let us examine the points in which it varies from pure democracy, and we shall comprehend both the nature of the cure and the efficacy which it must derive from the Union.

The two great points of difference between a democracy and a republic are: first, the delegation of the government, in the latter, to a small number of citizens elected by the rest; secondly, the greater number of citizens and greater sphere of country over which the latter may be extended.

The effect of the first difference is, on the one hand, to refine and enlarge the public views by passing them through the medium of a chosen body of citizens, whose wisdom may best discern the true interest of their country and whose patriotism and love of justice will be least likely to sacrifice it to temporary or partial considerations. Under such a regulation it may well happen that the public voice, pronounced by the representatives of the people, will be more consonant to the public good than if pronounced by the people themselves, convened for the purpose. On the other hand, the effect may be inverted. Men of factious tempers, of local prejudices, or of sinister designs, may, by intrigue, by corruption, or by other means, first obtain the suffrages, and then betray the interests of the people. The question resulting is, whether small or extensive republics are most favorable to the election of proper guardians of the public weal; and it is clearly decided in favor of the latter by two obvious considerations.

In the first place it is to be remarked that however small the republic may be the representatives must be raised to a certain number in order to guard against the cabals of a few; and that however large it may be they must be limited to a certain number in order to guard against the confusion of a multitude. Hence, the number of representatives in the two cases not being in proportion to that of the constituents, and being proportionally greatest in the small republic, it follows that if the proportion of fit characters be not less in the large than in the small republic, the former will present a greater option, and consequently a greater probability of a fit choice.

In the next place, as each representative will be chosen by a greater number of citizens in the large than in the small republic, it will be more difficult for unworthy candidates to practice with success the vicious arts by which elections are too often carried; and the suffrages of the people being more free, will be more likely to center on men who possess the most attractive merit and the most diffusive and established characters.

It must be confessed that in this, as in most other cases, there is a mean, on both sides of which inconveniencies will be found to lie. By enlarging too much the number of electors, you render the representative too little acquainted with all their local circumstances and lesser interests; as by reducing it too much, you render him unduly attached to these, and too little fit to comprehend and pursue great and national objects. The federal Constitution forms a happy combination in this respect; the great and aggregate interests being referred to the national, the local and particular to the State legislatures.

In the remaining passages of this essay, Madison looks at another "point of difference" between a republic and a democracy. Specifically, a republic can encompass a larger territory and a greater number of citizens than a democracy can. This fact, too, argues Madison, will help to control the influence of factions because the interests that draw people together to act in concert are typically at the local level and would be unlikely to affect or dominate the national government. As Madison states, "The influence of factious leaders may kindle a flame within their particular States but will be unable to spread a general conflagration through the other States." Generally, in a large republic, there will be numerous factions, and no particular faction will be able to "pervade the whole body of the Union."

The other point of difference is the greater number of citizens and extent of territory which may be brought within the compass of republican than of democratic government; and it is this circumstance principally which renders factious combinations less to be dreaded in the former than in the latter. The smaller the society, the fewer probably will be the distinct parties and interests composing it; the fewer the distinct parties and interests, the more frequently will a majority be found of the same party; and the smaller the number of individuals composing a majority, and the smaller the compass within which they are placed, the more easily will they concert and execute their plans of oppression. Extend the sphere and you take in a greater variety of parties and interests; you make it less probable that a majority of the whole will have a common motive to invade the rights of other citizens; or if such a common motive exists, it will be more difficult for all who feel it to discover their own strength and to act in unison with each other. Besides other impediments, it may be remarked that, where there is a consciousness of unjust or dishonorable purposes, communication is always checked by distrust in proportion to the number whose concurrence is necessary.

Hence, it clearly appears that the same advantage which a republic has over a democracy in controlling the effects of faction is enjoyed by a large over a small republic—is enjoyed by the Union over the States composing it. Does this advantage consist in the substitution of representatives whose enlightened views and virtuous sentiments render them superior to local prejudices and to schemes of injustice? It will not be denied that the representation of the Union will be most likely to possess these requisite endowments. Does it consist in the greater security afforded by a greater variety of parties, against the event of any one party being able to outnumber and oppress the rest? In an equal degree does the increased variety of parties comprised within the Union increase this security. Does it, in fine, consist in the greater obstacles opposed to the concert and accomplishment of the secret wishes of an unjust and interested majority? Here again the extent of the Union gives it the most palpable advantage.

The influence of factious leaders may kindle a flame within their particular States but will be unable to spread a general conflagration through the other States. A religious sect may degenerate into a political faction in a part of the Confederacy; but the variety of sects dispersed over the entire face of it must secure the national councils against any danger from that source. A rage for paper money, for an abolition of debts, for an equal division of property, or for any other improper or wicked project, will be less apt to pervade the whole body of the Union than a particular member of it, in the same proportion as such a malady is more likely to taint a particular county or district than an entire State.

In the extent and proper structure of the Union, therefore, we behold a republican remedy for the diseases most incident to republican government. And according to the degree of pleasure and pride we feel in being republicans ought to be our zeal in cherishing the spirit and supporting the character of federalists.

Publius
(James Madison)

#51

Federalist Paper No. 51, which was also authored by James Madison, is one of the classics in American political theory. Recall from Chapter 2 that a major concern of the founders was to create a relatively strong national government but one that would not be capable of tyrannizing over the populace. In the following essay, Madison sets forth the theory of "checks and balances." He explains that the new Constitution, by dividing the national government into three branches (executive, legislative, and judicial), offers protection against tyranny.

To what expedient, then, shall we finally resort, for maintaining in practice the necessary partition of power among the several departments as laid down in the Constitution? The only answer that can be given is that as all these exterior provisions are found to be inadequate the defect must be supplied, by so contriving the interior structure of the government as that its several constituent parts may, by their mutual relations, be the means of keeping each other in their proper places. Without presuming to undertake a full development of this important idea I will hazard a few general observations which may perhaps place it in a clearer light, and enable us to form a more correct judgment of the principles and structure of the government planned by the convention.

In the following two paragraphs, Madison explains that to ensure that the powers of government are genuinely separated, it is important that each of the three branches of government (executive, legislative, and judicial) should have a "will of its own." Among other things, this means that persons in one branch should not depend on persons in another branch for the "emoluments annexed to their offices" (pay, perks, and privileges). If they did, then the branches would not be truly independent of one another.

In order to lay a due foundation for that separate and distinct exercise of the different powers of government, which to a certain extent is admitted on all hands to be essential to the preservation of liberty, it is evident that each department should have a will of its own; and consequently should be so constituted that the members of each should have as little agency as possible in the appointment of the members of the others. Were this principle rigorously adhered to, it would require that all the appointments for the supreme executive, legislative, and judiciary magistracies should be drawn from the same fountain of authority, the people, through channels having no communication whatever with one another. Perhaps such a plan of constructing the several departments would be less difficult in practice than it may in contemplation appear. Some difficulties, however, and some additional expense would attend the execution of it. Some deviations, therefore, from the principle must be admitted. In the constitution of the judiciary department in particular, it might be inexpedient to insist rigorously on the principle: first, because peculiar qualifications being essential in the members, the primary consideration ought to be to select that mode of choice which best secures these qualifications; second, because the permanent tenure by which the appointments are held in that department must soon destroy all sense of dependence on the authority conferring them.

It is equally evident that the members of each department should be as little dependent as possible on those of the others for the emoluments annexed to their offices. Were the executive magistrate, or the judges, not independent of the legislature in this particular, their independence in every other would be merely nominal.

One of the striking qualities of the theory of checks and balances as posited by Madison is that it assumes that persons are not angels but driven by personal interests and motives. In the following two paragraphs, which are among the most widely quoted of Madison's writings, he stresses that the division of the government into three branches helps to check personal ambitions. Personal ambitions will naturally arise, but they will be linked to the constitutional powers of each branch. In effect, they will help to keep the three branches separate and thus serve the public interest.

But the great security against a gradual concentration of the several powers in the same department consists in giving to those who administer each department the necessary constitutional means and personal motives to resist encroachments of the others. The provision for defense must in this, as in all other cases, be made commensurate to the danger of attack. Ambition must be made to counteract ambition. The interest of the man must be connected with the constitutional rights of the place. It may be a reflection on human nature that such devices should be necessary to control the abuses of government. But what is government itself but the greatest of all reflections on human nature? If men were angels, no government would be necessary. If angels were to govern men, neither external nor internal controls on government would be necessary. In framing a government which is to be administered by men over men, the great difficulty lies in this: you must first enable the government to control the governed; and in the next place oblige it to control itself. A dependence on the people is, no doubt, the primary control on the government; but experience has taught mankind the necessity of auxiliary precautions.

This policy of supplying, by opposite and rival interests, the defect of better motives, might be traced through the whole system of human affairs, private as well as public. We see it particularly displayed in all the subordinate distributions of power, where the constant aim is to divide and arrange the several offices in such a manner as that each may be a check on the other—that the private interest of every individual may be a sentinel over the public rights. These inventions of prudence cannot be less requisite in the distribution of the supreme powers of the State.

In the next two paragraphs, Madison first points out that the "legislative authority necessarily predominates"

in a republican form of government. The "remedy" for this lack of balance with the other branches of government is to divide the legislative branch into two chambers with "different modes of election and different principles of action."

But it is not possible to give to each department an equal power of self-defense. In republican government, the legislative authority necessarily predominates. The remedy for this inconveniency is to divide the legislature into different branches; and to render them, by different modes of election and different principles of action, as little connected with each other as the nature of their common functions and their common dependence on the society will admit. It may even be necessary to guard against dangerous encroachments by still further precautions. As the weight of the legislative authority requires that it should be thus divided, the weakness of the executive may require, on the other hand, that it should be fortified. An absolute negative on the legislature appears, at first view, to be the natural defense with which the executive magistrate should be armed. But perhaps it would be neither altogether safe nor alone sufficient. On ordinary occasions it might not be exerted with the requisite firmness, and on extraordinary occasions it might be perfidiously abused. May not this defect of an absolute negative be supplied by some qualified connection between this weaker department and the weaker branch of the stronger department, by which the latter may be led to support the constitutional rights of the former, without being too much detached from the rights of its own department?

If the principles on which these observations are founded be just, as I persuade myself they are, and they be applied as a criterion to the several State constitutions, and to the federal Constitution, it will be found that if the latter does not perfectly correspond with them, the former are infinitely less able to bear such a test.

In the remaining passages of this essay, Madison discusses the importance of the division of government powers between the states and the national government. This division of powers, by providing additional checks and balances, offers a "double security" against tyranny.

There are, moreover, two considerations particularly applicable to the federal system of America, which place that system in a very interesting point of view.

First. In a single republic, all the power surrendered by the people is submitted to the administration of a single government; and the usurpations are guarded against by a division of the government into distinct and separate departments. In the compound republic of America, the power surrendered by the people is first divided between two distinct governments, and then the portion allotted to each subdivided among distinct and separate departments. Hence a double security arises to the rights of the people. The different governments will control each other, at the same time that each will be controlled by itself.

Second. It is of great importance in a republic not only to guard the society against the oppression of its rulers, but to guard one part of the society against the injustice of the other part. Different interests necessarily exist in different classes of citizens. If a majority be united by a common interest, the rights of the minority will be insecure. There are but two methods of providing against this evil: the one by creating a will in the community independent of the majority—that is, of the society itself; the other, by comprehending in the society so many separate descriptions of citizens as will render an unjust combination of a majority of the whole very improbable, if not impracticable. The first method prevails in all governments possessing an hereditary or self-appointed authority. This, at best, is but a precarious security; because a power independent of the society may as well espouse the unjust views of the major as the rightful interests of the minor party, and may possibly be turned against both parties. The second method will be exemplified in the federal republic of the United States. Whilst all authority in it will be derived from and dependent on the society, the society itself will be broken into so many parts, interests and classes of citizens, that the rights of individuals, or of the minority, will be in little danger from interested combinations of the majority. In a free government the security for civil rights must be the same as that for religious rights. It consists in the one case in the multiplicity of interests, and in the other in the multiplicity of sects. The degree of security in both cases will depend on the number of interests and sects; and this may be presumed to depend on the extent of country and number of people comprehended under the same government. This view of the subject must particularly recommend a proper federal system to all the sincere and considerate friends of republican government, since it shows that in exact proportion as the territory of the Union may be formed into more circumscribed Confederacies, or States, oppressive combinations of a majority will be facilitated; the best security, under the republican forms, for the rights of every class of citizen,

will be diminished; and consequently the stability and independence of some member of the government, the only other security, must be proportionally increased. Justice is the end of government. It is the end of civil society. It ever has been and ever will be pursued until it be obtained, or until liberty be lost in the pursuit. In a society under the forms of which the stronger faction can readily unite and oppress the weaker, anarchy may as truly be said to reign as in a state of nature, where the weaker individual is not secured against the violence of the stronger; and as, in the latter state, even the stronger individuals are prompted, by the uncertainty of their condition, to submit to a government which may protect the weak as well as themselves; so, in the former state, will the more powerful factions or parties be gradually induced, by a like motive, to wish for a government which will protect all parties, the weaker as well as the more powerful. It can be little doubted that if the State of Rhode Island was separated from the Confederacy and left to itself, the insecurity of rights under the popular form of government within such narrow limits would be displayed by such reiterated oppressions of factious majorities that some power altogether independent of the people would soon be called for by the voice of the very factions whose misrule had proved the necessity of it. In the extended republic of the United States, and among the great variety of interests, parties, and sects which it embraces, a coalition of a majority of the whole society could seldom take place on any other principles than those of justice and the general good; whilst there being thus less danger to a minor from the will of a major party, there must be less pretext, also, to provide for the security of the former, by introducing into the government a will not dependent on the latter, or, in other words, a will independent of the society itself. It is no less certain than it is important, notwithstanding the contrary opinions which have been entertained, that the larger the society, provided it lie within a practicable sphere, the more duly capable it will be of self-government. And happily for the *republican cause,* the practicable sphere may be carried to a very great extent by a judicious modification and mixture of the *federal principle.*

Publius
(James Madison)

8. bringing issues to the public's attention, affecting the vote, and providing a voice for voters who are frustrated with the Republican and Democratic parties (LearningOutcome 7–5)

Multiple Choice

9. a. (LearningOutcome 7–1)
10. b. (LearningOutcome 7–1)
11. c. (LearningOutcome 7–2)
12. b. (LearningOutcome 7–3)
13. c. (LearningOutcome 7–4)
14. b. (LearningOutcome 7–5)

Chapter 8

Fill-In

1. family, schools, churches, the media, opinion leaders, and peer groups (LearningOutcome 8–1)

2. each person within the entire population being polled has an equal chance of being chosen (LearningOutcome 8–2)

3. house effect (LearningOutcome 8–2)

4. push poll (LearningOutcome 8–2)

5. party identification (LearningOutcome 8–3)

6. policy voting (LearningOutcome 8–3)

7. educational attainment, occupation and income, age, gender, religion and ethnic background, and geographic region (LearningOutcome 8–3)

8. literacy tests, poll taxes, the grandfather clause, and white primaries (LearningOutcome 8–4)

Multiple Choice

9. c. (LearningOutcome 8–1)
10. b. (LearningOutcome 8–1)
11. b. (LearningOutcome 8–2)
12. a. (LearningOutcome 8–3)
13. a. (LearningOutcome 8–3)
14. b. (LearningOutcome 8–4)
15. a. (LearningOutcome 8–4)

Chapter 9

Fill-In

1. who receives the largest popular vote in a state is credited with all that state's electoral votes (LearningOutcome 9–1)

2. 270 (LearningOutcome 9–1)

3. direct (LearningOutcome 9–2)

4. the states moving their primaries to earlier in the year in an effort to make their primaries more prominent in the media and influential in the political process (LearningOutcome 9–2)

5. opposition (LearningOutcome 9–3)

6. collecting as much information as possible about voters in a database and then filtering out various groups for special attention (LearningOutcome 9–4)

7. federal income tax returns (LearningOutcome 9–5)

8. super PACs (LearningOutcome 9–5)

Multiple Choice

9. a. (LearningOutcome 9–1)
10. b. (LearningOutcome 9–1)
11. a. (LearningOutcome 9–2)
12. b. (LearningOutcome 9–2)
13. c. (LearningOutcome 9–3)
14. c. (LearningOutcome 9–4)
15. b. (LearningOutcome 9–5)

Chapter 10

Fill-In

1. Priming (LearningOutcome 10–1)

2. television (LearningOutcome 10–1)

3. televised comment, lasting for only a few seconds, that captures a thought or a perspective and has an immediate impact on the viewers (LearningOutcome 10–1)

4. they have lost a major share of their advertising revenue to online sites. (LearningOutcome 10–1)

5. John F. Kennedy and Richard Nixon (LearningOutcome 10–2)

6. political candidates' press advisers, who try to convince reporters to give a story or event concerning a candidate a particular interpretation or slant (LearningOutcome 10–2)

7. male, middle-aged, and conservative (LearningOutcome 10–3)

8. talk-show hosts often exaggerate their political biases for effect. Hosts sometimes appear to care more about the entertainment value of their statements than whether they are, strictly speaking, true. No journalistic conventions are observed (LearningOutcome 10–3)

9. losers (LearningOutcome 10–4)

10. the collection, analysis, and dissemination of information online by independent journalists, scholars, political activists, and the general citizenry (LearningOutcome 10–5)

Multiple Choice

11. a. (LearningOutcome 10–1)
12. c. (LearningOutcome 10–2)
13. c. (LearningOutcome 10–3)
14. c. (LearningOutcome 10–4)
15. b. (LearningOutcome 10–5)

CHAPTER 11

Fill-In

1. ten (LearningOutcome 11–1)
2. serve the broad interests of the entire society and act according to his or her perception of national needs (LearningOutcome 11–1)
3. fund-raising ability, franking privileges, professional staffs, lawmaking power, access to the media, and name recognition (LearningOutcome 11–2)
4. preside over sessions of the House, vote in the event of a tie, put questions to a vote, participate in making important committee assignments, and schedule bills for action (LearningOutcome 11–3)
5. cloture (LearningOutcome 11–3)
6. a meeting held by a congressional committee or subcommittee to approve, amend, or redraft a bill (LearningOutcome 11–4)
7. Rules (LearningOutcome 11–4)
8. the federal judiciary and to the cabinet (LearningOutcome 11–5)
9. authorization and appropriation (LearningOutcome 11–6)

Multiple Choice

10. c. (LearningOutcome 11–1)
11. a. (LearningOutcome 11–2)
12. b. (LearningOutcome 11–3)
13. b. (LearningOutcome 11–4)
14. c. (LearningOutcome 11–5)
15. a. (LearningOutcome 11–6)

CHAPTER 12

Fill-In

1. the legal profession (LearningOutcome 12–1)
2. commander in chief (LearningOutcome 12–2)

3. chief legislator (LearningOutcome 12–2)
4. presidential orders to carry out policies described in laws passed by Congress (LearningOutcome 12–3)
5. War Powers Resolution (LearningOutcome 12–3)
6. an inherent executive power claimed by presidents to withhold information from, or to refuse to appear before, Congress or the courts (LearningOutcome 12–4)
7. the heads of the executive departments and other officials whom the president may choose to appoint (LearningOutcome 12–5)
8. White House Office, the Office of Management and Budget, and the National Security Council (LearningOutcome 12–5)

Multiple Choice

9. c. (LearningOutcome 12–1)
10. c. (LearningOutcome 12–2)
11. a. (LearningOutcome 12–2)
12. a. (LearningOutcome 12–3)
13. a. (LearningOutcome 12–3)
14. b. (LearningOutcome 12–4)
15. c. (LearningOutcome 12–5)

CHAPTER 13

Fill-In

1. 16 (LearningOutcome 13–1)
2. secretary (LearningOutcome 13–2)
3. Commerce (LearningOutcome 13–2)
4. president; Senate (LearningOutcome 13–3)
5. merit through open, competitive examinations (LearningOutcome 13–3)
6. enabling legislation (LearningOutcome 13–4)
7. a three-way alliance among legislators, bureaucrats, and interest groups to make or preserve policies that benefit their respective interests (LearningOutcome 13–4)
8. reports on gross governmental inefficiency, illegal action, or other wrongdoing (LearningOutcome 13–5)

Multiple Choice

9. b. (LearningOutcome 13–1)
10. a. (LearningOutcome 13–2)
11. c. (LearningOutcome 13–2)
12. b. (LearningOutcome 13–2)
13. c. (LearningOutcome 13–3)

14. b. (LearningOutcome 13–4)

15. a. (LearningOutcome 13–5)

CHAPTER 14

Fill-In

1. constitutions, statutes, administrative agency rules and regulations, and decisions by courts (LearningOutcome 14–1)

2. writ of certiorari (LearningOutcome 14–2)

3. oral arguments (LearningOutcome 14–2)

4. concurring (LearningOutcome 14–2)

5. senatorial courtesy (LearningOutcome 14–3)

6. strict construction and originalism (LearningOutcome 14–4)

7. rewriting a statute to negate a court's ruling, proposing constitutional amendments to reverse Supreme Court decisions, or limiting the jurisdiction of the federal courts (LearningOutcome 14–5)

Multiple Choice

8. b. (LearningOutcome 14–1)

9. b. (LearningOutcome 14–2)

10. a. (LearningOutcome 14–3)

11. a. (LearningOutcome 14–4)

12. b. (LearningOutcome 14–5)

CHAPTER 15

Fill-In

1. issue identification and agenda setting, policy formulation and adoption, and policy implementation and evaluation (Learning Outcome 15–1)

2. Medicare (Learning Outcome 15–2)

3. all persons obtain health-care insurance from one source or another, or pay a penalty (LearningOutcome 15–2)

4. Canada and Mexico (LearningOutcome 15–3)

5. a rise in sea levels, changes in rainfall patterns, and increases in extreme weather (LearningOutcome 15–3)

6. solar power, hydropower, and wind power (LearningOutcome 15–3)

7. recession (LearningOutcome 15–4)

8. Federal Reserve System (LearningOutcome 15–4)

9. the People's Republic of China (LearningOutcome 15–4)

Multiple Choice

10. c. (LearningOutcome 15–1)

11. b. (LearningOutcome 15–2)

12. a. (LearningOutcome 15–2)

13. c. (LearningOutcome 15–3)

14. b. (LearningOutcome 15–4)

15. c. (LearningOutcome 15–4)

CHAPTER 16

Fill-In

1. departments of state and defense, and the National Security Council and the Central Intelligence Agency (LearningOutcome 16–1)

2. isolationism (LearningOutcome 16–2)

3. Cold War (LearningOutcome 16–2)

4. Afghanistan (LearningOutcome 16–3)

5. Pakistan (LearningOutcome 16–3)

6. Palestinian Authority (LearningOutcome 16–4)

7. North Korea and Iran (LearningOutcome 16–5)

8. Taiwan (LearningOutcome 16–6)

Multiple Choice

9. b. (LearningOutcome 16–1)

10. c. (LearningOutcome 16–2)

11. a. (LearningOutcome 16–2)

12. c. (LearningOutcome 16–3)

13. a. (LearningOutcome 16–4)

14. b. (LearningOutcome 16–5)

15. a. (LearningOutcome 16–6)

Chapter 1

1. Lasswell, *Politics: Who Gets What, When, and How* (New York: McGraw-Hill, 1936).

2. Charles Lewis, *The Buying of Congress* (New York: Avon Books, 1998), p. 346.

3. As quoted in Paul M. Angle and Earl Schenck Miers, *The Living Lincoln* (New York: Barnes & Noble, 1992), p. 155.

4. Martin J. Wade and William F. Russell, *The Short Constitution* (Iowa City: American Citizen Publishing, 1920), p. 38.

Chapter 2

1. The first *European* settlement in today's United States was St. Augustine, Florida, which was founded on September 8, 1565, by the Spaniard Pedro Menéndez de Ávilés.

2. Archaeologists recently discovered the remains of a colony at Popham Beach, on the southern coast of what is now Maine, that was established at the same time as the colony at Jamestown. The Popham colony disbanded after thirteen months, however, when the leader, after learning that he had inherited property back home, returned—with the other colonists—to England.

3 John Camp, *Out of the Wilderness: The Emergence of an American Identity in Colonial New England* (Middleton, Conn.: Wesleyan University Press, 1990).

4. Ironically, the colonists were in fact protesting a tax reduction. The British government believed that if tea were cheaper, Americans would be more willing to drink it, even though it was still taxed. The Americans viewed the tax reduction as an attempt to trick them into accepting the principle of taxation. If the tea had been expensive, it would have been easy to organize a boycott. Because the tea was cheap, the protesters destroyed it so that no one would be tempted to buy it. (Also, many of the protesters were in the business of smuggling tea, and they would have been put out of business by the cheap competition.)

5. Much of the colonists' fury over British policies was directed personally at King George III, who had ascended the British throne in 1760 at the age of twenty-two, rather than at Britain or British rule *per se*. If you look at the Declaration of Independence in Appendix A, you will note that much of that document focuses on what "He" (George III) has or has not done. George III's lack of political experience, his personality, and his temperament all combined to lend instability to the British government at this crucial point in history.

6. *The Political Writings of Thomas Paine*, Vol. 1 (Boston: J. P. Mendum Investigator Office, 1870), p. 46.

7. The equivalent in today's publishing world would be a book that sells between 9 million and 11 million copies in its first year of publication.

8. As quoted in Winthrop D. Jordan *et al.*, *The United States*, 6th ed. (Englewood Cliffs, N.J.: Prentice Hall, 1987).

9. Some scholars feel that Locke's influence on the colonists, including Thomas Jefferson, has been exaggerated. For example, Jay Fliegelman states that Jefferson's fascination with the ideas of Homer, Ossian, and Patrick Henry "is of greater significance than his indebtedness to Locke." Jay Fliegelman, *Declaring Independence: Jefferson, Natural Language, and the Culture of Performance* (Stanford, Calif.: Stanford University Press, 1993).

10. Well before the Articles were ratified, many of them had, in fact, already been implemented. The Second Continental Congress and the thirteen states conducted American military, economic, and political affairs according to the standards and form specified later in the Articles of Confederation. See Robert W. Hoffert, *A Politics of Tensions: The Articles of Confederation and American Political Ideas* (Niwot, Colo.: University Press of Colorado, 1992).

11. Shays' Rebellion was not merely a small group of poor farmers. The participants and their supporters represented whole communities, including some of the wealthiest and most influential families of Massachusetts. Leonard L. Richards, *Shays' Rebellion: The American Revolution's Final Battle* (Philadelphia: University of Pennsylvania Press, 2003).

12. Madison, however, was much more "republican" in his views—that is, less of a centralist—than Hamilton. See Lance Banning, *The Sacred Fire of Liberty: James Madison and the Founding of the Federal Republic* (Ithaca, N.Y.: Cornell University Press, 1995).

13. The State House was later named Independence Hall. The East Room was the same room in which the Declaration of Independence had been signed eleven years earlier.

14. Charles A. Beard, *An Economic Interpretation of the Constitution of the United States* (New York: Macmillan, 1913; New York: Free Press, 1986).

15. Morris was partly of French descent, which is why his first name may seem unusual. Note, however, that naming one's child *Gouverneur* was not common at the time in any language, including French.

16. Today, there are 100 senators in the Senate and 435 members of the House of Representatives. In addition, the District of Columbia has three electoral votes, as provided for by the Twenty-third Amendment to the Constitution.

17. This group includes those who support the National Popular Vote movement, a proposed interstate compact that would cast the electoral votes of each participating state for the candidate who won the national popular vote. The compact would go into effect if participating states controlled a majority of the votes in the electoral college.

18. Quoted in J. J. Spengler, "Malthusianism in Late Eighteenth-Century America," *American Economic Review* 25 (1935), p. 705.

19. For further detail on Wood's depiction of the founders' views, see Gordon S. Wood, *Revolutionary Characters: What Made the Founders Different* (New York: Penguin Press, 2006).

20. Some scholarship suggests that the *Federalist Papers* did not play a significant role in bringing about the ratification of the Constitution. Nonetheless, the papers have lasting value as an authoritative explanation of the Constitution.

21. The papers written by the Anti-Federalists are online at www.constitution.org/afp/afp.htm. For essays on the positions, arranged in topical order, see John P. Kaminski and Richard Leffler, *Federalists and Antifederalists: The Debate over the Ratification of the Constitution*, 2d ed. (Madison, Wis.: Madison House, 1998).

22. The concept of the separation of powers generally is credited to the French political philosopher Montesquieu (1689–1755), who included it in his monumental two-volume work entitled *The Spirit of the Laws*, published in 1748.

23. The Constitution does not explicitly mention the power of judicial review, but the delegates at the Constitutional Convention probably assumed that the courts would have this power. Indeed, Alexander Hamilton, in *Federalist Paper* No. 78, explicitly outlined the concept of judicial review. In any event, whether the founders intended for the courts to exercise this power is a moot point, because in an 1803 decision, *Marbury v. Madison*, the Supreme Court successfully claimed this power for the courts—see Chapter 14.

24. Eventually, Supreme Court decisions led to legislative reforms relating to apportionment. The amendment concerning compensation of members of Congress became the Twenty-seventh Amendment to the Constitution when it was ratified 203 years later, in 1992.

25. The Twenty-first Amendment repealed the Eighteenth Amendment, which had prohibited the manufacture or sale of alcoholic beverages nationwide (Prohibition). Special conventions were necessary because prohibitionist forces controlled too many state legislatures for the standard ratification method to work.

Chapter 3

1. Daniel J. Elazar, *American Federalism: A View from the States*, 3rd ed. (New York: Harper & Row, 1984), pp. 94–99.

2. Ibid.

3. The federal models used by the German and Canadian governments provide interesting comparisons with the U.S. system. See Arthur B. Gunlicks, *Laender and German Federalism* (Manchester, England: Manchester University Press, 2003); and Jennifer Smith, *Federalism* (Vancouver: University of British Columbia Press, 2004).

4. Text of an address by the president to the National Conference of State Legislatures, Atlanta, Georgia (Washington, D.C.: The White House, Office of the Press Secretary, July 30, 1981).

5. 133 S.Ct. 2675 (2013).

6. An excellent illustration of this principle was President Dwight Eisenhower's disciplining of Arkansas governor Orval Faubus when Faubus refused to allow a Little Rock high school to be desegregated in 1957. Eisenhower federalized the National Guard to enforce the court-ordered desegregation of the school.

7. 5 U.S. 137 (1803).

8. 17 U.S. 316 (1819).

9. 22 U.S. 1 (1824).

10. *Hammer v. Dagenhart*, 247 U.S. 251 (1918). This decision was overruled in *United States v. Darby*, 312 U.S. 100 (1941).

11. *Wickard v. Filburn,* 317 U.S. 111 (1942).

12. *McLain v. Real Estate Board of New Orleans, Inc.,* 444 U.S. 232 (1980).

13. 514 U.S. 549 (1995).

14. *Printz v. United States,* 521 U.S. 898 (1997).

15. *United States v. Morrison,* 529 U.S. 598 (2000).

16. 549 U.S. 497 (2007).

17. 567 U.S. ___ (2012).

18. 132 S.Ct. 2566 (2012).

19. 570 U.S. ___ (2013).

Chapter 4

1. 32 U.S. 243 (1833).

2. 572 U.S. ___ (2014).

3. *Everson v. Board of Education,* 330 U.S. 1 (1947).

4. 370 U.S. 421 (1962).

5. *Stone v. Graham,* 449 U.S. 39 (1980).

6. *Wallace v. Jaffree,* 472 U.S. 38 (1985).

7. See, for example, *Brown v. Gwinnett County School District,* 112 F.3d 1464 (1997).

8. *Santa Fe Independent School District v. Doe,* 530 U.S. 290 (2000).

9. *Epperson v. Arkansas,* 393 U.S. 97 (1968).

10. *Edwards v. Aguillard,* 482 U.S. 578 (1987).

11. *Kitzmiller v. Dover Area School District,* 400 F. Supp.2d 707 (M.D.Pa. 2005).

12. 403 U.S. 602 (1971).

13. *Zelman v. Simmons-Harris,* 536 U.S. 639 (2002).

14. *Holmes v. Bush* (Fla.Cir.Ct. 2002). For details about this case, see David Royse, "Judge Rules School Voucher Law Violates Florida Constitution," *USA Today,* August 6, 2002, p. 7D.

15. 98 U.S. 145 (1878).

16. *Police v. City of Newark,* 170 F.3d 359 (3d Cir. 1999).

17. 573 U.S. ___ (2014).

18. *Schenck v. United States,* 249 U.S. 47 (1919).

19. Ibid.

20. *Gitlow v. New York,* 268 U.S. 652 (1925).

21. 341 U.S. 494 (1951).

22. *Brandenburg v. Ohio,* 395 U.S. 444 (1969).

23. *Liquormart v. Rhode Island,* 517 U.S. 484 (1996).

24. 413 U.S. 15 (1973).

25. *Reno v. American Civil Liberties Union,* 521 U.S. 844 (1997); and *Ashcroft v. American Civil Liberties Union,* 542 U.S. 656 (2004). In *United States v. American Library Association,* 539 U.S. 194 (2003), the Court finally found that the government could require libraries that received certain federal subsidies to install filtering software to prevent minors from viewing pornographic material. The filters could be turned off at adult request. The subsidies were small, however, and about one-third of libraries nationwide rejected them and did not install the software.

26. *Morse v. Frederick,* 551 U.S. 393 (2007).

27. See, for example, *Doe v. University of Michigan,* 721 F.Supp. 852 (1989).

28. *Hazelwood School District v. Kuhlmeier,* 484 U.S. 260 (1988).

29. Brandeis made this statement in a dissenting opinion in *Olmstead v. United States,* 277 U.S. 438 (1928).

30. 381 U.S. 479 (1965).

31. 410 U.S. 113 (1973). Jane Roe was not the real name of the woman in this case. It is a common legal pseudonym used to protect a party's privacy.

32. See, for example, the Supreme Court's decision in *Lambert v. Wicklund,* 520 U.S. 1169 (1997). The Court held that a Montana law requiring a minor to notify one of her parents before getting an abortion was constitutional.

33. *Schenck v. ProChoice Network,* 519 U.S. 357 (1997); and *Hill v. Colorado,* 530 U.S. 703 (2000).

34. *McCullen v. Coakley,* 573 U.S. ___ (2014).

35. *Stenberg v. Carhart,* 530 U.S. 914 (2000).

36. *Gonzales v. Carhart,* 550 U.S. 124 (2007).

37. *Washington v. Glucksberg,* 521 U.S. 702 (1997).

38. *Gonzales v. Oregon,* 546 U.S. 243 (2006).

39. The state of South Carolina challenged the constitutionality of this act, claiming that the law violated states' rights under the Tenth Amendment. The Supreme Court, however, held that Congress had the authority, under its commerce power, to pass the act because drivers' personal information had become an article of interstate commerce. *Reno v. Condon,* 528 U.S. 141 (2000).

40. *Sorrell v. IMS Health,* 131 S.Ct. 857 (2011).

41. Initially, the data collection appeared to be limited to a single telephone service provider, but Internet experts soon concluded the program was almost certainly universal.

42. 372 U.S. 335 (1963).

43. *Mapp v. Ohio,* 367 U.S. 643 (1961).

44. 384 U.S. 436 (1966). In 1968, Congress passed legislation including a provision that reinstated the previous rule that statements made by defendants can be used against them as long as the statements were made voluntarily. This provision was never enforced, however, and only in 1999 did a court try to enforce it. The case ultimately came before the Supreme Court, which held that the *Miranda* rights were based on the Constitution and thus could not be overruled by legislative act. See *Dickerson v. United States,* 530 U.S. 428 (2000).

45. *Moran v. Burbine,* 475 U.S. 412 (1986).

46. *Arizona v. Fulminante,* 499 U.S. 279 (1991).

47. *Davis v. United States,* 512 U.S. 452 (1994).

48. *Berghuis v. Thompkins,* 130 S.Ct. 2250 (2010).

49. *J.D.B. v. North Carolina,* 564 U.S. ___ (2011).

50. Thomas P. Sullivan, *Police Experiences with Recording Custodial Interrogations* (Chicago: Northwestern University School of Law Center on Wrongful Convictions, Summer 2004), p. 4.

Chapter 5

1. *Michael M. v. Superior Court,* 450 U.S. 464 (1981).

2. See, for example, *Craig v. Boren,* 429 U.S. 190 (1976).

3. *Orr v. Orr,* 440 U.S. 268 (1979).

4. *Mississippi University for Women v. Hogan,* 458 U.S. 718 (1982).

5. 518 U.S. 515 (1996).

6. 163 U.S. 537 (1896).

7. 347 U.S. 483 (1954).

8. 349 U.S. 294 (1955).

9. *Swann v. Charlotte-Mecklenburg Board of Education,* 402 U.S. 1 (1971).

10. *Keyes v. School District No. 1,* 413 U.S. 189 (1973).

11. *Milliken v. Bradley,* 418 U.S. 717 (1974).

12. *Riddick v. School Board of City of Norfolk,* 627 F.Supp. 814 (E.D.Va. 1984).

13. 570 U.S. ___ (2013).

14. Emily Bazelon, "The Next Kind of Integration," *The New York Times Magazine,* July 20, 2008.

15. Claudia Goldin, "A Grand Gender Convergence: Its Last Chapter," *American Economic Review* 104, no. 4 (2014): 1091–1119.

16. *Oncale v. Sundowner Offshore Services,* 523 U.S. 75 (1998).

17. *Faragher v. City of Boca Raton,* 524 U.S. 775 (1998).

18. The Supreme Court upheld these actions in *Hirabayashi v. United States,* 320 U.S. 81 (1943); and *Korematsu v. United States,* 323 U.S. 214 (1944).

19. Historians in the early and mid-twentieth century gave much smaller figures for the pre-Columbian population—as low as 14 million people for the entire New World. Today, 40 million is considered a conservative estimate, and an estimate of 100 million has much support among demographers. If 100 million is correct, the epidemics that followed the arrival of the Europeans killed one out of every five people alive in the world at that time. See Charles C. Mann, *1491* (New York: Vintage, 2006).

20. The 1890 siege was the subject of Dee Brown's best-selling book *Bury My Heart at Wounded Knee* (New York: Holt, Rinehart & Winston, 1971).

21. *County of Oneida, New York v. Oneida Indian Nation,* 470 U.S. 226 (1985).

22. *Sutton v. United Airlines,* 527 U.S. 471 (1999); and *Toyota v. Williams,* 534 U.S. 184 (2002).

23. *Board of Trustees of the University of Alabama v. Garrett,* 531 U.S. 356 (2001).

24. 539 U.S. 558 (2003).

25. 517 U.S. 620 (1996).

26. *Goodridge v. Department of Public Health,* 798 N.E.2d 941 (Mass. 2003).

27. *Hollingsworth v. Perry,* 570 U.S. ___ (2013).

28. 570 U.S. ___ (2013).

29. *Log Cabin Republicans v. United States,* 716 F.Supp.2d 884 (C.D.Cal. 2010).

30. 438 U.S. 265 (1978).

31. 515 U.S. 200 (1995).

32. 84 F.3d 720 (5th Cir. 1996).

33. 539 U.S. 244 (2003).

34. 539 U.S. 306 (2003).

35. 551 U.S. 701 (2007).

36. *Schuette v. Coalition to Defend Affirmative Action,* 572 U.S. ___ (2014).

Chapter 6

1. David Bicknell Truman, *The Governmental Process: Political Interests and Public Opinion.* (Santa Barbara, Calif.: Praeger, 1981). This work is a political science classic.

2. Robert H. Salisbury, *Interests and Institutions: Substance and Structure in American Politics* (Pittsburgh: University of Pittsburgh Press, 1992).

3. Phillip Bradley, ed., *Democracy in America,* Vol. 1 (New York: Knopf, 1980), p. 191.

4. Mancur Olson, *The Logic of Collective Action: Public Goods and the Theory of Groups,* rev. ed. (Cambridge, Mass.: Harvard University Press, 1971).

5. Pronounced ah-*mee*-kus *kure*-ee-eye.

6. Martin Gilens and Benjamin I. Page, "Testing Theories of American Politics: Elites, Interest Groups, and Average Citizens," *Perspectives on Politics* 12, no. 3 (Fall 2014).

7. Fred McChesney, *Money for Nothing: Politicians, Rent Extraction and Political Extortion* (Cambridge, Mass.: Harvard University Press, 1997).

8. The Agricultural Adjustment Act of 1933 (declared unconstitutional) was replaced by the

1937 Agricultural Adjustment Act, which later was changed and amended several times.

9. 558 U.S. 50 (2010).

10. 567 U.S. ___ (2012).

11. *Caperton v. A. T. Massey Coal Co.*, 556 U.S. 868 (2009).

12. *United States v. Harriss*, 347 U.S. 612 (1954).

Chapter 7

1. Letter to Francis Hopkinson written from Paris while Jefferson was ambassador to France, as cited in John P. Foley, ed., *The Jeffersonian Cyclopedia* (New York: Russell & Russell, 1967), p. 677.

2. The U.S. Senate presents the text of the address at www.access.gpo.gov/congress/senate/farewell/sd106-21.pdf.

3. The association of red with the Republicans and blue with the Democrats is barely a decade old. The terms *red* and *blue* are derived from the colors used by the major television networks to show the states carried by the Republican and Democratic presidential candidates. This use of colors deliberately reverses a traditional pattern. In most European countries, the right-of-center party uses blue, while the left-of-center party employs red. The use of red originated in the socialist movement, from which most European left-of-center parties descend. From time to time, Republicans have accused Democrats of socialism. U.S. television networks thus assigned red to the Republicans precisely so that the networks would not appear to be endorsing that accusation.

4. For an interesting discussion of the pros and cons of patronage from a constitutional perspective, see the majority opinion versus the dissent in the Supreme Court case *Board of County Commissioners v. Umbehr*, 518 U.S. 668 (1996).

5. The term *third party*, although not literally accurate (because sometimes there has been a fourth party, a fifth party, and even more), is commonly used to refer to a minor party.

6. Today, twelve states have multimember districts for their state houses, and a handful also have multimember districts for their state senates.

Chapter 8

1. Doris A. Graber, *Mass Media and American Politics*, 8th ed. (Washington, D.C.: CQ Press, 2009).

2. Jimmy Carter, *Palestine: Peace Not Apartheid* (New York: Simon & Schuster, 2007).

3. The elections that Gallup predicted incorrectly were usually close ones. In 2004, Gallup reported a statistical tie—49 percent each—between Republican George W. Bush and Democrat John Kerry. In 1976, Gallup falsely predicted that Republican incumbent Gerald Ford would prevail over Democrat Jimmy Carter. In 1948, Gallup wrongly predicted that Republican Thomas Dewey would defeat Democratic incumbent Harry Truman. The 2012 elections, however, may have been Gallup's biggest embarrassment to date. Assuming very low Democratic voter turnout, Gallup had Romney well in the lead throughout October. It corrected its last poll to reflect greater turnout, but it still predicted a Romney victory.

4. John M. Benson, "When Is an Opinion Really an Opinion?" *Public Perspective*, September/October 2001, pp. 40–41.

5. As quoted in Karl G. Feld, "When Push Comes to Shove: A Polling Industry Call to Arms," *Public Perspective*, September/October 2001, p. 38.

6. Pew Research Center for the People and the Press, survey conducted September 21–October 4,

2006, and reported in "Who Votes, Who Doesn't, and Why," released October 28, 2006.

7. *Guinn v. United States*, 238 U.S. 347 (1915).

8. *Smith v. Allwright*, 321 U.S. 649 (1944).

9. For more information on voting systems, see the Web site of **verifiedvoting.org**.

10. The argument about the vote-eligible population was first made by Michael P. McDonald and Samuel L. Popkin, "The Myth of the Vanishing Voter," *American Political Science Review*, Vol. 95, No. 4 (December 2001), p. 963.

Chapter 9

1. These states award one electoral vote to the candidate who wins the popular vote in a congressional district and an additional two electoral votes to the winner of the statewide popular vote. Other states have considered similar plans.

2. The word *caucus* apparently was first used in the name of a men's club, the Caucus Club of colonial Boston, sometime between 1755 and 1765. (Many early political and government meetings took place in pubs.) We have no certain knowledge of the origin of the word, but it may be from an Algonquin term meaning "elder" or from the Latin name of a drinking vessel.

3. Today, the Democratic and Republican caucuses in the House and Senate (the Republicans now use the term *conference* instead of *caucus*) choose each party's congressional leadership and sometimes discuss legislation and legislative strategy.

4. Due to the customs of the time, none of the candidates could admit that he had made a personal decision to run. All claimed to have entered the race in response to popular demand.

5. Parties cannot use their freedom-of-association rights to practice racial discrimination in state-sponsored elections: *Smith v. Allwright*, 321 U.S. 649 (1944). When racial discrimination is not involved, the parties have regularly won freedom-of-association suits against state governments. Examples are *Tashjian v. Republican Party of Connecticut*, 479 U.S. 208 (1986), and *California Democratic Party v. Jones*, 530 U.S. 567 (2000).

6. In Washington, the state government holds presidential primaries for both parties. The Democratic Party, however, ignores the Democratic primary and chooses its national convention delegates through a caucus/convention system. In 1984, following a dispute with the state of Michigan over primary rules, the state Democratic Party organized a presidential primary election that was run completely by party volunteers. In 2008, after a similar dispute with its state, the Virginia Republican Party chose its candidate for the U.S. Senate at its state party convention instead of through the Virginia primary elections.

7. The case was *California Democratic Party v. Jones*, cited in footnote 5.

8. *Washington State Grange v. Washington State Republican Party et al.*, 552 U.S. 442 (2008).

9. This act is sometimes referred to as the Federal Election Campaign Act of 1972 because it became effective in that year. The official date of the act, however, is 1971.

10. *Buckley v. Valeo*, 424 U.S. 1 (1976).

11. This figure is from the Center for Responsive Politics.

12. *Colorado Republican Federal Campaign Committee v. Federal Election Commission*, 518 U.S. 604 (1996).

13. Quoted in George Will, "The First Amendment on Trial," *The Washington Post*, December 1, 2002, p. B7.

14. 540 U.S. 93 (2003).

15. 551 U.S. 449 (2007).

16. 558 U.S. 50 (2010).

17. 599 F.3d 686 (D.C.Cir. 2010).

18. 572 U.S. ___ (2014).

Chapter 10

1. *Mutual Film Corporation v. Industrial Commission of Ohio*, 236 U.S. 230 (1915).

2. *Joseph Burstyn, Inc. v. Wilson*, 343 U.S. 495 (1952).

3. *Reno v. American Civil Liberties Union*, 521 U.S. 844 (1997).

4. *United States v. Playboy Entertainment Group*, 529 U.S. 803 (2000).

5. Bernard Cohen, *The Press and Foreign Policy* (Princeton, N.J.: Princeton University Press, 1963), p. 81.

6. Interestingly, in the 2000 campaigns, a Texas group supporting George W. Bush's candidacy paid for a remake of the "daisy" commercial, but the target in the new ad was Al Gore.

7. As quoted in Michael Grunwald, "The Year of Playing Dirtier," *Washington Post*, October 27, 2006, p. A1.

8. John G. Geer, *In Defense of Negativity: Attack Ads in Presidential Campaigns* (Chicago: University of Chicago Press, 2006).

9. The commission's action was upheld by a federal court. See *Perot v. Federal Election Commission*, 97 F.3d 553 (D.C.Cir. 1996).

10. For more details on how political candidates manage news coverage, see Doris A. Graber, *Mass Media and American Politics*, 7th ed. (Washington, D.C.: CQ Press, 2005).

11. For suggestions on how to dissect spin and detect when language is steering one toward a conclusion, see Brooks Jackson and Kathleen Hall Jamieson, *unSpun: Finding Facts in a World of Disinformation* (New York: Random House, 2007).

12. *Red Lion Broadcasting Co. v. FCC*, 395 U.S. 367 (1969).

13. Kathleen Hall Jamieson, *Everything You Think You Know about Politics . . . and Why You're Wrong* (New York: Basic Books, 2000), pp. 187–195.

14. Debra Reddin van Tuyll and Hubert P. van Tuyll, "Political Partisanship," in William David Sloan and Jenn Burleson Mackay, eds., *Media Bias: Finding It, Fixing It* (Jefferson, N.C.: McFarland, 2007), pp. 35–49.

15. Jamieson, *Everything You Think You Know about Politics*, pp. xiii–xiv.

16. Pew Research Center for the People and the Press and the Project for Excellence in Journalism, *The State of the News Media 2007: An Annual Report on American Journalism*.

17. For details, search on "all your base wiki" and "revenue are belong to."

18. The term *podcasting* is used for this type of information delivery because initially podcasts were downloaded onto Apple's iPods.

Chapter 11

1. These states are Alaska, Delaware, Montana, North Dakota, South Dakota, Vermont, and Wyoming.

2. *Baker v. Carr*, 369 U.S. 186 (1962).

3. *Wesberry v. Sanders*, 376 U.S. 1 (1964).

4. See, for example, *Davis v. Bandemer*, 478 U.S. 109 (1986).

5. *Amicus curiae* brief filed by the American Civil Liberties Union (ACLU) in support of the appellants in *Easley v. Cromartie*, 532 U.S. 234 (2001).

6. See, for example, *Shaw v. Reno*, 509 U.S. 630 (1993); *Miller v. Johnson*, 515 U.S. 900 (1995); *Shaw v. Hunt*, 517 U.S. 899 (1996); and *Bush v. Vera*, 517 U.S. 952 (1996).

7. *Easley v. Cromartie*, 532 U.S. 234 (2001).

8. *Powell v. McCormack*, 395 U.S. 486 (1969).

9. Some observers maintain that another reason Congress stays in session longer is the invention of air-conditioning. Until the advent of air-conditioning, no member of Congress wanted to stay in session during the hot and sticky late spring, summer, and early fall months in Washington, D.C.

10. *U.S. Term Limits, Inc. v. Thornton*, 514 U.S. 779 (1995).

11. A term used by Woodrow Wilson in *Congressional Government* (New York: Meridian Books, 1956 [first published in 1885]).

Chapter 12

1. Lyndon B. Johnson, *The Vantage Point: Perspectives of the Presidency, 1963–1969* (New York: Henry Holt & Co., 1971).

2. *Ex parte Grossman*, 267 U.S. 87 (1925).

3. *Clinton v. City of New York*, 524 U.S. 417 (1998).

4. As cited in Lewis D. Eigen and Jonathan P. Siegel, *The Macmillan Dictionary of Political Quotations* (New York: Macmillan, 1993), p. 565.

5. The Constitution does not grant the president explicit power to remove from office officials who are not performing satisfactorily or who do not agree with the president. In 1926, however, the Supreme Court prevented Congress from interfering with the president's ability to fire those executive-branch officials whom he had appointed with Senate approval. See *Myers v. United States*, 272 U.S. 52 (1926).

6. Ironically, Lincoln believed that the actions of the president ought to be strictly limited when war powers were not concerned. He therefore left most domestic issues that did not involve the war entirely to Congress. In doing so, Lincoln was true to the ideas of his former party, the Whigs. That party advocated a limited role for the presidency in reaction to the sweeping assumption of authority by President Andrew Jackson, their great opponent. See David Donald's classic essay "Abraham Lincoln: Whig in the White House," in *Lincoln Reconsidered: Essays on the Civil War Era*, 3d ed. (New York: Vintage, 2001), pp. 133–147.

7. Richard E. Neustadt, *Presidential Power: The Politics of Leadership* (New York: John Wiley, 1960), p. 10.

8. As quoted in Richard M. Pious, *The American Presidency* (New York: Basic Books, 1979), pp. 51–52.

9. A phrase coined by Samuel Kernell in *Going Public: New Strategies of Presidential Leadership*, 2d ed. (Washington, D.C.: Congressional Quarterly Press, 1992).

10. Christopher S. Kelley and Bryan W. Marshall, "Assessing Presidential Power: Signing Statements and Veto Threats as Coordinated Strategies," *American Politics Research* 37, no. 3 (May 2009), pp. 508–533.

11. Congress used its power to declare war in the War of 1812, the Mexican War (1846–1848), the Spanish-American War (1898), and World War I (U.S. involvement lasted from 1916 until 1918) and on six different occasions during World War II (U.S. involvement lasted from 1941 until 1945).

12. As quoted in Thomas E. Cronin, *The State of the Presidency*, 2d ed. (Boston: Little, Brown, 1980), p. 11.

Chapter 13

1. This definition follows the classic model of bureaucracy put forth by German sociologist Max Weber. See Max Weber, *Theory of Social and Economic Organization*, ed. Talcott Parsons (New York: Oxford University Press, 1974).

2. It should be noted that although the president is technically the head of the bureaucracy, the president cannot always control the bureaucracy—as you will read later in this chapter.

3. Maury Gittleman and Brooks Pierce, "Compensation for State and Local Government Workers," *Journal of Economic Perspectives* 26, no. 1 (Winter 2012), pp. 217–242 (www.aeaweb.org/articles.php?doi=10.1257/jep.26.1.217).

4. Dennis Cauchon, "Federal Workers Earning Double Their Private Counterparts," *USA Today*, August 13, 2010. According to FactCheck.org, however, the total wage figure from which the $123,049 estimate was derived includes approximately $10,000 per current employee that was actually paid to other employees who retired earlier. Thus, the true average is closer to $113,000.

5. Alicia Munnell, Jean-Pierre Aubry, Josh Hurwitz, and Laura Quinby, *Comparing Compensation: State-Local Versus Private Sector Workers*, Center for Retirement Research at Boston College, September 2011 (slge.org/publications/comparing-compensation-state-local-versus-private-sectorworkers).

6. Congressional Budget Office, "Comparing the Compensation of Federal and Private-Sector Employees," January 30, 2012 (www.cbo.gov/publication/42921).

7. For an insightful analysis of the policymaking process in Washington, D.C., and the role played by various groups in the process, see Morton H. Halperin and Priscilla A. Clapp, with Arnold Kanter, *Bureaucratic Politics and Foreign Policy*, 2d ed. (Washington, D.C.: The Brookings Institution, 2006). Although the focus of the book is on foreign policy, the analysis applies in many ways to the general policymaking process.

Chapter 14

1. 347 U.S. 483 (1954).

2. See *Plessy v. Ferguson*, 163 U.S. 537 (1896).

3. 130 S.Ct. 876 (2010).

4. 494 U.S. 652 (1990).

5. 540 U.S. 93 (2003).

6. Although a state's highest court is often referred to as the state supreme court, there are exceptions. In the New York court system, for example, the supreme court is a trial court, and the highest court is called the New York Court of Appeals.

7. Between 1790 and 1891, Congress allowed the Supreme Court almost no discretion over which cases to decide. After 1925, in almost 95 percent of appealed cases the Court could choose whether to hear arguments and issue an opinion. Beginning in October 1988, mandatory review was nearly eliminated.

8. *McCutcheon v. Federal Election Commission*, 572 U.S. ___ (2014).

9. *Town of Greece v. Galloway*, 572 U.S. ___ (2014).

10. *McCullen v. Coakley*, 573 U.S. ___ (2014).

11. 573 U.S. ___ (2014).

12. 132 S.Ct. 2566 (2012).

13. 347 U.S. 483 (1954).

14. 5 U.S. 137 (1803). The Supreme Court had considered the constitutionality of an act of Congress in *Hylton v. United States*, 3 U.S. 171 (1796), in which Congress's power to levy certain taxes was challenged. That particular act was ruled constitutional, rather than unconstitutional, however, so this first federal exercise of judicial review was not clearly recognized as such. Also, during the decade before the adoption of the federal Constitution, courts in at least eight states had exercised the power of judicial review.

15. 539 U.S. 558 (2003).

16. 570 U.S. ___ (2013).

17. Antonin Scalia, *A Matter of Interpretation: Federal Courts and the Law* (Princeton, N.J.: Princeton University Press, 1997).

18. Letter by Thomas Jefferson to William C. Jarvis, 1820, in Andrew A. Lipscomb and Albert Ellery Bergh, *The Writings of Thomas Jefferson*, Memorial Edition (Washington, D.C.: Thomas Jefferson Memorial Association of the United States, 1904).

19. As quoted in Carl Hulse and David D. Kirkpatrick, "DeLay Says Federal Judiciary Has 'Run Amok,' Adding Congress Is Partly to Blame," *New York Times*, April 8, 2005, p. 5.

Chapter 15

1. Stan Dorn, *Uninsured and Dying because of It: Updating the Institute of Medicine Analysis on the Impact of Uninsurance on Mortality* (Washington, D.C.: Urban Institute, 2008).

2. *National Federation of Independent Business v. Sebelius*, 567 U.S. ___ (2012).

3. No. 14-5018, D.C. Circuit (2013).

4. A recent investigation has shown that hydraulic fracturing that takes place deep underground has no effect on underground water sources used for human consumption. The distance is too great. However, contamination *is* possible if the pipes leading down to the fracking are not properly sealed. A second study has linked the underground disposal of wastewater generated by fracking to an increase in the number of small earthquakes. Fracking itself rarely induces quakes.

5. Paul Krugman, "Romer and Bernstein on Stimulus," in the blog Conscience of a Liberal, *New York Times*, January 10, 2009.

6. www.chinadaily.com.cn/opinion/2011-08/08/content_13069554.htm.

7. Paul Krugman, "Currency Regimes, Capital Flows, and Crises" (keynote lecture, IMF Annual Research Conference, Washington, D.C., November 7, 2013).

Chapter 16

1. *Public Papers of the Presidents of the United States: Harry S. Truman, 1947* (Washington, D.C.: U.S. Government Printing Office, 1963), pp. 176–180.

2. The containment policy was outlined by George F. Kennan, the chief of the policy-planning staff for the Department of State at that time, in an article that appeared in *Foreign Affairs*, July 1947, p. 575. The author's name was given as "X."

3. The last war between great powers was the Korean War, in which American and Chinese troops met in combat. As of World War II, the "great powers" were conventionally considered to be China, France, Germany, Japan, the Soviet Union, the United Kingdom, and the United States. The five powers on the winning side of the war became the permanent members of the United Nations Security Council, a role they retain to this day (the Russian Federation has replaced the Soviet Union). Because of the overwhelming dominance of the Soviet Union and the United States after the war, however, the concept of "great powers" was largely displaced by the idea of two "superpowers."

A

action-reaction syndrome The principle that for every government action, there will be a reaction by the public.

adjudicate To render a judicial decision. In administrative law, it is the process in which an administrative law judge hears and decides issues that arise when an agency charges a person or firm with violating a law or regulation enforced by the agency.

administrative law The body of law created by administrative agencies (in the form of rules, regulations, orders, and decisions) in order to carry out their duties and responsibilities.

affirmative action A policy that gives special consideration, in jobs and college admissions, to members of groups that have been discriminated against in the past.

agenda setting Getting an issue on the political agenda to be addressed by Congress; part of the first stage of the policymaking process. Also, the media's ability to determine which issues are considered important by the public and by politicians.

agents of political socialization People and institutions that influence the political views of others.

Anti-Federalists A political group that opposed the adoption of the Constitution.

appellate court A court having appellate jurisdiction. An appellate court normally does not hear evidence or testimony but reviews the transcript of the trial court's proceedings, other records relating to the case, and attorneys' arguments as to why the trial court's decision should or should not stand.

apportionment The distribution of House seats among the states on the basis of their respective populations.

appropriation A part of the congressional budgeting process—the determination of how many dollars will be spent in a given year on a particular government activity.

Articles of Confederation The nation's first national constitution, which established a national form of government following the American Revolution. The Articles provided for a confederal form of government in which the central government had few powers.

Australian ballot A secret ballot that is prepared, distributed, and counted by government officials at public expense; used by all states in the United States since 1888.

authority The ability to legitimately exercise power, such as the power to make and enforce laws.

authorization A part of the congressional budgeting process—the creation of the legal basis for government programs.

autocracy A form of government in which the power and authority of the government are in the hands of a single person.

B

biased sample A poll sample that does not accurately represent the population.

bicameral legislature A legislature made up of two chambers, or parts.

bill of attainder A legislative act that inflicts punishment on particular persons or groups without granting them the right to a trial.

Bill of Rights The first ten amendments to the U.S. Constitution. They list the freedoms—such as the freedoms of speech, press, and religion—that a citizen enjoys and that cannot be infringed on by the government.

block grant A federal grant given to a state for a broad area, such as criminal justice or mental-health programs.

bureaucracy A large, complex, hierarchically structured administrative organization that carries out specific functions.

bureaucrat An individual who works in a bureaucracy. As generally used, the term refers to a government employee.

busing The transportation of public school students by bus to schools physically outside their neighborhoods to eliminate school segregation based on residential patterns.

C

cabinet An advisory group selected by the president to assist with decision making. Traditionally, the cabinet has consisted of the heads of the executive departments and other officers whom the president may choose to appoint.

campaign strategy The comprehensive plan developed by a candidate and his or her advisers for winning an election.

capitalism An economic system based on the private ownership of wealth-producing property, free markets, and freedom of contract. The privately owned corporation is the preeminent capitalist institution.

case law The rules of law announced in court decisions. Case law includes the aggregate of reported cases that interpret judicial precedents, statutes, regulations, and constitutional provisions.

categorical grant A federal grant targeted for a specific purpose as defined by federal law.

caucus A meeting held to choose political candidates or delegates.

checks and balances A major principle of American government in which each of the three branches is given the means to check (to restrain or balance) the actions of the others.

chief diplomat The role of the president of the United States in recognizing and interacting with foreign governments.

chief executive The head of the executive branch of government; in the United States, the president.

chief of staff The person who directs the operations of the White House Office and advises the president on important matters.

Children's Health Insurance Program (CHIP) A joint federal-state program that provides health-care insurance for low-income children.

citizen journalism The collection, analysis, and dissemination of information online by independent journalists, scholars, politicians, and the general citizenry.

civil disobedience The deliberate and public act of refusing to obey laws thought to be unjust.

civil law The branch of law that spells out the duties that individuals in society owe to other persons or to their governments, excluding the duty not to commit crimes.

civil liberties Individual rights protected by the Constitution against the powers of the government.

civil rights The rights of all Americans to equal treatment under the law, as provided by the Fourteenth Amendment to the Constitution.

civil rights movement The movement in the 1950s and 1960s, by minorities and concerned whites, to end racial segregation.

civil service Nonmilitary government employees.

closed primary A primary in which only party members can vote to choose that party's candidates.

cloture A procedure for ending filibusters in the Senate and bringing the matter under consideration to a vote.

coalition An alliance of individuals or groups with a variety of interests and opinions who join together to support all or part of a political party's platform.

coalition An alliance of nations formed to undertake a foreign policy action, particularly a military action. A coalition is often a temporary alliance that dissolves after the action is concluded.

Cold War The war of words, warnings, and ideologies between the Soviet Union and the United States that lasted from the late 1940s through the late 1980s.

colonial empire A group of dependent nations that are under the rule of an imperial power.

commander in chief The supreme commander of a nation's military force.

commerce clause The clause in Article I, Section 8, of the Constitution that gives Congress the power to regulate interstate commerce (commerce involving more than one state).

commercial speech Advertising statements that describe products. Commercial speech receives less protection under the First Amendment than ordinary speech.

common law The body of law developed from judicial decisions in English and U.S. courts, not attributable to a legislature.

competitive federalism A model of federalism in which state and local governments compete for businesses and citizens, who in effect "vote with their feet" by moving to jurisdictions that offer a competitive advantage.

concurrent powers Powers held by both the federal and the state governments in a federal system.

concurring opinion A statement written by a judge or justice who agrees (concurs) with the court's decision, but for reasons different from those in the majority opinion.

confederal system A league of independent sovereign states, joined together by a central government that has only limited powers over them.

confederation A league of independent states that are united only for the purpose of achieving common goals.

conference In regard to the Supreme Court, a private meeting of the justices in which they present their arguments concerning a case under consideration.

conference committee A temporary committee that is formed when the two chambers of Congress pass differing versions of the same bill. The conference committee consists of members from the House and the Senate who work out a compromise bill.

conference report A report submitted by a conference committee after it has drafted a single version of a bill.

congressional district The geographic area that is served by one member in the House of Representatives.

conservatism A set of political beliefs that include a limited role for the national government in helping individuals and in the economic affairs of the nation, as well as support for traditional values and lifestyles.

conservative movement An ideological movement that arose in the 1950s and 1960s and continues to shape conservative beliefs.

Constitutional Convention The convention of delegates from the states that was held in Philadelphia in 1787 for the purpose of amending the Articles of Confederation. In fact, the delegates wrote a new constitution (the U.S. Constitution) that established a federal form of government.

constitutional law Law based on the U.S. Constitution and the constitutions of the various states.

containment A U.S. policy designed to contain the spread of communism by offering military and economic aid to threatened nations.

contempt of court A ruling that a person has disobeyed a court order or has shown disrespect to the court or to a judicial proceeding.

continuing resolution A temporary resolution passed by Congress that enables executive agencies to continue work with the same funding that they had in the previous fiscal year.

cooperative federalism A model of federalism in which the states and the federal government cooperate in solving problems.

Corporate Average Fuel Economy (CAFE) standards A set of federal standards under which each vehicle manufacturer (or the industry as a whole) must meet a miles-per-gallon benchmark averaged across all new cars or trucks.

Credentials Committee A committee of each national political party that evaluates the claims of national party convention delegates to be the legitimate representatives of their states.

criminal law The branch of law that defines and governs actions that constitute crimes. Generally, criminal law has to do with wrongful actions committed against society for which society demands redress.

Cuban missile crisis A nuclear standoff that occurred in 1962 when the United States learned that the Soviet Union had placed nuclear warheads in Cuba.

D

dealignment Among voters, a growing detachment from both major political parties.

de facto **segregation** Racial segregation that occurs not as a result of government actions but because of social and economic conditions and residential patterns.

de jure **segregation** Racial segregation that occurs because of laws or decisions by government agencies.

delegate A person selected to represent the people of one geographic area at a party convention.

democracy A system of government in which the people have ultimate political authority. The word is derived from the Greek *demos* ("the people") and *kratia* ("rule").

détente A French word meaning a "relaxation of tensions." Détente characterized the relationship between the United States and the Soviet Union in the 1970s as they attempted to pursue cooperative dealings and arms control.

deterrence A policy of building up military strength for the purpose of discouraging (deterring) military attacks by other nations; the policy that supported the arms race between the United States and the Soviet Union during the Cold War.

devolution The surrender or transfer of powers to local authorities by a central government.

dictatorship A form of government in which absolute power is exercised by an individual or group whose power is not supported by tradition.

diplomat A person who represents one country in dealing with representatives of another country.

direct democracy A system of government in which political decisions are made by the people themselves rather than by elected representatives. This form of government was practiced in some parts of ancient Greece.

direct primary An election held within each of the two major parties—Democratic and Republican—to choose the party's candidates for the general election. Voters choose the candidate directly, rather than through delegates.

direct technique Any method used by an interest group to interact with government officials directly to further the group's goals.

dissenting opinion A statement written by a judge or justice who disagrees with the majority opinion.

diversity of citizenship A basis for federal court jurisdiction over a lawsuit that arises when (1) the parties in the lawsuit live in different states or when one of the parties is a foreign government or a foreign citizen, and (2) the amount in controversy is more than $75,000.

divine right theory The theory that a monarch's right to rule was derived directly from God rather than from the consent of the people.

division of powers A basic principle of federalism established by the U.S. Constitution, by which powers are divided between the national and state governments.

domestic policy Public policy concerning issues within a national unit, such as national policy concerning health care or the economy.

double jeopardy The prosecution of a person twice for the same criminal offense; prohibited by the Fifth Amendment in all but a few circumstances.

dual federalism A system of government in which the federal and the state governments maintain diverse but sovereign powers.

due process clause The constitutional guarantee, set out in the Fifth and Fourteenth Amendments, that the government will not illegally or arbitrarily deprive a person of life, liberty, or property.

due process of law The requirement that the government use fair, reasonable, and standard procedures whenever it takes any legal action against an individual; required by the Fifth and Fourteenth Amendments.

E

earmark Spending provision inserted into legislation that benefits only a small number of people.

easy-money policy A monetary policy that involves stimulating the economy by expanding the rate of growth of the money supply.

economic policy All actions taken by the national government to address ups and downs in the nation's level of business activity.

elector A member of the electoral college.

electoral college The group of electors who are selected by the voters in each state to officially elect the president and vice president. The number of electors in each state is equal to the number of that state's representatives in both chambers of Congress.

electorate All of the citizens eligible to vote in a given election.

electronic media Communication channels that involve electronic transmissions, such as radio, television, and the Internet.

enabling legislation A law enacted by a legislature to establish an administrative agency. Enabling legislation normally specifies the name, purpose, composition, and powers of the agency being created.

entitlement program A government program (such as Social Security) that allows, or entitles, a certain class of people (such as elderly persons) to receive benefits. Entitlement programs operate under open-ended budget authorizations that, in effect, place no limits on how much can be spent.

equality A concept that holds, at a minimum, that all people are entitled to equal protection under the law.

equal protection clause Section 1 of the Fourteenth Amendment, which states that no state shall "deny to any person within its jurisdiction the equal protection of the laws."

establishment clause The section of the First Amendment that prohibits Congress from passing laws "respecting an establishment of religion."

exclusionary rule A criminal procedural rule stating that illegally obtained evidence is not admissible in court.

executive agreement A binding international agreement, or pact, that is made between the president and another head of state and that does not require Senate approval.

Executive Office of the President (EOP) A group of staff agencies that assist the president in carrying out major duties.

executive order A presidential order to carry out a policy or policies described in a law passed by Congress.

executive privilege An inherent executive power claimed by presidents to withhold information from, or to refuse to appear before, Congress or the courts. The president can also accord the privilege to other executive officials.

***ex post facto* law** A criminal law that punishes individuals for committing an act that was legal when the act was committed.

expressed powers Constitutional or statutory powers that are expressly provided for by the U.S. Constitution; also called *enumerated powers.*

F

faction A group of persons forming a cohesive minority.

federalism A system of shared sovereignty between two levels of government—one national and one subnational—occupying the same geographic region.

Federalists A political group, led by Alexander Hamilton and John Adams, that supported the adoption of the Constitution and the creation of a federal form of government.

federal mandate A requirement in federal legislation that forces states and municipalities to comply with certain rules.

Federal Open Market Committee (FOMC) The most important body within the Federal Reserve System; decides how monetary policy should be carried out.

federal question A question that pertains to the U.S. Constitution, acts of Congress, or treaties. A federal question provides a basis for federal court jurisdiction.

federal system A form of government that provides for a division of powers between a central government and several regional governments.

feminism A doctrine advocating full political, economic, and social equality for women.

filibustering The Senate tradition of unlimited debate undertaken for the purpose of preventing action on a bill.

first budget resolution A budget resolution, which is supposed to be passed in May, that sets overall revenue goals and spending targets for the next fiscal year, beginning on October 1.

First Continental Congress A gathering of delegates from twelve of the thirteen colonies, held in 1774 to protest the Coercive Acts.

fiscal federalism The allocation of taxes collected by one level of government (typically the national government) to another level (typically state or local governments).

fiscal policy The use of changes in government expenditures and taxes to alter national economic variables.

fiscal year A twelve-month period that is established for bookkeeping or accounting purposes. The government's fiscal year runs from October 1 through September 30.

foreign policy A systematic and general plan that guides a country's attitudes and actions toward the rest of the world. Foreign policy includes all of the economic, military, commercial, and diplomatic positions and actions that a nation takes in its relationships with other countries.

fracking Technique for extracting oil or natural gas from underground rock by the high-power injection of a mixture of water, sand, and chemicals.

framing An agenda-setting technique that establishes the context of a media report. Framing can mean fitting events into a familiar story or filtering information through preconceived ideas.

free exercise clause The provision of the First Amendment stating that the government cannot pass laws "prohibiting the free exercise" of religion.

free rider problem The difficulty that exists when individuals can enjoy the outcome of an interest group's efforts without having to contribute, such as by becoming members of the group.

fundamental right A basic right of all Americans, such as First Amendment rights. Any law or action that prevents some group of persons from exercising a fundamental right is subject to the *strict scrutiny standard*.

G

gender gap The difference between the percentage of votes cast for a particular candidate by women and the percentage of votes cast for the same candidate by men.

general election A regularly scheduled election to choose the U.S. president, vice president, and senators and representatives in Congress. General elections are held in even-numbered years on the Tuesday after the first Monday in November.

gerrymandering The drawing of a legislative district's boundaries in such a way as to maximize the influence of a certain group or political party.

glass ceiling An invisible but real discriminatory barrier that prevents women and minorities from rising to top positions of power or responsibility.

global warming An increase in the average temperature of the Earth's surface over the last half century and its projected continuation; referred to more generally as *climate change*.

GOP A nickname for the Republican Party—"grand old party."

government The individuals and institutions that make society's rules and possess the power and authority to enforce those rules.

government corporation An agency of the government that is run as a business enterprise. Such agencies engage primarily in commercial activities, produce revenues, and require greater flexibility than most government agencies have.

grandfather clause A clause in a state law that had the effect of restricting voting rights to those whose ancestors had voted before the 1860s. It was one of the techniques used in the South to prevent African Americans from exercising their right to vote.

Great Compromise A plan for a bicameral legislature in which one chamber would be based on population and the other chamber would represent each state equally. Also known as the Connecticut Compromise.

greenhouse gas A gas that, when released into the atmosphere, traps the sun's heat and slows its release into outer space. Carbon dioxide (CO_2) is a major example.

H

head of state The person who serves as the ceremonial head of a country's government and represents that country to the rest of the world.

house effect In the case of a polling firm, a consistent tendency to report results more favorable to one of the political parties than the results reported by other pollsters.

I

ideology Generally, a system of political ideas that are rooted in religious or philosophical beliefs concerning human nature, society, and government.

imminent lawless action test The current Supreme Court doctrine for assessing the constitutionality of subversive speech. To be illegal, speech must be "directed to inciting . . . imminent lawless action."

implied powers The powers of the federal government that are implied by the expressed powers in the Constitution, particularly in Article I, Section 8.

independent executive agency A federal agency that is not located within a cabinet department.

independent expenditure An expenditure for activities that are independent from (not coordinated with) those of a political candidate or a political party.

independent regulatory agency A federal organization that is responsible for creating and implementing rules that regulate private activity and protect the public interest in a particular sector of the economy.

indirect technique Any method used by interest groups to influence government officials through third parties, such as voters.

individual mandate In the context of health-care reform, a requirement that all persons obtain health-care insurance from one source or another. Those failing to do so must pay a penalty.

inflation A sustained rise in average prices; equivalent to a decline in the value of the dollar.

inherent powers The powers of the national government that, although not always expressly granted by the Constitution, are necessary to ensure the nation's integrity and survival as a political unit.

institution An ongoing organization that performs certain functions for society.

instructed delegate A representative who deliberately mirrors the views of the majority of his or her constituents.

interest group An organized group of individuals sharing common objectives who actively attempt to influence policymakers.

interstate commerce Trade that involves more than one state.

interventionism Direct involvement by one country in another country's affairs.

iron curtain A phrase coined by Winston Churchill to describe the political boundaries between the democratic countries in Western Europe and the Soviet-controlled Communist countries in Eastern Europe.

iron triangle A three-way alliance among legislators, bureaucrats, and interest groups to make or preserve policies that benefit their respective interests.

ISIS The Islamic State in Iraq and Greater Syria; a terrorist organization that by 2014 had taken over substantial portions of Iraq and Syria. Also known as *ISIL* (the Islamic State in Iraq and the Levant) or the Islamic State.

isolationism A political policy of noninvolvement in world affairs.

issue ad A political advertisement that focuses on a particular issue. Issue ads can be used to support or attack a candidate's position or credibility.

issue networks Groups of individuals or organizations—which consist of legislators and legislative staff members, interest group leaders, bureaucrats, the media, scholars, and other experts—that support particular policy positions on a given issue.

J

judicial review The power of the courts to decide on the constitutionality of legislative enactments and of actions taken by the executive branch.

judiciary The courts; one of the three branches of government in the United States.

jurisdiction The authority of a court to hear and decide a particular case.

justiciable controversy A controversy that is not hypothetical or academic but real and substantial; a requirement that must be satisfied before a court will hear a case. *Justiciable* is pronounced jus-*tish*-a-bul.

K

Keynesian economics An economic theory proposed by British economist John Maynard Keynes that is typically associated with the use of fiscal policy to alter national economic variables.

kitchen cabinet The name given to a president's unofficial advisers. The term was coined during Andrew Jackson's presidency.

L

labor force All of the people over the age of sixteen who are working or actively looking for jobs.

legislative rule An administrative agency rule that carries the same weight as a statute enacted by a legislature.

***Lemon* test** A three-part test enunciated by the Supreme Court in the 1971 case of *Lemon v. Kurtzman* to determine whether government aid to parochial schools is constitutional.

libel A published report of a falsehood that tends to injure a person's reputation or character.

liberalism A set of political beliefs that include the advocacy of active government, including government intervention to improve the welfare of individuals and to protect civil rights.

libertarianism The belief that government should do as little as possible, not only in the economic sphere, but also in regulating morality and personal behavior.

liberty The freedom of individuals to believe, act, and express themselves as they choose so long as doing so does not infringe on the rights of other individuals in the society.

limited government A form of government based on the principle that the powers of government should be clearly limited either through a written document or through wide public understanding. It is characterized by institutional checks to ensure that government serves public rather than private interests.

literacy test A test given to voters to ensure that they could read and write and thus evaluate political information. This technique was used in many southern states to restrict African American participation in elections.

lobbying All of the attempts by organizations or by individuals to influence the passage, defeat, or contents of legislation or to influence the administrative decisions of government.

lobbyist An individual who handles a particular interest group's lobbying efforts.

M

Madisonian Model The model of government devised by James Madison, in which the powers of the government are separated into three branches: legislative, executive, and judicial.

majority leader The party leader elected by the majority party in the House or in the Senate.

majority party The political party that has more members in the legislature than the opposing party.

malapportionment A condition in which the voting power of citizens in one district is greater than the voting power of citizens in another district.

managed news coverage News coverage that is manipulated (managed) by a campaign manager or political consultant to gain media exposure for a political candidate.

markup session A meeting held by a congressional committee or subcommittee to approve, amend, or redraft a bill.

Marshall Plan A plan providing for U.S. economic assistance to European nations following World War II to help those nations recover from the war. The plan was named after George C. Marshall, secretary of state from 1947 to 1949.

mass media Communication channels, such as newspapers and radio and television broadcasts, through which people can communicate to large audiences.

material incentive A reason to join an interest group—practical benefits such as discounts, subscriptions, or group insurance.

Mayflower Compact A document drawn up by Pilgrim leaders in 1620 on the ship *Mayflower*. The document stated that laws were to be made for the general good of the people.

media Newspapers, magazines, television, radio, the Internet, and any other printed or electronic means of communication.

Medicaid A joint federal-state program that pays for health-care services for low-income persons.

Medicare A federal government program that pays for health-care insurance for Americans aged sixty-five years and over.

minority leader The party leader elected by the minority party in the House or in the Senate.

minority-majority district A district in which minority groups make up a majority of the population.

minority party The political party that has fewer members in the legislature than the opposing party.

Miranda warnings A series of statements informing criminal suspects, on their arrest, of their constitutional rights, such as the right to remain silent and the right to counsel; required by the Supreme Court's 1966 decision in *Miranda v. Arizona*.

moderates Persons whose views fall in the middle of the political spectrum.

monarchy A form of autocracy in which a king, queen, emperor, empress, tsar, or tsarina is the highest authority in the government. Monarchs usually obtain their power through inheritance.

monetary policy Actions taken by the Federal Reserve Board to change the amount of money in circulation to affect interest rates, credit markets, the rate of inflation, the rate of economic growth, and the rate of unemployment.

Monroe Doctrine A U.S. policy, announced in 1823 by President James Monroe, that the United States would not tolerate foreign intervention in the Western Hemisphere, and in return, the United States would stay out of European affairs.

moral idealism In foreign policy, the belief that the most important goal is to do what is right. Moral idealists think that it is possible for nations to cooperate as part of a rule-based community.

mutually assured destruction (MAD) A phrase referring to the assumption that if the forces of two nations are capable of destroying each other, neither nation will take a chance on war.

N

national convention The meeting held by each major party every four years to nominate presidential and vice-presidential candidates, write a party platform, and conduct other party business.

national health insurance A program, found in many of the world's economically advanced nations, under which the central government provides basic health-care insurance coverage to everyone in the country.

national party chairperson An individual who serves as a political party's administrative head at the national level and directs the work of the party's national committee.

national party committee The political party leaders who direct party business during the four years between the national party conventions, organize the next national convention, and plan how to support the party's candidate in the next presidential election.

National Security Council (NSC) A council that advises the president on domestic and foreign matters concerning the safety and defense of the nation.

natural rights Rights that are not bestowed by governments but are inherent within every man, woman, and child by virtue of the fact that he or she is a human being.

necessary and proper clause Article I, Section 8, Clause 18, of the Constitution, which gives Congress the power to make all laws "necessary and proper" for the federal government to carry out its responsibilities; also called the *elastic clause*.

negative political advertising Political advertising undertaken for the purpose of discrediting an opposing candidate in voters' eyes. Attack ads are one form of negative political advertising.

neutral competency The application of technical skills to jobs without regard to political issues.

neutrality The position of not being aligned with either side in a dispute or conflict, such as a war.

New Deal The policies ushered in by the Roosevelt administration in 1933 in an attempt to bring the United States out of the Great Depression.

new federalism A plan to limit the federal government's role in regulating state governments and to give the states increased power in deciding how they should spend government revenues.

nominating convention An official meeting of a political party to choose its candidates. Nominating conventions at the state and local levels also select delegates to represent the citizens of their geographic areas at a higher-level party convention.

representative democracy A form of democracy in which the will of the majority is expressed through groups of individuals elected by the people to act as their representatives.

republic Essentially, a representative democracy in which there is no king or queen and the people are sovereign.

reverse discrimination Discrimination against those who have no minority status.

right-to-work laws Laws that ban unions from collecting dues or other fees from workers whom they represent but who have not actually joined the union.

rulemaking The process undertaken by an administrative agency when formally proposing, evaluating, and adopting a new regulation.

rule of law A basic principle of government that requires those who govern to act in accordance with established law.

Rules Committee A standing committee in the House of Representatives that provides special rules governing how particular bills will be considered and debated by the House. The Rules Committee normally proposes time limits on debate for any bill.

S

sample In the context of opinion polling, a group of people selected to represent the population being studied.

sampling error In the context of opinion polling, the difference between what the sample results show and what the true results would have been had everybody in the relevant population been interviewed.

school voucher An educational certificate, provided by a government, that allows a student to use public funds to pay for a private or a public school chosen by the student or his or her parents.

secession The act of formally withdrawing from membership in an alliance; the withdrawal of a state from the federal Union.

second budget resolution A budget resolution, which is supposed to be passed in September, that sets "binding" limits on taxes and spending for the next fiscal year.

Second Continental Congress The congress of the colonies that met in 1775 to assume the powers of a central government and to establish an army.

seditious speech Speech that urges resistance to lawful authority or that advocates the overthrow of a government.

self-incrimination Providing damaging information or testimony against oneself in court.

senatorial courtesy A practice that allows a senator of the president's party to veto the president's nominee to a federal court judgeship within the senator's state.

separate-but-equal doctrine A Supreme Court doctrine holding that the equal protection clause of the Fourteenth Amendment did not forbid racial segregation as long as the facilities for blacks were equal to those for whites.

separation of powers The principle of dividing governmental powers among the legislative, the executive, and the judicial branches of government.

sexual harassment Unwanted physical contact, verbal conduct, or abuse of a sexual nature that interferes with a recipient's job performance, creates a hostile environment, or carries with it an implicit or explicit threat of adverse employment consequences.

Shays' Rebellion A rebellion of angry farmers in western Massachusetts in 1786, led by former Revolutionary War captain Daniel Shays.

signing statement A written statement, appended to a bill at the time the president signs it into law, indicating how the president interprets that legislation.

sit-in A tactic of nonviolent civil disobedience. Demonstrators enter a business, college building, or other public place and remain seated until they are forcibly removed or until their demands are met.

slander The public utterance (speaking) of a statement that holds a person up for contempt, ridicule, or hatred.

social conflict Disagreements among people in a society over what the society's priorities should be.

social contract A voluntary agreement among individuals to create a government and to give that government adequate power to secure the mutual protection and welfare of all individuals.

socialism A political ideology that lies to the left of liberalism on the traditional political spectrum. Socialists are scarce in the United States but common in many other countries.

soft money Campaign contributions not regulated by federal law, such as some contributions that are made to political parties instead of to particular candidates.

solidarity Mutual agreement among the members of a particular group.

solidary incentive A reason to join an interest group—pleasure in associating with like-minded individuals.

Solid South A term used to describe the tendency of the southern states to vote Democratic after the Civil War.

sound bite A televised comment, lasting for only a few seconds, that captures a thought or a perspective and has an immediate impact on viewers.

Soviet bloc The group of Eastern European nations that fell under the control of the Soviet Union following World War II.

Speaker of the House The presiding officer in the House of Representatives. The Speaker is a member of the majority party and is the most powerful member of the House.

special election An election that is held at the state or local level when the voters must decide an issue before the next general election or when vacancies occur by reason of death or resignation.

spin A reporter's slant on, or interpretation of, a particular event or action.

spin doctor A political candidate's press adviser who tries to convince reporters to give a story or event concerning the candidate a particular "spin" (interpretation, or slant).

standing committee A permanent committee in Congress that deals with legislation concerning a particular area, such as agriculture or foreign relations.

standing to sue The requirement that an individual must have a sufficient stake in a controversy before he or she can bring a lawsuit. The party bringing the suit must demonstrate that he or she has either been harmed or been threatened with a harm.

stare decisis A common law doctrine under which judges normally are obligated to follow the precedents established by prior court decisions. Pronounced *ster*-ay dih-*si*-sis.

statutory law The body of law enacted by legislatures (as opposed to constitutional law, administrative law, or case law).

straw poll A nonscientific poll in which there is no way to ensure that the opinions expressed are representative of the larger population.

strict scrutiny standard A standard under which a law or action must be necessary to promote a compelling state interest and must be narrowly tailored to meet that interest.

subcommittee A division of a larger committee that deals with a particular part of the committee's policy area. Most standing committees have several subcommittees.

suffrage The right to vote; the franchise.

supremacy clause Article VI, Clause 2, of the Constitution, which makes the Constitution and federal laws superior to all conflicting state and local laws.

suspect classification A classification, such as race, that provides the basis for a discriminatory law. Any law based on a suspect classification is subject to strict scrutiny by the courts, meaning that the law must be justified by a compelling state interest.

symbolic speech The expression of beliefs, opinions, or ideas through forms other than verbal speech or print; speech involving actions and other nonverbal expressions.

T

Tea Party movement A grassroots conservative movement that arose in 2009 after Barack Obama became president. The movement opposes big government and current levels of taxation, and also rejects political compromise.

third party In the United States, any party other than the two major parties (Republican and Democratic).

three-fifths compromise A compromise reached during the Constitutional Convention by which three-fifths of all slaves were to be counted for purposes of representation in the House of Representatives.

trade organization An association formed by members of a particular industry, such as the oil industry or the trucking industry, to develop common standards and goals for the industry. Trade organizations, as interest groups, lobby government for legislation or regulations that specifically benefit their members.

treaty A formal agreement between the governments of two or more countries.

trial court A court in which trials are held and testimony is taken.

trustee A representative who tries to serve the broad interests of the entire society and not just the narrow interests of his or her constituents.

two-party system A political system in which two strong and established parties compete for political offices.

tyranny The arbitrary or unrestrained exercise of power by an oppressive individual or government.

U

unemployment The state of not having a job even when actively seeking one.

unicameral legislature A legislature with only one chamber.

unitary system A centralized governmental system in which local or subdivisional governments exercise only those powers given to them by the central government.

V

veto A Latin word meaning "I forbid"; the refusal by an official, such as the president of the United States or a state governor, to sign a bill into law.

veto power A constitutional power that enables the chief executive (president or governor) to reject legislation and return it to the legislature with reasons for the rejection. This either prevents or delays the bill from becoming law.

vote-eligible population The number of people who are actually eligible to vote in an American election.

voting-age population The number of people residing in the United States who are at least eighteen years old.

W

ward A local unit of a political party's organization, consisting of a division or district within a city.

Watergate scandal A scandal involving an illegal break-in at the Democratic National Committee offices in 1972 by members of President Richard Nixon's reelection campaign staff.

weapons of mass destruction Chemical, biological, or nuclear weapons that can inflict massive casualties.

whip A member of Congress who assists the majority or minority leader in the House or in the Senate in managing the party's legislative program.

whistleblower In the context of government employment, someone who "blows the whistle" (reports to authorities or the press) on gross governmental inefficiency, illegal action, or other wrongdoing.

White House Office The personal office of the president. White House Office personnel handle the president's political needs and manage the media, among other duties.

white primary A primary election in which African Americans were prohibited from voting. The practice was banned by the Supreme Court in 1944.

winner-take-all system A system in which the candidate who receives the most votes wins. In contrast, proportional systems allocate votes to multiple winners.

writ of *certiorari* An order from a higher court asking a lower court for the record of a case. *Certiorari* is pronounced sur-shee-uh-*rah*-ree.

writ of *habeas corpus* An order that requires an official to bring a specified prisoner into court and explain to the judge why the person is being held in jail.

INDEX

D

Daily Show with Jon Stewart, 226
Dealignment, 152
Death penalty, as cruel and unusual punishment, 92
Debates
    Republican presidential primary debates of 2012, 201, 202
    television, 225
Debt, public debt, 350–352
Debt-ceiling crisis, 151, 259–260
Declaration of Independence
    equality and, 13
    political culture and, 12
    pursuit of happiness, 14
    significance of, 30
    slavery and, 38, 40
Declaration of Sentiments, 106
De facto segregation, 101
Defense, Department of, 284
    foreign policymaking and, 359–360
    principle duties of, 297
Defense Advanced Research Projects Agency (DARPA), 220
Defense of Marriage Act (DOMA), 57–58, 64, 116
Deferred Action for Childhood Arrivals (DACA), 97
De Jonge v. Oregon, 77
De jure segregation, 101
Delegates
    defined, 198
    national convention, 202–203
    to nominating convention, 198
    unpledged, 198
Democracy. *See also* American democracy
    American, 11–16
    defined, 8
    direct, 8–9
    free and unfree nations, 8
    parliamentary democracy, 9
    presidential democracy, 9
    representative, 9
Democratic Party
    African American support for, 18, 149, 181
    beginning of, 148
    business interest groups and, 129
    civil rights movement and, 18
    Civil rights plank of platform in 1948 election, 149
    control of Congress, 14, 150, 151, 239, 255, 282
    current condition of, 150–152
    dealignment, 152
    donkey mascot, 156
    global warming and, 343
    Great Depression and, 149, 172
    growing partisanship, 151
    health care proposal, 340–341
    Hispanics identification with, 110
    historical perspective of political parties, 146–150
    immigration issue and Latino voters, 110
    liberals identify with, 18, 19
    national committees, 158
    national conventions, 158–159
    Populist movement and, 149

raising taxes to reduce federal deficit, 3
    realignment elections, 150
    red state vs. blue state, 150–152
    shifting political fortunes, 150–151
    size of government and, 3
    socioeconomic factors
        age, 179, 181
        educational attainment, 179
        gender and, 181
        geographic region and, 181–182
        income and, 153
        moderates, 182–183
        occupation and income level, 179
        religion and ethnicity, 181
        Solid South, 182
        tipping, 152
        trouble for, 150–151
Democratic Republicans, 147
Dennis v. United States, 83
Depression. *See* Great Depression
Derbyshire, John, 79
Détente, 363–364
Deterrence, 363
Devolution, 63–64
Dictatorship, 7–8, 9
Die, right to, 87–88
Dingell, John, Jr., 203
Dingell, John, Sr., 203
Diplomat, 270
    role of president as chief, 270
Direct democracy
    Athenian model of, 8
    ballot proposals and, 10
    defined, 8
Direct-mail campaigns, 206
Direct payments, 123
    farm bill and, 338
Direct primary, 198
Direct techniques of interest groups, 134–136
Disabilities, persons with
    civil rights of, 113–114
    reasonable accommodations, 325–326
Disability payments, federal budget spent on, 294
Discretionary spending, 257–258
    compared to entitlement programs and, 340
Discrimination. *See also* Civil rights
    affirmative action, 116–119
    of African Americans, 100–106
    of Asian Americans, 110–112
    equal employment opportunity, 116–117
    equal protection clause and, 98–99
    of gays and lesbians, 114–116
    historical perspective on, 98
    of Native Americans, 111–113
    reverse, 117
    of women, 106–109
Disney, 222
Dissenting opinions, 321
District, 158
District courts, 318–319
District of Columbia, 240
Disturbance theory, 125
Diversity of citizenship, 317
Divided government
    Bush and, 273–274

    Obama and, 44, 274, 282
    parliamentary system and, 44
Divine right theory, 7
Division of powers, 56–59
Divorce, state power and, 57
Dixiecrat Party, 163
Domestic policy, 335–352
    defined, 336
    farm bill of 2014, 338
    health care, 338–342
    policymaking process, 336–338
"Don't ask, don't tell" policy, 116
Double jeopardy, 75, 77, 91
Drinking age debate, 69
Driver's Privacy Protection Act, 88
Drug Enforcement Administration, 295
Drugs, racial disparities for incarceration rates for, 105
Dual federalism, 61
Duckworth, Tammy, 114
Due process, 75, 76–77, 91
    of law, 76
    procedural, 76
    sodomy laws and, 115
    substantive, 76–77
Dukakis, Michael, 268
Dye, Thomas R., 68

E

Earmarks, 141, 244
Earned-Income Tax Credit, 135
East Germany
    Berlin Wall, 364
    Soviet bloc, 362
Easy-money policy, 346–347
Economic policy, 345–352
    easy-money policy, 346–347
    federal tax system, 348–350
    fiscal policy, 347–348
    goals of, 345–346
    inflation and, 346
    Keynesian economics, 347–348
    monetary policy, 346–347
    public debt, 350–352
    pushing on a string, 347
    tight-money policy, 347
    unemployment and, 346
Economic Report of the President, 276
Economic status, formation of political opinion and, 172
Economic Value Added program, 308
Economy. *See also* Great Recession
    as issue in 2008-2014 elections, 179
    president's power to influence, 276–277
Education. *See also* Schools
    affirmative action at colleges, 117–119
    African American challenges, 104–106
    aid to parochial schools, 80–81
    Asian Americans, 111, 112
    Brown decision and school integration, 100–102
    busing, 101–102
    cyberbullying, 88
    evolution vs. creationism, 79–80
    federal budget spent on, 294
    formation of political opinion and, 170–171

    free speech for students, 84–85
    intelligent design, 79–80
    land-grant colleges, 66
    persons with disabilities and, 113
    prayer in schools, 78–79
    race-blind admissions, 119
    Race to the Top, 337
    school voucher programs, 80–81
    sexual assaults on college campuses, 109
    socioeconomic class and, 104–106
    Title IX of Education Amendments, 109
    voter turnout and educational attainment, 188
    voting behavior and attainment of, 179
Education, Department of, 284, 297
E-fraud, 309
Egypt
    Arab Spring, 368
    elections in, 195
    Yom Kippur War and, 370
Eighth Amendment
    bails and fines, 91
    death penalty and, 92
    text of, 75
Eisenhower, Dwight D.
    school integration and, 101
    Supreme Court appointments, 324
Elastic clause, 56
Elections. *See also* Mid-term elections; Presidential elections; Primary elections (Primaries)
    ballots used in, 194
    conducting elections and counting votes, 194
    cost of, 208–213
    general, 194
    interest groups and election process, 134–136
    landslide, 196
    nominating candidates, 196–203
    nonpartisan, 161–162
    political action committees, 135–136
    primary, 198–200
    special, 194
Electoral college
    defined, 194
    electors, 194–196
    map of, 196
    winner-take-all system, 39, 160, 195–196
Electorate
    defined, 155
    red state vs. blue state, 150–152
Electors, 194–196
Electronic media, 218
Elite theory, 127–128
Ellsworth, Oliver, 40
EMILY's List, 133
Eminent domain, 75
Employment, immigrants and impact on, 16
Enabling legislation, 301–303
Energy, Department of, 284
    foreign policymaking and, 359
    principle duties of, 297

Energy policy, 342–345
    BP oil spill, 345
    expanded supplied of oil and
        natural gas, 343–344
    fracking, 344
    fuel efficiency standards, 342
    global warming and, 342–343
    greenhouse gas emissions and,
        343
    nuclear energy, 345
    offshore drilling and BP oil
        spill, 344–345
    price of, 342
    problem of imported oil, 342
    renewable energy, 345
Engel v. Vitale, 78–79
England. *See also* Great Britain;
    United Kingdom
    Bill of Rights, 11
    Irish Republic Army and peace
        process, 366
    limited government, 11
    Magna Carta, 11
    terrorist bombings in London's
        transportation system, 365
English Bill of Rights, 11
Entitlement programs
    characteristics of, 340
    defined, 257, 340
    liberals vs. conservatives views
        of, 340
    Obamacare as, 340
    Social Security and
        unemployment
        compensation, 340
Entrepreneurial theory, 125
Enumerated powers, 56
Environmental interest groups, 133
Environmental Protection Agency
    (EPA), 64, 299, 303
Equal employment opportunity,
    116–117
Equal Employment Opportunity
    Commission, 299
Equality
    defined, 13
    as political value, 13–14
    in voting, 12
Equal Pay Act, 108
Equal protection clause
    affirmative action and, 117, 118
    defined, 98
    gays and lesbians, 115
    intermediate scrutiny standard,
        99
    ordinary scrutiny, 99
    original intention of, 100
    racial gerrymandering, 242
    rational basis test, 99
    separate-but-equal doctrine,
        100
    strict scrutiny standard, 98
Equal Rights Amendment, 47, 106
Espionage Act, 82
Establishment clause, 77–80
Ethiopia, 52
Ethnicity
    distribution of US population
        by, 15–16
    voting behavior and, 181
Euro, 375
European Data Protection
    Directive, 89
European Union (EU)
    as confederal system, 53

European Data Protection
    Directive, 89
    future of euro, 375
Euthanasia, 87
Everson v. Board of Education, 77
Evolution
    vs. creationism, 79–80
    vs. intelligent design, 79–80
Exacting scrutiny, 99
Executive agreements, 359
    defined, 279
    presidential use of, 279
Executive branch. *See also*
    President of United States
    authority of, and Constitution,
        38
    bureaucracy as part of, 292
    checks and balances and, 43
    organization of, 283–286
    separation of powers, 42–43
Executive departments, 284. *See
    also* specific departments
    list of each with duties, 297
    organization of, 295, 296
    president's cabinet, 284
    types of structures, 295
Executive Office of the President,
    284–286
Executive orders, 278
Executive privilege, 282–283
Export taxes, 37, 57
Ex post facto law, 74
Expressed powers, 56, 60
Expression, freedom of, 82–85. *See
    also* Speech, freedom of

F

Facebook, 207, 219, 230
FactCheck, 229
Faction, 39, 133
Fairness doctrine, talk radio and,
    227
False Claims Act, 306
Family, formation of political
    opinion and, 170
Fannie Mae (Federal National
    Mortgage Association), 300
Farm bill, 338
Farm Bureau, 129
Farm subsidies, 123, 130
Faubus, Orval, 101
Federal Assault Weapons Ban, 73
Federal budget
    appropriation, 257
    authorization, 257
    budget deficit (*See* Public debt)
    budgeting process, 258–260
    by category, 294
    cost of maintaining government,
        293–294
    debt ceiling issue, 259–260
    defense spending, 294
    earmarks, 244
    entitlement programs, 257
    health care spending, 338–339,
        340
    pork barrel spending, 244
    projections of, 259
    public debt and, 350–352
    social program spending, 294
    steps in process, 257–260
Federal budget deficit. *See* Public
    debt

Federal Bureau of Investigation
    (FBI), National Security Letters,
    89–90
Federal Communications
    Commission (FCC), 233
    creation of, 298
    fairness doctrine, 227
    principle duties of, 299
Federal court system, 318–322
    appellate courts (courts of
        appeal), 319–320
    assessing role of, 330–331
    court procedures, 318
    diversity of citizenship, 317
    ideology and, 327–330
    judicial appointments, 322–325
    jurisdiction, 317
    organization of, 318
    as policymakers, 325–330
    senatorial courtesy, 324
    trial courts (U.S. district
        courts), 318–319
    U.S. Supreme Court, 320–322
Federal Deposit Insurance
    Corporation, principal duties
    of, 300
Federal Election Campaign Act,
    208–209
Federal Election Commission
    (FEC), 209, 233
*Federal Election Commission v.
    Wisconsin Right to Life Inc.,*
    210, 211
Federal government. *See also*
    Federalism
    bankruptcy and private
        corporations, 300
    federal spending as anticyclical,
        67
    organization of, 295–300
        executive departments, 295
        government corporations,
            298–300
        independent executive
            agencies, 295–296, 298,
            299
        independent regulatory
            agencies, 298, 299
        overview of, 296
    size of, 3
    term of, 53
Federal grants
    block, 67
    categorical, 66–67
    to control states, 67–68
    cross-cutting requirements, 67
    land-grant colleges and, 66
    minimum drinking age and, 69
    No Child Left Behind and, 68
    state budgets and, 67
Federal Home Loan Mortgage
    Corporation (Freddie Mac), 300
Federalism, 52–70. *See also*
    National government
    advantages of, 53–54
    alternatives to, 53
    Canadian vs. American, 55
    characteristics of, 52–53
    compared to unitary system, 53
    competitive, 68–69
    concurrent powers, 58
    confederal system, 53
    cooperative, 61–63
    defined, 52
    disadvantages of, 54–55

division of powers, 56–59
dual, 61
federal mandate, 64
fiscal side of, 66–69
    competitive federalism, 68–69
    cost of federal mandates, 68
    federal grants, 66–68
    fiscal federalism, 66
George W. Bush Administration
    and, 64
horizontal, 57
interstate relations, 57–58
minimum drinking age and, 69
nation-centered, 63
picket-fence federalism, 62
politics of, 64–65
preemption, 63
as principle of Constitution, 42
state-centered, 63
struggle for supremacy and,
    59–63
supremacy clause, 58–59
supremacy of national
    government
    Civil War, 60–61
    cooperative federalism, 61–63
    dual federalism, 61
    early Supreme Court
        decisions, 59–60
    struggle for, 59–63
today, 63–65
    economic crisis and, 67
    health-care reform, 65
    immigration, 65
    new federalism, 63–64
    shifting boundary between
        federal and state
        authority, 64–65
    Supreme Court and, 64
*Federalist Gazette of the United
    States,* 224
Federalist Papers, 39, 326
Federalists, 52, 197–198
    defined, 38
    as first political party, 146–147
    ratification of Constitution,
        38–39
Federal lands, 56–57
Federal mandates
    cost of, 68
    defined, 64
    examples of, 66
Federal National Mortgage
    Association (Fannie Mae), 300
Federal Open Market Committee
    (FOMC), 346
Federal question, 317
Federal Register, 308
Federal Regulation of Lobbying
    Act, 139
Federal Reserve System (Fed)
    easy-money policy, 346–347
    overview of, 346–347
    principal duties of, 299
    tight-money policy, 347
Federal system. *See also* Federalism
    defined, 42, 52
    other countries that have, 52
    of United States, 52–55
Federal tax system, 348–350
    action-reaction syndrome,
        348–350
    as progressive system, 348
    taxes under George W. Bush,
        349

election support, 134–136
  lobbying, 134–136
formation of, 125–127
  defending group's interest,
    125
  disturbance theory, 125
  entrepreneurial theory, 125
  free rider problem, 126–127
  importance of leaders, 125
  incentives to join group,
    125–126
  increase in government and,
    125
free rider problem, 126–127
functions of, 127–128
incentives to join, 125–126
indirect techniques of
  demonstrations, 138
  going to court, 137–138
  issues ads and 527s, 137
  mobilizing constituents, 137
  rating systems, 136
  shaping public opinion, 136
influence on policy, 134–138
iron triangle, 304–305
issue campaigns, 210
majoritarianism and elite
  theory, 127–128
percentage of Americans
  belonging to, 126
pluralist theory and, 127
policymaking vs. special
  interests, 338
political action committees
  (PACs), 135–136
vs. political parties, 128
professional lobbyists, 138–139
public good and, 126
regulation of, 139–141
tax breaks and, 127
today's lobbying establishment,
  138–141
types of, 128–133
  agricultural, 129–130
  business, 128–130
  consumer, 132
  identity, 132–133
  ideological, 133
  labor, 130–132
  professional, 131–132
  public-interest, 132
Intergovernmental Panel on
  Climate Change (IPCC), 343
Interior, Department of, 284, 295,
  297
Intermediate-scrutiny standard, 99
International Atomic Energy
  Agency (IAEA), 372
International Brotherhood of
  Electrical Workers, 130
International Trade, Court of, 319
Internet
  blogs, 231–232
  censorship of, 218, 220
  citizen journalism, 232
  creation of, 220
  First Amendment and, 219
  net neutrality, 233
  news organizations online,
    230–231
  newspaper circulation decline
    and, 217, 218
  obscenity and, 84
  online advertising revenues, 231
  podcasting news, 232

political campaigns and,
  232–234
  candidates' 24/7 exposure,
    234
  controlling netroots, 234
  fundraising on, 206
  microtargeting, 206–207
  Obama's campaign, 207
  online fundraising, 234
  rise of Internet campaign, 234
  support for local organizing,
    207
  targeting supporters, 207
privacy issues, 220
public opinion polls and, 174
revenge porn, 88–89
usage of, by consumers, 230
Internet survey, 174
Internment camps, 111
Inter-Services Intelligence (ISI),
  368
Interstate commerce, 61
  defined, 37
  regulated by Congress, 37,
    56, 63
  supremacy of national
    government and, 60
Interstate Commerce Commission
  (ICC), 298
Interstate compacts, 58
Interventionism, 361
Intolerable Acts, 29
Iran
  Council of Guardians, 10–11
  ISIS attacks on, 369
  Islamic government in, 10–11
  nuclear weapons and emerging
    threat of, 373–374
  as oil exporter, 342
  religious intolerance in, 78
  as theocracy, 10–11
Iraq
  elections in, 195
  First Gulf War, 367
  ISIS and air strikes against,
    265, 281
  Kuwait invaded by, 367
  as oil exporter, 342
  rise and fall of insurgency,
    367–368
  weapons of mass destruction
    thought to be in, 367
  WMD inspections, 367
Iraq War
  authorization of armed forces
    in, 280
  federal budget spent on, 294
  First Gulf War background, 367
  invasion of, 367
  Obama and, 368
  President Bush and, 280, 367
  public opinion of, 14
  rise and fall of insurgency,
    367–368
  withdrawal, 368
Ireland, Irish Republic Army and
  peace process England, 366
Irish Republican Army, 366
Iron curtain, 362
Iron triangle, 250
  policymaking and, 337
ISIS (Islamic State in Iraq and
  Greater Syria)
  air strikes against, 265, 281, 369
  attacks on Iraq, 369

rise of, 369
Islam, government based on, 10–11
Isolationism, 361
Israel, 366
  conflict with Palestinians,
    369–372
  Gaza Strip War, 371–372
  negotiations with, 371–372
  as unitary system, 52
Issue ads, 137
  defined, 224
  effectiveness of, 224
  influence of, 137
  limits for, 137
Issue campaigns, 210
Issue identification, 336–337
Issue networks, 250, 305–306
Issue-oriented parties, 163
Italy, 362

J

Jackson, Andrew, 25, 61, 198, 275
  Democrats and, 148
  election of 1828, 148
  kitchen cabinet, 284
Jamestown colony, 26
Jamieson, Kathleen Hall, 228–229
Japan
  aging population in, 16
  as debt holder of U.S. public
    debt, 351
  nuclear crisis in, 345
  Pearl Harbor attacked by, 362
  as unitary system, 52
World War II, 362
Japanese Americans, 111
Jay, John, 38
Jefferson, Thomas, 25, 31, 82, 198,
  224, 275, 330
  Constitutional Convention
    and, 35
  Declaration of Independence,
    30
  election of 1796, 147
  election of 1800, 147
  election of 1804, 147
  establishment clause, 77–78
  on political parties, 146
  on slavery, 40
  wall of separation, 78
Jeffersonian Republicans, 147, 197
Jeffords, James M., 330
Jews, voting behavior, 181
Jim Crow laws, 100
Job Corps, 62
John, King (England), 11
Johnson, Andrew
  impeachment, 255
  vetoes by, 273
Johnson, Lyndon B., 17, 62, 197,
  266, 273
  affirmative action, 116
  block grants, 67
  daisy girl ad, 224
  election of 1964, 150
  Great Society, 66
  legislative success of, 278
  Medicare and Medicaid, 17
Joint Chiefs of Staff, 359–360
Jordan, 370
JPMorgan Chase & Co., 129
Judicial activism, 326–327

Judicial branch
  authority of, and Constitution,
    38
  checks and balances and, 43
  judicial review, 43
  separation of powers, 42–43
Judicial restraint, 326–327, 330
Judicial review, 43, 60
  defined, 326
  power of, 326
Judiciary, 313–331
  broad language and, 325–326
  checks and balances, 326
  defined, 314
  electing judges, 313
  federal court system, 318–322
  federal judicial appointments,
    322–325
  ideology and, 327–330
  jurisdiction, 317
  origins and sources of American
    law, 314–318
  power of judicial review, 326
  standing to sue, 317–318
Jurisdiction, 317
Jury trials, 91
  common law tradition, 314–315
  impartial jury, 77
  right to, 75
Justice, Department of, 284, 295,
  297
Justiciable controversy, 317–318

K

Kagan, Elena, 107, 325, 327
Kennedy, Anthony, 327, 328
Kennedy, John F., 267, 268
  Cuban missile crisis, 363
  election of 1960, television
    debates, 206, 225
Kennedy, Patrick J., 203
Kerry, John, 268
Keynes, John Maynard, 347–348
Keynesian economics, 347–348
Kim Jong Il, 373
Kim Jong Un, 8, 372, 373
King, Martin Luther, Jr., 102, 103
King Caucus, 198
King's court, 314
Kitchen cabinet, 284
Klopfer v. North Carolina, 77
Klu Klux Klan, 100, 101
Koch, Charles, 156, 211
Koch, David, 156, 211, 213
Koch, Julia, 213
Korean War, 280, 363
Kosovo, 364
Krugman, Paul, 182
Kurds, 367
Kuwait, invaded by Iraq, 367

L

Labor, Department of, 284, 297
Laborers Union, 130
Labor force, 130
Labor interest groups, 130–132
Labor unions. *See* Unions
Land-grant colleges, 66
Landon, Alfred, 173
Landslide election, 196, 197

Sexual harassment, 108–109
Sharon, Ariel, 371
Shays, Daniel, 34
Shays' Rebellion, 34
Shelby, Richard, 251
Shelby County v. Holder, 65, 104
Sherman, Roger, 36
Shiite Muslims, 367
Sierra Club
    501(c)4 group, 137
    litigation used by, 137
Signing statements, 278–279
    defined, 278
    by George W. Bush, 279
Silver, Nate, 173
Single-member district, 160–161
Sit-ins, 102–103
Sixteenth Amendment, 56
Sixth Amendment, 75, 91
Skype, 174
Slander, 83
Slaves/slavery
    Civil War and, 60–61
    Constitutional Convention and, 36–37
    Constitution of United States and, 36–37
    Declaration of Independence, 38, 40
    importation of, 37
    as presidential election issue, 148–149
    Republican Party and, 148–149
    three-fifths compromise, 36–37
Small Business Administration, 299
Smith, Al, 268
Smith Act, 83
Smith v. Allwright, 186
SNAP, 135
    farm bill and, 338
Snowden, Edward, 90, 307
Social conflict, 4
Social contract, 11–12
Socialism, 19
Socialist Labor Party, 163
Socialist Party, 162
Social Security
    AARP preserving benefits for, 125
    as entitlement program, 340
    federal budget spent on, 294
    size of government and, 3
Social Security Administration (SSA), 299
Socioeconomic factors, voting behavior and, 179–182
Sodomy laws, 114–115
Soft money, 137, 209–210
Solidarity, 157
Solidary incentive, 126
Solid South, 182
Somalia, 364
Soros, George, 211–212
Sotomayor, Sonia, 107, 325, 327
Sound bite, 222
Southern Christian Leadership Conference (SCLC), 102, 132
Sovereignty
    Articles of Confederation, 32
    popular, 41
Soviet bloc, 362
Soviet Union. *See also* Russia
    arms race and deterrence, 363
    breakup of, 357
    Cold War and, 362–364

Cuban missile crisis, 363
détente and arms control, 363–364
dissolution of, 364
Soviet bloc, 362
Strategic Arms Limitation Treaty (SALT I), 363
World War II, 362
Spain
    Basque separatists terrorism in, 366
    constitutional monarchy in, 7
    Madrid commuter train bombing, 366
    Spanish-American War and, 361
Spanish-American War, 361
Speaker of the House, 107, 247
    presidential succession and, 287
Speaker *pro tempore* of the House, 247
Special districts, number of, in U.S., 54
Special election, 194
Special interest groups. *See* Interest groups
Speech
    commercial, 83
    libel and slander, 83
    obscene, 83–84
    seditious, 82–83
    symbolic, 82
    unprotected, 83–84
Speech, freedom of, 13, 75, 77, 82–85
    early restrictions on expression, 82
    libel and slander, 83
    limited protection for commercial speech, 83
    obscenity, 83–84
    for students, 84–85
    symbolic speech, 82
    unprotected speech, 83–84
Speechnow v. FEC, 211
Spin, 226
Spin doctors, 226
Splinter party, 163
Stalin, Joseph, 7
Stamp Act, 28
Standard operating procedures, 292
Standing committees, 249, 250
Standing to sue, 317–318
Stanton, Elizabeth Cady, 106
Stare decisis, 314–315, 330
State, Department of, 284
    foreign policymaking and, 359
    original size of, 292
    principle duties of, 297
State-centered federalism, 63
State court system
    court procedures, 318
    jurisdiction, 317
    supreme court, 317
State government. *See also* States
    affirmative action, 118–119
    authority of, and shifting boundary with federal authority, 64–65
    cooperative federalism, 61–63
    devolution, 64
    division of powers, 57
    dual federalism, 61
    federal grants to control, 67–68
    federal revenue for state spending, 67

Hispanics holding office in, 110
interstate relations, 57–58
Native American tribal governments and, 56
new federalism, 63
number of, in U.S., 54
powers of, 53
    concurrent powers, 58
    police power, 57
    prohibited, 57
privatization, 308
size of bureaucracy, 293
state spending as procyclical, 67
supremacy clause, 58–59
women holding office in, 107–108
State party organization, 157
States. *See also* State government
    competitive federalism, 68–69
    confederation of, 32–33
    constitutions of, 31
    electoral college, 194, 196
    federalism, 42
    general fund budget, 67
    Medicaid spending by, 339
    primaries and role in, 199
    rights of, and Civil War, 60–61
    secession of, 51
    transformed from colonies, 31
States' Rights Party, 163
Statistical modeling, public opinion polls and, 174–175
Statistical noise, 174
Statutory law, 315–316
Stewart, Jon, 156, 219
Stimulus package
    federal grants to states, 67
    government employment and, 293
    Medicaid payments and, 339
    Obama's ability to get passed, 277
    Race to the Top, 337
    size of, to have real impact, 348
Stone, Lucy, 106
Stonewall Inn incident, 114
Strategic Arms Limitation Treaty (SALT I), 363
Straw polls, 173
Strict construction, 328–329
Strict scrutiny standard, 98, 117
Student Nonviolent Coordinating Committee (SNCC), 102, 132
Subcommittees, 249–250
Subsidies, agricultural, 123, 130
Substantive due process, 76–77
Succession Act, 287
Sudan, 364
Suffrage, 106, 183–184
Sugar Act, 28
Suicide, assisted, 87–88
Sullivan, Thomas P., 93
Sunlight Foundation, 223
Sunni Muslims, 367
Sunshine laws, 308
Super PACs, 136, 208, 211–212
    myth of independence, 211
    role of individual donor, 211–212
Super Tuesday, 201
Supplemental Nutrition Assistance Program (SNAP), 135, 294
Supremacy clause, 58–59, 60, 63
Supreme court, state, 317
Supreme Court of the United States, 320–322

abortion, 86–87
affirmative action, 117–118
aid to parochial schools, 80
assessing role of, 330–331
bad tendency rule, 83
Bill of Rights, 75–76
busing, 101–102
campaign financing, 209, 210–211
cases that reach, 320–321
checks and balances and, 43
clear and present danger test, 83
commerce clause, 62–63, 64
commercial speech, 83
confirmation process, 256
congressional districts, 241, 242–243
cooperative federalism, 62–63
court-packing, 62
establishment clause, 78
establishment of, 38
evolution in schools, 79
gay rights, 328, 329–330
gender-based laws and intermediate-scrutiny standard, 99
grandfather clause, 185
healthcare reform, 65, 320–321, 328, 341
ideology and, 327–330
    original intent vs. modernism, 329–330
    partisan ideology and, 327–330
    Roberts Court, 327
    strict vs. broad construction, 328–329
immigration, 65
imminent lawless action test, 83
incorporating Bill of Rights into Fourteenth Amendment, 76–77
individual mandate, 328
judicial review, 60, 326
justices of
    background of, 323
    confirmation or rejection, 324–325
    judicial activism vs. restraint, 326–327
    nomination process, 323–324
    women, 107
legislation from the bench, 330, 331
line-item veto, 274
media and First Amendment, 219
Miranda warning, 92–93
Native American treaty rights, 113
new federalism and, 64
number of cases heard by, 321
Obamacare, 65
obscene speech, 84
prayer in schools, 78–79
prior restraint, 85
privacy rights, 325
public opinion of, 331
racial gerrymandering, 242–243
religious beliefs vs. practice, 81
right to bear arms, 5
right to die, 87–88
right to freedom of association, 199

LEARNING OUTCOMES

1–1

Explain what is meant by the terms *politics* and *government*.
1 Resolving conflicts over how the society should use its scarce resources and who should receive various benefits is the essence of **politics. 2 Government**—the individuals and institutions that make society's rules and possess the **power** and **authority** to enforce those rules—resolves **social conflicts,** provides **public services,** and defends the nation and its culture against attacks by other nations.

1–2

Identify the various types of government systems. 3 Authoritarian rule by an individual is called **autocracy. Monarchs** are hereditary autocrats. A **dictatorship** is authoritarian rule by an individual or group unsupported by tradition. **4 Democracy** is a system of government in which the people have ultimate political authority. One modern institution with some of the characteristics of **direct democracy** is the ballot proposal. In a **representative democracy,** the will of the people is expressed through groups of individuals elected by the people to act as their representatives. **5** Other forms of government include aristocracy and plutocracy. In a theocracy, the government rules according to religious precepts.

1–3

Summarize some of the basic principles of American democracy and basic American political values. 6 In writing the U.S. Constitution, the framers incorporated two basic principles of government that had evolved in England: **limited government** and representative government. Our democracy resulted from a type of **social contract** among early Americans to create and abide by a set of governing rules. **7** American democracy is based on several principles, including equality in voting, individual freedom, equal protection of the law, majority rule and minority rights, and collective voluntary consent to be governed. **8** The rights to **liberty, equality,** and property are fundamental political values shared by most Americans. Differences among Americans in interpreting these values underlie the division between the Democratic and Republican parties, as well as the **Tea Party movement.**

1–4

Define common American ideological positions, such as "conservatism" and "liberalism." 9 The emergence of the **conservative movement** in the 1950s and 1960s was essential to the development of modern American **conservatism.** Conservatives believe that individuals and families should take responsibility for their own economic circumstances, and they place a high value on the principle of order, on family values, and on patriotism. Religious conservatives believe that government should reflect traditional religious values. While tracing its roots to the New Deal programs of Franklin D. Roosevelt, American **liberalism** took its modern form in the 1960s. Support for minority rights of all

KEY TERMS

1–1

authority The ability to legitimately exercise power, such as the power to make and enforce laws.

government The individuals and institutions that make society's rules and possess the power and authority to enforce those rules.

institution An ongoing organization that performs certain functions for society.

politics The process of resolving conflicts over how society should use its scarce resources and who should receive various benefits, such as public health care and public higher education.

power The ability to influence the behavior of others, usually through the use of force, persuasion, or rewards.

public services Essential services that individuals cannot provide for themselves, such as building and maintaining roads, establishing welfare programs, operating public schools, and preserving national parks.

social conflict Disagreements among people in a society over what the society's priorities should be.

1–2

autocracy A form of government in which the power and authority of the government are in the hands of a single person.

democracy A system of government in which the people have ultimate political authority. The word is derived from the Greek *demos* ("the people") and *kratia* ("rule").

dictatorship A form of government in which absolute power is exercised by an individual or group whose power is not supported by tradition.

direct democracy A system of government in which political decisions are made by the people themselves rather than by elected representatives. This form of government was practiced in some parts of ancient Greece.

divine right theory The theory that a monarch's right to rule was derived directly from God rather than from the consent of the people.

monarchy A form of autocracy in which a king, queen, emperor, empress, tsar, or tsarina is the highest authority in the government. Monarchs usually obtain their power through inheritance.

parliament The name of the national legislative body in countries governed by a parliamentary system, such as Britain and Canada.

representative democracy A form of democracy in which the will of the majority is expressed through groups of individuals elected by the people to act as their representatives.

republic Essentially, a representative democracy in which there is no king or queen and the people are sovereign.

1–3

capitalism An economic system based on the private ownership of wealth-producing property, free markets, and freedom of contract. The privately owned corporation is the preeminent capitalist institution.

equality A concept that holds, at a minimum, that all people are entitled to equal protection under the law.

liberty The freedom of individuals to believe, act, and express themselves as they choose so long as doing so does not infringe on the rights of other individuals in the society.

limited government A form of government based on the principle that the powers of government should be clearly limited either through a written document or through wide public understanding. It is characterized by institutional checks to ensure that government serves public rather than private interests.

natural rights Rights that are not bestowed by governments but are inherent within every man, woman, and child by virtue of the fact that he or she is a human being.

political culture The set of ideas, values, and attitudes about government and the political process held by a community or a nation.

social contract A voluntary agreement among individuals to create a government and to give that government adequate power to secure the mutual protection and welfare of all individuals.

Tea Party movement A grassroots conservative movement that arose in 2009 after Barack Obama became president. The movement opposes big government and current levels of taxation, and also rejects political compromise.

1–4

conservatism A set of political beliefs that include a limited role for the national government in helping individuals and in the economic affairs of the nation, as well as support for traditional values and lifestyles.

kinds became an important part of liberal ideology. Liberals, or **progressives,** argue that big government is a necessary tool for promoting the common welfare, and strongly favor the separation of church and state. Liberals identify with the Democratic Party, and conservatives typically identify themselves as Republicans. People whose views fall in the middle are generally called **moderates. 10** Many Americans have opinions that do not fit neatly under the liberal or conservative label. Some Americans, for example, are both economic progressives and social conservatives. To the left of liberalism on the ideological spectrum lies **socialism. Libertarians,** on the right, oppose almost all forms of government regulation.

INTERNET RESOURCES

www.usa.gov

hosted.ap.org

www.pewresearch.org

www.realclearpolitics.com

www.vox.com

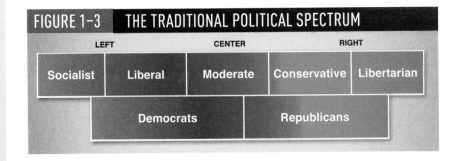

FIGURE 1–3	THE TRADITIONAL POLITICAL SPECTRUM

LEFT		CENTER		RIGHT
Socialist	Liberal	Moderate	Conservative	Libertarian
	Democrats		Republicans	

conservative movement An ideological movement that arose in the 1950s and 1960s and continues to shape conservative beliefs.

ideology Generally, a system of political ideas that are rooted in religious or philosophical beliefs concerning human nature, society, and government.

liberalism A set of political beliefs that include the advocacy of active government, including government intervention to improve the welfare of individuals and to protect civil rights.

libertarianism The belief that government should do as little as possible, not only in the economic sphere, but also in regulating morality and personal behavior.

moderates Persons whose views fall in the middle of the political spectrum.

progressivism An alternative, more popular term for the set of political beliefs also known as liberalism.

socialism A political ideology that lies to the left of liberalism on the traditional political spectrum. Socialists are scarce in the United States but common in many other countries.

LEARNING OUTCOMES

2–1

Point out some of the influences on the American political tradition in the colonial years. 1 American politics owes much to the English political tradition, but the colonists derived most of their understanding about limited government and representative government from their own experiences. In 1620, the Pilgrims drew up the **Mayflower Compact,** in which they set up a government and promised to obey its laws. Other colonies, in turn, established fundamental governing rules and principles that were later expressed in the U.S. Constitution and **Bill of Rights. 2** Colonial leaders became familiar with the practical problems of governing. They learned how to build coalitions among groups with diverse interests and how to make compromises.

2–2

Explain why the American colonies rebelled against Britain. 3 After the Seven Years' War (1756–1763), the British government decided to pay its war debts and to finance the defense of its North American empire by imposing taxes on the colonists. **4** The colonists protested, and Britain responded with even more repressive measures. The colonists established the **First Continental Congress** and sent a petition to King George III to explain their grievances. The congress also called for a continued boycott of British goods and required each colony to establish an army. **5** Soon after British soldiers fought colonial citizen soldiers in the first battles of the American Revolution in 1775, delegates gathered for the **Second Continental Congress,** which assumed the powers of a central government. The congress adopted the Declaration of Independence on July 4, 1776.

2–3

Describe the structure of government established by the Articles of Confederation and some of the strengths and weaknesses of the Articles. 6 The **Articles of Confederation** established the Congress of the Confederation as the central governing body. It was a unicameral assembly in which each state had one vote. Congress had several powers, including the power to declare war, to enter into treaties, and to settle disputes among the states under certain circumstances. Nevertheless, the central government created by the Articles was weak. Congress could not force the states to meet military quotas. It could not regulate commerce between the states or with other nations. There was no national judicial system and no executive branch. **7** Disruptions such as **Shays' Rebellion** persuaded American leaders that a true national government had to be created. Congress called on the states to send delegates to a meeting in Philadelphia in 1787 that became the **Constitutional Convention.**

KEY TERMS

2–1

Bill of Rights The first ten amendments to the U.S. Constitution. They list the freedoms—such as the freedoms of speech, press, and religion—that a citizen enjoys and that cannot be infringed on by the government.

Mayflower Compact A document drawn up by Pilgrim leaders in 1620 on the ship *Mayflower.* The document stated that laws were to be made for the general good of the people.

2–2

First Continental Congress A gathering of delegates from twelve of the thirteen colonies, held in 1774 to protest the Coercive Acts.

Second Continental Congress The congress of the colonies that met in 1775 to assume the powers of a central government and to establish an army.

unicameral legislature A legislature with only one chamber.

2–3

Articles of Confederation The nation's first national constitution, which established a national form of government following the American Revolution. The Articles provided for a confederal form of government in which the central government had few powers.

confederation A league of independent states that are united only for the purpose of achieving common goals.

Constitutional Convention The convention of delegates from the states that was held in Philadelphia in 1787 for the purpose of amending the Articles of Confederation. In fact, the delegates wrote a new constitution (the U.S. Constitution) that established a federal form of government.

Shays' Rebellion A rebellion of angry farmers in western Massachusetts in 1786, led by former Revolutionary War captain Daniel Shays.

2–4

Anti-Federalists A political group that opposed the adoption of the Constitution.

bicameral legislature A legislature made up of two chambers, or parts.

faction A group of persons forming a cohesive minority.

CHAPTER REVIEW 2

Federalists A political group, led by Alexander Hamilton and John Adams, that supported the adoption of the Constitution and the creation of a federal form of government.

Great Compromise A plan for a bicameral legislature in which one chamber would be based on population and the other chamber would represent each state equally. Also known as the Connecticut Compromise.

interstate commerce Trade that involves more than one state.

three-fifths compromise A compromise reached during the Constitutional Convention by which three-fifths of all slaves were to be counted for purposes of representation in the House of Representatives.

tyranny The arbitrary or unrestrained exercise of power by an oppressive individual or government.

2–5

checks and balances A major principle of American government in which each of the three branches is given the means to check (to restrain or balance) the actions of the others.

commerce clause The clause in Article I, Section 8, of the Constitution that gives Congress the power to regulate interstate commerce (commerce involving more than one state).

federal system A form of government that provides for a division of powers between a central government and several regional governments.

Madisonian Model The model of government devised by James Madison, in which the powers of the government are separated into three branches: legislative, executive, and judicial.

rule of law A basic principle of government that requires those who govern to act in accordance with established law.

separation of powers The principle of dividing governmental powers among the legislative, the executive, and the judicial branches of government.

veto power A constitutional power that enables the chief executive (president or governor) to reject legislation and return it to the legislature with reasons for the rejection. This either prevents or delays the bill from becoming law.

2–4

List some of the major compromises made by the delegates at the Constitutional Convention, and discuss the Federalist and Anti-Federalist positions on ratifying the Constitution. 8 Delegates resolved the small-state/large-state controversy over representation in Congress with the **Great Compromise,** which established a **bicameral legislature.** The **three-fifths compromise** settled a deadlock on how slaves would be counted to determine representation in the House of Representatives. The delegates also agreed that Congress could prohibit the importation of slaves beginning in 1808. The South agreed to let Congress have the power to regulate both **interstate commerce** and commerce with other nations in exchange for a ban on export taxes. **9 Federalists** favored a strong central government and the new Constitution. **Anti-Federalists** argued that the Constitution would lead to aristocratic **tyranny** or an overly powerful central government that would limit personal freedom. To gain support for ratification, the Federalists promised to add a bill of rights to the Constitution.

2–5

Summarize the Constitution's major principles of government, and describe how the Constitution can be amended. 10 The Constitution incorporated the principles of limited government, popular sovereignty, and the **rule of law.** A **federal system,** in which the national government shares powers with the state governments, was established. **Separation of powers** and a system of **checks and balances** ensure that no one branch—legislative, executive, or judicial—can exercise exclusive control. **11** An amendment to the Constitution can be proposed either by a two-thirds vote in each chamber of Congress or by a national convention called at the request of two-thirds of the state legislatures. Ratification of an amendment requires either approval by three-fourths of the state legislatures or by three-fourths of the states in special conventions.

INTERNET RESOURCES

www.law.cornell.edu/constitution

constitutioncenter.org

www.thisnation.com/library/madison

www.findlaw.com/casecode

www.servat.unibe.ch/icl

uselectionatlas.org

LEARNING OUTCOMES

3–1

Explain what federalism means, how federalism differs from other systems of government, and why it exists in the United States. 1 Government powers in a federal system are divided between a national government and subnational governments. The powers of both levels of government are specified and limited. Alternatives to **federalism** include a **unitary system,** in which subnational governments exercise only those powers given to them by the national government, and a **confederal system,** in which the national government exists and operates only at the direction of the subnational governments. **2** The Articles of Confederation failed because they did not allow for a sufficiently strong central government, but the framers of the Constitution were fearful of a too-powerful central government. The appeal of federalism was that it retained state powers and local traditions while establishing a strong national government capable of handling common problems.

3–2

Indicate how the Constitution divides governing powers in our federal system. 3 The national government possesses three types of powers: **expressed, implied,** and **inherent.** The Constitution expressly enumerates twenty-seven powers that Congress may exercise, while the **"necessary and proper" clause** is the basis for implied powers. The national government also enjoys certain inherent powers—powers that governments must have simply to ensure the nation's integrity and survival. In addition, the Constitution expressly prohibits the national government from undertaking certain actions. **4** The Tenth Amendment states that powers that are not delegated to the national government by the Constitution, or prohibited to the states, are "reserved" to the states or to the people. In principle, each state has **police powers**—the ability to regulate its internal affairs and to enact whatever laws are necessary to protect the health, safety, welfare, and morals of its people. **5** The Constitution also contains provisions, such as the full faith and credit clause, relating to interstate relations. **Concurrent powers** can be exercised by both the state governments and the federal government. The **supremacy clause** asserts that national government power takes precedence over any conflicting state action.

3–3

Summarize the evolution of federal–state relationships in the United States over time. 6 The Supreme Court, in *McCulloch v. Maryland* (1819) and *Gibbons v. Ogden* (1824), played a key role in establishing the constitutional foundations for the supremacy of the national government. An increase in the political power of the national government was also a result of the Civil War. **7** The relationship between the states and the national government has evolved through several stages. The model of **dual federalism,** which prevailed after the Civil War until the 1930s, assumes that the states and the national government are more or less equals, with each level of

KEY TERMS

3–1

confederal system A league of independent sovereign states, joined together by a central government that has only limited powers over them.

federalism A system of shared sovereignty between two levels of government—one national and one subnational—occupying the same geographic region.

unitary system A centralized governmental system in which local or subdivisional governments exercise only those powers given to them by the central government.

3–2

concurrent powers Powers held by both the federal and the state governments in a federal system.

division of powers A basic principle of federalism established by the U.S. Constitution, by which powers are divided between the national and state governments.

expressed powers Constitutional or statutory powers that are expressly provided for by the U.S. Constitution; also called *enumerated powers.*

implied powers The powers of the federal government that are implied by the expressed powers in the Constitution, particularly in Article I, Section 8.

inherent powers The powers of the national government that, although not always expressly granted by the Constitution, are necessary to ensure the nation's integrity and survival as a political unit.

necessary and proper clause Article I, Section 8, Clause 18, of the Constitution, which gives Congress the power to make all laws "necessary and proper" for the federal government to carry out its responsibilities; also called the *elastic clause.*

police powers The powers of a government body that enable it to create laws for the protection of the health, safety, welfare, and morals of the people. In the United States, most police powers are reserved to the states.

supremacy clause Article VI, Clause 2, of the Constitution, which makes the Constitution and federal laws superior to all conflicting state and local laws.

CHAPTER REVIEW 3

3-3

cooperative federalism A model of federalism in which the states and the federal government cooperate in solving problems.

dual federalism A system of government in which the federal and the state governments maintain diverse but sovereign powers.

New Deal The policies ushered in by the Roosevelt administration in 1933 in an attempt to bring the United States out of the Great Depression.

picket-fence federalism A model of federalism in which specific policies and programs are administered by all levels of government—national, state, and local.

preemption A doctrine rooted in the supremacy clause of the Constitution that provides that national laws or regulations governing a certain area take precedence over conflicting state laws or regulations governing that same area.

secession The act of formally withdrawing from membership in an alliance; the withdrawal of a state from the federal Union.

3-4

devolution The surrender or transfer of powers to local authorities by a central government.

federal mandate A requirement in federal legislation that forces states and municipalities to comply with certain rules.

new federalism A plan to limit the federal government's role in regulating state governments and to give the states increased power in deciding how they should spend government revenues.

3-5

block grant A federal grant given to a state for a broad area, such as criminal justice or mental-health programs.

categorical grant A federal grant targeted for a specific purpose as defined by federal law.

competitive federalism A model of federalism in which state and local governments compete for businesses and citizens, who in effect "vote with their feet" by moving to jurisdictions that offer a competitive advantage.

fiscal federalism The allocation of taxes collected by one level of government (typically the national government) to another level (typically state or local governments).

government having separate and distinct functions and responsibilities. The model of **cooperative federalism,** which views the national and state governments as complementary parts of a single governmental mechanism, grew out of the need to solve the pressing national problems caused by the Great Depression. The 1960s and 1970s saw an even greater expansion of the national government's role in domestic policy, but the massive social programs undertaken during this period also resulted in greater involvement by state and local governments. The model in which every level of government is involved in implementing a policy is sometimes referred to as **picket-fence federalism.**

3-4

Describe developments in federalism in recent years. 8 Starting in the 1970s, several administrations favored a shift from nation-centered federalism to state-centered federalism. One of the goals of the **"new federalism"** was to return to the states certain powers that had been exercised by the national government since the 1930s. **9** The federal government and the states seem to be in a constant tug-of-war over federal regulations, federal programs, and federal demands on the states. In the last several years, Supreme Court decisions regarding state immigration laws, health-care reform, same-sex marriage, and voting rights have affected the shape of our federal system.

3-5

Explain what is meant by the term *fiscal federalism.* 10 To help the states pay for the costs associated with implementing national policies, the national government gives back some of the tax dollars it collects to the states—in the form of **categorical** and **block grants.** States have come to depend on grants as an important source of revenue. By giving or withholding federal grant dollars, the federal government has been able to exercise control over matters that traditionally have been under the control of state governments. **11** Sometimes state and local governments engage in **competitive federalism** by offering lower taxes or more services to attract businesses and citizens.

INTERNET RESOURCES

www.supremecourt.gov

www.gutenberg.org/ebooks/1404

www.csg.org

www.nga.org

www.governing.com

CHAPTER REVIEW

Civil Liberties

4

LEARNING OUTCOMES

4–1

Define the term *civil liberties,* **explain how civil liberties differ from civil rights, and state the constitutional basis for our civil liberties. 1 Civil liberties** are legal and constitutional rights that protect citizens from government actions. Civil rights specify what the government *must* do. Civil liberties set forth what the government *cannot* do. **2** Many of our liberties were added by the Bill of Rights. The United States Supreme Court has used the **due process clause** to incorporate most of the protections guaranteed by the Bill of Rights into the liberties protected from state government actions under the Fourteenth Amendment.

4–2

List and describe the freedoms guaranteed by the First Amendment and explain how the courts have interpreted and applied these freedoms. 3 The First Amendment prohibits government from passing laws "respecting an establishment of religion, or prohibiting the free exercise thereof." Issues involving the **establishment clause** include prayer in the public schools, the teaching of evolution versus creationism or intelligent design, and government aid to parochial schools. The Supreme Court has ruled that public schools cannot sponsor religious activities and has held unconstitutional state laws forbidding the teaching of evolution in the schools. Some aid to parochial schools has been held to violate the establishment clause, while other forms of aid have been held permissible. **4** The Court has ruled consistently that the right to hold any religious belief is absolute, but the right to practice one's beliefs may have some limits. **5** Although the Supreme Court has zealously safeguarded the right to free speech under the First Amendment, at times it has imposed limits on speech in the interests of protecting other rights. These rights include security against harm to one's person or reputation, the need for public order, and the need to preserve the government. **6** The First Amendment freedom of the press generally protects the right to publish a wide range of opinions and information. Over the years, the Court has developed various guidelines and doctrines to use in deciding whether freedom of expression can be restrained.

4–3

Discuss why Americans are increasingly concerned about privacy rights. 7 The Supreme Court has held that a right to privacy is implied by other constitutional rights guaranteed in the Bill of Rights. The nature and scope of this right, however, are not always clear. **8** In 1973, the Court held that the right to privacy is broad enough to encompass a woman's decision to terminate a pregnancy, though the right is not absolute throughout pregnancy. Since that decision, the Court has upheld some restrictive state laws requiring certain actions prior to abortions. **9** Privacy issues have also been raised in the context of physician-assisted suicide. **10** A concern among Americans in recent years

KEY TERMS

4–1

bill of attainder A legislative act that inflicts punishment on particular persons or groups without granting them the right to a trial.

civil liberties Individual rights protected by the Constitution against the powers of the government.

due process clause The constitutional guarantee, set out in the Fifth and Fourteenth Amendments, that the government will not illegally or arbitrarily deprive a person of life, liberty, or property.

due process of law The requirement that the government use fair, reasonable, and standard procedures whenever it takes any legal action against an individual; required by the Fifth and Fourteenth Amendments.

ex post facto **law** A criminal law that punishes individuals for committing an act that was legal when the act was committed.

writ of *habeas corpus* An order that requires an official to bring a specified prisoner into court and explain to the judge why the person is being held in jail.

4–2

commercial speech Advertising statements that describe products. Commercial speech receives less protection under the First Amendment than ordinary speech.

establishment clause The section of the First Amendment that prohibits Congress from passing laws "respecting an establishment of religion."

free exercise clause The provision of the First Amendment stating that the government cannot pass laws "prohibiting the free exercise" of religion.

imminent lawless action test The current Supreme Court doctrine for assessing the constitutionality of subversive speech. To be illegal, speech must be "directed to inciting . . . imminent lawless action."

Lemon **test** A three-part test enunciated by the Supreme Court in the 1971 case of *Lemon v. Kurtzman* to determine whether government aid to parochial schools is constitutional.

libel A published report of a falsehood that tends to injure a person's reputation or character.

obscenity Indecency or offensiveness in speech, expression, behavior, or appearance.

school voucher An educational certificate, provided by a government, that allows a student to use public funds to pay for a private or a public school chosen by the student or his or her parents.

seditious speech Speech that urges resistance to lawful authority or that advocates the overthrow of a government.

slander The public utterance (speaking) of a statement that holds a person up for contempt, ridicule, or hatred.

symbolic speech The expression of beliefs, opinions, or ideas through forms other than verbal speech or print; speech involving actions and other nonverbal expressions.

4–4

double jeopardy The prosecution of a person twice for the same criminal offense; prohibited by the Fifth Amendment in all but a few circumstances.

exclusionary rule A criminal procedural rule stating that illegally obtained evidence is not admissible in court.

Miranda warnings A series of statements informing criminal suspects, on their arrest, of their constitutional rights, such as the right to remain silent and the right to counsel; required by the Supreme Court's 1966 decision in *Miranda v. Arizona.*

probable cause Cause for believing that there is a substantial likelihood that a person has committed or is about to commit a crime.

self-incrimination Providing damaging information or testimony against oneself in court.

is that their personal information could be collected by organizations that use the data improperly, and some laws have been passed to protect the privacy rights of individuals. Since the terrorist attacks of 9/11, the news media and Congress have debated how the United States can strengthen national security while still protecting civil liberties, particularly the right to privacy. The USA Patriot Act, the revelations regarding the NSA's collection of metadata, programs such as PRISM, and the tapping of foreign leaders' phones have all been part of the ongoing discussion.

4–4

Summarize how the Constitution and the Bill of Rights protect the rights of accused persons. 11 Constitutional safeguards include the Fourth Amendment protection from unreasonable searches and seizures and the requirement that no warrant for a search or an arrest be issued without **probable cause;** the Fifth Amendment prohibition against **double jeopardy** and the protection against **self-incrimination;** the Sixth Amendment guarantees of a speedy trial, a trial by jury, a public trial, the right to confront witnesses, and the right to counsel at various stages in some criminal proceedings; and the Eighth Amendment prohibitions against excessive bail and fines and against cruel and unusual punishments. The Constitution also provides for the **writ of *habeas corpus***—an order requiring that an official bring a specified prisoner into court and explain to the judge why the person is being held in jail.

INTERNET RESOURCES

www.aclu.org

ncac.org

www.lc.org

www.cdt.org

epic.org

www.stompoutbullying.org

LEARNING OUTCOMES

5–1

Explain the constitutional basis for our civil rights and for laws prohibiting discrimination. 1 Civil rights are the rights of all Americans to equal treatment under the law. The **equal protection clause** of the Fourteenth Amendment has been interpreted by the courts to mean that states may not discriminate unreasonably against a particular group or class of individuals. The amendment also provides a legal basis for federal civil rights legislation. The U.S. Supreme Court has developed various standards for determining whether the equal protection clause has been violated.

5–2

Discuss the reasons for the civil rights movement and the changes it caused in American politics and government. 2 The equal protection clause was originally intended to protect the newly freed slaves from discrimination after the Civil War. By the late 1880s, however, southern states had begun to pass a series of segregation laws. In 1896, the Supreme Court established the **separate-but-equal doctrine,** which was used to justify segregation for nearly sixty years. **3** In 1954, the Court held that segregation by race in public education was unconstitutional. One year later, the arrest of Rosa Parks for violating local segregation laws spurred a boycott of the bus system in Montgomery, Alabama. The protest was led by the Reverend Dr. Martin Luther King, Jr. In 1956, a federal court prohibited the segregation of buses in Montgomery, marking the beginning of the **civil rights movement. 4** Civil rights protesters in the 1960s applied the tactic of nonviolent **civil disobedience** in actions throughout the South. As the civil rights movement demonstrated its strength, Congress passed a series of civil rights laws, including the Civil Rights Act of 1964, the Voting Rights Act of 1965, and the Civil Rights Act of 1968. **5** Today, the percentages of voting-age blacks and whites registered to vote are nearly equal. Political participation by African Americans has increased, as has the number of African American elected officials. African Americans continue to struggle for income and educational parity with whites.

5–3

Describe the political and economic achievements of women in this country over time and identify some obstacles to equality that women continue to face. 6 The struggle of women for equal treatment initially focused on **suffrage.** In 1920, the Nineteenth Amendment was ratified, granting voting rights to women. **Feminism** shaped a new movement that began in the 1960s. Congress and several state legislatures enacted measures to provide equal rights for women, and the courts accepted the argument that gender discrimination violates the equal protection clause. Although women remain underrepresented in politics, increasingly women have gained power as public officials. **7** In spite of federal legislation to promote equal treatment of women in the workplace, women continue to face various forms

KEY TERMS

Introduction

civil rights The rights of all Americans to equal treatment under the law, as provided by the Fourteenth Amendment to the Constitution.

5–1

equal protection clause Section 1 of the Fourteenth Amendment, which states that no state shall "deny to any person within its jurisdiction the equal protection of the laws."

fundamental right A basic right of all Americans, such as First Amendment rights. Any law or action that prevents some group of persons from exercising a fundamental right is subject to the *strict scrutiny standard*.

rational basis test A test (also known as the *ordinary scrutiny standard*) used by the Supreme Court to decide whether a discriminatory law violates the equal protection clause of the Constitution. It is used only when there is no classification—such as race or gender—that would require a higher level of scrutiny.

strict scrutiny standard A standard under which a law or action must be necessary to promote a compelling state interest and must be narrowly tailored to meet that interest.

suspect classification A classification, such as race, that provides the basis for a discriminatory law. Any law based on a suspect classification is subject to strict scrutiny by the courts, meaning that the law must be justified by a compelling state interest.

5–2

busing The transportation of public school students by bus to schools physically outside their neighborhoods to eliminate school segregation based on residential patterns.

civil disobedience The deliberate and public act of refusing to obey laws thought to be unjust.

civil rights movement The movement in the 1950s and 1960s, by minorities and concerned whites, to end racial segregation.

***de facto* segregation** Racial segregation that occurs not as a result of government actions but because of social and economic conditions and residential patterns.

***de jure* segregation** Racial segregation that occurs because of laws or decisions by government agencies.

separate-but-equal doctrine A Supreme Court doctrine holding that the equal protection clause of the Fourteenth Amendment did not forbid racial segregation as long as the facilities for blacks were equal to those for whites.

sit-in A tactic of nonviolent civil disobedience. Demonstrators enter a business, college building, or other public place and remain seated until they are forcibly removed or until their demands are met.

5–3

feminism A doctrine advocating full political, economic, and social equality for women.

glass ceiling An invisible but real discriminatory barrier that prevents women and minorities from rising to top positions of power or responsibility.

sexual harassment Unwanted physical contact, verbal conduct, or abuse of a sexual nature that interferes with a recipient's job performance, creates a hostile environment, or carries with it an implicit or explicit threat of adverse employment consequences.

suffrage The right to vote; the franchise.

5–5

affirmative action A policy that gives special consideration, in jobs and college admissions, to members of groups that have been discriminated against in the past.

quota system A policy under which a specific number of jobs, promotions, or other types of placements, such as university admissions, are given to members of selected groups.

reverse discrimination Discrimination against those who have no minority status.

of discrimination, including a lingering bias that has been described as the **glass ceiling. 8** The prohibition of gender discrimination has been extended to prohibit **sexual harassment.**

5–4

Summarize the struggles for equality that other groups in America have experienced. 9 Latinos constitute the largest ethnic minority in the United States. Economically, Latino households are often members of this country's working poor. Immigration reform has been an important issue for many Latinos. **10** Asian Americans suffered from discriminatory treatment in the late 1800s and early 1900s, and again during World War II. Today, Asian Americans lead other minority groups in median income and median education. **11** Native Americans had no civil rights under U.S. laws until 1924. Beginning in the 1960s, some Native Americans formed organizations to strike back at the U.S. government and to reclaim their heritage, including their lands. **12** Persons with disabilities first became a political force in the 1970s. The Americans with Disabilities Act (ADA) of 1990 is the most significant legislation protecting the rights of this group of Americans. **13** In the decades following the 1969 Stonewall Inn incident, laws and court decisions protecting the rights of gay men and lesbians have reflected changing social attitudes. Same-sex marriage is legal in many states, and recent decisions by the Supreme Court have been supportive of same-sex couples.

5–5

Explain what affirmative action is and why it has been so controversial. 14 Affirmative action policies give special consideration, in jobs and college admissions, to members of groups that have been discriminated against in the past. Such policies have been tested in court cases involving claims of **reverse discrimination.** Some states have banned affirmative action or replaced it with alternative policies.

INTERNET RESOURCES

www.naacp.org

www.now.org

www.whoneedsfeminism.com

lulac.org

askjan.org

www.glaad.org

LEARNING OUTCOMES

6–1

Explain what an interest group is, why interest groups form, and how interest groups function in American politics. 1 An **interest group** is an organized group of people sharing common objectives who actively attempt to influence government policymakers through direct and indirect methods. The right to form interest groups and to lobby the government is protected by the First Amendment. Interest groups may form—and existing groups may become more politically active—when the government expands its scope of activities. Interest groups also come into existence in response to a perceived threat to a group's interests, or they can form in reaction to the creation of other groups. **Purposive incentives, solidary incentives,** and **material incentives** are among the reasons people join interest groups. **2** Interest groups (a) help bridge the gap between citizens and government; (b) help raise public awareness and inspire action on various issues; (c) provide public officials with specialized information that may be useful in making policy choices; and (d) serve as another check on public officials. The **pluralist theory** of American democracy views politics as a contest among various interest groups to gain benefits for their members. **3** Although both interest groups and political parties are groups of people joined together for political purposes, they differ in several ways.

6–2

Identify the various types of interest groups. 4 The most common interest groups are those that promote private interests. **5** Business has long been well organized for effective action. Hundreds of business groups operate at all levels of government, and there are also umbrella organizations, including the U.S. Chamber of Commerce, that represent business interests. **Trade organizations** support policies that benefit specific industries. Many groups work for general agricultural business interests at all levels of government, and producers of various specific farm commodities have formed their own organizations. **6** Interest groups representing labor have been some of the most influential groups in the nation's history. While the strength and political power of labor unions have waned in the last several decades, more than one-third of all public-sector workers are union members. Most professions that require advanced education or specialized training have organizations to protect and promote their interests. **7** Other types of groups include **public interest groups,** which are formed with the broader goal of working for the "public good." In reality, however, all lobbying groups represent special interests. Groups organized for the protection of consumer rights were very active in the 1960s and 1970s, and some are still active today. Americans who share the same race, ethnicity, gender, or other characteristic often have important common interests and form identity interest groups. Some interest groups, including environmental and religious groups, are organized to promote a shared political perspective or ideology. **8** Numerous interest groups focus on a single

KEY TERMS

6–1

free rider problem The difficulty that exists when individuals can enjoy the outcome of an interest group's efforts without having to contribute, such as by becoming members of the group.

interest group An organized group of individuals sharing common objectives who actively attempt to influence policymakers.

material incentive A reason to join an interest group—practical benefits such as discounts, subscriptions, or group insurance.

pluralist theory A theory that views politics as a contest among various interest groups—at all levels of government—to gain benefits for their members.

purposive incentive A reason to join an interest group—satisfaction resulting from working for a cause in which one believes.

solidary incentive A reason to join an interest group—pleasure in associating with like-minded individuals.

6–2

labor force All of the people over the age of sixteen who are working or actively looking for jobs.

public-interest group An interest group formed for the purpose of working for the "public good." Examples are the American Civil Liberties Union and Common Cause.

right-to-work laws Laws that ban unions from collecting dues or other fees from workers whom they represent but who have not actually joined the union.

trade organization An association formed by members of a particular industry, such as the oil industry or the trucking industry, to develop common standards and goals for the industry. Trade organizations, as interest groups, lobby government for legislation or regulations that specifically benefit their members.

6–3

direct technique Any method used by an interest group to interact with government officials directly to further the group's goals.

independent expenditure An expenditure for activities that are independent from (not coordinated with) those of a political candidate or a political party.

CHAPTER REVIEW 6

indirect technique Any method used by interest groups to influence government officials through third parties, such as voters.

lobbying All of the attempts by organizations or by individuals to influence the passage, defeat, or contents of legislation or to influence the administrative decisions of government.

lobbyist An individual who handles a particular interest group's lobbying efforts.

political action committee (PAC) A committee that is established by a corporation, labor union, or special interest group to raise funds and make campaign contributions on the establishing organization's behalf.

rating system A system by which a particular interest group evaluates (rates) the performance of legislators based on how often the legislators have voted with the group's position on particular issues.

issue. Efforts by state and local governments to lobby the federal government have escalated in recent years.

6–3

Discuss how the activities of interest groups help to shape government policymaking. 9 Interest groups operate at all levels of government and use a variety of strategies to steer policies in ways beneficial to their interests. Sometimes, they attempt to influence policymakers directly, but at other times they try to exert indirect influence on policymakers by shaping public opinion. **10 Lobbying** and providing election support are two important **direct techniques** used by interest groups. Groups also try to influence public policy through third parties or the general public. Indirect techniques include advertising, **rating systems,** issue advocacy through **independent expenditures,** mobilizing constituents, going to court, and organizing demonstrations.

6–4

Describe how interest groups are regulated by government. 11 In spite of legislation designed to reduce the "revolving door" syndrome, it remains common for those who leave positions with the federal government to become lobbyists or consultants for the interest groups they helped to regulate. **12** The Lobbying Disclosure Act of 1995 reformed a 1946 law in several ways, particularly by creating stricter definitions of who is a lobbyist. In the wake of lobbying scandals in the early 2000s, additional lobbying reform efforts were undertaken. The Honest Leadership and Open Government Act of 2007 increased lobbying disclosure and placed further restrictions on the receipt of gifts and travel by members of Congress paid for by lobbyists and the organizations they represent.

INTERNET RESOURCES

www.ipl.org/div/aon   www.nra.org

www.uschamber.com   www.aarp.org

www.nea.org   www.nrdc.org

TABLE 6–5	DIRECT LOBBYING TECHNIQUES
Technique	**Description**
Making Personal Contacts with Key Legislators	A lobbyist's personal contacts with key legislators or other government officials—in their offices, in the halls of Congress, or on social occasions such as dinners, boating expeditions, and the like—comprise one of the most effective direct lobbying techniques.
Providing Expertise and Research Results for Legislators	Lobbyists often have knowledge and expertise that are useful in drafting legislation, and this expertise can be a major strength for an interest group. Harried members of Congress cannot possibly be experts on everything they vote on and therefore eagerly seek information to help them make up their minds.
Offering "Expert" Testimony before Congressional Committees	Lobbyists often provide "expert" testimony before congressional committees for or against proposed legislation. Each expert offers as much evidence as possible to support her or his position.
Providing Legal Advice to Legislators	Many lobbyists assist legislators in drafting legislation or prospective regulations. Lobbyists are a source of ideas and sometimes offer legal advice on specific details.
Following Up on Legislation	Because executive agencies responsible for carrying out legislation can often change the scope of the new law, lobbyists may also try to influence the bureaucrats who implement the policy.

LEARNING OUTCOMES

7–1

Summarize the origins and development of the two-party system in the United States. **1** After the Constitution was ratified, the Federalist Party supported a strong central government that would encourage the development of commerce and manufacturing. The party's opponents, Jefferson's Republicans, favored a more limited role for government. After suffering electoral defeats in the early 1800s, the Federalists went out of existence, resulting in a **realignment** of the party system. In the mid-1820s, the Republicans split into two groups—the Democrats and the National Republicans (later the Whig Party). As the Democrats and Whigs competed for the presidency during the 1840s and 1850s, the **two-party system** as we know it today emerged. **2** By the mid-1850s, most northern Whigs were absorbed into the new Republican Party, which opposed the extension of slavery. After the Civil War, the Republicans and Democrats were roughly even in strength, although the Republicans were more successful in presidential contests. After the realigning election of 1896, many Americans viewed the **GOP** as the party that knew how to manage the nation's economy, and it remained dominant in national politics until the Great Depression. **3** The election of 1932 brought Franklin D. Roosevelt to the presidency and the Democrats back to power at the national level. In the 1960s, however, conservative Democrats did not like the direction in which their party seemed to be taking them, and over time most of them became Republican voters. The result of this "rolling realignment" was that by 2000, the two major parties were fairly evenly matched.

7–2

Describe the current status of the two major parties. **4** A key characteristic of recent politics has been the extreme partisanship of party activists and members of Congress. The rolling realignment after the elections of 1968 resulted in parties that were much more homogeneous. By 2009, the most conservative Democrat in the House was to the left of the most moderate Republican. **5** Ideological uniformity has made it easier for the parties to maintain discipline in Congress. Political polarization grew even more severe after the 2010 elections. Many of the new Republican members of Congress were pledged to the Tea Party philosophy of no-compromise conservatism. Also significant is the number of independent voters, contributing to a potential **dealignment** in the party system.

7–3

Explain how political parties function in our democratic system. **6** Political parties link the people's policy preferences to actual government policies. They recruit and nominate candidates for political office, coordinate campaigns, and take care of a number of tasks that are essential to the smooth functioning of the electoral process. Parties also help educate the public about important political issues. Parties coordinate policy among the various branches and levels

KEY TERMS

7–1

GOP A nickname for the Republican Party—"grand old party."

political party A group of individuals who organize to win elections, operate the government, and determine policy.

realignment A process in which the popular support for and relative strength of the parties shift and the parties are reestablished with different coalitions of supporters.

7–2

dealignment Among voters, a growing detachment from both major political parties.

7–3

coalition An alliance of individuals or groups with a variety of interests and opinions who join together to support all or part of a political party's platform.

majority party The political party that has more members in the legislature than the opposing party.

minority party The political party that has fewer members in the legislature than the opposing party.

primary A preliminary election held for the purpose of choosing a party's final candidate.

7–4

electorate All of the citizens eligible to vote in a given election.

national convention The meeting held by each major party every four years to nominate presidential and vice-presidential candidates, write a party platform, and conduct other party business.

national party chairperson An individual who serves as a political party's administrative head at the national level and directs the work of the party's national committee.

national party committee The political party leaders who direct party business during the four years between the national party conventions, organize the next national convention, and plan how to support the party's candidate in the next presidential election.

party activist A party member who helps to organize and oversee party functions and planning during and between campaigns, and may even become a candidate for office.

CHAPTER REVIEW 7

party identifier A person who identifies himself or herself as being a supporter of a particular political party.

party platform The document drawn up by each party at its national convention that outlines the policies and positions of the party.

party ticket A list of a political party's candidates for various offices. In national elections, the party ticket consists of the presidential and vice-presidential candidates.

patronage A system of rewarding the party faithful and workers with government jobs or contracts.

precinct A political district within a city, such as a block or a neighborhood, or a rural portion of a county; the smallest voting district at the local level.

solidarity Mutual agreement among the members of a particular group.

ward A local unit of a political party's organization, consisting of a division or district within a city.

7–5

third party In the United States, any party other than the two major parties (Republican and Democratic).

two-party system A political system in which two strong and established parties compete for political offices.

of government and balance the competing interests of those who support the party. In government, the minority party checks the actions of the party in power.

7–4

Discuss the structure of American political parties. 7 The party in the **electorate** consists of **party identifiers** and **party activists.** Each party is decentralized, with national, state, and local organizations. Delegates to the **national convention** nominate the party's presidential and vice-presidential candidates, and they adopt the **party platform.** The national party organization includes a **national party committee,** a **national party chairperson,** and congressional campaign committees. The party in government consists of all of the party's candidates who have won elections and now hold public office. The party in government helps to organize the government's agenda by convincing its own party members in office to vote for its policies.

7–5

Describe the different types of third parties and how they function in the American political system. 8 The United States has a two-party system in which the Democrats and the Republicans dominate national politics. American election laws and the rules governing campaign financing tend to favor the major parties. There are also institutional barriers that prevent third parties from enjoying electoral success. Because third parties normally do not win elections, Americans tend not to vote for them. **9** There are different kinds of third parties. An issue-oriented party is formed to promote a particular cause or timely issue. An ideological party supports a particular political doctrine or a set of beliefs. A splinter party develops out of a split within a major party, which may be part of an attempt to elect a specific person. **10** Third parties have brought many issues to the public's attention and can influence election outcomes. Third parties also provide a voice for voters who are frustrated with the Republican and Democratic parties.

INTERNET RESOURCES

www.politicalresources.net

www.politics1.com

www.democrats.org

www.gop.com

www.lp.org

www.greenparty.org

LEARNING OUTCOMES

8–1

Describe the political socialization process. 1 Most people acquire their political attitudes, opinions, beliefs, and knowledge through a complex learning process called **political socialization.** Most political socialization is informal. The strong early influence of the family later gives way to the multiple influences of schools, churches, the **media,** opinion leaders, major life events, **peer groups,** and economic status and occupation. People and institutions that influence the political views of others are called **agents of political socialization.**

8–2

Explain how public opinion polls are conducted, problems with polls, and how they are used in the political process. 2 A **public opinion poll** is a survey of the public's opinion on a particular topic at a particular moment, as measured through the use of **samples. 3** Early polling efforts often relied on **straw polls.** The opinions expressed in straw polls, however, usually represent an atypical subgroup of the population, or a **biased sample.** Over time, more scientific polling techniques were developed. Today, polling is used extensively by political candidates and policymakers. Polls can be quite accurate when conducted properly. In-person surveys have been replaced by telephone interviews, often with prerecorded messages that solicit responses. Some pollsters specialize in Internet surveys. **4** To achieve the most accurate results possible, pollsters use **random samples,** in which each person within the entire population being polled has an equal chance of being chosen. A properly drawn random sample will be representative of the population as a whole, though responses of various groups are sometimes weighted in an effort to achieve representativeness. Public opinion polls are fundamentally statistical. The true result of a poll is not a single figure, but a range of probabilities. Any poll contains a **sampling error**. Polling firms often use differing models that contribute to a **house effect. 5** Problems with polls can stem from the way questions are worded, and polls often reduce complex issues to questions that simply call for "yes" or "no" answers. Moreover, polls of voter preferences cannot reflect rapid shifts in public opinion unless they are taken frequently. **6** Many journalists base their political coverage during campaigns almost exclusively on poll findings, and media companies often report only the polls conducted by their affiliated pollsters. A tactic used in some political campaigns is a **push poll,** which asks "fake" polling questions that are designed to "push" voters toward one candidate or another.

8–3

Discuss the different factors that affect voter choices. 7 For established voters, party identification is one of the most important and lasting predictors of how a person will vote. Voters' choices often depend on the perceived character of the candidates rather than on their qualifications or policy positions. When people vote for candidates who share their positions on particular issues, they are engaging in policy voting. Historically, economic issues

KEY TERMS

8–1

agents of political socialization People and institutions that influence the political views of others.

media Newspapers, magazines, television, radio, the Internet, and any other printed or electronic means of communication.

peer group Associates, often close in age to one another; may include friends, classmates, co-workers, club members, or religious group members.

political socialization The learning process through which most people acquire their political attitudes, opinions, beliefs, and knowledge.

public opinion The views of the citizenry about politics, public issues, and public policies; a complex collection of opinions held by many people on issues in the public arena.

8–2

biased sample A poll sample that does not accurately represent the population.

house effect In the case of a polling firm, a consistent tendency to report results more favorable to one of the political parties than the results reported by other pollsters.

public opinion poll A survey of the public's opinion on a particular topic at a particular moment.

push poll A campaign tactic used to feed false or misleading information to potential voters, under the guise of taking an opinion poll, with the intent to "push" voters away from one candidate and toward another.

random sample In the context of opinion polling, a sample in which each person within the entire population being polled has an equal chance of being chosen.

sample In the context of opinion polling, a group of people selected to represent the population being studied.

sampling error In the context of opinion polling, the difference between what the sample results show and what the true results would have been had everybody in the relevant population been interviewed.

straw poll A nonscientific poll in which there is no way to ensure that the opinions expressed are representative of the larger population.

8–3

gender gap The difference between the percentage of votes cast for a particular candidate by women and the percentage of votes cast for the same candidate by men.

Solid South A term used to describe the tendency of the southern states to vote Democratic after the Civil War.

8–4

grandfather clause A clause in a state law that had the effect of restricting voting rights to those whose ancestors had voted before the 1860s. It was one of the techniques used in the South to prevent African Americans from exercising their right to vote.

literacy test A test given to voters to ensure that they could read and write and thus evaluate political information. This technique was used in many southern states to restrict African American participation in elections.

poll tax A fee of several dollars that had to be paid before a person could vote. This device was used in some southern states to discourage African Americans and low-income whites from voting.

white primary A primary election in which African Americans were prohibited from voting. The practice was banned by the Supreme Court in 1944.

vote-eligible population The number of people who are actually eligible to vote in an American election.

voting-age population The number of people residing in the United States who are at least eighteen years old.

have had the strongest influence on voters' choices. **8** Socioeconomic factors, including educational attainment, occupation and income, age, gender, religion, ethnic background, and geographic region, also influence how people vote. Ideology is another indicator of voting behavior.

8–4

Indicate some of the factors that affect voter turnout, and discuss what has been done to improve voter turnout and voting procedures. 9 The Fifteenth Amendment to the Constitution (1870) guaranteed suffrage to African American males. Yet, for many decades, African Americans were effectively denied the ability to exercise their voting rights. Today, devices used to restrict voting rights, such as the **poll tax, literacy tests,** the **grandfather clause,** and **white primaries,** are explicitly prohibited by constitutional amendments, by the Voting Rights Act of 1965, or by court decisions. The Nineteenth Amendment (1920) gave women the right to vote, and the Twenty-sixth Amendment (1971) reduced the minimum voting age to eighteen. **10** Some restrictions on voting rights, such as registration, residency, and citizenship requirements, still exist. Most states also do not permit prison inmates or felons to vote. Attempts to improve voter turnout and voting procedures include simplifying the voter-registration process, conducting voting by mail, updating voting equipment, and allowing early voting. In recent years, a number of states have passed laws that may have the effect of making it harder to vote, not easier. Voter turnout is affected by several factors, including educational attainment, income level, age, and minority status.

INTERNET RESOURCES

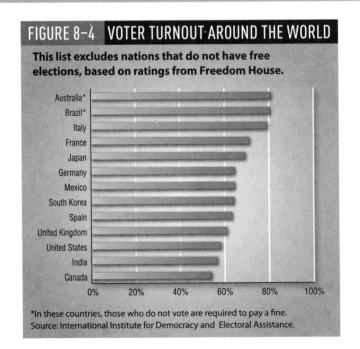

FIGURE 8–4   VOTER TURNOUT AROUND THE WORLD

This list excludes nations that do not have free elections, based on ratings from Freedom House.

*In these countries, those who do not vote are required to pay a fine.
Source: International Institute for Democracy and Electoral Assistance.

LEARNING OUTCOMES

9–1

Explain how elections are held and how the electoral college functions in presidential elections. 1 During **general elections,** voters decide who will be the U.S. president, vice president, and members of Congress. **2** An election board supervises the voting process in each precinct. **Poll watchers** from each of the two major parties typically monitor the polling place as well. **3** Citizens do not vote directly for the president and vice president. Instead, they vote for **electors** who will cast their ballots in the **electoral college.** Each state has as many electoral votes as it has U.S. senators and representatives. There are also three electors from the District of Columbia. **4** The electoral college system is primarily a **winner-take-all system** because, in nearly all states, the candidate who receives the most popular votes in the state is credited with all that state's electoral votes. To be elected through this system, a candidate must receive at least 270 electoral votes, a majority of the 538 electoral votes available.

9–2

Discuss how candidates are nominated. 5 The methods used by political parties to nominate candidates have changed over time, and have included **caucuses** and **nominating conventions.** Today, candidates who win **primary elections** go on to compete against the candidates from other parties in the general election. In a **direct primary,** which can be either **closed** or **open,** voters cast their ballots directly for candidates. The elections that nominate candidates for Congress and for state or local offices are almost always direct primaries. **6** Most of the states hold presidential primaries, which are indirect primaries used to choose **delegates** to the national nominating conventions. In some states, delegates are chosen through a caucus/convention system. Each political party holds a national convention where delegates adopt the party platform and nominate the party's presidential and vice-presidential candidates

9–3

Indicate what is involved in launching a political campaign today, and describe the structure and functions of a campaign organization. 7 To run a successful campaign, a candidate's campaign staff must be able to raise funds, get media coverage, produce and pay for political ads, schedule the candidate's time effectively with constituent groups and potential supporters, convey the candidate's position on the issues, conduct **opposition research,** and persuade the voters to go to the polls. Political party organizations are no longer as important as they once were in providing campaign services. Candidates now turn to political consultants who specialize in a particular area of the campaign such as conducting polls or developing the candidate's advertising. Most candidates have a campaign manager who coordinates and plans the **campaign strategy.**

KEY TERMS

9–1

Australian ballot A secret ballot that is prepared, distributed, and counted by government officials at public expense; used by all states in the United States since 1888.

elector A member of the electoral college.

electoral college The group of electors who are selected by the voters in each state to officially elect the president and vice president. The number of electors in each state is equal to the number of that state's representatives in both chambers of Congress.

general election A regularly scheduled election to choose the U.S. president, vice president, and senators and representatives in Congress. General elections are held in even-numbered years on the Tuesday after the first Monday in November.

poll watcher A representative from one of the political parties who is allowed to monitor a polling place to make sure that the election is run fairly and that fraud doesn't occur.

special election An election that is held at the state or local level when the voters must decide an issue before the next general election or when vacancies occur by reason of death or resignation.

winner-take-all system A system in which the candidate who receives the most votes wins. In contrast, proportional systems allocate votes to multiple winners.

9–2

caucus A meeting held to choose political candidates or delegates.

closed primary A primary in which only party members can vote to choose that party's candidates.

Credentials Committee A committee of each national political party that evaluates the claims of national party convention delegates to be the legitimate representatives of their states.

delegate A person selected to represent the people of one geographic area at a party convention.

direct primary An election held within each of the two major parties—Democratic and Republican—to choose the party's candidates for the general election. Voters choose the candidate directly, rather than through delegates.

CHAPTER REVIEW 9

nominating convention An official meeting of a political party to choose its candidates. Nominating conventions at the state and local levels also select delegates to represent the citizens of their geographic areas at a higher-level party convention.

open primary A primary in which voters can vote for a party's candidates regardless of whether they belong to the party.

primary election An election in which voters choose the candidates of their party, who will then run in the general election.

9-3

campaign strategy The comprehensive plan developed by a candidate and his or her advisers for winning an election.

opposition research The attempt to learn damaging information about an opponent in a political campaign.

political consultant A professional political adviser who, for a fee, works on an area of a candidate's campaign. Political consultants include campaign managers, pollsters, media advisers, and "get out the vote" organizers.

9-5

independent expenditure An expenditure for activities that are independent from (not coordinated with) those of a political candidate or a political party.

soft money Campaign contributions not regulated by federal law, such as some contributions that are made to political parties instead of to particular candidates.

9-4

Describe how the Internet has transformed political campaigns. 8 Today, the ability to make effective use of social media and the Internet is essential to a candidate. In 2008, Barack Obama gained an edge on his rivals in part because of his superior use of new technologies, and his 2012 campaign was even more sophisticated. Obama took Internet fund-raising to a new level. **9** Microtargeting, a technique that involves collecting as much information as possible about voters in a database and then filtering out various groups for special attention, was pioneered by the George W. Bush campaign in 2004. In 2012, Obama's microtargeting operation vastly outperformed Mitt Romney's. **10** Obama also took Web-based organizing to a new level. By 2012, the Obama campaign was able to create active local support groups in towns and counties across the country.

9-5

Summarize the current laws that regulate campaign financing and the role of money in modern political campaigns. 11 The modern campaign is an expensive undertaking. Campaign-financing laws enacted in the 1970s provided public funding for presidential primaries and general elections, limited individual and group contributions to candidates, and created the Federal Election Commission. Beginning in 2004, leading Democratic and Republican presidential candidates were refusing public funding for the primaries. By 2012, the public financing of presidential campaigns was effectively over. **12** The Bipartisan Campaign Reform Act of 2002 addressed the issues of **soft money** and **independent expenditures** to a certain extent. Several court decisions, however, have altered the rules of campaign financing. Notable consequences of these rulings include the rise of super PACs and fewer restrictions on wealthy individuals who wish to spend significant amounts of money during political campaigns. **13** Another campaign-finance issue arose after the creation of a new kind of organization, known as the 501c, which has the ability to spend money during campaigns and to conceal the identity of its donors.

INTERNET RESOURCES

frontloading.blogspot.com

www.fec.gov

www.politicalmoneyline.com

www.opensecrets.org

www.commoncause.org

www.votesmart.org

LEARNING OUTCOMES

10–1

Explain the role of the media in a democracy. 1 What the media say and do has an impact on what Americans think about political issues, but the media also reflect what Americans think about politics. While the new media based on the Internet are becoming increasingly important, the traditional media—radio, television, and print—remain important to American politics and government. **2** By helping to determine what people will talk and think about, the media play a role in setting the political agenda. Two techniques that are used are **priming** and **framing**. Of all the media, television still has the greatest impact on most Americans, but the medium of television imposes constraints on how political issues are presented.

10–2

Summarize how television influences the conduct of political campaigns. 3 Candidates for political office spend a great deal of time and money obtaining a TV presence through political ads, debates, and general news coverage. Televised **political advertising** consumes at least half of the total budget for a major political campaign. **Negative political advertising,** including **personal attack ads** and **issue ads,** is frequently used. Televised debates are a feature of presidential campaigns. They provide an opportunity for voters to find out how candidates differ on issues and allow candidates to capitalize on the power of television to improve their images or point out the failings of their opponents. **4** Candidates' campaigns have become increasingly sophisticated in **managing news coverage,** while press advisers try to convince reporters to give a story or event a **spin** that is favorable to the candidate.

10–3

Explain why talk radio has been described as the Wild West of the media. 5 Talk-show hosts do not attempt to hide their political biases; if anything, they exaggerate them for effect. Sometimes, hosts appear to care more about the entertainment value of their statements than whether they are, strictly speaking, true. No journalistic conventions are observed. **6** Those who think that talk radio is good for the country argue that talk shows, taken together, provide a great populist forum. Others fear that talk shows empower fringe groups, perhaps magnifying their rage.

10–4

Describe types of media bias and explain how such bias affects the political process. 7 Relatively few Americans believe that the news media are unbiased in their reporting, and there has been a notable decline in the public's confidence in news media in recent years. Nevertheless, the public does believe that the press is successful in fulfilling its role as a watchdog. While the majority of Americans think that the media reflect a bias in either a liberal or conservative direction, it is a media bias against losers that may play a significant

KEY TERMS

10–1

agenda setting The media's ability to determine which issues are considered important by the public and by politicians.

electronic media Communication channels that involve electronic transmissions, such as radio, television, and the Internet.

framing An agenda-setting technique that establishes the context of a media report. Framing can mean fitting events into a familiar story or filtering information through pre-conceived ideas.

mass media Communication channels, such as newspapers and radio and television broadcasts, through which people can communicate to large audiences.

priming An agenda setting technique in which a media outlet promotes specific facts or ideas that may affect the public's thinking on related topics.

print media Communication channels that consist of printed materials, such as newspapers and magazines.

sound bite A televised comment, lasting for only a few seconds, that captures a thought or a perspective and has an immediate impact on viewers.

10–2

issue ad A political advertisement that focuses on a particular issue. Issue ads can be used to support or attack a candidate's position or credibility.

managed news coverage News coverage that is manipulated (managed) by a campaign manager or political consultant to gain media exposure for a political candidate.

negative political advertising Political advertising undertaken for the purpose of discrediting an opposing candidate in voters' eyes. Attack ads are one form of negative political advertising.

personal attack ad A negative political advertisement that attacks the character of an opposing candidate.

political advertising Advertising undertaken by or on behalf of a political candidate to familiarize voters with the candidate and his or her views on campaign issues; advertising for or against policy issues.

spin A reporter's slant on, or interpretation of, a particular event or action.

spin doctor A political candidate's press adviser who tries to convince reporters to give a story or event concerning the candidate a particular "spin" (interpretation, or slant).

10–5

citizen journalism The collection, analysis, and dissemination of information online by independent journalists, scholars, politicians, and the general citizenry.

podcasting The distribution of audio or video files to personal computers or mobile devices such as smartphones.

role in shaping presidential campaigns and elections. The media use the winner-loser framework to describe events throughout the campaigns. **8** The expansion of the media universe to include cable channels and the Internet has increased the competition among news sources. News directors select programming they believe will attract the largest audiences and garner the highest advertising revenues. Many journalists believe that economic pressure is making significant inroads on independent editorial decision making. News organizations are redefining their purpose and looking for special niches in which to build their audiences.

10–5

Indicate the extent to which the Internet is reshaping news and political campaigns. 9 The Internet is a major source of information. Almost every major news organization, both print and broadcast, delivers news online. In addition, there has been a veritable explosion of **citizen journalism** in recent years. Blogs are offered by independent journalists, scholars, political activists, and the citizenry at large. **Podcasting** is another form of news distribution. **10** The Internet is an inexpensive way for candidates to contact, recruit, and mobilize supporters, as well as to disseminate information about their positions on issues. Candidates hire Web managers to create well-designed Web sites to attract viewers, manage their e-mails, and track their credit-card contributions. The Web manager also hires bloggers to promote the candidate's views, arranges for podcasting of campaign information, and hires staff to monitor the Web for news about the candidates and to track the online publications of netroots groups. **11** Citizen videos have also changed the traditional campaign. Comments a candidate makes may be caught on camera by someone with a cell phone or digital camera and published on the Internet for all to see.

INTERNET RESOURCES

refdesk.com/paper.html

hosted.ap.org

www.washingtonpost.com/blogs/fact-checker

polifact.com

www.aim.org

fair.org

LEARNING OUTCOMES

11–1

Explain how seats in the House of Representatives are apportioned among the states. 1 The Constitution provides for the **apportionment** of House seats among the states on the basis of their respective populations, though each state is guaranteed at least one seat. Every ten years, the 435 House seats are reapportioned based on the outcome of the census. **2** Each representative to the House is elected by voters in a **congressional district.** Within each state, districts must contain, as nearly as possible, equal numbers of people. This principle is known as the **"one person, one vote" rule. Gerrymandering** occurs when a district's boundaries are drawn to maximize the influence of a certain group or political party.

11–2

Describe the power of incumbency. 3 If legislators choose to run for reelection, they enjoy several advantages over their opponents, including name recognition, access to the media, congressional franking privileges, and lawmaking power. Members of Congress also have administrative staffs in Washington, D.C., and in their home districts. A key advantage is their fund-raising ability. Most incumbent members of Congress have a much larger network of contacts, donors, and lobbyists than their challengers have. While incumbents who run are usually reelected, there have been occasional periods of some turbulence when fewer incumbents than usual won reelection.

11–3

Identify the key leadership positions in Congress, describe the committee system, and indicate some important differences between the House of Representatives and the Senate. 4 The Constitution provides for the presiding officers of both the House and the Senate, and each chamber has added other leadership positions. The majority party in each chamber chooses the major officers of that chamber, selects committee chairpersons, and has a majority on all committees. **5** Chief among the leaders in the House of Representatives is the **Speaker of the House,** who has a great deal of power. Other leaders include the **majority and minority leaders,** and the **whips.** The vice president of the United States is the president of the Senate, and senators elect the president pro tempore ("pro tem"). The real power in the Senate is held by the majority and minority leaders, and their whips. **6** The committee system is a way to provide for specialization, or a division of legislative labor. Most of the work of legislating is performed by the **standing committees** and their **subcommittees** in the House and the Senate. Conference committees are formed for the purpose of achieving agreement between the House and Senate on the wording of legislative acts. **7** With its larger size, the House needs more rules and more formality than the Senate. The House **Rules Committee** proposes time limits on debate for most bills. The

KEY TERMS

11–1

apportionment The distribution of House seats among the states on the basis of their respective populations.

congressional district The geographic area that is served by one member in the House of Representatives.

earmark Spending provision inserted into legislation that benefits only a small number of people.

gerrymandering The drawing of a legislative district's boundaries in such a way as to maximize the influence of a certain group or political party.

instructed delegate A representative who deliberately mirrors the views of the majority of his or her constituents.

malapportionment A condition in which the voting power of citizens in one district is greater than the voting power of citizens in another district.

minority-majority district A district in which minority groups make up a majority of the population.

"one person, one vote" rule A rule, or principle, requiring that congressional districts have equal populations so that one person's vote counts as much as another's vote.

trustee A representative who tries to serve the broad interests of the entire society and not just the narrow interests of his or her constituents.

11–3

cloture A procedure for ending filibusters in the Senate and bringing the matter under consideration to a vote.

filibustering The Senate tradition of unlimited debate undertaken for the purpose of preventing action on a bill.

majority leader The party leader elected by the majority party in the House or in the Senate.

minority leader The party leader elected by the minority party in the House or in the Senate.

Rules Committee A standing committee in the House that provides special rules governing how particular bills will be considered and debated.

Speaker of the House The presiding officer in the House of Representatives. A member of the majority party and is the most powerful member of the House.

CHAPTER REVIEW 11

standing committee A permanent committee in Congress that deals with legislation concerning a particular area, such as agriculture or foreign relations.

subcommittee A division of a larger committee that deals with a particular part of the committee's policy area.

whip A member of Congress who assists the majority or minority leader in managing the party's legislative program.

11–4

conference committee A temporary committee that consists of members from the House and the Senate who work out a compromise bill.

conference report A report submitted by a conference committee after it has drafted a single version of a bill.

markup session A meeting held by a congressional committee or subcommittee to approve, amend, or redraft a bill.

pocket veto A special type of veto power used by the president after the legislature has adjourned.

11–5

nuclear option Changing Senate rules—in particular, rules that require a supermajority—by simple majority vote. Also know as the *constitutional option*.

11–6

appropriation The determination of how many dollars will be spent in a given year on a particular government activity.

authorization The creation of the legal basis for government programs.

fiscal year A twelve-month period (from October 1 through September 30, for the U.S. government) that is established for bookkeeping or accounting purposes.

first budget resolution A budget resolution, which is supposed to be passed in May, that sets overall revenue goals and spending targets for the next fiscal year, beginning on October 1.

second budget resolution A budget resolution, which is supposed to be passed in September, that sets "binding" limits on taxes and spending for the next fiscal year.

continuing resolution A temporary resolution that enables executive agencies to continue work with the same funding that they had in the previous fiscal year.

entitlement program A government program (such as Social Security) that allows, or entitles, a certain class of people (such as elderly persons) to receive benefits.

Senate normally permits extended debate. The use of unlimited debate to obstruct legislation is called **filibustering,** which may be ended by invoking **cloture.** There are other important differences between the House and the Senate as well.

11–4
Summarize the specific steps in the lawmaking process.

8 After a bill is introduced, it is sent to a standing committee. A committee chairperson will typically send the bill on to a subcommittee, where public hearings may be held. After a **markup session,** the bill goes to the full committee for further action. **9** After a bill is reported to the chamber, it is scheduled for floor debate. If, after votes are taken on the legislation, the House and Senate have passed differing versions of the same bill, a **conference committee** is formed to produce a compromise bill. A **conference report** is submitted to each chamber. If the bill is approved by both chambers, it is ready for action by the president.

11–5
Identify Congress's oversight functions and explain how Congress fulfills them.
10 Congress oversees the departments and agencies of the executive branch, and can rein in the power of the bureaucracy by refusing to fund government programs. Congress has the authority to investigate the actions of the executive branch, the need for certain legislation, and even the actions of its own members. It has the power to impeach federal officials and remove them from office. The Senate either confirms or fails to confirm the president's nominees for federal judgeships and top executive branch officers.

11–6
Indicate what is involved in the congressional budgeting process.
11 The budgeting process, which involves **authorization** and **appropriation,** begins when the president submits a proposed federal budget for the next **fiscal year.** In the **first budget resolution,** Congress sets overall revenue goals and spending targets. The **second budget resolution** sets "binding" limits on taxes and spending. When Congress is unable to pass a complete budget by October 1, it usually passes **continuing resolutions,** which enable executive agencies to work with the same funding they had in the previous year. **Entitlement programs** operate under open-ended budget authorizations.

INTERNET RESOURCES

www.politico.com

www.rollcall.com

thehill.com

Congress.gov

www.gpo.gov/fdsys

www.house.gov

www.senate.gov

LEARNING OUTCOMES

12–1

List the constitutional requirements for becoming president. 1 Article II of the Constitution sets forth relatively few requirements for becoming president. A person must be a natural born citizen, at least thirty-five years of age, and a resident within the United States for at least fourteen years.

12–2

Explain the roles that a president adopts while in office. 2 In the course of exercising his or her powers, the president performs a variety of roles. The president is the nation's **chief executive**—the head of the executive branch—and enforces laws and federal court decisions. The president leads the nation's armed forces as **commander in chief.** As **head of state,** the president performs ceremonial activities as a personal symbol of the nation. As **chief diplomat,** the president directs U.S. foreign policy and is the nation's most important representative in dealing with foreign governments. The president has become the chief legislator, informing Congress about the condition of the country and recommending legislative measures. As political party leader, the president chooses the chairperson of his or her party's national committee, attends party fund-raisers, and exerts influence within the party by using presidential appointment powers.

12–3

Indicate the scope of presidential powers. 3 The Constitution gives the president specific powers, such as the power to negotiate **treaties,** to grant reprieves and pardons, and to **veto** bills passed by Congress. The president also has inherent powers—powers that are necessary to carry out the specific constitutional duties of the presidency. **4** Several presidents have greatly expanded presidential powers. The president, for example, is now expected to develop a legislative program. The president's political skills, the ability to persuade others, and the strategy of "going public" all play a role in determining legislative success. **5** The president's executive authority has been expanded by the use of **executive orders** and **signing statements,** and the ability to make **executive agreements** has enhanced presidential power in foreign affairs. As commander in chief, the president can respond quickly to a military threat without waiting for congressional action, and since 1945, the president has been responsible for deciding if and when to use nuclear weapons.

12–4

Describe advantages enjoyed by Congress and by the president in their institutional relationship. 6 Congress has the advantage over the president in the areas of legislative authorization, the regulation of foreign and interstate commerce, and some budgetary matters. The president has the advantage over Congress in dealing with a national crisis, in setting foreign policy, and in influencing public opinion. **7** The relationship between Congress

KEY TERMS

12–2

- **chief diplomat** The role of the president of the United States in recognizing and interacting with foreign governments.
- **chief executive** The head of the executive branch of government; in the United States, the president.
- **commander in chief** The supreme commander of a nation's military force.
- **diplomat** A person who represents one country in dealing with representatives of another country.
- **head of state** The person who serves as the ceremonial head of a country's government and represents that country to the rest of the world.
- **patronage** The practice by which elected officials give government jobs to individuals who helped them gain office.

12–3

- **executive agreement** A binding international agreement, or pact, that is made between the president and another head of state and that does not require Senate approval.
- **executive order** A presidential order to carry out a policy or policies described in a law passed by Congress.
- **signing statement** A written statement, appended to a bill at the time the president signs it into law, indicating how the president interprets that legislation.
- **treaty** A formal agreement between the governments of two or more countries.
- **veto** A Latin word meaning "I forbid"; the refusal by an official, such as the president of the United States or a state governor, to sign a bill into law.

12–4

executive privilege An inherent executive power claimed by presidents to withhold information from, or to refuse to appear before, Congress or the courts. The president can also accord the privilege to other executive officials.

Watergate scandal A scandal involving an illegal break-in at the Democratic National Committee offices in 1972 by members of President Richard Nixon's reelection campaign staff.

12–5

cabinet An advisory group selected by the president to assist with decision making. Traditionally, the cabinet has consisted of the heads of the executive departments and other officers whom the president may choose to appoint.

chief of staff The person who directs the operations of the White House Office and advises the president on important matters.

Executive Office of the President (EOP) A group of staff agencies that assist the president in carrying out major duties.

kitchen cabinet The name given to a president's unofficial advisers. The term was coined during Andrew Jackson's presidency.

National Security Council (NSC) A council that advises the president on domestic and foreign matters concerning the safety and defense of the nation.

Office of Management and Budget (OMB) An agency in the Executive Office of the President that has the primary duty of assisting the president in preparing and supervising the administration of the federal budget.

press secretary A member of the White House staff who holds news conferences for reporters and makes public statements for the president.

White House Office The personal office of the president. White House Office personnel handle the president's political needs and manage the media, among other duties.

and the president is affected by their different constituencies and election cycles, and the fact that the president is limited to two terms in office. Their relationship is also affected when government is divided, with at least one house of Congress controlled by a different party than the White House.

12–5

Discuss the organization of the executive branch and the role of cabinet members in presidential administrations. 8 The heads of the fifteen executive departments are members of the president's **cabinet.** The president may add other officials to the cabinet as well. In general, presidents don't rely heavily on the advice of the formal cabinet. Department heads are often more responsive to the wishes of their own staffs, to their own political ambitions, or to obtaining resources for their departments than they are to the presidents they serve. **9** Since 1939, top advisers and assistants in the **Executive Office of the President (EOP)** have helped the president carry out major duties. Some of the most important staff agencies in the EOP are the **White House Office,** headed by the **chief of staff,** the **Office of Management and Budget,** and the **National Security Council.** In recent years, the responsibilities of the vice president have grown immensely, and the vice president has become one of the most important of the president's advisers.

INTERNET RESOURCES

www.whitehouse.gov

www.bartleby.com/124

millercenter.org/academic/americanpresident

www.archives.gov/presidential-libraries

www.gallup.com

www.foreignpolicy.com

TABLE 12–3	THE EXECUTIVE OFFICE OF THE PRESIDENT AS OF 2013

Agency
Council of Economic Advisers
Council on Environmental Quality
Executive Residence
National Security Staff
Office of Administration
Office of Management and Budget
Office of National Drug Control Policy
Office of Science and Technology Policy
Office of the U.S. Trade Representative
Office of the Vice President
White House Office

Source: www.whitehouse.gov.

LEARNING OUTCOMES

13–1

Describe the size and functions of the U.S. bureaucracy and the major components of federal spending. 1 A **bureaucracy** is a large, complex administrative organization that is structured hierarchically. In the federal government, the bureaucracy is part of the executive branch and its head is the president of the United States. The federal bureaucracy exists because Congress, over time, has delegated certain tasks to specialists. The three levels of government employ about 16 percent of the civilian labor force. **2** Over half of the federal budget consists of various social programs. Defense spending, including veterans' benefits, is almost 25 percent of total federal spending. Other categories of spending include military and economic foreign aid, as well as interest on the national debt.

13–2

Discuss the structure and basic components of the federal bureaucracy. 3 The fifteen executive departments are the major service organizations of the federal government. Each department was created by Congress as the perceived need for it arose, and each manages a specific policy area. Department heads are appointed by the president and confirmed by the Senate. Each department includes several subagencies. **4 Independent executive agencies** have a single function. Sometimes agencies are kept independent because of the sensitive nature of their functions, but at other times, Congress creates independent agencies to protect them from **partisan politics.** An **independent regulatory agency** is responsible for a specific type of policy. Its function is to create and implement rules that regulate private activity and protect the public interest in a particular sector of the economy. **5 Government corporations** are businesses owned by the government. They provide a service that could be handled by the private sector, and they charge for their services. A number of intermediate forms of organization exist that fall between a government corporation and a private one.

13–3

Describe how the federal civil service was established and how bureaucrats get their jobs. 6 Federal bureaucrats holding top-level positions are appointed by the president and confirmed by the Senate. The list of positions that are filled by appointments is published after each presidential election in a book that summarizes about eight thousand jobs. The rank-and-file bureaucrats—the rest of the federal bureaucracy—are part of the **civil service.** They obtain their jobs through the Office of Personnel Management (OPM). The OPM recruits, interviews, and tests potential government workers and makes recommendations to individual agencies as to which persons meet relevant standards. The Civil Service Reform Act of 1883 established the principle of government employment on the basis of merit through open, competitive examinations.

KEY TERMS

13–1

bureaucracy A large, complex, hierarchically structured administrative organization that carries out specific functions.

bureaucrat An individual who works in a bureaucracy. As generally used, the term refers to a government employee.

13–2

government corporation An agency of the government that is run as a business enterprise. Such agencies engage primarily in commercial activities, produce revenues, and require greater flexibility than most government agencies have.

independent executive agency A federal agency that is not located within a cabinet department.

independent regulatory agency A federal organization that is responsible for creating and implementing rules that regulate private activity and protect the public interest in a particular sector of the economy.

partisan politics Political actions or decisions that benefit a particular party.

13–3

civil service Nonmilitary government employees.

13–4

adjudicate To render a judicial decision. In administrative law, it is the process in which an administrative law judge hears and decides issues that arise when an agency charges a person or firm with violating a law or regulation enforced by the agency.

enabling legislation A law enacted by a legislature to establish an administrative agency. Enabling legislation normally specifies the name, purpose, composition, and powers of the agency being created.

iron triangle A three-way alliance among legislators, bureaucrats, and interest groups to make or preserve policies that benefit their respective interests.

issue networks Groups of individuals or organizations—which consist of legislators and legislative staff members, interest group leaders, bureaucrats, the media, scholars, and other experts—that support particular policy positions on a given issue.

CHAPTER REVIEW 13

legislative rule An administrative agency rule that carries the same weight as a statute enacted by a legislature.

neutral competency The application of technical skills to jobs without regard to political issues.

rulemaking The process undertaken by an administrative agency when formally proposing, evaluating, and adopting a new regulation.

13–5

privatization The transfer of the task of providing services traditionally provided by government to the private sector.

whistleblower In the context of government employment, someone who "blows the whistle" (reports to authorities or the press) on gross governmental inefficiency, illegal action, or other wrongdoing.

13–4

Explain how regulatory agencies make rules and how issue networks affect policymaking in government. 7 Regulatory agencies are sometimes regarded as the fourth branch of government. They make **legislative rules** that are as legally binding as laws passed by Congress. When they are engaging in rulemaking, agencies must follow certain procedural requirements and must also make sure that their rules are based on substantial evidence. Bureaucrats in federal agencies are expected to exhibit **neutral competency,** which means that they are supposed to apply their technical skills to their jobs without regard to political issues. In reality, however, each independent agency and each executive department is interested in its own survival and expansion. **8 Iron triangles** are well established in almost every part of the bureaucracy. In some policy areas, there are less structured relationships among experts who have strong opinions and interests regarding the direction of policy. These **issue networks** are able to exert a great deal of influence on legislators and bureaucratic agencies.

13–5

Identify some of the ways in which the government has attempted to curb waste and improve efficiency in the bureaucracy. 9 To encourage federal employees to report gross governmental inefficiency or wrongdoing, Congress has passed laws to protect **whistleblowers** and to make cash rewards to them. To improve efficiency, almost every federal agency has had to describe its goals and identify methods for evaluating how well those goals are met. President Obama created the position of a chief performance officer who works with other economic officials in an attempt to increase efficiency and eliminate waste in government. Other ideas for reforming government bureaucracies include **privatization** and allowing citizens to file forms and apply for services online.

INTERNET RESOURCES

www.nasa.gov

www.cdc.gov/phpr/documents/Zombie_GN_Final.pdf

www.census.gov

www.whitehouse.gov/omb

www.usgovernmentmanual.gov

www.gsa.gov

LEARNING OUTCOMES

14–1

Summarize the origins of the American legal system and the basic sources of American law. 1 The American legal system evolved from the **common law** tradition that developed in England. The practice of deciding new cases with reference to **precedents (*stare decisis*)** became a cornerstone of the American judicial system. **2** Various **primary sources of law** provide the basis for **constitutional law, statutory law, administrative law,** and **case law. 3 Civil law** spells out the duties that individuals in society owe to other persons or to their governments. **Criminal law** has to do with wrongs committed against the public as a whole. **4** A court must have **jurisdiction** to hear and decide a particular case. A **federal question** provides a basis for federal court jurisdiction. Federal courts can also hear **diversity-of-citizenship** cases. To bring a lawsuit before a court, a person must have **standing to sue,** and the issue must be a **justiciable controversy.** The courts have also established procedural rules that apply in all cases.

14–2

Delineate the structure of the federal court system. 5 The U.S. district courts are **trial courts**—the courts in which cases involving federal laws begin. There is at least one federal district court in every state, and there is one in the District of Columbia. The U.S. courts of appeals are **appellate courts** that hear cases on review from the U.S. district courts located within their respective judicial circuits. Some federal administrative agency decisions may also be appealed to these courts. The Court of Appeals for the Federal Circuit has national jurisdiction over certain types of cases. The United States Supreme Court has some original jurisdiction, but most of its work is as an appellate court. The Supreme Court may take appeals of decisions made by the U.S. courts of appeals as well as appeals of cases decided in the state courts when federal questions are at issue. **6** To bring a case before the Supreme Court, a party may request that the Court issue a **writ of *certiorari.*** If the Court grants cert., it will typically hear **oral arguments.** The justices will then discuss the case in **conference.** When the Court has reached a decision, the justices explain their reasoning in written **opinions.**

14–3

Say how federal judges are appointed. 7 Federal judges are appointed by the president with the advice and consent of the Senate. They receive lifetime appointments. The Senate Judiciary Committee holds hearings on judicial nominees and makes its recommendations to the Senate, where it takes a majority vote to confirm nominations. **Senatorial courtesy** gives home-state senators of the president's party influence over the president's choice of nominees for district courts (and, to a lesser extent, the U.S. courts of appeals). The process of nominating and confirming federal judges often involves political debate and controversy.

KEY TERMS

14–1

- **administrative law** The body of law created by administrative agencies (in the form of rules, regulations, orders, and decisions) in order to carry out their duties and responsibilities.

- **case law** The rules of law announced in court decisions. Case law includes the aggregate of reported cases that interpret judicial precedents, statutes, regulations, and constitutional provisions.

civil law The branch of law that spells out the duties that individuals in society owe to other persons or to their governments, excluding the duty not to commit crimes.

common law The body of law developed from judicial decisions in English and U.S. courts, not attributable to a legislature.

constitutional law Law based on the U.S. Constitution and the constitutions of the various states.

contempt of court A ruling that a person has disobeyed a court order or has shown disrespect to the court or to a judicial proceeding.

criminal law The branch of law that defines and governs actions that constitute crimes. Generally, criminal law has to do with wrongful actions committed against society for which society demands redress.

diversity of citizenship A basis for federal court jurisdiction over a lawsuit that arises when (1) the parties in the lawsuit live in different states or when one of the parties is a foreign government or a foreign citizen, and (2) the amount in controversy is more than $75,000.

federal question A question that pertains to the U.S. Constitution, acts of Congress, or treaties. A federal question provides a basis for federal court jurisdiction.

judiciary The courts; one of the three branches of government in the United States.

- **jurisdiction** The authority of a court to hear and decide a particular case.

justiciable controversy A controversy that is not hypothetical or academic but real and substantial; a requirement that must be satisfied before a court will hear a case. *Justiciable* is pronounced jus-*tish*-a-bul.

CHAPTER REVIEW 14

precedent A court decision that furnishes an example or authority for deciding subsequent cases involving identical or similar facts and legal issues.

primary source of law A source of law that establishes the law. Primary sources of law include constitutions, statutes, administrative agency rules and regulations, and decisions rendered by the courts.

stare decisis A common law doctrine under which judges normally are obligated to follow the precedents established by prior court decisions. Pronounced *ster*-ay dih-*si*-sis.

statutory law The body of law enacted by legislatures (as opposed to constitutional law, administrative law, or case law).

standing to sue The requirement that an individual must have a sufficient stake in a controversy before he or she can bring a lawsuit. The party bringing the suit must demonstrate that he or she has either been harmed or been threatened with a harm.

trial court A court in which trials are held and testimony is taken.

14–2

appellate court A court having appellate jurisdiction. An appellate court normally does not hear evidence or testimony but reviews the transcript of the trial court's proceedings, other records relating to the case, and attorneys' arguments as to why the trial court's decision should or should not stand.

concurring opinion A statement written by a judge or justice who agrees (concurs) with the court's decision, but for reasons different from those in the majority opinion.

conference In regard to the Supreme Court, a private meeting of the justices in which they present their arguments concerning a case under consideration.

dissenting opinion A statement written by a judge or justice who disagrees with the majority opinion.

opinion A written statement by a court expressing the reasons for its decision in a case.

oral argument A spoken argument presented to a judge in person by an attorney on behalf of her or his client.

writ of *certiorari* An order from a higher court asking a lower court for the record of a case. *Certiorari* is pronounced sur-shee-uh-*rah*-ree.

14–4

Explain how the federal courts make policy, and describe the role of ideology and judicial philosophies in judicial decision making. 8 It is unavoidable that courts influence or even establish policy when they interpret and apply the law, because the law does not always provide clear answers to questions that come before the courts. Federal judges can also decide on the constitutionality of laws or actions undertaken by the other branches of government through the power of **judicial review. 9** Generally, activist judges believe that the courts should actively use their powers to check the other two branches of government to ensure that they do not exceed their authority. Restraintist judges generally assume that the courts should defer to the decisions of the other branches. **10** There are numerous examples of ideology affecting Supreme Court decisions. Judicial decision making, however, can be complex. How much weight is given to the factors that may be taken into account depends, in part, on the approaches justices take toward the interpretation of laws and the Constitution. Important judicial philosophies include originalism, textualism, and modernism.

14–5

Identify some of the criticisms of the federal courts and some of the checks on the power of the courts. 11 Policymaking by unelected judges has important implications in a democracy. Critics, especially on the political right, frequently accuse the judiciary of "legislating from the bench." There are several checks on the courts, however, including judicial traditions and doctrines, the judiciary's lack of enforcement powers, and potential congressional actions in response to court decisions. The American public continues to have a fairly high regard for the federal **judiciary.**

INTERNET RESOURCES

www.oyez.org

www.law.cornell.edu/supct

www.supremecourt.gov

www.washlaw.edu

www.uscourts.gov

14–3

senatorial courtesy A practice that allows a senator of the president's party to veto the president's nominee to a federal court judgeship within the senator's state.

14–4

judicial review The power of the courts to decide on the constitutionality of legislative enactments and of actions taken by the executive branch.

LEARNING OUTCOMES

15–1

Explain what domestic policy is, and summarize the steps in the policymaking process. 1 Domestic policy consists of public policy concerning issues within a national unit. **2** The **policymaking process** involves several phases. Identifying a problem that can be solved politically (issue identification) and getting the issue on the political agenda (**agenda-setting**) begin the process. The second stage involves the formulation and adoption of specific plans for achieving a particular goal. The final stages of the process focus on the implementation of the policy and evaluating its success. Each phase of the policymaking process involves interactions among various individuals and groups.

15–2

Discuss the issue of health-care funding and recent legislation on universal health insurance. 3 Most federal spending on health care is accounted for by two **entitlement programs, Medicaid** and **Medicare,** which is the government's second largest domestic spending program. **4** In some countries, the government is responsible for providing basic health-care insurance to everyone through **national health insurance.** The plan that the United States has adopted provides a large role for the private sector. Under the Patient Protection and Affordable Care Act, signed into law in 2010 by President Obama, employer-provided health insurance continues, and a new health-insurance marketplace allows small businesses and individuals to shop for plans. The legislation also includes an **individual mandate**—most individuals are required to obtain coverage or pay an income-tax penalty. **5** One immediate change was that young people could remain covered by their parents' insurance until they turn 26, but the most important provisions of the new law were not to take effect until 2014, when subsidies would help eligible citizens purchase health-care insurance if they were not covered by Medicare, Medicaid, or an employer's plan. **6** Conservatives were opposed to the Affordable Care Act, but repeated attempts by Republicans in the House to repeal Obamacare were ineffectual. The roll-out of the federal health insurance exchange in 2013 was disastrous, but by the end of the sign-up period in April 2014, 8 million Americans had obtained insurance policies through the state and federal exchanges.

15–3

Summarize the issues of energy independence and alternative energy sources. 7 By 2016, our nation will import 25 percent of its petroleum supply. Fortunately, friendly neighbors, Canada and Mexico, supply 45 percent of our imports. In response to rising oil prices, the Obama administration has issued higher **Corporate Average Fuel Economy (CAFE) standards. 8** Most climatologists believe that **global warming** is the result of human activities,

KEY TERMS

15–1

agenda setting Getting an issue on the political agenda to be addressed by Congress; part of the first stage of the policymaking process.

domestic policy Public policy concerning issues within a national unit, such as national policy concerning health care or the economy.

policymaking process The procedures involved in getting an issue on the political agenda; formulating, adopting, and implementing a policy with regard to the issue; and then evaluating the results of the policy.

15–2

Children's Health Insurance Program (CHIP) A joint federal-state program that provides health-care insurance for low-income children.

entitlement program A government program that provides benefits to all persons who meet specified requirements.

individual mandate In the context of health-care reform, a requirement that all persons obtain health-care insurance from one source or another. Those failing to do so must pay a penalty.

Medicaid A joint federal-state program that pays for health-care services for low-income persons.

Medicare A federal government program that pays for health-care insurance for Americans aged sixty-five years and over.

national health insurance A program, found in many of the world's economically advanced nations, under which the central government provides basic health-care insurance coverage to everyone in the country.

15–3

Corporate Average Fuel Economy (CAFE) standards A set of federal standards under which each vehicle manufacturer (or the industry as a whole) must meet a miles-per-gallon benchmark averaged across all new cars or trucks.

fracking Technique for extracting oil or natural gas from underground rock by the high-power injection of a mixture of water, sand, and chemicals.

global warming An increase in the average temperature of the Earth's surface over the last half century and its projected continuation; referred to more generally as *climate change*.

greenhouse gas A gas that, when released into the atmosphere, traps the sun's heat and slows its release into outer space. Carbon dioxide (CO_2) is a major example.

renewable energy Energy from technologies that do not rely on extracted resources, such as oil and coal, that can run out.

15–4

action-reaction syndrome The principle that for every government action, there will be a reaction by the public.

easy-money policy A monetary policy that involves stimulating the economy by expanding the rate of growth of the money supply.

economic policy All actions taken by the national government to address ups and downs in the nation's level of business activity.

Federal Open Market Committee (FOMC) The most important body within the Federal Reserve System; decides how monetary policy should be carried out.

fiscal policy The use of changes in government expenditures and taxes to alter national economic variables.

inflation A sustained rise in average prices; equivalent to a decline in the value of the dollar.

Keynesian economics An economic theory proposed by British economist John Maynard Keynes that is typically associated with the use of fiscal policy to alter national economic variables.

monetary policy Actions taken by the Federal Reserve Board to change the amount of money in circulation to affect interest rates, credit markets, the rate of inflation, the rate of economic growth, and the rate of unemployment.

public debt The total amount of money that the national government owes as a result of borrowing; also called the *national debt*.

recession A period in which the level of economic activity falls; usually defined as two or more quarters of economic decline.

unemployment The state of not having a job even when actively seeking one.

especially the release of **greenhouse gases** into the atmosphere. The predicted outcomes of climate change vary, and attitudes toward it have become highly politicized. **9** The issues of U.S. energy security and climate change raise the question of whether we can develop new energy sources. Due, in part, to new techniques, such as **fracking,** there has recently been an increase in supplies of natural gas and oil. A key obstacle to the construction of new nuclear power plants is cost. The cost of some **renewable energy** technologies, such as solar power and wind energy, has been falling. As a result, the number of solar and wind-power installations has grown rapidly.

15–4

Describe the two major areas of economic policymaking, and discuss the issue of the public debt. 10 The national government has two main tools to smooth the business cycle and to reduce **unemployment** and **inflation. 11 Monetary policy** is under the control of the Federal Reserve System (the Fed), an independent regulatory agency. The Fed and its **Federal Open Market Committee** make decisions about monetary policy several times each year. In periods of recession and high unemployment, the Fed pursues an **easy-money policy.** In periods of rising inflation, the Fed adopts a tight-money policy. **12 Fiscal policy,** associated with **Keynesian economics,** involves the use of changes in government spending or taxes to stimulate or curb economic activity. **13** The government raises money to pay its expenses through taxes levied on business and personal income and through borrowing. Tax policy is plagued by the **action-reaction syndrome,** resulting in a complicated tax system that is politically difficult to reform. When the government spends more than it receives, it borrows to finance the shortfall. Every time there is a federal government deficit, there is an increase in the total accumulated **public debt.** Today, about half of the U.S. net public debt is held by foreign individuals, foreign businesses, and foreign central banks. The federal budget deficit has gone down in recent years, but it is still causing the the public debt to grow faster than the economy.

INTERNET RESOURCES

www.facebook.com/ArtistsAgainstFracking

quickfacts.census.gov

www.heritage.org

twitter.com/NYTimeskrugman

www.treasurydirect.gov

www.whitehouse.gov/administration/eop/cea/economic-report-of-the-president

CHAPTER REVIEW **16**
Foreign Policy

LEARNING OUTCOMES

16–1

Discuss how foreign policy is made, and identify the key players in this process. 1 The president oversees the military, guides defense policies, and represents the United States to the rest of the world. The Department of State is responsible for diplomatic relations with other nations and with multilateral organizations. The Department of Defense establishes and carries out defense policy and protects our national security. Two key agencies in the area of **foreign policy** are the National Security Council and the Central Intelligence Agency. Congress has the power to declare war and the power to appropriate funds to equip the armed forces and provide for foreign aid. The Senate has the power to ratify treaties. A few congressional committees are directly concerned with foreign affairs.

16–2

Summarize the history of American foreign policy through the years. 2 Early leaders sought to protect American interests through **isolationism.** The Spanish-American War of 1898 marked the first step toward **interventionism. 3** In World War I, the United States initially adopted a policy of **neutrality,** and after the war, returned to a policy of isolationism. That policy ended when Pearl Harbor was attacked in 1941. After World War II, the wartime alliance between the United States and the Soviet Union deteriorated. The Truman Doctrine and the **Marshall Plan** marked the beginning of a policy of **containment. 4** During the **Cold War,** the United States and the Soviet Union engaged in an arms race supported by a policy of **deterrence,** in keeping with the theory of **mutually assured destruction (MAD).** In 1962, the two countries came close to a nuclear confrontation during the **Cuban missile crisis.** The fall of the Berlin Wall in 1989 and the demise of the Soviet Union in 1991 altered the framework and goals of U.S. foreign policy.

16–3

Identify the foreign policy challenges presented by terrorism. 5 Terrorism is defined as the use of staged violence, often against civilians, to achieve political goals. Governments around the world face the challenges of dealing with local or regional terrorism, state-sponsored terrorism, and foreign terrorist networks. After the 9/11 terrorist attacks, the U.S. military, supported by a **coalition** of allies, attacked al Qaeda camps in Afghanistan and the ruling Taliban regime that harbored those terrorists. **6** In 2003, U.S. and British forces attacked the nation of Iraq, believing (though incorrectly) that Iraq's dictator, Saddam Hussein, was developing **weapons of mass destruction** and that the Iraqi regime was in some way responsible for the 9/11 terrorist attacks. After overthrowing Hussein and undermining an insurgency that included the newly organized al Qaeda in Iraq, U.S. combat forces left Iraq in 2011. **7** By 2006, the Taliban had regrouped and were waging a war of insurgency against the new government in Afghanistan. In 2011, U.S. Navy Seals killed al Qaeda leader

KEY TERMS

Introduction

foreign policy A systematic and general plan that guides a country's attitudes and actions toward the rest of the world. Foreign policy includes all of the economic, military, commercial, and diplomatic positions and actions that a nation takes in its relationships with other countries.

moral idealism In foreign policy, the belief that the most important goal is to do what is right. Moral idealists think that it is possible for nations to cooperate as part of a rule-based community.

political realism In foreign policy, the belief that nations are inevitably selfish and that we should seek to protect our national security, regardless of moral arguments.

16–2

Cold War The war of words, warnings, and ideologies between the Soviet Union and the United States that lasted from the late 1940s through the late 1980s.

colonial empire A group of dependent nations that are under the rule of an imperial power.

containment A U.S. policy designed to contain the spread of communism by offering military and economic aid to threatened nations.

Cuban missile crisis A nuclear standoff that occurred in 1962 when the United States learned that the Soviet Union had placed nuclear warheads in Cuba.

détente A French word meaning a "relaxation of tensions." Détente characterized the relationship between the United States and the Soviet Union in the 1970s as they attempted to pursue cooperative dealings and arms control.

deterrence A policy of building up military strength for the purpose of discouraging (deterring) military attacks by other nations; the policy that supported the arms race between the United States and the Soviet Union during the Cold War.

interventionism Direct involvement by one country in another country's affairs.

iron curtain A phrase coined by Winston Churchill to describe the political boundaries between the democratic countries in Western Europe and the Soviet-controlled Communist countries in Eastern Europe.

isolationism A political policy of noninvolvement in world affairs.

Marshall Plan A plan providing for U.S. economic assistance to European nations following World War II to help those nations recover from the war. The plan was named after George C. Marshall, secretary of state from 1947 to 1949.

Monroe Doctrine A U.S. policy, announced in 1823 by President James Monroe, that the United States would not tolerate foreign intervention in the Western Hemisphere, and in return, the United States would stay out of European affairs.

mutually assured destruction (MAD) A phrase referring to the assumption that if the forces of two nations are capable of destroying each other, neither nation will take a chance on war.

neutrality The position of not being aligned with either side in a dispute or conflict, such as a war.

Soviet bloc The group of Eastern European nations that fell under the control of the Soviet Union following World War II.

16–3

coalition An alliance of nations formed to undertake a foreign policy action, particularly a military action. A coalition is often a temporary alliance that dissolves after the action is concluded.

ISIS The Islamic State in Iraq and Greater Syria; a terrorist organization that by 2014 had taken over substantial portions of Iraq and Syria. Also known as *ISIL* (the Islamic State in Iraq and the Levant) or the Islamic State.

weapons of mass destruction Chemical, biological, or nuclear weapons that can inflict massive casualties.

16–4

Oslo Accords The first agreement signed between Israel and the PLO; led to the establishment of the Palestinian Authority in the occupied territories.

Palestine Liberation Organization (PLO) An organization formed in 1964 to represent the Palestinian people. The PLO has a long history of terrorism but for some years has functioned primarily as a political party.

16–6

normal trade relations (NTR) status A trade status granted through an international treaty by which each member nation must treat other members at least as well as it treats the country that receives its most favorable treatment. This status was formerly known as *most-favored-nation status*.

Osama bin Laden in his Pakistani compound. In the aftermath of the "Arab Spring," however, new terrorist groups emerged. The most radical faction fighting in Syria was **ISIS,** which also became active in Iraq. The brutality of ISIS and its desire to create an Islamist state prompted the United States and five Arab states to begin a bombing campaign in Syria and Iraq to weaken its forces.

16–4

Explain the principal issues dividing the Israelis and the Palestinians and the solutions proposed by the international community. 8 For years after Israel was founded in 1948, the neighboring Arab states did not accept its legitimacy as a nation, resulting in a series of wars. After the 1967 war, Palestinians living in the West Bank and Gaza strip became an occupied people. Israeli settlements there remain controversial, and Palestinian terrorist attacks on Israel have made peace negotiations nearly impossible. **9** The international community agrees that lands seized in the 1967 war should be restored to the Palestinians, who could organize their own independent nation-state there. In turn, the Palestinians would have to recognize Israel's right to exist and take concrete steps to guarantee Israel's security. After a new round of fighting in the Gaza Strip in 2014, any agreement between Israel and the Palestinians seems far off.

16–5

Outline some of the actions taken by the United States to curb the threat of nuclear weapons. 10 Neither weapons inspections nor negotiations have resolved the issue of North Korea's nuclear ambitions. That nation conducted nuclear tests in 2006, 2009, and 2013. **11** Iran has been engaged in a covert nuclear program, and, like North Korea, has been openly hostile to the United States. Efforts to address Iran's pursuit of nuclear weapons include talks involving Britain, France, Germany, Iran, Russia, and the United States, as well as sanctions imposed by the United Nations and the United States. A change in Iran's leadership in 2013 led to progress in freezing parts of its nuclear program in return for the lifting of some sanctions.

16–6

Describe China's emerging role as a world power. 12 China has one of the fastest-growing economies in the world, along with a population of 1.3 billion and a GDP that is expected to surpass that of the United States by 2020. Congress has granted China **normal trade relations status.** In recent years, China has exhibited nationalist tendencies that have alarmed some of its neighbors. In 2012, President Obama announced a "pivot" to East Asia involving shifting naval resources into the region and negotiating enhanced security relationships with area nations.

INTERNET RESOURCES

www.cia.gov/library/publications/the-world-factbook

www.un.org/en

www.imf.org

www.worldbank.org

www.oecd.org

www.iie.com

www.defense.gov

www.nato.int